McGraw Hill Education create™

Course	Tax Impact on Decisions ACIS 3314
Course Number	**Spring 2018**
	VIRGINIA TECH
	Accounting and Information Systems

AF854530

create™

http://create.mheducation.com

ISBN-10: 1307085504 ISBN-13: 9781307085501

Contents

Credits

Online Supplements 523

chapter

1 An Introduction to Tax

Learning Objectives

Upon completing this chapter, you should be able to:

LO 1-1 Demonstrate how taxes influence basic business, investment, personal, and political decisions.

LO 1-2 Discuss what constitutes a tax and the general objectives of taxes.

LO 1-3 Describe the different tax rate structures and calculate a tax.

LO 1-4 Identify the various federal, state, and local taxes.

LO 1-5 Apply appropriate criteria to evaluate alternative tax systems.

© Andrew Rich/Getty Images

Storyline Summary

Taxpayer:	Margaret
Employment status:	Margaret is a full-time student at the University of Georgia.
Current situation:	She is beginning her first tax class.

Margaret is a junior beginning her first tax course. She is excited about her career prospects as an accounting major but hasn't had much exposure to taxes. On her way to campus she runs into an old friend, Eddy, who is going to Washington, D.C., to protest recent proposed changes to the U.S. tax system. Eddy is convinced the IRS is evil and that the current tax system is blatantly unfair and corrupt. He advocates a simpler, fairer way of taxation. Margaret is intrigued by Eddy's passion but questions whether he has a complete understanding of the U.S. tax system. She decides to withhold all judgments about it (or about pursuing a career in taxation) until the end of her tax course. ■

LO 1-1 WHO CARES ABOUT TAXES AND WHY?

A clear understanding of the role of taxes in everyday decisions will help you make an informed decision about the value of studying taxation or pursuing a career in taxation. One view of taxation is that it represents an inconvenience every April 15th (the annual due date for filing federal individual tax returns without extensions). However, the role of taxation is much more pervasive than this view suggests. Your study of this subject will provide you a unique opportunity to develop an informed opinion about taxation. As a business student, you can overcome the mystery that encompasses popular impressions of the tax system and perhaps, one day, share your expertise with friends or clients.

What are some common decisions you face that taxes may influence? In this course, we alert you to situations in which you can increase your return on investments by up to one-third! Even the best lessons in finance courses can't approach the increase in risk-adjusted return that smart tax planning provides. Would you like to own your home someday? Tax deductions for home mortgage interest and real estate taxes can reduce the after-tax costs of owning a home relative to renting. Thus, when you face the decision to buy or rent, you can make an informed choice if you understand the relative tax advantages of home ownership. Would you like to retire someday? Understanding the tax-advantaged methods of saving for retirement can increase the after-tax value of your retirement nest egg—and thus increase the likelihood that you can afford to retire, and do so in style. Other common personal financial decisions that taxes influence include: choosing investments, evaluating alternative job offers, saving for education expenses, and doing gift or estate planning. Indeed, taxes are a part of everyday life and have a significant effect on many of the personal financial decisions all of us face.

The role of taxes is not limited to personal finance. Taxes play an equally important role in fundamental business decisions such as the following:

- What organizational form should a business use?
- Where should the business locate?
- How should business acquisitions be structured?
- How should the business compensate employees?
- What is the appropriate mix of debt and equity for the business?
- Should the business rent or own its equipment and property?
- How should the business distribute profits to its owners?

Savvy business decisions require owners and managers to consider all costs and benefits in order to evaluate the merits of a transaction. Although taxes don't necessarily dominate these decisions, they do represent large transaction costs that businesses should factor into the financial decision-making process.

Taxes also play a major part in the political process. U.S. presidential candidates often distinguish themselves from their opponents based upon their tax rhetoric. Indeed, the major political parties generally have very diverse views of the appropriate way to tax the public.[1] Determining who is taxed, what is taxed, and how much is taxed are tough questions with nontrivial answers. Voters must have a basic understanding of taxes to evaluate the merits of alternative tax proposals. Later in this chapter, we'll introduce criteria you can use to evaluate alternative tax proposals.

[1]The U.S. Department of the Treasury provides a "history of taxation" on its website (www.treasury.gov/resource-center/faqs/Taxes/Pages/historyrooseveltmessage.aspx). You may find it interesting to read this history in light of the various political parties in office at the time.

TAXES IN THE REAL WORLD Republicans vs. Democrats

Tax Policy: Republicans versus Democrats

Oliver Wendell Holmes said "taxes are the price we pay to live in a civilized society." Both Democrats and Republicans desire the same things: a civilized society and a healthy economy. However, neither party can agree on what defines a civilized society or which path best leads to a healthy economy. The U.S. national debt is $20 trillion dollars and growing, yet the only thing we might agree on is that something has gone wrong. Regardless of which party or candidate you support, each party's agenda will affect your income and taxes in various ways.

To explore the divide, let's examine excerpts from each party's National Platform from our most recent presidential election (2016).

Republicans

"We are the party of a growing economy that gives everyone a chance in life, an opportunity to learn, work, and realize the prosperity freedom makes possible."

"Government cannot create prosperity, though government can limit or destroy it. Prosperity is the product of self-discipline, enterprise, saving and investment by individuals, but it is not an end in itself. Prosperity provides the means by which citizens and their families can maintain their independence from government, raise their children by their own values, practice their faith, and build communities of cooperation and mutual respect."

"Republicans consider the establishment of a pro-growth tax code a moral imperative. More than any other public policy, the way government raises revenue—how much, at what rates, under what circumstances, from whom, and for whom—has the greatest impact on our economy's performance. It powerfully influences the level of economic growth and job creation, which translates into the level of opportunity for those who would otherwise be left behind."

"A strong economy is one key to debt reduction, but spending restraint is a necessary component that must be vigorously pursued." https://www.gop.com/platform/restoring-the-american-dream/

Democrats

"At a time of massive income and wealth inequality, we believe the wealthiest Americans and largest corporations must pay their fair share of taxes. Democrats will claw back tax breaks for companies that ship jobs overseas, eliminate tax breaks for big oil and gas companies, and crack down on inversions and other methods companies use to dodge their tax responsibilities ... We will then use the revenue raised from fixing the corporate tax code to reinvest in rebuilding America and ensuring economic growth that will lead to millions of good-paying jobs."

"We will ensure those at the top contribute to our country's future by establishing a multimillionaire surtax to ensure millionaires and billionaires pay their fair share. In addition, we will shut down the "private tax system" for those at the top, immediately close egregious loopholes like those enjoyed by hedge fund managers, restore fair taxation on multimillion dollar estates, and ensure millionaires can no longer pay a lower rate than their secretaries. At a time of near-record corporate profits, slow wage growth, and rising costs, we need to offer tax relief to middle-class families—not those at the top."

"We will offer tax relief to hard working, middle-class families for the cost squeeze they have faced for years from rising health care, childcare, education, and other expenses." https://www.democrats.org/party-platform#preamble

Conclusion

Each party fundamentally believes the government should create/maintain cities and states that form a civilized society, and that government should foster a healthy economy. However, they choose very different paths to reach this objective. Democrats want to raise taxes on the wealthy and create government programs which cost more money, while Republicans wish to lower taxes and decrease government size and spending. Both motives are pure; however, current and cumulative deficits indicate that current revenue is insufficient to meet government spending. Solving these problems will require civil discourse, education and research/information in order to find realistic, effective solutions.

In summary, taxes affect many aspects of personal, business, and political decisions. Developing a solid understanding of taxation should allow you to make informed decisions in these areas. Thus, Margaret can take comfort that her semester will likely prove useful to her personally. Who knows? Depending on her interest in business, investment, retirement planning, and the like, she may ultimately decide to pursue a career in taxation.

THE KEY FACTS

What Qualifies as a Tax?

- The general purpose of taxes is to fund government agencies.
- Unlike fines or penalties, taxes are not meant to punish or prevent illegal behavior; however, "*sin taxes*" are meant to discourage some behaviors.
- To qualify as a tax, three criteria must be met. The payment must be:
  - required;
  - imposed by a government;
  - and not tied directly to the benefit received by the taxpayer.

LO 1-2 WHAT QUALIFIES AS A TAX?

"Taxes are the price we pay for a civilized society." —Oliver Wendell Holmes, Jr.

Taxes have been described in many terms: some positive, some negative, some printable, some not. Let's go directly to a formal definition of a tax, which should prove useful in identifying alternative taxes and discussing alternative tax systems.

A **tax** *is a payment required by a government that is unrelated to any specific benefit or service received from the government.* The general purpose of a tax is to fund the operations of the government (to raise revenue). Taxes differ from fines and penalties in that taxes are not intended to punish or prevent illegal behavior. Nonetheless, by allowing deductions from income, our federal tax system does encourage certain behaviors like charitable contributions, retirement savings, and research and development. Thus, we can view it as discouraging other legal behavior. For example, **sin taxes** impose relatively high surcharges on alcohol and tobacco products.[2] Another example is the shared-responsibility payment introduced by the Affordable Care Act (see the nearby box). This payment was declared to be a "tax" by the Supreme Court. The tax is imposed on those who do not have minimum essential health care coverage.[3]

TAXES IN THE REAL WORLD Affordable Care Act

The Affordable Care Act requires individuals to be covered by a health insurance plan or to pay a tax—which is paid on the individual's income tax return. The adult annual dollar amount was phased in as follows: $95 in 2014; $325 in 2015; $695 in 2016 and is indexed by inflation thereafter. The Congressional Budget Office and the Joint Committee on Taxation jointly estimated that 5.9 million Americans will be subject to the penalty in 2016 and the provision will raise $6.9 billion in revenue in that year.

You may recall that one question the Supreme Court had to rule on was whether this provision is a "penalty" or a "tax." The Supreme Court held that the provision is a tax and answered as follows: "The payment is not so high that there is really no choice but to buy health insurance; the payment is not limited to willful violations, as penalties for unlawful acts often are; and the payment is collected solely by the (Internal Revenue Service) through the normal means of taxation," Chief Justice John Roberts wrote in the decision.

Source: National Federation of Independent Business v. Sebelius, 132 S. Ct. 2566 (2012).

Key components of the definition of a tax are that the payment is:

- Required (it is not voluntary);
- Imposed by a government agency (federal, state, or local); and
- Not tied directly to the benefit received by the taxpayer.

This last point is not to say that taxpayers receive no benefits from the taxes they pay. They benefit from national defense, a judicial system, law enforcement, government-sponsored social programs, an interstate highway system, public schools, and many other government-provided programs and services. The distinction is that taxes paid are not *directly* related to any specific benefit received by the taxpayer. For example, the price of admission to Yellowstone National Park is a fee rather than a tax because a specific benefit is received.

Can taxes be assessed for special purposes, such as a 1 percent sales tax for education? Yes. Why is an **earmarked tax,** a tax that is assessed for a specific purpose, still considered a tax? Because the payment made by the taxpayer does not directly relate to the specific benefit *received by the taxpayer.*

[2] Sin taxes represent an interesting confluence of incentives. On the one hand, demand for such products as alcohol, tobacco, and gambling is often relatively inelastic because of their addictive quality. Thus, taxing such a product can raise substantial revenues. On the other hand, one of the arguments for sin taxes is frequently the social goal of *reducing* demand for such products.

[3] For details on the computation of the shared-responsibility payment see Reg. §1.5000A-4.

Example 1-1

Margaret travels to Birmingham, Alabama, where she rents a hotel room and dines at several restaurants. The price she pays for her hotel room and meals includes an additional 2 percent city surcharge to fund roadway construction in Birmingham. Is this a tax?

Answer: Yes. The payment is required by a local government and does not directly relate to a specific benefit that Margaret receives.

Example 1-2

Margaret's parents, Bill and Mercedes, recently built a house and were assessed $1,000 by their county government to connect to the county sewer system. Is this a tax?

Answer: No. The assessment was mandatory and it was paid to a local government. However, the third criterion was not met since the payment directly relates to a specific benefit (sewer service) received by the payees. For the same reason, tolls, parking meter fees, and annual licensing fees are also not considered taxes.

HOW TO CALCULATE A TAX

LO 1-3

In its simplest form, the amount of tax equals the tax base multiplied by the tax rate:

Eq. 1-1

$$\text{Tax} = \text{Tax Base} \times \text{Tax Rate}$$

The **tax base** defines what is actually taxed and is usually expressed in monetary terms, whereas the **tax rate** determines the level of taxes imposed on the tax base and is usually expressed as a percentage. For example, a sales tax rate of 6 percent on a purchase of $30 yields a tax of $1.80 ($1.80 = $30 × .06).

Federal, state, and local jurisdictions use a large variety of tax bases to collect tax. Some common tax bases (and related taxes) include taxable income (federal and state income taxes), purchases (sales tax), real estate values (real estate tax), and personal property values (personal property tax).

Different portions of a tax base may be taxed at different rates. A single tax applied to an entire base constitutes a **flat tax.** In the case of **graduated taxes,** the base is divided into a series of monetary amounts, or **brackets,** and each successive bracket is taxed at a different (gradually higher or gradually lower) percentage rate.

Calculating some taxes—income taxes for individuals or corporations, for example—can be quite complex. Advocates of flat taxes argue that the process should be simpler. But as we'll see throughout the text, most of the difficulty in calculating a tax rests in determining the tax *base,* not the tax rate. Indeed, there are only three basic tax rate structures (proportional, progressive, and regressive), and each can be mastered without much difficulty.

THE KEY FACTS

How to Calculate a Tax

- Tax = Tax base × Tax rate
- The tax base defines what is actually taxed and is usually expressed in monetary terms.
- The tax rate determines the level of taxes imposed on the tax base and is usually expressed as a percentage.
- Different portions of a tax base may be taxed at different rates.

DIFFERENT WAYS TO MEASURE TAX RATES

Before we discuss the alternative tax rate structures, let's first define three different tax rates that will be useful in contrasting the different tax rate structures: the marginal, average, and effective tax rates.

The **marginal tax rate** is the tax rate that applies to the *next additional increment* of a taxpayer's taxable income (or deductions). Specifically,

Eq. 1-2

$$\text{Marginal Tax Rate} = \frac{\Delta\text{Tax}^*}{\Delta\text{Taxable Income}} = \frac{(\text{New Total Tax} - \text{Old Total Tax})}{(\text{New Taxable Income} - \text{Old Taxable Income})}$$

*Δ means *change in.*

where "old" refers to the current tax and "new" refers to the revised tax after incorporating the additional income (or deductions) in question. In graduated income tax systems, additional income (deductions) can push a taxpayer into a higher (lower) tax bracket, thus changing the marginal tax rate.

Example 1-3

Margaret's parents, Bill and Mercedes, file a joint tax return. They have $160,000 of taxable income this year (after all tax deductions). Assuming the following federal tax rate schedule applies, how much federal income tax will they owe this year?[4]

Married Filing Jointly (and Surviving Spouses)

Not over $18,650	10% of taxable income
$18,650 to $75,900	$1,865 + 15% of taxable income in excess of $18,650
$75,900 to $153,100	$10,462.50 + 25% of taxable income in excess of $75,900
$153,100 to $233,350	$29,752.50 + 28% of taxable income in excess of $153,100
$233,350 to $416,700	$52,222.50 + 33% of taxable income in excess of $233,350
$416,700 to $470,700	$112,728 + 35% of taxable income in excess of $416,700
Over $470,700	$131,628 + 39.6% of taxable income in excess of $470,700

Answer: Bill and Mercedes will owe $31,684.50 computed as follows:

$31,684.50 = $29,752.50 + 28% ($160,000 − $153,100)

Note that in this graduated tax rate structure, the first $18,650 of taxable income is taxed at 10 percent, the next $57,250 of taxable income (between $18,650 and $75,900) is taxed at 15 percent, and the next $77,200 of taxable income (between $75,900 and $153,100) is taxed at 25 percent. Bill and Mercedes's last $6,900 of taxable income (between $153,100 and $160,000) is taxed at 28 percent.

Many taxpayers incorrectly believe that all their income is taxed at their marginal rate. This mistake leads people to say, "I don't want to earn any additional money because it will put me in a higher tax bracket." Bill and Mercedes are currently in the 28 percent marginal tax rate bracket, but notice that not all their income is taxed at this rate. Their *marginal* tax rate is 28 percent. This means that small increases in income will be taxed at 28 percent, and small increases in tax deductions will generate tax *savings* of 28 percent. If Bill and Mercedes receive a large increase in income (or in deductions) such that they would change tax rate brackets, we cannot identify their marginal tax rate by simply identifying their current tax bracket.

Example 1-4

Bill, a well-known economics professor, signs a publishing contract with an $80,000 royalty advance. Using the rate schedule from Example 1-3, what would Bill and Mercedes's marginal tax rate be on this additional $80,000 of taxable income?

Answer: 28.42 percent, computed as follows:

Description	Amount	Explanation
(1) Taxable income with additional $80,000 of taxable income	$240,000.00	$80,000 plus $160,000 taxable income (Example 1-3)
(2) Tax on $240,000 taxable income	$ 54,417.00	Using the rate schedule in Example 1-3, $54,417.00 = $52,222.50 + 33% × ($240,000 − $233,350)

[4]The tax rate schedules for single, married filing jointly, married filing separately, and head of household are included in Appendix D.

Description	Amount	Explanation
(3) Taxable income before additional $80,000 of taxable income	$160,000.00	Example 1-3
(4) Tax on $160,000 taxable income	$ 31,684.50	Example 1-3
Marginal tax rate on additional $80,000 of taxable income	**28.42%**	$\frac{\Delta \text{Tax}}{\Delta \text{Taxable income}} = [(2) - (4)]/[(1) - (3)]$

Note that Bill and Mercedes's marginal tax rate on the $80,000 increase in taxable income rests between the 28 percent and 33 percent bracket rates because a portion of the additional income ($233,350 − $160,000 = $73,350) is taxed at 28 percent with the remaining income ($240,000 − $233,350 = $6,650) taxed at 33 percent.

Example 1-5

Assume now that, instead of receiving a book advance, Bill and Mercedes start a new business that loses $60,000 this year (it results in $60,000 of additional tax deductions). What would be their marginal tax rate for these deductions?

Answer: 25.26 percent, computed as follows:

Description	Amount	Explanation
(1) Taxable income with additional $60,000 of tax deductions	$100,000.00	$160,000 taxable income (Example 1-3) less $60,000
(2) Tax on $100,000 taxable income	$ 16,487.50	Using the rate schedule in Example 1-3, $100,000 − $75,900 = $24,100 × 25% = $6,025 + $10,462.50
(3) Taxable income before additional $60,000 of tax deductions	$160,000.00	Example 1-3
(4) Tax on $160,000 taxable income	$ 31,684.50	Example 1-3
Marginal tax rate on additional $60,000 of tax deductions	**25.33%**	$\frac{\Delta \text{Tax}}{\Delta \text{Taxable income}} = [(2)-(4)]/[(1) - (3)]$

Bill and Mercedes's marginal tax rate on $60,000 of additional deductions (25.33 percent) differs from their marginal tax rate on $80,000 of additional taxable income (28.42 percent) in these scenarios because the relatively large increase in deductions in Example 1-5 causes some of their income to be taxed in a lower tax rate bracket, while the relatively large increase in income in Example 1-4 causes some of their income to be taxed in a higher tax rate bracket. Taxpayers often will face the same marginal tax rates for small changes in income and deductions.

THE KEY FACTS

Different Ways to Measure Tax Rates

- Marginal tax rate
  - The tax that applies to the next increment of income or deduction.
  - $= \frac{\Delta \text{Tax}}{\Delta \text{Taxable income}}$
  - Useful in tax planning.
- Average tax rate
  - A taxpayer's average level of taxation on each dollar of *taxable* income.
  - $= \frac{\text{Total tax}}{\text{Taxable income}}$
  - Useful in budgeting tax expense.
- Effective tax rate
  - A taxpayer's average rate of taxation on each dollar of *total* income (taxable *and* nontaxable income).
  - $= \frac{\text{Total tax}}{\text{Total income}}$
  - Useful in comparing the relative tax burdens of taxpayers.

The marginal tax rate is particularly useful in tax planning because it represents the rate of taxation or savings that would apply to additional taxable income (or tax deductions). In the Tax Planning Strategies and Related Limitations chapter, we discuss basic tax planning strategies that use the marginal tax rate.

The **average tax rate** represents a taxpayer's average level of taxation on each dollar of taxable income. Specifically,

Eq. 1-3

$$\text{Average Tax Rate} = \frac{\text{Total Tax}}{\text{Taxable Income}}$$

The average tax rate is often used in budgeting tax expense as a portion of income (i.e, determining what percent of taxable income earned is paid in tax).

The **effective tax rate** represents the taxpayer's average rate of taxation on each dollar of total income (sometimes referred to as economic income), including taxable *and* nontaxable income. Specifically,

Eq. 1-4

$$\text{Effective Tax Rate} = \frac{\text{Total Tax}}{\text{Total Income}}$$

Relative to the average tax rate, the effective tax rate provides a better depiction of a taxpayer's tax burden because it depicts the taxpayer's total tax paid as a ratio of the sum of both taxable and nontaxable income earned.

Example 1-6

Assuming Bill and Mercedes have $160,000 of taxable income and $10,000 of nontaxable income, what is their average tax rate?

Answer: 19.80 percent, computed as follows:

Description	Amount	Explanation
(1) Taxable income	$160,000.00	
(2) Tax on $160,000 taxable income	$ 31,684.50	Example 1-3
Average tax rate	**19.80%**	$\frac{\text{Total tax}}{\text{Taxable income}} = (2)/(1)$

We should not be surprised that Bill and Mercedes's average tax rate is lower than their marginal tax rate because, although they are currently in the 28 percent tax rate bracket, not all of their taxable income is subject to tax at 28 percent. The first $18,650 of their taxable income is taxed at 10 percent, their next $57,250 is taxed at 15 percent, their next $77,200 is taxed at 25 percent, and only their last $6,900 of taxable income is taxed at 28 percent. Thus, their average tax rate is considerably lower than their marginal tax rate.

Example 1-7

Again, given the same income figures as in Example 1-6 ($160,000 of taxable income and $10,000 of nontaxable income), what is Bill and Mercedes's effective tax rate?

Answer: 18.64 percent, computed as follows:

Description	Amount	Explanation
(1) Total income	$170,000.00	$160,000 taxable income plus $10,000 in nontaxable income (Example 1-6)
(2) Tax on $160,000 taxable income	$ 31,684.50	Example 1-3
Effective tax rate	**18.64%**	$\frac{\text{Total tax}}{\text{Total income}} = (2)/(1)$

Should we be surprised that the effective tax rate is lower than the *average* tax rate? No, because except when the taxpayer has more nondeductible expenses (such as fines or penalties) than nontaxable income (such as tax-exempt interest), the effective tax rate will be equal to or less than the average tax rate.

TAX RATE STRUCTURES

There are three basic tax rate structures used to determine a tax: proportional, progressive, and regressive.

Proportional Tax Rate Structure

A **proportional tax rate structure,** also known as a flat tax, imposes a constant tax rate throughout the tax base. As the tax base increases, the taxes paid increase proportionally. Because this rate stays the same throughout all levels of the tax base, the marginal tax rate remains constant and, in fact, equals the average tax rate (see Exhibit 1-1). The most common example of a proportional tax is a sales tax, although Steve Forbes proposed a flat income tax as part of his 1996 and 2000 presidential campaigns.

To calculate the tax owed for a proportional tax, simply use Equation 1-1 to multiply the tax base by the tax rate.

$$\text{Proportional tax} = \text{Tax base} \times \text{Tax rate}$$

EXHIBIT 1-1 Proportional Tax Rate

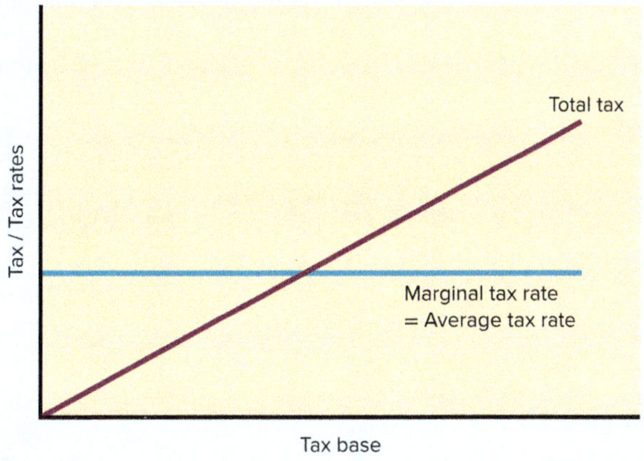

Example 1-8

Knowing her dad is a serious Bulldog fan, Margaret buys a $100 sweatshirt in downtown Athens. The city of Athens imposes a sales tax rate of 7 percent. How much tax does Margaret pay on the purchase?

Answer: $100 purchase (tax base) × 7% (tax rate) = $7

Progressive Tax Rate Structure

A **progressive tax rate structure** imposes an increasing marginal tax rate as the tax base increases. Thus as the tax base increases, both the marginal tax rate and the taxes paid increase. Common examples of progressive tax rate structures include federal and most state income taxes. The tax rate schedule in Example 1-3 is a progressive tax rate structure. As illustrated in Exhibit 1-2, the average tax rate in a progressive tax rate structure will always be less than or equal to the marginal tax rate.

EXHIBIT 1-2 **Progressive Tax Rate**

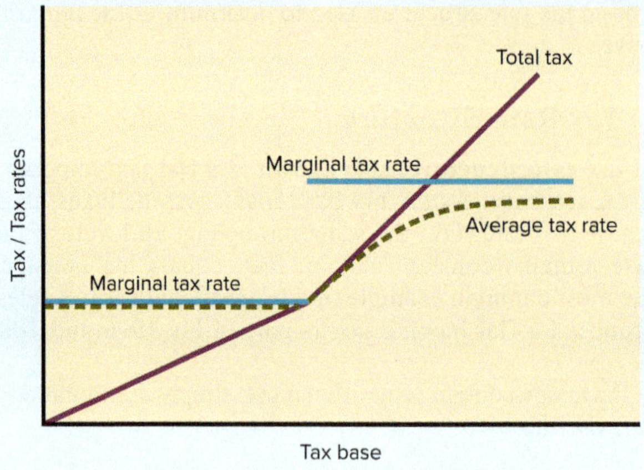

Regressive Tax Rate Structure

A **regressive tax rate structure** imposes a decreasing marginal tax rate as the tax base increases (see Exhibit 1-3). As the tax base increases, the taxes paid increase, but the marginal tax rate decreases. Regressive tax rate structures are not common. In the United States, the Social Security tax and federal and state unemployment taxes employ a regressive tax rate structure.[5]

However, some taxes are regressive when viewed in terms of effective tax rates. For example, a sales tax is a proportional tax by definition, because as taxable purchases increase, the sales tax rate remains constant.[6] Nonetheless, when you consider that the proportion of your total income spent on taxable purchases likely decreases as your total income increases, you can see the sales tax as a regressive tax.

EXHIBIT 1-3 **Regressive Tax Rate**

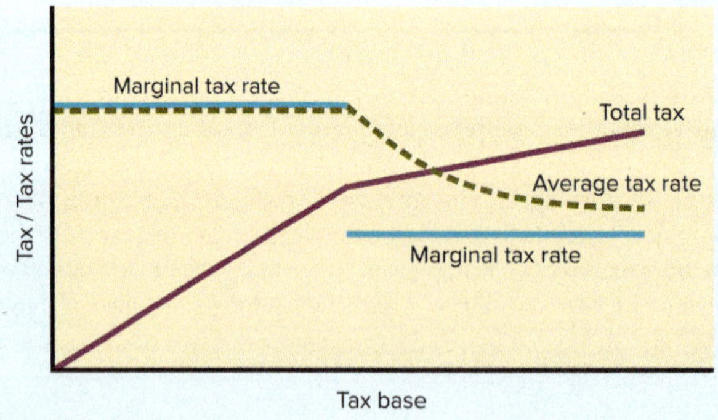

[5]Wages subject to the Social Security tax (6.2 percent in 2017) are capped each year ($127,200 in 2017). Wages in excess of the cap are not subject to the tax. As might be expected, the maximum Social Security retirement benefit is capped as a function of the maximum wage base. Likewise, the federal and state unemployment tax bases and related unemployment benefits are capped.

[6]For example, a destitute taxpayer likely spends all he makes on food and other items subject to the sales tax; thus, all of his income is subject to a sales tax. In contrast, a wealthy taxpayer likely spends only a small fraction of his income on items subject to sales tax (while saving the rest). Thus, less of wealthy taxpayers' total income is subject to the sales tax, which ultimately results in a lower effective tax rate.

Example 1-9

Bill and Mercedes have two single friends, Elizabeth and Marc, over for dinner. Elizabeth earns $300,000 as CFO of a company and spends $70,000 for purchases subject to the 7 percent sales tax. Marc, who earns $75,000 as a real estate agent, spends $30,000 of his income for taxable purchases. Let's compare their marginal, average, and effective tax rates for the sales tax with Bill and Mercedes, who spend $50,000 of their income for taxable purchases:

	Elizabeth	Bill and Mercedes	Marc
(1) Total income	$300,000	$170,000	$75,000
(2) Total purchases subject to 7% sales tax	$ 70,000	$ 50,000	$30,000
(3) Sales tax paid	$ 4,900	$ 3,500	$ 2,100
Marginal tax rate	7%	7%	7%
Average tax rate (3)/(2)	7%	7%	7%
Effective tax rate (3)/(1)	1.6%	2.1%	2.8%

Is the sales tax regressive?

Answer: Yes. In terms of *effective* tax rates, the sales tax is regressive.

THE KEY FACTS

Tax Rate Structures

- A proportional tax rate structure
  - Imposes a constant tax rate throughout the tax base.
  - As a taxpayer's tax base increases, the taxpayer's taxes increase proportionally.
  - The marginal tax rate remains constant and always equals the average tax rate.
- A progressive tax rate structure
  - Imposes an increasing marginal tax rate as the tax base increases.
  - As a taxpayer's tax base increases, both the marginal tax rate and the taxes paid increase.
- A regressive tax rate structure
  - Imposes a decreasing marginal tax rate as the tax base increases.
  - As a taxpayer's tax base increases, the marginal tax rate decreases while the total taxes paid increases.

When we consider the marginal and average tax rates in Example 1-9, the sales tax has a proportional tax rate structure. But when we look at the *effective* tax rates, the sales tax is a regressive tax. Indeed, Marc, who has the smallest total income, bears the highest effective tax rate, despite all three taxpayers being subject to the same marginal and average tax rates. Why do we see such a different picture when considering the effective tax rate? Because unlike the marginal and average tax rates, the effective tax rate captures the *incidence* of taxation, which relates to the ultimate economic burden of a tax. Thus, a comparison of effective tax rates is more informative about taxpayers' relative tax burdens.

TYPES OF TAXES

LO 1-4

"You can't live with 'em. You can't live without 'em." This statement has often been used in reference to bosses, parents, spouses, and significant others. To some degree, it applies equally as well to taxes. Although we all benefit in multiple ways from tax revenues, and all civilized nations impose them, it would be hard to find someone who *enjoys* paying them. Most people don't object to the idea of paying taxes. Instead, it's the way taxes are levied that many people, like Margaret's friend Eddy, dislike. Hence, the search for the "perfect" tax can be elusive. The following paragraphs describe the major types of taxes currently used by federal, state, and local governments. After this discussion, we describe the criteria for evaluating alternative tax systems.

THE KEY FACTS

Federal Taxes

- Income tax
  - The most significant tax assessed by the U.S. government.
  - Represents approximately 60 percent of all tax revenues collected in the United States.
  - Levied on individuals, corporations, estates, and trusts.
- Employment and unemployment taxes
  - Second largest group of taxes imposed by the U.S. government.

(continued)

Federal Taxes

The federal government imposes a variety of taxes to fund federal programs such as national defense, Social Security, an interstate highway system, educational programs, and Medicare. Major federal taxes include the individual and corporate income taxes, employment taxes, estate and gift taxes, and excise taxes (each discussed in detail in the following paragraphs). Noticeably absent from this list are a sales tax (a common tax for most state and local governments) and a **value-added tax** (a type of sales tax also commonly referred to as a VAT). Value-added taxes are imposed on the producers of goods

- Employment taxes consist of the Old Age, Survivors, and Disability Insurance (OASDI) tax, commonly called the Social Security tax, and the Medical Health Insurance (MHI) tax, also known as the Medicare tax.
- Unemployment taxes fund temporary unemployment benefits for individuals terminated from their jobs without cause.
- Excise taxes
  - Third largest group of taxes imposed by the U.S. government.
  - Levied on the *quantity* of products sold.
- Transfer taxes
  - Levied on the fair market values of wealth transfers upon death or by gift.

and services based on the value added to the goods and services at each stage of production. They are quite common in Europe.

Income Tax The most significant tax assessed by the U.S. government is the individual **income tax,** representing approximately 47.4 percent of all tax revenues collected in the United States in 2015. Despite the magnitude and importance of the federal income tax, its history is relatively short. Congress enacted the first U.S. personal income tax in 1861 to help fund the Civil War. This relatively minor tax (maximum tax rate of 5 percent) was allowed to expire in 1872. In 1892, Congress resurrected the income tax, but not without dissension among the states. In 1895, the income tax was challenged in *Pollock v. Farmers' Loan and Trust Company,* 157 U.S. 429 (1895). The U.S. Supreme Court ruled that the income tax was unconstitutional because direct taxes were prohibited by the Constitution unless the taxes were apportioned across states based upon their populations. This ruling, however, did not deter Congress. In July 1909, Congress sent a proposed constitutional amendment to the states to remove any doubt as to whether income taxes were allowed by the Constitution—and in February 1913, the 16th Amendment was ratified.

Congress then enacted the Revenue Act of 1913, which included a graduated income tax structure with a maximum rate of 6 percent. The income tax has been an important source of tax revenues for the U.S. government ever since. Today, income taxes are levied on individuals (maximum rate of 39.6 percent), corporations (maximum rate of 35 percent), estates (maximum rate of 39.6 percent), and trusts (maximum rate of 39.6 percent). Higher income taxpayers must also pay a 3.8 percent tax on their net investment income. As Exhibit 1-4 illustrates, the individual income tax and employment taxes represent the largest sources of federal tax revenues. We discuss each of these taxes in greater detail later in the text.

Employment and Unemployment Taxes Employment and unemployment taxes are the second largest group of taxes imposed by the U.S. government. **Employment taxes** consist of the Old Age, Survivors, and Disability Insurance (OASDI) tax, commonly called the Social Security tax, and the Medical Health Insurance (MHI) tax known as the Medicare tax. The **Social Security tax** pays the monthly retirement, survivor, and disability benefits for qualifying individuals, whereas the **Medicare tax** pays for medical insurance for individuals who are elderly or disabled. The tax base for the Social Security

EXHIBIT 1-4 U.S. Federal Tax Revenues

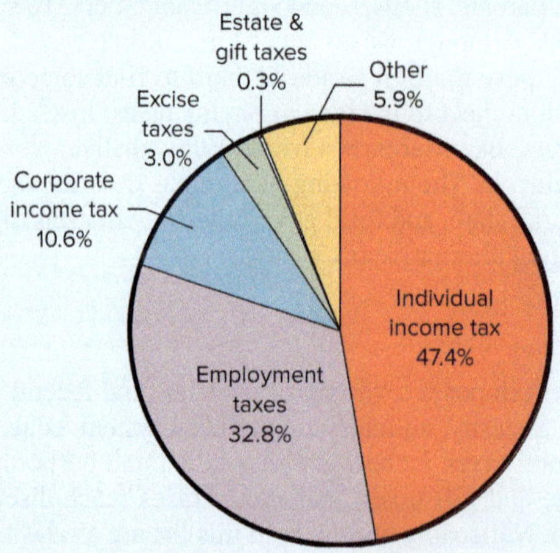

Source: Treasury Department (Fiscal Year 2015).

and Medicare taxes is wages or salary, and the rates are 12.4 percent and 2.9 percent, respectively, in 2017. In 2017, the tax base for the Social Security tax is capped at $127,200. The tax base for the Medicare tax is not capped. Employers and employees split these taxes equally. Self-employed individuals, however, must pay these taxes in their entirety. In this case, the tax is often referred to as the **self-employment tax.** We discuss these taxes in more depth later in the text. There is a .9 percent Additional Medicare Tax levied on income earned by employees (employers are exempt) and self-employed taxpayers on income exceeding a threshold amount (see Individual Income Tax Computation and Tax Credits for details).

In addition to the Social Security and Medicare taxes, employers are also required to pay federal and state **unemployment taxes,** which fund temporary unemployment benefits for individuals terminated from their jobs without cause. As you might expect, the tax base for the unemployment taxes is also wages or salary. Currently, the federal unemployment tax rate is 6.0 percent. The wage base is the first $7,000 of wages received during the year. The U.S. government allows a credit for state unemployment taxes paid up to 5.4 percent. Thus, the effective federal unemployment tax rate may be as low as 0.6 percent (6.0% – 5.4% = 0.6%).[7]

Excise Taxes **Excise taxes** are taxes levied on the retail sale of particular products. They differ from other taxes in that the tax base for an excise tax typically depends on the *quantity* purchased, rather than a monetary amount. The federal government imposes a number of excise taxes on goods such as alcohol, diesel fuel, gasoline, and tobacco products and on services such as telephone use, air transportation, and tanning beds. In addition, states often impose excise taxes on these same items.

Example 1-10

On the drive home from Athens, Georgia, Margaret stops at Gasup-n-Go. On each gallon of gasoline she buys, Margaret pays 18.4 cents of federal excise tax and 7.5 cents of state excise tax (plus 4 percent sales tax). Could Margaret have avoided paying excise tax had she stopped in Florida instead?

Answer: No. Had she stopped in Florida instead, Margaret would have paid the same federal excise tax. Additionally, Florida imposes higher state taxes on gas.

Because the producer of the product pays the excise tax to the government, many consumers are not even aware that businesses build these taxes into the prices consumers pay. Nonetheless, consumers bear the burden of the taxes because of the higher price.

THE KEY FACTS

State and Local Taxes

- Sales and use taxes
  - The tax base for a sales tax is the retail sales of goods and some services.
  - The tax base for the use tax is the retail price of goods owned, possessed, or consumed within a state that were *not* purchased within the state.
- Property taxes
  - Property taxes are ad valorem taxes, meaning that the tax base for each is the fair market value of the property.

(*continued*)

Transfer Taxes Although they are a relatively minor tax compared to the income tax in terms of revenues collected, federal **transfer taxes**—estate and gift taxes—can be substantial for certain individual taxpayers and have been the subject of much debate in recent years. The **estate tax** (labeled the "death tax" by its opponents) and **gift taxes** are based on the fair market values of wealth transfers upon death or by gift, respectively. The estate and gift tax rates have traditionally been high (the maximum tax rate through 2009 was 45 percent) compared to income tax rates and can be burdensome without proper planning. In 2017, the maximum rate imposed on gifts is 40 percent. Most taxpayers, however, are not subject to estate and gift taxation because of the annual gift exclusion and gift and estate unified tax credits. The annual gift exclusion allows a taxpayer to transfer $14,000 of gifts per donee (gift recipient) each year without gift taxation. In 2017, the unified tax credit exempts from taxation

[7]Although employers pay both federal and state unemployment taxes, all unemployment benefits actually are administered and paid by state governments.

- Real property taxes consist of taxes on land, structures, and improvements permanently attached to land.
- Personal property taxes include taxes on all other types of property, both tangible and intangible.
- Income taxes
  - Most state taxable income calculations largely conform to the federal taxable income calculations, with a limited number of modifications.
- Excise taxes
  - States typically impose excise taxes on items subject to federal excise tax.

EXHIBIT 1-5 Average State Tax Revenues

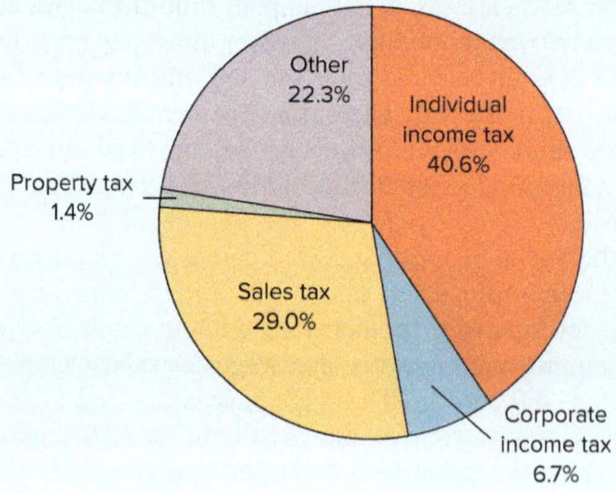

Source: U.S. Bureau of Census (2015).

$5,490,000 in bequests (transfers upon death) and gifts. Thus, only large transfers are subject to the gift and estate taxes.

State and Local Taxes

Like the federal government, state and local governments (such as counties, cities, and school districts) use a variety of taxes to generate revenues for their programs (such as education, highways, and police and fire departments). Some of the more common **state** and **local taxes** include income taxes, sales and use taxes, excise taxes, and property taxes. Typically, as shown in Exhibit 1-5, the largest state tax revenues are generated by individual income taxes and state sales taxes—in contrast to federal revenues, which rely primarily on income and employment taxes. Local tax revenues are predominantly from sales and property taxes.

Income Taxes Currently, most states and the District of Columbia impose income taxes on individuals and corporations who either reside in or earn income within the state.[8] This requires individuals living in these states to file a state tax return in addition to the federal return they already file. Calculations of individual and corporate taxable income vary with state law. Nonetheless, most state taxable income calculations largely conform to the federal taxable income calculations, with a limited number of modifications, although the tax rates are significantly less than the federal rate. The state of California is a notable exception because it has numerous modifications. Certain local governments such as New York City also impose an income tax and, again, the local calculations generally follow the respective state taxable income calculation.

Sales and Use Taxes Most states, the District of Columbia, and local governments impose sales and use taxes. The tax base for a **sales tax** is the retail sales of goods and some services, and retailers are responsible for collecting and remitting the tax;

[8]Currently, Alaska, Florida, Nevada, South Dakota, Texas, Washington, and Wyoming have no personal income tax, and New Hampshire and Tennessee only tax individual dividend and interest income. Nevada and Wyoming do not impose taxes on corporate income, and South Dakota only taxes banks. Washington imposes a gross receipts tax instead of a corporate income tax. Texas and Ohio have an activity-based tax that is based on net income or gross receipts.

typically, sales tax is collected at the point of sale. The tax base for the **use tax** is the retail price of goods owned, possessed, or consumed within a state that were *not* purchased within the state. The purpose of a use tax is to discourage taxpayers from buying goods out of state in order to avoid or minimize the sales tax in their home state. At the same time, by eliminating the incentive to purchase goods out of state, a use tax removes any competitive disadvantage a retailer may incur from operating in a state with a high sales tax. States with a sales tax allow taxpayers to take a use tax credit on goods purchased out of state to mitigate the potential for double taxation on goods subject to sales tax in another state.

Example 1-11

Margaret buys three new Lands' End shirts for her dad for $100. Because Lands' End does not have a business presence in Florida, it does not collect Florida sales tax on the $100 purchase. Does Margaret's purchase escape Florida taxation?

Answer: No. Because Florida has a 6 percent use tax, Margaret is liable for $6 in use tax on the purchase ($6 = $100 × .06).

Despite the potential importance of the use tax as a source of state tax revenue, states have only recently begun to enforce it. Poor compliance is therefore not surprising; indeed, many individuals have never heard of the use tax. While it is relatively easy to enforce it on goods obtained out of state if they are subject to a registration requirement, such as automobiles, it is quite difficult for states to tax most other out-of-state purchases. The state of Florida is not likely to search your closet to look for tax-evaded Lands' End shirts. Note, however, that the majority of states have joined together (www.streamlinedsalestax.org) to try to subject all Internet sales to sales taxes.

Property Taxes State and local governments commonly use two types of property taxes as sources of revenue: **real property taxes** and **personal property taxes.** Both are **ad valorem taxes,** meaning that the tax base for each is the fair market value of the property, and both are generally collected annually (if imposed at all).

Real property consists of land, structures, and improvements permanently attached to land, whereas *personal property* includes all other types of property, both tangible and intangible. Common examples of tangible personal property potentially subject to state and local taxation include automobiles, boats, private planes, business inventory, equipment, and furniture. Intangible personal property potentially subject to state and local taxation includes stocks, bonds, and intellectual property. Relative to personal property tax, real property taxes are easier to administer because real property is not movable and purchases often have to be registered with the state, thereby making it easy to identify the tax base and taxpayer. Furthermore, the taxing body can estimate market values for real property without much difficulty. In contrast, personal property is generally mobile (easier to hide) and may be more difficult to value; therefore, personal property taxes are difficult to enforce. Accordingly, whereas all states and the District of Columbia provide for a real property tax, only a majority of states currently impose personal property taxes, most of which are assessed at the time of licensing or registration. However, most states do collect personal property taxes on business property.

Excise Taxes We've said that the tax base for excise taxes is typically the quantity of an item or service purchased. States typically impose excise taxes on items subject to federal excise tax. Transactions subject to state excise tax often include the sale of alcohol, diesel fuel, gasoline, tobacco products, and telephone services.

Implicit Taxes

All the taxes discussed above are **explicit taxes;** that is, they are taxes directly imposed by a government and are easily quantified. **Implicit taxes,** on the other hand, are indirect taxes—not paid directly to the government—that result from a tax advantage the government grants to certain transactions to satisfy social, economic, or other objectives. Implicit taxes are defined as the reduced before-tax return that a tax-favored asset produces because of its tax-advantaged status. Let's examine this concept more closely.

First of all, what does it mean to be *tax-favored*? An asset is said to be tax-favored when the income the asset produces is either excluded from the tax base or subject to a lower (preferential) tax rate, or if the asset generates some other tax benefit such as large tax deductions. These tax benefits, *all other things equal,* result in higher after-tax profits (or lower after-tax costs) from investing in the tax-advantaged assets.

Why do tax-advantaged assets bear an implicit tax, or a reduced before-tax return as a result of the tax advantage? The answer is simple economics. The tax benefits associated with the tax-favored asset increase the demand for the asset. Increased demand drives up the price of the asset, which in turn reduces its before-tax return, which is an implicit tax by definition. Consider Example 1-12.

Example 1-12

Consider two bonds, one issued by the Coca-Cola Co. and the other issued by the state of Georgia. Both bonds have similar nontax characteristics (risk, for example), the same face value of $10,000, and the same market interest rate of 10 percent. The only difference between the two bonds is that the interest income from the Coca-Cola Co. bond is subject to a 20 percent income tax rate, whereas the interest income from the State of Georgia bond is tax-exempt with a 0 percent tax rate. Which of the two bonds is a better investment and should therefore have a higher demand?

	Price	Before-Tax* Return	Interest Income	Income† Tax	After-Tax Income	After-Tax* Return
Coca-Cola Bond	$10,000	10%	$1,000	$200	$ 800	8%
State of GA Bond	$10,000	10%	$1,000	$ 0	$1,000	10%

*Before-tax return is calculated as the before-tax income divided by the price of the bond. Likewise, after-tax return is calculated as the after-tax income divided by the price of the bond.
†Income tax equals the taxable interest income ($1,000) multiplied by the assumed income marginal tax rate (20 percent).

Answer: Compare the after-tax returns of the bonds. Given the difference between the return after taxes (10 percent vs. 8 percent), the better investment—again, all other investment features being equal—is the State of Georgia bond because it provides a higher *after*-tax return. Because all investors in this example should prefer to buy the State of Georgia bond, the demand for the bond will be high, and its price should increase. This increase in price leads to a lower before-tax return due to the bond's tax-favored status (this is an implicit tax).

Example 1-12 is a basic illustration of the need to consider the role of taxes in investment decisions. Without understanding the relative tax effects associated with each bond, we cannot correctly compare their after-tax returns.

At what point in Example 1-12 would you be indifferent between investing in the Coca-Cola Co. bond and the State of Georgia bond? Assuming each bond has the same nontax characteristics, you would be indifferent between them when they both provide the same after-tax rate of return. This could occur if the state of Georgia raised the price of its bond from $10,000 to $12,500 ($1,000 interest/$12,500 price = 8% return). Or the state of Georgia could lower its bond interest payment from $1,000 to $800 ($800 interest/$10,000 price = 8% return). Either way, the state of Georgia benefits from selling the tax-exempt bonds—either at a higher price or at a lower interest rate relative to other bonds. Let's look more closely at this latter option, because it is, in fact, what many tax-exempt bond issuers choose to do.

	Price	Before-Tax Return	Interest Income	Income Tax	After-Tax Income	After-Tax Return
Coca-Cola Bond	$10,000	10%	$1,000	$200	$800	8%
State of GA Bond	$10,000	8%	$ 800	$ 0	$800	8%

At this point, assuming each bond has the same nontax characteristics, an investor should be indifferent between the Coca-Cola Co. bond and the State of Georgia bond. What is the tax burden on investors choosing the Coca-Cola Co. bond? Coca-Cola Co. bond investors are paying $200 of income taxes (explicit taxes). What is the tax burden on investors choosing the State of Georgia bond? While it is true they are subject to zero income taxes (explicit taxes), they are subject to implicit taxes in the form of the $200 less in interest income they accept. This $200 reduced interest income (2 percent reduced before-tax rate of return) is an implicit tax. Although the investors in the State of Georgia bond are not paying this tax directly, they are paying it indirectly.

Does this happen in real life? Yes. Municipal bond interest income (interest income paid on bonds issued by state and local governments) generally is not subject to federal income taxation. Because of their tax-advantaged status, municipalities are able to pay a lower interest rate on their bond issuances and investors are willing to accept the lower rate. This type of indirect federal subsidy allows municipalities to raise money at a reduced cost without the need of direct federal subsidy or approval.

Although we were able to quantify the implicit taxes paid in the above example, in reality it is very difficult to estimate the amount of implicit taxes paid. For example, the federal government subsidizes housing by allowing taxpayers to deduct mortgage interest on their principal residence. Does this subsidy result in an implicit tax in the form of higher housing prices? Probably. Nonetheless, it would be difficult to quantify this implicit tax.

Despite the difficulty in quantifying implicit taxes, you should understand the concept of implicit taxes so you can make informed judgments about the attractiveness of alternative investments and the relative total tax burdens of tax-advantaged investments (considering both explicit and implicit taxes).

THE KEY FACTS

Implicit Taxes

- Implicit taxes are indirect taxes that result from a tax advantage the government grants to certain transactions to satisfy social, economic, or other objectives.
- Implicit taxes are defined as the reduced before-tax return that a tax-favored asset produces because of its tax-advantaged status.
- Implicit taxes are difficult to quantify but important to understand in evaluating the relative tax burdens of tax-advantaged investments.

EVALUATING ALTERNATIVE TAX SYSTEMS

LO 1-5

Although it may appear that tax systems are designed without much forethought, in truth lawmakers engage in continuous debate over the basic questions of whom to tax, what to tax, and how much to tax. Margaret's friend Eddy is obviously upset with what he views as an unfair tax system. But fairness, as we will discuss shortly, is often like beauty—it is in the eye of the beholder. What is fair to one may seem blatantly unfair to others. In the following paragraphs, we offer various criteria (sufficiency, equity, certainty, convenience, and economy) you can use to evaluate alternative tax systems.[9] Satisfying everyone at the same time is difficult. Hence, the spirited debate on tax reform.

[9]Adam Smith identified and described the latter four criteria in *The Wealth of Nations.*

THE KEY FACTS

Evaluating Alternative Tax Systems—Sufficiency

- Sufficiency involves assessing the aggregate size of the tax revenues that must be generated and ensuring that the tax system provides these revenues.
- Static forecasting ignores how taxpayers may alter their activities in response to a proposed tax law change and bases projected tax revenues on the existing state of transactions.
- Dynamic forecasting attempts to account for possible taxpayer responses to a proposed tax law change.

Sufficiency

Judging the **sufficiency** of a tax system means assessing the size of the tax revenues it must generate and ensuring that it provides them. For a tax system to be successful, it must provide sufficient revenues to pay for governmental expenditures for a defense system, social services, and so on. This sounds easy enough: Estimate the amount of government expenditures that will be required, and then design the system to generate enough revenues to pay for these expenses. In reality, however, accurately estimating governmental expenditures and revenues is a rather daunting and imprecise process. Estimating governmental expenditures is difficult because it is impossible to predict the unknown. For example, in recent years governmental expenditures have increased due to the terrorist attacks of September 11, 2001, the Afghanistan and Iraq Wars, natural disasters, economic stimulus, and health care. Likewise, estimating governmental revenues is difficult because tax revenues are the result of transactions influenced by these same national events, the economy, and other factors. Thus, precisely estimating and matching governmental expenditures with tax revenues is nearly impossible.

The task of estimating tax revenues becomes even more daunting when the government attempts to make significant changes to the existing tax system or design a new one. Whenever Congress proposes changing who is taxed, what is taxed, or how much is taxed, its members must consider the taxpayer response to the change. That affects the amount of tax collected, and how forecasters predict what taxpayers will do affects how much revenue they estimate.

Static versus Dynamic Forecasting One option in forecasting revenue is to ignore how taxpayers may alter their activities in response to a tax law change and to base projected tax revenues on the existing state of transactions, a process referred to as **static forecasting.** However, this type of forecasting may result in a large discrepancy in projected versus actual tax revenues if taxpayers do change their behavior. The other choice is to attempt to account for possible taxpayer responses to the tax law change, a process referred to as **dynamic forecasting.** Dynamic forecasting is ultimately only as good as the assumptions underlying the forecasts and does not guarantee accurate results. Nonetheless, considering how taxpayers may alter their activities in response to a tax law change is a useful exercise to identify the potential ramifications of the change, even if the revenue projections ultimately miss the mark. For more information on the Congressional Revenue Estimating Process, including dynamic scoring, see the Joint Committee on Taxation explanation at https://www.jct.gov/publications.html?func=startdown&id=3720.

In some cases, static forecasting can lead to a tax consequence opposite the desired outcome. In Example 1-13, we might estimate that given Heflin's close proximity to other cities with a $1.00 cigarette tax, the number of packs of cigarettes sold within the city would drop significantly to, say, 50,000. In this case, the tax increase would actually *decrease* tax revenues by $100,000 ($400,000 existing tax − $300,000 new tax)—not a good outcome if the goal was to increase tax revenues.

Example 1-13

The city of Heflin would like to increase tax revenues by $2,000,000 to pay for needed roadwork. A concerned taxpayer recently proposed increasing the cigarette excise tax from $1.00 per pack of cigarettes to $6.00 per pack to raise the additional needed revenue. Last year, 400,000 packs of cigarettes were sold in the city. Will the tax be successful in raising the $2,000,000 revenue?

Answer: Not likely. The proposed tax increase of $5, and the assumption that 400,000 packs will still be sold, is an example of static forecasting: It ignores that many taxpayers may respond to the tax change by quitting, cutting down, or buying cheaper cigarettes in the next town.

Income versus Substitution Effects Example 1-13 described proposed changes in an excise tax, which is a proportional tax. In terms of a progressive tax such as an *income* tax, a tax rate increase or an expansion of the tax base can result in one of two taxpayer responses, both of which are important for dynamic forecasting. The **income effect** predicts that when taxpayers are taxed more (when, say, a tax rate increases from 25 to 28 percent), they will work harder to generate the same after-tax dollars. The **substitution effect** predicts that when taxpayers are taxed more, rather than work more, they will substitute nontaxable activities like leisure pursuits for taxable ones because the marginal value of taxable activities has decreased. Which view is accurate? The answer depends on the taxpayer. Consider the following examples.

Example 1-14

Margaret's friend George, who earns $40,000 taxable income as a mechanic, is taxed at an average rate of 10 percent ($4,000 of tax). If Congress increases the income tax rate such that George's average tax rate increases from 10 percent to 25 percent, how much more income tax will he pay?

Answer: It depends on whether the income effect or the substitution effect is operating. Assuming George is single and cannot afford a net decrease in his after-tax income, he will likely work more (the income effect rules). Prior to the tax rate increase, George had $36,000 of after-tax income ($40,000 taxable income less $4,000 tax). With the increased tax rate, George will have to earn $48,000 of taxable income to keep $36,000 after taxes [$48,000 – ($48,000 × .25) = $36,000]. Thus, if the income effect rules, the government will collect $12,000 of federal income tax from George, or $8,000 more than under the previous lower tax rate. In this scenario, the tax change increases government revenues because of the increased tax rate *and* the increased tax base.

Whether the substitution effect or the income effect will describe any individual taxpayer's reaction to a tax increase is something we can only guess. But some factors—such as having higher disposable income—are likely to correlate with the substitution effect.

Example 1-15

What if: Now let's assume that George is married and has two young children. Both he and his wife work, and they file a tax return jointly with a 10 percent average tax rate. Either of their incomes is sufficient to meet necessities, even after the tax rate increase. But fixed child care costs make the marginal wage rate (the after-tax hourly wage less hourly child care cost) more sensitive to tax rate increases. In this case, the lower-earning spouse may choose to work less. Suppose George quits his full-time job and takes a part-time position that pays $10,000 to spend more time with his kids and to pursue his passion, reading sports novels. What are the taxes on George's income?

Answer: In this case, George will owe $2,500 tax ($10,000 × .25 = $2,500). Here, the substitution effect operates, and the government collects much less than it would have if George had maintained his full-time position, because the tax rate increase had a negative effect on the tax base.

As Examples 1-14 and 1-15 illustrate, the response to a tax law change can vary by taxpayer and can greatly affect the magnitude of tax revenues generated by the change. Herein lies one of the challenges in significantly changing an existing tax system or designing a new one: If a tax system fails to generate sufficient revenues, the government must seek other sources to pay for governmental expenditures. The most common source of these additional funds for the federal government is the issuance of debt instruments such as Treasury bonds. This, however, is only a short-term solution to a budget deficit. Debt issuances require both interest and principal payments, which require the federal government to identify even more sources of revenue to service the debt issued or to cut governmental spending (both of which may be unpopular choices with voters). A third option is for the government to default on its debt obligations. However, the costs of this option are potentially devastating. If the historical examples of Mexico, Brazil, Argentina, and Greece are any guide, a U.S. government default on its debt obligations would likely devalue the U.S. dollar severely and have extreme negative consequences for the U.S. capital markets.

The best option is for the government to match its revenues with its expenses—that is, not to spend more than it collects. State governments seem to be more successful in this endeavor than the U.S. federal government. Indeed, all states except Vermont require a balanced budget each year, whereas the federal government has had deficit spending for most of the last 40 years.

TAXES IN THE REAL WORLD National Debt

How much debt does the U.S. have today? About $19.8 trillion. Almost $14.3 trillion of the national debt is held by public investors, including individual bondholders; institutional investors; and foreign governments such as China, the United Kingdom, and Brazil. The $5.5 trillion remaining amount represents intragovernmental holdings—primarily Social Security.

Is $19.8 trillion too much to handle? The key issue is fiscal sustainability: the ability to pay off a debt in the future. Rising debt also has other negative consequences, such as higher interest payments, a need for higher taxes, restricting policy makers' fiscal policy choices, and increasing the probability of a sudden fiscal crisis. If nothing is done to change the national debt trajectory, the debt will grow faster than the economy.

Is the national debt sustainable? The federal government has been recording budget deficits that are a larger share of the economy than any year since the end of World War II. With an aging population, Social Security and other benefits will require larger expenditures. By the end of the current decade, barring any significant policy shifts, the vast majority of federal tax revenue will be consumed by just four expenditures: interest on the debt, Medicare, Medicaid, and Social Security. To finance other government expenditures, including defense and all other discretionary programs, policy makers will have to borrow the money to pay for them.

Equity

We've looked at the challenges of designing a tax system that provides sufficient revenues to pay for governmental expenditures. An equally challenging issue is how the tax burden should be distributed across taxpayers. At the heart of this issue is the concept of **equity,** or fairness. Fairness is inherently subject to personal interpretation, and informed minds often disagree about what is fair. There is no "one-size-fits-all" definition of equity or fairness. Nonetheless, it is informative to consider in broad terms what makes a fair or equitable tax system.

In general terms, a tax system is considered fair or equitable if the tax is based on the taxpayer's ability to pay. Taxpayers with a greater ability to pay tax, pay more tax. In broad terms, each of the federal, state, and local taxes we've discussed satisfies this criterion. For example, those individuals with greater taxable income, purchases, property, and estates (upon death) generally pay higher dollar amounts in federal income tax, sales tax, property tax, and estate tax. If this is the case, why is there so much debate over the fairness of the U.S. income tax system? The answer is that equity is more complex than our first definition suggests. Let's take a closer look.

Horizontal versus Vertical Equity Two basic types of equity are relevant to tax systems. **Horizontal equity** means that two taxpayers in similar situations pay the same tax. In broad terms, each of the federal, state, and local taxes discussed satisfy this definition. Two individual taxpayers with the same taxable income, same purchases, same value of property, and same estate value pay the same federal income tax, sales tax, property tax, and estate tax. However, on closer inspection we might argue that each of these tax systems is *not* horizontally equitable. Here are some examples:

- Two individual taxpayers with the same income will not pay the same federal income tax if one individual's income was earned as salary and the other individual's income was tax-exempt municipal bond interest income, dividend income, or capital gain(s) income, which can be subject to a lower tax rate.
- Two individuals with the same dollar amount of purchases will not pay the same sales tax if one buys a higher proportion of goods that are subject to a lower sales tax rate, such as groceries.
- Two individuals with real estate of the same value will not pay the same property tax if one individual owns farmland, which is generally subject to a lower property tax rate.
- Finally, two individuals with estates of the same value will not pay the same estate tax if one individual bequeaths more of her property to charity or a spouse, because these transfers are not subject to estate tax.

THE KEY FACTS

Evaluating Alternative Tax Systems—Equity

- Equity considers how the tax burden should be distributed across taxpayers.
- Horizontal equity means that two taxpayers in similar situations pay the same tax.
- Vertical equity is achieved when taxpayers with greater ability to pay tax, pay more tax relative to taxpayers with a lesser ability to pay tax.

These failures of horizontal equity are due to what we call *tax preferences*. Governments provide tax preferences for a variety of reasons, such as to encourage investment or further social objectives. Whether we view these tax preferences as appropriate greatly influences whether we consider a tax system to be fair in general and horizontally equitable in particular.

The second type of equity to consider in evaluating a tax system is **vertical equity.** Vertical equity is achieved when taxpayers with greater ability to pay tax, pay more tax than taxpayers with less ability to pay. We can think of vertical equity in terms of tax dollars paid or in terms of tax rates. Proponents of a flat income tax or of a sales tax—both of which are proportional tax rate structures—are more likely to argue that vertical equity is achieved when taxpayers with a greater ability to pay tax, simply pay more in tax *dollars*. Proponents of a progressive tax system are more likely to argue that taxpayers with a greater ability to pay should be subject to a higher tax *rate*. This view is based upon the argument that the *relative* burden of a flat tax rate decreases as a taxpayer's income increases. Which is the correct answer? There is no correct answer. Nonetheless, many feel very strongly regarding one view or the other.

Our discussion has focused on how we can view alternative tax rate structures in terms of vertical equity, ignoring the role that the tax base plays in determining vertical equity. Indeed, focusing on the tax rate structure in evaluating a tax system is appropriate only if the tax base chosen—whether it's taxable income, purchases, property owned, or something else—accurately portrays a taxpayer's ability to pay. This can be a rather strong assumption. Consider the sales tax in Example 1-9. Although taxable purchases in this example increase as the taxpayers' total incomes increase, total incomes increase at a much faster rate than taxable purchases. Thus, the gap between taxable purchases and total income widens as total income increases. The end result is that the effective tax rates for those with a greater ability to pay are *lower* than for those taxpayers with a lesser ability to pay, making this tax regressive. Regressive tax rate structures are generally considered not to satisfy vertical equity, unless you strongly believe that those with a greater ability to pay do so simply by paying more tax dollars, albeit at a lower tax rate. In sum, evaluating vertical equity in terms of effective tax rates may be much more informative than simply evaluating tax rate structures.

Certainty

Certainty means that taxpayers should be able to determine when to pay the tax, where to pay the tax, and how to determine the tax. Determining when and where to pay each of the taxes previously discussed is relatively easy. For example, individual federal income tax returns and the remaining balance of taxes owed must be filed with the Internal Revenue Service each year on or before April 15th. Likewise, sales taxes, property taxes, and excise taxes are each determined with relative ease: Sales taxes are based on the value of taxable purchases, property taxes are generally based on assessed property values, and excise taxes are based on the number of taxable units purchased. Indeed, these taxes are calculated for the taxpayer and often charged at regular intervals or at the point of purchase; they do not require a tax return.

In contrast, income taxes are often criticized as being too complex. What are taxable versus nontaxable forms of income? What are deductible/nondeductible expenses? When should income or expenses be reported? For wage earners with few investments, the answers to these questions are straightforward. For business owners and individuals with a lot of investments, the answers are nontrivial. Yearly tax law changes enacted by Congress can make it more difficult to determine a taxpayer's current tax liability, much less plan for the future.

THE KEY FACTS

Evaluating Alternative Tax Systems—Certainty, Convenience, and Economy

- Certainty
  - Means taxpayers should be able to determine when, where, and how much tax to pay.
  - Determining when and where to pay each of the taxes previously discussed is relatively easy.
  - The income tax has been criticized for its complexity in determining how much to pay.
- Convenience
  - Means a tax system should be designed to facilitate the collection of tax revenues without undue hardship on the taxpayer or the government.
  - Various tax systems meet this criterion by tying the collection of the tax as closely as possible to the transaction that generates it.
- Economy
  - Means a tax system should minimize its compliance and administration costs.
  - May be viewed from both the taxpayers' and the government's perspectives.

Convenience

Convenience suggests that a tax system should be designed to facilitate the collection of tax revenues without undue hardship on the taxpayer or the government. Various tax systems meet this criterion by tying the collection of the tax as closely as possible to the transaction that generates it (when it is most convenient to pay the tax). For example, retailers collect sales taxes when buyers purchase goods. Thus, it is difficult for the buyer to avoid paying sales tax, assuming she is transacting with an ethical retailer. Likewise, employers withhold federal income and Social Security taxes directly from wage earners' paychecks, which speeds the government's collection of the taxes and makes it difficult for the taxpayer to evade the taxes. If tax withholdings are not sufficient relative to the taxpayer's anticipated income tax liability, the taxpayer is required to make quarterly estimated tax installments. Individual quarterly estimated payments are due on April 15, June 15, September 15, and January 15, whereas corporate estimated tax payments are due on the 15th day of the third, sixth, ninth, and twelfth months of the corporation's fiscal year.

Economy

Economy requires that a good tax system should minimize the compliance and administration costs associated with the tax system. We can view economy from both the taxpayers' and the government's perspectives. Believe it or not, most tax systems fare well in terms of economy, at least from the government's perspective. For example, the current IRS budget represents approximately $\frac{1}{2}$ of a percent of every tax dollar collected. Compared to the typical costs of a collection agency, this is quite low.

How about from the taxpayer's perspective? Here the picture is a bit different. The sales tax imposes no administrative burden on the taxpayer and only small administrative costs on the local retailer. However, out-of-state sellers argue that collecting and remitting use taxes for thousands of state and city jurisdictions would be a substantial burden. Other taxes such as excise taxes and property taxes also impose minimal administrative costs on the taxpayer. In contrast, as we've seen, the income tax is often criticized for the compliance costs imposed on the taxpayer. Indeed, for certain taxpayers, record-keeping costs, accountant fees, attorney fees, and so on can be substantial. Advocates of alternative tax systems often challenge the income tax on this criterion.

Evaluating Tax Systems—The Trade-Off

At the heart of any debate on tax reform are fundamental decisions and concessions based on the five criteria we've just discussed. Interestingly enough, much of the debate regarding alternative tax systems can be reduced to a choice between simplicity and fairness. Those taxes that generally are simpler and easier to administer, such as the sales tax, are typically viewed as less fair. Those taxes that may be viewed as more fair, such as the federal income tax, often are more complex to administer. Thus, Margaret's friend Eddy faces a difficult choice about which type of tax system to advocate, as do all taxpayers. An understanding of the evaluative criteria should be helpful to anyone trying to reconcile the trade-offs among alternative tax proposals.

CONCLUSION

In almost any society, taxes are a part of life. They influence decisions about personal finance, investment, business, and politics. In this chapter, we introduced the basic concepts of why one should study tax, what is a tax, and how to calculate a tax. We also discussed various tax rates, tax rate structures, and different types of taxes imposed by federal, state, and local governments. Finally, we discussed the criteria that one might use to evaluate alternative tax rate systems. To make informed personal finance, investment, business, and political decisions, one must have a basic understanding of these items. In the following chapters we expand the discussion of how taxes influence these decisions while providing a basic understanding of our federal income tax system. Read on and learn more!

Summary

Demonstrate how taxes influence basic business, investment, personal, and political decisions. **LO 1-1**

- Taxes are significant costs that influence many basic business, investment, and personal decisions.
  - *Business decisions:* What organizational form to take; where to locate; how to compensate employees; appropriate debt mix; owning versus renting equipment and property; how to distribute profits; and so forth.
  - *Investment decisions:* Alternative methods for saving for education or retirement, and so forth.
  - *Personal finance decisions:* Evaluating job offers; gift or estate planning; owning a home versus renting; and so forth.
- Taxes also play a major part in the political process. Major parties typically have very diverse views on whom, what, and how much to tax.

Discuss what constitutes a tax and the general objectives of taxes. **LO 1-2**

- The general purpose of taxes is to fund the government. Unlike fines or penalties, taxes are not meant to punish or prevent illegal behavior; but "sin taxes" (on alcohol, tobacco, tanning beds, etc.) are meant to discourage some behaviors.
- To qualify as a tax, three criteria are necessary: the payment must be (1) required (it is not voluntary), (2) imposed by a government (federal, state, or local), and (3) not tied directly to the benefit received by the taxpayer.

Describe the different tax rate structures and calculate a tax. **LO 1-3**

- Tax = Tax rate × Tax base, where the tax base is what is taxed and the tax rate is the level of taxes imposed on the base. Different portions of a tax base may be taxed at different rates.

- There are three different tax rates that are useful in contrasting the different tax rate structures, tax planning, and/or assessing the tax burden of a taxpayer: the marginal, average, and effective tax rates.
- The *marginal* tax rate is the tax that applies to the next increment of income or deduction. The *average* tax rate represents a taxpayer's average level of taxation on each dollar of taxable income. The *effective* tax rate represents the taxpayer's average rate of taxation on each dollar of total income (taxable *and* nontaxable income).
- The three basic tax rate structures are proportional, progressive, and regressive.
  - A *proportional tax rate* structure imposes a constant tax rate throughout the tax base. As a taxpayer's tax base increases, the taxpayer's taxes increase proportionally. The marginal tax rate remains constant and always equals the average tax rate. A common example is a sales tax.
  - A *progressive tax rate* imposes an increasing marginal tax rate as the tax base increases. As a taxpayer's tax base increases, both the marginal tax rate and the taxes paid increase. A common example is the U.S. federal income tax.
  - A *regressive tax rate* imposes a decreasing marginal tax rate as the tax base increases. As a taxpayer's tax base increases, the marginal tax rate decreases while the total taxes paid increases.

LO 1-4 Identify the various federal, state, and local taxes.

- Federal taxes include the income tax, employment taxes (Social Security and Medicare taxes), unemployment taxes, excise taxes (levied on quantity purchased), and transfer taxes (estate and gift taxes).
- State and local taxes include the income tax (levied by most states), sales tax (levied on retail sales of goods and some services), use tax (levied on the retail price of goods owned or consumed within a state that were purchased out of state), property taxes (levied on fair market value of real and personal property), and excise taxes.
- Implicit taxes are indirect taxes that result from a tax advantage the government grants to certain transactions to satisfy social, economic, or other objectives. They are defined as the reduced before-tax return that a tax-favored asset produces because of its tax-advantaged status.

LO 1-5 Apply appropriate criteria to evaluate alternative tax systems.

- Sufficiency involves assessing the aggregate size of the tax revenues that must be generated and ensuring that the tax system provides these revenues. Static forecasting ignores how taxpayers may alter their activities in response to a proposed tax law change and bases projected tax revenues on the existing state of transactions. Dynamic forecasting attempts to account for possible taxpayer responses to a proposed tax law change.
- Equity considers how the tax burden should be distributed across taxpayers. Generally, a tax system is considered fair or equitable if the tax is based on the taxpayer's ability to pay—that is, taxpayers with a greater ability to pay tax, pay more tax. Horizontal equity means that two taxpayers in similar situations pay the same tax. Vertical equity is achieved when taxpayers with greater ability to pay tax, pay more tax relative to taxpayers with a lesser ability to pay tax.
- Certainty means taxpayers should be able to determine when, where, and how much tax to pay.
- Convenience means a tax system should be designed to facilitate the collection of tax revenues without undue hardship on the taxpayer or the government.
- Economy means a tax system should minimize its compliance and administration costs.

KEY TERMS

ad valorem taxes (1-15)
average tax rate (1-7)
bracket (1-5)
certainty (1-22)
convenience (1-22)
dynamic forecasting (1-18)
earmarked tax (1-4)
economy (1-22)
effective tax rate (1-8)
employment taxes (1-12)
equity (1-20)
estate tax (1-13)

excise taxes (1-13)
explicit taxes (1-16)
flat tax (1-5)
gift tax (1-13)
graduated taxes (1-5)
horizontal equity (1-21)
implicit taxes (1-16)
income effect (1-19)
income tax (1-12)
local tax (1-14)
marginal tax rate (1-5)
Medicare tax (1-12)
personal property tax (1-15)
progressive tax rate structure (1-9)
proportional tax rate structure (1-9)
real property tax (1-15)
regressive tax rate structure (1-10)
sales tax (1-14)
self-employment tax (1-13)
sin taxes (1-4)
Social Security tax (1-12)
state tax (1-14)
static forecasting (1-18)
substitution effect (1-19)
sufficiency (1-18)
tax (1-4)
tax base (1-5)
tax rate (1-5)
transfer taxes (1-13)
unemployment tax (1-13)
use tax (1-15)
value-added tax (1-11)
vertical equity (1-21)

DISCUSSION QUESTIONS

Discussion Questions are available in Connect®.

1. Jessica's friend Zachary once stated that he couldn't understand why someone would take a tax course. Why is this a rather naïve view? LO 1-1
2. What are some aspects of business that require knowledge of taxation? What are some aspects of personal finance that require knowledge of taxation? LO 1-1
3. Describe some ways in which taxes affect the political process in the United States. LO 1-1
4. Courtney recently received a speeding ticket on her way to the university. Her fine was $200. Is this considered a tax? Why or why not? LO 1-2
5. Marlon and Latoya recently started building a house. They had to pay $300 to the county government for a building permit. Is the $300 payment a tax? Why or why not? LO 1-2
6. To help pay for the city's new stadium, the city of Birmingham recently enacted a 1 percent surcharge on hotel rooms. Is this a tax? Why or why not? LO 1-2
7. As noted in Example 1-2, tolls, parking meter fees, and annual licensing fees are not considered taxes. Can you identify other fees that are similar? LO 1-2
8. If the general objective of our tax system is to raise revenue, why does the income tax allow deductions for charitable contributions and retirement plan contributions? LO 1-2
9. One common argument for imposing so-called sin taxes is the social goal of *reducing* demand for such products. Using cigarettes as an example, is there a segment of the population that might be sensitive to price and for whom high taxes might discourage purchases? LO 1-2
10. Dontae stated that he didn't want to earn any more money because it would "put him in a higher tax bracket." What is wrong with Dontae's reasoning? LO 1-3
11. Describe the three different tax rates discussed in the chapter and how taxpayers might use them. LO 1-3
12. Which is a more appropriate tax rate to use to compare taxpayers' tax burdens—the average or the effective tax rate? Why? LO 1-3
13. Describe the differences between proportional, progressive, and regressive tax rate structures. LO 1-3
14. Arnold and Lilly have recently had a heated discussion about whether a sales tax is a proportional tax or a regressive tax. Arnold argues that a sales tax is regressive. Lilly counters that the sales tax is a flat tax. Who is correct? LO 1-3
15. Which is the largest tax collected by the U.S. government? What types of taxpayers are subject to this tax? LO 1-4

LO 1-4 16. What is the tax base for the Social Security and Medicare taxes for an employee or employer? What is the tax base for Social Security and Medicare taxes for a self-employed individual? Is the self-employment tax in addition to or in lieu of federal income tax?

LO 1-4 17. What are unemployment taxes?

LO 1-4 18. What is the distinguishing feature of an excise tax?

LO 1-4 19. What are some of the taxes that currently are unique to state and local governments? What are some of the taxes that the federal, state, and local governments each utilize?

LO 1-4 20. The state of Georgia recently increased its tax on a pack of cigarettes by $2. What type of tax is this? Why might Georgia choose this type of tax?

LO 1-4 21. What is the difference between a sales tax and a use tax?

LO 1-4 22. What is an ad valorem tax? Name an example of this type of tax.

LO 1-4 23. What are the differences between an explicit and an implicit tax?

LO 1-4 24. When we calculate average and effective tax rates, do we consider implicit taxes? What effect does this have on taxpayers' perception of equity?

LO 1-4 25. Benjamin recently bought a truck in Alabama for his business in Georgia. What different types of federal and state taxes may affect this transaction?

LO 1-5 26. Kobe strongly dislikes SUVs and is appalled that so many are on the road. He proposes to eliminate the federal income tax and replace it with a $50,000 annual tax per SUV. Based on the number of SUVs currently owned in the United States, he estimates the tax will generate exactly the amount of tax revenue currently collected from the income tax. What is wrong with Kobe's proposal? What type of forecasting is Kobe likely using?

LO 1-5 27. What is the difference between the income and substitution effects? For which types of taxpayers is the income effect more likely descriptive? For which types of taxpayers is the substitution effect more likely descriptive?

LO 1-5 28. What is the difference between horizontal and vertical equity? How do tax preferences affect people's view of horizontal equity?

LO 1-3 LO 1-5 29. Montel argues that a flat income tax rate system is vertically equitable. Oprah argues that a progressive tax rate structure is vertically equitable. How do their arguments differ? Who is correct?

LO 1-3 LO 1-5 30. Discuss why evaluating vertical equity simply based on tax rate structure may be less than optimal.

LO 1-4 LO 1-5 31. Compare the federal income tax to sales taxes using the "certainty" criterion.

LO 1-5 32. Many years ago a famous member of Congress proposed eliminating federal income tax withholding. What criterion for evaluating tax systems did this proposal violate? What would likely have been the result of eliminating withholding?

LO 1-5 33. "The federal income tax scores very high on the economy criterion because the current IRS budget is relatively low compared to the costs of a typical collection agency." Explain why this statement may be considered wrong.

PROBLEMS

Select problems are available in Connect®. connect

LO 1-3 34. Chuck, a single taxpayer, earns $75,000 in taxable income and $10,000 in interest from an investment in City of Heflin bonds. Using the U.S. tax rate schedule, how much federal tax will he owe? What is his average tax rate? What is his effective tax rate? What is his current marginal tax rate?

35. Using the facts in problem 34, if Chuck earns an additional $40,000 of taxable income, what is his marginal tax rate on this income? What is his marginal rate if, instead, he had $40,000 of additional deductions? LO 1-3

36. In reviewing the tax rate schedule for a single taxpayer, Chuck notes that the tax on $75,000 is $5,226.25 plus 25 percent of the taxable income over $37,950. What does the $5,226.25 represent? LO 1-3

37. Campbell, a single taxpayer, earns $400,000 in taxable income and $2,000 in interest from an investment in State of New York bonds. Using the U.S. tax rate schedule, how much federal tax will she owe? What is her average tax rate? What is her effective tax rate? What is her current marginal tax rate? LO 1-3

38. Using the facts in problem 37, if Campbell earns an additional $15,000 of taxable income, what is her marginal tax rate on this income? What is her marginal rate if, instead, she had $15,000 of additional deductions? LO 1-3

39. Jorge and Anita, married taxpayers, earn $150,000 in taxable income and $40,000 in interest from an investment in City of Heflin bonds. Using the U.S. tax rate schedule for married filing jointly (see Example 1-3), how much federal tax will they owe? What is their average tax rate? What is their effective tax rate? What is their current marginal tax rate? LO 1-3

40. Using the facts in problem 39, if Jorge and Anita earn an additional $100,000 of taxable income, what is their marginal tax rate on this income? What is their marginal rate if, instead, they report an additional $100,000 in deductions? LO 1-3

41. Scot and Vidia, married taxpayers, earn $240,000 in taxable income and $5,000 in interest from an investment in City of Tampa bonds. Using the U.S. tax rate schedule for married filing jointly (see Example 1-3), how much federal tax will they owe? What is their average tax rate? What is their effective tax rate? What is their current marginal tax rate? LO 1-3

42. Using the facts in problem 41, if Scot and Vidia earn an additional $70,000 of taxable income, what is their marginal tax rate on this income? How would your answer differ if they, instead, had $70,000 of additional deductions? LO 1-3

43. Melinda invests $200,000 in a City of Heflin bond that pays 6 percent interest. Alternatively, Melinda could have invested the $200,000 in a bond recently issued by Surething Inc. that pays 8 percent interest and has risk and other nontax characteristics similar to the City of Heflin bond. Assume Melinda's marginal tax rate is 25 percent. LO 1-3 LO 1-4
    a) What is her after-tax rate of return for the City of Heflin bond?
    b) How much explicit tax does Melinda pay on the City of Heflin bond?
    c) How much implicit tax does she pay on the City of Heflin bond?
    d) How much explicit tax would she have paid on the Surething Inc. bond?
    e) What would have been her after-tax rate of return on the Surething Inc. bond?

44. Hugh has the choice between investing in a City of Heflin bond at 6 percent or investing in a Surething bond at 9 percent. Assuming that both bonds have the same nontax characteristics and that Hugh has a 40 percent marginal tax rate, in which bond should he invest? LO 1-3 LO 1-4 planning

45. Using the facts in problem 44, what interest rate does Surething Inc. need to offer to make Hugh indifferent between investing in the two bonds? LO 1-3 LO 1-4 planning

46. Fergie has the choice between investing in a State of New York bond at 5 percent and a Surething bond at 8 percent. Assuming that both bonds have the same nontax characteristics and that Fergie has a 30 percent marginal tax rate, in which bond should she invest? LO 1-3 LO 1-4 planning

LO 1-3 LO 1-4 planning

47. Using the facts in problem 46, what interest rate does the State of New York bond need to offer to make Fergie indifferent between investing in the two bonds?

LO 1-3

48. Given the following tax structure, what minimum tax would need to be assessed on Shameika to make the tax progressive with respect to average tax rates?

Taxpayer	Salary	Muni-Bond Interest	Total Tax
Mihwah	$10,000	$10,000	$600
Shameika	$50,000	$30,000	$???

LO 1-3

49. Using the facts in problem 48, what minimum tax would need to be assessed on Shameika to make the tax progressive with respect to effective tax rates?

LO 1-3 LO 1-5

50. Song earns $100,000 taxable income as an interior designer and is taxed at an average rate of 20 percent (i.e., $20,000 of tax). If Congress increases the income tax rate such that Song's average tax rate increases from 20 percent to 25 percent, how much more income tax will she pay assuming that the income effect is descriptive? What effect will this tax rate change have on the tax base and tax collected?

LO 1-3 LO 1-5

51. Using the facts from problem 50, what will happen to the government's tax revenues if Song chooses to spend more time pursuing her other passions besides work in response to the tax rate change and earns only $75,000 in taxable income? What is the term that describes this type of reaction to a tax rate increase? What types of taxpayers are likely to respond in this manner?

LO 1-5

52. Given the following tax structure, what tax would need to be assessed on Venita to make the tax horizontally equitable?

Taxpayer	Salary	Total Tax
Mae	$10,000	$ 600
Pedro	$20,000	$1,500
Venita	$10,000	$???

LO 1-5

53. Using the facts in problem 52, what is the minimum tax that Pedro should pay to make the tax structure vertically equitable based on the tax rate paid? This would result in what type of tax rate structure?

LO 1-5

54. Using the facts in problem 52, what is the minimum tax that Pedro should pay to make the tax structure vertically equitable with respect to the amount of tax paid? This would result in what type of tax rate structure?

LO 1-5

55. Consider the following tax rate structure. Is it horizontally equitable? Why or why not? Is it vertically equitable? Why or why not?

Taxpayer	Salary	Total Tax
Rajiv	$10,000	$600
LaMarcus	$20,000	$600
Dory	$10,000	$600

LO 1-5

56. Consider the following tax rate structure. Is it horizontally equitable? Why or why not? Is it vertically equitable? Why or why not?

Taxpayer	Salary	Total Tax
Marilyn	$10,000	$ 600
Kobe	$20,000	$3,000
Alfonso	$30,000	$6,000

57. Consider the following tax rate structure. Is it horizontally equitable? Why or why not? Is it vertically equitable? Why or why not? LO 1-5

Taxpayer	Salary	Total Tax
Rodney	$10,000	$600
Keisha	$10,000	$600

58. Lorenzo is considering starting a trucking company either in Texas or Oklahoma. He will relocate his family, which includes his wife, children, and parents, to reside in the same state as his business. What types of taxes may influence his decision of where to locate his business? LO 1-1 LO 1-4 planning

59. Congress would like to increase tax revenues by 10 percent. Assume that the average taxpayer in the United States earns $65,000 and pays an average tax rate of 15 percent. If the income effect is in effect for all taxpayers, what average tax rate will result in a 10 percent increase in tax revenues? This is an example of what type of forecasting? LO 1-3 LO 1-5 planning

60. Locate the IRS website at www.irs.gov/. For every $100 the IRS collected, how much was spent on the IRS's collection efforts? What tax system criterion does this information help you to evaluate with respect to the current U.S. tax system? LO 1-5 research

61. Using the Internet, find a comparison of income tax rates across states. What state currently has the highest income tax rate? In considering individual tax burdens across states, what other taxes should you consider? LO 1-4 research

ROGER | CPA Review

Sample CPA Exam questions from Roger CPA Review are available in Connect as support for the topics in this text. These Multiple Choice Questions and Task-Based Simulations include expert-written explanations and solutions, and provide a starting point for students to become familiar with the content and functionality of the actual CPA Exam.

chapter 2 Tax Compliance, the IRS, and Tax Authorities

Learning Objectives

Upon completing this chapter, you should be able to:

- LO 2-1 Identify the filing requirements for income tax returns and the statute of limitations for assessment.
- LO 2-2 Outline the IRS audit process, how returns are selected, the different types of audits, and what happens after the audit.
- LO 2-3 Evaluate the relative weights of the various tax law sources.
- LO 2-4 Describe the legislative process as it pertains to taxation.
- LO 2-5 Perform the basic steps in tax research and evaluate various tax law sources when faced with ambiguous statutes.
- LO 2-6 Describe tax professional responsibilities in providing tax advice.
- LO 2-7 Identify taxpayer and tax professional penalties.

©Jose Luis Pelaez Inc/Blend Images LLC

Storyline Summary

Taxpayers:	Bill and Mercedes
Family description:	Bill and Mercedes are married with one daughter, Margaret, and live in Tampa, Florida.
Employment status:	Bill is an economics professor; Mercedes is a small business owner.
Filing status:	Married, filing jointly
Current situation:	Bill and Mercedes face an IRS audit involving a previous year's interest deductions.

Bill and Mercedes received a notice from the Internal Revenue Service (IRS) that their return is under audit for certain interest deductions. As you might expect, they are quite concerned, especially because it has been several years since they claimed the deductions and they worry that all their supporting documentation may not be in place. Several questions run through their minds. How could the IRS audit a return that was filed so long ago? Why was their tax return selected, and what should they expect during the audit? The interest deductions they reported were based on advice from their CPA. What would cause the IRS and a CPA to interpret the law differently? What is their financial exposure if the deductions are ultimately disallowed?

Will they have to pay interest and penalties in addition to the tax they might owe? ■

Even the most conservative taxpayer is likely to feel anxiety after receiving an IRS notice. This chapter will help answer Bill and Mercedes's questions and provide an overview of the audit process and tax research. While all taxpayers should understand these basics of our tax system, aspiring accountants should be especially familiar with them.

LO 2-1

TAXPAYER FILING REQUIREMENTS

To file or not to file? Unlike Hamlet's "to be or not to be," this question has a pretty straightforward answer. Filing requirements are specified by law for each type of taxpayer. All corporations must file a tax return annually regardless of their taxable income. Estates and trusts are required to file annual income tax returns if their gross income exceeds $600.[1]

The filing requirements for individual taxpayers are a little more complex. Specifically, they depend on the taxpayer's filing status (single, married filing jointly, and so on, discussed in more detail in the Individual Income Tax Overview, Exemptions, and Filing Status chapter), age, and gross income (income before deductions). Exhibit 2-1 lists the 2017 gross income thresholds for taxpayers based on their filing status, gross income, and age. As detailed in Exhibit 2-1, the gross income thresholds are calculated as the sum of the standard deduction, additional deductions for taxpayers age 65 or older, and personal exemption(s) that apply to each respective filing status.[2] These amounts are indexed for inflation and thus change each year. For certain taxpayers such as the self-employed and those claimed as dependents by another taxpayer, lower gross income thresholds apply.

EXHIBIT 2-1 2017 Gross Income Thresholds by Filing Status

Filing Status and Age (in 2017)	2017 Gross Income	Explanation
Single	$10,400	$6,350 standard deduction + $4,050 personal exemption
Single, 65 or older	$11,950	$6,350 standard deduction + $1,550 additional deduction + $4,050 personal exemption
Married, filing a joint return	$20,800	$12,700 standard deduction + $8,100 personal exemptions (2)
Married, filing a joint return, one spouse 65 or older	$22,050	$12,700 standard deduction + $1,250 additional deduction (2) + $8,100 personal exemptions (2)
Married, filing a joint return, both spouses 65 or older	$23,300	$12,700 standard deduction + $2,500 additional deductions (2) + $8,100 personal exemptions (2)
Married, filing a separate return	$ 4,050	$4,050 personal exemption
Head of household	$13,400	$9,350 standard deduction + $4,050 personal exemption
Head of household, 65 or older	$14,950	$9,350 standard deduction + $1,550 additional deduction + $4,050 personal exemption
Surviving spouse with a dependent child	$16,750	$12,700 standard deduction + $4,050 personal exemption
Surviving spouse, 65 or older, with a dependent child	$18,000	$12,700 standard deduction + $1,250 additional deduction + $4,050 personal exemption

Whether a taxpayer is due a refund (which occurs when taxes paid exceed tax liability) does *not* determine whether a taxpayer must file a tax return. Gross income determines whether a tax return is required. Further, note that a taxpayer whose gross income falls below the respective threshold is not precluded from filing a tax return. Indeed,

[1]Estates file income tax returns during the administration period (i.e., before all of the estate assets are distributed).

[2]IRC §6012. We describe the standard deduction and personal exemptions in detail later in the text.

taxpayers due a refund *should* file a tax return to receive the refund (or claim a refundable tax credit), even if they are not required to file a tax return.

Tax Return Due Date and Extensions

Like the filing requirements, due dates for tax returns vary based on the type of taxpayer. Individual tax returns are due on the fifteenth day of the fourth month following year-end—that is, April 15 for calendar-year individuals. (Due dates that fall on a Saturday, Sunday, or holidays are automatically extended to the next day that is not a Saturday, Sunday, or holiday.) Similarly, tax returns for taxable corporations ("C" corporations) are generally due on the fifteenth day of the fourth month following the corporation's year-end. The exception is for tax returns for C corporations with a June 30 year-end, which are due on the fifteenth day of the third month (September 15th). For both partnerships and S corporations (generally nontaxable corporations), tax returns must be filed by the fifteenth day of the third month following the entity's year-end (March 15 for calendar-year partnerships or S corporations). Any individual, partnership, or S corporation unable to file a tax return by the original due date can, by that same deadline, request a six-month extension to file, which is granted automatically by the IRS. Similarly, C corporations may request an automatic six- or seven-month extension to file depending on the corporation's year-end.[3]

An extension allows the taxpayer to delay filing a tax return but does *not* extend the due date for tax payments. Thus, when a taxpayer files an extension, she must estimate how much tax will be owed. If a taxpayer fails to pay the entire balance of tax owed by the original due date of the tax return, the IRS charges the taxpayer interest on the underpayment from the due date of the return until the taxpayer pays the tax.[4] The interest rate charged depends on taxpayer type (individual or corporation) and varies quarterly with the federal short-term interest rate.[5] For example, the interest rate for tax underpayments for individuals equals the federal short-term rate plus three percentage points.[6]

What happens if the taxpayer does not file a tax return by the time required, whether April 15 or an extended deadline? As you might guess, the IRS imposes penalties on taxpayers failing to comply with the tax law. In many cases, the penalties can be quite substantial (see later discussion in this chapter). In the case of failure to file a tax return, the penalty equals 5 percent of the tax due for each month (or partial month) that the return is late. However, the maximum penalty is generally 25 percent of the tax owed, and the failure-to-file penalty does not apply if the taxpayer owes no tax.

THE KEY FACTS

Filing Requirements and Due Dates

- Filing requirements
  - Specified by law for each type of taxpayer.
  - For individuals, filing requirements vary by filing status, gross income, and age.
  - Gross income thresholds are indexed each year for inflation.
- Due dates
  - The due date for tax returns varies based on the type of taxpayer.
  - Individual tax returns are due on April 15 for calendar-year individuals.
  - Due dates that fall on a Saturday, Sunday, or holiday are automatically extended to the next day that is not a Saturday, Sunday, or holiday.
  - Any taxpayer unable to file a tax return by the original due date can request an extension to file.
  - An extension allows the taxpayer to delay filing a tax return but does *not* extend the due date for tax payments.

Statute of Limitations

Despite the diligent efforts of taxpayers and tax professionals, it is quite common for tax returns to contain mistakes. Some may be to the taxpayer's advantage and others may be to the government's advantage. Regardless of the nature of the mistake, the taxpayer is obligated to file an amended return to correct the error (and request a refund or pay a deficiency) if the statute of limitations has not expired for the tax return. Likewise, the IRS can propose adjustments to the taxpayer's return if the statute of limitations for the return has not expired.

By law, the **statute of limitations** defines the period in which the taxpayer can file an amended tax return or the IRS can assess a tax deficiency for a specific tax year. For both amended tax returns filed by a taxpayer and proposed tax assessments by the IRS, the statute of limitations generally ends three years from the *later* of (1) the date the tax return was actually filed or (2) the tax return's original due date.

[3]June 30 year-end C corporations may request a seven-month extension. All other C corporations may request a six-month extension.

[4]The tax law also imposes a penalty for late payment in addition to the interest charged on the underpayment. We briefly discuss this penalty later in the chapter and in the Individual Income Tax Computation and Tax Credits chapter.

[5]The federal short-term rate is determined from a one-month average of the market yields from marketable obligations of the United States with maturities of three years or less.

[6]This same interest rate applies to individuals who overpay their taxes (i.e., receive a tax refund and interest payment as a result of an IRS audit or from filing an amended tax return).

The statute of limitations for IRS assessment can be extended in certain circumstances. For example, a six-year statute of limitations applies to IRS assessments if the taxpayer omits items of gross income that exceed 25 percent of the gross income reported on the tax return. For fraudulent returns, or if the taxpayer fails to file a tax return, the news is understandably worse. The statute of limitations remains open indefinitely in these cases.

Example 2-1

Bill and Mercedes file their 2013 federal tax return on September 6, 2014, after receiving an automatic extension to file their return by October 15, 2014. In 2017, the IRS selects their 2013 tax return for audit. When does the statute of limitations end for Bill and Mercedes's 2013 tax return?

Answer: Assuming the six-year and "unlimited" statute of limitation rules do not apply, the statute of limitations ends on September 6, 2017 (three years after the later of the actual filing date and the *original* due date).

What if: When would the statute of limitations end for Bill and Mercedes for their 2013 tax return if the couple filed the return on March 22, 2014 (before the original due date of April 15, 2014)?

Answer: In this scenario the statute of limitations would end on April 15, 2017, because the later of the actual filing date and the original due date is April 15, 2014.

Taxpayers should prepare for the possibility of an audit by retaining all supporting documents (receipts, cancelled checks, etc.) for a tax return until the statute of limitations expires. After the statute of limitations expires, taxpayers can discard the majority of supporting documents but should still keep a copy of the tax return itself, as well as any documents that may have ongoing significance, such as those establishing the taxpayer's *basis* or original investment in existing assets like personal residences and long-term investments.

LO 2-2 IRS AUDIT SELECTION

Why me? This is a recurring question in life and definitely a common taxpayer question after receiving an IRS audit notice. The answer, in general, is that a taxpayer's return is selected for audit because the IRS has data suggesting the taxpayer's tax return has a high probability of a significant understated tax liability. Budget constraints limit the IRS's ability to audit a majority or even a large minority of tax returns. Currently, fewer than 1 percent of all tax returns are audited. Thus, the IRS must be strategic in selecting returns for audit in an effort to promote the highest level of voluntary taxpayer compliance and increase tax revenues.

Specifically, how does the IRS select tax returns for audit? The IRS uses a number of computer programs and outside data sources (newspapers, financial statement disclosures, informants, and other public and private sources) to identify tax returns that may have an understated tax liability. Common computer initiatives include the **DIF (Discriminant Function) system,** the **document perfection program,** and the **information matching program.** The most important of these initiatives is the DIF system. The DIF system assigns a score to each tax return that represents the probability the tax liability on the return has been underreported (a higher score = a higher likelihood of underreporting). The IRS derives the weights assigned to specific tax return attributes from historical IRS audit adjustment data from the National Research Program.[7] The DIF system then uses these (undisclosed) weights to score each tax return based on the tax return's characteristics. Returns with higher DIF scores are then reviewed to determine whether an audit is the best course of action.

[7]Similar to its predecessor, the Taxpayer Compliance Measurement Program, the National Research Program (NRP) analyzes a large sample of tax returns that are randomly selected for audit. From these randomly selected returns, the IRS identifies tax return characteristics (e.g., deductions for a home office, unusually high tax deductions relative to a taxpayer's income) associated with underreported liabilities, weights these characteristics, and then incorporates them into the DIF system. The NRP analyzes randomly selected returns to ensure that the DIF scorings are representative of the population of tax returns.

All returns are checked for mathematical and tax calculation errors, a process referred to as the document perfection program. Individual returns are also subject to the information matching program. This program compares the taxpayer's tax return to information submitted to the IRS from other taxpayers like banks, employers, mutual funds, brokerage companies, and mortgage companies. Information matched includes items such as wages (Form W-2 submitted by employers), interest income (Form 1099-INT submitted by banks), and dividend income (Form 1099-DIV submitted by brokerage companies). For tax returns identified as incorrect via the document perfection and information matching programs, the IRS recalculates the taxpayer's tax liability and sends a notice explaining the adjustment. If the taxpayer owes tax, the IRS will request payment of the tax due. If the taxpayer overpaid tax, the IRS will send the taxpayer a refund of the overpayment.

In addition to computer-based methods for identifying tax returns for audit, the IRS may use a number of other audit initiatives that target taxpayers in certain industries, engaged in certain transactions like the acquisition of other companies, or having specific attributes like home office deductions. Taxpayers of a given size and complexity, such as large publicly traded companies, may be audited every year.

THE KEY FACTS

IRS Audit Selection

- The IRS uses a number of computer programs and outside data sources to identify tax returns that may have an understated tax liability.
- Common computer initiatives include the DIF (Discriminant Function) system, the document perfection program, and the information matching program.
- The DIF system assigns a score to each tax return that represents the probability the tax liability on the return has been underreported.
- The document perfection program checks all returns for mathematical and tax calculation errors.
- The information matching program compares the taxpayer's tax return to information submitted to the IRS from other taxpayers.

TAXES IN THE REAL WORLD Turning in Your Neighbor Can Pay Big Bucks

The Wall Street Journal reported that in April 2011 the IRS paid its first payment under its new taxpayer whistleblower program that promises large rewards for turning in tax cheats. Under the large-award whistleblower program (where unpaid taxes, interest, and penalties exceed $2 million and the tax cheat, if an individual, had gross income exceeding $200,000 in at least one year), whistleblowers can be paid between 15 and 30 percent of the taxes, interest, and penalties collected by the IRS. Under the small-award whistleblower program (tax, interest, and penalty underpayments of $2 million or less), the IRS may pay whistleblowers up to 15 percent of the unpaid taxes and interest collected. Whistleblowers use IRS Form 211 (www.IRS.gov) to apply for the program, and as you might expect, all whistleblower payments received are fully taxable. In its first payment, the IRS paid $4.5 million to a former in-house accountant for a large financial services firm. Given the potential windfall to whistleblowers, you might expect a long line of "concerned" citizens applying for the program. You would be correct. As of February 2016, the IRS Commissioner announced that the IRS has paid out more than $403 million in awards since 2007, on collection of more than $3 billion based on whistleblower information.

Based on: "Taxes: How to Turn in Your Neighbor to the IRS," *The Wall Street Journal*, WSJ.com, September 3, 2011.

How was Bill and Mercedes's tax return selected for audit? Given the audit focus on certain deductions, the IRS likely selected their return for audit because the amount or type of the deductions resulted in a high DIF score. IRS personnel then determined that the deductions warranted further review and, thus, selected the tax return for audit.

ETHICS

After Bill and Mercedes's tax return was selected for audit, Bill read on the Internet speculation that filing a paper copy tax return (instead of filing electronically) and extending a tax return decrease the chance of IRS audit. Bill has convinced Mercedes that they need to use these strategies going forward and look for other ways to avoid audit. Has Bill crossed an ethical boundary?

Types of Audits

The three types of IRS audits are correspondence, office, and field examinations. **Correspondence examinations** are the most common. These audits, as the name suggests, are conducted by mail and generally are limited to one or two items on the taxpayer's return. Of the three types of audits, correspondence audits are generally the narrowest in scope and the least complex. The IRS typically requests supporting documentation for one or more items on the taxpayer's return, like charitable contributions deducted, for example. When appropriate documentation is promptly supplied, these audits typically can be concluded relatively quickly. Of course, they can also be expanded to address other issues that arise as a result of the IRS's inspection of taxpayer documents.

Office examinations are the second most common audit. As the name suggests, the IRS conducts them at its local office. These audits are typically broader in scope and more complex than correspondence examinations. Small businesses, taxpayers operating sole proprietorships, and middle- to high-income individual taxpayers are more likely, if audited, to have office examinations. In these examinations, the taxpayer receives a notice that identifies the items subject to audit; requests substantiation for these items as necessary; and notifies the taxpayer of the date, time, and location of the exam. Taxpayers may attend the examination alone, with representation, such as their tax adviser or attorney, or simply let their tax adviser or attorney attend on the taxpayer's behalf.

Field examinations are the least common audit. The IRS conducts these at the taxpayer's place of business or the location where the taxpayer's books, records, and source documents are maintained. Field examinations are generally the broadest in scope and the most complex of the three audit types. They can last months to years and generally are limited to business returns and the most complex individual returns.

What type of exam do you think Bill and Mercedes will have? Because their return is an individual tax return and the audit is restricted to a relatively narrow set of deductions, their return will likely be subject to a correspondence audit. If the audit were broader in scope, an office examination would be more likely.

THE KEY FACTS

IRS Audits

- The three types of IRS audits are correspondence, office, and field examinations.
- After the audit, the IRS will send the taxpayer a 30-day letter, which provides the taxpayer the opportunity to pay the proposed assessment or request an appeals conference.
- If an agreement is not reached at appeals or the taxpayer does not pay the proposed assessment, the IRS will send the taxpayer a 90-day letter.
- After receiving the 90-day letter, the taxpayer may pay the tax or petition the U.S. Tax Court to hear the case.
- If the taxpayer chooses to pay the tax, the taxpayer may then request a refund of the tax and eventually sue the IRS for refund in the U.S. District Court or the U.S. Court of Federal Claims.

After the Audit After the examination, the IRS agent provides a list of proposed adjustments (if any) to the taxpayer for review. If he or she agrees to the proposed changes, the taxpayer signs an agreement form (Form 870) and pays the additional tax owed or receives the proposed refund. If the taxpayer disputes the proposed changes, the taxpayer will receive a **30-day letter** giving him or her 30 days to either (1) request a conference with an appeals officer, who is independent and resides in a separate IRS division from the examining agent, or (2) agree to the proposed adjustment. An appeals officer would consider the merits of the unresolved issues as well as the "hazards of litigation"—that is, the probability that the IRS will lose if the case is brought to court and the resulting costs of a taxpayer-favorable ruling. If the taxpayer chooses the appeals conference and reaches an agreement with the IRS there, the taxpayer can then sign Form 870. If the taxpayer and IRS still do not agree on the proposed adjustment at the appeals conference, or the taxpayer chooses not to request an appeals conference, the IRS will send the taxpayer a 90-day letter. See Exhibit 2-2.

The **90-day letter** (also known as a *statutory notice of deficiency*) explains that the taxpayer has 90 days to either (1) pay the proposed deficiency or (2) file a petition in the U.S. Tax Court to hear the case.[8] The **U.S. Tax Court** is a national court whose judges are tax experts and who hear only tax cases. If the taxpayer would like to litigate the case but prefers it to be heard in the local **U.S. District Court** or the **U.S. Court of Federal Claims,** the taxpayer must pay the tax deficiency first, then request a refund from the IRS, and then sue the IRS for refund in the court after the IRS denies the refund claim.

Why would a taxpayer prefer one trial court over others? To understand this, we must appreciate the basic distinguishing factors of each. First and foremost, it is relatively common for the U.S. Tax Court, local U.S. District Court, or the U.S. Court of Federal

[8]If the taxpayer lacks the funds to pay the assessed tax, there is legitimate doubt as to whether the taxpayer owes part or all of the assessed tax, or collection of the tax would cause the taxpayer economic hardship or be unfair or inequitable, the taxpayer can request an offer in compromise with the IRS to settle the tax liability for less than the full amount assessed by completing Form 656.

EXHIBIT 2-2 **IRS Appeals/Litigation Process**

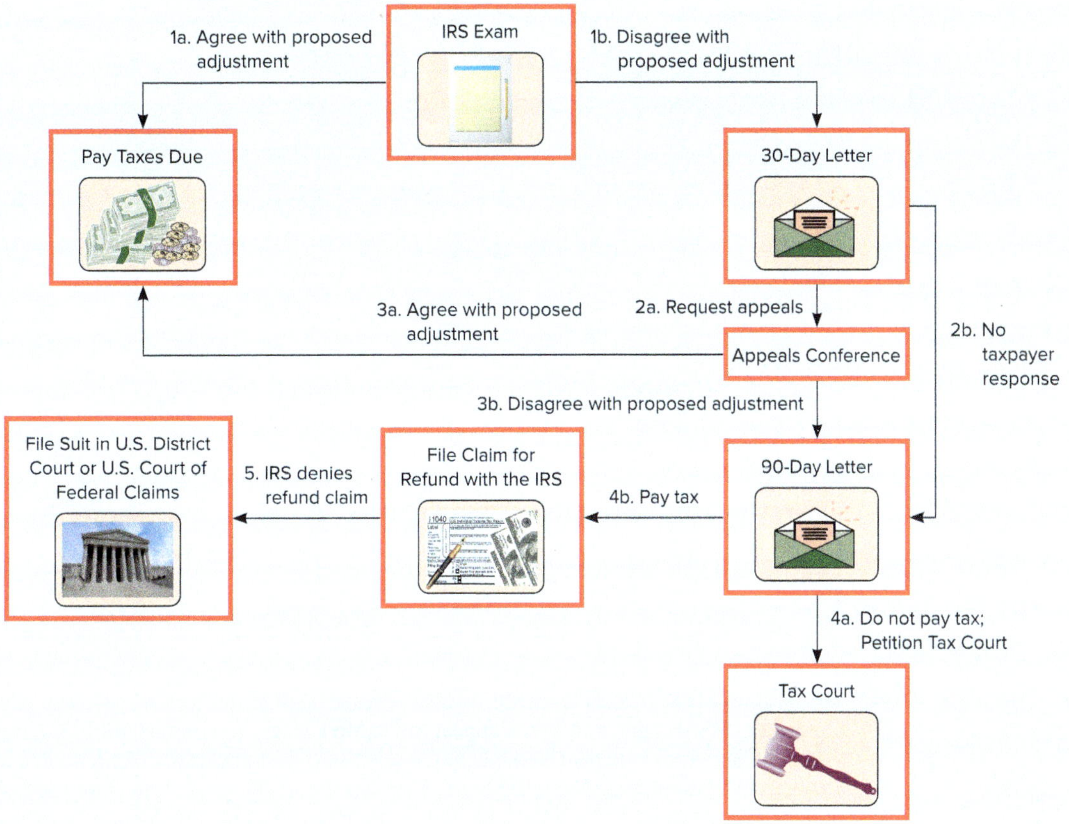

IRS Exam: © Royalty-Free/Corbis, Supreme Court: © McGraw-Hill Education/Jill Braaten, photographer, File Claim: © Michael A. Keller/Corbis

Claims to interpret and rule differently on the same basic tax issue. Given a choice of courts, the taxpayer should prefer the court most likely to rule favorably on his or her particular issues. The courts also differ in other ways. For example, the U.S. District Court is the only court that provides for a jury trial; the U.S. Tax Court is the only court that allows tax cases to be heard *before* the taxpayer pays the disputed liability and the only court with a small claims division (hearing claims involving disputed liabilities of $50,000 or less); the U.S. Tax Court judges are tax experts, whereas the U.S. District Court and U.S. Court of Federal Claims judges are generalists. The taxpayer should consider each of these factors in choosing a trial court. For example, if the taxpayer feels very confident in her tax return position but does not have sufficient funds to pay the disputed liability, she will prefer the U.S. Tax Court. If, instead, the taxpayer is litigating a tax return position that is low on technical merit but high on emotional appeal, a jury trial in the local U.S. District Court may be the best option.

What happens after the taxpayer's case is decided in a trial court? The process may not be quite finished. After the trial court's verdict, the losing party has the right to request one of the 13 **U.S. Circuit Courts of Appeals** to hear the case. Exhibit 2-3 depicts the specific appellant courts for each lower-level court. Both the U.S. Tax Court and local U.S. District Court cases are appealed to the specific U.S. Circuit Court of Appeals based on the taxpayer's residence.[9] Cases litigated in Alabama, Florida, and Georgia, for example,

[9]Decisions rendered by the U.S. Tax Court Small Claims Division cannot be appealed by the taxpayer or the IRS.

EXHIBIT 2-3 Federal Judicial System

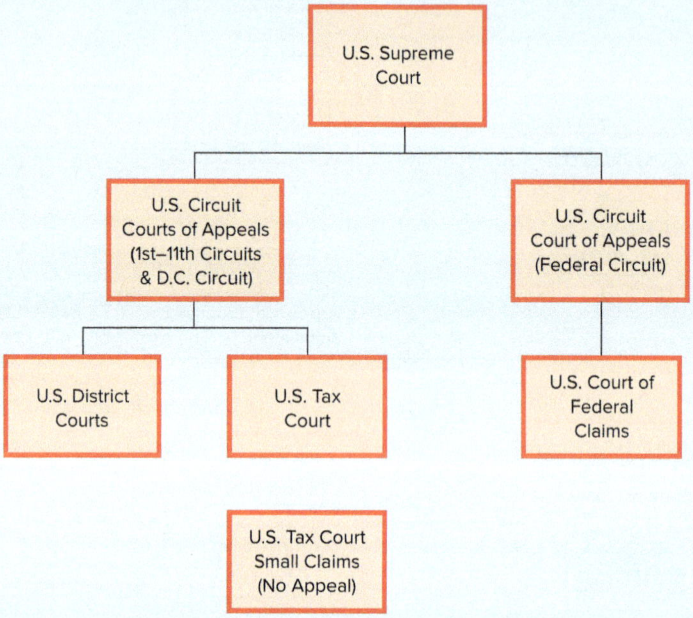

appeal to the U.S. Circuit Court of Appeals for the 11th Circuit; whereas those tried in Louisiana, Mississippi, and Texas appeal to the 5th Circuit. In contrast, all U.S. Court of Federal Claims cases appeal to the U.S. Circuit Court of Appeals for the Federal Circuit (located in Washington, D.C.). Exhibit 2-4 depicts the geographic regions for each of the 11 U.S. Circuit Courts of Appeals defined by numerical region. Not depicted are the U.S. Circuit Court of Appeals for the District of Columbia and the U.S. Circuit Court of Appeals for the Federal Circuit.

Through the initial selection of a trial court—U.S. District Court, U.S. Tax Court, or U.S. Court of Federal Claims—the taxpayer has the ability to determine which circuit court would hear an appeal of the case (the U.S. Circuit Court of Appeals based on residence or the U.S. Circuit Court of Appeals for the Federal Circuit). Because alternative circuit courts may interpret the law differently, the taxpayer should consider in choosing a trial-level court the relevant circuit courts' judicial histories to determine which circuit court (and thus, which trial court) would be more likely to rule in his or her favor.

After an appeals court hears a case, the losing party has one last option to receive a favorable ruling: a petition to the **U.S. Supreme Court** to hear the case. However, given the quantity of other cases appealed to the U.S. Supreme Court that are of national importance, the Supreme Court agrees to hear only a few tax cases a year with great significance to a broad cross-section of taxpayers, or cases litigating issues in which there has been disagreement among the circuit courts. For most tax cases, the Supreme Court refuses to hear the case (denies the ***writ of certiorari***) and litigation ends with the circuit court decision.

Although litigation of tax disputes is quite common, taxpayers should carefully consider the pros and cons. Litigation can be very costly financially and emotionally, and thus it is more appropriately used as an option of last resort, after all other appeal efforts have been exhausted.

What is the likely course of action for Bill and Mercedes's audit? It is too soon to tell. Before you can assess the likely outcome of their audit, you need a better understanding of both the audit issue and the relevant tax laws that apply to the issue. The next section explains alternative tax law sources. After we discuss the various sources of our tax laws,

EXHIBIT 2-4 Geographic Boundaries for the U.S. Circuit Courts of Appeals

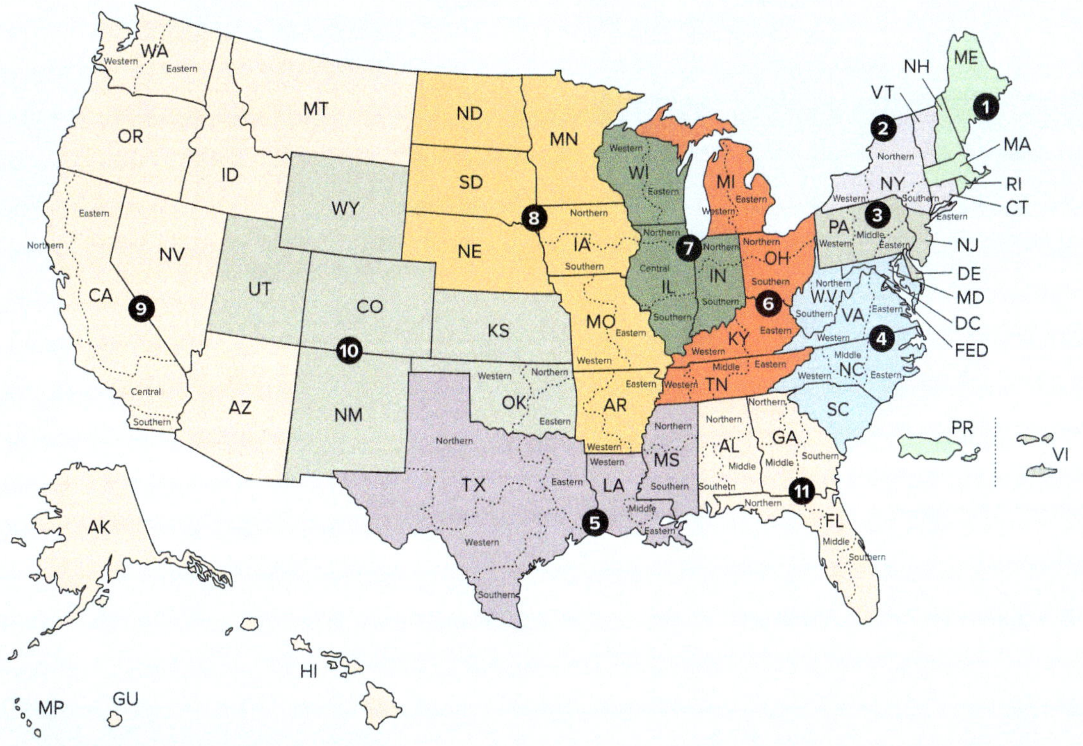

Source: www.uscourts.gov/courtlinks

*U.S. District Court jurisdictions for those states with more than one U.S. District Court are also depicted (for example, the state of Washington is divided into Eastern and Western Districts).

†Not depicted are the U.S. Circuit Court of Appeals for the District of Columbia and the U.S. Circuit Court of Appeals for the Federal Circuit.

we'll describe how Bill and Mercedes (or their CPA) can research the sources to identify the best possible course of action.[10]

TAX LAW SOURCES

LO 2-3 LO 2-4

There are two broad categories of tax authorities: primary authorities and secondary authorities. **Primary authorities** are official sources of the tax law generated by the legislative branch (statutory authority issued by Congress), judicial branch (rulings by the U.S. District Courts, U.S. Tax Court, U.S. Court of Federal Claims, U.S. Circuit Courts of Appeals, or U.S. Supreme Court), and executive/administrative branch (Treasury and IRS pronouncements). Exhibit 2-5 displays the most common primary sources, their respective citations, and related explanations. We'll discuss each of these authorities below.

Secondary authorities are unofficial tax authorities that interpret and explain the primary authorities, such as tax research services (discussed below), tax articles from professional journals and law reviews, newsletters, and textbooks. For quick questions, practitioners often use the *CCH Master Tax Guide* or *RIA Federal Tax Handbook.*

[10]Accountants should be mindful to not engage in the unauthorized practice of law. In years past, several court cases have addressed this issue without providing a clear understanding between practicing tax accounting and the unauthorized practice of law. At present, tax accountants are not likely to overstep their responsibilities if they limit their advice to tax issues and leave the general legal advice and drafting of legal documents to attorneys.

EXHIBIT 2-5 Citations to Common Primary Authorities

Statutory Authorities:	***Citation:***	***Explanation:***
Internal Revenue Code	IRC Sec. 162(e)(2)(B)(i)	Section number 162, subsection e, paragraph 2, subparagraph B, clause i
Committee Reports: Senate Finance Committee Report	S. Rep. No. 353, 82d Cong., 1st Sess. 14 (1951)	Senate report number 353, Congress number 82, Congressional session 1, page number 14, year 1951
House Ways and Means Committee Report	H. Rep. No. 242, 82d Cong., 1st Sess. 40 (1951)	House report number 242, Congress number 82, Congressional session 1, page number 40, year 1951
Administrative Authorities:	***Citation:***	***Explanation:***
Final Regulation	Reg. Sec. 1.217-2(c)(1)	Type of regulation (1 = income tax), code section 217, regulation number 2, paragraph number c, subparagraph number 1
Temporary Regulation	Temp. Reg. Sec. 1.217-2(c)(1)	Same as final regulation
Proposed Regulation	Prop. Reg. Sec. 1.217-2(c)(1)	Same as final regulation
Revenue Ruling	Rev. Rul. 77-262, 1977-2 C.B. 41	Ruling number 77-262 (262nd ruling of 1977), volume number of cumulative bulletin 1977-2, page number 41
Revenue Procedure	Rev. Proc. 99-10, 1999-1 C.B. 272	Procedure number 99-10 (10th procedure of 1999), volume number of cumulative bulletin 1999-1, page number 272
Private Letter Ruling	PLR 200601001	Year 2006, week number 01 (1st week of 2006), ruling number 001 (1st ruling of the week)
Technical Advice Memorandum	TAM 200402001	Year 2004, week number 02 (2nd week of 2004), ruling number 001 (1st ruling of the week)
Judicial Authorities:	***Citation:***	***Explanation:***
U.S. Supreme Court	*Comm. v. Kowalski,* 434 U.S. 77 (S. Ct., 1977)	Volume 434 of the United States Reporter, page 77, year 1977
	Comm. v. Kowalski, 98 S. Ct. 315 (S. Ct., 1977)	Volume 98 of the West court reporter, page 315, year 1977
	Comm. v. Kowalski, 77-2 USTC par. 9,748 (S. Ct., 1977)	Volume 77-2 of the CCH court reporter, paragraph 9,748, year 1977
	Comm. v. Kowalski, 40 AFTR2d 77-6128 (S. Ct., 1977)	Volume 40 of the RIA AFTR2d court reporter, paragraph 77-6128, year 1977
U.S. Circuit Court of Appeals	*Azar Nut Co. v. Comm.,* 931 F.2d 314 (5th Cir., 1991)	Volume 931 of the West F.2d court reporter, page 314, circuit 5th, year 1991
	Azar Nut Co. v. Comm., 91-1 USTC par. 50,257 (5th Cir., 1991)	Volume 91-1 of the CCH USTC court reporter, paragraph 50,257, circuit 5th, year 1991
	Azar Nut Co. v. Comm., 67 AFTR2d 91-987 (5th Cir., 1991)	Volume 67 of the RIA AFTR2d court reporter, paragraph 91-987, year 1991
U.S. Tax Court—Regular decision	*L.A. Beeghly,* 36 TC 154 (1962)	Volume 36 of the Tax Court reporter, page 154, year 1962
U.S. Tax Court—Memorandum decision	*Robert Rodriguez,* RIA TC Memo 2005-012	Paragraph number 2005-012 of the RIA Tax Court Memorandum reporter
	Robert Rodriguez, 85 TCM 1162 (2005)	Volume 85 of the CCH Tax Court Memorandum reporter, page 1162, year 2005
U.S. Court of Federal Claims	*J.R. Cohen v. U.S.,* 510 F. Supp. 297 (Fed. Cl., 1993)	Volume 510 of the West F. Supp. court reporter, page 297, year 1993
	J.R. Cohen v. U.S., 72 AFTR2d 93-5124 (Fed. Cl., 1993)	Volume 72 of the RIA AFTR2d court reporter, paragraph 93-5124, year 1993
	J.R. Cohen v. U.S., 93-1 USTC par. 50,354 (Fed. Cl., 1993)	Volume 93-1 of the CCH USTC court reporter, paragraph 50,354, year 1993
U.S. District Court	*Waxler Towing Co., Inc. v. U.S.,* 510 F. Supp. 297 (W.D, TN, 1981)	Volume 510 of the West F. Supp. court reporter, page 297, Western District (W.D.), state Tennessee, year 1981
	Waxler Towing Co., Inc. v. U.S., 81-2 USTC par. 9,541 (W.D., TN, 1981)	Volume 81-2 of the CCH USTC court reporter, paragraph 9,541, Western District (W.D.), state Tennessee, year 1981
	Waxler Towing Co., Inc. v. U.S., 48 AFTR2d 81-5274 (W.D., TN, 1981)	Volume 48 of the RIA AFTR2d court reporter, paragraph 81-5274, Western District (W.D.), state Tennessee, year 1981

EXHIBIT 2-6 Common Secondary Tax Authorities

Tax Research Services:	Professional Journals:
BNA Tax Management Portfolios	*Journal of Accountancy*
CCH Standard Federal Tax Reporter	*Journal of Taxation*
CCH Tax Research Consultant	*Practical Tax Strategies*
RIA Federal Tax Coordinator	*Taxes*
RIA United States Tax Reporter	*Tax Adviser*
Newsletters:	**Quick Reference Sources:**
Daily Tax Report	*IRS Publications*
Federal Tax Weekly Alert	*CCH Master Tax Guide*
Tax Notes	*RIA Federal Tax Handbook*
Law Reviews:	**Textbooks:**
Tax Law Review (New York University School of Law)	*McGraw-Hill's Taxation of Individuals and Business Entities*
Virginia Tax Review (University of Virginia School of Law)	*McGraw-Hill's Essentials of Federal Taxation*

Secondary authorities may be very helpful in understanding a tax issue, but they hold little weight in a tax dispute (hence their "unofficial" status). Thus, tax advisers should always be careful to verify their understanding of tax law by examining primary authorities directly and to *never* cite secondary authority in a research memo. Exhibit 2-6 lists some of the common sources of secondary authority.

TAXES IN THE REAL WORLD Google: Not Authoritative on Tax Matters

While Internet super giant Google may be the king of all cyberspace knowledge, the Tax Court ruled in *Woodard v. Comm.*, TC Summary Opinion 2009-150, that a Google search does not constitute reasonable cause to excuse a Harvard MBA/CPA from taking an incorrect tax return position. The Tax Court noted that although the taxpayer had not worked as an accountant for years before filing his tax return, "his accounting degree, MBA, and CPA training, no matter how stale, undoubtedly taught him what sources could be relied upon as definitive; such as, for example, the Internal Revenue Code and the income tax regulations, both of which are readily available on the Internet."

Legislative Sources: Congress and the Constitution

The three legislative or statutory tax authorities are the U.S. Constitution, the Internal Revenue Code, and tax treaties. The **U.S. Constitution** is the highest authority in the United States, but it provides very little in the way of tax law since it contains no discussion of tax rates, taxable income, or other details. Instead, the 16th Amendment provides Congress the ability to tax income directly, from whatever source derived, without apportionment across the states.

Various attempts to amend the U.S. Constitution with regard to taxation—for example, one effort to repeal the 16th Amendment entirely and one to require a two-thirds majority in both houses to raise taxes—have so far met with failure.

Internal Revenue Code The second (and main) statutory authority is the **Internal Revenue Code of 1986,** as amended, known as the Code. The Internal Revenue Code has the same authoritative weight as tax treaties and Supreme Court rulings. Thus, a taxpayer should feel very confident in a tax return position, such as taking a deduction that is specifically allowed by the Code. The Internal Revenue Code is unique in that every other authority—all administrative and judicial authorities except tax treaties and the

EXHIBIT 2-7 Tax Legislation Process

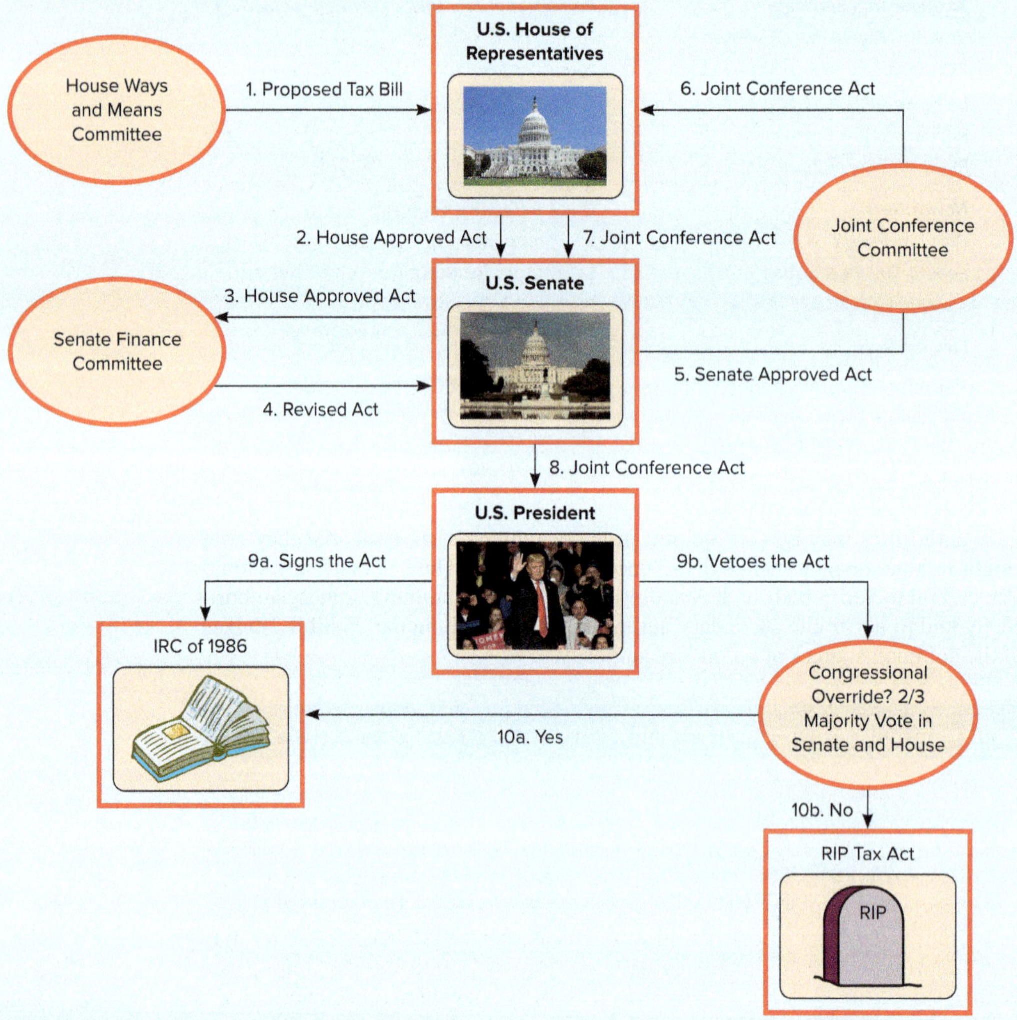

U.S. House: © Dwight Nadig/Getty Images, U.S. Senate: © Brand X Pictures/PunchStock, President: © Evan El/Shutterstock

Constitution—can be seen as an interpretation of it. Hence, understanding the relevant code section(s) is critical to being an efficient and effective tax professional.

Congress enacts tax legislation virtually every year that changes the Code; 1986 was simply the last major overhaul. Prior to 1986, tax law changes were incorporated into the Internal Revenue Code of 1954, the year a new numbering system and other significant changes were introduced. Before that, tax law changes were incorporated into the Internal Revenue Code of 1939, which was the year the tax law was first codified.

The Legislative Process for Tax Laws Exhibit 2-7 illustrates the legislative process for enacting tax laws. As required by the U.S. Constitution (Article 1, Section 7), "All bills for raising revenue shall originate in the House of Representatives." The Senate may propose tax legislation, but the first to formally consider a bill will be the House, typically within its Ways and Means Committee. After the committee debates the proposed legislation and drafts a bill, the bill goes to the House of Representatives floor for debate and ultimately a vote (either yea or nay without modification). If the bill is approved, it becomes an *act* and is sent to the Senate, which typically refers the act to the Senate Finance Committee. Not to be outdone by the House, the Senate Finance Committee usually amends the act during its deliberations. After the revised act passes the Senate Finance Committee, it goes to the Senate for debate and vote. Unlike representatives, senators may modify the proposed legislation during their debate.

If the Senate passes the act, both the House and Senate versions of the legislation are sent to the Joint Conference Committee, which consists of members of the House Ways and Means Committee and the Senate Finance Committee. During the Joint Conference Committee deliberations, committee members debate the two versions of the proposed legislation. Possible outcomes for any specific provision in the proposed legislation include adoption of the Senate version, the House version, or some compromise version of the two acts. Likewise, the Joint Conference Committee may simply choose to eliminate specific provisions from the proposed legislation or fail to reach a compromise, thereby terminating the legislation.

After the Joint Conference Committee approves the act, the revised legislation is sent to the House and Senate for vote. If both the House and Senate approve it, the act is sent to the president for his or her signature. If the president signs the act, it becomes law and is incorporated into the Internal Revenue Code of 1986 (Title 26 of the U.S. Code, which contains *all* codified laws of the United States). If the president vetoes the legislation, Congress may override the veto with a two-thirds positive vote in both the House and the Senate.

The House Ways and Means Committee, Senate Finance Committee, and Joint Conference Committee each produce a committee report that explains the current tax law, proposed change in the law, and reasons for the change. These committee reports are considered statutory sources of the tax law and may be very useful in interpreting tax law changes and understanding congressional intent. This is especially important after new legislation has been enacted because, with the exception of the Code, there will be very little authority interpreting the new law (i.e., no judicial or administrative authorities because of the time it takes for the new law to be litigated or for the IRS to issue interpretative guidance).

Basic Organization of the Code The Internal Revenue Code is segregated into subtitles, chapters, subchapters, parts, subparts, and sections. All existing and any new tax laws are placed in the Code within a specific subtitle, chapter, subchapter, part, subpart, and section of the Code. When referencing a tax law, the researcher generally refers to the law simply by its code section. Code sections are numbered from 1 to 9834, with gaps in the section numbers to allow new code sections to be added to the appropriate parts of the Code as needed. Each code section is further segregated into subsections, paragraphs, subparagraphs, and clauses to allow more specific reference or citation. See Exhibit 2-5 for an example code citation and explanation.

Memorizing the various subtitles and chapters of the Code has limited value (except to impress your friends at parties). However, understanding the *organization* of the Code is important, especially for the aspiring tax accountant. (See Exhibit 2-8.) First, you must understand the organization of a code section, its subsections, paragraphs, subparagraphs, and clauses to be able to cite the respective law correctly as, for example, IRC Sec. 162(b)(2). Second, note that many provisions in the Code apply only to specific parts of the Code. For example, it is quite common for a code section to include the phrase "for purposes of this chapter, ..." If you do not understand what laws are encompassed in the chapter, it would be very difficult for you to interpret the code section and determine its applicability to a research question.

Finally, remember that code sections addressing similar transactions, such as deductions, or topics, such as C corporations, are grouped together. Consider a researcher faced with the question of whether an item of income is taxable. If the researcher understands the organization of the Code, she can quickly focus her research on code sections 61–140, which provide a broad definition of gross income, list items specifically included in gross income, and identify items specifically excluded from gross income.

THE KEY FACTS

Statutory Authorities

- U.S. Constitution
  - The 16th Amendment provides Congress the ability to tax income directly, from whatever source derived, without apportionment across the states.
- Internal Revenue Code
  - The main statutory authority is the Internal Revenue Code of 1986.
  - The Internal Revenue Code has the same authoritative weight as tax treaties and Supreme Court rulings.
  - Changes to the Code are passed by the House of Representatives and Senate and signed into law by the president.
  - The House Ways and Means Committee and Senate Finance Committee oversee tax legislation in the House of Representatives and Senate, respectively.
  - When referencing a tax law, the researcher generally refers to the law by its code section.
- Treaties
  - Tax treaties are agreements negotiated between countries that describe the tax treatment of entities subject to tax in both countries.

EXHIBIT 2-8 Example of Code Organization

Subtitle A—Income Taxes
Chapter 1—Income Taxes
Subchapter A—Determination of Tax Liability
Part I—Definition of Gross Income, Adjusted Gross Income, Taxable Income, etc. (Sec. 61–68)
Sec. 61—Gross Income Defined
Sec. 62—Adjusted Gross Income Defined
Sec. 63—Taxable Income Defined
Subsection 63(c)—Standard Deduction
Paragraph 63(c)(2)—Basic Standard Deduction
Subparagraph 63(c)(2)(A)
Clause 63(c)(2)(A)(i)
Part II—Items Specifically Included in Gross Income (Sec. 71–90)
Sec. 71—Alimony
Sec. 72—Annuities
Sec. 73—Services of Child
Sec. 74—Prizes & Awards
Part III—Items Specifically Excluded from Gross Income (Sec. 101–140)
Sec. 101—Certain Death Benefits
Sec. 102—Gifts and Inheritances
Sec. 103—Interest on State & Local Bonds

Tax Treaties **Tax treaties** are negotiated agreements between countries that describe the tax treatment of entities subject to tax in both countries, such as U.S. citizens earning investment income in Spain. The U.S. president has the authority to enter into a tax treaty with another country after receiving the Senate's advice. If you are a U.S. citizen earning income abroad or an accountant with international clients, you need knowledge of U.S. tax laws, the foreign country's tax laws, and the respective tax treaty between the U.S. and the foreign country for efficient tax planning. Because the focus in this text is on U.S. tax laws, we only briefly mention the importance of tax treaties as a statutory authority.

Example 2-2

Bill recently spent a summer in Milan, Italy, teaching a graduate level economics course. While in Italy he earned a $20,000 stipend from Bocconi University and some interest in a temporary banking account that he established for the trip. What tax laws must Bill consider to determine the taxation of his $20,000 stipend?

Answer: U.S. tax laws, Italian tax laws, and the U.S.–Italy tax treaty will determine the tax consequences of the amounts Bill earned in Italy.

Judicial Sources: The Courts

Our judicial system has the ultimate authority to interpret the Internal Revenue Code and settle disputes between the IRS and taxpayers. As Exhibit 2-3 illustrates, there are five basic sources of judicial authority (three trial-level courts, 13 U.S. Circuit Courts of Appeals, and the Supreme Court). We've noted that the Supreme Court, along with the Code, represents the highest tax-specific authority. An important distinction between the two, however, is that the Supreme Court does not establish law, but instead simply interprets and applies the Code (along with other authorities). Thus, the Code and the Supreme Court should never be in conflict.[11]

THE KEY FACTS

Judicial Authorities

- Our judicial system is tasked with the ultimate authority to interpret the Internal Revenue Code and settle disputes between taxpayers and the IRS.
- The Supreme Court is the highest judicial authority.
- Beneath the Supreme Court, the decisions of the 13 Circuit Courts of Appeals represent the next highest judicial authority.

(continued)

[11]The Supreme Court does have the authority to declare a Code provision unconstitutional.

Below the Supreme Court, the decisions of the 13 U.S. Circuit Courts of Appeals represent the next highest judicial authority. The lowest level of judicial authority consists of three different types of trial-level courts (94 U.S. District Courts that hear cases involving taxpayers that reside within their respective district, the U.S. Court of Federal Claims, and the U.S. Tax Court). Given that the U.S. Tax Court hears only tax cases and that its judges are "tax experts," its decisions typically have more weight than those rendered by a district court or the U.S. Court of Federal Claims.[12] Likewise, because the U.S. Court of Federal Claims hears a much narrower set of issues than U.S. District Courts (only monetary claims against the U.S. government), its decisions have more weight than district court decisions.

In rendering court decisions, all courts apply the judicial doctrine of ***stare decisis.*** This doctrine means that a court will rule consistently with (a) its previous rulings (unless, due to evolving interpretations of the tax law over time, the court decides to overturn an earlier decision) and (b) the rulings of higher courts with appellate jurisdiction (the courts its cases are appealed to). The implication of *stare decisis* is that a circuit court will abide by Supreme Court rulings and its own rulings, whereas a trial-level court will abide by Supreme Court rulings, its respective circuit court's rulings, and its own rulings. For example, a district court in California would follow U.S. 9th Circuit and Supreme Court rulings as well as the court's own rulings.

The doctrine of *stare decisis* presents a special problem for the U.S. Tax Court because it appeals to different circuit courts based on the taxpayer's residence. To implement the doctrine of *stare decisis,* the tax court applies the **Golsen rule.**[13] The Golsen rule simply states that the tax court will abide by rulings of the circuit court that has appellate jurisdiction for a case.

- The lowest level of judicial authority consists of three different types of trial-level courts (U.S. District Courts, U.S. Court of Federal Claims, and the U.S. Tax Court).
- U.S. Tax Court decisions typically are considered to have more authoritative weight than decisions rendered by a district court or the U.S. Court of Federal Claims.
- All courts apply the judicial doctrine of *stare decisis,* which means that a court will rule consistently with its previous rulings and the rulings of higher courts with appellate jurisdiction.

Example 2-3

What if: If Bill and Mercedes opt to litigate their case in the U.S. Tax Court, by which circuit court's rulings will the court abide?

Answer: Because Bill and Mercedes live in Florida, the U.S. Tax Court will abide the circuit court with appellate jurisdiction in Florida, which happens to be the U.S. 11th Circuit Court.

Administrative Sources: The U.S. Treasury

Regulations, Revenue Rulings, and Revenue Procedures

The Treasury Department, of which the IRS is a bureau, is charged with administering and interpreting the tax laws of the United States, among other duties such as printing money and advising the president on economic issues. **Regulations** are the Treasury Department's official interpretation of the Internal Revenue Code, have the highest authoritative weight, and often contain examples of the application of the Code that may be particularly helpful to the tax researcher. Regulations are issued in three different forms: final, temporary, and proposed. The names are very descriptive. **Final regulations** are regulations that have been issued in final form, and thus, unless or until revoked, they represent the Treasury's interpretation of the Code. **Temporary regulations** have a limited life (three years for regulations issued after November 20, 1988). Nonetheless, during their life, they carry the same authoritative weight as final regulations. Finally, all regulations are issued in the form of **proposed regulations** first, to allow public comment on them. Proposed regulations do not carry the same authoritative weight as temporary or final regulations.

In addition to being issued in three different forms, regulations also serve three basic purposes: interpretative, procedural, and legislative. Most regulations are issued as

THE KEY FACTS

Administrative Authorities

- The Treasury Department is charged with administering and interpreting the tax laws.
- Regulations
  - Regulations are the Treasury Department's official interpretation of the Internal Revenue Code and have the highest authoritative weight.
  - Regulations are issued in three different forms (proposed, temporary, and final) and serve three basic purposes (interpretative, procedural, and legislative).

(continued)

[12]The Tax Court renders both "regular" and "memorandum" decisions. Regular decisions involve new or unusual points of law, whereas memorandum decisions involve questions of fact or the application of existing law. Both decisions have similar authoritative weight. Decisions issued by the Tax Court's Small Claims division may not be cited as precedent.

[13]54 TC 742 (1970).

- Revenue rulings and revenue procedures
  - Revenue rulings and revenue procedures are second in administrative authoritative weight after regulations.
  - Revenue rulings address the application of the Code and regulations to a specific factual situation.
  - Revenue procedures explain in greater detail IRS practice and procedures in administering the tax law.
- Letter rulings
  - Letter rulings are less authoritative but more specific than revenue rulings and regulations.
  - Private letter rulings represent the IRS's application of the Code and other tax authorities to a specific transaction and taxpayer.

interpretative or procedural regulations. As the names suggest, **interpretative regulations** represent the Treasury's interpretation of the Code. In Bill and Mercedes's case, these might be the regulations issued under IRC Sec. 163, which discuss interest deductions. **Procedural regulations** explain Treasury Department procedures as they relate to administering the Code. Again, for Bill and Mercedes's case, these might be the regulations issued under IRC Sec. 6501 regarding the statute of limitations for IRS assessment and collection. **Legislative regulations,** the rarest type, are issued when Congress specifically directs the Treasury Department to create regulations to address an issue in an area of law. In these instances, the Treasury is actually writing the law instead of interpreting the Code. Because legislative regulations represent tax law instead of an interpretation of tax law, legislative regulations generally have been viewed to have more authoritative weight than interpretative and procedural regulations. However, in *Mayo Foundation for Medical Education & Research v. U.S.,* 131 S.Ct. 704 (2011), the Supreme Court held (subject to specific conditions) that all Treasury regulations warrant deference. Accordingly, it is a very difficult process to challenge any regulation and thus, taxpayers are cautioned not to take tax return positions inconsistent with regulations.

Revenue rulings and revenue procedures are second in administrative authoritative weight after regulations. But unlike regulations, revenue rulings address the application of the Code and regulations to a specific factual situation. Thus, while **revenue rulings** have less authoritative weight, they provide a much more detailed interpretation of the Code as it applies to a specific transaction and fact pattern. For example, Rev. Rul. 87-22 discusses the deductions of prepaid interest (points) a taxpayer may claim when refinancing the mortgage for a principal residence, whereas the Code and regulations do not specifically address this issue. Although revenue rulings are binding on the IRS (until revoked, superseded, or modified), courts may agree or disagree with a revenue ruling. Thus, while revenue rulings should be carefully evaluated as they represent the IRS's interpretation, courts may provide a different interpretation of the tax law that a taxpayer might choose to follow. **Revenue procedures** are also much more detailed than regulations. They explain in greater detail IRS practice and procedures in administering the tax law. For example, Rev. Proc. 87-56 provides the specific depreciation lives for depreciable assets (discussed in the Property Acquisition and Cost Recovery chapter). As with revenue rulings, revenue procedures are binding on the IRS until revoked, modified, or superseded.

Letter Rulings Below revenue rulings and revenue procedures in authoritative weight rest letter rulings. As you might guess, letter rulings are less authoritative but more specific than revenue rulings and regulations. Letter rulings generally may not be used as precedent by taxpayers. However, they may be cited as authority to avoid the substantial understatement of tax penalty under IRC Sec. 6662 imposed on taxpayers and the related tax practitioner penalty under IRC Sec. 6694 (discussed later in this chapter). **Private letter rulings** represent the IRS's application of the Code and other tax authorities to a specific transaction and taxpayer. Private letter rulings are issued in response to a taxpayer request and are common for proposed transactions with potentially large tax implications. For example, companies commonly request a private letter ruling to ensure that a proposed corporate acquisition meets the definition of a tax-free exchange. However, the IRS also maintains a list of certain issues on which it refuses to rule, such as the tax consequences of proposed federal tax legislation. Each year, the IRS publishes an updated list of these transactions in a revenue procedure.

Other types of letter rulings include determination letters and technical advice memorandums. **Determination letters,** issued by local IRS directors, are generally not controversial. An example of a determination letter is the request by an employer for the IRS to rule that the taxpayer's retirement plan is a "qualified plan." **Technical advice memorandums** differ from private letter rulings in that they are generated for completed transactions and usually are requested by an IRS agent during an IRS audit.

Is this a comprehensive list of IRS pronouncements? No. In addition to the pronouncements listed above, the IRS issues several less common types, which are beyond the scope of this text. A couple of other pronouncements, however, warrant some discussion. As we mentioned above, the IRS and taxpayers litigate tax cases in a number of courts and jurisdictions. Obviously, the IRS wins some and loses some of these cases. Except for Supreme Court cases, whenever the IRS loses, it may issue an **acquiescence** or **nonacquiescence** as guidance for how the IRS intends to respond to the loss. Although an acquiescence indicates that the IRS has decided to *follow* the court's adverse ruling in the future, it does not mean that the IRS *agrees* with it. Instead, it simply means that the IRS will no longer litigate this issue. A nonacquiescence has the exact opposite implications and alerts taxpayers that the IRS does plan to continue to litigate this issue. Finally, the IRS also issues **actions on decisions,** which explain the background reasoning behind an IRS acquiescence or nonacquiescence.[14] What are noticeably absent from the list of administrative authorities? IRS publications and tax return form instructions. *Neither are considered primary authorities and should not be cited as precedent. Likewise, it is not advisable to rely on either to avoid taxpayer or tax practitioner penalties.*

TAX RESEARCH

LO 2-5

Now that you have a basic understanding of the different types of tax authority, why do you think that the IRS and taxpayers disagree with respect to the tax treatment of a transaction? In other words, why would the IRS and Bill and Mercedes's CPA reach different conclusions regarding the deductibility of certain expenses? The answer is that, because the Code does not specifically address the tax consequences of each transaction type or every possible variation of a particular transaction, the application of the tax law is subject to debate and differing interpretations by the IRS, courts, tax professionals, taxpayers, and so on. Tax research, therefore, plays a vital role in allowing us to identify and understand the varying authorities that provide guidance on an issue, to assess the relative weights of differing authorities, to understand the risks associated with different tax return positions, and ultimately to draw an appropriate conclusion regarding the application of the tax law to the issue. The following paragraphs describe the basic process of tax research that tax professionals use to identify and analyze tax authorities to answer tax questions. We will then revisit Bill and Mercedes's issue and view the research memo prepared by their CPA.

Step 1: Understand Facts

To answer a tax question, you must understand the question. To understand the question, you must know the facts. There are two basic types of facts: open facts and closed facts. Open facts have not yet occurred, such as the facts associated with a proposed transaction. Closed facts have already occurred. The distinction between open and closed facts is important because, unlike closed facts, open facts can be altered, and different facts may result in very different tax consequences. Open facts allow the taxpayer to arrange a transaction to achieve the most advantageous outcome. Thus, they are especially important in tax planning.

How do you determine the facts for a research question? Interview clients, speak with third parties such as attorneys and brokers, and review client documents such as contracts, prior tax returns, wills, trust documents, deeds, and corporate minutes. When interviewing clients, remember that not many are tax experts. Thus, it is up to the tax professional to ask the correct initial and follow-up questions to obtain all the relevant facts. Also consider nontax factors, such as a client's personal values or objectives, as these often put constraints on tax planning strategies.

Step 2: Identify Issues

A tax professional's ability to identify issues is largely a function of his or her type of tax expertise. A tax expert in a particular area will typically be able to identify quickly the

[14]Actions on decisions have no precedential value but may be cited as authority to avoid the substantial understatement of tax penalty under IRC Sec. 6662 imposed on taxpayers and the related tax practitioner penalty under IRC Sec. 6694 (discussed later in this chapter).

THE KEY FACTS

Tax Research

- The five steps in tax research are (1) understand the facts, (2) identify issues, (3) locate relevant authorities, (4) analyze the tax authorities, and (5) document and communicate research results.
- The two types of tax services that tax professionals use in tax research are annotated tax services, arranged by code section, and topical services, arranged by topic.
- Research questions often consist of questions of fact or questions of law.
  - The answer to a question of fact hinges upon the facts and circumstances of the taxpayer's transaction.
  - The answer to a question of law hinges upon the interpretation of the law, such as interpreting a particular phrase in a code section.
- When the researcher identifies that different authorities have conflicting views, she should evaluate the "hierarchy," jurisdiction, and age of the authorities.
- Once the tax researcher has identified relevant authorities, she must make sure that the authorities are still valid and up to date.

(continued)

- The most common end product of a research question is a research memo, which has five basic parts: (1) facts, (2) issues, (3) authority list, (4) conclusion, and (5) analysis.

specific tax issues that relate to transactions in that area. For example, an expert in corporate acquisitions would quickly identify the tax consequences and specific issues of alternative acquisition types. A novice, on the other hand, would likely identify broader issues first and then more specific issues as he or she researched the relevant tax law.

What's the best method to identify tax issues? First of all, get a good understanding of the client's facts. Then, combine your understanding of the facts with your knowledge of the tax law. Let's consider the example of Bill and Mercedes's interest deduction. For an expert in this particular area, the issues will be immediately evident. For a novice, the initial response may take the form of a series of general questions: (1) Is this item of expense deductible? (2) Is that item of income taxable? (3) In what year should the expense be deducted? (4) In what year should the item of income be taxed? After you identify these types of general issues, your research will enable you to identify the more specific issues that ultimately determine the tax ramifications of the transaction.

Example 2-4

Elizabeth, Bill and Mercedes's friend who is a shareholder and the CFO of a company, loaned money to her company to help prevent the company from declaring bankruptcy. Despite Elizabeth's loan, the company did file bankruptcy, and Elizabeth was not repaid the loan. What issues would a researcher consider?

Answer: The first questions to ask are whether Elizabeth can deduct the bad debt expense and, if so, as what type of deduction? As the researcher delves more into the general issue, he would identify that the type of deduction depends on whether Elizabeth's debt is considered a business or nonbusiness bad debt. This more specific issue depends on whether Elizabeth loaned the money to the company to protect her job (business bad debt) or to protect her stock investment in the company (nonbusiness bad debt). Bad debt expenses incurred for nonbusiness debts (investment-related debts) are deducted as capital losses and thus subject to limitations (discussed in Investments), whereas bad debt expenses for business debts (business-related debts) are ordinary deductions and not limited.

Why might this case be a good one to litigate in U.S. District Court?

Answer: Because a jury might be more likely to be convinced to assess Elizabeth's motives favorably.

Step 3: Locate Relevant Authorities

Step three in the research process is to locate the relevant authorities (code sections, regulations, court cases, revenue rulings) that address the tax issue. Luckily, tax services can aid the researcher in identifying relevant authorities. Most, if not all, of these services are available on the Internet (with a subscription) and thus offer the flexibility to conduct research almost anywhere.[15]

There are two basic types of tax services: annotated and topical. **Annotated tax services** are arranged by Internal Revenue Code section. That is, for each code section, an annotated service includes the code section; a listing of the code section history; copies of congressional committee reports that explain changes to the code section; a copy of all the regulations issued for the specific code section; the service's unofficial explanation of the code section; and brief summaries (called annotations) of relevant court cases, revenue rulings, revenue procedures, and letter rulings that address issues specific to the code section. Two examples of annotated tax services are Commerce Clearing House's (CCH) Standard Federal Tax Reporter and Research Institute of America's (RIA) United States Tax Reporter.

[15]www.IRS.gov contains a lot of information (tax forms, IRS publications, etc.) that may be especially useful for answering basic tax questions. In addition, tax publishers, such as CCH and RIA, produce quick reference tax guides (e.g., the *CCH Master Tax Guide* or the *RIA Federal Tax Handbook*) that may be used to answer basic tax questions.

Topical tax services are arranged by topic, such as taxable forms of income, tax-exempt income, and trade or business expenses. For each topic, the services identify tax issues that relate to each topic and then explain and cite authorities relevant to the issue (code sections, regulations, court cases, revenue rulings, etc.). Beginning tax researchers often prefer topical services, because they generally are easier to read. Some examples of topical federal tax services include BNA's Tax Management Portfolios, CCH's Tax Research Consultant, and RIA's Federal Tax Coordinator.

How does a researcher use these services? An expert would probably go directly to the relevant portions of an annotated or topical service. A novice may conduct a keyword search in the service, use the tax service's topical index, or "browse" the tax service to identify the relevant portions. Some suggestions for identifying keywords: Try to describe the transaction in three to five words. An ideal keyword search typically includes (1) the relevant area of law and (2) a fact or two that describes the transaction. Try to avoid keywords that are too broad (income, deduction, taxable) or that may be too narrow.

Example 2-5

Bill and Mercedes refinanced the mortgage on their principal residence a couple of years ago when their original mortgage's four-year balloon payment came due. Their mortgage institution charged Bill and Mercedes $3,000 of points (prepaid interest) upon the refinancing in order to give them a reduced interest rate. On their CPA's advice, Bill and Mercedes deducted the $3,000 in the year they paid it, but upon audit, the IRS disallowed the deduction. What is the research issue?

Answer: The issue is, should Bill and Mercedes have deducted the $3,000 of points in the year they paid it?

What are some keywords that could identify the relevant tax authority?

Answer: Points (area of law), interest (area of law), refinancing (fact that describes the transaction).

Keyword searching is more an art than an exact science. As you gain a better understanding of different areas of the tax law, you'll become much more efficient at using keywords. If keyword searching is not proving beneficial, check your spelling, make sure you're searching within the correct database, rethink your keywords, use another research method, use another tax service, or as a last resort, take a break.

While utilizing keyword searches or other research methods to identify potentially relevant areas of law and tax authorities, constantly ask yourself whether you are indeed in the correct area of law. Once the answer to this question is an authoritative yes, you can delve deeper into the area of law and related authorities to answer the question.

Step 4: Analyze Tax Authorities

Once a researcher identifies relevant authorities, she must read carefully to ensure she fully understands them, as well as their application to the research problem. Two basic types of issues researchers will encounter are questions of fact and questions of law.

The answer to a **question of fact** hinges upon the facts and circumstances of the taxpayer's transaction. For example, whether a trade or business expense is "ordinary," "necessary," "reasonable," and thus deductible, is a question of fact. If you're researching a question of fact, understand *which* facts determine the answer—in this case, which facts make an expense "ordinary," "necessary," and "reasonable" and which do not. In this type of question, the researcher will focus on understanding how various facts affect the research answer and identifying authorities with fact patterns similar to her client's.

The answer to a **question of law** hinges upon the interpretation of the law, such as interpreting a particular phrase in a code section (see the sample research memo in Exhibit 2-9 for an example of a question of law). If a researcher is faced with this type of

EXHIBIT 2-9 Sample Internal Research Memo

Below is the memo that Bill and Mercedes's CPA drafted after researching their issue.

Date: July 8, 2017

Preparer: Joe Staff

Reviewer: Sandra Miller

Subject: Deductibility of Points Paid in Refinancing

Facts: Four years ago Bill and Mercedes's credit union provided them a $250,000 mortgage loan for their new home. The mortgage loan was a four-year interest-only note with a balloon payment at the end of four years. Bill and Mercedes (Floridians residing in the 11th Circuit) chose this type of loan to allow them to minimize their mortgage payment until their previous house was sold. After 18 months, Bill and Mercedes sold their previous house and refinanced their original short-term loan with a 15-year conventional mortgage. The credit union charged Bill and Mercedes $3,000 in points (prepaid interest) upon the refinancing.

Issue: Can Bill and Mercedes deduct the points in the year they paid them?

Authorities: IRC Sec. 461(g)
Rev. Rul. 87-22, 1987-1 CB 146.
J.R. Huntsman v. Comm. (8 Cir., 1990), 90-2 USTC par. 50,340, rev'g 91 TC 917 (1988).
AOD 1991-002.
P.G. Cao v. Comm. (9 Cir., 1996), 96-1 USTC par. 50,167, aff'g 67 TCM 2171 (1994).

Conclusion: Because Bill and Mercedes's refinancing represents an integrated step in securing permanent financing for their home, substantial authority supports their deduction of the $3,000 in points this year.

Analysis: IRC Sec. 461(g)(1) provides that cash-method taxpayers (Bill and Mercedes) must amortize prepaid interest (points) over the life of the loan instead of receiving a current deduction. IRC Sec. 461(g)(2) provides an exception to the general rule of Sec. 461(g)(1). Specifically, IRC Sec. 461(g)(2) allows cash-method taxpayers to deduct points in the year paid if the related debt was incurred "in connection with the purchase or improvement of," and secured by, the taxpayer's principal residence. The question whether Bill and Mercedes should amortize or currently deduct the points paid to refinance the mortgage on their principal residence depends upon the interpretation of "in connection with the purchase or improvement of" found in IRC Sec. 461(g)(2).

There are two basic interpretations of "in connection with the purchase or improvement of." In Revenue Ruling 87-22, the IRS rules that points incurred in refinancing a mortgage on a taxpayer's residence are deductible in the year paid to the extent that the taxpayer uses the loan proceeds to improve the taxpayer's residence. Thus, points paid to simply refinance an existing mortgage without improving the residence must be amortized over the life of the loan.

In contrast, in *J.R. Huntsman v. Comm.*, the 8th Circuit Court interpreted the phrase "in connection with the purchase or improvement of" much more broadly and held that points incurred to refinance a mortgage on the taxpayer's principal residence are currently deductible if the refinancing represents an *integrated step to secure permanent financing* for the taxpayer's residence. The facts in *J.R. Huntsman v. Comm.* are very similar to Bill and Mercedes's facts. Like Bill and Mercedes, the taxpayers in *J.R. Huntsman v. Comm.* also purchased their principal residence using a short-term loan with a "balloon" payment. When the balloon payment came due, the taxpayers obtained a permanent mortgage on their home (a 30-year conventional mortgage). The 8th Circuit Court held that in this case the permanent mortgage was acquired to extinguish the short-term financing and finalize the purchase of the home. "Thus, where taxpayers purchase a principal residence with a short-term three-year loan secured by a mortgage on the residence, and replace the loan with permanent financing . . . , the permanent mortgage obtained is sufficiently in connection with the purchase of the home to fall within the exception provided for by section 461(g)(2)."

In Action on Decision 1991-002, the IRS has indicated that it will not follow the *J.R. Huntsman v. Comm.* decision outside the 8th Circuit (in the 11th Circuit where Bill and Mercedes live). Nonetheless, other courts (the 9th Circuit in *P.G. Cao v. Comm.*) have indicated a willingness to apply the 8th Circuit's interpretation of IRC Sec. 461(g)(2). That is, they have allowed deductibility of points incurred in refinancing if the refinancing occurred to secure permanent financing, instead of for some other reason such as to secure a lower interest rate.

Given the similarity in facts between Bill and Mercedes's refinancing and those in *J.R. Huntsman v. Comm.* (refinancing of a short-term note to secure permanent financing), substantial authority supports a current deduction of the points paid.

question, she will spend much of her time researching the various interpretations of the code section and take note of which authorities interpret the code differently and why.

For many tax questions, the answer is clear with no opposing interpretations or contrary authorities. For other questions, the researcher may identify that different authorities have conflicting views. In this situation, the tax researcher should evaluate the hierarchical level, jurisdiction, and age of the authorities, placing more weight on higher and newer authorities that have jurisdiction over the taxpayer. A tax researcher will become more adept at this process as she gains experience.

Once the tax researcher has identified relevant authorities, she must make sure the authorities are still valid and up to date. For court cases, a **citator,** which is a research tool that allows you to check the status of several types of tax authorities, will review the history of the case to find out, for example, whether it was subsequently appealed and overturned, and to identify subsequent cases that cite the case. Favorable citations strengthen a case, while unfavorable ones weaken it. Citators can also check the status of revenue rulings, revenue procedures, and other IRS pronouncements. Checking the status of the Code is fairly simple: just locate the current version. Checking the status of regulations is a little more complicated. Most tax services alert researchers if a regulation has not been updated for certain changes in the Code. If this is the case, the researcher should evaluate whether the changes in the Code make the regulation obsolete.

As you will see in the analysis section of the sample research memo drafted by Bill and Mercedes's CPA (see Exhibit 2-9), the question whether they should amortize or currently deduct the points paid to refinance the mortgage on their principal residence is a question of law that ultimately depends upon the interpretation of a particular phrase: "in connection with the purchase or improvement of" found in IRC Sec. 461(g)(2). Is there a correct answer to this question? No. There is no clear-cut answer. Rather, this is a situation where the tax professional must use professional judgment. Because there is substantial authority supporting the current deduction of the points (discussed in detail in the sample memo), Bill and Mercedes should be able to deduct the points currently without risk of penalty. However, Bill and Mercedes should be aware that the IRS has clearly stated in an action on decision that it will fight this issue outside the 8th Circuit—for example, in the 11th Circuit, where Bill and Mercedes live.

Step 5: Document and Communicate the Results

After a researcher finishes her research, the final step of the process is to document and communicate the results. The most common end product of a research question is the internal research memo the researcher drafts for her supervisor's attention. The memo has five basic parts: (1) facts, (2) issues, (3) authority list, (4) conclusion, and (5) analysis. The purpose of the memo is to inform the reader of the answer to a research question, and thus, it should be written in an objective manner by discussing all relevant authorities to the research question, including those authorities that support, as well as those that conflict with, the answer. Below are some suggestions for each part of the memo. Compare these to the execution within the sample internal research memo presented in Exhibit 2-9.

Facts Discuss facts relevant to the question presented—that is, facts that provide necessary background of the transaction (generally, who, what, when, where, and how much) and those facts that may influence the research answer. Keeping the fact discussion relatively brief will focus the reader's attention on the relevant characteristics of the transaction.

Issues State the specific issues that the memo addresses. This section confirms that you understand the research question, reminds the reader of the question being analyzed, and allows future researchers to determine whether the analysis in the memo is relevant. Issues should be written as specifically as possible and limited to one or two sentences per issue.

Authorities In this section, the researcher cites the relevant tax authorities that apply to the issue, such as the IRC, court cases, and revenue rulings. How many authorities should you cite? Enough to provide a clear understanding of the issue and interpretation of the law. Remember, in order to reach an accurate assessment of the strength of your conclusion, you should consider authorities that may support your desired conclusion, as well as those that may go against it.

Conclusion There should be one conclusion per issue. Each conclusion should answer the question as briefly as possible and, preferably, indicate why the answer is what it is.

Analysis The goal of the analysis is for the researcher to provide the reader a clear understanding of the area of law and specific authorities that apply. Typically, an analysis will be organized to discuss the general area(s) of law first (the code section) and then the specific authorities (court cases, revenue rulings) that apply to the research question. How many authorities should you discuss? As many as necessary to provide the reader an understanding of the issue and relevant authorities. After you discuss the relevant authorities, apply the authorities to your client's transaction and explain how the authorities result in your conclusion.

Client Letters In addition to internal research memos, tax professionals often send their clients letters that summarize their research and recommendations. Basic components of the client letter include: (1) research question and limitations, (2) facts, (3) analysis, and (4) closing. Below are some suggestions for each part of the client letter. Compare these to the execution within the sample client letter presented in Exhibit 2-10.

Research Question and Limitations After the salutation (Dear Bill and Mercedes) and social graces (I enjoyed seeing you last week at the Tampa Bay Boys and Girls Clubs charity auction. What a great event for such a worthy cause!), clearly state the research question addressed and any disclaimers related to the work performed. This portion of the letter ensures that the tax professional and client have a mutual understanding of the question researched and any limitations on the research performed. As with a memo, issues should be written as specifically as possible and be limited to one or two sentences. Most accounting firms have standard boilerplate language regarding the limitations on work performed that is included in every client letter.

Facts Briefly summarize the facts relevant to the question presented—that is, facts that provide necessary background of the transaction and those facts that may influence the research answer. Keeping the fact discussion relatively brief will focus the client's attention on the relevant characteristics of the transaction.

Analysis Summarize the relevant authorities (including citations in most situations) and their implications for the client's research question using precise language appropriate for the client's level of tax expertise. The length of this portion of the letter will vary with the complexity of the research question and the client's interest in understanding the specific research details.

Closing In this section, summarize the key outcome(s) of the research conducted and any recommended client action, thank the client for requesting your service, and remind the client to contact you with additional questions or for further assistance.

In the case of Bill and Mercedes's interest deduction, their CPA recommended a tax return position that the IRS disallowed upon audit. Did their CPA violate her professional responsibilities by recommending a position the IRS disallowed? Good question. Let's take a look at the rules governing tax professional responsibilities.

EXHIBIT 2-10 Sample Client Letter

Below is the client letter that Bill and Mercedes's CPA sent to them.

Dear Bill and Mercedes,

I enjoyed seeing you last week at the Tampa Bay Boys and Girls Clubs charity auction. What a great event for such a worthy cause!

Thank you for requesting my advice concerning the tax treatment of the points paid when refinancing your mortgage.

My research is based upon the federal income tax laws that apply as of the date of this letter and the facts that you have provided as follows: Four years ago your credit union provided you a $250,000 interest-only note on your home that required a balloon payment at the end of four years. You chose this type of loan to minimize your mortgage payment until your previous house sold. After 18 months, you sold your previous house and refinanced the original short-term loan with a 15-year conventional mortgage. The credit union charged you $3,000 in points upon the refinancing.

After a thorough review of the applicable tax authority, there is substantial authority that supports a current deduction of the $3,000 points paid. IRC Sec. 461(g)(2) allows cash-method taxpayers to deduct points in the year paid if the related debt was incurred "in connection with the purchase or improvement of," and secured by, the taxpayer's principal residence. There are two basic interpretations of "in connection with the purchase or improvement of." The IRS has ruled (Revenue Ruling 87-22) that points paid to simply refinance an existing mortgage without improving the residence must be amortized over the life of the loan. In contrast, in *J.R. Huntsman v. Comm.*, the 8th Circuit Court held that points incurred to refinance a mortgage on the taxpayer's principal residence are currently deductible if the refinancing represents an *integrated step to secure permanent financing* for the taxpayer's residence.

The facts in *J.R. Huntsman v. Comm.* are very similar to your facts. Like you, the taxpayers in *J.R. Huntsman v. Comm.* purchased their principal residence using a short-term loan with a "balloon" payment. When the balloon payment came due, the taxpayers obtained a permanent mortgage on their home. The 8th Circuit Court held that in this case the permanent mortgage was acquired to finalize the purchase of the home and allowed the current deduction of the points.

J.R. Huntsman v. Comm. provides substantial authority to support a current deduction of the $3,000 points paid to refinance your initial short-term mortgage. In addition, other courts have applied the 8th Circuit's interpretation of IRC Sec. 461(g)(2), which adds "strength" to the 8th Circuit decision. However, the IRS has indicated that it will not follow the *J.R. Huntsman v. Comm.* decision outside the 8th Circuit (in the 11th Circuit where you live). Accordingly, the IRS would likely disallow the $3,000 deduction upon audit, and thus, while you have substantial authority to deduct the points currently, there is risk in doing so.

I would be happy to discuss this issue with you in more depth as these types of issues are always difficult. Likewise, if you have any other questions or issues with which I may assist you, please do not hesitate to contact me. Thank you again for requesting my advice.

Sincerely,

Sandra Miller, CPA

TAX PROFESSIONAL RESPONSIBILITIES

LO 2-6

Tax practitioners are subject to a variety of statutes, rules, and codes of professional conduct. Some examples include the American Institute of CPAs (AICPA) Code of Professional Conduct, the AICPA **Statements on Standards for Tax Services (SSTS),** the IRS's Circular 230, and statutes enacted by a CPA's specific state board of accountancy. Tax practitioners should absolutely have a working knowledge of these statutes, rules, and guidelines because (1) they establish the professional standards for the practitioner and (2) failure to comply with the standards could result in adverse consequences for the tax professional, such as being admonished, suspended, or barred from practicing before the IRS; being admonished, suspended, or expelled from the AICPA; or suffering suspension or revocation of the CPA license. Given the voluminous nature of applicable statutes, rules, and codes, we will simply provide a brief overview of the major common sources of tax professional standards.

CPAs who are members of the AICPA are bound by the AICPA Code of Professional Conduct and Statements on Standards for Tax Services. Other tax professionals use these provisions as guidance of professional standards. The AICPA Code of Professional Conduct is not specific to tax practice and provides broader professional standards that are especially relevant for auditors—that is, for those independent CPAs charged with examining an entity's financial statements. Provisions included in the Code of Professional Conduct address the importance of a CPA maintaining independence from the client and using due professional care in carrying out responsibilities. Additional provisions limit the acceptance of contingent fees, preclude discreditable acts such as signing a false return, and prohibit false advertising and charging commissions. Most of these provisions rightly fall under the heading of common sense. Nonetheless, a regular review should prove useful to the practicing CPA.

The AICPA's Statements on Standards for Tax Services (SSTS) recommend appropriate standards of practice for tax professionals and are intended to complement other provisions that govern tax practice (e.g., Circular 230 discussed below). One objective of these standards is to encourage increased understanding by the Treasury, IRS, and the public of a CPA's professional standards. Many state boards of accountancy have adopted similar standards, thus making the SSTS especially important. Currently, seven SSTS describe the tax professional standards when recommending a tax return position, answering questions on a tax return, preparing a tax return using data supplied by a client, using estimates on a tax return, taking a tax return position inconsistent with a previous year's tax return, discovering a tax return error, and giving tax advice to taxpayers. Exhibit 2-11 provides a brief summary of each SSTS. Most important from a research perspective, SSTS No. 1 provides that a tax professional must comply with the standards imposed by the applicable tax authority when recommending a tax return position or preparing or signing a tax return. IRC Sec. 6694 provides these standards for federal tax purposes.

IRC Sec. 6694 imposes a penalty on a *tax practitioner* for any position that is not supported by **substantial authority.**[16] A good tax professional evaluates whether supporting authority is substantial based upon the supporting and opposing authorities' weight and relevance. Substantial authority suggests the probability that the taxpayer's position will be sustained upon audit or litigation is in the 35 to 40 percent range or above. The tax practitioner can also avoid penalty under IRC Sec. 6694 if the tax return position has at least a reasonable basis (i.e., is supported by one or more tax authorities) and the position is disclosed on the taxpayer's return.

Example 2-6

Did Bill and Mercedes's CPA meet her professional standards as provided by SSTS No. 1?

Answer: Yes. Based on *J.R. Huntsman v. Comm.*, it is safe to conclude that there is a 35 to 40 percent or greater probability that the current points deduction will be sustained upon judicial review. Specifically, Bill and Mercedes's facts are very similar to those in *J.R. Huntsman v. Comm.*, and subsequent courts have interpreted the phrase "in connection with" consistently with *J.R. Huntsman v. Comm.*

Circular 230, issued by the IRS, provides regulations governing tax practice and applies to all persons practicing before the IRS. There are five parts of Circular 230: Subpart A describes who may practice before the IRS (CPAs, attorneys, enrolled agents) and

[16]The "more likely than not" standard, defined as a greater than 50 percent chance of a position being sustained on its merits, applies to tax shelters and other reportable transactions specified by the IRS.

EXHIBIT 2-11 Summary of the AICPA Statements on Standards for Tax Services

SSTS No 1: Tax Return Positions

A tax professional should comply with the standards, if any, imposed by the applicable tax authority for recommending a tax return position, or preparing or signing a tax return. If the tax authority has no written standards (or if they are lower than the following standard), the tax professional may recommend a tax return position or prepare or sign a return when she has a good-faith belief that the position has a realistic possibility of being sustained if challenged, or if there is a reasonable basis for the position and it is *adequately disclosed* on the tax return.

SSTS No. 2: Answers to Questions on Returns

A tax professional should make a reasonable effort to obtain from the taxpayer the information necessary to answer all questions on a tax return.

SSTS No. 3: Certain Procedural Aspects of Preparing Returns

In preparing or signing a tax return, a tax professional may rely without verification on information that a taxpayer or a third party has provided, unless the information appears to be incorrect, incomplete, or inconsistent.

SSTS No. 4: Use of Estimates

Unless prohibited by statute or rule, a tax professional may use taxpayer estimates in preparing a tax return if it is impractical to obtain exact data and if the estimated amounts appear reasonable based on the facts and circumstances known by the professional.

SSTS No. 5: Departure from a Position Previously Concluded in an Administrative Proceeding or Court Decision

A tax professional may sign a tax return that contains a departure from a position previously concluded in an administrative or court proceeding if the tax professional adheres to the standards of SSTS No. 1. This rule does not apply if the taxpayer is bound to a specific tax treatment in the later year, such as by a formal closing agreement with the IRS.

SSTS No. 6: Knowledge of Error: Return Preparation and Administrative Proceedings

A tax professional must advise the taxpayer promptly of an error and its potential consequences when she learns of an error in a previously filed tax return, an administrative hearing (such as an audit), or the taxpayer's failure to file a required return. The tax professional should include a recommendation for appropriate measures the taxpayer should take. The professional is not obligated to inform the IRS of the error, nor may she do so without the taxpayer's permission, except when required by law. However, in an administrative proceeding only, the tax professional should request the taxpayer's agreement to disclose the error to the IRS. If the taxpayer refuses to disclose the error to the IRS, the professional may consider terminating the professional relationship with the taxpayer.

SSTS No. 7: Form and Content of Advice to Taxpayers

In providing advice to taxpayers, tax professionals must use judgment that reflects professional competence and serves the taxpayer's needs. The professional should ensure that the standards under SSTS No. 1 are satisfied for all advice rendered. The professional is not obligated to communicate with a taxpayer when subsequent events affect advice previously provided except when implementing plans associated with the advice provided or when the professional is obligated to do so by specific agreement.

what practicing before the IRS means (tax return preparation, representing clients before the IRS, and so on).[17] Subpart B describes the duties and restrictions that apply to individuals governed by Circular 230. Included in Subpart B are provisions discussing the submission of records to the IRS, guidelines when a practitioner discovers a tax return error, restrictions on charging contingency fees, prohibition of sharing employment with someone suspended from practicing before the IRS, stringent rules relating to providing

THE KEY FACTS

Tax Professional Responsibilities

- Tax practitioners are subject to a variety of statutes, rules, and codes of professional conduct.
- The AICPA's seven Statements on Standards for Tax Services (SSTS) recommend appropriate standards of practice for tax professionals.
  - Many state boards of accountancy have adopted similar standards to the SSTS standards.
- Circular 230 provides regulations governing tax practice and applies to all persons practicing before the IRS.
  - There is a good bit of overlap between Circular 230 and the AICPA SSTS.

[17]Similar to attorneys and CPAs, enrolled agents and registered tax return preparers can represent taxpayers before the IRS. To become an enrolled agent, you must have either worked for the IRS for five years or pass a comprehensive examination.

advice for tax shelters, and standards for when a practitioner can recommend a tax return position.[18] Subparts C and D explain sanctions and disciplinary proceedings for practitioners violating the Circular 230 provisions. Subpart E concludes with a few miscellaneous provisions (such as the Circular 230 effective date). There is a good bit of overlap between Circular 230 and the AICPA SSTS.

Although Circular 230 provides many rules governing tax practice, the Internal Revenue Code and other Treasury Regulations often contain requirements specific to tax professionals. Thus, it is important for tax professionals to keep abreast of all applicable guidance, regardless of the specific authoritative source. A good example of this is the tax-preparer registration requirement in Reg. §1.6109-2, which requires that all paid tax-return preparers apply for and receive a preparer tax identification number (PTIN) and pay an annual fee, as prescribed by the IRS. Although not a particularly daunting registration requirement, it is important nonetheless as failure to include the tax-return preparer's PTIN on tax returns is subject to a $50 penalty per violation.

LO 2-7

TAXPAYER AND TAX PRACTITIONER PENALTIES

THE KEY FACTS

Taxpayer and Tax Practitioner Penalties

- The IRS can impose both criminal and civil penalties to encourage tax compliance by both tax professionals and taxpayers.
- The standard of conviction is higher in a criminal trial, but the penalties are also much higher.
- A taxpayer will not be subject to an underpayment penalty if there is substantial authority that supports the tax return position.
- A tax practitioner will also not be subject to penalty for recommending a tax return position if there is substantial authority that supports the position.

In addition to motivating good behavior via tax professional standards, the IRS can impose both criminal and civil penalties to encourage tax compliance by both tax professionals and taxpayers. **Civil penalties** are much more common, generally come in the form of monetary penalties, and may be imposed when tax practitioners or taxpayers violate tax statutes without reasonable cause—say, as the result of negligence, intentional disregard of pertinent rules, willful disobedience, or outright fraud. Some common examples of civil penalties are listed in Exhibit 2-12.

Criminal penalties are much less common than civil penalties, although they have been used to incarcerate some of the most notorious criminals. (Notorious mobster Al Capone was convicted and put in prison for tax evasion.) They are commonly charged in tax evasion cases, which include willful intent to defraud the government, but are imposed only after normal due process, including a trial. Compared to civil cases, the standard of conviction is higher in a criminal trial; guilt must be proven beyond a reasonable doubt (versus a "clear and convincing evidence" standard for civil tax fraud). However, the penalties are also much higher, such as fines up to $100,000 for individuals plus a prison sentence.

Assuming the IRS assesses additional tax upon audit, will the taxpayer always be subject to penalty? No. While the taxpayer will have to pay interest on the underpayment, he or she will *not* be subject to an underpayment penalty *if there is substantial authority that supports the tax return position.*[19] As previously discussed, substantial authority suggests that the probability that the taxpayer's position will be sustained upon audit or litigation is in the 35 to 40 percent range or above.

Example 2-7

What is Bill and Mercedes's exposure to penalties in their IRS audit?

Answer: None. Why? Because "substantial tax authority" supports their tax return position and the disputed tax liability is relatively small (the tax savings on a $3,000 tax deduction), Bill and Mercedes have no penalty exposure. Nonetheless, Bill and Mercedes will owe interest on the disputed tax liability unless the IRS recants its position in the audit or appeals process (or if the case is litigated and Bill and Mercedes win).

[18] Circular 230 imposes the same tax practitioner standards as in IRC Sec. 6694 for when a tax practitioner generally may recommend a tax return position (substantial authority and no disclosure or reasonable basis with disclosure).

[19] The taxpayer can also avoid penalty if the tax return position has at least a reasonable basis (i.e., supported by one or more tax authorities) and the position is disclosed on the taxpayer's return (IRC Sec. 6662).

EXHIBIT 2-12 Civil Penalties Imposed for Tax Violations

Taxpayers		Tax Practitioners	
Failure to file a tax return	5% of tax due per month (or partial month). Maximum penalty is 25% of net tax due. If the tax return is not filed within 60 days of the due date (including extensions), the minimum penalty is the smaller of $210 or 100% of the unpaid tax.	Failure to provide a copy of the tax return to a taxpayer	$50 per violation
Failure to pay tax owed	0.5% of tax due per month (or partial month). Reduces the failure to file a tax return penalty, if applicable. Maximum combined failure to file and failure to pay tax penalty is 5% of net tax due per month not to exceed 25% of net tax due. Minimum combined penalty if the tax return is not filed within 60 days of the due date (including extensions) is the smaller of $210 or 100% of the unpaid tax.	Failure to sign a tax return	$50 per violation
Failure to make estimated payments	Penalty varies with federal short-term interest rate and underpayment.	Failure to include the tax practitioner's ID number on the tax return	$50 per violation
Substantial understatement of tax	20% of understatement	Failure to keep a listing of taxpayers or tax returns	$50 per violation
Underpayment of tax due to transactions lacking economic substance	20% or 40% of understatement		
Providing false withholding information	$500	Failure to keep a listing of employees	$50 per violation
Fraud	75% of liability attributable to fraud.	Understatement due to unreasonable position	Greater of $1,000 or 50% of income derived from preparing the taxpayer's tax return.
		Willful understatement of tax	Greater of $5,000 or 75% of income derived from preparing the taxpayer's tax return.
		Organizing, promoting, etc. an abusive tax shelter	Lesser of $1,000 or 100% of gross income derived from tax shelter. If activity is based on fraudulent statements, the penalty equals 50% of gross income derived from tax shelter.
		Aiding and abetting the understatement of a tax liability	$1,000 ($10,000 if related to corporate taxes).

As we explained in Example 2-6, Bill and Mercedes's CPA met her professional standards (as defined currently in SSTS No. 1) by recommending a tax return position that meets the "Substantial Authority" standard. Likewise, because substantial tax authority supports the tax return position, Bill and Mercedes's CPA should also not have penalty exposure under IRC Sec. 6694.

CONCLUSION

Now that we have a full understanding of the issue under audit for Bill and Mercedes, what is their likely outcome? Another good question. The IRS has stated that it will continue to disallow a current deduction for points incurred for refinanced mortgages. Nonetheless, the courts appear to follow *J.R. Huntsman v. Comm.,* and therefore, the IRS stands a strong possibility of losing this case if litigated. In an IRS appeals conference, the appeals officer may consider the hazards of litigation. Accordingly, Bill and Mercedes have a good likelihood of a favorable resolution at the appeals conference.

In this chapter we discussed several of the fundamentals of tax practice and procedure: taxpayer filing requirements, the statute of limitations, the IRS audit process, the primary tax authorities, tax research, tax professional standards, and taxpayer and tax practitioner penalties. For the tax accountant, these fundamentals form the basis for much of her work. Likewise, tax research forms the basis of much of a tax professional's compliance and planning services. Even for the accountant who doesn't specialize in tax accounting, gaining a basic understanding of tax practice and procedure is important. Assisting clients with the IRS audit process is a valued service that accountants provide, and clients expect all accountants to understand basic tax procedure issues and how to research basic tax issues.

Summary

LO 2-1 Identify the filing requirements for income tax returns and the statute of limitations for assessment.

- All corporations must file a tax return annually regardless of their taxable income. Estates and trusts are required to file annual income tax returns if their gross income exceeds $600. The filing requirements for individual taxpayers depend on the taxpayer's filing status, age, and gross income.
- Individual and C corporation tax returns (except for C corporations with a June 30 year-end) are due on the fifteenth day of the fourth month following year-end. For C corporations with a June 30 year-end, partnerships and S corporations, tax returns must be filed by the fifteenth day of the third month following the entity's fiscal year-end. Any taxpayer unable to file a tax return by the original due date can request an extension to file.
- For both amended tax returns filed by a taxpayer and proposed tax assessments by the IRS, the statute of limitations generally ends three years from the *later* of (1) the date the tax return was actually filed or (2) the tax return's original due date.

LO 2-2 Outline the IRS audit process, how returns are selected, the different types of audits, and what happens after the audit.

- The IRS uses a number of computer programs and outside data sources to identify tax returns that may have an understated tax liability. Common computer initiatives include the DIF (Discriminant Function) system, the document perfection program, and the information matching program.
- The three types of IRS audits consist of correspondence, office, and field examinations.
- After the audit, the IRS will send the taxpayer a 30-day letter, which provides the taxpayer the opportunity to pay the proposed assessment or request an appeals conference. If an agreement is not reached at appeals or the taxpayer does not pay the proposed

assessment, the IRS will send the taxpayer a 90-day letter. At this time, the taxpayer may pay the tax or petition the U.S. Tax Court to hear the case. If the taxpayer chooses to pay the tax, the taxpayer may then request a refund of the tax and eventually sue the IRS for a refund in the U.S. District Court or the U.S. Court of Federal Claims.

Evaluate the relative weights of the various tax law sources. LO 2-3

- Primary authorities are official sources of the tax law generated by the legislative branch (statutory authority issued by Congress), judicial branch (rulings by the U.S. District Court, U.S. Tax Court, U.S. Court of Federal Claims, U.S. Circuit Court of Appeals, or U.S. Supreme Court), or executive/administrative branch (Treasury and IRS pronouncements). Secondary authorities are unofficial tax authorities that interpret and explain the primary authorities.

Describe the legislative process as it pertains to taxation. LO 2-4

- Exhibit 2-7 illustrates the legislative process for enacting tax law changes. Bills proceed from the House Ways and Means Committee to the House of Representatives. If approved, the act is sent to the Senate Finance Committee with a revised version then sent to the U.S. Senate. If approved, the Joint Conference Committee considers the acts passed by the House of Representatives and Senate. If a compromise is reached, the revised act is sent to the House of Representatives; if approved, it is then sent to the Senate; and if approved by the Senate, it is then sent to the president. If signed by the president, the act is incorporated into the IRC of 1986. If the president vetoes the legislation, Congress may override the veto with a two-thirds positive vote in both the House of Representatives and Senate.

Perform the basic steps in tax research and evaluate various tax law sources when faced with ambiguous statutes. LO 2-5

- The five basic steps in tax research are (1) understand the facts, (2) identify issues, (3) locate relevant authorities, (4) analyze the tax authorities, and (5) document and communicate research results.
- When the researcher identifies that different authorities have conflicting views, she should evaluate the "hierarchy," jurisdiction, and age of the authorities, placing more weight on higher and newer authorities that have jurisdiction over the taxpayer.

Describe tax professional responsibilities in providing tax advice. LO 2-6

- Tax practitioners are subject to a variety of statutes, rules, and codes of professional conduct. Some examples include the American Institute of CPAs (AICPA) Code of Professional Conduct, the AICPA Statements on Standards for Tax Services (SSTS), the IRS's Circular 230, and statutes enacted by a CPA's specific state board of accountancy.
- The AICPA's Statements on Standards for Tax Services (SSTS) recommend appropriate standards of practice for tax professionals. Many state boards of accountancy have adopted similar standards, thus making the SSTS especially important. Currently, there are seven SSTS (summarized in Exhibit 2-11) that describe the tax professional standards.
- Circular 230 provides regulations governing tax practice and applies to all persons practicing before the IRS. There is a good bit of overlap between Circular 230 and the AICPA SSTS.

Identify taxpayer and tax professional penalties. LO 2-7

- The IRS can impose both criminal and civil penalties to encourage tax compliance by both tax professionals and taxpayers. Civil penalties are much more common, generally come in the form of monetary penalties, and may be imposed when tax practitioners or taxpayers violate tax statutes without reasonable cause. Some common examples of civil penalties are listed in Exhibit 2-12.
- Criminal penalties are much less common than civil penalties and are commonly charged in tax evasion cases. Compared to civil cases, the standard of conviction is higher in a criminal trial, but the penalties are also much higher.
- A taxpayer will not be subject to an underpayment penalty if there is substantial authority that supports the tax return position.
- A tax practitioner will also not be subject to penalty for recommending a tax return position if there is substantial authority that supports the position.

KEY TERMS

30-day letter (2-6)
90-day letter (2-6)
acquiescence (2-17)
action on decision (2-17)
annotated tax service (2-18)
Circular 230 (2-24)
citator (2-21)
civil penalties (2-26)
correspondence examination (2-5)
criminal penalties (2-26)
determination letters (2-16)
DIF (Discriminant Function) system (2-4)
document perfection program (2-4)
field examination (2-6)
final regulations (2-15)
Golsen rule (2-15)
information matching program (2-4)
Internal Revenue Code of 1986 (2-11)
interpretative regulations (2-16)
legislative regulations (2-16)
nonacquiescence (2-17)
office examination (2-6)
primary authorities (2-9)
private letter rulings (2-16)
procedural regulations (2-16)
proposed regulations (2-15)
question of fact (2-19)
question of law (2-19)
regulations (2-15)
revenue procedures (2-16)
revenue rulings (2-16)
secondary authorities (2-9)
***stare decisis* (2-15)**
Statements on Standards for Tax Services (SSTS) (2-23)
statute of limitations (2-3)
substantial authority (2-24)
tax treaties (2-14)
technical advice memorandum (2-16)
temporary regulations (2-15)
topical tax service (2-19)
U.S. Circuit Courts of Appeals (2-7)
U.S. Constitution (2-11)
U.S. Court of Federal Claims (2-6)
U.S. District Court (2-6)
U.S. Supreme Court (2-8)
U.S. Tax Court (2-6)
***writ of certiorari* (2-8)**

DISCUSSION QUESTIONS

Discussion Questions are available in Connect®. connect

LO 2-1 1. Name three factors that determine whether a taxpayer is required to file a tax return.

LO 2-1 2. Benita is concerned that she will not be able to complete her tax return by April 15. Can she request an extension to file her return? By what date must she do so? Assuming she requests an extension, what is the latest date that she could file her return this year without penalty?

LO 2-1 3. Agua Linda Inc. is a calendar-year corporation. What is the original due date for the corporate tax return? What happens if the original due date falls on a Saturday?

LO 2-2 4. Approximately what percentage of tax returns does the IRS audit? What are the implications of this number for the IRS's strategy in selecting returns for audit?

LO 2-2 5. Explain the difference between the DIF system and the National Research Program. How do they relate to each other?

LO 2-2 6. Describe the differences between the three types of audits in terms of their scope and taxpayer type.

LO 2-2 7. Simon just received a 30-day letter from the IRS indicating a proposed assessment. Does he have to pay the additional tax? What are his options?

LO 2-2 8. Compare and contrast the three trial-level courts.

LO 2-3 9. Compare and contrast the three types of tax law sources and give examples of each.

LO 2-3 10. The U.S. Constitution is the highest tax authority but provides very little in the way of tax laws. What are the next highest tax authorities beneath the U.S. Constitution?

LO 2-3 11. Jackie has just opened her copy of the Code for the first time. She looks at the table of contents and wonders why it is organized the way it is. She questions whether it makes sense to try and understand the Code's organization. What are some reasons why understanding the organization of the Internal Revenue Code may prove useful?

12. Laura Li, a U.S. resident, worked for three months this summer in Hong Kong. What type of tax authority may be especially useful in determining the tax consequences of her foreign income? LO 2-3
13. What are the basic differences between regulations, revenue rulings, and private letter rulings? LO 2-3
14. Under what circumstance would the IRS issue an acquiescence? A nonacquiescence? An action on decision? LO 2-3
15. Carlos has located a regulation that appears to answer his tax research question. He is concerned because the regulation is a temporary regulation. Evaluate the authoritative weight of this type of regulation. Should he feel more or less confident in his answer if the regulation is a proposed regulation? LO 2-3
16. Tyrone recently read a regulation that Congress specifically requested the IRS to issue. What type of regulation is this? How does this regulation's authoritative weight compare to other regulations? LO 2-3
17. In researching a tax question, you find only one authority (a trial-level court opinion) that is directly on point. Which court would you least prefer to have hear this case and why? LO 2-3
18. What is *stare decisis* and how does it relate to the Golsen rule? LO 2-3
19. Mason was shocked to learn that the current Code is the Internal Revenue Code of 1986. He thought that U.S. tax laws change more frequently. What is wrong with Mason's perception? LO 2-4
20. Describe in general the process by which new tax legislation is enacted. LO 2-4
21. What are the three committees that debate proposed tax legislation? What documents do these committees generate, and how might they be used? LO 2-4
22. The president recently vetoed a tax act passed by the House and Senate. Is the tax act dead? If not, what will it take for the act to be passed? LO 2-4
23. What are the five basic parts of an internal research memo? LO 2-5
24. What is the difference between primary and secondary authorities? Explain the role of each authority type in conducting tax research. LO 2-5
25. Jorge is puzzled that the IRS and his CPA could legitimately reach different conclusions on a tax issue. Why does this happen? LO 2-5
26. What is the difference between open and closed facts? How is this distinction important in conducting tax research? LO 2-5
27. In writing a research memo, what types of facts should be included in the memo? LO 2-5
28. Amber is a tax expert, whereas Rob is a tax novice. Explain how their process in identifying tax issues may differ. LO 2-5
29. Discuss the basic differences between annotated and topical tax services. How are these services used in tax research? LO 2-5
30. In constructing a keyword search, what should the keyword search include? LO 2-5
31. Lindley has become very frustrated in researching a tax issue using keyword searches. What suggestions can you give her? LO 2-5
32. Nola, a tax novice, has a fairly simple tax question. Besides tax services, what are some sources that she can use to answer her question? LO 2-5
33. Armando identifies a tax research question as being a question of fact. What types of authorities should he attempt to locate in his research? LO 2-5
34. How are citators used in tax research? LO 2-5
35. What is the general rule for how many authorities a research memo should discuss? LO 2-5
36. Identify some of the sources for tax professional standards. What are the potential ramifications of failing to comply with these standards? LO 2-6

LO 2-6 37. Levi is recommending a tax return position to his client. What standard must he meet to satisfy his professional standards? What is the source of this professional standard?

LO 2-6 38. What is Circular 230?

LO 2-7 39. What are the basic differences between civil and criminal tax penalties?

LO 2-7 40. What are some of the most common civil penalties imposed on taxpayers?

LO 2-7 41. What are the taxpayer's standards to avoid the substantial understatement of tax penalty?

LO 2-7 42. What are the tax practitioner's standards to avoid a penalty for recommending a tax return position?

PROBLEMS

Select problems are available in Connect®. connect

LO 2-1 43. Ahmed does not have enough cash on hand to pay his taxes. He was excited to hear that he can request an extension to file his tax return. Does this solve his problem? What are the ramifications if he doesn't pay his tax liability by April 15?

LO 2-1 44. Molto Stancha Corporation had zero earnings this fiscal year; in fact, it lost money. Must the corporation file a tax return?

LO 2-1 45. The estate of Monique Chablis earned $450 of income this year. Is the estate required to file an income tax return?

LO 2-1 46. Jamarcus, a full-time student, earned $2,500 this year from a summer job. He had no other income this year and will have zero federal income tax liability this year. His employer withheld $300 of federal income tax from his summer pay. Is Jamarcus required to file a tax return? Should Jamarcus file a tax return?

LO 2-1 47. Shane has never filed a tax return despite earning excessive sums of money as a gambler. When does the statute of limitations expire for the years in which Shane has not filed a tax return?

LO 2-1 48. Latoya filed her tax return on February 10 this year. When will the statute of limitations expire for this tax return?

LO 2-1 49. Using the facts from the previous problem, how would your answer change if Latoya understated her income by 40 percent? How would your answer change if Latoya intentionally failed to report as taxable income any cash payments she received from her clients?

LO 2-2 50. Paula could not reach an agreement with the IRS at her appeals conference and has just received a 90-day letter. If she wants to litigate the issue but does not have sufficient cash to pay the proposed deficiency, what is her best court choice?

LO 2-2 51. In choosing a trial-level court, how should a court's previous rulings influence the choice? How should circuit court rulings influence the taxpayer's choice of a trial-level court?

LO 2-2 52. Sophia recently won a tax case litigated in the 7th Circuit. She recently heard that the Supreme Court denied the *writ of certiorari*. Should she be happy or not, and why?

LO 2-2 53. Campbell's tax return was audited because she failed to report interest she earned on her tax return. What IRS audit selection method identified her tax return?

LO 2-2 54. Yong's tax return was audited because he calculated his tax liability incorrectly. What IRS audit procedure identified his tax return for audit?

LO 2-2 55. Randy deducted a high level of itemized deductions two years ago relative to his income level. He recently received an IRS notice requesting documentation for his itemized deductions. What audit procedure likely identified his tax return for audit?

56. Jackie has a corporate client that has recently received a 30-day notice from the IRS with a $100,000 tax assessment. Her client is considering requesting an appeals conference to contest the assessment. What factors should Jackie advise her client to consider before requesting an appeals conference? LO 2-2 planning

57. The IRS recently completed an audit of Shea's tax return and assessed $15,000 additional tax. Shea requested an appeals conference but was unable to settle the case at the conference. She is contemplating which trial court to choose to hear her case. Provide a recommendation based on the following alternative facts: LO 2-2 planning
    a) Shea resides in the 2nd Circuit, and the 2nd Circuit has recently ruled against the position Shea is litigating.
    b) The Federal Circuit Court of Appeals has recently ruled in favor of Shea's position.
    c) The issue being litigated involves a question of fact. Shea has a very appealing story to tell but little favorable case law to support her position.
    d) The issue being litigated is highly technical, and Shea believes strongly in her interpretation of the law.
    e) Shea is a local elected official and would prefer to minimize any local publicity regarding the case.

58. Juanita, a Texas resident (5th Circuit), is researching a tax question and finds a 5th Circuit case ruling that is favorable and a 9th Circuit case that is unfavorable. Which circuit case has more "authoritative weight" and why? How would your answer change if Juanita were a Kentucky resident (6th Circuit)? LO 2-3

59. Faith, a resident of Florida (11th Circuit) recently found a circuit court case that is favorable to her research question. Which two circuits would she prefer to have issued the opinion? LO 2-3

60. Robert has found a "favorable" authority directly on point for his tax question. If the authority is a court case, which court would he prefer to have issued the opinion? Which court would he least prefer to have issued the opinion? LO 2-3

61. Jamareo has found a "favorable" authority directly on point for his tax question. If the authority is an administrative authority, which specific type of authority would he prefer to answer his question? Which administrative authority would he least prefer to answer his question? LO 2-3

62. For each of the following citations, identify the type of authority (statutory, administrative, or judicial) and explain the citation. LO 2-3
    a) Reg. Sec. 1.111-1(b)
    b) IRC Sec. 469(c)(7)(B)(i)
    c) Rev. Rul. 82-204, 1982-2 C.B. 192
    d) *Amdahl Corp.*, 108 TC 507 (1997)
    e) PLR 9727004
    f) *Hills v. Comm.*, 50 AFTR2d 82-6070 (11th Cir., 1982)

63. For each of the following citations, identify the type of authority (statutory, administrative, or judicial) and explain the citation. LO 2-3
    a) IRC Sec. 280A(c)(5)
    b) Rev. Proc. 2004-34, 2004-1 C.B. 911
    c) *Lakewood Associates,* RIA TC Memo 95-3566
    d) TAM 200427004
    e) *U.S. v. Muncy,* 2008-2 USTC par. 50,449 (E.D., AR, 2008)

64. Justine would like to clarify her understanding of a code section recently enacted by Congress. What tax law sources are available to assist Justine? LO 2-4

65. Aldina has identified conflicting authorities that address her research question. How should she evaluate these authorities to make a conclusion? LO 2-5

LO 2-5

66. Georgette has identified a 1983 court case that appears to answer her research question. What must she do to determine if the case still represents "current" law?

LO 2-5

67. Sandy has determined that her research question depends upon the interpretation of the phrase "not compensated by insurance." What type of research question is this?

LO 2-5 research

68. J. C. has been a professional gambler for many years. He loves this line of work and believes the income is tax-free.
    a) Use an available tax research service to determine whether J. C.'s thinking is correct. Is the answer to this question found in the Internal Revenue Code? If not, what type of authority answers this question?
    b) Write a memo communicating the results of your research.

LO 2-5 research

69. Katie recently won a ceramic dalmatian valued at $800 on a television game show. She questions whether this prize is taxable since it was a "gift" she won on the show.
    a) Use an available tax research service to answer Katie's question.
    b) Write a letter to Katie communicating the results of your research.

LO 2-5 research

70. Pierre recently received a tax penalty for failing to file a tax return. He was upset to receive the penalty, but he was comforted by the thought that he will get a tax deduction for paying the penalty.
    a) Use an available tax research service to determine if Pierre is correct.
    b) Write a memo communicating the results of your research.

LO 2-5 research

71. Paris was happy to provide a contribution to her friend Nicole's campaign for mayor, especially after she learned that charitable contributions are tax deductible.
    a) Use an available tax service to determine whether Paris can deduct this contribution.
    b) Write a memo communicating the results of your research.

LO 2-5 research

72. Matt and Lori recently were divorced. Although grief stricken, Matt was at least partially comforted by his monthly receipt of $10,000 alimony. He was particularly excited to learn from his friend, Denzel, that the alimony was not taxable. Use an available tax service to determine if Denzel is correct. Would your answer change if Matt and Lori continued to live together?

LO 2-5 research

73. Shaun is a huge college football fan. In the past, he has always bought football tickets on the street from ticket scalpers. This year, he decided to join the university's ticket program, which requires a $2,000 contribution to the university for the "right" to purchase tickets. Shaun will then pay $400 per season ticket. Shaun understands that the price paid for the season tickets is not tax deductible as a charitable contribution. However, contributions to a university are typically tax deductible.
    a) Use an available tax service to determine how much, if any, of Shaun's $2,000 contribution for the right to purchase tickets is tax deductible.
    b) Write a letter to Shaun communicating the results of your research.

LO 2-5 research

74. Latrell recently used his Delta Skymiles to purchase a free round-trip ticket to Milan, Italy (value $1,200). The frequent flyer miles used to purchase the ticket were generated from Latrell's business travel as a CPA. Latrell's employer paid for his business trips, and he was not taxed on the travel reimbursement.
    a) Use an available tax research service to determine how much income, if any, Latrell will have to recognize as a result of purchasing an airline ticket with Skymiles earned from business travel.
    b) Write a memo communicating the results of your research.

75. Benjamin, a new staff accountant for Local Firm CPAs LLC, takes a CPA review course to help prepare for the CPA exam. Benjamin is not reimbursed for the cost of the course ($1,500), but his firm expects him to take and pass the exam. LO 2-5 research
    a) Use an available tax research service to determine if Benjamin may deduct the cost of the CPA exam course.
    b) Write a memo communicating the results of your research.
76. Randy has found conflicting authorities that address a research question for one of his clients. The majority of the authorities provide an unfavorable answer for his client. According to Randy's estimates, if the client takes the more favorable position on its tax return then there is approximately a 48 percent chance that the position will be sustained upon audit or judicial proceeding. If the client takes this position on its tax return, will Randy be subject to penalty? Will the client potentially be subject to penalty? LO 2-6
77. Using the same facts from the previous problem, how would your answer change if Randy estimates that there is only a 20 percent chance that the position will be sustained upon audit or judicial proceeding? LO 2-6
78. Sasha owes additional tax imposed in a recent audit. In addition to the tax, will she be assessed other amounts? If so, how will these amounts be determined? LO 2-7
79. Maurice has a client that recently asked him about the odds of the IRS detecting cash transactions not reported on a tax return. What are some of the issues that Maurice should discuss with his client? LO 2-7

ROGER | CPA Review

Sample CPA Exam questions from Roger CPA Review are available in Connect as support for the topics in this text. These Multiple Choice Questions and Task-Based Simulations include expert-written explanations and solutions, and provide a starting point for students to become familiar with the content and functionality of the actual CPA Exam.

chapter 3

Tax Planning Strategies and Related Limitations

Learning Objectives

Upon completing this chapter, you should be able to:

- LO 3-1 Identify the objectives of basic tax planning strategies.
- LO 3-2 Apply the timing strategy and describe its applications and limitations.
- LO 3-3 Apply the concept of present value to tax planning.
- LO 3-4 Apply the strategy of income shifting, provide examples, and describe its limitations.
- LO 3-5 Apply the conversion strategy, provide examples, and describe its limitations.
- LO 3-6 Describe basic judicial doctrines that limit tax planning strategies.
- LO 3-7 Contrast tax avoidance and tax evasion.

© Cultura RF/Getty Images

Storyline Summary

Taxpayers:	Bill and Mercedes
Family description:	Bill and Mercedes are married with one daughter, Margaret.
Employment status:	Bill is an economics professor; Mercedes is a small-business owner.
Filing status:	Married, filing jointly
Current situation:	Bill and Mercedes want to engage in less risky tax planning strategies.

While working with their CPA during their audit, Bill and Mercedes decide to inquire about less risky tax planning opportunities. Specifically, they would like to gain a better understanding of how to maximize their after-tax returns without increasing their potential for another audit. (Although it was fun and educational, one audit is enough!) Mercedes is convinced that, as a small-business owner (Lavish Interior Designs Inc.), she pays more than her fair share of taxes. Likewise, Bill, an avid investor, wonders whether he is missing the mark by not considering taxes in his investment decisions. ■

Bill and Mercedes have come to the right place. This chapter describes the basic tax planning concepts that form the basis of the simplest to most complex tax planning transactions. In the process we also discuss the judicial doctrines that serve as basic limits on tax planning.

LO 3-1

BASIC TAX PLANNING OVERVIEW

Effective tax planning requires a basic understanding of the roles that taxes and nontax factors play in structuring business, investment, and personal decisions. Although taxes may not be the sole or even the primary determinant of a transaction or its structure, taxes can significantly affect the costs or benefits associated with business, investment, and personal transactions. Thus, the tax implications of competing transactions warrant careful consideration. Likewise, nontax factors, such as the taxpayer's financial goals or legal constraints, are an integral part of every transaction.

In general terms, effective tax planning maximizes the taxpayer's after-tax wealth while achieving the taxpayer's nontax goals. Maximizing after-tax wealth is not necessarily the same as minimizing taxes. Specifically, maximizing after-tax wealth requires us to consider both the tax and nontax costs and benefits of alternative transactions, whereas tax minimization focuses solely on a single cost—taxes. Indeed, if the goal of tax planning were simply to minimize taxes, the simplest way to achieve it would be to earn no income at all. Obviously, this strategy has potential limitations—most notably, the unattractive nontax consequence of poverty. Thus, it is necessary to consider the nontax ramifications of any planning strategy.

THE KEY FACTS

The Basics of Tax Planning

- Effective tax planning maximizes the taxpayer's after-tax wealth while achieving the taxpayer's nontax goals.
- Virtually every transaction includes three parties: the taxpayer, the other transacting party, and the uninvited silent party that specifies the tax consequences of the transaction—the government.
- Astute tax planning requires an understanding of the tax and nontax costs from the taxpayer's *and* the other party's perspectives.

Virtually every transaction includes three parties: the taxpayer, the other transacting party, and the uninvited silent party that specifies the tax consequences of the transaction—the government. Astute tax planning requires an understanding of the tax and nontax costs from the taxpayer's *and* the other party's perspective. For example, as discussed in the Compensation chapter, it would be impossible for an employer to develop an effective compensation plan without considering the tax and nontax costs associated with different compensation arrangements from both the employer's and the employees' perspectives. With sound tax planning, the employer can design a compensation package that generates value for employees while reducing costs for the employer. (One way to achieve this goal is through the use of nontaxable fringe benefits, such as health insurance, which are deductible by the employer but not taxable income to employees.) Throughout the text, we highlight situations where this multilateral approach to tax planning is especially important.

In this chapter we discuss three basic tax planning strategies that represent the building blocks of tax planning:

1. *Timing* (deferring or accelerating taxable income and tax deductions).
2. *Income shifting* (shifting income from high- to low-tax-rate taxpayers).
3. *Conversion* (converting income from high- to low-tax-rate activities).

LO 3-2 LO 3-3 LO 3-6

TIMING STRATEGIES

One of the cornerstones of basic tax planning is the idea of *timing*. *When* income is taxed or an expense is deducted affects the associated "real" tax costs or savings. This is true for two reasons. First, the timing of when income is taxed or an expense is deducted affects the *present value* of the taxes paid on income or the tax savings on deductions. Second, the tax costs of income and tax savings of deductions vary as *tax rates* change. The tax costs on income are higher when tax rates are higher and lower when tax rates are lower. Likewise, the tax savings on deductions are higher when tax rates are higher and lower when tax rates are lower. Let's look at the effects of present value and tax rates on the timing strategy.

Present Value of Money

The concept of **present value**—also known as the time value of money—basically states that \$1 today is worth *more* than \$1 in the future. Is this true, or is this some type of new math?

It's true. Assuming an investor can earn a positive **after-tax rate of return** such as 5 percent, \$1 invested today should be worth \$1.05 in one year.[1] Specifically,

Eq. 3-1

$$\begin{aligned}\text{Future Value} &= \text{Present Value} \times (1 + r)^n \\ &= \$1 \times (1 + .05)^1 = \$1.05\end{aligned}$$

where \$1 is the present value, r is the after-tax rate of return (5 percent), and n is the investment period (1 year). Hence, \$1 today is equivalent to \$1.05 in one year. The implication of the time value of money for tax planning is that the timing of a cash inflow or a cash outflow affects the present value of the income or expense.

Example 3-1

Bill is given the choice of receiving a \$1,000 nontaxable gift today or a \$1,000 nontaxable gift in one year. Which would Bill prefer? Assume Bill could invest \$1,000 today and earn an 8 percent return after taxes in one year. If he receives the gift today, how much would the \$1,000 be worth in one year?

Answer: The \$1,000 gift today would be worth \$1,080 in one year and thus, Bill should prefer to receive the gift today. Specifically,

$$\begin{aligned}\text{Future Value} &= \text{Present Value} \times (1 + r)^n \\ &= \$1{,}000 \times (1 + .08)^1 = \$1{,}080\end{aligned}$$

In terms of *future value,* the choice in the above example of receiving either \$1,000 today or \$1,000 in one year simplifies to a choice of \$1,080 or \$1,000. For even the least materialistic individual, choosing \$1,080—that is, \$1,000 *today*—should be straightforward.

Often tax planners find it useful to consider sums not in terms of future value, but rather in terms of present value. How would we restate the choice in Example 3-1 in terms of present value? Obviously, the present value of receiving \$1,000 today is \$1,000, but what is the *present value* of \$1,000 received in one year? The answer depends on the **discount factor,** which we derive from the taxpayer's expected after-tax rate of return. The discount factor is very useful for calculating the present value of future inflows or outflows of cash. We can derive the discount factor for a given rate of return simply by rearranging the future value equation (Eq. 3-1) from above:

Eq. 3-2

$$\begin{aligned}\text{Present Value} &= \text{Future Value}/(1 + r)^n \\ &= \$1/(1 + .08)^1 = \$0.926\end{aligned}$$

Therefore, the discount factor = 0.926

THE KEY FACTS

Present Value of Money

- The concept of present value—also known as the time value of money—states that \$1 today is worth *more* than \$1 in the future.
- The implication of the time value of money for tax planning is that the timing of a cash inflow or a cash outflow affects the present value of the income or expense.
- Present Value = Future Value/$(1 + r)^n$
- When considering cash inflows, higher present values are preferred; when considering cash outflows, lower present values are preferred.

[1]Assuming a constant marginal tax rate (t), after-tax rate of return (r) may be calculated as follows: $r = R \times (1 - t)$, where R is the taxpayer's before-tax rate of return.

EXHIBIT 3-1 Present Value of a Single Payment at Various Annual Rates of Return

Year	4%	5%	6%	7%	8%	9%	10%	11%	12%
1	.962	.952	.943	.935	.926	.917	.909	.901	.893
2	.925	.907	.890	.873	.857	.842	.826	.812	.797
3	.889	.864	.840	.816	.794	.772	.751	.731	.712
4	.855	.823	.792	.763	.735	.708	.683	.659	.636
5	.822	.784	.747	.713	.681	.650	.621	.593	.567
6	.790	.746	.705	.666	.630	.596	.564	.535	.507
7	.760	.711	.665	.623	.583	.547	.513	.482	.452
8	.731	.677	.627	.582	.540	.502	.467	.434	.404
9	.703	.645	.592	.544	.500	.460	.424	.391	.361
10	.676	.614	.558	.508	.463	.422	.386	.352	.322
11	.650	.585	.527	.475	.429	.388	.350	.317	.287
12	.625	.557	.497	.444	.397	.356	.319	.286	.257
13	.601	.530	.469	.415	.368	.326	.290	.258	.229
14	.577	.505	.442	.388	.340	.299	.263	.232	.205
15	.555	.481	.417	.362	.315	.275	.239	.209	.183

Applying the discount factor, we can see that $1,000 received in one year is worth $926 in today's dollars. Thus, in terms of present value, Bill's choice in Example 3-1 simplifies to a choice between a cash inflow of $1,000 today and a cash inflow worth $926 today. Again, choosing $1,000 today is pretty straightforward.

Exhibit 3-1 provides the discount factors for a lump sum (single payment) received in *n* periods using various rates of return. Tax planners frequently utilize such tables for quick reference in calculating present value for sums under consideration.

Example 3-2

At a recent holiday sale, Bill and Mercedes purchased $1,000 worth of furniture with "no money down and no payments for one year!" How much money is this deal really worth? (Assume their after-tax rate of return on investments is 10 percent.)

Answer: The discount factor of .909 (Exhibit 3-1, 10% Rate of Return column, Year 1 row) means the present value of $1,000 is $909 ($1,000 × .909 = $909)—so Bill and Mercedes save $91 ($1,000 − $909 = $91).

While Example 3-1 considers a $1,000 cash inflow, Example 3-2 addresses a $1,000 cash *outflow*. In terms of present value, a choice between $1,000 paid today and $1,000 paid in a year simplifies to incurring a cash outflow of either $1,000 (by paying today) or $909 (by paying in one year). Most people would prefer to pay $909. Indeed, financial planners always keep the following general rule of thumb in mind: When considering *cash inflows, prefer higher present values;* when considering *cash outflows, prefer lower present values.*

The Timing Strategy When Tax Rates Are Constant

In terms of tax planning, remember that *taxes paid* represent cash *outflows,* while *tax savings* generated from tax deductions are cash *inflows*. This perspective leads us to two basic tax-related timing strategies when tax rates are constant (not changing):

1. Accelerate tax deductions (deduct in an earlier period).
2. Defer recognizing taxable income (recognize in a later period).

Accelerating tax deductions to an earlier period increases the present value of the tax savings from the deduction. That is, tax savings received now have a higher present value than the same amount received a year from now.

Deferring income to a later period decreases the present value of the tax cost of the income. That is, taxes paid a year from now have a lower present value than taxes paid today. These two strategies are summarized in Exhibit 3-2.

EXHIBIT 3-2 The Timing Tax Strategy When Tax Rates Are Constant

Item	Recommendation	Why?
Tax deductions	Accelerate tax deductions into earlier years.	Maximizes the present value of tax savings from deductions.
Taxable income	Defer taxable income into later tax years.	Minimizes the present value of taxes paid.

Example 3-3

Mercedes, a calendar-year taxpayer, uses the cash method of accounting for her small business.[2] On December 28, she receives a $10,000 bill from her accountant for consulting services related to her small business. She can avoid late payment charges by paying the $10,000 bill before January 10 of next year. Let's assume that Mercedes's marginal tax rate is 30 percent *this year and next* and that she can earn an after-tax rate of return of 10 percent on her investments. When should she pay the $10,000 bill—this year or next?

Answer: If Mercedes pays the bill this year, she will receive a tax deduction on this year's tax return.[3] If she pays the bill in January, she will receive a tax deduction on next year's tax return (one year later). She needs to compare the after-tax cost of the accounting service using the present value of the tax savings for each scenario:

Present Value Comparison

Description	Option 1: Pay $10,000 bill *this year*	Option 2: Pay $10,000 bill *next year*
Tax deduction	$10,000	$10,000
Marginal tax rate	× 30%	× 30%
Tax savings	$ 3,000	$ 3,000
Discount factor	× 1	× .909
Present value tax savings	$ 3,000	$ 2,727
After-tax cost of accounting services:		
Before-tax cost	$10,000	$10,000
Less: Present value tax savings	− 3,000	− 2,727
After-tax cost of accounting services	$ 7,000	$ 7,273

Since Mercedes would surely rather spend $7,000 than $7,273 for accounting services, paying the bill in December is the clear winner.

[2] In the Business Income, Deductions, and Accounting Methods chapter, we discuss the basic accounting methods (e.g., cash vs. the accrual method), which influence the timing of when income and deductions are recognized for tax purposes.

[3] Accelerating her payment from January 10 to December 31 will increase the present value of the $10,000 cash outflow by 10 days. Thus, there is a minor present value cost associated with accelerating her payment.

In terms of accelerating deductions, the intent of the timing strategy is to accelerate the tax deduction significantly *without* accelerating the actual cash outflow that generates the expense. Indeed, if we assume a marginal rate of 30 percent and an after-tax return of 8 percent, accelerating a $1,000 cash outflow by one year to realize $300 in tax savings actually *increases* the after-tax *cost* of the expense from $648.20 to $700.

Present Value Comparison

Description	Present value of net cash outflow *today*	Present value of net cash outflow in *one year*
Cash outflow	$1,000	$1,000.00
Less: Tax savings (outflow × 30% tax rate)	− 300	− 300.00
Net cash outflow	$ 700	$ 700.00
Present value factor	× 1	× .926
Present value of net cash outflow today	$ 700	$ 648.20

Generally speaking, whenever a taxpayer can accelerate a deduction without also accelerating the cash outflow, the timing strategy will be more beneficial.

Is the accelerating deductions strategy utilized in the real world? Yes. While the strategy is particularly effective for cash-method taxpayers who can often control the year in which they pay their expenses, all taxpayers have *some* latitude in timing deductions. Common examples of the timing strategy include accelerating depreciation deductions for depreciable assets, using LIFO instead of FIFO for inventory, and accelerating the deduction of certain prepaid expenses.[4] For large corporations, the benefits associated with this timing strategy can be quite substantial. Thus, tax planners spend considerable time evaluating the proper period in which to recognize expenses and identifying opportunities to accelerate deductions.

Are there certain taxpayer or transaction attributes that enhance the advantages of accelerating deductions? Absolutely. Higher tax rates, higher rates of return, larger transaction amounts, and the ability to accelerate deductions by two or more years all increase the benefits of accelerating deductions. To demonstrate this for yourself, simply rework Example 3-3 and substitute any of the following: 50 percent tax rate, 12 percent after-tax rate of return, $100,000 expense, or a five-year period difference in the timing of the expense deduction. The benefits of accelerating deductions become much more prominent with these changes.

Deferring income recognition is an equally beneficial timing strategy, especially when the taxpayer can defer the recognition of income significantly without deferring the actual receipt of income very much. Consider the following example.

Example 3-4

In early December, Bill decides he would like to sell $100,000 of his Dell Inc. stock, which cost $20,000 10 years ago. Assume Bill's tax rate on the $80,000 gain will be 15 percent and his typical after-tax rate of return on investments is 7 percent. What effect would deferring the sale to January have on Bill's after-tax income on the sale?

[4]See the discussion of accounting methods in the Business Income, Deductions, and Accounting Methods chapter.

Answer:

Present Value Comparison

Description	Option 1: Sell the $100,000 stock in *December*[5]	Option 2: Sell the $100,000 stock in *January*[6]
Sales price	$100,000	$100,000
Less: Cost of stock	− 20,000	− 20,000
Gain on sale	$ 80,000	$ 80,000
Marginal tax rate	× 15%	× 15%
Tax on gain	$ 12,000	$ 12,000
Discount factor	× 1	× .935
Present value tax cost	$ 12,000	$ 11,220
After-tax income from sale:		
Before-tax income	$100,000	$100,000
Less: Present value tax cost	− 12,000	− 11,220
After-tax income from sale	$ 88,000	$ 88,780

Bill would doubtlessly prefer to earn $88,780 to $88,000, so from a tax perspective, selling the Dell Inc. stock in January is preferable. An important nontax issue for Bill to consider is the possibility that the stock price may fluctuate between December and January.

Income deferral represents an important aspect of investment planning (Investments chapter), retirement planning (Retirement Savings and Deferred Compensation chapter), and certain property transactions (Property Dispositions chapter). Income-related timing considerations also affect tax planning for everyday business operations, such as determining the appropriate period in which to recognize sales income (upon product shipment, on delivery, or on customer acceptance).

Do certain taxpayer or transaction attributes enhance the advantages of deferring income? Yes. The list is very similar to that for accelerating deductions: Higher tax rates, higher rates of return, larger transaction amounts, and the ability to defer revenue recognition for longer periods of time increase the benefits of deferral. To demonstrate this for yourself, simply rework Example 3-4 using any of the following: 50 percent tax rate, 12 percent after-tax rate of return on investments, or $200,000 gain.[7]

THE KEY FACTS

The Timing Strategy

- The timing of when income is taxed or an expense is deducted affects the *present value* of the taxes paid on income or tax savings on deductions.
- The tax costs of income and tax savings of deductions vary as *tax rates* change.
- When tax rates are constant, tax planners prefer to defer income and accelerate deductions.
- When tax rates are increasing, the taxpayer must calculate the optimal tax strategies for deductions and income.
- When tax rates are decreasing, taxpayers should accelerate tax deductions into earlier years and defer taxable income to later years.

The Timing Strategy When Tax Rates Change

When tax rates change, the timing strategy requires a little more consideration because the tax costs of income and the tax savings from deductions will now vary. The higher the tax rate, the higher the tax savings for a tax deduction. The lower the tax rate, the lower

[5]This will require Bill to pay the tax on the gain no later than April 15 of the following year (i.e., three months after the sale). If Bill and Mercedes's current-year withholding and estimated payments do not equal or exceed 110 percent of their previous year's tax liability, they will have to make an estimated payment by January 15 to avoid the failure to make estimated tax payment penalty (discussed later in the Individual Income Tax Computation and Tax Credits chapter). This example assumes that Bill and Mercedes can avoid the underpayment of estimated tax penalty discussed in the Individual Income Tax Computation and Tax Credits chapter by paying 110 percent of their previous year's tax liability in both options 1 and 2. Thus, they can defer paying the tax on the gain until April 15 of the year following the sale.

[6]This will require Bill to pay the tax on the gain no later than April 15 of the following year (i.e., 15 months after the sale).

[7]In Example 3-4, increasing the deferral period (e.g., from one to five years) also increases the benefits of tax deferral but requires additional assumptions regarding the expected five-year return of the Dell Inc. stock (assuming he does not sell the stock for five years) and his new investment (assuming he sells the Dell Inc. stock and immediately reinvests the after-tax proceeds).

EXHIBIT 3-3 Historical Maximum Ordinary and Capital Gains Tax Rates for Individuals Since 1982

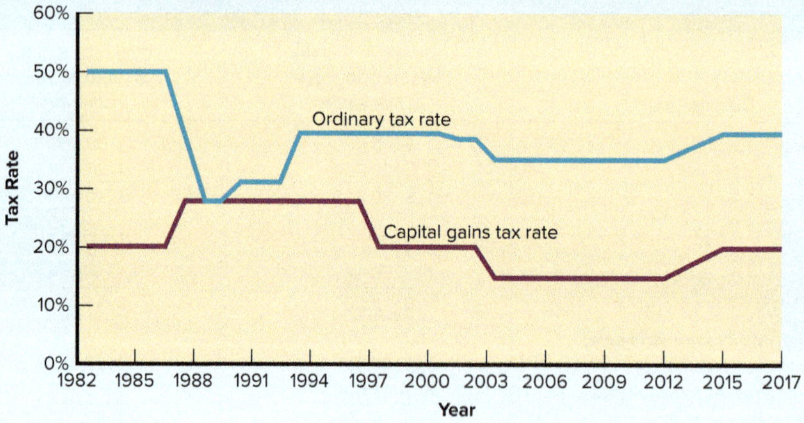

the tax costs for taxable income. *All other things being equal, taxpayers should prefer to recognize deductions during high-tax-rate years and income during low-tax-rate years.* The implication is that before a taxpayer implements the timing strategies suggested above (accelerate deductions, defer income), she should consider whether her tax rates are likely to change. In fact, as we discuss below, increasing tax rates may even suggest the taxpayer should *accelerate* income and *defer* deductions.

What would cause a taxpayer's marginal tax rate to change? The taxpayer's taxable income can change, perhaps due to changing jobs, retiring, or starting a new business. Indeed, in the Introduction to Tax chapter, we demonstrated how a taxpayer's marginal tax rate changes as income or deductions change. Marginal tax rates can also change because of tax legislation. We discussed the tax legislative process in the Tax Compliance, the IRS, and Tax Authorities chapter and noted that Congress frequently enacts tax legislation because lawmakers use taxes to raise revenue, stimulate the economy, and so on. In the last 35 years, Congress has changed the maximum statutory tax rates that apply to ordinary income, such as wages and business income, or capital gains, such as gains from the sale of stock, for individual taxpayers no fewer than nine times (see Exhibit 3-3).

Let's take a look at how changing tax rates affect the timing strategy recommendations. Exhibit 3-4 presents recommendations when tax rates are increasing. The taxpayer must actually calculate the optimal tax strategies for deductions and income when tax rates are increasing. Specifically, because accelerating deductions

EXHIBIT 3-4 The Timing Tax Strategy When Tax Rates Are Increasing

Item	Recommendation	Why?
Tax deductions	Requires calculation to determine optimal strategy.	The taxpayer must calculate whether the benefit of accelerating deductions outweighs the disadvantage of recognizing deductions in a *lower*-tax-rate year.
Taxable income	Requires calculation to determine optimal strategy.	The taxpayer must calculate whether the benefit of deferring income outweighs the disadvantage of recognizing income in a *higher*-tax-rate year.

causes them to be recognized in a *lower*-tax-rate year, the taxpayer must calculate whether the benefit of accelerating the deduction outweighs the disadvantage. Likewise, because deferring income causes income to be recognized in a *higher*-tax-rate year, the taxpayer must calculate whether the benefit of deferring income outweighs the disadvantage.

Example 3-5

Having decided she needs new equipment for her business, Mercedes is now considering whether to make the purchase and claim a corresponding $10,000 deduction at year-end or next year. Mercedes anticipates that, with the new machinery, her business income will rise such that her marginal rate will increase from 20 percent this year to 28 percent next year. Assuming her after-tax rate of return is 8 percent, what should Mercedes do?

Answer: Given rising tax rates, Mercedes must calculate the after-tax cost of the equipment for *both* options and compare present values.

Present Value Comparison

Description	Option 1: Pay $10,000 bill *this year*	Option 2: Pay $10,000 bill *next year*
Tax deduction	$10,000	$10,000
Marginal tax rate	× 20%	× 28%
Tax savings	$ 2,000	$ 2,800
Discount factor	× 1	× .926
Present value tax savings	$ 2,000	$ 2,593
After-tax cost of equipment:		
Before-tax cost	$10,000	$10,000
Less: Present value tax savings	− 2,000	− 2,593
After-tax cost of equipment	$ 8,000	$ 7,407

Paying the $10,000 next year is the clear winner.

In the above example, if the choice were either to recognize $10,000 of *income* this year or next, the *amounts* would be exactly the same but the conclusion would be different, and Mercedes would prefer to receive $8,000 of after-tax income this year instead of $7,407. (Remember, when considering cash *inflows,* we prefer the *higher* present value.) Are these always the answers when tax rates are increasing? No, the answer will depend both on the taxpayer's after-tax rate of return and on the magnitude of the tax rate increase.

Now let's consider the recommendations when tax rates are *decreasing*—a common scenario when an individual reaches retirement. Exhibit 3-5 presents the timing

EXHIBIT 3-5 The Timing Tax Strategy When Tax Rates Are Decreasing

Item	Recommendation	Why?
Tax deductions	Accelerate tax deductions into earlier years.	Maximizes the present value of tax savings from deductions due to the acceleration of the deductions into *earlier* years with a *higher* tax rate.
Taxable income	Defer taxable income into later tax years.	Minimizes the present value of taxes paid due to the deferral of the income to later years with a *lower* tax rate.

strategy recommendations in this case. The recommendations are clear. Taxpayers should accelerate tax deductions into earlier years to reap the tax savings from *accelerating* deductions to *higher*-tax-rate years. Likewise, taxpayers should defer taxable income to later years to enjoy the tax benefits of *deferring* taxable income to *lower*-tax-rate years.

THE KEY FACTS

Limitation on the Timing Strategy

- Timing strategies contain several inherent limitations.
- Whenever a taxpayer is unable to accelerate a deduction without also accelerating the cash outflow, the timing strategy will be less beneficial.
- Tax law generally requires taxpayers to continue their investment in an asset in order to defer income recognition for tax purposes.
- A deferral strategy may not be optimal if the taxpayer has severe cash flow needs, if continuing the investment would generate a low rate of return compared to other investments, if the current investment would subject the taxpayer to unnecessary risk, and so on.
- The constructive receipt doctrine, which provides that a taxpayer must recognize income when it is actually *or* constructively received, also restricts income deferral for cash-method taxpayers.

Limitations to Timing Strategies Timing strategies contain certain inherent limitations. First, tax laws generally require taxpayers to continue their investment in an asset in order to defer income recognition for tax purposes. In other words, deferral is generally not an option if a taxpayer has "cashed out" of an investment.[8] For example, Bill could not sell his Dell stock in December and then choose not to recognize the income until January. A deferral strategy may not be optimal (1) if the taxpayer has severe cash flow needs, (2) if continuing the investment would generate a low rate of return compared to other investments, or (3) if the current investment would subject the taxpayer to unnecessary risk. For example, the risk that the value of Bill's investment in Dell Inc. will decline from December to January in Example 3-4 may lead Bill to forgo deferring his stock sale until January. Again, the astute taxpayer considers both the tax *and* nontax ramifications of deferring income.

A second limitation results from the **constructive receipt doctrine,** which also restricts income deferral for cash-method taxpayers.[9] Unlike accrual-method taxpayers, cash-method taxpayers report income for tax purposes when the income is *received,* whether it is in the form of cash, property, or services.[10] The cash method affords taxpayers some leeway in determining when to recognize income because such taxpayers can control when they bill their clients. However, the constructive receipt doctrine provides that a taxpayer must recognize income when it is actually *or* constructively received. Constructive receipt is deemed to have occurred if the income has been credited to the taxpayer's account or if the income is unconditionally available to the taxpayer, the taxpayer is aware of the income's availability, and there are no restrictions on the taxpayer's control over the income.

Example 3-6

Mercedes's brother-in-law, Carlos, works for King Acura, which recently instituted a bonus plan that pays year-end bonuses each December to employees rated above average for their customer service. Carlos is expecting a $10,000 bonus this year that will be paid on December 31. Thinking he'd prefer to defer this income until next year, Carlos plans to take a vacation on December 30 so that he will not receive his bonus check until January. Will Carlos's strategy work?

Answer: No, the constructive receipt doctrine applies here. Because Carlos's check was unconditionally available to him on December 31, he was aware of its availability, and there were no restrictions on his control over the income on that date, Carlos must report the income in the current year.

[8] See the discussions of like-kind exchanges in the Property Dispositions chapter, investment planning in the Investments chapter, and retirement planning in the Retirement Savings and Deferred Compensation chapter.

[9] Later in this chapter we discuss other judicial doctrines that apply to all planning strategies.

[10] As we discuss in depth in the Business Income, Deductions, and Accounting Methods chapter, accrual-method taxpayers report income when it is earned. In general, income is deemed earned when all events have occurred that fix the taxpayer's right to the income and the income can be estimated with reasonable accuracy. Thus, income recognition for accrual-method taxpayers generally is not tied to payment. Receipt of prepaid income by accrual-method taxpayers may trigger income recognition in certain circumstances. The constructive receipt doctrine may apply in these situations.

What could taxpayers do to avoid Carlos's problem in the future? They could request that their employer institute a company policy of paying bonuses on January 1, which would allow all employees to report the bonus income in that year. However, if the employer is a cash-method taxpayer, this creates a potential conflict with its employees.[11] Such an employer would most likely prefer to deduct the bonus in the current year, which requires the bonuses to be paid in December. This conflict would not exist if the employer were an accrual-method taxpayer, because paying the bonuses in January would not affect its ability to deduct the bonuses in the previous year.[12]

INCOME-SHIFTING STRATEGIES

LO 3-4 LO 3-6

We've seen that the value of a tax deduction, or the tax cost of income, varies with the marginal tax rate. We've also seen that tax rates can vary across time, which leads to basic tax planning strategies regarding when to recognize deductions and income. Tax rates can also vary across *taxpayers* or *jurisdictions* (states, countries), which leads to still other tax planning strategies—for example, shifting income from high-tax-rate taxpayers to low-tax-rate taxpayers or shifting deductions from low-tax-rate taxpayers to high-tax-rate taxpayers.

The type of taxpayers who benefit most from this strategy are (1) related parties, such as family members or businesses and their owners, who have varying marginal tax rates and are willing to shift income for the benefit of the group; and (2) taxpayers operating in multiple jurisdictions with different marginal tax rates. In any case, tax planners should seek only legitimate methods of shifting income that will withstand IRS scrutiny. In the following section we discuss transactions between family members, followed by a discussion of transactions between owners and their businesses, and finally a discussion of income shifting across jurisdictions.

Transactions between Family Members and Limitations

One of the most common examples of income shifting is high-tax-rate parents shifting income to low-tax-rate children. For example, Bill and Mercedes have a 30 percent marginal tax rate, whereas their daughter, Margaret, has a 10 percent marginal tax rate. Assuming their marginal tax rates remain constant with relatively modest changes in income, every $1 of income that Bill and Mercedes shift to Margaret reduces the family's tax liability by 20 cents [$1 × (30% − 10%)]. Thus, if Bill and Mercedes shift $10,000 of taxable income to Margaret, the family's after-tax income will increase by $2,000. Can taxpayers legally do this? Yes and no. As you might expect, there are limitations on this type of income shifting.

The **assignment of income doctrine** requires income to be taxed to the taxpayer who actually earns it.[13] Merely attributing your paycheck or dividend to another

[11]Because King Acura carries inventory, the cash method is not allowed for transactions related to its inventory (e.g., cost of goods sold, sales, etc.). However, King Acura is permitted to use the cash method for other transactions. This mixed method is referred to as the "hybrid" method of accounting.

[12]§267(a)(2). When an employee/shareholder and an employer/corporation are related (i.e., the employee/shareholder owns more than 50 percent of the value of the employer corporation), the corporation is not allowed to deduct the compensation expense until the employee/shareholder includes the payment in income.

[13]Later in this chapter we discuss other judicial doctrines that apply to all planning strategies.

taxpayer does not transfer the tax liability associated with the income. The assignment of income doctrine implies that, in order to shift income to a taxpayer, that taxpayer must actually earn the income. For example, if Mercedes would like to shift some of her business income to Margaret, Margaret must actually earn it. One way to accomplish this would be for Mercedes to employ Margaret in her business and pay her a $10,000 salary. The effects of this transaction are to decrease Mercedes's taxable income by $10,000 because of tax-deductible salary expense, and increase Margaret's income by the $10,000 taxable salary. What if Margaret is paid $10,000 to answer Mercedes's business phone one Saturday afternoon every month? Does this seem reasonable? Not likely. The IRS frowns upon this type of aggressive strategy.

Indeed, the IRS closely scrutinizes such **related-party transactions**—that is, financial activities among family members (also among owners and their businesses, or among businesses owned by the same owners). Unlike **arm's-length transactions**, where each transacting party negotiates for his or her own benefit, related-party transactions involve taxpayers who are much more willing to negotiate for their own common good to the detriment of the IRS. For example, would Mercedes pay an unrelated party $10,000 to answer the phone once a month? Doubtful.[14]

Are there other ways to shift income to children? For example, could Bill shift some of his investment income to Margaret? Yes, but there's a catch. The assignment of income applies what is referred to as the "fruit and the tree" analogy [*Lucas v. Earl* (S. Ct., 1930), 8 AFTR 10287]. For the owner to avoid being taxed on the fruit from the tree (the income), the owner must transfer the tree. Thus, to shift investment income, Bill would also have to transfer ownership in the underlying investment assets to Margaret.[15] Is there a problem with this requirement? Not for Margaret. However, Bill would likely prefer to maintain his wealth. The nontax disadvantages of transferring wealth to implement the income-shifting strategy often outweigh the tax benefits of the transfer. For example, most parents either could not afford to or would have serious reservations about transferring significant wealth to their children—a prime example of how nontax costs may override tax considerations.

Transactions between Owners and Their Businesses and Limitations

Income shifting is not limited to transactions within a family unit. One of the most common examples occurs between owners and their businesses. Let's consider Mercedes's interior design business. Currently, Mercedes operates her business as a sole proprietorship. A sole proprietorship (unlike a C corporation) is not a separate reporting entity, and thus, Mercedes reports her business income and deductions on her individual tax return. Shifting income to or from her sole proprietorship offers little benefit, because all of her sole proprietorship income is reported on her tax return regardless of whether it is attributed to her personally or to her business. On the other hand, if Mercedes operated her interior design business as a C corporation, shifting income to or from the C corporation may make good financial sense because the corporation would be a separate entity

[14]The Internal Revenue Code also contains specific provisions to curtail benefits from related-party transactions. For example, as we discuss in the Property Dispositions chapter, §267 disallows a tax deduction for losses on sales to related parties (even if the sale was consummated at the asset's fair market value).

[15]Further, as we discuss in the Individual Income Tax Computation and Tax Credits chapter, the "kiddie tax" may apply when parents shift too much investment income to children. The kiddie tax restricts the amount of a child's investment income that can be taxed at the child's (lower) tax rate instead of the parents' (higher) tax rate.

with tax rates distinct from Mercedes's individual tax rate. Shifting income to herself may allow Mercedes to decrease the tax on her business profits, thereby increasing her after-tax income. Example 3-7 illustrates the savings obtainable from this strategy.

Example 3-7

Mercedes is considering incorporating her interior design business. She projects $200,000 of business profit next year. Excluding this profit, Bill and Mercedes expect $160,000 of taxable income next year. If Mercedes would like to minimize her current-year tax liability, should she incorporate her business? [Use the married filing jointly and corporate tax rates in Appendix D to answer this question.]

Answer: If Mercedes does not incorporate her business, the first $73,350 of her business profits will be taxed at 28 percent (from $160,000 to $233,350 of taxable income, the marginal tax rate is 28 percent). The remaining $126,650 (from $233,350 to $360,000 of taxable income) would be taxed at 33 percent. Upon reviewing the corporate tax rate schedule, you should note that the first two corporate tax rates (15 and 25 percent) are lower than Bill and Mercedes's current marginal tax rate of 33 percent. Thus, there appears to be some opportunity for Mercedes to reduce her current-year tax liability by incorporating her business.[16]

In order to shift income from the corporation to the owner, the corporation must create a tax deduction for itself in the process. Compensation paid to employee–owners is the most common method of shifting income from corporations to their owners. Compensation expense is deductible by the corporation and is generally taxable to the employee. (See the Compensation chapter for a broader discussion of nontaxable compensation benefits.) Having the business owner rent property to the corporation or loan money to the corporation are also effective income-shifting methods, because both transactions generate tax deductions for the corporation and income for the shareholder. Because corporations don't get a tax deduction for dividends paid, paying dividends is *not* an effective way to shift income. Having a corporation pay dividends actually results in "double taxation"—the profits generating the dividends are taxed first at the corporate level, and then at the shareholder level. Recommending this tax planning strategy may not be a good way to keep your job as a tax consultant.

After a taxpayer identifies the opportunity and appropriate method to shift income (compensation paid to a related party), he or she can easily determine the optimal amount to shift depending on the taxpayers' marginal tax rates.

Example 3-8

Assuming Mercedes's goal is to minimize her current-year federal income tax liability, how much of the $200,000 business income should her corporation report?

Answer: It should report $75,000. Comparing the two tax rate schedules reveals how to calculate this number.

Step 1: Would Mercedes rather have income taxed at 15 percent (the corporation's marginal tax rate from $0 to $50,000 taxable income) or 28 percent (Bill and Mercedes's marginal tax rate

(continued on page 3-14)

[16]Note that this is a simplified discussion of one of many tax issues associated with incorporating a business. For example, as discussed later in this chapter, Mercedes must consider the judicial doctrines (economic substance, business purpose, etc.) in making this decision. She also needs to consider further tax planning opportunities described in the following example.

before recognizing any profit from Mercedes's business)? Fifteen percent is the obvious answer. To take advantage of the 15 percent corporate tax bracket, Mercedes should retain $50,000 of the expected $200,000 in profits in the corporation, because $50,000 is the width of the 15 percent corporate tax bracket.

Step 2: Assuming the corporation reports $50,000 of income, its marginal tax rate will now be 25 percent, and thus Mercedes's choice is to have any additional income taxed at 25 percent (the corporation's marginal tax rate) or at 28 percent (Bill and Mercedes's marginal tax rate before recognizing any profit from Mercedes's business). Twenty-five percent is the clear answer. To take advantage of the 25 percent corporate tax bracket, the corporation should retain another $25,000 of the expected $200,000 in profits ($25,000 is the width of the 25 percent corporate tax bracket). The corporation's marginal tax rate will now be 34 percent.

Step 3: Continuing this same decision process, Mercedes should shift the remaining $125,000 of profits ($73,350 taxed at 28 percent and $51,650 taxed at 33 percent) to herself and Bill—via a salary paid to Mercedes—because their marginal tax rates (28 percent and 33 percent) will be lower than the corporation's marginal tax rate (34 percent).

How much current federal income tax does this strategy save Bill and Mercedes? The corporation's and Bill and Mercedes's combined federal income tax liability will be $83,017 ($13,750 for the corporation plus $69,267 for Bill and Mercedes) compared to $94,017 for Bill and Mercedes if the business is operated as a sole proprietorship. Thus, they will save $11,000.[17]

Are there nontax disadvantages of the income-shifting-via-incorporating strategy? Yes. For example, one nontax disadvantage for Mercedes is that her new corporation now has $61,250 of her after-tax profits ($75,000 profits less $13,750 of corporate tax). If Mercedes has personal cash-flow needs that require use of the $61,250, this is not a viable strategy. Indeed, it's advantageous only if the business owner intends to reinvest the business profits into the business. Furthermore, any subsequent transactions between Mercedes and the corporation would clearly be related-party transactions. Thus, Mercedes should be prepared for IRS scrutiny.[18] If the salary, rent, and other costs are deemed to be unreasonable, the IRS may reclassify any excess payments above the value of services and property provided as nondeductible corporate dividends. In this scenario, the corporation and Mercedes would both pay income tax on each dollar of deemed dividend payment. This is not a good outcome for Mercedes or any business owner.

Example 3-9

Upon reviewing Bill and Mercedes's tax return, the IRS reclassifies $65,000 of Mercedes's $125,000 salary in Example 3-8 as a dividend. What are the tax consequences of this reclassification?

Answer: (1) The corporation's taxable income will increase from $75,000 to $140,000 because dividends are not deductible, thereby increasing the corporation's tax liability from $13,750 to $37,850; and (2) Bill and Mercedes's taxable income will remain the same, except $65,000 of their

[17]This strategy will result in the eventual double taxation of the income retained in Mercedes's corporation. Specifically, Mercedes will eventually have to pay tax on the income retained by the corporation, either in the form of taxable dividends from the corporation or a taxable gain when she sells or liquidates the corporation. The present value of this additional layer of tax reduces the tax savings from this strategy. The longer that the second layer of tax is deferred, the more advantageous this strategy will be. This calculation is beyond the scope of this chapter.

[18]The taxpayer should maintain documentation for related-party transactions (e.g., notes for related-party loans and contemporaneous documentation of reasonable compensation paid to related parties).

$285,000 of taxable income will be dividends taxed at a preferential 15 percent tax rate.[19] Thus, Bill and Mercedes will have $220,000 of taxable income taxed at their ordinary tax rates ($48,485 of tax) and $65,000 of dividend income taxed at 15 percent ($9,750 of tax), resulting in a tax liability of $58,235.

Under this scenario, the combined tax liabilities of the corporation and Bill and Mercedes will be $96,085, which is $2,068 *higher* than Bill and Mercedes's $94,017 tax liability had they not incorporated Mercedes's business.[20]

As the above examples illustrate, tax-avoiding strategies can be quite beneficial, but they also entail some financial risks if the structure fails to pass muster with the IRS.

ETHICS

Agnes Meher is the owner of LuPat, a profitable construction company that she operates as a sole proprietorship. As a sole proprietor, Agnes reports the business income from LuPat on her individual tax return. Agnes expects the business to generate $400,000 of taxable income this year, which in combination with her other income will put her in the top tax bracket (39.6%). Agnes has two children named Ellie Mae and Spencer, ages 9 and 11 respectively, who do not currently have any taxable income. Agnes would like to shift some of her income from LuPat to Ellie Mae and Spencer to reduce the overall tax burden from the business income. To shift the income, Agnes hired Ellie Mae and Spencer to perform some janitorial and clerical services for LuPat, paying each child $20,000. What do you think of Agnes's strategy?

Income Shifting across Jurisdictions and Limitations

Taxpayers that operate in multiple jurisdictions (states, countries) also apply the income-shifting strategy. Specifically, income earned in different jurisdictions—whether in the United States or abroad, and for state income tax purposes, income earned in different states—is often taxed very differently. With a proper understanding of the differences in tax laws across jurisdictions, taxpayers can use these differences to maximize their after-tax wealth.

Example 3-10

Carlos's employer, King Acura, has two locations. Its main location is in South Dakota (a state with no corporate tax), with a secondary location in North Dakota (maximum corporate state tax rate of 4.31 percent). What tax planning strategy may save money for King Acura?

Answer: The most obvious strategy is to shift income from the North Dakota location to the South Dakota location, thereby reducing King Acura's state income tax liability by about 4.31 cents for every dollar of income shifted.[21]

[19]Bill and Mercedes may also be subject to an additional 3.8% net investment income tax on some of the reclassified dividends, which would increase the combined tax liabilities if Bill and Mercedes incorporate the business.

[20]The Compensation chapter discusses the consequences of unreasonable compensation to employee–owners.

[21]Because state taxes are deductible for federal tax purposes, every dollar of state taxes reduced with this strategy will increase King Acura's federal income tax liability by its federal marginal tax rate (e.g., 35 percent). Thus, the net tax savings for every dollar of income shifted from North Dakota to South Dakota will be 2.8 percent, which equals the state tax savings (4.31 percent) less the federal tax increase resulting from the lost state tax deduction (4.31% × 35%).

THE KEY FACTS

The Income-Shifting Strategy

- Income shifting exploits the differences in tax rates across taxpayers or jurisdictions.
- Common examples of income shifting include high-tax-rate parents shifting income to low-tax-rate children, businesses shifting income to their owners, and taxpayers shifting income from high-tax jurisdictions to low-tax jurisdictions. The assignment of income doctrine requires income to be taxed to the taxpayer who actually earns the income.
- The IRS also closely monitors income-shifting strategies that involve related-party transactions.

A number of possibilities exist to execute a strategy such as King Acura's in Example 3-10. Assuming that the North Dakota and South Dakota locations exchange cars, the firm could shift income via *transfer pricing* (using the price the South Dakota location charges the North Dakota location for cars transferred to North Dakota). Likewise, if the South Dakota location (the corporate headquarters) provides a legitimate support function for the North Dakota location, the firm should allocate a portion of the overhead and administrative expenses from the South Dakota location to the North Dakota location.

What are some of the limitations of income shifting across jurisdictions? First, taxing authorities are fully aware of the tax benefits of strategically structuring transactions across tax borders (across countries or states). Thus, the IRS closely examines transfer pricing on international transactions. Similarly, state tax authorities scrutinize interstate transactions between related taxpayers. Second, when taxpayers locate in low-tax-rate jurisdictions to, in effect, shift income to a tax-advantaged jurisdiction, they may bear **implicit taxes** (i.e., additional costs attributable to the jurisdiction's tax advantage). For example, the demand for workers, services, or property in low-tax-rate jurisdictions, whether a foreign country or a low-tax state, may increase the nontax costs associated with operating a business there enough to offset the tax advantages. Finally, negative publicity from moving operations (and jobs) from the United States to a lower-tax jurisdiction may more than offset any tax benefits associated with these strategies.

LO 3-5

CONVERSION STRATEGIES

THE KEY FACTS

The Conversion Strategy

- The conversion strategy is based on the understanding that the tax law does not treat all types of income or deductions the same.
- To implement the conversion strategy, one must be aware of the underlying differences in tax treatment across various types of income, expenses, and activities and have some ability to alter the nature of the income or expense to receive the more advantageous tax treatment.
- The Internal Revenue Code contains specific provisions that prevent the taxpayer from changing the nature of expenses, income, or activities to a more tax-advantaged status.
- Implicit taxes may also reduce or eliminate the advantages of conversion strategies.

We've now seen how tax rates can vary across time and taxpayers. They can also vary across different *activities*. For example, ordinary income such as salary, interest income, and business income received by individual taxpayers is taxed at their ordinary marginal tax rates, whereas long-term capital gains, which are gains from the sale of investment assets held longer than one year, and dividends are taxed at lower tax rates (currently a maximum of 20 percent), and still other forms of income like nontaxable compensation benefits and municipal bond interest are tax-exempt. Expenses from different types of activities may also be treated very differently for tax purposes. Business expenses are generally fully tax deductible, whereas tax deductions for investment expenses may be limited, and tax deductions for personal expenses may be completely disallowed. In sum, the tax law does not treat all types of income or deductions the same. This understanding forms the basis for the conversion strategy—recasting income and expenses to receive the most favorable tax treatment.

To implement the conversion strategy, the taxpayer must be aware of the underlying differences in tax treatment across various types of income, expenses, and activities and have some ability to alter the nature of the income or expense to receive the more advantageous tax treatment. What are some common examples of the conversion strategy? In the Individual Income Tax Overview, Exemptions, and Filing Status chapter, we explain character differences in income and deductions. In the Investments chapter, we consider investment planning and the advantages of investing in assets that generate preferentially taxed income. In the Business Income, Deductions, and Accounting Methods chapter, we explain the basic differences between business and investment activities and what characteristics result in the more favorable "business" designation for expense deductions. In the Compensation chapter and the Retirement Savings and Deferred Compensation chapters, we discuss compensation planning and the benefits of restructuring employee compensation from currently taxable compensation to nontaxable or tax-deferred forms of compensation, such as employer-provided health insurance and retirement contributions.

To analyze the benefits of the conversion strategy, you often compare the after-tax returns of alternative investments rather than the **before-tax rate of returns.** Given a stationary marginal tax rate, you can calculate an investment's after-tax rate of return as follows:

Eq. 3-3

$$\text{After-Tax Return} = \text{Before-Tax Return} - (\text{Before-Tax Return} \times \text{Marginal Tax Rate})$$

which simplifies to

Eq. 3-4

$$\text{After-Tax Return} = \text{Before-Tax Return} \times (1 - \text{Marginal Tax Rate})$$

Example 3-11

Bill is contemplating three different investments, each with the same amount of risk:

1. A high-dividend stock that pays 8.5 percent dividends annually but has no appreciation potential.
2. Taxable corporate bonds that pay 9 percent interest annually.
3. Tax-exempt municipal bonds that pay 6 percent interest annually.

Assuming that dividends are taxed at 20 percent and that Bill's marginal tax rate on ordinary income is 30 percent, which investment should Bill choose?

Answer: To answer this question, we must compute Bill's after-tax rate of return for each investment. The after-tax returns for the three investments are

Investment Choice	Computation	After-Tax Return
High-dividend stock	8.5% × (1 − 20%) =	6.8%
Corporate bond	9% × (1 − 30%) =	6.3
Municipal bond	6% × (1 − 0%) =	6.0

Accordingly, Bill should choose the dividend-yielding stock.

What marginal tax rate on ordinary income would make Bill indifferent between the dividend-yielding stock and the corporate bond?

Answer: The dividend-yielding stock has an after-tax rate return of 6.8 percent. For Bill to be indifferent between this stock and the corporate bond, the corporate bond would need a 6.8 percent after-tax rate of return. We can use Eq. 3-4 above to solve for the marginal tax rate.

$$\text{After-Tax Return} = \text{Before-Tax Return} \times (1 - \text{Marginal Tax Rate})$$
$$6.8\% = 9\% \times (1 - \text{Marginal Tax Rate})$$
$$\text{Marginal Tax Rate} = 24.44\%$$

Let's check this answer: After-Tax Return = 9% × (1 − 24.44%) = 6.8%

The example above shows how taxpayers may compare investments when the investment period is one year. However, when taxpayers hold investments for more than a year they potentially receive benefits from combining the timing strategy and the conversion strategy. First, they may be able to defer recognizing gains on the assets until they sell them—the longer the deferral period, the lower the present value of the tax when taxpayers ultimately sell the assets. Second, they may pay taxes on the gains at preferential rates. For example, taxpayers who invest in a corporate stock (capital asset) that does not pay dividends will defer gain on any stock appreciation until they sell the stock; and because it is a capital asset held longer than one year, gains will be taxed at the lower preferential tax rate for long-term capital gains. These tax advantages provide taxpayers with a greater after-tax rate of return on these investments than they would obtain from less tax-favored assets that earn equivalent before-tax rates of return. Investors who quickly sell investments pay taxes on gains at higher, ordinary rates and incur significantly greater transaction costs. Nevertheless, taxpayers should balance the tax benefits available for holding assets with the risk that the asset values will have declined by the time they want to sell the assets.

To enable comparison of investments with differing time horizons, taxpayers use the annualized after-tax rate of return. In general, the after-tax rate of return on any investment is $(FV/I)^{1/n} - 1$ where *FV* is the future value after taxes, *I* is the investment, and *n* is the number of investment periods.[22]

Example 3-12

What if: Assume Bill decides to purchase Intel stock for $50,000 and hold the shares for five years. If the Intel stock grows at a constant 8 percent before-tax rate and does not pay any dividends, how much cash will Bill accumulate after taxes after five years assuming a long-term capital gains tax rate of 20 percent?

Answer: $68,773, computed as follows:

Description	Amount	Explanation
(1) Proceeds from sale	$ 73,466	[$50,000 × (1 + 0.08)^5]
(2) Basis in shares	50,000	This is the investment in the shares.
(3) Gain realized on sale	$ 23,466	(1) − (2)
(4) Tax rate on gain	× 20%	Low rate for long-term capital gain*
(5) Tax on gain	$ 4,693	(3) × (4)
After-tax cash after 5 years	**$68,773**	(1) − (5)

*Assumes Bill doesn't have any capital losses.

What annual after-tax rate of return will Bill earn on the money invested?

Answer: 6.58 percent [($68,773/$50,000)^{1/5} − 1].

What if: What would be the after-tax rate of return if Bill held the stock for 18 years?

Answer: 7.03 percent, computed as follows:

Description	Amount	Explanation
(1) Proceeds from sale	$199,801	[$50,000 × (1 + 0.08)^18]
(2) Basis in shares	50,000	This is the investment in the shares.
(3) Gain realized on sale	$149,801	(1) − (2)
(4) Tax rate on gain	× 20%	Low rate for long-term capital gain*
(5) Tax on gain	$ 29,960	(3) × (4)
After-tax cash after 18 years	$169,841	(1) − (5)
After-tax rate of return after 18 years	**7.03**	[($169,841/$50,000)^{1/18} − 1]

*Assumes Bill doesn't have any capital losses.

What if: How does Bill's rate of return on the Intel stock held for five years compare to a taxable corporate bond that pays 9 percent interest annually and is held for five years?

Answer: The annualized rate of return on the stock held for five years is 6.58 percent as shown above. Because the interest on the taxable corporate bond is taxed annually, the annual after-tax rate of return does not change with the investment horizon and will equal 6.3 percent as shown in Example 3-11 [9% × (1 − 30%)]. In this situation, the combined tax benefits from the timing and conversion strategies cause the stock investment to generate a higher annualized after-tax return than the taxable corporate bond even though its pretax return is lower.

[22]Financial calculators designate this calculation as the IRR or internal rate of return.

TAXES IN THE REAL WORLD Deducting Losses on Residences Is Tricky

The conversion tax planning strategy can involve converting ordinary income into capital gains, taxable income into tax-exempt income, or even nondeductible losses into deductible losses. Taxpayers often look to employ this strategy when they sell a home at a loss. The tax law disallows losses on the sale of personal use assets so any loss generated upon the sale of a personal residence is nondeductible. However, the tax law permits deductions for losses on the sale of rental property (including residences).

Suppose that you would like to sell your home but you are facing a large nondeductible loss if you sell it. Can you simply move out, convert the home to a rental property, and then sell the house and deduct the loss? It seems the answer is yes, subject to a couple of important caveats. First, the law prevents taxpayers from deducting losses that were incurred while the home was used for personal purposes. That is, only the losses generated while the house was a rental property are deductible. Second, if you claim that you converted the house to rental property, you should actually rent the house.

In a recent court case (*Redisch v. Commissioner*, TC Memo 2015-95), the taxpayers had a beachfront condo they used personally for four years. Had they sold it at that time, they would have realized a large nondeductible loss. Instead they decided to convert the condo to a rental. They hired a realtor to help in finding a renter but rather than finding a tenant, the realtor used the condo for a "model" of other units in the community. The following year, the taxpayers listed the home for sale and it sold the next year at a loss. The taxpayers deducted a loss on the sale of the home claiming they had converted the home from personal use to rental. The IRS disagreed and argued that the taxpayers had not successfully converted the home to rental because it was never rented. The Tax Court agreed with the IRS and disallowed the loss on the sale of the home, arguing that the taxpayers did not rent the home and, more importantly, did not really even put forth a good effort to rent it.

Drawn from: "Tax Court: In Order to Convert a Home to a Rental, You Should Probably Rent It." *Forbes*, May 20, 2015, http://www.forbes.com/sites/anthonynitti/2015/05/20/tax-court-in-order-to-convert-a-home-to-a-rental-you-should-probably-rent-it/#3bd41d2f4469

Limitations of Conversion Strategies

Like other tax planning strategies, conversion strategies face potential limitations. The Code itself also contains several specific provisions that prevent the taxpayer from changing the nature of expenses, income, or activities to a more tax-advantaged status, including (among many others) the depreciation recapture rules discussed in the Property Dispositions chapter and the luxury auto depreciation rules discussed in the Property Acquisition and Cost Recovery chapter. In addition, as discussed in the Introduction to Tax chapter, implicit taxes may reduce or eliminate the advantages of tax-preferred investments (such as municipal bonds or any investment taxed at preferential tax rates) by decreasing their before-tax rate of returns. Thus, implicit taxes may reduce the advantages of the conversion strategy.

ADDITIONAL LIMITATIONS TO TAX PLANNING STRATEGIES: JUDICIAL DOCTRINES

LO 3-6

The IRS also has several other doctrines at its disposal for situations where it expects taxpayer abuse. These doctrines apply across a wide variety of transactions and planning strategies (timing, income shifting, and conversion). The **business purpose doctrine,** for instance, allows the IRS to challenge and disallow business expenses for transactions with no underlying business motivation, such as the travel cost of a spouse accompanying a taxpayer on a business trip. The **step-transaction doctrine** allows the IRS to collapse a series of related transactions into one transaction to determine the tax consequences of the transaction. The **substance-over-form doctrine** allows

THE KEY FACTS

Additional Limitations to Tax Planning Strategies: Judicial Doctrines

- Certain judicial doctrines restrict the common tax planning strategies (timing, income shifting, and conversion).
  - The business purpose doctrine allows the IRS to challenge and disallow business expenses for transactions with no underlying business motivation.
  - The step-transaction doctrine allows the IRS to collapse a series of related transactions into one transaction to determine the tax consequences of the transaction.
  - The substance-over-form doctrine allows the IRS to reclassify a transaction according to its substance.

the IRS to consider the transaction's substance regardless of its form, and where appropriate, to reclassify the transaction according to its substance. Finally, the **economic substance doctrine** requires transactions to meet two criteria to obtain tax benefits. First, a transaction must meaningfully change a taxpayer's economic position (excluding any federal income tax effects). Second, the taxpayer must have a substantial purpose (other than tax avoidance) for the transaction. Economic substance is clearly related to several other doctrines such as the business purpose, step-transaction, and substance-over-form doctrines; however, its codification standardizes the requirement for transactions to meet both tests. The courts had been inconsistent with the application of the tests, with some requiring the transaction to meet either the business purpose or economic substance and others requiring that both tests be met. A key part of the codification is the strict penalty of 40 percent—reduced to 20 percent if the taxpayer makes adequate disclosure—of the underpayment for failing to meet the requirements. In the Tax Compliance, the IRS, and Tax Authorities chapter, we noted that the Internal Revenue Code is the ultimate tax authority. The business purpose, step-transaction, substance-over-form, and economic substance doctrines allow the IRS to determine the tax consequences of transactions that follow only the form of the Internal Revenue Code and not the spirit.

You can often assess whether the business purpose, step-transaction, or substance-over-form doctrines apply by using the "smell test." If the transaction "smells bad," one of these doctrines likely applies. (Transactions usually smell bad when the primary purpose is to avoid taxes and not to accomplish an independent business objective.) For example, using the substance-over-form doctrine, the IRS would likely reclassify most of the $10,000 paid to Margaret for answering the phone one Saturday afternoon a month as a gift from Mercedes to Margaret (see the earlier discussion of income shifting and transactions between family members), even though the transaction was structured as compensation and Margaret did do some work for her mother. This recharacterization would unwind the income-shifting benefits for the amount considered to be a gift, as gifts to family members are not tax deductible. In sum, the *substance* of the transaction must be justifiable, not just the form.

LO 3-7

TAX AVOIDANCE VERSUS TAX EVASION

Each of the tax planning strategies discussed in this book falls within the confines of legal **tax avoidance.** Tax avoidance has long been endorsed by the courts and even Congress. For example, remember that Congress specifically encouraged tax avoidance by excluding municipal bond income from taxation, preferentially taxing dividend and capital gain income, and other strategies. Likewise, the courts have often made it quite clear that taxpayers are under no moral obligation to pay more taxes than required by law. As an example, in *Commissioner v. Newman,* 159 F.2d 848 (2 Cir., 1947), which considered a taxpayer's ability to shift income to his children using trusts, Judge Learned Hand included the following statement in his dissenting opinion:

> Over and over again courts have said that there is nothing sinister in so arranging one's affairs as to keep taxes as low as possible. Everybody does so, rich or poor; and all do right, for nobody owes any public duty to pay more than the law demands: taxes are enforced exactions, not voluntary contributions. To demand more in the name of morals is mere cant.

THE KEY FACTS

Tax Evasion versus Tax Avoidance

- Tax avoidance is the legal act of arranging one's transactions to minimize taxes paid.
- Tax evasion is the willful attempt to defraud the government by not paying taxes legally owed.
- Tax evasion falls outside the confines of legal tax avoidance.

In contrast to tax avoidance, **tax evasion**—that is, the willful attempt to defraud the government—falls outside the confines of legal tax avoidance and thus may land the perpetrator within the confines of a federal prison. (Recall from the Tax Compliance, the IRS, and Tax Authorities chapter that the rewards of tax evasion include stiff monetary penalties and imprisonment.) When does tax avoidance become tax evasion? Very good question. In many cases a clear distinction exists between avoidance (such as not paying tax on municipal bond interest) and evasion (not paying tax on a $1,000,000 game show prize). In other cases, the line is less clear. In these situations, professional judgment, the use of a smell test, and consideration of the business purpose, step-transaction, and substance-over-form doctrines may prove useful.

TAXES IN THE REAL WORLD Cheating the IRS

Few people like to pay taxes, but most of us do so. Some, however, try to cheat the IRS, including the rich and famous (Lindsay Lohan, Nicholas Cage, Willie Nelson). Folks who are trying to escape the reach of the IRS may fail to file tax returns, claim deductions to which they're not entitled, make up fake business expenses, or otherwise try to disguise how much money they really made. These tax evaders cost the government a lot of money. In 2006, the latest year for which statistics are available, the IRS reported a gross "tax gap"—the amount of owed taxes that weren't paid on time—of $385 billion.

The main cause of the tax gap is underreporting income, accounting for $376 billion of the IRS's missing money. Not filing returns and underpaying taxes owed were two other causes. Some of that money fails to make it into the hands of the government through innocent accounting mistakes or because taxpayers want to pay but aren't able to. But some of that money goes missing due to deliberate fraud.

For the past three years, the IRS has launched roughly 4,500 criminal investigations related to tax code violations (these aren't the same as audits, which are much more common—1.2 million people were audited in 2014). The number of criminal investigations is relatively small, especially considering the millions of taxpayers in the U.S. But once the IRS starts an investigation, there's a good chance that it will lead to a conviction and prison time for the offender. Of the 3,853 investigations in 2015, 75 percent, eventually led to a conviction.

Source: "Avoid an Audit: 6 Tax Lessons from Celebrities." http://www.cheatsheet.com/personal-finance/5-lessons-from-celebrity-tax-cheats.html/?a=viewall April 4, 2016.

As you might expect, tax evasion is a major area of concern and focus for the IRS. While the IRS vigorously prosecutes suspected tax evaders, its actions alone have not been able to solve this problem. Is tax evasion a victimless crime? No. Because the federal government must replace lost tax revenues by imposing higher taxes on others, honest taxpayers are the true victims of tax evasion. Currently, the federal government estimates that tax evasion costs the federal government annually more than $450 billion in lost tax revenues. As citizens and residents of the United States, each of us must recognize our obligation to support our country. As future accountants and business professionals, we also must recognize the inherent value of high ethical standards, which call for us to do the right thing in *all* situations. As business professionals have learned over and over, the costs of doing otherwise far exceed any short-term gains.

CONCLUSION

In this chapter we discussed three basic tax planning strategies—timing, income shifting, and conversion—and their related limitations. Each of these strategies exploits the variation in taxation across different dimensions. The timing strategy exploits the variation in taxation across time: The "real" tax costs of income decrease as taxation is deferred; the "real" tax savings associated with tax deductions increase as tax deductions are accelerated. However, because tax rates may change over time and the tax costs of income and tax savings of deductions vary with tax rates, tax planning should consider the effects of such changes on the timing strategy. The income-shifting strategy exploits the variation in taxation across taxpayers or jurisdictions. The assignment of income doctrine limits aggressive attempts to shift income across taxpayers. In addition, related-party transactions receive close IRS attention given the increased likelihood of taxpayer abuses in these transactions. Finally, the conversion strategy exploits the variation in taxation rates across activities although implicit taxes may reduce the advantages of this strategy. In addition to limitations specific to each planning strategy, the judicial doctrines of business purpose, step-transaction, and substance-over-form broadly apply to a wide range of transactions and planning strategies.

The timing, income-shifting, and conversion strategies represent the building blocks for the more sophisticated tax strategies that tax professionals employ on a daily basis. Combining an understanding of these basic tax planning strategies with knowledge of our tax law will provide you with the tools necessary to identify, evaluate, and implement tax planning strategies. Throughout the remainder of the text, we will discuss how these strategies can be applied to different transactions.

Summary

LO 3-1 Identify the objectives of basic tax planning strategies.

- Effective tax planning maximizes the taxpayer's after-tax wealth while achieving the taxpayer's nontax goals. Maximizing after-tax wealth is not necessarily the same as tax minimization. Maximizing after-tax wealth requires one to consider both the tax and nontax costs and benefits of alternative transactions, whereas tax minimization focuses solely on a single cost (i.e., taxes).
- Virtually every transaction involves three parties: the taxpayer, the other transacting party, and the uninvited silent party that specifies the tax consequences of the transaction (i.e., the government). Astute tax planning requires an understanding of the tax and nontax costs from the taxpayer's *and* the other party's perspectives.

LO 3-2 Apply the timing strategy and describe its applications and limitations.

- One of the cornerstones of basic tax planning involves the idea of *timing*—that is, *when* income is taxed or an expense is deducted affects the associated "real" tax costs or savings. This is true for two reasons. First, the timing of when income is taxed or an expense is deducted affects the *present value* of the taxes paid on income or tax savings on deductions. Second, the tax costs of income and tax savings income vary as *tax rates* change.
- When tax rates are constant, tax planners prefer to defer income (i.e., to reduce the present value of taxes paid) and accelerate deductions (i.e., to increase the present value of tax savings). Higher tax rates, higher rates of return, larger transaction amounts, and the ability to accelerate deductions or defer income by two or more years increase the benefits of the timing strategy.
- When tax rates change, the timing strategy requires a little more consideration because the tax costs of income and the tax savings from deductions vary as *tax rates* change. When tax rates are increasing, the taxpayer must calculate the optimal tax strategies for deductions and income. When tax rates are decreasing, the recommendations are clear. Taxpayers should accelerate tax deductions into earlier years and defer taxable income to later years.
- Timing strategies contain several inherent limitations. Generally speaking, whenever a taxpayer must accelerate a cash outflow to accelerate a deduction, the timing strategy will be less beneficial. Tax law generally requires taxpayers to continue their investment in an asset in order to defer income recognition for tax purposes. A deferral strategy may not be optimal if the taxpayer has severe cash flow needs, if continuing the investment would generate a low rate of return compared to other investments, if the current investment would subject the taxpayer to unnecessary risk, and so on. The constructive receipt doctrine, which provides that a taxpayer must recognize income when it is actually or constructively received, also restricts income deferral for cash-method taxpayers.

Apply the concept of present value to tax planning. LO 3-3

- The concept of present value—also known as the time value of money—basically states that $1 today is worth *more* than $1 in the future. For example, assuming an investor can earn a positive return (e.g., 5 percent after taxes), $1 invested today should be worth $1.05 in one year. Hence, $1 today is equivalent to $1.05 in one year.
- The implication of the time value of money for tax planning is that the timing of a cash inflow or a cash outflow affects the present value of the income or expense.

Apply the strategy of income shifting, provide examples, and describe its limitations. LO 3-4

- The income-shifting strategy exploits the differences in tax rates across taxpayers or jurisdictions. Three of the most common examples of income shifting are high-tax-rate parents shifting income to low-tax-rate children, businesses shifting income to their owners, and taxpayers shifting income from high-tax jurisdictions to low-tax jurisdictions.
- The assignment of income doctrine requires income to be taxed to the taxpayer who actually earns the income. In addition, the IRS closely monitors such related-party transactions—that is, financial activities among family members, among owners and their businesses, or among businesses owned by the same owners. Implicit taxes may also limit the benefits of income shifting via locating in tax-advantaged jurisdictions.

Apply the conversion strategy, provide examples, and describe its limitations. LO 3-5

- Tax law does not treat all types of income or deductions the same. This understanding forms the basis for the conversion strategy—recasting income and expenses to receive the most favorable tax treatment. To implement the conversion strategy, one must be aware of the underlying differences in tax treatment across various types of income, expenses, and activities and have some ability to alter the nature of the income or expense to receive the more advantageous tax treatment.
- Common examples of the conversion strategy include investment planning to invest in assets that generate preferentially taxed income; compensation planning to restructure employee compensation from currently taxable compensation to nontaxable or tax-deferred forms of compensation; and corporate distribution planning to structure corporate distributions to receive the most advantageous tax treatment.
- The Internal Revenue Code contains specific provisions that prevent the taxpayer from changing the nature of expenses, income, or activities to a more tax-advantaged status. Implicit taxes may also reduce or eliminate the advantages of conversion strategies.

Describe basic judicial doctrines that limit tax planning strategies. LO 3-6

- The constructive receipt doctrine, which may limit the timing strategy, provides that a taxpayer must recognize income when it is actually *or* constructively received. Constructive receipt is deemed to have occurred if the income has been credited to the taxpayer's account or if the income is unconditionally available to the taxpayer, the taxpayer is aware of the income's availability, and there are no restrictions on the taxpayer's control over the income.
- The assignment of income doctrine requires income to be taxed to the taxpayer who actually earns the income. The assignment of income doctrine implies that, in order to shift income to a taxpayer, that taxpayer must actually earn the income.
- The business purpose, step-transaction, and substance-over-form doctrines apply across a wide variety of transactions and planning strategies (timing, income shifting, and conversion).
- The business purpose doctrine allows the IRS to challenge and disallow business expenses for transactions with no underlying business motivation, such as the travel cost of a spouse accompanying a taxpayer on a business trip.
- The step-transaction doctrine allows the IRS to collapse a series of related transactions into one transaction to determine the tax consequences of the transaction.
- The substance-over-form doctrine allows the IRS to consider the transaction's substance regardless of its form and, where appropriate, reclassify the transaction according to its substance.

- The codified economic substance doctrine requires transactions to have a substantial purpose and to meaningfully change a taxpayer's economic position in order for a taxpayer to obtain tax benefits.

LO 3-7 Contrast tax avoidance and tax evasion.

- Tax avoidance is the legal act of arranging one's transactions, and so on, to minimize taxes paid. Tax evasion is the willful attempt to defraud the government (i.e., by not paying taxes legally owed). Tax evasion falls outside the confines of legal tax avoidance.
- In many cases a clear distinction exists between avoidance (e.g., not paying tax on municipal bond interest) and evasion (e.g., not paying tax on a $1,000,000 game show prize). In other cases, the line between tax avoidance and evasion is less clear. In these situations, professional judgment, the use of a "smell test," and consideration of the business purpose, step-transaction, and substance-over-form doctrines may prove useful.

KEY TERMS

after-tax rate of return (3-3)
arm's-length transaction (3-12)
assignment of income doctrine (3-11)
before-tax rate of return (3-17)
business purpose doctrine (3-19)
constructive receipt doctrine (3-10)
discount factor (3-3)
economic substance doctrine (3-20)
implicit tax (3-16)
present value (3-3)
related-party transaction (3-12)
step-transaction doctrine (3-19)
substance-over-form doctrine (3-19)
tax avoidance (3-20)
tax evasion (3-20)

DISCUSSION QUESTIONS

Discussion Questions are available in Connect®. connect

LO 3-1 1. "The goal of tax planning is to minimize taxes." Explain why this statement is not true.

LO 3-1 2. Describe the three parties engaged in every business transaction and how understanding taxes may aid in structuring transactions.

LO 3-1 3. In this chapter we discuss three basic tax planning strategies. What different features of taxation does each of these strategies exploit?

LO 3-2 4. What are the two basic timing strategies? What is the intent of each?

LO 3-2 5. Why is the timing strategy particularly effective for cash-method taxpayers?

LO 3-2 6. What are some common examples of the timing strategy?

LO 3-2 7. What factors increase the benefits of accelerating deductions or deferring income?

LO 3-2 LO 3-3 8. How do changing tax rates affect the timing strategy? What information do you need to determine the appropriate timing strategy when tax rates change?

LO 3-2 LO 3-6 9. Describe the ways in which the timing strategy has limitations.

LO 3-3 10. The concept of the time value of money suggests that $1 today is not equal to $1 in the future. Explain why this is true.

LO 3-3 11. Why is understanding the time value of money important for tax planning?

LO 3-3 12. What two factors increase the difference between present and future values?

LO 3-4 13. What factors have to be present for income shifting to be a viable strategy?

LO 3-4 14. Name three common types of income shifting.

LO 3-4 15. What are some ways that a parent could effectively shift income to a child? What are some of the disadvantages of these methods?

LO 3-4 16. What is the key factor in shifting income from a business to its owners? What are some methods of shifting income in this context?

17. Explain why paying dividends is not an effective way to shift income from a corporation to its owners. LO 3-4
18. What are some of the common examples of the conversion strategy? LO 3-5
19. What is needed to implement the conversion strategy? LO 3-5
20. Explain how implicit taxes may limit the benefits of the conversion strategy. LO 3-5
21. Clark owns stock in BCS Corporation that he purchased in January of the current year. The stock has appreciated significantly during the year. It is now December of the current year, and Clark is deciding whether or not he should sell the stock. What tax and nontax factors should Clark consider before making the decision on whether to sell the stock now? LO 3-5 LO 3-6 planning
22. Do after-tax rates of return for investments in either interest- or dividend-paying securities increase with the length of the investment? Why or why not? LO 3-5
23. Cameron purchases stock in both Corporation X and Corporation Y. Neither corporation pays dividends. The stocks both earn an identical before-tax rate of return. Cameron sells stock in Corporation X after three years and he sells the stock in Corporation Y after five years. Which investment likely earned a greater after-tax return? Why? LO 3-5
24. Under what circumstances would you expect the after-tax return from an investment in a capital asset to approach that of tax-exempt assets (assuming equal before-tax rates of return)? LO 3-5
25. Laurie is thinking about investing in one or several of the following investment options: LO 3-5 planning

    Corporate bonds (ordinary interest paid annually)
    Dividend-paying stock (qualified dividends)
    Life insurance (tax-exempt)
    Savings account
    Growth stock

    a) Assuming all of the options earn similar returns before taxes, rank Laurie's investment options from highest to lowest according to their after-tax returns.
    b) Which of the investments employ the deferral and/or conversion tax planning strategies?
    c) How does the time period of the investment affect the returns from these alternatives?
    d) How do these alternative investments differ in terms of their nontax characteristics?
26. What is an "implicit tax" and how does it affect a taxpayer's decision to purchase municipal bonds? LO 3-5
27. Several judicial doctrines limit basic tax planning strategies. What are they? Which planning strategies do they limit? LO 3-6
28. What is the constructive receipt doctrine? What types of taxpayers does this doctrine generally affect? For what tax planning strategy is the constructive receipt doctrine a potential limitation? LO 3-6
29. Explain the assignment of income doctrine. In what situations would this doctrine potentially apply? LO 3-6
30. Relative to arm's-length transactions, why do related-party transactions receive more IRS scrutiny? LO 3-6
31. Describe the business purpose, step-transaction, and substance-over-form doctrines. What types of tax planning strategies may these doctrines inhibit? LO 3-6

LO 3-7 32. What is the difference between tax avoidance and tax evasion?

LO 3-7 33. What are the rewards of tax avoidance? What are the rewards of tax evasion?

LO 3-7 34. "Tax avoidance is discouraged by the courts and Congress." Is this statement true or false? Please explain.

PROBLEMS

Select problems are available in Connect®.

LO 3-2 planning 35. Yong recently paid his accountant $10,000 for elaborate tax planning strategies that exploit the timing strategy. Assuming this is an election year and there could be a power shift in the White House and Congress, what is a potential risk associated with Yong's strategies?

LO 3-2 LO 3-3 planning 36. Billups, a physician and cash-method taxpayer, is new to the concept of tax planning and recently learned of the timing strategy. To implement the timing strategy, Billups plans to establish a new policy that allows all his clients to wait two years to pay their co-pays. Assume that Billups does not expect his marginal tax rates to change. What is wrong with his strategy?

LO 3-2 LO 3-3 planning 37. Tesha works for a company that pays a year-end bonus in January of each year (instead of December of the preceding year) to allow employees to defer the bonus income. Assume Congress recently passed tax legislation that decreases individual tax rates as of next year. Does this increase or decrease the benefits of the bonus deferral this year? What if Congress passed legislation that increased tax rates next year? Should Tesha ask the company to change its policy this year? What additional information do you need to answer this question?

LO 3-2 LO 3-3 planning 38. Isabel, a calendar-year taxpayer, uses the cash method of accounting for her sole proprietorship. In late December she received a $20,000 bill from her accountant for consulting services related to her small business. Isabel can pay the $20,000 bill anytime before January 30 of next year without penalty. Assume her marginal tax rate is 40 percent this year and next year, and that she can earn an after-tax rate of return of 12 percent on her investments. When should she pay the $20,000 bill—this year or next?

LO 3-2 LO 3-3 planning 39. Using the facts from the previous problem, how would your answer change if Isabel's after-tax rate of return were 8 percent?

LO 3-2 LO 3-3 planning 40. Manny, a calendar-year taxpayer, uses the cash method of accounting for his sole proprietorship. In late December he performed $20,000 of legal services for a client. Manny typically requires his clients to pay his bills immediately upon receipt. Assume Manny's marginal tax rate is 40 percent this year and next year, and that he can earn an after-tax rate of return of 12 percent on his investments. Should Manny send his client the bill in December or January?

LO 3-2 LO 3-3 planning 41. Using the facts from the previous problem, how would your answer change if Manny's after-tax rate of return were 8 percent?

LO 3-2 LO 3-3 planning 42. Reese, a calendar-year taxpayer, uses the cash method of accounting for her sole proprietorship. In late December, she received a $20,000 bill from her accountant for consulting services related to her small business. Reese can pay the $20,000 bill anytime before January 30 of next year without penalty. Assume Reese's marginal tax rate is 30 percent this year and will be 40 percent next year, and that she can earn an after-tax rate of return of 12 percent on her investments. When should she pay the $20,000 bill—this year or next?

LO 3-2 LO 3-3 planning 43. Using the facts from the previous problem, when should Reese pay the bill if she expects her marginal tax rate to be 33 percent next year? 25 percent next year?

44. Hank, a calendar-year taxpayer, uses the cash method of accounting for his sole proprietorship. In late December, he performed $20,000 of legal services for a client. Hank typically requires his clients to pay his bills immediately upon receipt. Assume his marginal tax rate is 30 percent this year and will be 40 percent next year, and that he can earn an after-tax rate of return of 12 percent on his investments. Should Hank send his client the bill in December or January? LO 3-2 LO 3-3 planning
45. Using the facts from the previous problem, when should Hank send the bill if he expects his marginal tax rate to be 33 percent next year? 25 percent next year? LO 3-2 LO 3-3 planning
46. Geraldo recently won a lottery and chose to receive $100,000 today instead of an equivalent amount in 10 years, computed using an 8 percent rate of return. Today, he learned that interest rates are expected to increase in the future. Is this good news for Geraldo given his decision? LO 3-3
47. Assume Rafael can earn an 8 percent after-tax rate of return. Would he prefer $1,000 today or $1,500 in five years? LO 3-3 planning
48. Assume Ellina earns a 10 percent after-tax rate of return, and that she owes a friend $1,200. Would she prefer to pay the friend $1,200 today or $1,750 in four years? LO 3-3 planning
49. Jonah has the choice of paying Rita $10,000 today or $40,000 in 10 years. Assume Jonah can earn a 12 percent after-tax rate of return. Which should he choose? LO 3-3 planning
50. Bob's Lottery Inc. has decided to offer winners a choice of $100,000 in 10 years or some amount currently. Assume that Bob's Lottery Inc. earns a 10 percent after-tax rate of return. What amount should Bob offer lottery winners currently, in order for him to be indifferent between the two choices? LO 3-3 planning
51. Tawana owns and operates a sole proprietorship and has a 40 percent marginal tax rate. She provides her son, Jonathon, $8,000 a year for college expenses. Jonathon works as a pizza delivery person every fall and has a marginal tax rate of 15 percent. LO 3-4 planning
    a) What could Tawana do to reduce her family tax burden?
    b) How much pretax income does it currently take Tawana to generate the $8,000 (after taxes) given to Jonathon?
    c) If Jonathon worked for his mother's sole proprietorship, what salary would she have to pay him to generate $8,000 after taxes (ignoring any Social Security, Medicare, or self-employment tax issues)?
    d) How much money would the strategy in part (c) save?
52. Moana is a single taxpayer who operates a sole proprietorship. She expects her taxable income next year to be $250,000, of which $200,000 is attributed to her sole proprietorship. Moana is contemplating incorporating her sole proprietorship. Using the single individual tax brackets and the corporate tax brackets, find out how much current tax this strategy could save Moana (ignore any Social Security, Medicare, or self-employment tax issues). How much income should be left in the corporation? LO 3-4 planning
53. Orie and Jane, husband and wife, operate a sole proprietorship. They expect their taxable income next year to be $300,000, of which $125,000 is attributed to the sole proprietorship. Orie and Jane are contemplating incorporating their sole proprietorship. Using the married-joint tax brackets and the corporate tax brackets, find out how much current tax this strategy could save Orie and Jane. How much income should be left in the corporation? LO 3-4 planning
54. Hyundai is considering opening a plant in two neighboring states. One state has a corporate tax rate of 10 percent. If operated in this state, the plant is expected to generate $1,000,000 pretax profit. The other state has a corporate tax rate of 2 percent. If operated in this state, the plant is expected to generate $930,000 of pretax profit. Which state should Hyundai choose? Why do you think the plant in the state with a lower tax rate would produce a lower before-tax income? LO 3-4 planning

LO 3-4 LO 3-6 planning

55. Bendetta, a high-tax-rate taxpayer, owns several rental properties and would like to shift some income to her daughter, Jenine. Bendetta instructs her tenants to send their rent checks to Jenine so Jenine can report the rental income. Will this shift the income from Bendetta to Jenine? Why, or why not?

LO 3-4 LO 3-6 planning

56. Using the facts in the previous problem, what are some ways that Bendetta could shift some of the rental income to Jenine? What are the disadvantages associated with these income-shifting strategies?

LO 3-5 planning

57. Daniel is considering selling two stocks that have not fared well over recent years. A friend recently informed Daniel that one of his stocks has a special designation, which allows him to treat a loss up to $50,000 on this stock as an ordinary loss rather than the typical capital loss. Daniel figures that he has a loss of $60,000 on each stock. If Daniel's marginal tax rate is 35 percent and he has $120,000 of other capital gains (taxed at 15 percent), what is the tax savings from the special tax treatment?

LO 3-5 planning

58. Dennis is currently considering investing in municipal bonds that earn 6 percent interest, or in taxable bonds issued by the Coca-Cola Company that pay 8 percent. If Dennis's tax rate is 20 percent, which bond should he choose? Which bond should he choose if his tax rate is 30 percent? At what tax rate would he be indifferent between the bonds? What strategy is this decision based upon?

LO 3-5 planning

59. Helen holds 1,000 shares of Fizbo Inc. stock that she purchased 11 months ago. The stock has done very well and has appreciated $20/share since Helen bought the stock. When sold, the stock will be taxed at capital gains rates (the long-term rate is 15 percent and the short-term rate is the taxpayer's marginal tax rate). If Helen's marginal tax rate is 35 percent, how much would she save by holding the stock an additional month before selling? What might prevent Helen from waiting to sell?

LO 3-5

60. Anne's marginal income tax rate is 30 percent. She purchases a corporate bond for $10,000 and the maturity, or face value, of the bond is $10,000. If the bond pays 5 percent per year before taxes, what is Anne's annual after-tax rate of return from the bond if the bond matures in one year? What is her annual after-tax rate of return if the bond matures in 10 years?

LO 3-5 planning

61. Irene is saving for a new car she hopes to purchase either four or six years from now. Irene invests $10,000 in a growth stock that does not pay dividends and expects a 6 percent annual before-tax return (the investment is tax deferred). When she cashes in the investment after either four or six years, she expects the applicable marginal tax rate on long-term capital gains to be 25 percent.
    a) What will be the value of this investment four years from now? Six years from now?
    b) When Irene sells the investment, how much cash will she have after taxes to purchase the new car (four and six years from now)?

LO 3-5 planning

62. Komiko Tanaka invests $12,000 in LymaBean, Inc. LymaBean does not pay any dividends. Komiko projects that her investment will generate a 10 percent before-tax rate of return. She plans to invest for the long term.
    a) How much cash will Komiko retain, after taxes, if she holds the investment for five years and then sells it when the long-term capital gains rate is 15 percent?
    b) What is Komiko's after-tax rate of return on her investment in part (a)?
    c) How much cash will Komiko retain, after taxes, if she holds the investment for five years and then sells when the long-term capital gains rate is 25 percent?
    d) What is Komiko's after-tax rate of return on her investment in part (c)?
    e) How much cash will Komiko retain, after taxes, if she holds the investment for 15 years and then sells when the long-term capital gains rate is 15 percent?
    f) What is Komiko's after-tax rate of return on her investment in part (e)?

63. Alan inherited $100,000 with the stipulation that he "invest it to financially benefit his family." Alan and his wife Alice decided they would invest the inheritance to help them accomplish two financial goals: purchasing a Park City vacation home and saving for their son Cooper's education. LO 3-5 planning

	Vacation Home	Cooper's Education
Initial investment	$50,000	$50,000
Investment horizon	5 years	18 years

Alan and Alice have a marginal income tax rate of 30 percent (capital gains rate of 15 percent) and have decided to investigate the following investment opportunities.

	5 Years	Annual After-Tax Rate of Return	18 Years	Annual After-Tax Rate of Return
Corporate bonds (ordinary interest taxed annually)	5.75%		4.75%	
Dividend-paying stock (no appreciation and dividends are taxed at 15%)	3.50%		3.50%	
Growth stock	FV = $65,000		FV = $140,000	
Municipal bond (tax-exempt)	3.20%		3.10%	

Complete the two annual after-tax rates of return columns for each investment and provide investment recommendations for Alan and Alice.

64. Duff is really interested in decreasing his tax liability, and by his very nature he is somewhat aggressive. A friend of a friend told him that cash transactions are more difficult for the IRS to identify and, thus, tax. Duff is contemplating using this "strategy" of not reporting cash collected in his business to minimize his tax liability. Is this tax planning? What are the risks with this strategy? LO 3-7

65. Using the facts from the previous problem, how would your answer change if, instead, Duff adopted the cash method of accounting to allow him to better control the timing of his cash receipts and disbursements? LO 3-7

66. Using an available tax service or the Internet, identify three basic tax planning ideas or tax tips suggested for year-end tax planning. Which basic tax strategy from this chapter does each planning idea employ? LO 3-2 LO 3-4 LO 3-5 planning research

67. Jayanna, an advertising consultant, is contemplating instructing some of her clients to pay her in cash so that she does not have to report the income on her tax return. Use an available tax service to identify the three basic elements of tax evasion and penalties associated with tax evasion. Write a memo to Jayanna explaining tax evasion and the risks associated with her actions. LO 3-7 research

68. Using the IRS website (https://www.irs.gov/uac/The-Tax-Gap), how large is the current estimated "tax gap" (i.e., the amount of tax underpaid by taxpayers annually)? What group of taxpayers represents the largest "contributors" to the tax gap? LO 3-7 research

ROGER | CPA Review

Sample CPA Exam questions from Roger CPA Review are available in Connect as support for the topics in this text. These Multiple Choice Questions and Task-Based Simulations include expert-written explanations and solutions, and provide a starting point for students to become familiar with the content and functionality of the actual CPA Exam.

chapter 4

Individual Income Tax Overview, Exemptions, and Filing Status

Learning Objectives

Upon completing this chapter, you should be able to:

LO 4-1 Describe the formula for calculating an individual taxpayer's taxes payable or refund and generally explain each formula component.

LO 4-2 Explain the requirements for determining a taxpayer's personal and dependency exemptions.

LO 4-3 Determine a taxpayer's filing status.

© Creatas Images/Getty Images

Tara Hall just completed a unit on individual taxation in her undergraduate tax class at South Dakota State University. She was excited to share her knowledge with her parents, Rodney and Anita Hall, as they prepared their tax return. Rodney and Anita have been married for over 25 years, and they have filed a joint tax return each year. The Halls' 12-year-old son Braxton lives at home but Tara, who is 21, lives nearby in the university dorms. Further, in January of this year, Rodney's younger brother Shawn moved in with the Halls. They expect Shawn to live with them for at least one year and maybe two. Every year Rodney and Anita use tax-preparation software to complete their tax return, but they are not always sure they understand the final result. This year, with Tara's help, they hope that will change. ■

Storyline Summary

Taxpayers:	Rodney and Anita Hall
Other household members:	Tara, their 21-year-old daughter, and Braxton, their 12-year-old son. Shawn, Rodney's brother, also lives with the Halls.
Location:	Brookings, South Dakota
Employment status:	Rodney is a manager for a regional grocery chain. His annual salary is $74,000. Anita works as a purchasing-card auditor at South Dakota State University. Her annual salary is $56,000.
Current situation:	Determining their tax liability

This chapter and the next four discuss the fundamental elements of the individual income tax formula. This is the overview chapter; the other chapters provide more depth on individual income tax topics. Here we introduce the individual income tax formula, summarize its components, describe requirements for dependency exemptions, and explain how to determine a taxpayer's filing status. The Gross Income and Exclusions chapter explains gross income, the Individual Deductions chapter describes deductible expenses to determine adjusted gross income and taxable income, and the Investments chapter discusses tax issues associated with investments. Finally, the Individual Income Tax Computation and Tax Credits chapter addresses issues associated with calculating a taxpayer's tax liability and discusses tax return filing concerns.

LO 4-1

THE INDIVIDUAL INCOME TAX FORMULA

Each year, individuals file tax returns to report their **taxable income,** the tax base for the individual income tax, to the Internal Revenue Service.[1] Exhibit 4-1 presents a simplified formula for calculating taxable income.

EXHIBIT 4-1 Individual Tax Formula

	Gross income
Minus:	*For AGI (above the line) deductions*
Equals:	Adjusted gross income (AGI)
Minus:	*From AGI (below the line) deductions*
	(1) *Greater* of
	(a) Standard deduction or
	(b) Itemized deductions and
	(2) Personal and dependency exemptions
Equals:	Taxable income
Times:	Tax rates
Equals:	Income tax liability
Plus:	Other taxes
Equals:	Total tax
Minus:	Credits
Minus:	Prepayments
Equals:	Taxes due or (refund)

Beginning with gross income, this formula is embedded in the first two pages of the individual income tax Form 1040, the form individuals generally use to report their taxable income.[2] Exhibit 4-2 presents the first two pages of the form (throughout the text we use 2016 tax forms because 2017 forms were unavailable when the book went to press). The last line on page 1 of Form 1040 is **adjusted gross income (AGI),** an important reference point in the income tax formula.

Let's look at the components of the individual tax formula and provide a brief description of each of the key elements.

Gross Income

The U.S. tax laws are based on the **all-inclusive income concept.** Under this concept, **gross income** generally includes all **realized income** from *whatever source derived.*[3] Realized income is generated in a transaction with a second party in which there is a measurable change in property rights between parties (for example, appreciation in a stock investment would not represent realized income unless the taxpayer sold the stock).

[1]See Exhibit 1 in the Tax Compliance, the IRS, and Tax Authorities chapter for a description of who must file a tax return.

[2]To see the 1913 version of the individual tax form, go to http://www.irs.gov/pub/irs-utl/1913.pdf

[3]§61(a).

EXHIBIT 4-2 **Form 1040, pages 1 and 2**

Form **1040** Department of the Treasury—Internal Revenue Service (99)
U.S. Individual Income Tax Return **2016** OMB No. 1545-0074 IRS Use Only—Do not write or staple in this space.

For the year Jan. 1–Dec. 31, 2016, or other tax year beginning , 2016, ending , 20 See separate instructions.

Your first name and initial	Last name	**Your social security number**
If a joint return, spouse's first name and initial	Last name	**Spouse's social security number**
Home address (number and street). If you have a P.O. box, see instructions.	Apt. no.	▲ Make sure the SSN(s) above and on line 6c are correct.
City, town or post office, state, and ZIP code. If you have a foreign address, also complete spaces below (see instructions).		**Presidential Election Campaign** Check here if you, or your spouse if filing jointly, want $3 to go to this fund. Checking a box below will not change your tax or refund. ☐ You ☐ Spouse
Foreign country name	Foreign province/state/county / Foreign postal code	

Filing Status

Check only one box.

1 ☐ Single
2 ☐ Married filing jointly (even if only one had income)
3 ☐ Married filing separately. Enter spouse's SSN above and full name here. ▶
4 ☐ Head of household (with qualifying person). (See instructions.) If the qualifying person is a child but not your dependent, enter this child's name here. ▶
5 ☐ Qualifying widow(er) with dependent child

Exemptions

6a ☐ **Yourself.** If someone can claim you as a dependent, **do not** check box 6a . . . . .
b ☐ **Spouse** . . . .

Boxes checked on 6a and 6b

c **Dependents:**

(1) First name Last name	(2) Dependent's social security number	(3) Dependent's relationship to you	(4) ✓ if child under age 17 qualifying for child tax credit (see instructions)
			☐
			☐
			☐
			☐

No. of children on 6c who:
• lived with you
• did not live with you due to divorce or separation (see instructions)
Dependents on 6c not entered above

If more than four dependents, see instructions and check here ▶ ☐

d Total number of exemptions claimed . . . . **Add numbers on lines above ▶**

Income

Attach Form(s) W-2 here. Also attach Forms W-2G and 1099-R if tax was withheld.

If you did not get a W-2, see instructions.

7	Wages, salaries, tips, etc. Attach Form(s) W-2		7
8a	**Taxable** interest. Attach Schedule B if required		8a
b	**Tax-exempt** interest. **Do not** include on line 8a . . .	8b	
9a	Ordinary dividends. Attach Schedule B if required		9a
b	Qualified dividends	9b	
10	Taxable refunds, credits, or offsets of state and local income taxes		10
11	Alimony received		11
12	Business income or (loss). Attach Schedule C or C-EZ		12
13	Capital gain or (loss). Attach Schedule D if required. If not required, check here ▶ ☐		13
14	Other gains or (losses). Attach Form 4797		14
15a	IRA distributions . 15a	b Taxable amount . . .	15b
16a	Pensions and annuities 16a	b Taxable amount . . .	16b
17	Rental real estate, royalties, partnerships, S corporations, trusts, etc. Attach Schedule E		17
18	Farm income or (loss). Attach Schedule F		18
19	Unemployment compensation		19
20a	Social security benefits 20a	b Taxable amount . . .	20b
21	Other income. List type and amount		21
22	Combine the amounts in the far right column for lines 7 through 21. This is your **total income** ▶		22

Adjusted Gross Income

23	Educator expenses	23	
24	Certain business expenses of reservists, performing artists, and fee-basis government officials. Attach Form 2106 or 2106-EZ	24	
25	Health savings account deduction. Attach Form 8889 .	25	
26	Moving expenses. Attach Form 3903	26	
27	Deductible part of self-employment tax. Attach Schedule SE .	27	
28	Self-employed SEP, SIMPLE, and qualified plans . .	28	
29	Self-employed health insurance deduction	29	
30	Penalty on early withdrawal of savings	30	
31a	Alimony paid b Recipient's SSN ▶	31a	
32	IRA deduction	32	
33	Student loan interest deduction	33	
34	Tuition and fees. Attach Form 8917	34	
35	Domestic production activities deduction. Attach Form 8903	35	
36	Add lines 23 through 35		36
37	Subtract line 36 from line 22. This is your **adjusted gross income** . . . . . ▶		37

For Disclosure, Privacy Act, and Paperwork Reduction Act Notice, see separate instructions. Cat. No. 11320B Form **1040** (2016)

(continued)

EXHIBIT 4-2 Form 1040, pages 1 and 2 (*continued*)

Form 1040 (2016) Page **2**

Tax and Credits

38	Amount from line 37 (adjusted gross income)		38
39a	Check if: ☐ **You** were born before January 2, 1952, ☐ Blind. ☐ **Spouse** was born before January 2, 1952, ☐ Blind. **Total boxes checked ▶ 39a** ☐		
b	If your spouse itemizes on a separate return or you were a dual-status alien, check here▶ 39b☐		
40	**Itemized deductions** (from Schedule A) **or** your **standard deduction** (see left margin)		40
41	Subtract line 40 from line 38		41
42	**Exemptions.** If line 38 is $155,650 or less, multiply $4,050 by the number on line 6d. Otherwise, see instructions		42
43	**Taxable income.** Subtract line 42 from line 41. If line 42 is more than line 41, enter -0-		43
44	**Tax** (see instructions). Check if any from: **a** ☐ Form(s) 8814 **b** ☐ Form 4972 **c** ☐		44
45	**Alternative minimum tax** (see instructions). Attach Form 6251		45
46	Excess advance premium tax credit repayment. Attach Form 8962		46
47	Add lines 44, 45, and 46 ▶		47
48	Foreign tax credit. Attach Form 1116 if required	48	
49	Credit for child and dependent care expenses. Attach Form 2441	49	
50	Education credits from Form 8863, line 19	50	
51	Retirement savings contributions credit. Attach Form 8880	51	
52	Child tax credit. Attach Schedule 8812, if required	52	
53	Residential energy credits. Attach Form 5695	53	
54	Other credits from Form: **a** ☐ 3800 **b** ☐ 8801 **c** ☐	54	
55	Add lines 48 through 54. These are your **total credits**		55
56	Subtract line 55 from line 47. If line 55 is more than line 47, enter -0- ▶		56

Standard Deduction for—
- People who check any box on line 39a or 39b **or** who can be claimed as a dependent, see instructions.
- All others:

Single or Married filing separately, $6,300

Married filing jointly or Qualifying widow(er), $12,600

Head of household, $9,300

Other Taxes

57	Self-employment tax. Attach Schedule SE		57
58	Unreported social security and Medicare tax from Form: **a** ☐ 4137 **b** ☐ 8919		58
59	Additional tax on IRAs, other qualified retirement plans, etc. Attach Form 5329 if required		59
60a	Household employment taxes from Schedule H		60a
b	First-time homebuyer credit repayment. Attach Form 5405 if required		60b
61	Health care: individual responsibility (see instructions) Full-year coverage ☐		61
62	Taxes from: **a** ☐ Form 8959 **b** ☐ Form 8960 **c** ☐ Instructions; enter code(s)		62
63	Add lines 56 through 62. This is your **total tax** ▶		63

Payments

If you have a qualifying child, attach Schedule EIC.

64	Federal income tax withheld from Forms W-2 and 1099	64	
65	2016 estimated tax payments and amount applied from 2015 return	65	
66a	**Earned income credit (EIC)**	66a	
b	Nontaxable combat pay election 66b		
67	Additional child tax credit. Attach Schedule 8812	67	
68	American opportunity credit from Form 8863, line 8	68	
69	Net premium tax credit. Attach Form 8962	69	
70	Amount paid with request for extension to file	70	
71	Excess social security and tier 1 RRTA tax withheld	71	
72	Credit for federal tax on fuels. Attach Form 4136	72	
73	Credits from Form: **a** ☐ 2439 **b** ☐ Reserved **c** ☐ 8885 **d** ☐	73	
74	Add lines 64, 65, 66a, and 67 through 73. These are your **total payments** ▶		74

Refund

Direct deposit? See instructions.

75	If line 74 is more than line 63, subtract line 63 from line 74. This is the amount you **overpaid**		75
76a	Amount of line 75 you want **refunded to you.** If Form 8888 is attached, check here ▶ ☐		76a
▶ b	Routing number ▶ c Type: ☐ Checking ☐ Savings		
▶ d	Account number		
77	Amount of line 75 you want **applied to your 2017 estimated tax** ▶	77	

Amount You Owe

78	**Amount you owe.** Subtract line 74 from line 63. For details on how to pay, see instructions ▶		78
79	Estimated tax penalty (see instructions)	79	

Third Party Designee

Do you want to allow another person to discuss this return with the IRS (see instructions)? ☐ **Yes.** Complete below. ☐ **No**

Designee's name ▶ Phone no. ▶ Personal identification number (PIN) ▶

Sign Here

Joint return? See instructions. Keep a copy for your records.

Under penalties of perjury, I declare that I have examined this return and accompanying schedules and statements, and to the best of my knowledge and belief, they are true, correct, and accurately list all amounts and sources of income I received during the tax year. Declaration of preparer (other than taxpayer) is based on all information of which preparer has any knowledge.

Your signature	Date	Your occupation	Daytime phone number
Spouse's signature. If a joint return, **both** must sign.	Date	Spouse's occupation	If the IRS sent you an Identity Protection PIN, enter it here (see inst.)

Paid Preparer Use Only

Print/Type preparer's name	Preparer's signature	Date	Check ☐ if self-employed	PTIN
Firm's name ▶			Firm's EIN ▶	
Firm's address ▶			Phone no.	

www.irs.gov/form1040 Form **1040** (2016)

Certain tax provisions allow taxpayers to permanently exclude specific types of realized income from gross income (the income items are never taxable) and other provisions allow taxpayers to defer including certain types of realized income items in gross income until a subsequent year (the income item is included in gross income in a later year). Realized income items that taxpayers permanently exclude from taxation are referred to as **exclusions.** Realized income items that taxpayers include in gross income in a subsequent year are called **deferrals.** Exhibit 4-3 provides a partial listing of common income items included in gross income, their character (discussed below), and where in the text we provide more detail on each income item. Exhibit 4-4 provides a partial listing of common exclusions and deferrals and indicates where in the text we discuss each in more detail.

EXHIBIT 4-3 Partial Listing of Common Income Items

Income Item	Character	Discussed in More Detail in These Chapters
Compensation for services including fringe benefits	Ordinary	Gross Income and Exclusions and Compensation
Business income	Ordinary	Business Income, Deductions, and Accounting Methods
Gains from selling property	Ordinary or capital[4]	Investments and Property Dispositions
Interest and dividends	Ordinary or qualified dividend	Gross Income and Exclusions and Investments
Rents and royalties	Ordinary	Gross Income and Exclusions, Investments, and Tax Consequences of Home Ownership
Alimony received and annuities	Ordinary	Gross Income and Exclusions
Retirement income	Ordinary	Retirement Savings and Deferred Compensation
Income from the discharge of indebtedness	Ordinary	Gross Income and Exclusions

EXHIBIT 4-4 Partial Listing of Common Exclusions and Deferrals

Exclusion or Deferral Item	Exclusion or Deferral	Discussed in These Chapters
Interest income from municipal bonds	Exclusion	Gross Income and Exclusions
Gifts and inheritances	Exclusion	Gross Income and Exclusions
Gain on sale of personal residence	Exclusion	Gross Income and Exclusions and Tax Consequences of Home Ownership
Life insurance proceeds	Exclusion	Gross Income and Exclusions
Installment sale	Deferral	Property Dispositions
Like-kind exchange	Deferral	Property Dispositions

Character of Income While gross income increases taxable income dollar for dollar, it is important to note that certain types of income are treated differently than other types of income for purposes of computing a taxpayer's taxable income and income tax liability. For example, one type of income may be taxed at a different rate than another type of

[4]Dispositions of assets used in a trade or business for more than a year generate an intermediate character of income called §1231 gain or loss. Ultimately, §1231 gains and losses are treated as either ordinary or capital on the tax return.

income. The *type* of income is commonly referred to as the **character of income.** The most common characters of income are as follows:

- Ordinary: This is income or loss that is taxed at the ordinary rates provided in the tax rate schedules in Appendix D, or offsets income taxed at these rates, and is not capital in character.
- Capital: These are gains or losses on the disposition or sale of capital assets. In general, capital assets are all assets *other than*
    1. Accounts receivable from the sale of goods or services.
    2. Inventory and other assets held for sale in the ordinary course of business.
    3. Assets used in a trade or business, including supplies.[5]

  Nonbusiness assets such as personal-use automobiles or personal residences and assets held for investment such as stocks and bonds are capital assets.

  Capital gains and losses are further characterized as long-term (when the taxpayer owns the capital asset for more than one year before selling it) or as short-term (when the taxpayer owns the capital asset for one year or less before selling it). A gain on a sale of a capital asset is generally included in gross income. If the gain is a long-term capital gain, it is taxed at a 15 percent tax rate (20 percent for high income taxpayers and 0 percent for low income taxpayers). If the gain is a short-term capital gain, the gain is taxed at ordinary income rates. Note that even though a short-term capital gain is taxed at ordinary rates, it is still considered to be a capital gain and not ordinary income.

  A loss on the sale of a capital asset (no matter how long the taxpayer holds the asset before selling) generates a deduction for the taxpayer in the year of sale (a *for* AGI deduction, as discussed below). However, the deduction for the loss is limited to $3,000 for the year (losses in excess of the limit are carried forward indefinitely). If the taxpayer sells a personal-use asset (like a personal automobile or personal residence) at a loss, the loss is not deductible.

  When a taxpayer sells more than one capital asset during the year, the gains and losses are netted together. A net loss is subject to the $3,000 annual deduction limit. A net gain may be taxed at 15, 20, or 0 percent or at the ordinary rates depending on the outcome of the netting process and the taxpayer's taxable income. We discuss the netting process in detail in the Investments chapter.[6]
- Qualified dividend: Shareholders receiving dividends from corporations include the dividend income in gross income. If the dividend meets the qualified dividend requirements, it is taxed at a rate of 15 percent (20 percent for high income taxpayers and 0 percent for low income taxpayers).[7] If a dividend does not meet the qualified dividend requirement, it is taxed at ordinary rates. Because qualified dividends (and long-term capital gains) are taxed at a **preferential tax rate** (a rate lower than the ordinary income rate), qualified dividends (and long-term capital gains) can be referred to as **preferentially taxed income.** While qualified dividends are taxed at the same rate as long-term capital gains, qualified dividends are not included in the capital gain and loss netting process. Therefore, qualified dividend is a separate and distinct character from capital.

Example 4-1

Rodney earned a salary of $74,000, and Anita earned a salary of $56,000. The Halls also received $600 of interest income from investments in corporate bonds and $300 of interest income from investments in municipal bonds. This was their only income during the year. What is the Halls' gross income?

[5]See §1221(a) for the definition of a capital asset.

[6]As we discover in the Investments chapter, some certain capital gains may be taxed at a maximum rate of 25 percent and others may be taxed at a maximum rate of 28 percent.

[7]A qualified dividend generally includes dividends distributed by a U.S. corporation if the shareholder meets certain holding requirements for the stock. These requirements are discussed in more detail in the Investments chapter.

Answer: $130,600, computed as follows:

Description	Amount	Explanation
(1) Rodney's salary	$ 74,000	
(2) Anita's salary	56,000	
(3) Interest from corporate bonds	600	
Gross income	**$130,600***	(1) + (2) + (3)

*The $300 of interest income from municipal bonds is excluded from gross income.

What is the character of the salary, the interest income from the corporate bonds, and the interest income from the investments in municipal bonds?

Answer: The salary and interest income from corporate bonds are ordinary income. The interest income from the municipal bonds is excluded from gross income.

What if: Suppose this year the Halls sold shares of stock in XYZ corporation at a $4,000 gain (their only transaction involving a capital asset). They purchased the stock three years ago. What would be the character of the gain? At what rate would the gain be taxed?

Answer: This is a long-term capital gain because stock is a capital asset and the Halls owned the stock for more than a year before selling. Given their income level, the gain would be taxed at a maximum rate of 15 percent.

What if: Suppose this year the Halls sold stock at a $4,000 loss (their only transaction involving a capital asset). They purchased the stock three years ago. What would be the character of the loss? How much of the loss may the Halls deduct this year?

Answer: This is a long-term capital loss because the stock is a capital asset and the Halls owned the stock for more than a year before selling. The Halls can deduct $3,000 of the loss as a *for* AGI deduction this year. The remaining $1,000 loss is carried over to next year.

What if: Suppose this year the Halls sold a personal automobile at a $4,000 loss. They purchased the automobile three years ago. What is the character of the loss? How much of the loss may the Halls deduct in the current year?

Answer: This is a long-term capital loss because the automobile is a capital asset and the Halls owned the auto for more than a year before selling. However, the Halls are not allowed to deduct any of the $4,000 loss this year or any year because the automobile is a personal-use asset.

Deductions

Deductions reduce a taxpayer's taxable income. However, they are not necessarily easy to come by because, in contrast to the all-inclusive treatment of income, taxpayers are *not allowed to deduct anything unless a specific tax provision allows them to do so*. Thus, deductions are a matter of **legislative grace.** The tax laws provide for two distinct types of deductions in the individual tax formula: *for adjusted gross income (AGI) deductions* and *from AGI deductions.* As indicated in the individual tax formula, gross income minus ***for* AGI deductions** equals AGI and AGI minus ***from* AGI deductions** equals taxable income. Congress identifies whether the deductions are *for* or *from* AGI when it enacts new legislation that grants deductions. The distinction between the deduction types is particularly important because AGI is an important reference point that is often used in other tax-related calculations. Specifically, limits on certain *from* AGI deductions depend on AGI (certain *from* AGI deductions are reduced as a taxpayer's AGI increases). Because *for* AGI deductions decrease AGI, they *increase* the deductibility of *from* AGI deductions subject to AGI limitations.

THE KEY FACTS

***For* and *From* AGI Deductions**

- *For* AGI deductions
  - Deduct in determining AGI.
  - Deduction "above the line."
  - Generally more valuable than *from* AGI deductions.
- *From* AGI deductions
  - Deducted *from* AGI to determine taxable income.
  - Deduction "below the line."
  - Generally less valuable than *for* AGI deductions.

For AGI Deductions

For AGI deductions tend to be deductions associated with business activities and certain investing activities. Because *for* AGI deductions are subtracted in determining AGI (deducted on page 1 of Form 1040), they are referred to as **"deductions above the line."** The "line" in this case is AGI, which is the last line on page 1 of Form 1040 (see Exhibit 4-2). Exhibit 4-5 provides a partial listing of common *for* AGI deductions and indicates where in the text we discuss them.

EXHIBIT 4-5 Partial Listing of Common *for* AGI Deductions

***For* AGI Deduction**	**Discussed in More Detail in These Chapters**
Alimony paid	Individual Deductions
Health insurance deduction for self-employed taxpayers	Individual Deductions
Moving expenses	Individual Deductions
Rental and royalty expenses	Individual Deductions and Tax Consequences of Home Ownership
Capital losses (*net* losses limited to $3,000 for the year)	Investments
One-half of self-employment taxes paid	Individual Income Tax Computation and Tax Credits
Business expenses	Business Income, Deductions, and Accounting Methods
Losses on dispositions of assets used in a trade or business	Property Dispositions
Contributions to qualified retirement accounts	Retirement Savings and Deferred Compensation

Example 4-2

The Halls paid $5,000 of deductible moving expenses (*for* AGI) when the family relocated due to an employment transfer for Rodney. What is the Halls' adjusted gross income?

Answer: $125,600, computed as follows:

Description	Amount	Explanation
(1) Gross income	$ 130,600	Example 4-1
(2) Moving expenses	(5,000)	*For* AGI deduction (see Exhibit 4-5)
Adjusted gross income	**$125,600**	(1) + (2)

From AGI Deductions In contrast to *for* AGI deductions, *from* AGI deductions tend to be personal in nature. *From* AGI deductions are commonly referred to as **"deductions below the line"** because they are deducted after AGI has been determined (deducted on page 2 of Form 1040). *From* AGI deductions include **itemized deductions,** the **standard deduction,** and **exemptions.** In a given year, individuals have the choice of deducting *either* their itemized deductions *or* a fixed amount called the standard deduction. As we discuss in the Individual Deductions chapter, itemized deductions are partially phased out for taxpayers with AGI over a certain threshold. Taxpayers generally deduct the higher of the standard deduction or itemized deductions (after the itemized deductions phase out, if any). Exhibit 4-6 identifies the primary categories of itemized deductions.

EXHIBIT 4-6 Primary Categories of Itemized Deductions

- *Medical and dental expenses:* Deductible to the extent these expenses exceed 10 percent of AGI for taxpayers under age 65 (through 2016 not extended to 2017 as of press time) at year-end and 7.5 percent otherwise.
- *Taxes:* State and local income taxes, sales taxes, real estate taxes, personal property taxes, and other taxes.
- *Interest expense:* Mortgage, home equity, and investment interest expense.
- *Gifts to charity (charitable contributions).*
- *Casualty and theft losses:* Deductible to the extent they exceed 10 percent of AGI.
- *Job expenses and certain miscellaneous deductions:* Deductible to the extent the sum of these expenses exceeds 2 percent of AGI.
- *Other miscellaneous deductions:* Gambling losses (to the extent of gambling winnings) and certain other deductions not subject to AGI limitation.

Note: Itemized deductions are detailed on Schedule A of Form 1040. We discuss itemized deductions in more depth in the Individual Deductions chapter.

The amount of the standard deduction varies by taxpayer filing status (we discuss filing status in more detail later in the chapter); the government indexes this deduction for inflation. Exhibit 4-7 presents the basic standard deduction amounts by filing status for 2016 and 2017. Special rules may alter the allowable standard deduction for certain taxpayers. We discuss these departures from the basic standard deduction amounts in the Individual Deductions chapter.

EXHIBIT 4-7 Standard Deduction Amounts by Filing Status*

	2016	2017
Married filing jointly	$12,600	$12,700
Qualifying widow or widower	12,600	12,700
Married filing separately	6,300	6,350
Head of household	9,300	9,350
Single	6,300	6,350

*Married taxpayers 65 years of age or over and/or blind are entitled to an additional standard deduction of $1,250 ($1,250 for age and another $1,250 for blindness); single and head of household taxpayers 65 years of age or over and/or blind are entitled to an additional standard deduction of $1,550 (one for age and another for blindness). (See the Individual Deductions chapter for more detail.) For individuals claimed as a dependent on another tax return, the 2017 standard deduction is the greater of (1) $1,050 or (2) $350 plus earned income not to exceed the standard deduction amount for those who are not dependents (see the Individual Income Tax Computation and Tax Credits chapter for more detail).

The final *from* AGI deduction is the deduction for exemptions. An exemption is a flat deduction allowed for the taxpayer, the taxpayer's spouse, and each person who qualifies as a dependent of the taxpayer. The exemptions for the taxpayer(s) filing the tax return are called **personal exemptions,** while the others are referred to as **dependency exemptions.** In 2017, the amount of the exemption deduction is $4,050 for both exemption types. As we discuss in the Individual Deductions chapter, deductions for exemptions are phased out over a range of AGI for taxpayers with AGI over a certain threshold. We discuss the dependency qualification requirements later in this chapter.

Example 4-3

Rodney and Anita Hall annually file a joint tax return. They paid a total of $14,000 for expenditures that qualified as itemized deductions. Assuming Tara and her younger brother Braxton qualify as Rodney and Anita's dependents, what is the total amount of *from* AGI deductions Rodney and Anita are allowed to deduct on their tax return?

Answer: $30,200, computed as follows:

Description	Amount	Explanation
(1) Standard deduction	$12,700	Married filing joint filing status (see Exhibit 4-7).
(2) Itemized deductions	14,000	
(3) Greater of (1) or (2)	14,000	Itemized deductions exceed the standard deduction.
(4) Personal and dependency exemptions	16,200	($4,050 × 4) One exemption each for Rodney, Anita, Tara, and Braxton.
Total deductions from AGI	**$30,200**	(3) + (4). (Also referred to as deductions "below the line.")

What if: What would be the amount of the Halls' *from* AGI deductions if, instead of the original facts, Rodney and Anita had paid a total of $8,000 in expenditures that qualified as itemized deductions?

(continued on page 4-10)

Answer: $28,900, computed as follows:

Description	Amount	Explanation
(1) Standard deduction	$12,700	Married filing joint filing status (see Exhibit 4-7).
(2) Itemized deductions	8,000	
(3) Greater of (1) or (2)	12,700	The standard deduction exceeds itemized deductions.
(4) Personal and dependency exemptions	16,200	($4,050 × 4) One personal exemption each for Rodney, Anita, Tara, and Braxton.
Total deductions from AGI	**$28,900**	(3) + (4)

Income Tax Calculation

After determining taxable income, taxpayers can generally calculate their regular income tax liability using either a **tax table** or a **tax rate schedule,** depending on their filing status and income level (see Appendix D for the regular tax rate schedules). Taxpayers with taxable income under $100,000 generally must use the tax tables.[8] However, as we discussed above, certain types of income that are included in taxable income are taxed at rates different from the rates embedded in the tables or published in the tax rate schedules.

Example 4-4

With Tara's help, the Halls have determined their taxable income to be $95,400, as follows:

Description	Amount	Explanation
(1) Adjusted gross income	$125,600	Example 4-2
(2) *From* AGI deductions	(30,200)	Example 4-3
Taxable income	**$ 95,400**	(1) + (2)

They have also determined that all of their income is ordinary income. What is their tax liability? (Use the tax rate schedule rather than the tax tables to answer the question.)

Answer: $15,327.50. See the married filing jointly tax rate schedule in Appendix D. {$10,452.50 + $4,875 [25% × ($95,400 − $75,900)]}.

What if: Using the tax rate schedules, what would the Halls' tax liability be if their taxable income was $12,000 (all ordinary income)?

Answer: $1,200 ($12,000 × 10%).

What if: Assume that in addition to the $95,400 of ordinary income, the Halls also reported $5,000 of long-term capital gain subject to a 15 percent tax rate. How much tax would they pay on the additional $5,000 gain?

Answer: $750 ($5,000 × 15%). Long-term capital gains (gains on the sale of a capital asset owned for more than a year) are generally taxed at a 15 percent rate. Note that the Halls' taxable income is $100,400. $95,400 of the income is taxed at ordinary rates and $5,000 is taxed at the preferential 15 percent rate.

Other Taxes

In addition to the individual income tax, individuals may also be required to pay other taxes such as the **alternative minimum tax (AMT)** or **self-employment taxes.** These taxes are imposed on tax bases other than the individual's regular taxable income.

[8]For administrative convenience and to prevent low- and middle-income taxpayers from making mathematical errors using a rate schedule, the IRS provides tax tables that present the gross tax for various amounts of taxable income. For simplicity, we use the tax rate schedule to determine tax liabilities in the examples presented in this text.

Furthermore, taxpayers with relatively high AGI are subject to a 3.8 percent net investment income tax on unearned (investment) income and a .9 percent additional Medicare tax on earned income. We discuss these taxes in more detail in the Individual Income Tax Computation and Tax Credits chapter.

Tax Credits

Individual taxpayers may reduce their tax liabilities by **tax credits** to determine their total taxes payable. Like deductions, tax credits are specifically granted by Congress and are narrowly defined. Unlike deductions, which reduce *taxable income,* tax credits *directly reduce taxes payable*. Thus, a $1 deduction reduces taxes payable by $1 times the marginal tax rate while a $1 credit reduces taxes payable by $1. Common credits include the child tax credit ($1,000 per child that qualifies for the credit), the child and dependent care credit, the earned income credit, the American opportunity credit, and the lifetime learning credit. We discuss credits in more detail in the Individual Income Tax Computation and Tax Credits chapter.

Tax Prepayments

After calculating the total tax and subtracting their available credits, taxpayers determine their taxes due (or tax refund) by subtracting tax prepayments from the total tax remaining after credits. Tax prepayments include (1) **withholdings,** or income taxes withheld from the taxpayer's salary or wages by her employer; (2) **estimated tax payments** the taxpayer makes for the year (paid directly to the IRS), and (3) taxes the taxpayer overpaid on the prior year tax return that the taxpayer elects to apply as an estimated payment for the current tax year instead of receiving the overpayment as a refund.

If tax prepayments exceed the total tax after subtracting credits, the taxpayer receives a tax refund for the difference. If tax prepayments are less than the total tax after credits, the taxpayer owes additional tax and potentially a penalty for the underpayment.

Example 4-5

Based on their calculation in Example 4-4, Rodney and Anita Hall's tax liability is $15,327.50. The Halls had $13,920 of federal income taxes withheld by their employers from their paychecks and are able to claim a $1,000 child tax credit for their 12-year-old son Braxton (Tara is too old to qualify). What is the Halls' tax due or tax refund?

Answer: $407.50 tax refund, computed as follows:

Description	Amount	Explanation
(1) Tax liability	$ 15,327.50	Example 4-4
(2) Tax credits	(1,000.00)	$1,000 child tax credit for 12-year old son Braxton.
(3) Tax prepayments	(14,735.00)	
Tax refund	**($ 407.50)**	(1) + (2) + (3)

Although not explicitly stated in the individual tax formula, a taxpayer's filing status affects many parts of the tax formula, including the standard deduction amount and the applicable income tax rate schedule, among others. In the next section, we describe the rules for determining a taxpayer's filing status. However, because a taxpayer's filing status may depend on whether the taxpayer has dependents for tax purposes, we discuss how to determine who qualifies as a taxpayer's dependent before we address filing status.

LO 4-2

PERSONAL AND DEPENDENCY EXEMPTIONS

Individual taxpayers generally may deduct a personal exemption for themselves. Married couples filing jointly may claim two personal exemptions (one for each spouse).[9] Further, to provide some tax relief for those supporting others, a taxpayer may claim an additional exemption for each person who qualifies as the taxpayer's dependent.[10] In 2017, taxpayers are allowed to deduct $4,050 for each personal and dependency exemption they are entitled to claim. Individuals who qualify as a dependent of another taxpayer may *not* claim a personal exemption for themselves on their own individual tax returns and they may not claim a dependency exemption for someone else.[11,12]

Example 4-6

Assume that Tara (the Halls' 21-year-old daughter who is a full-time college student) qualifies as Rodney and Anita's dependent. Tara earned $9,000 at a summer job this year, and she files her own tax return. Is Tara allowed to claim a personal exemption for herself on her own tax return?

Answer: No. Because Tara qualifies as the Halls' dependent, the Halls may deduct a dependency exemption for Tara, but Tara may *not* deduct a personal exemption for herself.

Dependency Requirements

Taxpayers (who are not dependents of another) may claim exemptions only for persons qualifying as their **dependents.** To qualify as a dependent of another, an individual:

1. Must be a citizen of the United States or a resident of the United States, Canada, or Mexico.
2. Must *not* file a joint return with the individual's spouse unless there is no tax liability on the couple's joint return and there would not have been any tax liability on either spouse's tax return if they had filed separately.[13]
3. Must be considered either a **qualifying child** of the taxpayer *or* a **qualifying relative** of the taxpayer.[14]

While the requirements for determining a qualifying child and a qualifying relative have some similarities, the qualifying relative requirements are broader in scope than the qualifying child requirements.

Qualifying Child To be considered a qualifying child of a taxpayer, an individual must satisfy the following four tests: (1) relationship, (2) age, (3) residence, and (4) support.[15]

[9]§151(b).

[10]§151(c).

[11]§151(b)

[12]See Publication 17, "Your Federal Income Tax," for information relating to personal and dependency exemptions.

[13]Rev. Rul. 54-567, 1954-2 C.B. 108.

[14]§152.

[15]Technically, an individual is not eligible to be a qualifying child of another if she filed a joint return with her spouse (other than to claim a refund) [see §151(c)(2)(e)]. However, because this is also a requirement to be claimed as a dependent, we do not discuss the requirement separately here.

Relationship test. A qualifying child must be an eligible relative of the taxpayer. Eligible relatives include the taxpayer's:

- Child or descendant of a child. For this purpose, a child includes a taxpayer's adopted child, stepchild, and eligible foster child.
- Sibling or descendant of sibling. For this purpose, a sibling includes a taxpayer's half-brother, half-sister, stepbrother, or stepsister.

Under this definition, the taxpayer's grandchild would qualify as an eligible relative as would the taxpayer's sister's grandchild.

Age test. A qualifying child must be younger than the taxpayer and *either* (1) under age 19 at the end of the year or (2) under age 24 at the end of the year *and* a full-time student.[16] A person is a full-time student if she was in school full-time during any part of each of five calendar months during the calendar year.[17] An individual who is permanently and totally disabled is deemed to have met the age test.[18]

Residence test. A qualifying child must have the same principal residence as the taxpayer for *more* than half the year. Time that a child (or the taxpayer) is temporarily (not permanently) away from the taxpayer's home because the child (or taxpayer) is ill, is pursuing an education, or has other special circumstances is counted as though the child (or taxpayer) were living in the taxpayer's home.[19]

Support test. A qualifying child must *not* have provided more than half of his or her *own* support (living expenses) for the year. Support generally includes:

- Food, school lunches, toilet articles, and haircuts.
- Clothing.
- Recreation—including toys, summer camp, horseback riding, entertainment, and vacation expenses.
- Medical and dental care.
- Child care expenses.
- Allowances and gifts.
- Wedding costs.
- Lodging.
- Education—including board, uniforms at military schools, and tuition. When determining who provided the support for a *child* of the taxpayer who is a full-time student, scholarships are excluded from the computation (neither the parent nor the child are treated as providing the support for the child).[20]

Example 4-7

Rodney and Anita have two children: Braxton, age 12, who lives at home, and Tara, age 21, who is a full-time student and does not live at home. Tara earned $9,000 in a summer job, but she did *not* provide more than half of her own support during the year. Are Braxton and Tara qualifying children of Rodney and Anita?

(continued on page 4-14)

[16] §152(c)(3)(A).
[17] §152(f)(2).
[18] §151(c)(3)(B).
[19] Reg. §1.152-1(b).
[20] §152(f)(5) and §152(f)(1). This provision requires that the student be a son, daughter, stepson, stepdaughter, or an eligible foster child of the taxpayer.

Answer: Yes, see analysis of factors below:

Test	Braxton	Tara
Relationship	Yes, son.	Yes, daughter.
Age	Yes, under age 19 at end of year (and younger than his parents).	Yes, under age 24 at year-end *and* full-time student (and younger than her parents).
Residence	Yes, lived at home entire year.	Yes, time away at college is considered as time at home if Tara plans to live in her parents' home again at some point (it is a temporary absence).
Support	Yes, does not provide more than half of own support.	Yes, does not provide more than half of own support.

Because they both meet all the requirements, Braxton and Tara are qualifying children to the Halls. So, the Halls may claim one dependency exemption for Braxton and one for Tara.

What if: Suppose Tara provided more than half of her own support. Would she be considered a qualifying child of her parents?

Answer: No. She would fail the support test.

What if: Assume the original facts except now suppose that Tara is age 25. Would Tara be considered a qualifying child of her parents?

Answer: No. She would fail the age test. Note, however, that Tara could still qualify as her parents' dependent as a qualifying relative (see Example 4-9 below).

What if: Assume the original facts except now suppose that Braxton is Anita's stepbrother's son. Would Braxton be considered a qualifying child of Rodney and Anita?

Answer: Yes. Braxton meets the relationship test because he is the descendant of Anita's stepbrother (sibling).

Tiebreaking rules. The requirements for determining who is a qualifying child leave open the possibility that one person could be a qualifying child to more than one taxpayer. In these circumstances, the taxpayer who has priority for claiming the dependency exemption is based on the following tiebreaking rules:

1. If the person is a qualifying child of a parent, the parent is entitled to the dependency exemption for the child. This situation could arise, for example, when a child lives with her mother *and* her grandparents. In this case, the mother has priority for claiming the dependency exemption over the grandparents.
2. If the individual is a qualifying child to both parents, the parent with whom the child has resided for the longest period of time during the year has priority for claiming the dependency exemption. This situation may arise in a year when the child lives with both parents for more than half of the year, but the parents separate or divorce in the latter part of the year. Note, however, that the dependency exemption for a child of divorced parents can be claimed by the noncustodial parent if the custodial parent (the parent entitled to claim the exemption) releases the exemption to the noncustodial parent through a written declaration and the noncustodial parent attaches the declaration to his or her tax return.[21]
3. Finally, if the child resides with both parents for the same amount of time during the year or the qualifying child resides with a taxpayer who is not the child's parent, the taxpayer with the *highest AGI* has priority for claiming the dependency exemption for the child.[22]

[21]See §152(e). The custodial parent releases the exemption to the noncustodial parent with a signature on Form 8332.

[22]However, if the parents may claim the child as a qualifying child but no parent does so, another taxpayer may claim the individual as a qualifying child but only if the other individual's AGI is higher than the AGI of any parent of the child [§152(c)(4)(C)].

Example 4-8

In the previous example, we determined that Braxton (Rodney and Anita's son) is Rodney and Anita's qualifying child. Braxton's Uncle Shawn (Rodney's brother) lived in the Halls' home (the same home Braxton lived in) for more than 11 months during the year. Does Braxton meet the requirements to be considered Shawn's qualifying child?

Answer: Yes, see analysis of factors below.

Test	Braxton
Relationship	Yes, son of Shawn's brother.
Age	Yes, under age 19 at end of year (and younger than Shawn).
Residence	Yes, lived in same residence as Shawn for more than half the year.
Support	Yes, does not provide more than half of his own support.

Thus, Braxton is considered to be Rodney and Anita's qualifying child *and* he is considered to be Shawn's qualifying child. Under the tiebreaker rules, who is allowed to claim Braxton as a dependent for the year?

Answer: Rodney and Anita. Under the first tiebreaking rule, Rodney and Anita are allowed to claim the dependency exemption for Braxton because they are Braxton's parents.

What if: Suppose that Shawn is Rodney's cousin. Would Braxton be Shawn's qualifying child?

Answer: No, Braxton does not meet the relationship test for Shawn if he is Rodney's cousin. Braxton is not the descendant of Shawn's sibling.

Qualifying Relative A qualifying relative is a person who is *not* a qualifying child *and* satisfies (1) a relationship test, (2) a support test, and (3) a gross income test.

Relationship test. As you might expect, the relationship test for a qualifying relative is more inclusive than the relationship test for a qualifying child. A person meets the qualifying relative relationship test if the person either (1) has a qualifying family relationship with the taxpayer or (2) meets the qualifying relative "member of the household" test. A qualifying family relationship with the taxpayer includes the following:

- A descendant or ancestor of the taxpayer. For this purpose, a child includes a taxpayer's adopted child, stepchild, and eligible foster child; and a parent includes a stepmother and stepfather.
- A sibling of the taxpayer, including a stepbrother or a stepsister.
- A son or daughter of the brother or sister of the taxpayer (cousins do not qualify).
- A sibling of the taxpayer's mother or father.
- An in-law (mother-in-law, father-in-law, sister-in-law, brother-in-law, son-in-law, or daughter-in-law) of the taxpayer.
- A person meets the qualifying relative "member of the household" test if that person has the same principal place of abode as the taxpayer for the entire year (*even if the person does not have a qualifying family relationship with the taxpayer*).[23]

Support test. The support test generally requires that the taxpayer pay more than half the qualifying relative's living expenses (note that this is a different support test than the support test for a qualifying child). As we discussed above, living expenses

[23]A person is considered to live with the taxpayer for the entire year if he or she was either born during the year or died during the year and resided with the taxpayer for the remaining part of the year.

include rent, food, medicine, and clothes, among other things. Just as with the qualifying child support test, scholarships of children of a taxpayer who are full-time students are excluded from the support test.[24] Under a multiple support agreement, taxpayers who don't pay over half of an individual's support may still be allowed to claim the individual as a dependent under the qualifying relative rules if the following apply:[25]

1. No one taxpayer paid over one-half of the individual's support.
2. The taxpayer and at least one other person provided more than half the support of the individual, and the taxpayer and the other person(s) would have been allowed to claim the individual as a dependent except for the fact that they did not provide over half of the support of the individual.
3. The taxpayer contributed *over* 10 percent of the individual's support for the year.
4. Each other person who provided *over* 10 percent of the individual's support (see requirement (2) above) provides a signed statement to the taxpayer agreeing not to claim the individual as a dependent. The taxpayer includes the names, addresses, and Social Security numbers of each other person on Form 2120, which the taxpayer attaches to her Form 1040.

Multiple support agreements are commonly used in situations when siblings support elderly parents.

Gross income test. The gross income test requires that a qualifying relative's gross income for the year be *less* than the personal exemption amount. As we noted above, the personal exemption amount for 2017 is $4,050.

Example 4-9

What if: Suppose Tara is age 25, is a full-time student, and does not live with her parents. Tara earned $3,000 in a summer job, and her parents provided more than half her support. Does Tara qualify as her parents' dependent?

Answer: Yes, as their qualifying relative. She is too old to be their qualifying child.

Test	Explanation
Relationship	Yes, Rodney and Anita's daughter.
Support	Yes, the Halls provide more than half of Tara's support.
Gross income	Yes, Tara's gross income for the year is less than the exemption amount.

Tara's parents may claim a dependency exemption for Tara. Tara is not allowed to claim a personal exemption for herself. Note that if Tara's gross income exceeded the exemption amount, she would *not* qualify as her parents' dependent, and she would claim a personal exemption for herself.

Example 4-10

In determining their dependency exemptions for the year, Rodney and Anita evaluated whether Shawn is their *qualifying relative*. Assuming Shawn's gross income for the year is $42,000, the Halls provided food and lodging for Shawn valued at $8,000, and Shawn paid for his other living expenses valued at $14,000, is Shawn a qualifying relative of the Halls?

[24]§152(f)(5) and §152(f)(1). Just as with a qualifying child, this provision requires that the student be a son, daughter, stepson, stepdaughter, or an eligible foster child of the taxpayer.

[25]§152(d)(3).

Answer: No, as analyzed below.

Test	Explanation
Relationship	Yes, Rodney's brother.
Support	No, the Halls provided $8,000 of support to Shawn, but Shawn provided $14,000 of his own support. Because the Halls provided less than half of Shawn's support, Shawn does not pass the support test.
Gross income	No, Shawn's gross income for the year is $42,000, which exceeds the exemption amount, so Shawn fails the gross income test.

Because Shawn fails the support test and the gross income test, he is not a qualifying relative of the Halls. Consequently, they cannot claim a dependency exemption for him. Thus, Shawn can claim a personal exemption for himself on his own tax return.

What if: Assume that Shawn received $5,000 of tax-exempt interest during the year and that this is his only source of income. Does he fail the gross income test? Note, however, that Shawn would still fail the support test so he still would not be a qualifying relative of the Halls.

Answer: No. Because tax-exempt interest is excluded from gross income, Shawn's gross income is $0, so he passes the gross income test.

What if: Assume the original facts in the example except now suppose that Shawn paid for his $14,000 of living expenses with interest he had received from tax-exempt bonds. Would Shawn pass the support test?

Answer: No. The Halls would not have provided more than half of Shawn's support. The fact that Shawn received the money he spent on his support from tax-exempt income does not matter. All that matters is that he provided more than half of his own support.

What if: Assume that Anita's 92-year-old grandfather Juan lives in an apartment by himself near the Halls' residence. His gross income for the year is $3,000. Assuming the Halls provide more than half of Juan's living expenses for the year, would Juan be a qualifying relative of the Halls?

Answer: Yes, as analyzed below.

Test	Explanation
Relationship	Yes, Anita's grandfather.
Support	Yes, as assumed in the facts, the Halls provide more than half of Juan's support.
Gross income	Yes, Juan's gross income for the year is $3,000, which is below the exemption amount, so Juan passes the gross income test.

What if: Assume that Anita's 92-year-old grandfather Juan lives in an apartment by himself and reports gross income for the year of $3,000. Anita provided 40 percent of Juan's support, Juan provided 25 percent of his own support, Anita's brother Carlos provided 30 percent of the support, and Anita's sister Kamella provided 5 percent of Juan's support. Who is eligible to claim Juan as a dependent under a multiple support agreement?

Answer: Anita and Carlos. Anita and Carlos are eligible because (1) no one taxpayer provided more than half of Juan's support, (2) Anita and Carlos together provided more than half of Juan's support and Juan would have been both Anita's and Carlos's qualifying relative except for the fact that neither provided over half of Juan's support, and (3) Anita and Carlos each provided over 10 percent of Juan's support (Kamella provided only 5 percent of Juan's support so she is not eligible). Anita and Carlos will need to agree on who will claim the dependency exemption for Juan. Assuming they agree that Anita will claim the exemption, she will need to receive a signed statement from Carlos agreeing not to claim the exemption and she will need to attach Form 2120 to her (and Rodney's) tax return providing Carlos's name, address, and Social Security number.

What if: Assume Juan lives in an apartment by himself and is a friend of the family but not related to either Rodney or Anita. His gross income is $3,000 and the Halls provide over half of his support. Is Juan a qualifying relative of the Halls?

(continued on page 4-18)

Answer: No, as analyzed below.

Test	Explanation
Relationship	No, not related to the Halls and his principal place of abode is not in the Halls' household for the *entire* year. If the Halls' home was his principal place of abode for the entire year, he would have met the relationship test even though he's not actually related to anyone in the Hall family.
Support	Yes, as assumed in the facts, the Halls provide more than half of Juan's support.
Gross income	Yes, Juan's gross income for the year is $3,000, which is below the exemption amount, so Juan passes the gross income test.

The Halls would not be able to claim an exemption for Juan as a qualifying relative because he fails the relationship test under this set of facts.

The rules for determining who qualifies as a dependent as a qualifying child and who qualifies as a dependent as a qualifying relative overlap to some extent. The primary differences between the two are:

1. The relationship requirement is more broadly defined for qualifying relatives than for qualifying children.
2. Qualifying children are subject to age restrictions while qualifying relatives are not.
3. Qualifying relatives are subject to a gross income restriction while qualifying children are not.
4. Taxpayers need not provide more than half a qualifying child's support (though the child cannot provide more than half of her own support), but they must provide more than half of the support of a qualifying relative.
5. Qualifying children are subject to a residence test (they must have the same primary residence as the taxpayer for more than half the year), while qualifying relatives are not. Exhibit 4-8 summarizes the dependency requirements.

EXHIBIT 4-8 Summary of Dependency Requirements

Test	Qualifying Child	Qualifying Relative
Relationship	Taxpayer's child, stepchild, foster child, sibling, half-brother or half-sister, stepbrother or stepsister, or a descendant of any of these relatives.	Taxpayer's descendant or ancestor, sibling, stepmother, stepfather, stepbrother or stepsister, son or daughter of taxpayer's sibling, sibling of the taxpayer's mother or father, in-laws, and anyone else who has the same principal place of abode as the taxpayer for the entire year (even if not otherwise related).
Age	Younger than the taxpayer claiming the individual as a qualifying child and under age 19 or a full-time student under age 24. Also anyone totally and permanently disabled.	Not applicable.
Residence	Lives with taxpayer for more than half of the year (includes temporary absences for things such as illness and education).	Not applicable.
Support	The qualifying child must not provide more than half of his or her own support.	Taxpayer must have provided more than half of the support for the qualifying relative.
Gross income	Not applicable.	Gross income less than exemption amount ($4,050 in 2017).
Other	Not applicable.	Not a qualifying child.

Appendix A at the end of this chapter provides a flowchart for determining whether an individual qualifies as the taxpayer's dependent.

ETHICS

Blake is 21 years of age at the end of the year. During the year, Blake was a full-time college student. He also worked part-time and earned $8,000, which he used to pay all of his $6,000 of living expenses. Blake's parents, Troy and Camille, claimed Blake as a dependent on their joint tax return. After filing the joint tax return, Troy told Blake they owed him $3,001 for his annual living expenses. What do you think of Troy and Camille's strategy to claim a dependency exemption for Blake?

FILING STATUS

LO 4-3

Each year taxpayers determine their **filing status** according to their marital status at year-end and whether they have any dependents. A taxpayer's filing status is important because, as we discussed above, it determines:

- The applicable tax rate schedule for determining the taxpayer's tax liability.
- The taxpayer's standard deduction amount.
- The AGI threshold for reductions in certain tax benefits such as itemized deductions and certain tax credits, among others.

Each year, all taxpayers filing tax returns file under one of the following five filing statuses:

1. Married filing jointly
2. Married filing separately
3. Qualifying widow or widower (surviving spouse)
4. Single
5. Head of household

Married Filing Jointly and Married Filing Separately

Married couples may file tax returns jointly **(married filing jointly)** or separately **(married filing separately).** To be married for filing status purposes, taxpayers must be married on the last day of the year. When one spouse dies during the year, the surviving spouse is considered to be *married* to the spouse who died at the end of the year unless the surviving spouse remarries during the year. Married couples filing joint returns combine their income and deductions and agree to share joint and several liability for the resulting tax. That is, they are both ultimately responsible to see that the tax is paid.

When married couples file separately, each spouse reports the income he or she received during the year and the deductions he or she is claiming on a tax return separate from that of the other spouse.[26] So that married taxpayers can't file separately to gain more combined tax benefits than they would be entitled to if they were to file jointly, tax-related items for married filing separate (MFS) taxpayers—such as tax rate schedules and standard deduction amounts, among others—are generally one-half what they are for married filing joint (MFJ) taxpayers. Also, if one spouse deducts itemized deductions, the other spouse is required to deduct itemized deductions even if his or her standard deduction amount is more than the total itemized deductions. Thus, only in unusual circumstances does it make economic sense for *tax* purposes for married couples to file separately.

THE KEY FACTS

Filing Status for Married Taxpayers

- Married filing jointly
  - Taxpayers are legally married as of the last day of the year.
  - When one spouse dies during the year the surviving spouse is still considered to be married for tax purposes during the year of the spouse's death.
  - Both spouses are ultimately responsible for paying the joint tax.
- Married filing separately
  - Taxpayers are legally married as of the last day of the year.
  - Generally no tax advantage to filing separately (usually a disadvantage).
  - Each spouse is ultimately responsible for paying own tax.
  - Couples may choose to file separately (generally for nontax reasons).
- Qualifying widow or widower
  - When a taxpayer's spouse dies, the surviving spouse can file as a qualifying widow or widower for two years after the year of the spouse's death if the surviving spouse remains unmarried and maintains a household for a dependent child.

[26]As we discuss in the next chapter, under community property laws of certain states, one spouse may be treated as receiving income earned by the other spouse.

However, it may be wise for married couples to file separately for *nontax* reasons. For example, a spouse who does not want to be liable for the other spouse's income tax liability, or a spouse who is not in contact with the other spouse, may want to file separately (see abandoned spouse discussion below).

Example 4-11

Rodney and Anita Hall are married at the end of the year. What is their filing status?

Answer: Married filing jointly, unless they choose to file separately.

What if: Assume that in 2017 the Halls file a joint return. In 2018, Rodney and Anita divorce and the IRS audits their 2017 tax return and determines that due to overstating their deductions, the Halls underpaid their taxes by $2,000. Who must pay the tax?

Answer: Both Rodney and Anita are responsible for paying. If the IRS can't locate Rodney, it can require Anita to pay the full $2,000 even though Anita earned $56,000 and Rodney earned $74,000.

What if: Assume that in 2017 the Halls file separate tax returns. In 2018, Rodney and Anita divorce and the IRS audits the Halls' separate tax returns. It determines that by overstating deductions, Rodney understated his tax liability by $1,500 and Anita understated her tax liability by $500. Further, the IRS cannot locate Rodney. What is the maximum amount of taxes Anita is liable for?

Answer: $500. Because she filed a separate return, she is responsible for the tax liability associated with her separate tax return, and she is not responsible for the taxes associated with Rodney's tax return.

TAXES IN THE REAL WORLD Tax Status for Same-Sex Married Couples

In June of 2013, the Supreme Court struck down the federal "Defense of Marriage Act" (DOMA) which meant that same-sex couples who were married in a state that authorized and recognized same-sex marriages would now be treated as married for federal income tax purposes. However, couples who were in a registered domestic partnership, civil union, or other similar formal relationship recognized under state law were *not* recognized as married for federal income tax purposes. In June of 2015, the Supreme Court ruled that the 14th Amendment of the Constitution guarantees a right to same-sex marriage. This ruling unifies marital status at both the federal and state levels. A taxpayer's marital status is important for determining income tax filing status and has implications for other areas of the tax law (estate and gift tax, for example).

See *Obergefell vs. Hodges*, 576 U.S. ____ (2015).

Qualifying Widow or Widower (Surviving Spouse)

When a taxpayer's spouse dies, the taxpayer is no longer legally married. However, to provide tax relief for widows and widowers *with dependents,* taxpayers who meet certain requirements qualify for the **qualifying widow or widower** (also referred to as surviving spouse) filing status for up to two years *after* the end of the year in which the other spouse died (recall that for tax purposes, they are still considered to be married for the year of the spouse's death). Taxpayers are eligible for qualifying widow or widower filing status if they (1) remain unmarried and (2) pay over half the cost of maintaining a household where a dependent child lived for the entire year (except for temporary absences).[27] The dependent child must be a child or stepchild (including an adopted child) for whom the taxpayer may claim an exemption (not a foster child). A qualifying widow or widower is

[27]§2(a).

not considered to be married for tax purposes. Consequently, a qualifying widow or widower is allowed to claim one personal exemption (recall that taxpayers who are married filing jointly are allowed to claim two personal exemptions). Nevertheless, this filing status is advantageous because qualifying widows and widowers use the same tax rate schedule and standard deduction amounts as married taxpayers filing joint tax returns.

Example 4-12

What if: Assume that last year Rodney passed away, and during the current year Anita did not remarry but maintained a household for Braxton and Tara, her dependent children. Under these circumstances, what would Anita's filing status be?

Answer: Qualifying widow. Last year, the year of Rodney's death, Anita qualified to file a joint return with Rodney. This year, Anita qualifies as a qualifying widow (also referred to as a surviving spouse) because she has not remarried and she has maintained a household for the entire year for her dependent children. She will qualify as a surviving spouse next year (two years after Rodney's death) if she does not remarry and she continues to maintain a household for Braxton and/or Tara for the entire year. Anita will claim three exemptions. One personal exemption and two dependency exemptions (for Braxton and Tara).

Single

Unmarried taxpayers who do not qualify for head of household status (discussed below) file as **single** taxpayers. As we discuss below, an unmarried taxpayer generally must be able to claim an exemption for a dependent in order to qualify for head of household status.

Example 4-13

Shawn Hall, Rodney's brother, was divorced in January and is unmarried at the end of the year. Shawn does not claim any dependency exemptions. What is his filing status?

Answer: Single. Because Shawn is unmarried at the end of the year, and he does not have any dependents, his filing status is single.

Head of Household

In terms of tax rate schedules and standard deduction amounts, the **head of household** filing status is less favorable than the married filing jointly and qualifying widow or widower filing statuses. However, it is more favorable than married filing separately and single filing statuses (see tax rates and standard deduction amounts provided in Appendix D). To qualify for head of household filing status, a taxpayer must:

- Be unmarried (or considered to be unmarried under the provisions discussed below) at the end of the year.
- Not be a qualifying widow or widower.
- Pay more than half the costs of keeping up a home for the year.
- Have a "qualifying person" live in the taxpayer's home for more than half the year (except for temporary absences such as military service, illness, or schooling). However, if the qualifying person is the taxpayer's *dependent* parent, the parent is not required to live with the taxpayer. A qualifying person may not qualify more than one person for head of household filing status. Exhibit 4-9 describes who is a qualifying person for purposes of head of household filing status.[28]

THE KEY FACTS

Filing Status for Unmarried Taxpayers

- Single
  - Unmarried taxpayers at year-end who do not qualify for head of household.
- Head of household
  - Unmarried taxpayers or taxpayers considered to be unmarried at year-end.
  - Must pay more than half of the costs of maintaining a household in which a qualifying person lives for more than half of the tax year or must pay more than half of the costs for maintaining a separate household for a parent who qualifies as taxpayer's dependent.

[28]§2(b).

EXHIBIT 4-9 Who Is a Qualifying Person for Determining Head of Household Filing Status? (Adapted from Table 4 in IRS Publication 501)

IF the person is the taxpayer's . . .	And . . .	THEN, the person is . . .
qualifying child	the person is single,	a qualifying person, whether or not the taxpayer can claim an exemption for the person.**
	the person is married and the taxpayer may claim a dependency exemption for the person,	a qualifying person.**
	the person is married and the taxpayer may not claim a dependency exemption for the person,	a qualifying person.**
qualifying relative who is the taxpayer's mother or father	the taxpayer may not claim a dependency exemption for the mother or father,	not a qualifying person.
	the taxpayer may claim a dependency exemption for the taxpayer's father or mother,	a qualifying person even if the taxpayer's mother or father did not live with the taxpayer. However, the taxpayer must have paid more than half the costs to maintain the household of the mother or father.
qualifying relative other than the taxpayer's mother or father	the person did not live with the taxpayer for more than half the year,	not a qualifying person.
	the taxpayer can claim a dependency exemption for the person, the person lived with the taxpayer for more than half the year, and the person is related to the taxpayer through a qualifying family relationship,	a qualifying person.
	the person is the taxpayer's qualifying relative only because the person lived with the taxpayer as a member of the taxpayer's household for the entire year (the person does not have a qualifying family relationship with the taxpayer),	not a qualifying person.
	the taxpayer cannot claim a dependency exemption for the person or the taxpayer can claim a dependency exemption only because of a multiple support agreement,	not a qualifying person.

*Appendix B at the end of this chapter includes a flowchart for determining whether a person is a qualifying person for head of household filing status.
**If a custodial parent releases the exemption for the person to a noncustodial parent under a divorce decree, the release is ignored for purposes of this test.

Example 4-14

What if: Assume Rodney and Anita divorced last year. During the current year, Braxton lives with Anita for the entire year and Anita pays all the costs of maintaining the household for herself and Braxton. Under these circumstances, what is Anita's filing status for the year?

Answer: Head of household. Anita is unmarried at the end of the year, she provides more than half the costs of maintaining her household, Braxton lives with her for more than half the year, and Braxton is her qualifying child.

What if: Assume Rodney and Anita divorced last year. During the current year, Braxton lives with Anita for the entire year, and Anita pays all the costs of maintaining the household for herself and Braxton. Assume that Anita released the dependency exemption to Rodney under the divorce decree. Under these circumstances, what is Anita's filing status for the year?

Answer: Head of household. Braxton is a qualifying person for Anita (the custodial parent) even though Anita is not claiming the dependency exemption for Braxton. Braxton is not a qualifying person for Rodney (the noncustodial parent).

What if: Assume that Rodney and Anita divorced last year. If Braxton is Anita's cousin (rather than her son) and he lives with Anita in her home from June 15 through December 31, what is Anita's filing status for the year?

Answer: Single. Anita does not qualify for head of household filing status because Braxton is not Anita's qualifying child (he fails the relationship test) or her qualifying relative (he fails the relationship test because he did not live in Anita's home for the entire year and he does not have a qualifying family relationship with Anita because he is Anita's cousin).

What if: Assume that Rodney and Anita divorced last year, Braxton is Anita's cousin, and Braxton lives with Anita in her home for the entire year. What is Anita's filing status for the year?

Answer: Single. Even though Braxton is Anita's qualifying relative, Braxton meets the qualifying relative relationship test only because he lived with Anita for the entire year (not because he had a qualifying family relationship with Anita). Therefore, while Anita may claim a dependency exemption for Braxton, she does not qualify for the head of household filing status.

What if: Assume Shawn (Rodney's brother) lived with the Halls, but Shawn paid more than half the costs of maintaining a separate apartment that is the principal residence of his mother, Sharon, whose gross income is $1,500. Because Shawn provided more than half of Sharon's support during the year, and because Sharon's gross income was only $1,500, she qualifies as Shawn's dependent (as a qualifying relative). In these circumstances, what is Shawn's filing status?

Answer: Head of household. Shawn paid more than half the costs of maintaining a separate household where his mother resides, and his mother qualifies as his dependent.

If Sharon's gross income exceeded the exemption amount she would fail the dependency gross income test and would not qualify as Shawn's dependent. If she did not qualify as his dependent she would not be a qualifying person, and Shawn would not qualify for the head of household filing status. Also, if Sharon were Shawn's grandmother rather than his mother, she would not be a qualifying person (no matter the amount of her gross income) and Shawn would not qualify for head of household status—Sharon must be Shawn's parent in order for her to qualify Shawn as a head of household.

Married Individuals Treated as Unmarried (Abandoned Spouse) In certain situations a couple may be legally married at the end of the year, but living apart. Although the couple could technically file a joint tax return, this is often not desirable from a nontax perspective, because each spouse would be assuming responsibility for paying tax on income earned by either spouse whether it was reported or not. However, because both spouses are married at the end of the year, their only other option is to file under the tax-unfavorable married filing separately filing status.

To provide tax relief in these situations, the tax laws treat a married taxpayer *as though he or she were unmarried* at the end of the year if the taxpayer meets the following requirements:

- The taxpayer is married at the end of the year (or is not *legally* separated from the other spouse).
- The taxpayer does not file a joint tax return with the other spouse.
- The taxpayer pays *more than half* the costs of maintaining his or her home for the entire year, and this home is the principal residence for a child (who qualifies as the taxpayer's dependent[29]) for *more than half* the year (the child must be a child of the taxpayer, including adopted child, stepchild, or eligible foster child[30]).
- The taxpayer lived apart from the other spouse for the last six months of the year (the other spouse did not live at all in the taxpayer's home during the last six months—temporary absences due to illness, education, business, vacation, or military service count as though the spouse still lived in the taxpayer's home).

If the taxpayer meets these requirements, he or she also meets the head of household filing status requirements and may file as head of household for the year. The primary objective of this tax rule is to provide tax relief to one spouse who has been abandoned by or separated from the other spouse and left to care for a dependent child. Thus, a married taxpayer who qualifies as unmarried under this provision is

[29]A taxpayer meets this test if the taxpayer (custodial parent) cannot claim an exemption for the child only because he or she released the exemption to the noncustodial parent under a divorce agreement.

[30]§152(f).

frequently referred to as an **abandoned spouse.** Nevertheless, the provision may still apply even when no spouse has been abandoned. For example, a couple may separate by mutual consent. Further, if both spouses meet the requirements, both spouses may qualify as being unmarried in the same year and thus both may qualify for head of household filing status.

Example 4-15

What if: Assume that last year, Rodney and Anita informally separated (they did not *legally* separate). Rodney moved out of the home and into his own apartment. Anita stayed in the Halls' home with Braxton. During the current year, Anita paid more than half the costs of maintaining the home for herself and Braxton. Even though Rodney and Anita were legally married at the end of the year, they filed separate tax returns. Under these circumstances, is Anita considered to be married or unmarried for tax purposes?

Answer: Unmarried. Anita meets the requirements for being treated as unmarried determined as follows (see requirements above):

- Anita is married to Rodney at the end of the year.
- Anita filed a tax return separate from Rodney's.
- Anita paid more than half the costs of maintaining her home, and her home was the principal residence for Braxton, who is her dependent child.
- Rodney did not live in Anita's home for the last six months of the year (in fact, he didn't live there at any time during the entire year).

What if: Given that Anita meets the requirements for being treated as unmarried, what is her filing status?

Answer: Head of household. Since Anita meets the abandoned spouse requirements she also meets the head of household filing status requirements. Without the abandoned spouse rule, Anita would have been required to file as married filing separately. Rodney's filing status, however, is married filing separately. Note, however, that if Rodney's new residence became Tara's principal residence, Rodney would also be treated as unmarried and would be eligible for head of household filing status.

Appendix C at the end of this chapter includes a flowchart for determining a taxpayer's filing status.

SUMMARY OF INCOME TAX FORMULA

Tara crunched some numbers and put together a summary of her parents' taxable income calculation. She determined that her parents will receive a $407.50 tax refund when they file their tax return. Tara's summary is provided in Exhibit 4-10, and Exhibit 4-11 presents pages 1 and 2 of the Halls' Form 1040.

EXHIBIT 4-10 Taxable Income and Tax Calculation Summary for Rodney and Anita Hall

Description	Amount	Explanation
(1) Gross income	130,600.00	Example 4-1
(2) *For* AGI deductions	(5,000.00)	Example 4-2, line (2)
(3) Adjusted gross income	$125,600.00	(1) + (2)
(4) Itemized deductions	(14,000.00)	Example 4-3, line (2)
(5) Personal and dependency exemptions	(16,200.00)	Example 4-3, line (4)
(6) Taxable income	$ 95,400.00	(3) + (4) + (5)
(7) Income tax liability	$ 15,327.50	Example 4-4
(8) Other taxes	0.00	
(9) Total tax	$ 15,327.50	(7) + (8)
(10) Credits	(1,000.00)	Example 4-5, line (2)
(11) Tax prepayments	(14,735.00)	Example 4-5, line (3)
Tax refund	($407.50)	(9) + (10) + (11)

EXHIBIT 4-11

Form 1040 Department of the Treasury—Internal Revenue Service (99)
U.S. Individual Income Tax Return **2016** OMB No. 1545-0074 IRS Use Only—Do not write or staple in this space.

For the year Jan. 1–Dec. 31, 2016, or other tax year beginning , 2016, ending , 20 | See separate instructions.

Your first name and initial	Last name	Your social security number
Rodney	Hall	224-56-1245
If a joint return, spouse's first name and initial	Last name	Spouse's social security number
Anita	Hall	324-43-3478

Home address (number and street). If you have a P.O. box, see instructions. Apt. no.
665 Henry Avenue

▲ Make sure the SSN(s) above and on line 6c are correct.

City, town or post office, state, and ZIP code. If you have a foreign address, also complete spaces below (see instructions).
Brookings, SD, 57007

Foreign country name | Foreign province/state/county | Foreign postal code

Presidential Election Campaign
Check here if you, or your spouse if filing jointly, want $3 to go to this fund. Checking a box below will not change your tax or refund. ☐ You ☐ Spouse

Filing Status

Check only one box.

1 ☐ Single
2 ☑ Married filing jointly (even if only one had income)
3 ☐ Married filing separately. Enter spouse's SSN above and full name here. ▶
4 ☐ Head of household (with qualifying person). (See instructions.) If the qualifying person is a child but not your dependent, enter this child's name here. ▶
5 ☐ Qualifying widow(er) with dependent child

Exemptions

6a ☑ **Yourself.** If someone can claim you as a dependent, **do not** check box 6a
b ☑ **Spouse**

Boxes checked on 6a and 6b: 2

c **Dependents:**

(1) First name Last name	(2) Dependent's social security number	(3) Dependent's relationship to you	(4) ✓ if child under age 17 qualifying for child tax credit (see instructions)
Tara Hall	242-68-9945	Daughter	☐
Braxton Hall	242-23-7845	Son	☑
			☐
			☐

No. of children on 6c who:
• lived with you: 2
• did not live with you due to divorce or separation (see instructions):
Dependents on 6c not entered above:

If more than four dependents, see instructions and check here ▶ ☐

d Total number of exemptions claimed — Add numbers on lines above ▶ 4

Income

Attach Form(s) W-2 here. Also attach Forms W-2G and 1099-R if tax was withheld.

If you did not get a W-2, see instructions.

7	Wages, salaries, tips, etc. Attach Form(s) W-2	7	130,000
8a	**Taxable** interest. Attach Schedule B if required	8a	600
b	**Tax-exempt** interest. **Do not** include on line 8a — 8b: 300		
9a	Ordinary dividends. Attach Schedule B if required	9a	
b	Qualified dividends — 9b		
10	Taxable refunds, credits, or offsets of state and local income taxes	10	
11	Alimony received	11	
12	Business income or (loss). Attach Schedule C or C-EZ	12	
13	Capital gain or (loss). Attach Schedule D if required. If not required, check here ▶ ☐	13	
14	Other gains or (losses). Attach Form 4797	14	
15a	IRA distributions — 15a; b Taxable amount	15b	
16a	Pensions and annuities — 16a; b Taxable amount	16b	
17	Rental real estate, royalties, partnerships, S corporations, trusts, etc. Attach Schedule E	17	
18	Farm income or (loss). Attach Schedule F	18	
19	Unemployment compensation	19	
20a	Social security benefits — 20a; b Taxable amount	20b	
21	Other income. List type and amount	21	
22	Combine the amounts in the far right column for lines 7 through 21. This is your **total income** ▶	22	130,600

Adjusted Gross Income

23	Educator expenses	23			
24	Certain business expenses of reservists, performing artists, and fee-basis government officials. Attach Form 2106 or 2106-EZ	24			
25	Health savings account deduction. Attach Form 8889	25			
26	Moving expenses. Attach Form 3903	26	5,000		
27	Deductible part of self-employment tax. Attach Schedule SE	27			
28	Self-employed SEP, SIMPLE, and qualified plans	28			
29	Self-employed health insurance deduction	29			
30	Penalty on early withdrawal of savings	30			
31a	Alimony paid b Recipient's SSN ▶	31a			
32	IRA deduction	32			
33	Student loan interest deduction	33			
34	Tuition and fees. Attach Form 8917	34			
35	Domestic production activities deduction. Attach Form 8903	35			
36	Add lines 23 through 35			36	5,000
37	Subtract line 36 from line 22. This is your **adjusted gross income** ▶			37	125,600

For Disclosure, Privacy Act, and Paperwork Reduction Act Notice, see separate instructions. Cat. No. 11320B Form **1040** (2016)

(continued)

EXHIBIT 4-11 *(continued)*

Form 1040 (2016) Page **2**

Section	Line	Description			Line	Amount
	38	Amount from line 37 (adjusted gross income)			38	125,600
Tax and Credits	39a	Check if: ☐ **You** were born before January 2, 1952, ☐ Blind. ☐ **Spouse** was born before January 2, 1952, ☐ Blind. **Total boxes checked ▶ 39a** ☐				
	b	If your spouse itemizes on a separate return or you were a dual-status alien, check here ▶ 39b ☐				
	40	**Itemized deductions** (from Schedule A) **or** your **standard deduction** (see left margin)			40	14,000
	41	Subtract line 40 from line 38			41	111,600
	42	**Exemptions.** If line 38 is $155,650 or less, multiply $4,050 by the number on line 6d. Otherwise, see instructions			42	16,200
	43	**Taxable income.** Subtract line 42 from line 41. If line 42 is more than line 41, enter -0-			43	95,400
	44	**Tax** (see instructions). Check if any from: **a** ☐ Form(s) 8814 **b** ☐ Form 4972 **c** ☐			44	15,328
	45	**Alternative minimum tax** (see instructions). Attach Form 6251			45	
	46	Excess advance premium tax credit repayment. Attach Form 8962			46	
	47	Add lines 44, 45, and 46 ▶			47	15,328
	48	Foreign tax credit. Attach Form 1116 if required	48			
	49	Credit for child and dependent care expenses. Attach Form 2441	49			
	50	Education credits from Form 8863, line 19	50			
	51	Retirement savings contributions credit. Attach Form 8880	51			
	52	Child tax credit. Attach Schedule 8812, if required	52	1,000		
	53	Residential energy credits. Attach Form 5695	53			
	54	Other credits from Form: **a** ☐ 3800 **b** ☐ 8801 **c** ☐	54			
	55	Add lines 48 through 54. These are your **total credits**			55	1,000
	56	Subtract line 55 from line 47. If line 55 is more than line 47, enter -0- ▶			56	14,328
Other Taxes	57	Self-employment tax. Attach Schedule SE			57	
	58	Unreported social security and Medicare tax from Form: **a** ☐ 4137 **b** ☐ 8919			58	
	59	Additional tax on IRAs, other qualified retirement plans, etc. Attach Form 5329 if required			59	
	60a	Household employment taxes from Schedule H			60a	
	b	First-time homebuyer credit repayment. Attach Form 5405 if required			60b	
	61	Health care: individual responsibility (see instructions) Full-year coverage ☐			61	
	62	Taxes from: **a** ☐ Form 8959 **b** ☐ Form 8960 **c** ☐ Instructions; enter code(s)			62	
	63	Add lines 56 through 62. This is your **total tax** ▶			63	14,328
Payments	64	Federal income tax withheld from Forms W-2 and 1099	64	14,735		
	65	2016 estimated tax payments and amount applied from 2015 return	65			
	66a	**Earned income credit (EIC)**	66a			
	b	Nontaxable combat pay election	66b			
	67	Additional child tax credit. Attach Schedule 8812	67			
	68	American opportunity credit from Form 8863, line 8	68			
	69	Net premium tax credit. Attach Form 8962	69			
	70	Amount paid with request for extension to file	70			
	71	Excess social security and tier 1 RRTA tax withheld	71			
	72	Credit for federal tax on fuels. Attach Form 4136	72			
	73	Credits from Form: **a** ☐ 2439 **b** ☐ Reserved **c** ☐ 8885 **d** ☐	73			
	74	Add lines 64, 65, 66a, and 67 through 73. These are your **total payments** ▶			74	14,735
Refund	75	If line 74 is more than line 63, subtract line 63 from line 74. This is the amount you **overpaid**			75	407
	76a	Amount of line 75 you want **refunded to you.** If Form 8888 is attached, check here ▶ ☐			76a	407
Direct deposit? See instructions.	▶ b	Routing number ▶ c Type: ☐ Checking ☐ Savings				
	▶ d	Account number				
	77	Amount of line 75 you want **applied to your 2017 estimated tax** ▶	77			
Amount You Owe	78	**Amount you owe.** Subtract line 74 from line 63. For details on how to pay, see instructions ▶			78	
	79	Estimated tax penalty (see instructions)	79			

Standard Deduction for—
- People who check any box on line 39a or 39b **or** who can be claimed as a dependent, see instructions.
- All others:

Single or Married filing separately, $6,300

Married filing jointly or Qualifying widow(er), $12,600

Head of household, $9,300

If you have a qualifying child, attach Schedule EIC.

Third Party Designee Do you want to allow another person to discuss this return with the IRS (see instructions)? ☐ **Yes.** Complete below. ☐ **No**

Designee's name ▶ Phone no. ▶ Personal identification number (PIN) ▶

Sign Here Under penalties of perjury, I declare that I have examined this return and accompanying schedules and statements, and to the best of my knowledge and belief, they are true, correct, and accurately list all amounts and sources of income I received during the tax year. Declaration of preparer (other than taxpayer) is based on all information of which preparer has any knowledge.

Joint return? See instructions. Keep a copy for your records.

Your signature	Date	Your occupation	Daytime phone number
Spouse's signature. If a joint return, **both** must sign.	Date	Spouse's occupation	If the IRS sent you an Identity Protection PIN, enter it here (see inst.)

Paid Preparer Use Only

Print/Type preparer's name	Preparer's signature	Date	Check ☐ if self-employed	PTIN
Firm's name ▶			Firm's EIN ▶	
Firm's address ▶			Phone no.	

www.irs.gov/form1040 Form **1040** (2016)

CONCLUSION

This chapter presents an overview of the individual income tax formula and provides rules for determining who qualifies as a taxpayer's dependents and for determining a taxpayer's filing status. In the Gross Income and Exclusions chapter, we turn our attention to determining gross income. In the Individual Deductions chapter, we describe deductions available to taxpayers when computing their taxable income. In the Individual Income Tax Computation and Tax Credits chapter, we conclude our review of the individual income tax formula by determining how to compute a taxpayer's tax liability and her taxes due or tax refund.

Appendix A Dependency Exemption Flowchart (Part I)

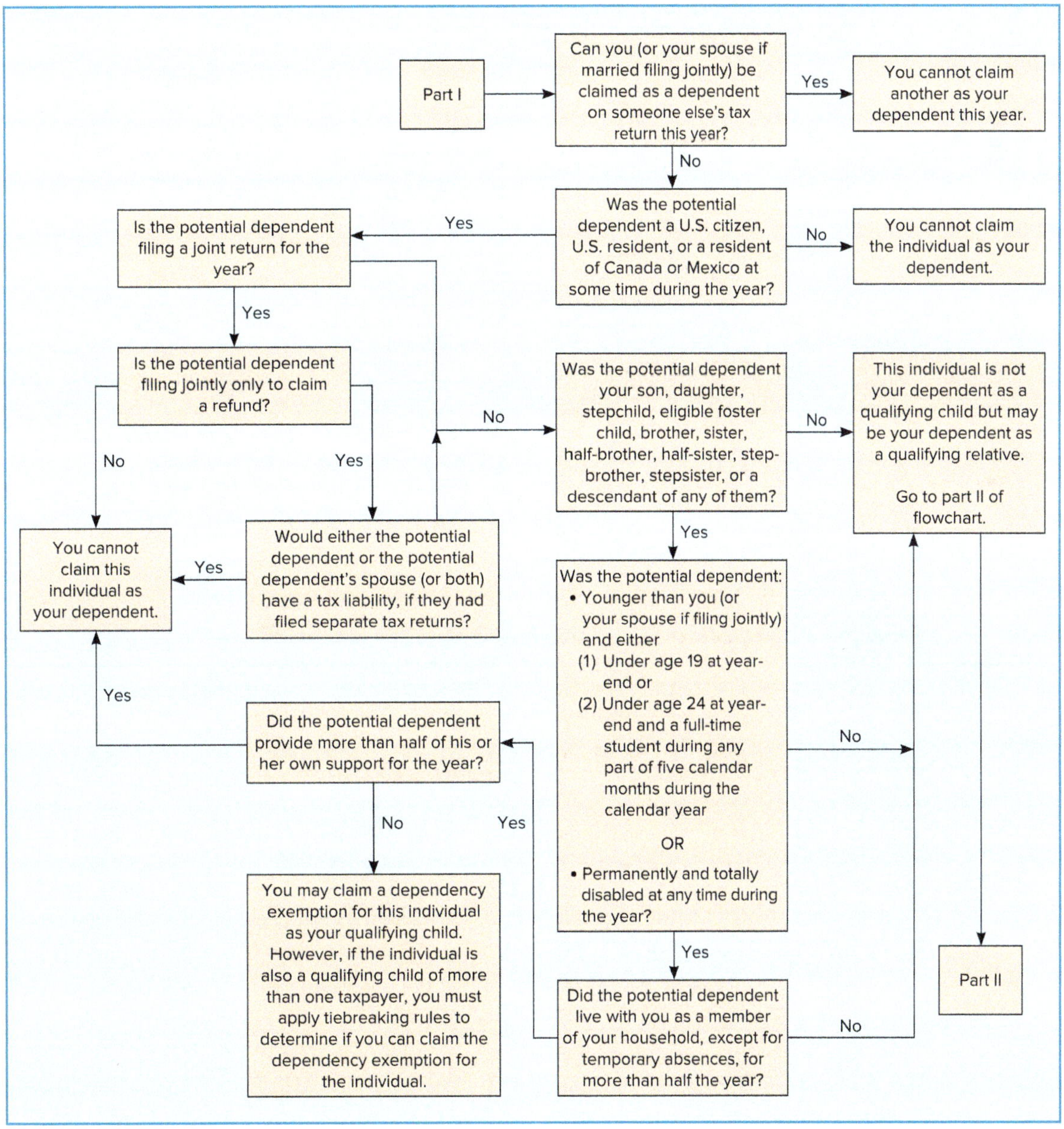

Appendix A (Part II)

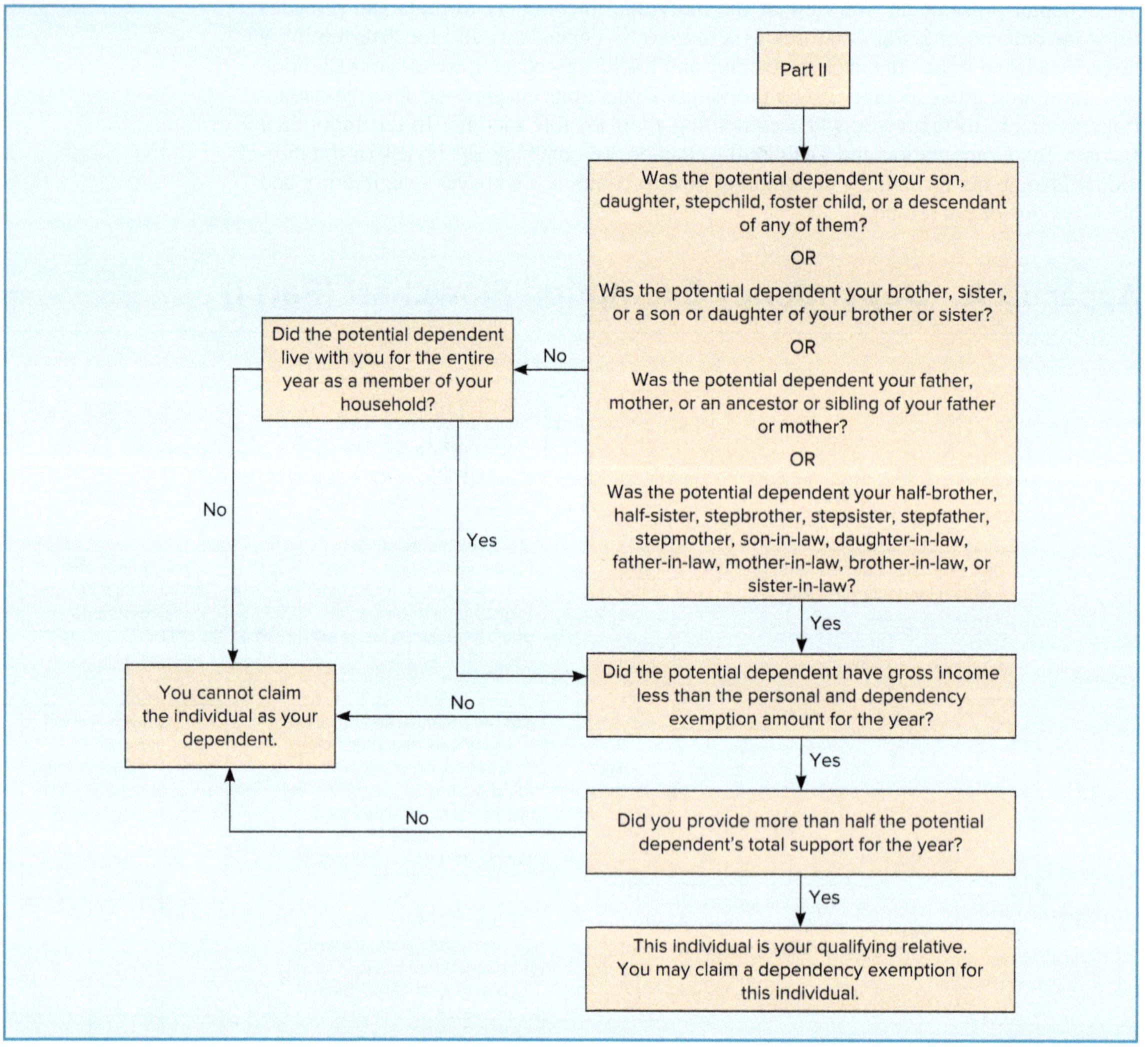

Appendix B Qualifying Person for Head of Household Filing Status Flowchart

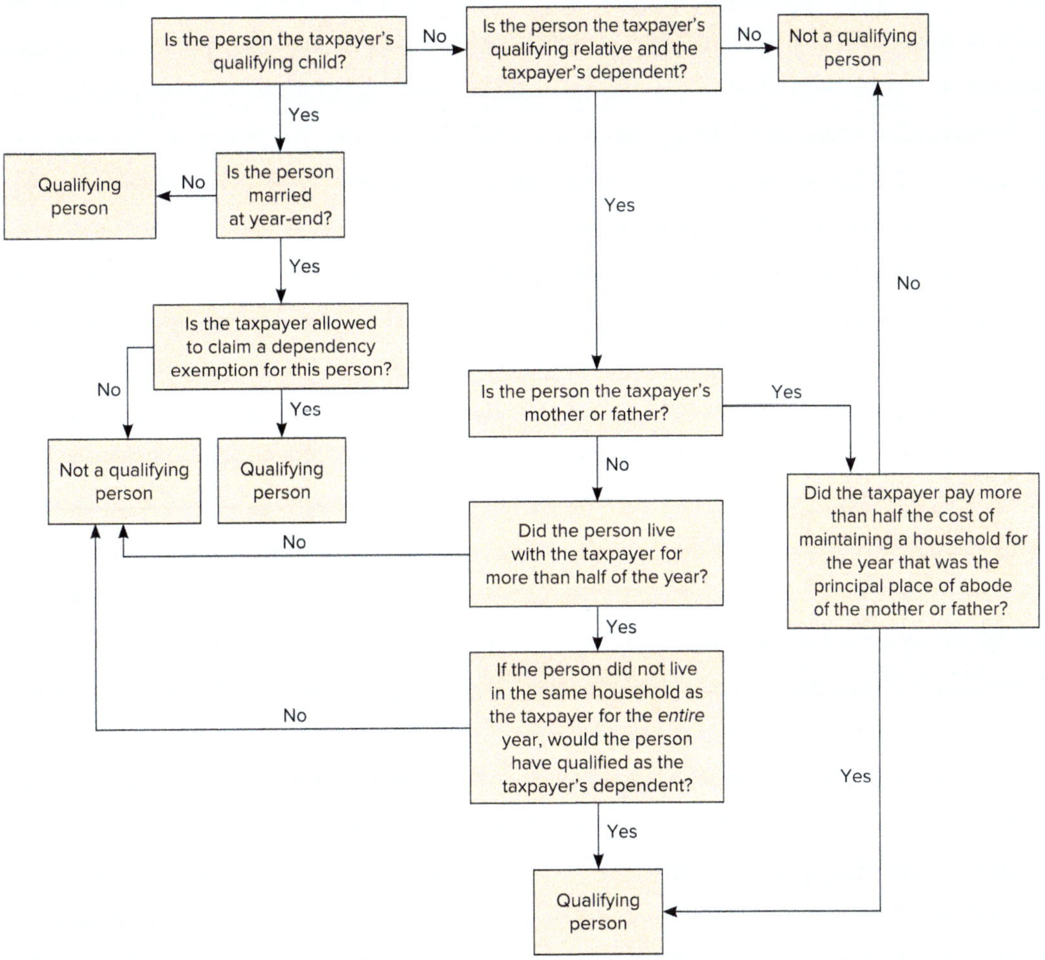

Notes:

- If a custodial parent releases the exemption for the person to a noncustodial parent under a divorce decree, the release is ignored for purposes of this text.
- If the taxpayer can claim an exemption for the person only because of a multiple support agreement, that person is not a qualifying person.
- One qualifying person may not qualify more than one person for head of household filing status.

Appendix C Determination of Filing Status Flowchart

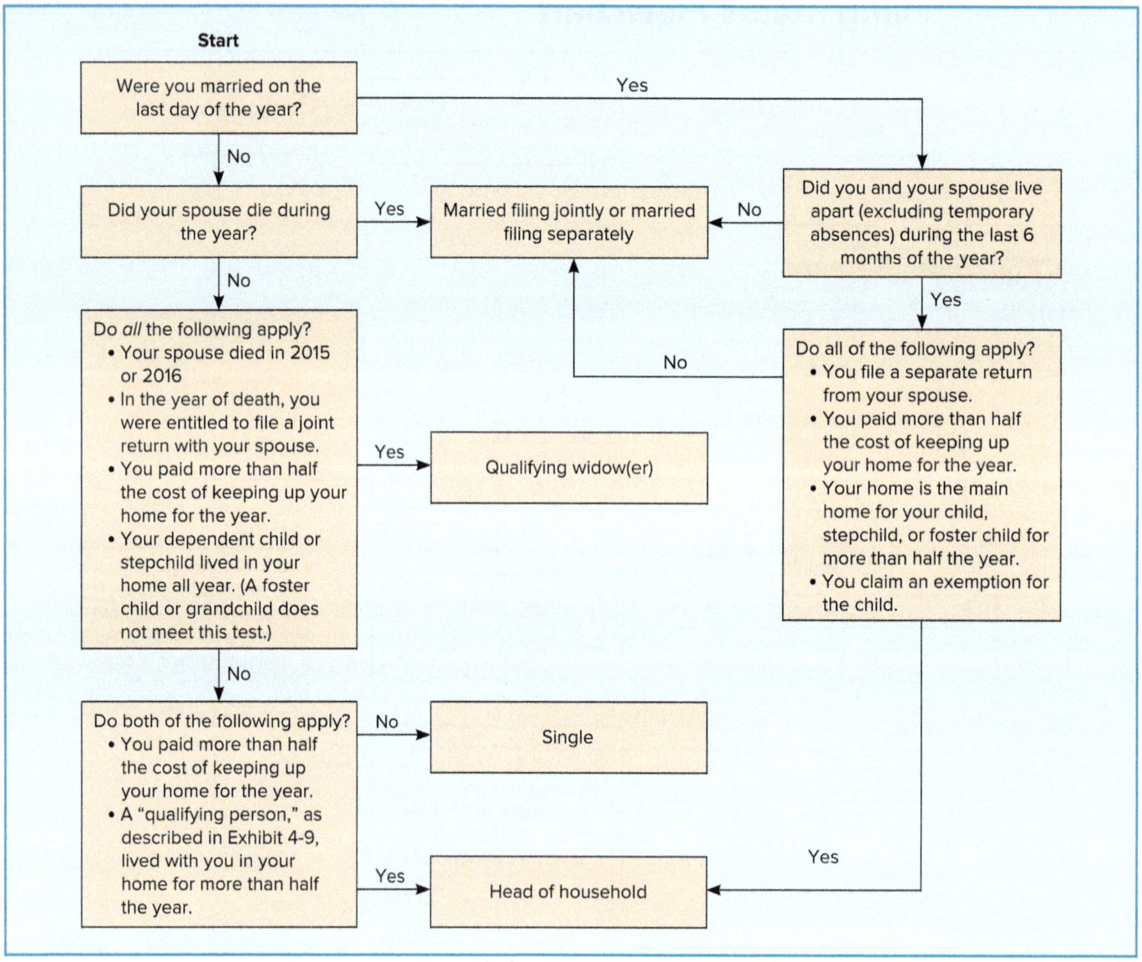

Summary

LO 4-1 Describe the formula for calculating an individual taxpayer's taxes payable or refund and generally explain each formula component.

- Generally, taxpayers are taxed on all income they realize during the year, no matter the source. However, the tax laws allow taxpayers to permanently exclude or to defer to a later year certain types of income they realize during the year.
- Income items that taxpayers are allowed to permanently exclude from income are called *exclusions*. Realized income items that taxpayers are not taxed on until a future period are called *deferrals*.
- Taxpayers include gross income on their tax returns.
- The character of the income determines how the income is treated for tax purposes, including, potentially, the rate at which the income is taxed.

- Ordinary income is taxed at the rates provided in the tax rate schedules; long-term capital gains (after a netting process) and qualified dividends are taxed at a maximum rate of 0, 15, or 20 percent, depending on the taxpayer's taxable income.
- Capital gains and losses arise from the sale or disposition of capital assets. In general a capital asset is any asset other than accounts receivable from the sale of goods or services, inventory, and assets used in a trade or business. If a capital asset is owned for more than a year before it is sold, the capital gain or loss is long-term. Otherwise, it is short-term.
- Taxpayers may deduct up to $3,000 of net capital loss for the year (excess of capital losses over capital gains for the year) against ordinary income. The remainder is suspended and carried over to the next year.
- Even though a personal-use asset meets the capital asset definition, a taxpayer is not allowed to deduct a loss on the sale or disposition of a personal-use asset.
- Deductions reduce a taxpayer's taxable income. The two types of deductions are *for* AGI deductions and *from* AGI deductions.
- Gross income minus *for* AGI deductions equals adjusted gross income (AGI). *For* AGI deductions are deductions "above the line," the last line on the front page of the individual tax form, Form 1040.
- *For* AGI deductions tend to relate to business activities and certain investment activities.
- AGI minus *from* AGI deductions equals taxable income.
- *From* AGI deductions include itemized deductions, the standard deduction, and exemptions. *From* AGI deductions are referred to as "deductions below the line."
- AGI is an important reference point in the individual tax formula because it is often used in other tax-related calculations, including determining limitations on *from* AGI deductions.
- Taxpayers generally deduct itemized deductions when the amount of the itemized deductions exceeds the standard deduction. The standard deduction varies by filing status and is indexed for inflation. Special rules may alter the standard deduction amount for certain taxpayers.
- Taxpayers are allowed to deduct personal exemptions for themselves (and their spouses if they file jointly) and dependency exemptions for those who qualify as their dependents.
- Taxpayers generally calculate the tax on their taxable income by referring to tax tables or tax rate schedules.
- Taxpayers may be required to pay the alternative minimum tax (AMT), self-employment tax, the 3.8 percent net investment income tax on unearned (investment) income, and/or the .9 percent additional Medicare tax on earned income in addition to their regular income tax.
- Tax credits reduce taxpayers' tax liability dollar for dollar, while deductions decrease taxable income dollar for dollar.
- Taxpayers prepay taxes during the year through withholdings by employers, estimated tax payments, or prior year overpayments applied toward the current-year tax liability.
- If tax prepayments exceed the taxpayer's total tax after credits, the taxpayer receives a refund. If tax prepayments are less than the total tax after credits, the taxpayer owes additional tax with his or her tax return.

Explain the requirements for determining a taxpayer's personal and dependency exemptions. **LO 4-2**

- For 2017, taxpayers are allowed to deduct $4,050 for each personal and dependency exemption they are entitled to claim.
- Individuals may claim a personal exemption for themselves (and for their spouses if they are married and file jointly). They may also claim dependency exemptions for each person who qualifies as their dependent.
- If an individual qualifies as a dependent of another taxpayer, the individual may not deduct a personal exemption for him- or herself on his or her individual return. Also, the individual may not claim any dependency exemptions.

- Taxpayers may claim dependency exemptions for those who (1) are citizens of the United States or residents of the United States, Canada, or Mexico and (2) meet the joint tax return test, and are considered either a qualifying child or a qualifying relative of the taxpayer.
- A child must meet a relationship test, an age test, a residence test, and a support test to qualify as a qualifying child.
- A person who is not a qualifying child may be considered a qualifying relative by meeting a relationship test, a support test, and a gross income test.

LO 4-3 Determine a taxpayer's filing status.

- Taxpayers may file their tax returns as married filing jointly, married filing separately, qualifying widow or widower (also referred to as surviving spouse), single, or head of household.
- Married taxpayers may file a joint return or they may file separately. It is generally more advantageous for tax purposes to file jointly, if married. However, for nontax reasons, it may be advantageous to file separately.
- Each spouse is ultimately responsible for paying the tax on a joint return no matter who received the income.
- For two years after the year in which one spouse dies, the surviving spouse may file as a qualifying widow or widower as long as he or she (1) remains unmarried and (2) maintains a household for a dependent child (child, stepchild, or adopted child). However, the surviving spouse is not allowed to claim a dependency exemption for the deceased spouse beyond the year of the spouse's death. That is, a qualifying widow or widower (surviving spouse) may claim only one personal exemption.
- Unmarried taxpayers who do not qualify for head of household status file as single taxpayers.
- An unmarried taxpayer who is not a qualifying widow or widower may file as head of household if the person pays more than half the costs of maintaining a household that is, for *more* than half the taxable year, the principal place of abode for a qualifying person (if the qualifying person is a parent, the parent need not reside with the taxpayer). In general, for an individual to be a qualifying person, the taxpayer must be able to claim an exemption for that individual and the individual must be considered to be related to the taxpayer even if the individual does not live with the taxpayer for the entire year. That is, the taxpayer and the individual must be related through a qualifying family relationship. See Exhibit 4-9 for a flowchart for determining whether an individual is a qualifying person for purposes of determining head of household filing status.

KEY TERMS

abandoned spouse (4-24)
adjusted gross income (AGI) (4-2)
all-inclusive income concept (4-2)
alternative minimum tax (AMT) (4-10)
character of income (4-6)
deductions (4-7)
deductions above the line (4-7)
deductions below the line (4-8)
deferrals (4-5)
dependency exemptions (4-9)
dependent (4-12)
estimated tax payments (4-11)
exclusions (4-5)
exemptions (4-8)
filing status (4-19)
***for* AGI deductions (4-7)**
***from* AGI deductions (4-7)**
gross income (4-2)
head of household (4-21)
itemized deductions (4-8)
legislative grace (4-7)
married filing jointly (4-19)
married filing separately (4-19)
personal exemptions (4-9)
preferential tax rate (4-6)
preferentially taxed income (4-6)
qualifying child (4-12)
qualifying relative (4-12)
qualifying widow or widower (4-20)
realized income (4-2)
single (4-21)
self-employment taxes (4-10)
standard deduction (4-8)
taxable income (4-2)
tax credits (4-11)
tax rate schedule (4-10)
tax tables (4-10)
withholdings (4-11)

DISCUSSION QUESTIONS

Discussion Questions are available in Connect®.

connect

1. How are realized income, gross income, and taxable income similar, and how are they different? LO 4-1
2. Are taxpayers required to include all realized income in gross income? Explain. LO 4-1
3. All else being equal, should taxpayers prefer to exclude income or to defer it? Why? LO 4-1
4. Why should a taxpayer be interested in the character of income received? LO 4-1
5. Is it easier to describe what a capital asset is or what it is not? Explain. LO 4-1
6. Are all capital gains (gains on the sale or disposition of capital assets) taxed at the same rate? Explain. LO 4-1
7. Are taxpayers allowed to deduct net capital losses (capital losses in excess of capital gains)? Explain. LO 4-1
8. Compare and contrast *for* and *from* AGI deductions. Why are *for* AGI deductions likely more valuable to taxpayers than *from* AGI deductions? LO 4-1
9. What is the difference between gross income and adjusted gross income, and what is the difference between adjusted gross income and taxable income? LO 4-1
10. How do taxpayers determine whether they should deduct their itemized deductions or utilize the standard deduction? LO 4-1
11. Why are some deductions called "above the line" deductions and others called "below the line" deductions? What is the "line"? LO 4-1
12. What is the difference between a tax deduction and a tax credit? Is one more beneficial than the other? Explain. LO 4-1
13. What types of federal income-based taxes, other than the regular income tax, might taxpayers be required to pay? In general terms, what is the tax base for each of these other taxes on income? LO 4-1
14. Identify three ways taxpayers can pay their income taxes to the government. LO 4-1
15. If a person is considered to be a qualifying child or qualifying relative of a taxpayer, is the taxpayer automatically entitled to claim a dependency exemption for the person? LO 4-1
16. Emily and Tony are recently married college students. Can Emily qualify as her parents' dependent? Explain. LO 4-2
17. Compare and contrast the relationship test requirements for a qualifying child with the relationship requirements for a qualifying relative. LO 4-2
18. In general terms, what are the differences in the rules for determining who is a qualifying child and who qualifies as a dependent as a qualifying relative? Is it possible for someone to be a qualifying child and a qualifying relative of the same taxpayer? Why or why not? LO 4-2
19. How do two taxpayers determine who has priority to claim the dependency exemption for a qualifying child of both taxpayers when neither taxpayer is a parent of the child (assume the child does not qualify as a qualifying child of either parent)? How do parents determine who gets to deduct the dependency exemption for a qualifying child of both parents when the parents are divorced or file separate returns? LO 4-2
20. Isabella provides 30 percent of the support for her father Hastings, who lives in an apartment by himself and has no gross income. Is it possible for Isabella to claim a dependency exemption for her father? Explain. LO 4-2

LO 4-3 21. What requirements do an abandoned spouse and a qualifying widow or widower have in common?

LO 4-3 22. True or False. For purposes of determining head of household filing status, the taxpayer's mother or father is considered to be a qualifying person of the taxpayer (even if the mother or father does not qualify as the taxpayer's dependent) as long as the taxpayer pays more than half the costs of maintaining the household of the mother or father. Explain.

LO 4-3 23. Is a qualifying relative always a qualifying person for purposes of determining head of household filing status?

LO 4-3 24. For tax purposes, why is the married filing jointly tax status generally preferable to the married filing separately filing status? Why might a married taxpayer prefer *not* to file a joint return with the taxpayer's spouse?

LO 4-3 25. What does it mean to say that a married couple filing a joint tax return has joint and several liability for the taxes associated with the return?

PROBLEMS

Select problems are available in Connect®. connect

LO 4-1 26. Jeremy earned $100,000 in salary and $6,000 in interest income during the year. Jeremy has two qualifying dependent children who live with him. He qualifies to file as head of household and has $17,000 in itemized deductions. Neither of his dependents qualifies for the child tax credit.

a) Use the 2017 tax rate schedules to determine Jeremy's taxes due.

b) Assume that in addition to the original facts, Jeremy has a long-term capital gain of $4,000. What is Jeremy's tax liability including the tax on the capital gain?

c) Assume the original facts except that Jeremy had only $7,000 in itemized deductions. What is Jeremy's total income tax liability?

LO 4-1 27. David and Lilly Fernandez have determined their tax liability on their joint tax return to be $1,700. They have made prepayments of $1,500 and also have a child tax credit of $1,000. What is the amount of their tax refund or taxes due?

LO 4-1 planning 28. Rick, who is single, has been offered a position as a city landscape consultant. The position pays $125,000 in cash wages. Assume Rick files single and is entitled to one personal exemption. Rick deducts the standard deduction instead of itemized deductions.

a) What is the amount of Rick's after-tax compensation (ignore payroll taxes)?

b) Suppose Rick receives a competing job offer of $120,000 in cash compensation and nontaxable (excluded) benefits worth $4,000. What is the amount of Rick's after-tax compensation for the competing offer? Which job should he take if taxes are the only concern?

LO 4-1 planning 29. Through November, Tex has received gross income of $120,000. For December, Tex is considering whether to accept one more work engagement for the year. Engagement 1 will generate $7,000 of revenue at a cost of $4,000 which is deductible *for* AGI. In contrast, engagement 2 will generate $7,000 of revenue at a cost of $3,000, which is deductible as an itemized deduction. Tex files as a single taxpayer.

a) Calculate Tex's taxable income assuming he chooses engagement 1 and assuming he chooses engagement 2. Assume he has no itemized deductions other than those generated by engagement 2.

b) Calculate Tex's taxable income assuming he chooses engagement 1 and assuming he chooses engagement 2. Assume he has $4,500 of itemized deductions other than those generated by engagement 2.

c) Calculate Tex's taxable income assuming he chooses engagement 1 and assuming he chooses engagement 2. Assume he has $7,000 of itemized deductions other than those generated by engagement 2.

30. Matteo, who is single and has no dependents, was planning on spending the weekend repairing his car. On Friday, Matteo's employer called and offered him $500 in overtime pay if he would agree to work over the weekend. Matteo could get his car repaired over the weekend at Autofix for $400. If Matteo works over the weekend, he will have to pay the $400 to have his car repaired but he will earn $500. Assume Matteo pays tax at a flat 15 percent rate. LO 4-1 planning

a) Strictly considering tax factors, should Matteo work or repair his car if the $400 he must pay to have his car fixed is not deductible?

b) Strictly considering tax factors, should Matteo work or repair his car if the $400 he must pay to have his car fixed is deductible *for* AGI?

31. Rank the following three single taxpayers in order of the magnitude of taxable income (from lowest to highest) and explain your results. LO 4-1 LO 4-2

	Ahmed	Baker	Chin
Gross income	$80,000	$80,000	$80,000
Deductions *for* AGI	8,000	4,000	0
Itemized deductions	0	4,000	8,000

32. Aishwarya's husband passed away in 2016. She needs to determine whether Jasmine, her 17-year-old stepdaughter, who is single, qualifies as her dependent in 2017. Jasmine is a resident but not a citizen of the United States. She lived in Aishwarya's home from June 15 through December 31, 2017. Aishwarya provided more than half of Jasmine's support for 2017. LO 4-2

a) Is Aishwarya allowed to claim a dependency exemption for Jasmine for 2017?

b) Would Aishwarya be allowed to claim a dependency exemption for Jasmine for 2017 if Aishwarya provided more than half of Jasmine's support in 2017, Jasmine lived in Aishwarya's home from July 15 through December 31 of 2017, and Jasmine reported gross income of $5,000 in 2017?

c) Would Aishwarya be allowed to claim a dependency exemption for Jasmine for 2017 if Aishwarya provided more than half of Jasmine's support in 2017, Jasmine lived in Aishwarya's home from July 15 through December 31 of 2017, and Jasmine reported gross income of $2,500 in 2017?

33. The Samsons are trying to determine whether they can claim their 22-year-old adopted son, Jason, as a dependent. Jason is currently a full-time student at an out-of-state university. Jason lived in his parents' home for three months of the year and he was away at school for the rest of the year. He received $9,500 in scholarships this year for his outstanding academic performance and earned $4,800 of income working a part-time job during the year. The Samsons paid a total of $5,000 to support Jason while he was away at college. Jason used the scholarship, the earnings from the part-time job, and the money from the Samsons as his only sources of support. LO 4-2

a) Can the Samsons claim Jason as their dependent?

b) Assume the original facts except that Jason's grandparents, not the Samsons, provided him with the $5,000 worth of support. Can the Samsons (Jason's parents) claim Jason as their dependent? Why or why not?

c) Assume the original facts except substitute Jason's grandparents for his parents. Determine whether Jason's grandparents can claim Jason as a dependent.

d) Assume the original facts except that Jason earned $5,500 while working part-time and used this amount for his support. Can the Samsons claim Jason as their dependent? Why or why not?

LO 4-2 34. John and Tara Smith are married and have lived in the same home for over 20 years. John's uncle Tim, who is 64 years old, has lived with the Smiths since March of this year. Tim is searching for employment but has been unable to find any—his gross income for the year is $2,000. Tim used all $2,000 toward his own support. The Smiths provided the rest of Tim's support by providing him with lodging valued at $5,000 and food valued at $2,200.

a) Are the Smiths able to claim a dependency exemption for Tim?

b) Assume the original facts except that Tim earned $10,000 and used all the funds for his own support. Are the Smiths able to claim Tim as a dependent?

c) Assume the original facts except that Tim is a friend of the family and not John's uncle.

d) Assume the original facts except that Tim is a friend of the family and not John's uncle and Tim lived with the Smiths for the entire year.

LO 4-2 35. Francine's mother Donna and her father Darren separated and divorced in September of this year. Francine lived with both parents until the separation. Francine does *not* provide more than half of her own support. Francine is 15 years old at the end of the year.

a) Is Francine a qualifying child to Donna?

b) Is Francine a qualifying child to Darren?

c) Assume Francine spends more time living with Darren than Donna after the separation. Who may claim Francine as a dependency exemption for tax purposes?

d) Assume Francine spends an equal number of days with her mother and her father and that Donna has AGI of $52,000 and Darren has AGI of $50,000. Who may claim a dependency exemption for Francine?

LO 4-2 36. Jamel and Jennifer have been married 30 years and have filed a joint return every year of their marriage. Their three daughters, Jade, Lindsay, and Abbi, are ages 12, 17, and 22, respectively, and all live at home. None of the daughters provides more than half of her own support. Abbi is a full-time student at a local university and does not have any gross income.

a) How many personal and dependency exemptions are Jamel and Jennifer allowed to claim?

b) Assume the original facts except that Abbi is married. She and her husband live with Jamel and Jennifer while attending school and they file a joint return. Abbi and her husband reported a $1,000 tax liability on their tax return. If all parties are willing, can Jamel and Jennifer claim Abbi as a dependent on their tax return? Why or why not?

c) Assume the same facts as part (b), except that Abbi and her husband report a $0 tax liability on their joint tax return. Also, if the couple had filed separately, Abbi would not have had a tax liability on her return but her husband would have had a $250 tax liability on his separate return. Can Jamel and Jennifer claim Abbi as a dependent on their tax return? Why or why not?

d) Assume the original facts except that Abbi is married. Abbi files a separate tax return. Abbi's husband files a separate tax return and reports a $250 tax liability on the return. Can Jamel and Jennifer claim Abbi as a dependent?

LO 4-2 LO 4-3 37. Dean Kastner is 78 years old and lives by himself in an apartment in Chicago. Dean's gross income for the year is $2,500. Dean's support is provided as follows: Himself (5 percent), his daughters Camille (25 percent) and Rachel (30 percent), his son Zander (5 percent), his friend Frankie (15 percent), and his niece Sharon (20 percent).

a) Absent a multiple support agreement, of the parties mentioned in the problem, who may claim a dependency exemption for Dean as a qualifying relative?

b) Under a multiple support agreement, who is eligible to claim a dependency exemption for Dean as a qualifying relative? Explain.

c) Assume that Camille is allowed to claim Dean as a dependent under a multiple support agreement. Camille is single, and Dean is her only dependent. What is Camille's filing status?

38. Mel and Cindy Gibson's 12-year-old daughter Rachel was abducted on her way home from school on March 15, 2017. Police reports indicated that a stranger had physically dragged Rachel into a waiting car and sped away. Everyone hoped that the kidnapper and Rachel would be located quickly. However, as of the end of the year, Rachel was still missing. The police were still pursuing several promising leads and had every reason to believe that Rachel was still alive. In 2018, Rachel was returned safely to her parents. LO 4-2 research

a) Are the Gibsons allowed to claim an exemption deduction for Rachel in 2017 even though she only lived in the Gibsons' home for two-and-one-half months? Explain and cite your authority.

b) Assume the original facts except that Rachel is unrelated to the Gibsons but she has been living with them since January 2012. The Gibsons have claimed a dependency exemption for Rachel for the years 2012 through 2016. Are the Gibsons allowed to claim a dependency exemption for Rachel in 2017? Explain and cite your authority.

39. Bob Ryan filed his tax return and claimed a dependency exemption for his 16-year-old son Dylan. Both Bob and Dylan are citizens and residents of the United States. Dylan meets all the necessary requirements to be considered a qualifying child; however, when Bob filed the tax return he didn't know Dylan's Social Security number and, therefore, didn't include an identifying number for his son on the tax return. Instead, Bob submitted an affidavit with his tax return stating he had requested Dylan's Social Security number from Dylan's birth state. Is Bob allowed to claim a dependency exemption for Dylan without including Dylan's identifying number on the return? LO 4-2 research

40. Kimberly is divorced and the custodial parent of a 3-year-old girl named Bailey. Kimberly and Bailey live with Kimberly's parents, who pay all the costs of maintaining the household (such as mortgage, property taxes, and food). Kimberly pays for Bailey's clothing, entertainment, and health insurance costs. These costs comprised only a small part of the total costs of maintaining the household. Kimberly does not qualify as her parents' dependent. LO 4-2 LO 4-3

a) Determine the appropriate filing status for Kimberly.

b) What if Kimberly lived in her own home and provided all the costs of maintaining the household?

c) Assume Kimberly qualifies as her parents' dependent. How many personal and dependency exemptions may Kimberly claim on her tax return?

41. Lee is 30 years old and single. Lee paid all the costs of maintaining his household for the entire year. Determine Lee's filing status in each of the following alternative situations: LO 4-2 LO 4-3

a) Lee is Ashton's uncle. Ashton is 15 years old and has gross income of $5,000. Ashton lived in Lee's home from April 1 through the end of the year.

b) Lee is Ashton's uncle. Ashton is 20 years old, not a full-time student, and has gross income of $7,000. Ashton lived in Lee's home from April 1 through the end of the year.

c) Lee is Ashton's uncle. Ashton is 22 years old and was a full-time student from January through April. Ashton's gross income was $5,000. Ashton lived in Lee's home from April 1 through the end of the year.

d) Lee is Ashton's cousin. Ashton is 18 years old, has gross income of $3,000, and is not a full-time student. Ashton lived in Lee's home from April 1 through the end of the year.

e) Lee and Ashton are cousins. Ashton is 18 years old, has gross income of $3,000, and is not a full-time student. Ashton lived in Lee's home for the entire year.

LO 4-2 LO 4-3

42. Ray Albertson is 72 years old and lives by himself in an apartment in Salt Lake City. Ray's gross income for the year is $3,000. Ray's support is provided as follows: himself (11 percent), his daughters Diane (20 percent) and Karen (15 percent), his sons Mike (20 percent) and Kenneth (10 percent), his friend Milt (14 percent), and his cousin Henry (12 percent).

a) Absent a multiple support agreement, of the parties mentioned in the problem, who may claim a dependency exemption for Ray as a qualifying relative?

b) Under a multiple support agreement, who is eligible to claim a dependency exemption for Ray as a qualifying relative? Explain.

c) Assume that under a multiple support agreement, Diane claims a dependency exemption for Ray. Diane is single with no other dependents. What is her filing status?

LO 4-3

43. Juan and Bonita are married and have two dependent children living at home. This year, Juan is killed in an avalanche while skiing.

a) What is Bonita's filing status this year?

b) Assuming Bonita doesn't remarry and still has two dependent children living at home, what will her filing status be next year?

c) Assuming Bonita doesn't remarry and doesn't have any dependents next year, what will her filing status be next year?

LO 4-3

44. Gary and Lakesha were married on December 31 last year. They are now preparing their taxes for the April 15 deadline and are unsure of their filing status.

a) What filing status options do Gary and Lakesha have for last year?

b) Assume instead that Gary and Lakesha were married on January 1 of this year. What is their filing status for last year (neither has been married before and neither had any dependents last year)?

LO 4-3

45. Elroy, who is single, has taken over the care of his mother Irene in her old age. Elroy pays the bills relating to Irene's home. He also buys all her groceries and provides the rest of her support. Irene has no gross income.

a) What is Elroy's filing status?

b) Assume the original facts except that Elroy has taken over the care of his grandmother, Renae, instead of his mother. What is Elroy's filing status?

c) Assume the original facts except that Elroy's mother, Irene, lives with him and receives an annual $5,700 taxable distribution from her retirement account. Elroy still pays all the costs to maintain the household. What is his filing status?

LO 4-3

46. Kano and his wife, Hoshi, have been married for 10 years and have two children under the age of 12. The couple has been living apart for the last two years and both children live with Kano. Kano has provided all the means necessary to support himself and his children. Kano and Hoshi do not file a joint return.

a) What is Kano's filing status?

b) Assume the original facts except that Kano and Hoshi separated in May of the current year. What is Kano's filing status?

c) Assume the original facts except that Kano and Hoshi separated in November of this year. What is Kano's filing status?

d) Assume the original facts except that Kano's parents, not Kano, paid more than half of the cost of maintaining the home in which Kano and his children live. What is Kano's filing status?

47. Horatio and Kelly were divorced at the end of last year. Neither Horatio nor Kelly remarried during the current year and Horatio moved out of state. Determine the filing status of Horatio and Kelly for the current year in the following independent situations: LO 4-3
    a) Horatio and Kelly did not have any children and neither reported any dependents in the current year.
    b) Horatio and Kelly had one child, Amy, who turned 10 years of age in the current year. Amy lived with Kelly for all of the current year and Kelly provided all of her support.
    c) Assume the same facts as in part (b), but Kelly released the exemption for Amy to Horatio even though Amy did not reside with him at all during the current year.
    d) Assume the original facts except that during the current year Madison, a 17-year-old friend of the family, lived with Kelly (for the entire year) and was fully supported by Kelly.
    e) Assume the original facts except that during the current year Kelly's mother, Janet, lived with Kelly. For the current year, Kelly was able to claim a dependency exemption for her mother under a multiple support agreement.
48. In each of the following *independent* situations, determine the taxpayer's filing status and the number of personal and dependency exemptions the taxpayer is allowed to claim. LO 4-2 LO 4-3
    a) Frank is single and supports his 17-year-old brother, Bill. Bill earned $3,000 and did not live with Frank.
    b) Geneva and her spouse reside with their son, Steve, who is a 20-year-old undergraduate student at State University. Steve earned $13,100 at a part-time summer job, but he deposited this money in a savings account for graduate school. Geneva paid all of the $12,000 cost of supporting Steve.
    c) Hamish's spouse died last year and Hamish has not remarried. Hamish supports his father, Reggie, age 78, who lives in a nursing home and had interest income this year of $2,500.
    d) Irene is married but has not seen her spouse since February. She supports her spouse's 18-year-old child, Dolores, who lives with Irene. Dolores earned $4,500 this year.
    e) Assume the same facts as in part (d). Also, assume that Craig is Irene's husband. Craig supports his 12-year-old son Ethan, who lives with Craig. Ethan did not earn any income.
49. In each of the following *independent* cases, determine the taxpayer's filing status and the number of personal and dependency exemptions the taxpayer is allowed to claim. LO 4-2 LO 4-3
    a) Alexandra is a blind widow (her spouse died five years ago) who provides a home for her 18-year-old nephew, Newt. Newt's parents are dead and so Newt supports himself. Newt's gross income is $5,000.
    b) Bharati supports and maintains a home for her daughter, Daru, and son-in-law, Sam. Sam earned $15,000 and filed a joint return with Daru, who had no income.
    c) Charlie intended to file a joint return with his spouse, Sally. However, Sally died in December. Charlie has not remarried.
    d) Deshi cannot convince his spouse to consent to signing a joint return. The couple has not separated.
    e) Edith and her spouse support their 35-year-old son, Slim. Slim is a full-time college student who earned $5,500 over the summer in part-time work.
50. Jasper and Crewella Dahvill were married in year 0. They filed joint tax returns in years 1 and 2. In year 3, their relationship was strained and Jasper insisted on filing LO 4-3

a separate tax return. In year 4, the couple divorced. Both Jasper and Crewella filed single tax returns in year 4. In year 5, the IRS audited the couple's joint year 2 tax return and each spouse's separate year 3 tax returns. The IRS determined that the year 2 joint return and Crewella's separate year 3 tax return understated Crewella's self-employment income, causing the joint return year 2 tax liability to be understated by $4,000 and Crewella's year 3 separate return tax liability to be understated by $6,000. The IRS also assessed penalties and interest on both of these tax returns. Try as it might, the IRS has not been able to locate Crewella, but they have been able to find Jasper.

a) What amount of tax can the IRS require Jasper to pay for the Dahvill's year 2 joint return? Explain.

b) What amount of tax can the IRS require Jasper to pay for Crewella's year 3 separate tax return? Explain.

LO 4-3 research

51. Janice Traylor is single. She has an 18-year-old son named Marty. Marty is Janice's only child. Marty has lived with Janice his entire life. However, Marty recently joined the Marines and was sent on a special assignment to Australia. During the current year, Marty spent nine months in Australia. Marty was extremely homesick while in Australia, since he had never lived away from home. However, Marty knew this assignment was only temporary, and he couldn't wait to come home and find his room just the way he left it. Janice has always filed as head of household, and Marty has always been considered a qualifying child (and he continues to meet all the tests with the possible exception of the residence test due to his stay in Australia). However, this year Janice is unsure whether she qualifies as head of household due to Marty's nine-month absence during the year. Janice has come to you for advice on whether she qualifies for head of household filing status. What do you tell her?

LO 4-3 research

52. Doug Jones submitted his 2017 tax return on time and elected to file a joint tax return with his wife, Darlene. Doug and Darlene did not request an extension for their 2017 tax return. Doug and Darlene owed and paid the IRS $124,000 for their 2017 tax year. Two years later, Doug amended his return and claimed married filing separate status. By changing his filing status, Doug sought a refund for an overpayment for the tax year 2017 (he paid more tax in the original joint return than he owed on a separate return). Is Doug allowed to change his filing status for the 2017 tax year and receive a tax refund with his amended return?

COMPREHENSIVE PROBLEMS

Select problems are available in Connect®. connect

tax forms

53. Marc and Michelle are married and earned salaries this year of $64,000 and $12,000, respectively. In addition to their salaries, they received interest of $350 from municipal bonds and $500 from corporate bonds. Marc and Michelle also paid $2,500 of qualifying moving expenses, and Marc paid alimony to a prior spouse in the amount of $1,500. Marc and Michelle have a 10-year-old son, Matthew, who lived with them throughout the entire year. Thus, Marc and Michelle are allowed to claim a $1,000 child tax credit for Matthew. Marc and Michelle paid $6,000 of expenditures that qualify as itemized deductions and they had a total of $5,500 in federal income taxes withheld from their paychecks during the course of the year.

a) What is Marc and Michelle's gross income?

b) What is Marc and Michelle's adjusted gross income?

c) What is the total amount of Marc and Michelle's deductions *from* AGI?

d) What is Marc and Michelle's taxable income?

e) What is Marc and Michelle's taxes payable or refund due for the year? (Use the tax rate schedules.)

f) Complete the first two pages of Marc and Michelle's Form 1040 (use 2016 forms if 2017 forms are unavailable).

54. Demarco and Janine Jackson have been married for 20 years and have four children who qualify as their dependents (Damarcus, Janine, Michael, and Candice). The couple received salary income of $100,000, and they sold their home this year. They initially purchased the home three years ago for $200,000 and they sold it for $250,000. The gain on the sale qualified for the exclusion from the sale of a principal residence. The Jacksons incurred $16,500 of itemized deductions, and they had $6,250 withheld from their paychecks for federal taxes. They are also allowed to claim a child tax credit for each of their children.

tax forms

   a) What is the Jacksons' taxable income, and what is their tax liability or (refund)?
   b) Complete the first two pages of the Jacksons' Form 1040 (use 2016 forms if 2017 forms are unavailable).
   c) What would their taxable income be if their itemized deductions totaled $6,000 instead of $16,500?
   d) What would their taxable income be if they had $0 itemized deductions and $6,000 of *for* AGI deductions?
   e) Assume the original facts but now suppose they also incurred a loss of $5,000 on the sale of some of their investment assets. What effect does the $5,000 loss have on their *taxable income*?
   f) Assume the original facts but now suppose the Jacksons own investments that appreciated by $10,000 during the year. The Jacksons believe the investments will continue to appreciate, so they did not sell the investments during this year. What is the Jacksons' taxable income?

55. Camille Sikorski was divorced last year. She currently provides a home for her 15-year-old daughter, Kaly, and 18-year-old son, Parker. Both children lived in Camille's home, which she owns, for the entire year, and Camille paid for all the costs of maintaining the home. She received a salary of $105,000 and contributed $6,000 of it to a qualified retirement account (a *for* AGI deduction). She also received $10,000 of alimony from her former husband. Finally, Camille paid $5,000 of expenditures that qualified as itemized deductions.
   a) What is Camille's taxable income?
   b) What would Camille's taxable income be if she incurred $14,000 of itemized deductions instead of $5,000?
   c) Assume the original facts but now suppose Camille's daughter, Kaly, is 25 years old and a full-time student. Kaly's gross income for the year was $5,000. Kaly provided $3,000 of her own support, and Camille provided $5,000 of support. What is Camille's taxable income?

56. Tiffany is unmarried and has a 15-year-old qualifying child. Tiffany has determined her tax liability to be $3,525, and her employer has withheld $1,500 of federal taxes from her paycheck. Tiffany is allowed to claim a $1,000 child credit for her qualifying child. What amount of taxes will Tiffany owe (or what amount will she receive as a refund) when she files her tax return?

ROGER | CPA Review

Sample CPA Exam questions from Roger CPA Review are available in Connect as support for the topics in this text. These Multiple Choice Questions and Task-Based Simulations include expert-written explanations and solutions, and provide a starting point for students to become familiar with the content and functionality of the actual CPA Exam.

chapter 5

Gross Income and Exclusions

Learning Objectives

Upon completing this chapter, you should be able to:

LO 5-1 Apply the concept of realization and explain when taxpayers recognize gross income.

LO 5-2 Understand the distinctions between the various sources of income, including income from services and property.

LO 5-3 Apply basic income exclusion provisions to compute gross income.

© Image Source

Storyline Summary

Taxpayers:	Courtney Wilson, age 40 Courtney's mother, Dorothy "Gram" Weiss, age 70
Family description:	Courtney is divorced with a son, Deron, age 10, and a daughter, Ellen, age 20. Gram is currently residing with Courtney.
Location:	Kansas City, Missouri
Employment status:	Courtney works as an architect for EWD. Her salary is $118,000. Gram is unemployed.
Current situation:	Determining what income is taxable

The past year was a year of change for Courtney Wilson. After her divorce from Al Wilson, Courtney assumed sole custody of their 10-year-old son, Deron, and their 20-year-old daughter, Ellen. Looking for a fresh start in January, Courtney quit her job as an architect in Cincinnati, Ohio, and moved to Kansas City, Missouri. Courtney wanted to pursue several promising job opportunities in Kansas City and be close to Ellen while she attends the University of Missouri–Kansas City. Courtney's 70-year-old mother "Gram" also lives in Kansas City and is in relatively good health. However, Courtney's father, "Gramps," passed away last December from cancer. At Courtney's insistence, Gram moved in with Courtney and Deron in April.

In late April, Courtney broke her wrist in a mountain biking accident and was unable to work for two weeks. Thankfully, Courtney's disability insurance paid her for lost wages during her time away from work.

While her personal life has been in disarray, Courtney's financial prospects have been improving. Shortly after arriving in Kansas City, Courtney was fortunate to land a job as an architect with Earth Wise Design (EWD). EWD provided Courtney the following compensation and benefits this year:

- Salary $118,000.
- Medical and life insurance premiums.
- Contribution of 10 percent of her base salary to her qualified retirement account.
- No-interest loan with a promise to forgive the loan principal over time if she continues her employment with EWD.
- Performance bonus for her first year on the job.

Courtney also received other payments unrelated to her employment with EWD as follows:

- Alimony from her ex-husband Al.
- Child support from her ex-husband Al.
- Consulting income.
- Dividend, interest, and rental income.
- Refund of state taxes she paid last year.

Before Gram moved in with Courtney, she lived alone in an apartment in Kansas City. After Gramps died, Gram was dependent on her Social Security benefits. In March, Gram's landlord agreed to allow Gram to babysit his infant son in lieu of paying rent. In early April, Gram received the proceeds from Gramps's life insurance policy. She invested part of the proceeds in an annuity contract that will pay Gram a fixed amount per year. Gram also invested some of the proceeds in the stock of a local corporation. She used the rest of the life insurance proceeds to purchase a certificate of deposit and start a savings account. Gram also spent some of her spare time completing sweepstakes entries. Her hard work paid off when she won a WaveRunner in a sweepstakes contest.

Until their divorce, Courtney's husband always prepared their income tax return. Since EWD hired her, Courtney has become anxious about her income tax and whether her withholding will be sufficient to cover her tax bill. Courtney is also worried about Gram's tax situation, because Gram did not make any tax payments this year. ■

In the previous chapter, we presented an overview of individual taxation. In this chapter, we begin to dig deeper into the tax formula to determine a taxpayer's gross income. We focus on whether income is included or excluded from a taxpayer's gross income rather than the rate at which the income is taxed. In the next three chapters, we continue to work through the individual tax formula to determine the tax liabilities for Courtney and Gram. The Individual Deductions chapter describes deductible expenses to determine adjusted gross income and taxable income, the Investments chapter discusses the taxation of investments, and the Individual Income Tax Computation and Tax Credits chapter addresses issues associated with calculating the tax liability, tax credits, and tax return filing concerns.

LO 5-1 REALIZATION AND RECOGNITION OF INCOME

As we learned in the previous chapter, **gross income** is income that taxpayers realize, recognize, and report on their tax returns for the year. In the previous chapter, we discussed gross income in general terms. In this chapter we explain the requirements for taxpayers to recognize gross income, and we discuss the most common sources of gross income.

What Is Included in Gross Income?

The definition of gross income for tax purposes is provided in §61(a) as follows:

> GENERAL DEFINITION.—Except as otherwise provided in this subtitle, gross income means all income *from whatever source derived* (emphasis added).

In addition to providing this all-inclusive definition of income, §61 includes a list of examples of gross income such as compensation for services, business income, rents, royalties, interest, and dividends. However, it is clear that unless a tax provision says otherwise, gross income includes *all* income. Thus, gross income is *broadly* defined. Reg. §1.61-(a) provides further insight into the definition of gross income as follows:

> Gross income means all income from whatever source derived, unless excluded by law. Gross income includes income realized in any form, whether in money, property, or services.

Based on §61(a), Reg. §1.61-(a), and various judicial rulings, taxpayers *recognize* gross income when (1) they receive an economic benefit, (2) they realize the income, *and* (3) no tax provision allows them to exclude or defer the income from gross income for that year.[1] Let's address each of these three requirements for recognizing gross income.

Economic Benefit Taxpayers must receive an economic benefit (i.e., receive an item of value) to have gross income. Common examples where a taxpayer receives economic benefit include receiving compensation for services (the compensation could be in the form of cash, other property, or even services received), proceeds from property sales (typically cash, property, or debt relief), and income from investments or business activities (such as business income, rents, interest, and dividends). How about when a taxpayer borrows money? Is the economic benefit criterion met? No, because when a taxpayer borrows money, the economic benefit received (the cash received) is completely offset by the liability the taxpayer is required to pay from borrowing the funds (the debt amount).

Realization Principle As indicated in Reg. §1.61-(a), the tax definition of income adopts the **realization principle.** Under this principle, income is realized when (1) a taxpayer engages in a transaction with another party, and (2) the transaction results in a measurable change in property rights. In other words, assets or services are exchanged for cash, claims to cash, or other assets with determinable value.

The concept of realization for tax purposes closely parallels the concept of realization for financial accounting purposes. Requiring a transaction to trigger realization reduces the uncertainty associated with determining the *amount* of income because a change in rights can typically be traced to a specific moment in time and is generally accompanied by legal documentation.

Example 5-1

In April, Gram used part of the life insurance proceeds she received from Gramps's death to purchase 50 shares in Acme Corporation for $30 per share. From April to the end of December, the value of the shares fluctuated between $40 and $25, but on December 31, the shares were worth $35. If Gram does *not* sell the shares, how much income from her stockholdings in Acme Corporation does she *realize for* the year?

Answer: $0. Unless Gram sells the stock, she does not enter into a transaction resulting in a measurable change of property rights with a second party. Thus, she does not realize income even though she experienced an economic benefit from the appreciation of the stock from $30 per share to $35 per share.

Adopting the realization principle for defining gross income provides two major advantages. First, because parties to the transaction must agree to the value of the exchanged property rights, the transaction allows the income to be measured objectively. Second, the transaction often provides the taxpayer with the **wherewithal to pay** taxes (at least when the taxpayer receives cash in the transaction). That is, the transaction itself provides the taxpayer with the funds to pay taxes on income generated by the transaction. Thus, it reduces the possibility that the taxpayer will be required to sell other assets to pay the taxes on the income from the transaction. Note, however, when taxpayers receive property or services in a transaction (instead of cash), realization has also occurred (despite the absence of wherewithal to pay).

[1]For tax purposes it matters not whether income is obtained through legal or illegal activities (e.g., embezzlement). See *Eugene James v. U.S.* (1961, S. Ct.), 7 AFTR 2d 1361.

Recognition Taxpayers who realize an economic benefit must include the benefit in gross income unless a specific provision of the tax code says otherwise. That is, taxpayers are generally required to *recognize* all realized income by reporting it as gross income on their tax returns. However, as we describe later in this chapter, through exclusions Congress allows taxpayers to permanently exclude certain types of income from gross income and through deferrals it allows taxpayers to defer certain types of income from gross income until a subsequent year. Thus, it is important to distinguish between realized and recognized income.

Other Income Concepts

The tax laws, administrative authority, and judicial rulings have established several other concepts important for determining an individual's gross income.

Form of Receipt A common misperception is that taxpayers must receive cash to realize and recognize gross income. However, Reg. §1.61-(a) indicates that taxpayers realize income whether they receive money, property, *or* services in a transaction. For example, **barter clubs** facilitate the exchange of rights to goods and services between members, many of whom have the mistaken belief that they need not recognize income on the exchanges. However, when members exchange property, they realize and recognize income at the market price, the amount that outsiders are willing to pay for the goods or services. Also, other taxpayers who exchange or trade goods or services with each other must recognize the value of the goods or services as income, even when they do not receive any cash. Indeed, taxpayers have the legal and ethical responsibility to report realized income no matter the form of its receipt or whether the IRS knows the taxpayer received the income.

Example 5-2

During March, Gram paid no rent to her neighbor (also her landlord). Although the neighbor typically charges $350 per month for rent, he allowed Gram to live rent-free in exchange for babysitting his infant son. What income must Gram and Gram's neighbor realize and recognize on this exchange?

Answer: $350. Gram and the neighbor each must recognize $350 of income for March. The neighbor recognizes $350 of rental receipts because this is the value of the babysitting services the neighbor received in lieu of a cash payment for rent from Gram (an economic benefit the neighbor realized through the exchange). Gram recognizes $350 of babysitting income, because this is the value of the services provided to her neighbor (an economic benefit was realized because Gram was not required to pay rent).

Return of Capital Principle When taxpayers sell assets, they must determine the extent to which they include the sale proceeds in gross income. Initially, the IRS was convinced that Congress's all-inclusive definition of income required taxpayers to include *all* sale proceeds in gross income. Taxpayers, on the other hand, argued that a portion of proceeds from a sale represented a return of the cost or capital investment in the underlying property (called **tax basis**). The courts determined that when receiving a payment for property, taxpayers are allowed to recover the cost of the property tax-free. Consequently, when taxpayers sell property, they are allowed to reduce the sale proceeds by their unrecovered investment in the property to determine the realized gain from the sale.[2] When the tax basis exceeds the sale proceeds, the **return of capital** principle generally applies

[2]§1001(a).

to the extent of the sale proceeds. The excess of basis over sale proceeds is generally not considered to be a return of capital, but rather a loss that is deductible only if specifically authorized by the tax code. Below, we revisit the return of capital principle when we discuss asset dispositions.

The return of capital principle gets complicated when taxpayers sell assets and collect the sale proceeds over several periods. In these cases, the principle is usually modified by law to provide that the return of capital occurs pro rata as the proceeds are collected over time. We discuss this issue in more detail later in this chapter when we discuss the taxation of annuities.

Recovery of Amounts Previously Deducted A refund is not typically included in gross income because it usually represents a return of capital. For example, a refund of $1,000 on an auto purchased for $12,000 simply reduces the net cost of the vehicle to $11,000. Likewise, a $200 refund of a $700 business expense is not included in gross income but instead reduces the net expense to $500. However, if the refund is made for an expenditure deducted in a *previous* year, then under the **tax benefit rule** the refund is included in gross income to the extent that the prior deduction produced a tax benefit.[3] For example, suppose an individual paid a $1,000 business expense claimed as a *for* AGI deduction in 2016, but $250 of the expense was subsequently reimbursed in 2017. Because the $250 business deduction produced a tax benefit in 2016 (reduced taxable income), the $250 refund in 2017 would be included in income.

The application of the tax benefit rule is more complex for individuals who itemize deductions. An itemized deduction only produces a tax benefit to the extent that total itemized deductions exceed the standard deduction. For example, suppose that an individual's total itemized deductions exceeded the standard deduction by $100. A refund of $150 of itemized deductions would cause the individual's itemized deductions to fall $50 beneath the standard deduction. If the refund occurred in the same year as the expense, the individual would have elected the standard deduction, and the refund would have only caused taxable income to increase by $100 (the difference between claiming the standard deduction and the total itemized deductions that would have been claimed in the absence of any refund). If the refund occurs the year after the deduction is claimed, then only $100 of the $150 refund would be included in gross income under the tax benefit rule. The $100 is added to taxable income in the year of the refund because this is the increment in taxable income that would have resulted if the refund was issued in the year the itemized deduction was claimed.

Example 5-3

In 2016 Courtney paid $3,500 in Ohio state income taxes, and she included this payment with her other itemized deductions when she filed her federal income tax return in March of 2017. Courtney filed her 2016 federal return as a head of household and claimed $15,550 of itemized deductions. She also filed an Ohio state income tax return in March of 2017 and discovered she only owed $3,080 in Ohio income tax for 2016. Hence, Courtney received a $420 refund of her Ohio income tax in June of 2017. How much of the $420 refund, if any, is Courtney required to include in her gross income in 2017? The answer depends upon the standard deduction for 2016. Help Courtney apply the tax benefit rule (the standard deduction for head of household filing status in 2016 was $9,300).

Answer: All $420. Courtney is required to include the entire refund in her 2017 gross income because her itemized deduction for the $420 of state income taxes that she overpaid last year reduced her taxable income by $420. Accordingly, because she received a tax benefit (deduction) for the entire $420

(continued on page 5-6)

[3]§111.

overpayment, she must include it all in gross income in 2017. See the following for the calculation of the amount of tax benefit Courtney received from the $420 overpayment of taxes in 2016.

Deduction	Amount	Explanation
(1) Itemized deduction	$15,550	
(2) 2016 standard deduction	9,300	Head of household filing status
(3) Reduction in taxable income	15,550	Greater of (1) and (2)
(4) Itemized deductions adjusted for the $420 refund	15,130	(1) – $420
(5) Reduction in taxable income after adjustment for the $420 refund	15,130	Greater of (2) and (4)
Tax benefit due to prior deduction or $420 refund	**$ 420**	(3) – (5)

What if: Let's consider *alternative* fact patterns provided in Scenarios A and B to further illustrate the application of the tax benefit rule.

Scenario A: In 2016 Courtney's itemized deductions, including $3,500 in state taxes, were $5,500.

Scenario B: In 2016 Courtney's itemized deductions, including $3,500 in state taxes, were $9,500.

How much of the $420 refund would Courtney include in her 2017 gross income in Scenarios A and B?

Answer Scenario A: $0. As computed below, Courtney received $0 tax benefit from the $420 tax overpayment in 2016, so she need not include any of the refund in her gross income.

Answer Scenario B: $200. As computed below, Courtney received a $200 tax benefit (reduction in taxable income) from the $420 state tax overpayment in 2016, so she must include $200 of the refund in her 2017 gross income.

Deduction	Scenario A Amount	Scenario B Amount	Explanation
(1) Itemized deductions	$5,500	$9,500	
(2) 2016 standard deduction	9,300	9,300	Head of household filing status
(3) Reduction in taxable income	9,300	9,500	Greater of (1) and (2)
(4) Itemized deductions adjusted for the $420 refund	5,080	9,080	(1) – $420
(5) Reduction in taxable income adjusted for the $420 refund	9,300	9,300	Greater of (2) and (4)
Tax benefit due to prior deduction of $420 refund	**$ 0**	**$ 200**	(3) – (5)

When Do Taxpayers Recognize Income?

Individual taxpayers generally file tax returns reporting their taxable income for a calendar-year period, whereas corporations often use a fiscal year-end. In either case, the taxpayer's method of accounting generally determines the year in which realized income is recognized and included in gross income.

Accounting Methods Most large corporations use the accrual method of accounting. Under the **accrual method,** income is generally recognized when earned, and expenses are generally deducted in the period when liabilities are incurred. In contrast, most individuals use the **cash method** as their overall method of accounting.[4] Under the cash method, taxpayers recognize income in the period they receive it (in the form of cash, property, or services), rather than when they actually earn it. Likewise, cash-method taxpayers claim

[4]Taxpayers involved in a business may use the accrual or hybrid overall method of accounting. We discuss these methods in the Business Income, Deductions, and Accounting Methods chapter.

deductions when they make expenditures, rather than when they incur liabilities. The cash method greatly simplifies the computation of income for the overwhelming majority of individuals, many of whom have neither the time nor the training to apply the accrual method. Another advantage of the cash method is that taxpayers may have some control over when income is received and expenses are paid. Because of this control, taxpayers can more easily use the timing tax planning strategy (described in the Tax Planning Strategies and Related Limitations chapter) to lower the present value of their tax bill.

THE KEY FACTS

Income Recognition

- Cash-method taxpayers recognize income when it is received.
- Income is realized regardless of whether payments are received in money, property, *or* services.
- Income is taxed in the period in which a cash-method taxpayer has a right to receive payment without substantial restrictions.

Constructive Receipt Taxpayers using the cash method of accounting may try to shift income from the current year to the next year when they receive payments near year-end. For instance, taxpayers may merely delay cashing a check or avoid picking up a compensation payment until after year-end. The courts responded to this ploy by devising the **constructive receipt doctrine.**[5] The constructive receipt doctrine states that a taxpayer realizes and recognizes income when it is actually or *constructively* received. Constructive receipt is deemed to occur when the income has been credited to the taxpayer's account or when the income is unconditionally available to the taxpayer, the taxpayer is aware of the income's availability, and there are no restrictions on the taxpayer's control over the income.

Example 5-4

Courtney is a cash-method taxpayer. Based on her outstanding performance, Courtney earned a $4,800 year-end bonus. On December 28, Courtney's supervisor told her that her bonus was issued as a separate check and that Courtney could pick up the check in the accounting office anytime. Courtney did not pick up the check until January 2 of the next year, and she did not cash it until late January. When does Courtney realize and recognize the $4,800 income?

Answer: On December 28 of the tax year in question. Courtney *constructively* received the check that year because it was unconditionally available to her on December 28, she was aware of the check's availability, and there were no restrictions on her control over the check. Courtney must include the $4,800 bonus in gross income for that year, even though she did not actually receive the funds until late January of the next year.[6]

Claim of Right The **claim of right doctrine** is another judicial doctrine created to address the timing of income recognition. Specifically, this doctrine addresses when a taxpayer receives income in one period but is required to return the payment in a subsequent period. The claim of right doctrine states that income has been realized if a taxpayer receives income and there are no restrictions on the taxpayer's use of the income (e.g., the taxpayer does not have an obligation to repay the amount). A common example of the claim of right doctrine is a cash bonus paid to employees based on company earnings. Despite *potentially* having to repay the bonuses (e.g., if there is a "clawback" provision that requires repayment if the company has an earnings restatement), the employees would include the bonuses in gross income in the year received because there are no restrictions on their use of the income.[7]

[5]Justice Holmes summarized this doctrine as follows: "The income that is subject to a man's unfettered command and that he is free to enjoy at his own option may be taxed to him as his income, whether he sees fit to enjoy it or not." *Corliss v. Bowers,* 281 US 378 (1930).

[6]Note also that Courtney's employer would include her bonus on Courtney's W-2 for the year in which it issued the check.

[7]§1341 provides relief for a taxpayer who recognizes taxable income because of the claim of right doctrine and in a later year determines that she does not have a claim of right. Specifically, §1341 provides that if a taxpayer recognizes taxable income in an earlier year because she has a "claim of right" (unrestricted right) to the income received, a deduction is then allowable in a later year because she did not have an unrestricted right to the income, and the related tax deduction exceeds $3,000, then the tax imposed in the later year is the lesser of (1) the tax for the taxable year computed with the deduction or (2) the tax for the taxable year computed without the deduction, less a tax credit for the previous tax paid on the item of income.

Who Recognizes the Income?

In addition to determining when taxpayers realize and recognize income, it is important to consider *who* (which taxpayer) recognizes the income. This question often arises when taxpayers attempt to shift income to other related taxpayers through the income-shifting strategy. For example, a father (with a high marginal income tax rate) might wish to assign his paycheck to his baby daughter (with a low marginal income tax rate) to minimize their collective tax burden.

Assignment of Income The courts developed the **assignment of income doctrine** to prevent taxpayers from arbitrarily transferring the taxation on their income to others. In essence, the assignment of income doctrine holds that the taxpayer who earns income from services must recognize the income. Likewise, income from property, such as dividends and interest, is taxable to the person who actually owns the income-producing property.[8] For example, interest income from a bond is taxable to the person who owns the bond during the time the interest income accrues. Thus, to shift income from property to another person, a taxpayer must also transfer the *ownership* in the property to the other person.

Example 5-5

What if: Courtney would like to begin saving for Deron's college tuition. If Courtney were to direct EWD to deposit part of her salary in Deron's bank account, who would pay tax on the salary income?

Answer: Courtney would be taxed on her entire salary as income because she earned the income.[9] The payment to Deron would be treated as a gift and would not be taxable to him (gifts are excluded from the recipient's income as discussed later in the chapter).

What if: Suppose that Courtney wanted to shift her rental income to Deron. What would Courtney need to do to ensure that her rental income is taxed to Deron?

Answer: Courtney would have to transfer her ownership in the rental property to Deron in order for Deron to be taxed on the rental income.[10]

Community Property Systems While most states use a common law system, nine states (Arizona, California, Idaho, Louisiana, Nevada, New Mexico, Texas, Washington, and Wisconsin) implement **community property systems.** Under community property systems, the income earned from services by one spouse is treated as though it was earned equally by both spouses. Also, property acquired by either spouse during the marriage is usually community property and is treated as though it is owned equally by each spouse.[11] Property that a spouse brings into a marriage is treated as that spouse's separate property. For federal income tax purposes, the community property system has the following consequences:

- Half of the income earned from the *services* of one spouse is included in the gross income of the other spouse.
- Half of the income from property held as *community* property by the married couple is included in the gross income of each spouse.

[8]This rule of thumb is also referred to as the "fruit and the tree" doctrine because of the analogy to fruit belonging to the tree upon which it was grown. See *Lucas v. Earl* (1930) 281 US 111 and *Helvering v. Horst* (1940) 311 US 112.

[9]Note also that EWD has the responsibility of issuing a W-2 to the taxpayer who provided the services—Courtney in this case.

[10]As explained in Chapter 8, the tax savings from such a transfer would be mitigated in the calculation of Deron's tax by the so-called "kiddie" tax. Likewise, Courtney should consider the gift tax implications of this transfer before transferring the property to Deron.

[11]Property acquired during the marriage via gift or inheritance or purchased with a spouse's separate property is considered separate property.

- In five community property states (Arizona, California, Nevada, New Mexico, and Washington), all of the income from property owned *separately* by one spouse is included in that spouse's gross income.
- In Texas, Louisiana, Wisconsin, and Idaho, half of the income from property owned *separately* by one spouse is included in the gross income of each spouse.

In contrast, for federal income tax purposes, the common law system has the following consequences:

- All of the income earned from the *services* of one spouse is included in the gross income of the spouse who earned it.
- For property owned *separately,* all of the income from the separately owned property is included in that spouse's gross income.
- For property owned *jointly* (i.e., not separately), each co-owner is taxed on the income attributable to his or her share of the property. For example, suppose that a parcel of property is jointly owned by husband and wife. One-half would be included in the gross income of each spouse. Similarly, income from property owned by three or more persons would be included in the gross income of each co-owner based on his or her respective ownership share.

Example 5-6

In the year of their divorce, Courtney and Al Wilson lived in Ohio, a common law state. The divorce was finalized on October 1 of that year, and up to that date Al had earned $90,000 of annual salary and Courtney had earned $60,000. How much of the income earned by Al and by Courtney in the year of the divorce did Al report on his individual tax return? How much income did Courtney report on her individual tax return?

Answer: Because they resided in a common law state, Al reports the $90,000 that he earned through September (and all the income he earned through the end of the year) on his own return, and Courtney reports the entire $60,000 she earned through September (and all the income she earned through the rest of the year) on her own tax return.

What if: How much of this income would Al have been required to include on his individual tax return, and how much of this income would Courtney have been required to report on her individual tax return if they lived in California, a community property state?

Answer: If they resided in a community property state, both Al and Courtney would have included $75,000 of the $150,000 the couple had jointly earned through September [(Al's $90,000 + Courtney's $60,000)/2] on their respective individual tax returns. Whether they resided in a community property state or not, Al and Courtney also would have included on their respective individual tax returns the income they individually earned and received from October through December.

If a couple files a joint tax return, the community property rules do not affect the aggregate taxes payable by the couple, because the income of both spouses is aggregated on the return. However, when couples file separate tax returns, their combined tax liability may depend on whether they live in a common law state, a community property state that shares income from separate property equally between spouses, or a community property state that does not split income from separate property between spouses.[12]

TYPES OF INCOME

LO 5-2

Now that we have a basic understanding of the general definition of gross income and related concepts, let's turn our attention to specific *types* of income subject to taxation. Our discussion is organized around income from services, income from property, and other sources of income.

[12]§66 provides rules that allow spouses living apart in community property states to be taxed on his or her own income from services if (1) the taxpayers live apart for the entire year, (2) they do not file a joint tax return with each other, and (3) they do not transfer any of the income from services between each other.

Income from Services

Income from labor is one of the most common sources of gross income, and it is rarely exempt from taxation. Payments for services including salary, wages, and fees that a taxpayer earns through services in a nonemployee capacity are all considered income from services and so is unemployment compensation. Income from services is often referred to as **earned income** because it is generated by the efforts of the taxpayer (this also includes business income earned by a taxpayer even if the taxpayer's business is selling inventory).

Example 5-7

EWD pays Courtney a salary of $118,000. In addition, Courtney earned and received $19,500 of fees from consulting work she did on weekends independent of her employment with EWD. She incurred $1,500 of miscellaneous expenses for supplies and transportation while doing the consulting work. What is Courtney's *income* from services (earned income) from her employment and her self-employment activities?

Answer: $136,000, consisting of her $118,000 salary and her $19,500 business income from her consulting activities, less the $1,500 of expenses related to her consulting activities. Note that business deductions are *for* AGI deductions that taxpayers subtract from their gross business income to derive net business income or loss reported on page 1 of Form 1040. We discuss *for* AGI deductions in greater detail in the Individual Deductions chapter.

Income from Property

Income from property, often referred to as **unearned income,** may take different forms, such as gains or losses from the sale of property, dividends, interest, rents, royalties, and annuities.[13] The tax treatment of unearned income depends upon the type of income and, in some circumstances, the type of the transaction generating the income. For example, as discussed in the Individual Income Tax Overview, Exemptions, and Filing Status chapter, qualified dividends and long-term capital gains are taxed at preferential tax rates, whereas other unearned income is generally taxed at ordinary tax rates. Likewise, while gains or losses are typically recognized in the current period, certain types of gains and losses are postponed indefinitely. We discuss annuity income and property dispositions briefly in the following paragraphs. We discuss income from property in more detail in subsequent chapters.

Example 5-8

Courtney owns 1,000 shares of GE stock that she registered in a dividend reinvestment plan. Under this plan, all dividends are automatically used to purchase more shares of the stock. This year, GE declared and paid $700 in dividends on Courtney's stock. Must Courtney include the dividend in her gross income for the year?

Answer: Yes. Courtney includes the $700 of dividends (unearned income) in her gross income. The fact that Courtney chose to reinvest the dividends does not affect their taxability because she received an economic benefit and change in property rights associated with the dividend.

Example 5-9

Gram purchased a $100,000, three-year certificate of deposit (CD) with a portion of the life insurance proceeds she received on Gramps's death. At year-end, her CD account is credited with $4,100 of interest, and her savings account is credited with $300 of interest. Courtney had a total of $567 of interest credited to her savings account and $50 credited to her checking account during the year. How much interest must Gram and Courtney include in their gross income for the year?

[13]The tax definition of unearned income is different from the financial accounting definition. Unearned income for financial accounting purposes is a liability that represents advance payments for goods or services.

Answer: Gram must include the $4,100 of interest credited to her CD account and the $300 of interest credited to her savings account this year regardless of whether she withdraws the interest or not. Courtney must include the $567 of interest credited to her savings account and the $50 credited to her checking account regardless of whether she withdraws the interest or not.

Example 5-10

Courtney owns a condo in town that she rents to tenants. This year, the condo generated $14,000 of rental revenue. Courtney incurred $4,000 in real estate taxes, $2,500 in utility expenses, $500 in advertising expenses, and $2,000 of depreciation and other expenses associated with the rental. What effect does the rental have on Courtney's *gross income*? What effect does the rental have on Courtney's *taxable income*?

Answer: The rent increases Courtney's *gross income* by $14,000. However, after considering her allowable deductions for the rental, Courtney will report only $5,000 of *taxable income* from rental activities, computed as follows:

Description	Amount	
Rental revenue		$14,000
Less allowable deductions:		
Real estate taxes	(4,000)	
Utilities	(2,500)	
Advertising	(500)	
Depreciation and other expenses	(2,000)	
Total rental expenses		(9,000)
Net rental income		**$ 5,000**

Annuities An **annuity** is an investment that pays a stream of equal payments over time. Individuals often purchase annuities as a means of generating a fixed income stream during retirement. There are two basic types of annuities: (1) annuities paid over a fixed period and (2) annuities paid over a person's life (for as long as the person lives). The challenge from a tax perspective is to determine how much of each annuity payment represents gross income (income taxed at ordinary tax rates) and how much represents a nontaxable *return of capital* (return of the original investment). For both types of annuities, the tax law deems a *portion* of each annuity payment as a nontaxable return of capital and the remainder as gross income. Taxpayers use the *annuity exclusion ratio* to determine the portion of each payment that is a nontaxable return of capital.

$$\text{Annuity exclusion ratio} = \frac{\text{Original investment}}{\text{Expected value of annuity}} = \text{Return of capital percentage}$$

For fixed annuities, the expected value is the number of payments times the amount of the payment. In other words, for an annuity payable over a fixed term, the return of capital is simply the original investment divided by the number of payments. The number of payments, however, is uncertain for annuities paid over a person's life. For these annuities, taxpayers must use IRS tables to determine the expected value based upon the taxpayer's life expectancy at the start of the annuity.[14]

[14]See Reg. §1.72-9. Special rules under §72(d) apply to annuities from qualified retirement plans. These rules only apply when a taxpayer makes an after-tax contribution to a qualified employer retirement plan (which is uncommon). In most cases, taxpayers only make pretax contributions to qualified retirement plans, which results in fully taxable annuity distributions.

To calculate the expected value of the annuity, the number of annual payments from the table (referred to as the expected return multiple) is multiplied by the annual payment amount. Taxpayers with an annuity paid over the life of one person (a single-life annuity) use the expected return multiple from the table, a portion of which is presented in Exhibit 5-1.

EXHIBIT 5-1 Table for Expected Return Multiple for Ordinary Single-Life Annuity

Age at Annuity Starting Date	Expected Return Multiple
68	17.6
69	16.8
70	16.0
71	15.3
72	14.6

Some annuities provide payments over the lives of two people. For example, a taxpayer may purchase an annuity that provides an annual payment each year until both the taxpayer *and* the taxpayer's spouse pass away. This type of annuity is called a joint-life annuity. The IRS provides a separate table for determining the expected number of payments from joint-life annuities.

A taxpayer receiving a life annuity who lives longer than his or her estimated life expectancy will ultimately receive more than the expected number of payments. The entire amount of these "extra" payments is included in the taxpayer's gross income because the taxpayer has completely recovered her investment in the annuity by the time she receives them. If the taxpayer dies *before* receiving the expected number of payments, the amount of the unrecovered investment (the initial investment less the amounts received, which is treated as a nontaxable return of capital) is deducted on the taxpayer's final income tax return.[15]

Example 5-11

In January of this year, Gram purchased an annuity from UBET Insurance Co. that will pay her $10,000 per year for the next 15 years. Gram received the first $10,000 payment in December. Gram paid $99,000 for the annuity and will receive $150,000 over the life of the annuity (15 years × $10,000 per year). How much of the $10,000 payment received by Gram in December should she include in her gross income?

Answer: $3,400. Because Gram purchased a fixed-payment annuity, the portion of the annuity payment included in gross income is calculated as follows:

Description	Amount	Explanation
(1) Investment in annuity contract	$99,000	
(2) Number of payments	15	
(3) Return of capital per payment	$ 6,600	(1)/(2)
(4) Amount of each payment:	$10,000	
Gross income per payment	**$ 3,400**	(4) – (3)

What if: Assume the annuity Gram purchased pays her $1,000 per month over the remainder of her life. Gram (70 years old) paid $99,000 for the annuity, and she received her first $1,000 payment in December of this year. How much income would she recognize on the $1,000 payment?

[15]The unrecovered cost of the annuity is deducted as a miscellaneous itemized deduction not subject to the 2 percent of AGI floor. See §72(b)(3) and §67(b)(10).

Answer: $484.40, computed as follows:

Description	Amount	Explanation
(1) Investment in annuity contract	$ 99,000	
(2) Expected return multiple	16	Exhibit 5-1, 70 years old
(3) Amount of each payment	$ 1,000	
(4) Expected return	$192,000	(2) × (3) × 12 months
(5) Return of capital percentage	51.56%	(1)/(4)
(6) Return of capital per payment	$ 515.60	(3) × (5)
Taxable income per payment	**$ 484.40**	(3) – (6)

After Gram receives her entire $99,000 as a return of capital, each subsequent $1,000 annuity payment would be fully taxable.

Property Dispositions Taxpayers can realize a gain or loss when disposing of an asset. Consistent with the return of capital principle we discussed above, taxpayers are allowed to recover their investment in property (tax basis) before they realize any gain. A loss is realized when the proceeds are less than the tax basis in the property. Because the return of capital principle generally applies only to the extent of the sale proceeds, a loss does not necessarily reduce the taxpayer's taxable income. A loss will only reduce the taxpayer's taxable income if the loss is deductible. Exhibit 5-2 presents a general formula for computing the gain or loss from a sale of an asset.

THE KEY FACTS

Return of Capital

- Taxpayers are allowed to recover the capital invested in property tax-free.
- Payments from purchased annuities are part income and part return of capital.
- When property is sold or disposed of, the realized gain or loss equals the sale proceeds reduced by the tax basis of the property.

EXHIBIT 5-2 Formula for Calculating Gain (Loss) from Sale of an Asset

Sales proceeds
Less: Selling expenses
= Amount realized
Less: Tax basis (investment) in property sold
= Gain (loss) on sale

The rate at which taxpayers are taxed on *gains* from property dispositions and the extent to which they can deduct *losses* from property dispositions depends on whether the taxpayer used the asset for business purposes, investment purposes, or personal purposes. For example, as we discussed in the Individual Income Tax Overview, Exemptions, and Filing Status chapter, long-term capital gains realized by individuals are taxed at preferential tax rates, and deductions for net capital losses realized by individuals are limited to $3,000 per year. In contrast, losses realized on assets used for personal purposes are generally not deductible. We discuss specific rules associated with property dispositions in the Investments and Property Dispositions chapters.

Example 5-12

On December 31, Gram sold her 50 shares of Acme Corporation stock for $40 per share. Gram also paid $150 in broker's commissions on the sale. Gram originally purchased the shares in April of this year for $30 per share. How much gross income does Gram recognize from the stock sale?

Answer: Gram recognizes $350 gross income on the sale, computed as follows:

Sales proceeds ($40 × 50 shares)	$2,000
Less: Selling expenses	−150
= Amount realized	$1,850
Less: Tax basis (investment) in property sold ($30 × 50 shares)	−1,500
Gain (loss) on sale	**$ 350**

Other Sources of Gross Income

Taxpayers may receive income from sources other than their efforts (earned income from wages or business) and their property (unearned income such as dividends and interest). In this section we briefly summarize other common types of gross income. If by chance you encounter other types of income that are not specifically discussed here, remember that the tax law is based upon the all-inclusive income concept. That is, unless a specific provision grants exclusion or deferral, economic benefits that are realized generate gross income. This basic understanding of the structure of our tax law (and research skills to investigate the taxability of specific income types) will serve you well as you evaluate whether realized income should be included in gross income.

Income from Flow-Through Entities Individuals may invest in various business entities. The legal form of the business affects how the income generated by the business is taxed. For example, income earned by a corporation (other than an S corporation) is taxed at the entity level as opposed to the owner level. In contrast, the income and deductions from a **flow-through entity,** such as a partnership or S corporation (a corporation electing S corporation status), "flow through" to the owners of the entity (partners or shareholders). That is, the owners report income or deductions as though they operated a portion of the business personally. Specifically, each partner or S corporation shareholder reports his or her share of the entity's income and deductions, generally in proportion to his or her ownership percentage, on his or her individual tax return.[16]

Because different types of income and deductions may be treated differently for tax purposes (e.g., qualified dividends are eligible for a special low tax rate), each item the partners or shareholders report on their tax returns retains its underlying tax characteristics. That is, the partners are treated as if they personally received their share of each item of the flow-through entity's income. For example, corporate dividend income paid to a partnership is reported and taxed as dividend income on the partners' individual tax returns. Also, it is important to note that owners of flow-through entities are taxed on their share of the entity's income whether or not cash is distributed to them. When owners receive cash distributions from the entity, the distributions are generally treated as a return of capital to the extent of their investment (tax basis) in the entity and, therefore, are not included in the owner's gross income. Distributions in excess of basis are taxable. Partnerships and S corporations report to each partner or shareholder that partner's or shareholder's share of partnership and S corporation income (or loss) on Schedule K-1, which is filed with the partnership and S corporation's annual information returns (Form 1065 and 1120S, respectively).[17]

Example 5-13

What if: Suppose that Courtney is a 40 percent partner in KJZ partnership. KJZ reported $20,000 of business income and $3,000 of interest income for the year. KJZ also distributed $1,000 of cash to Courtney. What amount of gross income from her ownership in KJZ partnership would Courtney report for the current year?

Answer: $9,200, consisting of $8,000 of business income ($20,000 × 40%) and $1,200 of interest income ($3,000 × 40%). Courtney would not include the $1,000 distribution in her gross income because it was a return of her investment.

Alimony When couples legally separate or divorce, one spouse may be required to provide financial support to the other in the form of **alimony.** The tax law defines alimony as (1) a transfer of *cash* made under a written separation agreement or divorce decree and stipulates that (2) the separation or divorce decree does not designate the payment as

[16]The deduction of losses from partnerships and S corporations are subject to several limitations that we discuss in the Investments chapter.

[17]See Forms 1065 and 1120S on the IRS website, www.irs.gov.

something other than alimony, (3) in the case of legally separated (or divorced) taxpayers under a separation or divorce decree, the spouses do not live together when the payment is made, and (4) the payments cannot continue after the death of the recipient.[18]

For tax purposes, a transfer between former spouses represents alimony only if it meets this definition. If the payment is alimony, then the amount of the payment is included in the gross income of the person receiving it and is deductible *for* AGI by the person paying it. Thus, alimony shifts income from one spouse to the other.

Example 5-14

In addition to paying child support, under the divorce decree Al is required to pay Courtney $20,000 cash each year until she dies. The decree does not designate the payment as a payment for something other than alimony, and Al and Courtney do not live together. Does this payment qualify as alimony?

Answer: Yes. These payments qualify as alimony for tax purposes because they are (1) cash payments made under a divorce decree, (2) the payments are not designated as something other than alimony, (3) Al and Courtney do not live together, and (4) the payments cease on Courtney's death. In the current year, Al made a $20,000 alimony payment to Courtney. Courtney includes all $20,000 in her gross income. To ensure that the income is taxed only once, Al is allowed to deduct the entire payment as a deduction *for* AGI.

There may be other types of payments that *do not qualify as alimony*. These include (1) property divisions (e.g., who gets the car, house, or china?) and (2) child support payments fixed by the divorce or separation agreement.[19] In any event, if a transfer of property between spouses does *not* meet the definition of alimony, the *recipient* of the transfer *excludes* the value of the transfer from income, and the person transferring the property is not allowed to deduct the value of the property transferred.

Example 5-15

As required by the divorce decree, Al made $10,000 in child support payments during the year to Courtney to help her support Deron. Al is required to make child support payments until Deron is 18 years old. Is the current-year payment considered alimony?

Answer: No. The $10,000 of child support payments are not income to Courtney. The payments are not alimony because the divorce decree specifies that the payments are for child support. Consequently, Courtney does not include these payments in gross income, and Al does not deduct them.

The objective definition of alimony eliminates uncertainty regarding which transfers are treated as alimony. However, it creates a second problem. Since the purpose of the transfer is irrelevant to the tax consequences, it is possible to use alimony transfers to assign income from the (higher tax rate) payer of the alimony to the (lower tax rate) recipient. For example, instead of transferring ownership of an asset to the recipient as a nondeductible/nontaxable property settlement, the payer could claim an alimony deduction by making a transfer that meets the alimony requirements. The spouses can share the tax savings from this transaction if they can agree on structuring the payments to qualify as alimony (although cooperation may be a little difficult for a couple going through a divorce). To address this tax-avoidance opportunity, Congress enacted a complex set of restrictions called the *anti-front loading* rules that make it difficult for taxpayers to disguise property payments as alimony payments. In general terms, when taxpayers attempt to disguise property payments as alimony payments (large alimony payments shortly after the divorce, followed by smaller alimony payments in subsequent years), the tax laws

[18]§71(b). In addition, certain payments to third parties on behalf of the spouse, such as mortgage payments, can also qualify as payments in cash.

[19]§71(c). A payment that is not specifically designated as child support may nonetheless be treated as child support if the payment is reduced on the happening of a specific contingency related to the child. For example, a payment that ceases once a child reaches the age of 18 would be treated as child support.

may require the taxpayers to recharacterize (or "recapture") part of the alimony payments as nondeductible property transfers.[20]

Example 5-16

As part of the divorce agreement, Al transferred his interest in their joint residence to Courtney. The couple did not have any outstanding debt on the home. At the time of the divorce, the home was valued at $500,000 and Al's share was valued at $250,000. What are the tax consequences of the home ownership transfer to Courtney?

Answer: Because the transfer is not a cash transfer, it does not qualify as alimony. Consequently, Courtney does not recognize the $250,000 as income, and Al is not allowed to deduct the $250,000 transfer.

What if: Assume that Al's marginal tax rate is 35 percent and Courtney's marginal tax rate is 15 percent. To generate tax savings, in lieu of transferring his share of the ownership in the home, Al and Courtney agreed that Al would make a $250,000 cash transfer to Courtney. The divorce agreement stipulated that this payment was alimony. What are Al and Courtney trying to accomplish under this arrangement? Will they be successful?

Answer: They are trying to convert a property payment into alimony that is deductible by Al (at a high tax rate) and includable in Courtney's income (at a lower tax rate). As we discussed above, under a complex set of alimony recapture rules, it is likely that a portion of this payment will be treated as a nonalimony property settlement.

Prizes, Awards, and Gambling Winnings Prizes, awards, and gambling winnings, such as raffle or sweepstakes prizes or lottery winnings, are included in gross income.

Example 5-17

After devoting much of her free time during the year to filling out sweepstakes entries, Gram hit the jackpot. She won a WaveRunner worth $7,500 in a sweepstakes sponsored by *Reader's Digest.* How much of the prize, if any, must Gram include in her gross income?

Answer: Gram must include the full $7,500 value of the WaveRunner in her gross income. Note that because she must pay taxes on the winnings, she's not really getting the WaveRunner for "free."

There are three specific, narrowly defined exceptions to this rule. First, awards for scientific, literary, or charitable achievement such as the Nobel Prize are excluded from gross income, *but only if* (1) the recipient was selected without any action on his part to enter the contest or proceeding, (2) the recipient is not required to render substantial future services as a condition to receive the prize or award, and (3) the payer of the prize or award transfers the prize or award to a federal, state, or local governmental unit or qualified charity such as a church, school, or charitable organization designated by the taxpayer.[21] The obvious downside of this exception is that the award recipient does not actually get to receive or keep the cash from the award. However, for tax purposes it is more beneficial for the recipient to exclude the award from income entirely by immediately transferring it to a charitable organization than it is to receive the award, recognize the income, and then contribute funds to a charity for a charitable deduction. Designating the award for payment to a federal, state, or local governmental unit or qualified charity has the same effect as claiming the transfer as a deduction *for* AGI. However, by receiving the award, recognizing the income, and then contributing funds to a charity, the taxpayer is deducting the donation as a deduction *from* AGI. As we discussed in the Individual Income Tax Overview, Exemptions, and Filing Status chapter, deductions *for* AGI are likely more advantageous than deductions *from* AGI.

[20]These rules apply when alimony decreases by more than $15,000 between years 1 and 2, or between years 2 and 3 after the divorce. See §71(f) for details.

[21]§74(b).

The second exception is for employee *awards for length of service or safety achievement.*[22] These nontaxable awards are limited to $400 of tangible property *other than cash* per employee per year.[23] The award is not excluded from the employee's income if circumstances suggest it is disguised compensation.[24]

The third narrowly defined exception is for the value of any awards (medals) and prize money received by Team USA athletes from the U.S. Olympic Committee on account of competition in the Olympic and Paralympic games. While there is no limit on the exclusion amount, the exclusion does *not* apply to a taxpayer for any year in which the taxpayer's AGI (after excluding the award) exceeds $1 million ($500,000 for a married individual filing a separate return).[25]

TAXES IN THE REAL WORLD You Get a Car! And You Get a Car!

Remember when Oprah gave out cars like other people give out refrigerator magnets and foam cup holders? Audience members were thrilled with her generosity—until they realized that they had to pay income tax on their newfound luck. That's because there's literally no such thing as a free lunch—unless that lunch is served up with a heap of exceptions that make the IRS happy.

So in her last go-round, Oprah had her ducks in a row. When she gave her entire audience an all-expenses-paid trip to Australia in honor of her 25th and final season, she really meant *all* expenses. Including taxes. A CPA was said to be waiting in the wings to settle all of the tax issues associated with the trip. Reportedly, Oprah took care of paying the taxes associated with the fabulous prize.

Source: Kelly Phillips Erb, "The Oprah of Oz," TaxGirl .com, September 18, 2010. Copyright © 2010 by Kelly Phillips Erb. Used with permission.

Taxpayers must include the *gross* amount of their gambling winnings for the year in gross income.[26] Taxpayers are allowed to deduct their gambling losses to the extent of their gambling winnings, but the losses are usually deductible as miscellaneous itemized deductions.[27] For professional gamblers, however, the losses are deductible (to the extent of gambling winnings) *for* AGI.

ETHICS

While vacationing you find a $100 bill on the beach. Nobody saw you find it. Assuming the find meets the definition of gross income, would you report it as taxable income? Why or why not? Would your answer differ if you found $100,000 instead of $100?

Social Security Benefits Over the last 40 years, the taxation of Social Security benefits has changed considerably. Forty years ago, Social Security benefits were completely excluded from income. Today, taxpayers may be required to include *up to* 85 percent of the benefits in gross income *depending* on the amount of the taxpayer's filing status, Social Security benefits, and *modified* AGI.[28] Modified AGI is regular AGI (excluding Social

[22]Prizes or awards from an employer-sponsored contest are fully taxable.

[23]§74(c).

[24]The $400 limit is increased to $1,600 for qualified award plans (written plans that do not discriminate in favor of highly compensated employees). However, the *average* cost of all qualified plan awards from an employer is limited to $400. Managers, administrators, clerical employees, or professional employees are not eligible for an exclusion for a safety award.

[25]§74(d).

[26]Subject to de minimis rules, payers of gambling winnings report winnings to recipients and the IRS on Form W-2G.

[27]See Rev. Rul. 83-130, 1983-2 CB 148.

[28]§86(d) applies to monthly benefits under title II of the Social Security Act and tier 1 railroad retirement benefits. The Social Security Administration reports Social Security benefits on Form SSA-1099.

Security benefits) plus tax-exempt interest income, excluded foreign income (discussed later in the chapter), and certain other deductions *for* AGI.[29] The calculation of the amount of Social Security benefits to be included in income is depicted on the IRS worksheet in the appendix at the end of this chapter.[30] The calculation is complex, to say the least. However, the taxability of Social Security benefits can be summarized as follows:

Single taxpayers:

1. If modified AGI + 50 percent of Social Security benefits ≤ $25,000, Social Security benefits are not taxable.
2. If $25,000 < modified AGI + 50 percent of Social Security benefits ≤ $34,000, taxable Social Security benefits are the lesser of (a) 50 percent of the Social Security benefits or (b) 50 percent of (modified AGI + 50 percent of Social Security benefits − $25,000).
3. If modified AGI + 50 percent of Social Security benefits > $34,000, taxable Social Security benefits are the lesser of (a) 85 percent of Social Security benefits or (b) 85 percent of (modified AGI + 50 percent of Social Security benefits − $34,000), plus the lesser of (1) $4,500 or (2) 50 percent of Social Security benefits.

Taxpayers filing married separate:

Taxable Social Security benefits are the lesser of (a) 85 percent of the Social Security benefits or (b) 85 percent of the taxpayer's modified AGI + 50 percent of Social Security benefits.

Taxpayers filing married joint:

1. If modified AGI + 50 percent of Social Security benefits ≤ $32,000, Social Security benefits are not taxable.
2. If $32,000 < modified AGI + 50 percent of Social Security benefits ≤ $44,000, taxable Social Security benefits are the lesser of (a) 50 percent of the Social Security benefits or (b) 50 percent of (modified AGI + 50 percent of Social Security benefits − $32,000).
3. If modified AGI + 50 percent of Social Security benefits > $44,000, taxable Social Security benefits are the lesser of (a) 85 percent of Social Security benefits or (b) 85 percent of (modified AGI + 50 percent of Social Security benefits − $44,000), plus the lesser of (1) $6,000 or (2) 50 percent of Social Security benefits.

The implications of the above calculations are that the Social Security benefits of taxpayers with relatively low taxable income are not taxable and that 85 percent of the Social Security benefits of taxpayers with moderate to high taxable income are taxable.

Example 5-18

Gram received $7,200 of Social Security benefits this year. Suppose that Gram's modified AGI is $16,000. What amount of the Social Security benefits must Gram include in her gross income?

Answer: $0. Gram's modified AGI plus one-half of her Social Security benefits is $19,600 [$16,000 modified AGI + ($7,200 Social Security benefits × 50%)], which is below $25,000. Hence, Gram may *exclude* the entire $7,200 of Social Security income from gross income.

What if: Assume that Gram received $7,200 of Social Security benefits this year and that her modified AGI is $50,000. What amount of benefits must Gram include in her gross income?

Answer: $6,120 ($7,200 × 85%).

What if: Assume that Gram received $7,200 of Social Security benefits this year and that her modified AGI is $26,400. What amount of benefits must Gram include in her gross income?

Answer: $2,500. Gram is single and her modified AGI + 50 percent of Social Security benefits falls between $25,000 and $34,000. Her taxable Social Security benefits are the lesser of (a) 50 percent of the Social Security benefits ($7,200 × 50% = $3,600) or (b) 50 percent of [$26,400 modified AGI + $3,600

[29]See §86(b)(2).

[30]Because the 2017 worksheet was not available at the time the book went to press, we include the 2016 worksheet in the appendix at the end of the chapter. The 2016 worksheet can be used to determine the taxable portion of Social Security benefits received in 2017.

(50 percent of Social Security benefits) – $25,000] = $2,500. Thus, her taxable Social Security benefits are $2,500.

What if: Assume that Gram received $7,200 of Social Security benefits this year and that her modified AGI is $31,400. What amount of benefits must Gram include in her gross income?

Answer: $4,450. Gram is single and her modified AGI + 50 percent of Social Security benefits exceeds $34,000. Her taxable Social Security benefits are the lesser of (a) 85 percent of Social Security benefits ($7,200 × 85% = $6,120) or (b) 85 percent of [$31,400 modified AGI + $3,600 (50 percent of Social Security benefits) – $34,000] = $850, plus the lesser of (1) $4,500 or (2) 50 percent of Social Security benefits (50% × $7,200 = $3,600). This calculation simplifies to the lesser of (a) $6,120 or (b) $4,450 [$850 + lesser of (1) $4,500 or (2) $3,600]. Thus, Gram's taxable Social Security benefits are $4,450.

Imputed Income Besides realizing *direct* economic benefits like wages and interest, taxpayers sometimes realize *indirect* economic benefits that they must include in gross income as **imputed income.** Bargain purchases (such as an employer selling a good to an employee at a discount) and below-market loans (such as an employer lending an employee money at a zero or unusually low interest rate) are two common examples of taxable indirect economic benefits. Both bargain purchases and below-market loans generally result in gross income if the purchase or loan transaction takes place between related parties (such as an employer and employee, owner and entity, or transactions among family members). For bargain purchases, the general rule is that the discount received on the purchase from a related party is taxable, but the tax consequences vary based on the relationship of the parties. For example, a bargain purchase by an employee from an employer results in taxable compensation income to the employee, a bargain purchase by a shareholder from a corporation results in a taxable dividend to the shareholder, and a bargain purchase between family members is deemed to be a gift from one family member to the other (as discussed later in the chapter, gifts are nontaxable for income tax purposes but potentially subject to gift tax to be paid by the person making the gift).

Although the general rule is that bargain purchases by an employee from an employer create taxable compensation income to the employee, the tax law does provide a limited exclusion for employee bargain purchases. Specifically, employees may exclude (a) a discount on employer-provided goods as long as the discount does not exceed the employer's gross profit percentage on all property offered for sale to customers and (b) up to 20 percent employer-provided discounts on services. Discounts in excess of these amounts are taxable as compensation.[31]

Example 5-19

As part of her compensation package, EWD agreed to provide Courtney with EWD architectural design services (to create more space for Gram) at a substantial discount. EWD provided Courtney with services valued at $35,000 but charged her only $22,000 for the services. How much of the discount must Courtney include in gross income?

Answer: $6,000, computed as follows:

Description	Amount	Explanation
(1) Value of services EWD provided to Courtney	$35,000	
(2) Courtney's cost of the services	22,000	
(3) Discount on services	$13,000	(1) – (2)
(4) Excludable discount	7,000	(1) × 20%
Discount in excess of 20% is included in gross income	**$ 6,000**	(3) – (4)

For below-market loans, the indirect economic benefit conveyed to the borrower (such as an employee, shareholder, or family member) is a function of the amount of the loan and the difference in the market interest rate and the rate actually charged by the lender (such as an employer, corporation, or family member). To eliminate any tax

[31]§132(a)(2).

advantages of below-market loans, the tax law generally requires the lender and borrower to treat the transaction as if:

1. The borrower paid the lender the difference between the applicable federal interest rate (compounded semiannually) and the actual interest paid (this difference is called *imputed interest*).
2. The lender then returned the imputed interest to the borrower.

The deemed "payment" of the imputed interest in these transactions is treated as interest income to the lender and interest expense to the borrower. The deductibility of the interest expense for the borrower depends on how she used the loan proceeds (for business, investment, or personal purposes). As we learn in the next chapter, business interest expense is a deduction *for* AGI, investment interest expense is an itemized deduction subject to limitations, and personal interest is generally not deductible. The tax consequences of the "return" of the imputed interest from the lender to the borrower vary based on the relationship of the parties (similar to a bargain purchase). For example, the return of the imputed interest from an employer lender to an employee borrower is treated by both parties as taxable compensation paid to the employee, the return of the imputed interest from a corporation to a shareholder is considered a dividend, and a return of imputed interest by a family member to another family member is considered a gift. The imputed interest rules generally do not apply to aggregate loans of $10,000 or less between the lender and borrower [§7872(c)].[32]

Example 5-20

At the beginning of January, EWD provides Courtney with a $100,000 zero-interest loan. Assume that the applicable federal interest rate (compounded semiannually) is 4 percent. Courtney used the loan proceeds to acquire several personal-use assets (an automobile and other items). What amount is Courtney required to include in gross income in the current year?

Answer: $4,000, computed as follows:

Description	Amount	Explanation
(1) Loan principal	$100,000	
(2) Applicable federal interest rate compounded semiannually	4%	
(3) Interest on loan principal at federal rate	$ 4,000	(1) × (2)
(4) Interest paid by Courtney	0	
Imputed interest included in Courtney's gross income	**$ 4,000**	(3) − (4)

Courtney will include the $4,000 imputed interest in gross income as compensation and will also incur an imputed interest expense of $4,000 for the year. EWD will (a) deduct $4,000 of compensation expense and (b) report $4,000 of interest income. In this example, we assume Courtney used the proceeds for personal purposes so she is not allowed to deduct the interest expense.

What if: Assume the same facts except that EWD had loaned Courtney $10,000 at a zero-interest rate. How much imputed interest income would Courtney be required to include in her gross income for the year?

Answer: $0. The imputed interest rules don't apply because the loan did not exceed $10,000.

THE KEY FACTS

Other Sources of Income

- Alimony is taxable to the recipient when paid in cash, pursuant to written agreement or decree, the spouses do not live together, and the payment is contingent on the life of the recipient.
- Awards are included in gross income unless they meet one of three narrowly defined exceptions.
- A maximum of 85 percent of Social Security benefits are included in gross income depending on level of AGI.
- Discharge of debt is included in gross income unless the taxpayer is insolvent before and after forgiveness.

Discharge of Indebtedness In general, when a taxpayer's debt is forgiven by a lender (the debt is discharged), the taxpayer must include the amount of debt relief in gross income.[33]

[32]For "gift" loans (loans between family members), the $10,000 de minimis exception is not available for loan proceeds used to purchase or carry income-producing assets. Likewise, the $10,000 de minimis exception is not available for compensation-related loans or corporate-shareholder loans where the principal purpose of the loans is to avoid federal tax. For gift loans of $100,000 or less, the imputed interest is limited to the borrower's net investment income (investment income, such as interest income or other investment income not taxed at preferential rates, less related investment expenses). If the borrower's net investment income is $1,000 or less, the imputed interest rules do not apply. §7872(d). The exception for gift loans of $100,000 or less is not available for loans where the principal purpose of the loans is to avoid federal tax.

[33]§61(a)(12). Income from discharge of indebtedness is also realized when debt is forgiven by lenders other than employers such as banks and credit card companies.

To provide tax relief for insolvent taxpayers—taxpayers with liabilities, including tax liabilities, exceeding their assets—a **discharge of indebtedness** is *not* taxable if the taxpayer is insolvent before *and* after the debt forgiveness.[34] If the discharge of indebtedness makes the taxpayer solvent, the taxpayer recognizes gross income to the extent of his solvency.[35] For example, if a taxpayer is discharged of $30,000 of debt and this causes him to be solvent by $10,000 (after the debt relief, the taxpayer's assets exceed his liabilities by $10,000), the taxpayer must include $10,000 in gross income.[36]

Example 5-21

In the previous example, Courtney borrowed $100,000 from EWD. Because EWD wants to keep Courtney as an employee, it agreed to forgive $10,000 of loan principal at the end of each year that Courtney stays on board. On December 31 of this year, EWD formally cancels $10,000 of Courtney's indebtedness. How much of this debt relief is Courtney required to include in gross income?

Answer: All $10,000 is included in Courtney's gross income.

EXCLUSION PROVISIONS

LO 5-3

So far in this chapter, we've discussed various types of income taxpayers must realize and recognize by reporting it on their tax returns in the current year. However, there are specific types of income that taxpayers realize but are allowed to permanently *exclude* from gross income or temporarily defer from gross income until a subsequent period. As we discussed in the previous chapter, *exclusions* and *deferrals* are the result of *specific congressional action* and are *narrowly defined*. Because taxpayers are not required to recognize income that is excluded or deferred, we refer to tax laws allowing exclusions or deferrals as **nonrecognition provisions.** Nonrecognition provisions result from various policy objectives. In very general terms, Congress allows most exclusions and deferrals for two primary reasons: (1) to subsidize or encourage particular activities or (2) to be fair to taxpayers (such as mitigating the inequity of double taxation). Our discussion in this chapter focuses on exclusions.

Common Exclusions

Because exclusion provisions allow taxpayers to permanently remove certain income items from their tax base, they are particularly taxpayer friendly. We begin by introducing three common exclusion provisions, the exclusions of municipal interest, gain on the sale of a personal residence, and fringe benefits. We continue with a survey of other exclusion provisions based on their underlying purpose: education, double taxation, and sickness and injury.[37]

Municipal Interest The most common example of an exclusion provision is the exclusion of interest on **municipal bonds.** Municipal bonds include bonds issued by state and local governments located in the United States, and this exclusion is generally recognized as a subsidy to state and local governments (the exclusion allows state and local

[34]§108(a)(1)(B).

[35]§108(a)(3).

[36]Other circumstances in which taxpayers may exclude a discharge of indebtedness are beyond the scope of this chapter. See §108(f)(2) for discussion of the limited exclusion of student loan forgiveness for loans requiring students to work for a specified time in certain professions. See §108(a)(1)(E) for discussion of the exclusion of up to $2,000,000 of home mortgage forgiveness from 2007 through 2016. See §108(i) for a discussion for the deferral of debt forgiveness income for businesses reacquiring debt at a discounted price in 2009 and 2010. This provision allows taxpayer to recognize the debt forgiveness income ratably over the five-year period 2014 through 2018.

[37]Another common exclusion we discuss in detail in the Retirement Savings and Deferred Compensation chapter is the exclusion of earnings on Roth retirement savings accounts.

governments to offer bonds at a lower before-tax interest rate). In contrast, interest on U.S. government obligations (such as Treasury bills) is taxable for federal tax purposes but is tax-exempt for state and local tax purposes.

Example 5-22

Courtney holds a $10,000 City of Cincinnati municipal bond. The bond pays 5 percent interest annually. Courtney acquired the bond a few years ago. The city used the proceeds from the bond issuance to help pay for renovations on a major league baseball stadium. In late December, Courtney received $500 of interest income from the bond for the year. How much of the $500 interest from the municipal bond may Courtney *exclude* from her gross income?

Answer: All $500 because the interest is from a municipal bond.

Gains on the Sale of Personal Residence The tax law provides several provisions that encourage or subsidize home ownership, and the exclusion of the gain on the sale of a personal residence is a common example of one such provision. Specifically, taxpayers meeting certain home ownership *and* use requirements can permanently exclude up to $250,000 ($500,000 if married filing jointly) of realized gain on the sale of their principal residence.[38] Gain in excess of the excludable amount generally qualifies as long-term capital gain subject to tax at preferential rates. To satisfy the ownership test, the taxpayer must have owned the residence (house, condominium, trailer, or houseboat) for a total of two or more years during the five-year period ending on the date of the sale. To satisfy the use test, the taxpayer must have *used* the property as her principal residence for a total of two or more years (noncontiguous use is permissible) during the five-year period ending on the date of the sale. The tax law limits each taxpayer to one exclusion every two years. Married couples filing joint returns are eligible for the full $500,000 exclusion if *either* spouse meets the ownership test and *both* spouses meet the principal-use test. However, if *either* spouse is ineligible for the exclusion because he or she personally used the $250,000 exclusion on another home sale during the two years before the date of the current sale, the couple's available exclusion is reduced to $250,000.[39]

Example 5-23

What if: Assume that in October of this year, Courtney sold her prior home in Cincinnati. Courtney and her ex-husband purchased the home four years ago for $400,000, and Courtney received the house in the divorce. Courtney lived in the home until she moved to Kansas City in January. Courtney sold the home for $550,000. How much taxable gain does she recognize on the sale of the home?

Answer: $0. Because Courtney satisfies the two-year ownership and two-year use test, she may exclude up to $250,000 of gain from the sale of her home. Thus, Courtney may exclude the entire $150,000 gain that she realized on the sale ($550,000 sales price less $400,000 basis).

What if: Assume the same facts except Courtney sold the home for $700,000. How much taxable gain does she recognize on the sale of the home?

Answer: $50,000. Because Courtney satisfies the two-year ownership and two-year use test, she may exclude $250,000 of the $300,000 gain from the sale of her home ($700,000 sales price less $400,000 basis). Thus, Courtney recognizes a $50,000 taxable gain on the sale.

[38]§121.

[39]We discuss the rules for sale of principal residence in more detail in the Tax Consequence of Home Ownership chapter, including relief rules for taxpayers who cannot meet the ownership and use test due to unusual or hardship circumstances and the limitation on the gain exclusion for taxpayers using a home for something other than a principal residence for a period (nonqualified use) before using the home as a principal residence.

Fringe Benefits In addition to paying salary and wages, many employers provide employees with **fringe benefits.** For example, an employer may provide an employee with an automobile to use for personal purposes, pay for an employee to join a health club, or pay for an employee's home security. In general, the value of these benefits is *included* in the employee's gross income as compensation for services. However, certain fringe benefits, called "qualifying" fringe benefits, are excluded from gross income.[40] Exhibit 5-3 lists some of the most common fringe benefits that are excluded from an employee's gross income. In addition to excluded fringe benefits, many employers make contributions to retirement plans on behalf of their employees. Subject to specific rules that we discuss in the Retirement Savings and Deferred Compensation chapter, these contributions (as well as employee contributions from salary) are not currently included in the employee's gross income but are deferred until the employee withdraws the contributions and related earnings from the plan. We discuss fringe benefits in more depth in the Compensation chapter.

Example 5-24

EWD paid $6,000 this year for Courtney's health insurance premiums and $150 in premiums for her $40,000 group-term life insurance policy. How much of the $6,150 in benefits can Courtney exclude from her gross income?

Answer: Courtney can exclude all $6,150 in benefits from her gross income. All health insurance premiums paid by an employer on an employee's behalf are excluded from the employee's income. In addition, premiums employers pay on an employee's behalf for group-term life insurance (up to $50,000 of coverage) are also excluded from the employee's gross income.

Example 5-25

In December, Courtney mailed a newsletter to several dozen friends and relatives with a recent picture of her son, daughter, and mother. Courtney printed both the newsletter and the photos on printers at work (with permission of EWD). Courtney would have paid $55 for the duplicate newsletters and photos at a nearby copy center. How much of this $55 benefit that Courtney received from EWD may Courtney *exclude* from her gross income?

Answer: All $55 is excluded. The $55 benefit is considered a nontaxable de minimis fringe benefit because it is small in amount and infrequent.

TAXES IN THE REAL WORLD Have Phone, Will Call Tax-Free

In years past, the IRS classified employee cell phones issued by employers as a taxable benefit (i.e., taxable compensation) and required employees to keep detailed records to substantiate business versus personal use of the phone. As you might expect, the classification and record-keeping requirements were not met with great enthusiasm. In 2011, the IRS reversed its course and now considers an employer-issued cell phone as an excludible fringe benefit (both for business and personal use) when the phone is provided primarily for noncompensatory business reasons. Even better, the IRS no longer requires record keeping to receive the tax-free treatment. See Notice 2011-72.

[40]Most nontaxable fringe benefits are listed with "items specifically excluded from gross income" in §§101–140 of the Internal Revenue Code. Employers are generally prohibited from discriminating among employees with respect to nontaxable fringe benefits (i.e., they cannot offer them only to executives).

EXHIBIT 5-3 Common Qualifying Fringe Benefits (excluded from employee's gross income)

Item	Description
Medical and dental health insurance coverage [§106]	An employee may exclude from income the cost of medical and insurance coverage and dental health insurance premiums the employer pays on an employee's behalf.[41]
Life insurance coverage [§79]	Employees may exclude from income the value of life insurance premiums the employer pays on an employee's behalf for up to $50,000 of group-term life insurance.
De minimis (small) benefits [§132(a)(4)]	As a matter of administrative convenience, Congress allows employees to exclude from income relatively small and infrequent benefits employees receive at work (such as limited use of a business copy machine).
Meals and lodging for the employer's provided convenience [§119]	Employees may exclude employer-provided meals and lodging if they (1) are provided on the employer's business premises to the employee (and spouse and dependents); (2) are provided for the employer's convenience (such as allowing the employee to be on-call 24 hours a day or continue working on-site over lunch); and (3) for lodging only, the employee must accept the lodging as a condition of employment.
Employee educational assistance programs [§127]	Employees may exclude up to $5,250 of employer-provided educational assistance benefits covering tuition, books, and fees for any instruction that improves the taxpayer's capabilities, whether or not job-related or part of a degree program.
No additional cost services [§132(a)(1)]	Employees may exclude the value of services provided by an employer that generate no substantial costs to the employer (such as free flight benefits for airline employees on a space-available basis or free hotel service for hotel employees).
Qualified employee discounts [§132(a)(2)]	Employees may exclude (a) a discount on employer-provided goods as long as the discount does not exceed the employer's gross profit percentage on all property offered for sale to customers and (b) up to 20 percent employer-provided discount on services. Discounts in excess of these amounts are taxable as compensation. See Example 5-19.
Dependent care benefits [§129]	Employees may exclude up to $5,000 for benefits paid or reimbursed by employers for caring for children under age 13 or dependents or spouses who are physically or mentally unable to care for themselves.
Working condition fringe benefits [§132(a)(3)]	Employees may exclude from income any benefit or reimbursement of a benefit provided by an employer that would be deductible as an ordinary and necessary expense by the employee if the employee had paid the expense.
Qualified transportation benefits [§132(a)(5)]	Employees may exclude up to $255 per month of employer-provided parking and up to $255 per month of the combined value of employer-provided mass transit passes and the value of a car pool vehicle for employee use.
Qualified moving expenses [§132(a)(6)]	Employees may exclude employer reimbursement for qualified moving expenses (cost of moving household items and costs of travel, including lodging, to a new home for employee and dependents) that would otherwise be deductible by the employee. We discuss deductible moving expenses in the Individual Deductions chapter.
Cafeteria plans [§125]	A plan where employees choose among various nontaxable fringe benefits (such as health insurance and dental insurance) or cash. Tax-free to the extent the taxpayer chooses nontaxable fringe benefits; taxable to the extent the employee receives cash.
Flexible spending accounts [§125]	Allow employees to set a portion of their before-tax salary for payment of either health and/or dependent-care benefits. Amounts set aside must be used by the end of the year or within the first two and a half months of the next plan year, or employees forfeit the unused balance. In lieu of the two-and-a-half month grace period each year for health care flexible spending accounts, employers instead can allow employees to carry over up to $500 of unused amounts to be used anytime during the next year (i.e., it is the employer's choice). This option does not apply to dependent-care flexible spending accounts. For 2017, the amount of before-tax salary that an employee may set aside for medical expenses is limited to $2,600 and for dependent-care expenses is limited to $5,000.

[41]The cost of medical coverage paid by an employer and offered through a health insurance exchange is not an excludible benefit unless the employer is a small employer that elects to make all of its full-time employees eligible for plans offered through the small business health options program (SHOP). For this purpose, a small employer is an employer that employs an average of at least one but 100 or fewer employees during business days in the prior year, and employs at least one employee on the first day of the plan year. In 2015, SHOP is open to employers with 50 or fewer full-time equivalent employees. Beginning in 2016, some states opened SHOPs to employers with up to 100 full-time equivalent employees.

Education-Related Exclusions

As an incentive for taxpayers to participate in higher education (education beyond high school), Congress excludes certain types of income if the funds are used for higher education. In the following paragraphs, we discuss exclusions for scholarships and exclusions for certain types of investment plans used to save for college.[42]

Scholarships College students seeking a degree can exclude from gross income scholarships (including Pell grants) that pay for tuition, fees, books, supplies, and other equipment *required* for the student's courses.[43] Any excess scholarship amounts (such as for room or meals) are fully taxable. The scholarship exclusion applies only if the recipient is *not* required to perform services in exchange for receiving the scholarship. "Scholarships" that represent compensation for past, current, or future services are fully taxable. However, tuition waivers or reductions provided by an educational institution for undergraduate courses for student employees or for graduate courses for teaching or research assistants are not taxable.

What about athletic scholarships? Good question. The IRS has ruled that the value of athletic scholarships—which may not exceed expenses for tuition, fees, room, board, and necessary supplies; are awarded to students by a university that *expects* but *does not require* the students to participate in a particular sport; require no particular activity in lieu of participation; and are not canceled if the student cannot participate—is excludable from gross income.[44]

Example 5-26

Ellen, Courtney's daughter, received a $700 scholarship from the University of Missouri–Kansas City that pays $400 of her tuition and provides $300 cash for books. Ellen spent $350 on books. How much of the scholarship may she exclude from gross income?

Answer: All $700 is excluded. Ellen may exclude all of the scholarship for tuition and she may exclude the $300 cash she received for books because she spent all $300 purchasing her books for school.

What if: How much is Ellen allowed to exclude if she spent only $250 on books?

Answer: $650 is excluded. Ellen excludes all of the scholarship for her tuition and $250 of the $300 in cash payments because she spent $250 on books. She must include the excess cash payment of $50 ($300 – $250) in her gross income.

THE KEY FACTS

Education Exclusions

- Students seeking a college degree can exclude scholarships that pay for required tuition, fees, books, and supplies.
- Taxpayers can elect to exclude interest earned on Series EE savings bonds when the redemption proceeds are used to pay qualified higher education expenses.
- The exclusion of interest on Series EE savings bonds is restricted to taxpayers with modified AGI below specific limits.

Other Educational Subsidies Taxpayers are allowed to exclude from gross income earnings on investments in qualified education plans such as 529 plans and Coverdell education savings accounts as long as they use the earnings to pay for qualifying educational expenditures.

With 529 plans, parents, grandparents, and other individuals are allowed to contribute up to the maximum allowed by state-sponsored 529 plans to fund the qualified educational costs of future *college* students.[45] Earnings in 529 plans are distributed tax-free provided they are used for qualified *higher* education expenses. If, on the other hand, distributions are made to the beneficiary for other purposes, the earnings distributed are taxed to the beneficiary at the beneficiary's tax rate and are subject to an additional 10 percent penalty while distributions of the original investment (contributions)

[42]A detailed explanation is available in IRS Publication 970 *Tax Benefits for Education* available on the IRS website at www.irs.gov.

[43]§117(b)(2).

[44]Rev. Rul. 77-263, 1977-2 CB 47.

[45]Contribution limits vary according to the state administering the 529 plan. In addition, more than half the states offer a state tax deduction or credit to residents contributing to the 529 plan sponsored by the state in which the contributors reside.

to the beneficiary are treated as gifts.[46] Similarly, distributions to contributors (e.g., parents, grandparents) that represent earnings on their contributions are included in contributors' gross income and are also subject to the 10 percent penalty.

With a Coverdell account, yearly contributions to the account are limited to $2,000 for each beneficiary, and distributions may be used to pay for qualified educational costs of kindergarten through 12th grade and qualified higher education expenses such as tuition, books, fees, supplies, and reasonable room and board.[47] The $2,000 contribution limit for Coverdell accounts phases out as AGI (modified to include certain types of excluded foreign income) increases from $190,000 to $220,000 for married filing jointly taxpayers, and from $95,000 to $110,000 for all other taxpayers.

U.S. Series EE Bonds The federal government issues bonds that allow taxpayers to acquire the bonds at a discount and redeem the bonds for a fixed amount over stated time intervals. These bonds don't generate any cash in the form of interest until the taxpayer redeems the bond. At redemption, the amount of the redemption price in excess of the acquisition price is interest included in gross income.[48] U.S. Series EE bonds fall into this category. However, an exclusion is available for interest from Series EE bonds. This exclusion requires that the redemption proceeds be used to pay for higher education expenses of the taxpayer, the taxpayer's spouse, or a dependent of the taxpayer. Qualified higher education expenses include the tuition and fees required for enrollment or attendance at an eligible educational institution. Taxpayers may also exclude the interest income if they contribute the proceeds to a qualified tuition program.

The exclusion is partially reduced or eliminated for taxpayers exceeding a fixed level of modified adjusted gross income (adjusted gross income before the educational savings bond exclusion, the foreign-earned income exclusion, discussed below, and certain other deductions).[49] If the taxpayer's modified AGI exceeds the thresholds in the redemption year, the exclusion is phased out (gradually reduced) until all of the interest from the bonds is taxed.[50]

Exclusions That Mitigate Double Taxation

Congress provides certain exclusions that eliminate the potential double tax that may arise for gifts, inheritances, and life insurance proceeds.

Gifts and Inheritances Individuals may transfer property to other taxpayers without receiving or expecting to receive value in return. If the *transferor* is alive at the time of the transfer, the property transfer is called a **gift.** If the property is transferred from the decedent's estate (*transferor* is deceased), it is called an **inheritance.** These transfers are generally subject to a federal transfer tax, *not* the income tax. Gifts are typically subject to the federal gift tax and inheritances are typically subject to a federal estate tax.[51] Thus, gift and estate taxes are imposed on *transfer* of the property

[46]Under §529(c)(3), multiple distributions received under these circumstances are treated as annuities. As a result, a portion of each distribution would be treated as a gift with the remainder treated as income.

[47]§530(b). This definition of qualified higher education expenses is consistent with the definition used in §221(d)(2) to determine if interest paid on education-related loans is deductible (see the Individual Deductions chapter).

[48]Alternatively, taxpayers can elect to include the annual increase in the redemption value in gross income rather than waiting to recognize all the income on redemption. See §454(a).

[49]§135(c)(4).

[50]In 2017, the phase-out range begins at $117,250 of modified adjusted gross income for married taxpayers filing joint returns. For all other taxpayers, the phase-out range begins at $78,150.

[51]As a general rule, for 2017, the federal gift tax does not apply to relatively small gifts ($14,000 or less), and the federal estate tax does not apply to transfers from relatively small estates (under $5,490,000).

and *not included in income by the recipient.* The exclusion of gifts and inheritances from income taxation avoids the potential double taxation (transfer and income taxation) on these transfers.

Example 5-27

Ellen graduated from high school last year. As a graduation present, Gram purchased a $1,500 travel package for Ellen, so that Ellen could go on a Caribbean cruise. Last year, Ellen also received an inheritance of $2,000 from Gramps's estate. How much gross income does Ellen recognize on the $1,500 gift she received from Gram and the $2,000 inheritance she received from Gramps's estate?

Answer: $0. Ellen is allowed to exclude the entire gift and the entire amount of the inheritance from her gross income. Consequently, she does not recognize any gross income from these transactions.

Life Insurance Proceeds In some ways, life insurance proceeds are similar to inheritances. When the owner of the life insurance policy dies, the beneficiary receives the death benefit proceeds. The decedent (or the decedent's estate) is generally subject to estate taxation on the amount of the insurance proceeds. In order to avoid potential double taxation on the life insurance proceeds, the tax laws allow taxpayers receiving life insurance proceeds to exclude the proceeds from gross income.[52] However, when the insurance proceeds are paid over a period of time rather than in a lump sum, a portion of the payments represents interest and must be included in gross income. In addition, the life insurance proceeds exclusion generally does not apply when a life insurance policy is transferred to another party for valuable consideration. In this case, the eventual life insurance proceeds collected by the purchaser are excluded up to the sum of the purchase price of the policy and any subsequent premiums with remaining proceeds taxable as ordinary income.[53]

What happens if a taxpayer cashes out a policy before death? The tax treatment varies based on the specific facts. Generally, if a taxpayer simply cancels a life insurance contract and is paid the policy's cash surrender value, she would recognize ordinary income to the extent the proceeds received exceed previous premiums paid. If premiums paid exceed the proceeds received, the loss is not deductible. If, however, the taxpayer is terminally ill (medically certified with an illness expected to cause death within 24 months), early receipt of life insurance proceeds **(accelerated death benefits)** are not taxable. If a taxpayer is chronically ill (medically certified to require substantial assistance for daily living activities or due to cognitive impairment), life insurance proceeds are not taxable to the extent they are used to pay for the taxpayer's long-term care.

Example 5-28

What if: Gramps received $200,000 of accelerated death benefits from a life insurance policy last year when he was diagnosed with terminal cancer with an expected life of less than one year. How much gross income would the $200,000 payment generate?

Answer: None, because Gramps was medically certified as terminally ill with an illness expected to cause death within 24 months.

(continued on page 5-28)

[52]§101. The exclusion does not apply if the insurance policy is sold by the owner.

[53]This exception to the exclusion does not apply if the recipient of the policy is the insured, a partner of the insured, a partnership in which the insured is a partner, or a corporation in which the insured is an officer or shareholder. This exception also does not apply to policies transferred by gift or tax-free exchange. §101(a)(2).

What if: Due to financial issues, several years ago Gramps transferred a $100,000 life insurance policy on his life to a business associate for $5,000. Since that time, the business associate has continued to pay the annual premiums on the policy (totaling $20,000 before Gramps's death). Upon Gramps's death, the life insurance company paid the business associate the policy's $100,000 face value. How much of the $100,000 payment is taxable?

Answer: $75,000. Because the business associate purchased the life insurance policy from Gramps for valuable consideration, she may exclude the $100,000 proceeds up to the sum of the purchase price of the policy ($5,000) and any subsequent premiums ($20,000), with the remaining proceeds ($100,000 − $5,000 − $20,000 = $75,000) taxable as ordinary income.

THE KEY FACTS

Exclusions to Mitigate Double Taxation

- Gifts and inheritances are subject to federal transfer taxes and are, therefore, excluded from the income of the recipient.
- A maximum of $102,100 (2017) of foreign-earned income can be excluded from gross income for qualifying individuals.
- To be eligible for the foreign-earned income exclusion, the taxpayer must live in the foreign country for 330 days in a consecutive 12-month period.

Foreign-Earned Income U.S. citizens are subject to tax on all income whether it is generated in the United States or in foreign countries. Because most foreign countries also impose tax on income earned within their borders, U.S. citizens could be subject to both U.S. and foreign taxation on income earned abroad. To provide relief from this potential double taxation, Congress allows taxpayers to exclude foreign-earned income (income from foreign sources for personal services performed) up to an annual maximum amount. Income from pensions, annuities, salary paid by the U.S. government, or deferred compensation does not qualify for the exclusion. The maximum exclusion is indexed for inflation, and in 2017 the maximum is $102,100. Rather than claim this exclusion, taxpayers may deduct foreign taxes paid as itemized deductions or they may claim the foreign tax credit for foreign taxes paid on their foreign-earned income.[54] To determine whether claiming the annual exclusion, the deduction, or the foreign tax credit is most advantageous, taxpayers should compare the tax effects of each option. To claim the annual exclusion instead of the foreign tax deduction or credit, the taxpayer must elect to do so using Form 2555. Taxpayers who elect to use the exclusion may revoke the election for later years and use the foreign tax credit or deduct foreign taxes paid. However, once a taxpayer revokes the exclusion election, she may not reelect to use the exclusion before the sixth tax year after the tax year the revocation was made.

As you might expect, individuals must meet certain requirements to qualify for the foreign-earned income exclusion. To be eligible for the annual exclusion, a taxpayer must have her tax home in a foreign country and (1) be considered a resident of the foreign country by living in the country for the entire year (calendar year) or (2) live in the foreign country for 330 days in a consecutive 12-month period, which might occur over two tax years. The *maximum* exclusion is reduced pro rata for each day during the calendar year that is not part of the qualifying 12-month period. Taxpayers meeting the requirement for the foreign-earned income exclusion may also exclude from income reasonable housing costs (provided by an employer) that exceed 16 percent of the statutory foreign-earned income exclusion amount for the year (exceed 16 percent × $102,100 = $16,336 in 2017). The exclusion, however, is limited to a maximum of 14 percent of the statutory exclusion amount (14 percent × $102,100 = $14,294 in 2017). Thus, in 2017, if a taxpayer incurs housing costs (provided by an employer) exceeding $16,336, she may exclude such excess costs up to $14,294 (thus, the first $16,336 of employer-provided housing costs are included in gross income).[55] The housing exclusion limit is also subject to daily proration if the taxpayer's qualifying 12-month period occurs over two tax years.

[54]See §911(b)(2) and the Individual Deductions chapter and Individual Income Tax Computation and Credits chapter.

[55]§911(c).

Example 5-29

What if: Assume that Courtney is considering a transfer to EWD's overseas affiliate. If Courtney transfers, she anticipates she will earn approximately $120,000 in salary. How much of her expected $120,000 annual salary will Courtney be allowed to exclude from her gross income, assuming she meets the residency requirements?

Answer: She is eligible to exclude $102,100 of her $120,000 of compensation from U.S. taxation in 2017. However, her entire $120,000 salary may be subject to the foreign country's income tax.

What if: Assume that Courtney decides to transfer but she expects her 12-month qualifying period to include only 200 days in the first year and 140 days in the second year. How much of her expected $65,000 salary in the first year will she be allowed to exclude from gross income?

Answer: $55,945 [$102,100 full exclusion × 200/365 (days in foreign country/days in year)].

What if: Assume that Courtney expects her 12-month qualifying period to include 200 days in the first year and that she expects her salary to be $45,000 during this period. How much of her expected $45,000 salary will she be allowed to exclude from gross income?

Answer: All $45,000. She can exclude up to $55,945 of salary from income (see above computation).

What if: Assume that if Courtney transfers, EWD's overseas affiliate will also pay for her housing while overseas ($25,000 per year). How much of the $25,000 housing payments may Courtney exclude assuming she lives in the country for the entire year?

Answer: $8,664. Since Courtney meets the requirements for the foreign-earned income exclusion, she may exclude the employer-provided housing costs that exceed $16,336 (16% × $102,100), up to a maximum exclusion of $14,294 (14% × $102,100). Thus, Courtney may exclude $8,664 [the lesser of (a) $8,664 ($25,000 housing cost less $16,336) or (b) $14,294].

Sickness and Injury-Related Exclusions

The tax laws provide several exclusion provisions for taxpayers who are sick or injured. One explanation for these exclusions is that payments for sickness or injury are considered returns of (human) capital.

Workers' Compensation The provision for workers' compensation is relatively straightforward. Taxpayers receive workers' compensation benefits when they are unable to work because of a work-related injury. Any payments a taxpayer receives from a state-sponsored workers' compensation plan are excluded from the taxpayer's income.[56] Note that this treatment is *opposite* that of *unemployment* compensation, which is fully taxable.

Payments Associated with Personal Injury Historically, the question of which payments associated with a personal injury were excludable was controversial. In 1996 Congress settled the matter by deciding that all payments associated with compensating a taxpayer for a *physical* injury (including payments for past, current, and future lost wages) are excluded from gross income. That is, the tax laws specify that any *compensatory damages* on account of a *physical injury* or *physical sickness* are nontaxable. Thus, damages taxpayers receive for emotional distress associated with a physical injury are excluded. In contrast, *punitive damages* are *fully taxable,* because they are intended to punish the harm-doer rather than to compensate the taxpayer for injuries. Likewise, taxpayers receiving damages for emotional distress that are not associated with a physical injury must include those payments in income. In general, all other awards (those that do not relate to physical injury or sickness or are payments for the medical costs of treating emotional distress) are included in gross income.

[56]§104.

Example 5-30

In February, Courtney's cousin, Kelsey, was struck and injured by a bus while walking in a crosswalk. Because the bus driver was negligent, the bus company settled Kelsey's claim by paying her $1,500 for medical expenses and $500 for emotional distress associated with the accident. How much of the $2,000 Kelsey received from the bus company may she *exclude* from her gross income?

Answer: All $2,000. Kelsey may exclude the $1,500 she received for medical expenses and the $500 payment she received for emotional distress because these damages were associated with Kelsey's physical injury.

What if: Assume Kelsey sued the bus company and was awarded $5,000 in punitive damages. How much of the $5,000 would Kelsey be able to exclude from her gross income?

Answer: $0. Payments for punitive damages are not excludable. Kelsey would be required to include the entire $5,000 in her gross income.

THE KEY FACTS

Exclusions Related to Sickness and Injury

- Payments from workers' compensation plans are excluded from gross income.
- Payments received as compensation for a *physical* injury are excluded from gross income, but punitive damages are included in gross income.
- Reimbursements by health and accident insurance policies for medical expenses paid by the taxpayer are excluded from gross income.
- Disability payments received from an *employee-purchased* policy are excluded from gross income.

Health Care Reimbursement Any reimbursement a taxpayer receives from a health and accident insurance policy for medical expenses paid by the taxpayer during the current year is excluded from gross income. The exclusion applies regardless of whether the taxpayer, her employer, or someone else purchased the health and accident policy for the taxpayer. Of course, the tax benefit rule may require inclusion of reimbursements of medical expenses that were deducted by the taxpayer in a prior year.

Disability Insurance The exclusion provisions for **disability insurance** are more restrictive than those for workers' compensation payments or reimbursements from a health and accident insurance plan. Disability insurance, sometimes called wage replacement insurance, pays the insured individual for wages lost when the individual misses work due to injury or disability. If an individual purchases disability insurance directly, the cost of the policy is not deductible, but any disability benefits are excluded from gross income.

Disability insurance may also be purchased on an individual's behalf by an employer. When an employer pays disability insurance premiums, the employer may allow employees to choose whether the payments on their behalf are to be considered taxable compensation or a nontaxable fringe benefit. If the premiums paid on the employee's behalf are taxable compensation to the employee, the policy is considered to have been purchased by the employee. If the premium paid for by the employer is a nontaxable fringe benefit to the employee, the policy is considered to have been purchased by the employer. This distinction is important because only payments taxpayers receive from an *employee-purchased* policy are excluded from an employee's gross income. If the employer pays the premiums for an employee as a nontaxable fringe benefit, the employee must include all disability benefits in gross income.

Example 5-31

Courtney purchased disability insurance last year. In late April of this year, she broke her wrist in a mountain biking accident and could not work for two weeks. Courtney's doctor bills totaled $2,000, of which $1,600 was reimbursed by her health insurance purchased by EWD. How much of the $1,600 health insurance reimbursement for medical expenses is Courtney allowed to *exclude* from her gross income?

Answer: All $1,600 is excluded. All medical expense reimbursements from health insurance are excluded from a taxpayer's gross income.

Courtney also received $600 for lost wages due to the accident from her disability insurance policy. How much of the $600 is Courtney allowed to exclude from her gross income?

Answer: All $600 is excluded. Courtney can exclude the entire amount because she paid the premiums on the policy.

What if: How much of the $600 payment for lost wages from the disability insurance policy would Courtney exclude if EWD paid the disability insurance premium on her behalf as a nontaxable fringe benefit?

Answer: $0 would be excluded. In this circumstance the policy would be considered to be purchased by the employer, so Courtney would not be allowed to exclude any of the payment from gross income. She would include the payment in gross income and be taxed on the entire $600.

What if: How much of the $600 payment for lost wages from the disability insurance policy would Courtney be allowed to exclude if she paid half the cost of the policy with after-tax dollars and EWD paid the other half as a taxable fringe benefit?

Answer: All $600 would be excluded. Because Courtney paid for the entire cost of the policy with after-tax dollars, she would be allowed to exclude all of the disability insurance benefit. Note that if EWD had paid for half the cost of the policy as a nontaxable fringe benefit, Courtney would have been able to exclude $300, not $600.

Deferral Provisions

We've described exclusion provisions that allow taxpayers to permanently eliminate certain types of income from their tax base. Other code sections, called *deferral provisions,* allow taxpayers to defer (but not permanently exclude) the recognition of certain types of realized income. Transactions generating deferred income include **installment sales,** like-kind exchanges, involuntary conversions, and contributions to non-Roth **qualified retirement accounts.** We "defer" our detailed discussion of these transactions to subsequent chapters.

INCOME SUMMARY

At the end of the year, Courtney calculated her income and Gram's income. Exhibit 5-4 presents Courtney's income calculation, Exhibit 5-5 displays how this income would be reported on the front page of Courtney's tax return, and Exhibit 5-6 presents Gram's income calculation. Note that Courtney's actual *gross* income equals her total income on page 1 of her Form 1040 plus her $1,500 consulting expenses (see Example 5-7) and her $9,000 deductions for rental expenses (see Example 5-10), which are both *for* AGI deductions. Because Gram doesn't have any business, rental, or royalty deductions, her gross income is equal to her total income on line 22 of page 1 of her tax return.

EXHIBIT 5-4 Courtney's Income

Description	Amount	Reference
(1) Salary (line 7, 1040 page 1)	$ 118,000	Example 5-7
(2) Employment bonus award (line 7, 1040 page 1)	4,800	Example 5-4
(3) Discount architectural design services (line 7, 1040 page 1)	6,000	Example 5-19
(4) Compensation on below-market loan from EWD (line 7, 1040 page 1)	4,000	Example 5-20
(5) Discharge of indebtedness (line 7, 1040 page 1)	10,000	Example 5-21
(6) Interest income (line 8a, 1040 page 1)	617	Example 5-9
(7) Dividends (lines 9a and 9b, 1040 page 1)	700	Example 5-8
(8) State tax refund (line 10, 1040 page 1)	420	Example 5-3
(9) Alimony (line 11, 1040 page 1)	20,000	Example 5-14
(10) Net business income (line 12, 1040 page 1)	18,000	Example 5-7
(11) Net rental income (line 17, 1040 page 1)	5,000	Example 5-10
Total income as presented on line 22 of front page of 1040 (see Exhibit 5-5)	**$187,537**	Sum of (1) through (11)

EXHIBIT 5-5 Courtney's Tax Return
(total income as reported on 1040 page 1, lines 7–22)

If more than four dependents, see instructions and check here ▶ ☐				(see instructions)	
				Dependents on 6c not entered above	
	d	Total number of exemptions claimed		Add numbers on lines above ▶	
Income	7	Wages, salaries, tips, etc. Attach Form(s) W-2		7	142,800
	8a	**Taxable** interest. Attach Schedule B if required		8a	617
	b	**Tax-exempt** interest. **Do not** include on line 8a	8b 500		
Attach Form(s) W-2 here. Also attach Forms W-2G and 1099-R if tax was withheld.	9a	Ordinary dividends. Attach Schedule B if required		9a	700
	b	Qualified dividends	9b 700		
	10	Taxable refunds, credits, or offsets of state and local income taxes		10	420
	11	Alimony received		11	20,000
	12	Business income or (loss). Attach Schedule C or C-EZ		12	18,000
	13	Capital gain or (loss). Attach Schedule D if required. If not required, check here ▶ ☐		13	
If you did not get a W-2, see instructions.	14	Other gains or (losses). Attach Form 4797		14	
	15a	IRA distributions 15a	b Taxable amount	15b	
	16a	Pensions and annuities 16a	b Taxable amount	16b	
	17	Rental real estate, royalties, partnerships, S corporations, trusts, etc. Attach Schedule E		17	5,000
	18	Farm income or (loss). Attach Schedule F		18	
	19	Unemployment compensation		19	
	20a	Social security benefits 20a	b Taxable amount	20b	
	21	Other income. List type and amount		21	
	22	Combine the amounts in the far right column for lines 7 through 21. This is your **total income** ▶		22	187,537
Adjusted Gross Income	23	Educator expenses	23		
	24	Certain business expenses of reservists, performing artists, and fee-basis government officials. Attach Form 2106 or 2106-EZ	24		
	25	Health savings account deduction. Attach Form 8889	25		
	26	Moving expenses. Attach Form 3903	26		

EXHIBIT 5-6 Gram's Income

Deduction	Amount	Reference
Babysitting services	$ 350	Example 5-2
Interest income	4,400	Example 5-9
Annuity income	3,400	Example 5-11
Gain on stock sale	350	Example 5-12
Sweepstakes winnings (WaveRunner)	7,500	Example 5-17
Income for current year	$16,000	

CONCLUSION

In this chapter we explained the basic concepts of income realization and recognition, identified and discussed the major types of income, and described the most common income exclusions. We discovered that many exclusions are related to specific congressional objectives, but that absent a specific exclusion, realized income should be included in gross income. In the next chapter, we turn our attention to the deductions available to taxpayers when computing their taxable income. We will continue to follow Courtney and Gram in their quest to determine their taxable income and corresponding tax liability.

Appendix 2016 Social Security Worksheet from Form 1040

2016 Form 1040—Lines 20a and 20b

Social Security Benefits Worksheet—Lines 20a and 20b

Keep for Your Records

Before you begin:
- ✓ Complete Form 1040, lines 21 and 23 through 32, if they apply to you.
- ✓ Figure any write-in adjustments to be entered on the dotted line next to line 36 (see the instructions for line 36).
- ✓ If you are married filing separately and you lived apart from your spouse for all of 2016, enter "D" to the right of the word "benefits" on line 20a. If you do not, you may get a math error notice from the IRS.
- ✓ Be sure you have read the **Exception** in the line 20a and 20b instructions to see if you can use this worksheet instead of a publication to find out if any of your benefits are taxable.

1. Enter the total amount from **box 5** of **all** your **Forms SSA-1099** and **Forms RRB-1099.** Also, enter this amount on Form 1040, line 20a .... **1.** ______
2. Multiply line 1 by 50% (0.50) .... **2.** ______
3. Combine the amounts from Form 1040, lines 7, 8a, 9a, 10 through 14, 15b, 16b, 17 through 19, and 21 .... **3.** ______
4. Enter the amount, if any, from Form 1040, line 8b .... **4.** ______
5. Combine lines 2, 3, and 4 .... **5.** ______
6. Enter the total of the amounts from Form 1040, lines 23 through 32, plus any write-in adjustments you entered on the dotted line next to line 36 .... **6.** ______
7. Is the amount on line 6 less than the amount on line 5?
   - ☐ **No.** STOP None of your social security benefits are taxable. Enter -0- on Form 1040, line 20b.
   - ☐ **Yes.** Subtract line 6 from line 5 .... **7.** ______
8. If you are:
   - Married filing jointly, enter $32,000
   - Single, head of household, qualifying widow(er), or married filing separately and you **lived apart** from your spouse for all of 2016, enter $25,000
   - Married filing separately and you lived with your spouse at any time in 2016, skip lines 8 through 15; multiply line 7 by 85% (0.85) and enter the result on line 16. Then, go to line 17

   .... **8.** ______
9. Is the amount on line 8 less than the amount on line 7?
   - ☐ **No.** STOP None of your social security benefits are taxable. Enter -0- on Form 1040, line 20b. If you are married filing separately and you **lived apart** from your spouse for all of 2016, be sure you entered "D" to the right of the word "benefits" on line 20a.
   - ☐ **Yes.** Subtract line 8 from line 7 .... **9.** ______
10. Enter: $12,000 if married filing jointly; $9,000 if single, head of household, qualifying widow(er), or married filing separately and you **lived apart** from your spouse for all of 2016 .... **10.** ______
11. Subtract line 10 from line 9. If zero or less, enter -0- .... **11.** ______
12. Enter the **smaller** of line 9 or line 10 .... **12.** ______
13. Enter one-half of line 12 .... **13.** ______
14. Enter the **smaller** of line 2 or line 13 .... **14.** ______
15. Multiply line 11 by 85% (0.85). If line 11 is zero, enter -0- .... **15.** ______
16. Add lines 14 and 15 .... **16.** ______
17. Multiply line 1 by 85% (0.85) .... **17.** ______
18. **Taxable social security benefits.** Enter the **smaller** of line 16 or line 17. Also enter this amount on Form 1040, line 20b .... **18.** ______

TIP *If any of your benefits are taxable for 2016* ***and*** *they include a lump-sum benefit payment that was for an earlier year, you may be able to reduce the taxable amount. See* Lump-Sum Election *in Pub. 915 for details.*

Summary

LO 5-1 Apply the concept of realization and explain when taxpayers recognize gross income.

- Income is typically realized with a transaction that allows economic benefit to be identified and measured.
- Unless realized income is deferred or excluded, it is included in gross income in the period dictated by the taxpayer's accounting method.
- The accrual method of accounting recognizes income in the period it is earned, and this method is typically used by large corporations.
- The cash method of accounting recognizes income in the period received, and this method offers a simple and flexible method of accounting typically used by individuals.
- The return of capital principle, constructive receipt doctrine, and assignment of income doctrine affect how much income is recognized, when income is recognized, and who recognizes income, respectively.

LO 5-2 Understand the distinctions between the various sources of income, including income from services and property.

- Income from services is called earned income, whereas income from property is called unearned income.
- A portion of annuity payments and proceeds from sales of property is a nontaxable return of capital.
- Earned and unearned income generated by flow-through business entities is reported by partners and Subchapter S shareholders.
- Other sources of income include alimony payments, unemployment compensation, Social Security benefits, prizes and awards, bargain purchases, imputed interest on below-market loans, and discharge of indebtedness.

LO 5-3 Apply basic income exclusion provisions to compute gross income.

- Interest received from holding state and local indebtedness (municipal interest) is excluded from gross income.
- A taxpayer satisfying certain home ownership and use requirements can permanently exclude up to $250,000 ($500,000 if married filing jointly) of realized gain on the sale of her principal residence.
- Employment-related nonrecognition provisions include a variety of excludable fringe benefits.
- Gifts, inheritances, life insurance proceeds, and foreign-earned income up to $102,100 are excluded from gross income in order to mitigate the effects of double taxation.
- Common injury-related nonrecognition provisions include the exclusions for worker's compensation, personal injury payments and reimbursements from health insurance policies, and certain payments from disability policies.

KEY TERMS

accelerated death benefits (5-27)
accrual method (5-6)
alimony (5-14)
annuity (5-11)
assignment of income doctrine (5-8)
barter clubs (5-4)
cash method (5-6)
claim of right doctrine (5-7)
community property systems (5-8)
constructive receipt doctrine (5-7)
disability insurance (5-30)
discharge of indebtedness (5-21)
earned income (5-10)
flow-through entity (5-14)
fringe benefits (5-23)
gift (5-26)
gross income (5-2)
imputed income (5-19)
inheritance (5-26)
installment sale (5-31)
municipal bond (5-21)
nonrecognition provisions (5-21)
qualified retirement accounts (5-31)
realization principle (5-3)
return of capital (5-4)
tax basis (5-4)
tax benefit rule (5-5)
unearned income (5-10)
wherewithal to pay (5-3)

DISCUSSION QUESTIONS

Discussion Questions are available in Connect®. connect

1. Based on the definition of gross income in §61 and related regulations, what is the general presumption regarding the taxability of income realized? LO 5-1
2. Based on the definition of gross income in §61, related regulations, and judicial rulings, what are the three criteria for recognizing taxable income? LO 5-1
3. Describe the concept of realization for tax purposes. LO 5-1
4. Compare and contrast realization of income with recognition of income. LO 5-1
5. Tim is a plumber who joined a barter club. This year Tim exchanges plumbing services for a new roof. The roof is properly valued at $2,500, but Tim would have only billed $2,200 for the plumbing services. What amount of income should Tim recognize on the exchange of his services for a roof? Would your answer change if Tim would have normally billed $3,000 for his services? LO 5-1
6. Andre constructs and installs cabinets in homes. Blair sells and installs carpet in apartments. Andre and Blair worked out an arrangement whereby Andre installed cabinets in Blair's home and Blair installed carpet in Andre's home. Neither Andre nor Blair believes they are required to recognize any gross income on this exchange because neither received cash. Do you agree with them? Explain. LO 5-1
7. What issue precipitated the return of capital principle? Explain. LO 5-1
8. Compare how the return of capital principle applies when: (1) a taxpayer sells an asset and collects the sale proceeds immediately, and (2) a taxpayer sells an asset and collects the sale proceeds over several periods (an installment sale). If Congress wanted to maximize revenue from installment sales, how would it have applied the return of capital principle for installment sales? LO 5-1
9. This year Jorge received a refund of property taxes that he deducted on his tax return last year. Jorge is not sure whether he should include the refund in his gross income. What would you tell him? LO 5-1
10. Describe in general how the cash method of accounting differs from the accrual method of accounting. LO 5-1
11. Janet is a cash-method calendar-year taxpayer. She received a check for services provided in the mail during the last week of December. However, rather than cash the check, Janet decided to wait until the following January because she believes that her delay will cause the income to be realized and recognized next year. What would you tell her? Would it matter if she didn't open the envelope? Would it matter if she refused to check her mail during the last week of December? Explain. LO 5-1
12. The cash method of accounting means that taxpayers don't recognize income unless they receive cash or cash equivalents. True or false? Explain. LO 5-1
13. Contrast the constructive receipt doctrine with the claim of right doctrine. LO 5-1
14. Dewey is a lawyer who uses the cash method of accounting. Last year Dewey provided a client with legal services worth $55,000, but the client could not pay the fee. This year Dewey requested that in lieu of paying Dewey $55,000 for the services, the client could make a $45,000 gift to Dewey's daughter. Dewey's daughter received the check for $45,000 and deposited it in her bank account. How much of this income is taxed, if any, to Dewey? Explain. LO 5-1
15. Clyde and Bonnie were married this year. Clyde has a steady job that will pay him about $37,000, while Bonnie does odd jobs that will produce about $28,000 of income. They also have a joint savings account that will pay about $400 of interest. If Clyde and Bonnie reside in a community property state and file married-separate tax returns, how much gross income will Clyde and Bonnie each report? Any difference if they reside in a common law state? Explain. LO 5-2

LO 5-2 16. Distinguish earned income from unearned income, and provide an example of each.

LO 5-2 17. Jim purchased 100 shares of stock this year and elected to participate in a dividend reinvestment program. This program automatically uses dividends to purchase additional shares of stock. This year Jim's shares paid $350 of dividends and he used these funds to purchase additional shares of stock. These additional shares are worth $375 at year-end. What amount of dividends, if any, should Jim declare as income this year? Explain.

LO 5-2 18. Jerry has a certificate of deposit at the local bank. The interest on this certificate was credited to his account on December 31 of last year, but he didn't withdraw the interest until January of this year. When is the interest income taxed?

LO 5-2 19. Conceptually, when taxpayers receive annuity payments, how do they determine the amount of the payment they must include in gross income?

LO 5-2 20. George purchased a life annuity to provide him monthly payments for as long as he lives. Based on IRS tables, George's life expectancy is 100 months. Is George able to recover his cost of the annuity if he dies before he receives 100 monthly payments? Explain. What happens for tax purposes if George receives more than 100 payments?

LO 5-2 21. Brad purchased land for $45,000 this year. At year-end Brad sold the land for $51,700 and paid a sales commission of $450. What effect does this transaction have on Brad's gross income? Explain.

LO 5-2 22. Tomiko is a 50 percent owner (partner) in the Tanaka partnership. During the year, the partnership reported $1,000 of interest income and $2,000 of dividends. How much of this income must Tomiko include in her gross income?

LO 5-2 23. Clem and Ida have been married for several years, but this year they decided to get divorced. In the divorce decree, Clem agreed to deed his car to Ida and pay Ida $10,000 per year for four years. Will either of these transfers qualify as alimony for tax purposes? Explain.

LO 5-2 planning 24. Otto and Fiona are negotiating the terms of their divorce. Otto has agreed to transfer property to Fiona over the next two years, but he has reserved the right to make cash payments in lieu of property transfers. Will tax considerations play a role in Otto's decision to transfer property or pay cash? How will Otto's choice affect the combined gross income and income taxes paid by Otto and Fiona? Explain.

LO 5-2 25. Larry Bounds has won the gold bat award for hitting the longest home run in major league baseball this year. The bat is worth almost $35,000. Under what conditions can Larry exclude the award from his gross income? Explain.

LO 5-2 26. Rory and Nicholi, single taxpayers, each annually receive Social Security benefits of $15,000. Rory's taxable income from sources other than Social Security exceeds $200,000. In contrast, the Social Security benefits are Nicholi's only source of income. What percentage of the Social Security benefits must Rory include in his gross income? What percentage of Social Security benefits is Nicholi required to include in his gross income?

LO 5-2 27. Rolando purchases a golf cart from his employer, E-Z-Go Golf Carts, for a sizable discount. Explain the rules for determining if Rolando's purchase results in taxable income for him.

LO 5-2 28. When an employer makes a below-market loan to an employee, what are the tax consequences to the employer and employee?

LO 5-2 29. Explain why an insolvent taxpayer is allowed to exclude income from the discharge of indebtedness if the taxpayer remains insolvent after receiving the debt relief.

LO 5-3 30. What are the basic requirements to exclude the gain on the sale of a personal residence?

31. Cassie works in an office and has access to several professional color printers. Her employer allows Cassie and her fellow employees to use the printers to print color postcards for the holidays. This year Cassie printed out two dozen postcards worth almost $76. Must Cassie include this amount in her gross income this year? Explain your answer. LO 5-3
32. What are some common examples of taxable and tax-free fringe benefits? LO 5-3
33. Explain how state and local governments benefit from the provisions that allow taxpayers to exclude interest on state and local bonds from their gross income. LO 5-3
34. Explain why taxpayers are allowed to exclude gifts and inheritances from gross income even though these payments are realized and clearly provide taxpayers with the wherewithal to pay. LO 5-3
35. Describe the kinds of insurance premiums an employer can pay on behalf of an employee without triggering includible compensation to the employee. LO 5-3
36. How are state-sponsored 529 educational savings plans taxed if investment returns are used for educational purposes? Are the returns taxed differently if they are not ultimately used to pay for education costs? LO 5-3
37. Jim was injured in an accident and his surgeon botched the medical procedure. Jim recovered $5,000 from the doctors for pain and suffering and $2,000 for emotional distress. Determine the taxability of these payments and briefly explain to Jim the apparent rationale for including or excluding these payments from gross income. LO 5-3
38. Tom was just hired by Acme Corporation and has decided to purchase disability insurance. This insurance promises to pay him weekly benefits to replace his salary should he be unable to work because of disability. Disability insurance is also available through Acme as part of its compensation plan. Acme pays these premiums as a nontaxable fringe benefit, but the plan promises to pay about 10 percent less in benefits. If Tom elects to have Acme pay the premiums, then his compensation will be reduced by an equivalent amount. Should tax considerations play a role in Tom's choice to buy disability insurance through Acme or on his own? Explain. LO 5-3

PROBLEMS

Select problems are available in Connect®. connect

39. For the following independent cases, determine whether economic income is present and, if so, whether it must be included in gross income (i.e., is it realized and recognized for tax purposes?). LO 5-1
    a) Asia owns stock that is listed on the New York Stock Exchange, and this year the stock increased in value by $20,000.
    b) Ben sold stock for $10,000 and paid a sales commission of $250. Ben purchased the stock several years ago for $4,000.
    c) Bessie is a partner in SULU Enterprises LLC. This year SULU reported that Bessie's share of rental income was $2,700 and her share of municipal interest was $750.
40. Devon owns 1,000 shares of stock worth $10,000. This year he received 200 additional shares of this stock from a stock dividend. His 1,200 shares are now worth $12,500. Must Devon include the dividend paid in stock in income? LO 5-1 research
41. XYZ declared a $1 per share dividend on August 15. The date of record for the dividend was September 1 (the stock began selling *ex-dividend* on September 2). The dividend was paid on September 10. Ellis is a cash-method taxpayer. Determine if he must include the dividends in gross income under the following independent circumstances. LO 5-1 research
    a) Ellis bought 100 shares of XYZ stock on August 1 for $21 per share. Ellis received $100 on September 10. Ellis still owns the shares at year-end.

b) Ellis bought 100 shares of XYZ stock on August 1 for $21 per share. Ellis sold his XYZ shares on September 5 for $23 per share. Ellis received the $100 dividend on September 10 (note that even though Ellis didn't own the stock on September 10, he still received the dividend because he was the shareholder on the record date).

c) Ellis bought 100 shares of XYZ stock for $22 per share on August 20. Ellis received the $100 dividend on September 10. Ellis still owns the shares at year-end.

LO 5-1 research

42. For the following independent cases, determine whether economic income is present and, if so, whether it must be included in gross income. Identify a tax authority that supports your analysis.
   a) Hermione discovered a gold nugget (valued at $10,000) on her land.
   b) Jay embezzled $20,000 from his employer and has not yet been apprehended.
   c) Keisha found $1,000 inside an old dresser. She purchased the dresser at a discount furniture store at the end of last year and found the money after the beginning of the new year. No one has claimed the money.

LO 5-1

43. Although Hank is retired, he is an excellent handyman and often works part-time on small projects for neighbors and friends. Last week his neighbor, Mike, offered to pay Hank $500 for minor repairs to his house. Hank completed the repairs in December of this year. Hank uses the cash method of accounting and is a calendar-year taxpayer. Compute Hank's gross income for this year from each of the following alternative transactions:
   a) Mike paid Hank $200 in cash in December of this year and promised to pay the remaining $300 with interest in three months.
   b) Mike paid Hank $100 in cash in December of this year and gave him a negotiable promissory note for $400 due in three months with interest. Hank sold the note in January for $350.
   c) Mike gave Hank tickets to the big game in January. The tickets have a face value of $50 but Hank could sell them for $400. Hank went to the game with his son.
   d) Mike bought Hank a new set of snow tires. The tires typically sell for $500, but Mike bought them on sale for $450.

LO 5-1

44. Jim recently joined the Austin Barter Club, an organization that facilitates the exchange of services between its members. This year Jim provided lawn-mowing services to other club members. Jim received the following from the barter club. Determine the amount, if any, Jim should include in his gross income in each of the following situations:
   a) Jim received $275 of car repair services from another member of the club.
   b) Jim received a $150 credit that gave him the option of receiving a season pass at a local ski resort from another member of the club. However, he forgot to request the pass by the end of the ski season and his credit expired.
   c) Jim received a $450 credit that can only be applied for goods or services from club members next year.

LO 5-1 research

45. Last year Acme paid Ralph $15,000 to install a new air-conditioning unit at its headquarters building. The air conditioner did not function properly, and this year Acme requested that Ralph return the payment. Because Ralph could not repair one critical part in the unit, he refunded the cost of the repair, $5,000, to Acme.
   a) Is Ralph required to include the $15,000 payment he received last year in his gross income from last year?
   b) What are the tax implications of the repayment if Ralph was in the 35 percent tax bracket when he received the $15,000 payment from Acme, but was in the 28 percent tax bracket when he refunded $5,000 to Acme?
   c) How would you answer the question in part (b) if Ralph refunded $2,500 to Acme and not $5,000?

46. Louis files as a single taxpayer. In April of this year he received a $900 refund of state income taxes that he paid last year. How much of the refund, if any, must Louis include in gross income under the following independent scenarios? Assume the standard deduction last year was $6,300. LO 5-1
    a) Last year Louis claimed itemized deductions of $6,550. Louis's itemized deductions included state income taxes paid of $1,750.
    b) Last year Louis had itemized deductions of $4,800 and he chose to claim the standard deduction. Louis's itemized deductions included state income taxes paid of $1,750.
    c) Last year Louis claimed itemized deductions of $7,740. Louis's itemized deductions included state income taxes paid of $2,750.
47. L. A. and Paula file as married taxpayers. In August of this year, they received a $5,200 refund of state income taxes that they paid last year. How much of the refund, if any, must L. A. and Paula include in gross income under the following independent scenarios? Assume the standard deduction last year was $12,600. LO 5-1
    a) Last year L. A. and Paula had itemized deductions of $10,200, and they chose to claim the standard deduction.
    b) Last year L. A. and Paula claimed itemized deductions of $23,200. Their itemized deductions included state income taxes paid of $7,500.
    c) Last year L. A. and Paula claimed itemized deductions of $15,400. Their itemized deductions included state income taxes paid of $10,500.
48. Clyde is a cash-method taxpayer who reports on a calendar-year basis. This year Paylate Corporation has decided to pay Clyde a year-end bonus of $1,000. Determine the amount Clyde should include in his gross income this year under the following circumstances: LO 5-1
    a) Paylate Corporation wrote the check and put it in his office mail slot on December 30 of this year, but Clyde did not bother to stop by the office to pick it up until after year-end.
    b) Paylate Corporation mistakenly wrote the check for $100. Clyde received the remaining $900 after year-end.
    c) Paylate Corporation mailed the check to Clyde before the end of the year (and it was delivered before year-end). Although Clyde expected the bonus payment, he decided not to collect his mail until after year-end.
    d) Clyde picked up the check in December, but the check could not be cashed immediately because it was postdated January 10.
49. Identify the amount, if any, that these individuals must include in gross income in the following independent cases. Assume that the individuals are on the cash method of accounting and report income on a calendar-year basis. LO 5-2
    a) Elmer was an extremely diligent employee this year and his employer gave him three additional days off with pay (Elmer's gross pay for the three days totaled $1,200, but his net pay was only $948).
    b) Amax purchased new office furniture and allowed each employee to take home old office furniture valued at $250.
50. Ralph owns a building that he is trying to lease. Ralph is a calendar-year, cash-method taxpayer and is trying to evaluate the tax consequences of three different lease arrangements. Under lease 1, the building rents for $500 per month, payable on the first of the next month, and the tenant must make a $500 security deposit that is refunded at the end of the lease. Under lease 2, the building rents for $5,500 per year, payable at the time the lease is signed, but no security deposit is required. Under lease 3, the building rents for $500 per month, payable at the beginning of each month, and the tenant must pay a security deposit of $1,000 that is to be applied toward the rent for the last two months of the lease. LO 5-2 research

a) What amounts are included in Ralph's gross income this year if a tenant signs lease 1 on December 1 and makes timely payments under that lease?

b) What amounts are included in Ralph's gross income this year if the tenant signs lease 2 on December 31 and makes timely payments under that lease?

c) What amounts are included in Ralph's gross income this year if the tenant signs lease 3 on November 30 and makes timely payments under that lease?

LO 5-2

51. Anne purchased an annuity from an insurance company that promised to pay her $20,000 per year for the next 10 years. Anne paid $145,000 for the annuity, and in exchange she will receive $200,000 over the term of the annuity.

a) How much of the first $20,000 payment should Anne include in gross income?

b) How much income will Anne recognize over the term of the annuity?

LO 5-2

52. Larry purchased an annuity from an insurance company that promises to pay him $1,500 per month for the rest of his life. Larry paid $170,820 for the annuity. Larry is in good health and he is 72 years old. Larry received the first annuity payment of $1,500 this month. Use the expected number of payments in Exhibit 5-1 for this problem.

a) How much of the first payment should Larry include in gross income?

b) If Larry lives more than 15 years after purchasing the annuity, how much of each additional payment should he include in gross income?

c) What are the tax consequences if Larry dies just after he receives the 100th payment?

LO 5-2
research

53. Gramps purchased a joint survivor annuity that pays $500 monthly over his remaining life and that of his wife, Gram. Gramps is 70 years old and Gram is 65 years old. Gramps paid $97,020 for the contract. How much income will Gramps recognize on the first payment?

LO 5-2

54. Lanny and Shirley are recently divorced and do not live together. Shirley has custody of their child, Art, and Lanny pays Shirley $22,000 per year. All property was divided equally.

a) How much should Shirley include in income if Lanny's payments are made in cash but will cease if Shirley dies or remarries?

b) How much should Shirley include in income if $12,000 of Lanny's payments is designated as "nonalimony" in the divorce decree?

c) How much should Shirley include in income if Lanny's payments drop to $15,000 once Art reaches the age of 18?

LO 5-2
planning

55. Todd and Margo are seeking a divorce and no longer live together. Margo has offered to pay Todd $42,000 per year for five years if Margo receives sole title to the art collection. This collection cost them $100,000 but is now worth $360,000. All other property is to be divided equally.

a) If Margo's payments cease in the event of Todd's death, how are the payments treated for tax purposes?

b) How much of the gain would be taxed to Todd if Margo sells the art at the end of five years?

c) Compute the tax cost (benefit) to Todd (Margo) if the payments qualify as alimony. Assume that Todd (Margo) has a marginal tax rate of 15 percent (35 percent), and ignore the time value of money.

d) How much more over the five-year period should Todd demand in order to agree to allow the payments to cease in the event of his death? (How much more will make him indifferent between receiving $42,000 a year in nonalimony payments and receiving higher payments that are considered to be alimony?)

56. For each of the following independent situations, indicate the amount the taxpayer must include in gross income and explain your answer: LO 5-2
   a) Phil won $500 in the scratch-off state lottery. There is no state income tax.
   b) Ted won a compact car worth $17,000 in a TV game show. Ted plans to sell the car next year.
   c) Al Bore won the Nobel Peace Prize of $500,000 this year. Rather than take the prize, Al designated that the entire award should go to Weatherhead Charity, a tax-exempt organization.
   d) Jerry was awarded $2,500 from his employer, Acme Toons, when he was selected most handsome employee for Valentine's Day this year.
   e) Ellen won a $1,000 cash prize in a school essay contest. The school is a tax-exempt entity, and Ellen plans to use the funds to pay her college education.
   f) Gene won $400 in the office March Madness pool.

57. Grady received $8,200 of Social Security benefits this year. Grady also reported salary and interest income this year. What amount of the benefits must Grady include in his gross income under the following five independent situations? LO 5-2
   a) Grady files single and reports salary of $12,100 and interest income of $250.
   b) Grady files single and reports salary of $22,000 and interest income of $600.
   c) Grady files married joint and reports salary of $75,000 and interest income of $500.
   d) Grady files married joint and reports salary of $44,000 and interest income of $700.
   e) Grady files married separate and reports salary of $22,000 and interest income of $600.

58. George and Weezy received $30,200 of Social Security benefits this year ($12,000 for George; $18,200 for Weezy). They also received $5,000 of interest from jointly owned City of Ranburne bonds and dividend income. What amount of the Social Security benefits must George and Weezy include in their gross income under the following independent situations? LO 5-2
   a) George and Weezy file married joint and receive $8,000 of dividend income from stocks owned by George.
   b) George and Weezy file married separate and receive $8,000 of dividend income from stocks owned by George.
   c) George and Weezy file married joint and receive $30,000 of dividend income from stocks owned by George.
   d) George and Weezy file married joint and receive $15,000 of dividend income from stocks owned by George.

59. Nikki works for the Shine Company, a retailer of upscale jewelry. How much taxable income does Nikki recognize under the following scenarios? LO 5-2
   a) Nikki buys a diamond ring from Shine Company for $10,000 (normal sales price, $14,000; Shine Company's gross profit percentage is 40%).
   b) Nikki receives a 25 percent discount on jewelry restoration services offered by Shine Company. This year, Nikki had Shine Company repair a set of antique earrings (normal repair cost $500; discounted price $375).

60. Wally is employed as an executive with Pay More Incorporated. To entice Wally to work for Pay More, the corporation loaned him $20,000 at the beginning of the year at a simple interest rate of 1 percent. Wally would have paid interest of $2,400 this year if the interest rate on the loan had been set at the prevailing federal interest rate. LO 5-2

a) Wally used the funds as a down payment on a speedboat and repaid the $20,000 loan (including $200 of interest) at year-end. Does this loan result in any income to either party, and if so, how much?

b) Assume instead that Pay More forgave the loan and interest on December 31. What amount of gross income does Wally recognize this year? Explain.

LO 5-3

61. Jimmy has fallen on hard times recently. Last year he borrowed $250,000 and added an additional $50,000 of his own funds to purchase $300,000 of undeveloped real estate. This year the value of the real estate dropped dramatically, and Jimmy's lender agreed to reduce the loan amount to $230,000. For each of the following independent situations, indicate the amount Jimmy must include in gross income and explain your answer:

a) The real estate is worth $175,000 and Jimmy has no other assets or liabilities.

b) The real estate is worth $235,000 and Jimmy has no other assets or liabilities.

c) The real estate is worth $200,000 and Jimmy has $45,000 in other assets but no other liabilities.

LO 5-3 research

62. Grady is a 45-year-old employee with AMUCK Garbage Corporation. AMUCK pays group-term life insurance premiums for employees, and Grady chose the maximum face amount of $120,000. What amount, if any, of the premium AMUCK paid on his behalf must Grady include in his gross income for the year? Provide a tax authority to support your answer.

LO 5-3

63. Fred currently earns $9,000 per month. Fred has been offered the chance to transfer for three to five years to an overseas affiliate. His employer is willing to pay Fred $10,000 per month if he accepts the assignment. Assume that the maximum foreign-earned income exclusion for next year is $102,100.

a) How much U.S. gross income will Fred report if he accepts the assignment abroad on January 1 of next year and works overseas for the entire year? If Fred's employer also provides him free housing (cost of $20,000), how much of the $20,000 is excludable from Fred's income?

b) Suppose that Fred's employer has offered Fred a six-month overseas assignment beginning on January 1 of next year. How much U.S. gross income will Fred report next year if he accepts the six-month assignment abroad and returns home on July 1 of next year?

c) Suppose that Fred's employer offers Fred a permanent overseas assignment beginning on March 1 of next year. How much U.S. gross income will Fred report next year if he accepts the permanent assignment abroad? Assume that Fred will be abroad for 305 days out of 365 days next year. If Fred's employer also provides him free housing (cost of $16,000 next year), how much of the $16,000 is excludable from Fred's income?

LO 5-3

64. For each of the following situations, indicate how much the taxpayer is required to include in gross income and explain your answer:

a) Steve was awarded a $5,000 scholarship to attend State Law School. The scholarship pays Steve's tuition and fees.

b) Hal was awarded a $15,000 scholarship to attend State Hotel School. All scholarship students must work 20 hours per week at the school residency during the term.

LO 5-3

65. Cecil cashed in a Series EE savings bond with a redemption value of $14,000 and an original cost of $9,800. For each of the following independent scenarios, calculate the amount of interest Cecil will include in his gross income assuming he files as a single taxpayer:

a) Cecil plans to spend all of the proceeds to pay his son's tuition at State University. Cecil's son is a full-time student, and Cecil claims his son as a dependent. Cecil estimates his modified adjusted gross income at $63,100.

b) Assume the same facts in part (a), except Cecil plans to spend $4,200 of the proceeds to pay his son's tuition at State University, and Cecil estimates his modified adjusted gross income at $60,600.

66. Grady is a member of a large family and received the following payments this year. For each payment, determine whether the payment constitutes realized income and determine the amount of each payment Grady must include in his gross income. LO 5-3

a) A gift of $20,000 from Grady's grandfather.

b) One thousand shares of GM stock worth $120 per share inherited from Grady's uncle. The uncle purchased the shares for $25 each, and the shares are worth $125 at year-end.

c) A gift of $50,000 of Ford Motor Bonds. Grady received the bonds on October 31, and he received $1,500 of semiannual interest from the bonds on December 31.

d) A loan of $5,000 for school expenses from Grady's aunt.

67. Bart is the favorite nephew of his aunt Thelma. Thelma transferred several items of value to Bart. For each of the following transactions, determine the effect on Bart's gross income. LO 5-3

a) Thelma gave Bart an auto worth $22,000. Thelma purchased the auto three years ago for $17,000.

b) Thelma elects to cancel her life insurance policy, and she gives the cash surrender value of $15,000 to Bart.

c) Bart is the beneficiary of a $100,000 whole life insurance policy on the life of Thelma. Thelma died this year, and Bart received $100,000 in cash.

d) Bart inherited 500 shares of stock from Thelma's estate. Thelma purchased the shares many years ago for $1,200, and the shares are worth $45,000 at her death.

68. Terry was ill for three months and missed work during this period. During his illness, Terry received $4,500 in sick pay from a disability insurance policy. What amounts are included in Terry's gross income under the following independent circumstances? LO 5-3

a) Terry has disability insurance provided by his employer as a nontaxable fringe benefit. Terry's employer paid $2,800 in disability premiums for Terry this year.

b) Terry paid $2,800 in premiums for his disability insurance this year.

c) Terry's employer paid the $2,800 in premiums for Terry, but Terry elected to have his employer include the $2,800 as compensation on Terry's W-2.

d) Terry has disability insurance whose cost is shared with his employer. Terry's employer paid $1,800 in disability premiums for Terry this year as a nontaxable fringe benefit, and Terry paid the remaining $1,000 of premiums from his after-tax salary.

69. Tim's parents plan to provide him with $50,000 to support him while he establishes a new landscaping business. In exchange for the support, Tim will maintain the landscape at his father's business. Under what conditions will the transfer of $50,000 be included in Tim's gross income? Explain. Do you have a recommendation for Tim and his parents? LO 5-3 planning

70. What amounts are included in gross income for the following taxpayers? Explain your answers. LO 5-3

a) Janus sued Tiny Toys for personal injuries from swallowing a toy. Janus was paid $30,000 for medical costs and $250,000 for punitive damages.

b) Carl was injured in a car accident. Carl's insurance paid him $500 to reimburse his medical expenses and an additional $250 for the emotional distress Carl suffered as a result of the accident.

c) Ajax published a story about Pete and as a result Pete sued Ajax for damage to his reputation. Ajax lost in court and paid Pete an award of $20,000.

d) Bevis was laid off from his job last month. This month he drew $800 in unemployment benefits.

LO 5-3 71. This year, Janelle received $200,000 in life insurance proceeds. Under the following scenarios, how much of the $200,000 is taxable?

a) Janelle received the proceeds upon the death of her father, Julio.

b) Janelle received the $200,000 proceeds because she was diagnosed with colon cancer (life expectancy of six months), and she needed the proceeds for her care.

c) The proceeds related to a life insurance policy she purchased for $35,000 from a friend in need. After purchase, Janelle paid annual premiums that total $22,000.

LO 5-3 72. This year, Leron and Sheena sold their home for $750,000 after all selling costs. Under the following scenarios, how much taxable gain does the home sale generate for Leron and Sheena?

a) Leron and Sheena bought the home three years ago for $150,000 and lived in the home until it sold.

b) Leron and Sheena bought the home one year ago for $600,000 and lived in the home until it sold.

c) Leron and Sheena bought the home five years ago for $500,000. They lived in the home for three years until they decided to buy a smaller home. Their home has been vacant for the past two years.

LO 5-3 73. Dontae's employer has offered him the following employment package. What is Dontae's gross income from his employment?

Salary	$400,000
Health insurance	10,000
Dental insurance	1,500
Membership to Heflin Country Club	20,000
Season tickets to Atlanta Braves games	5,000
Tuition reimbursement for graduate courses	4,000
Housing allowance (for a McMansion in his neighborhood of choice)	40,000

COMPREHENSIVE PROBLEMS

Select problems are available in Connect®. connect

74. Charlie was hired by Ajax this year as a corporate executive and a member of the board of directors. During the current year, Charlie received the following payments or benefits paid on his behalf.

Salary payments	$92,000
Contributions to qualified pension plan	10,200
Qualified health insurance premiums	8,400
Year-end bonus	15,000
Annual director's fee	10,000
Group-term life insurance premiums (face = $40,000)	750
Whole life insurance premiums (face = $100,000)	1,420
Disability insurance premiums (no special elections)	4,350

a) Charlie uses the cash method and calendar year for tax purposes. Calculate Charlie's gross income for the current year.

b) Suppose that Ajax agrees to pay Charlie an additional $100,000 once Charlie completes five years of employment. Will this agreement alter Charlie's gross income this year relative to your part (a) answer? Explain.

c) Suppose that in exchange for his promise to remain with the firm for the next four years, Ajax paid Charlie four years of director's fees in advance. Will this arrangement alter Charlie's gross income this year relative to your part (a) answer? Explain.

d) Assume that in lieu of a year-end bonus Ajax transferred 500 shares of Bell stock to Charlie as compensation. Further assume that the stock was listed at $35 per share and Charlie would sell the shares by year-end, at which time he expected the price to be $37 per share. Will this arrangement alter Charlie's gross income this year relative to your part (a) answer? Explain.

e) Suppose that in lieu of a year-end bonus Ajax made Charlie's house payments (a total of $23,000). Will this arrangement alter Charlie's gross income this year relative to your part (a) answer? Explain.

75. Irene is disabled and receives payments from a number of sources. The interest payments are from bonds that Irene purchased over past years and a disability insurance policy that Irene purchased herself. Calculate Irene's gross income.

Interest, bonds issued by City of Austin, Texas	$ 2,000
Social Security benefits	8,200
Interest, U.S. Treasury bills	1,300
Interest, bonds issued by Ford Motor Company	1,500
Interest, bonds issued by City of Quebec, Canada	750
Disability insurance benefits	19,500
Distributions from qualified pension plan	5,400

76. Ken is 63 years old and unmarried. He retired at age 55 when he sold his business, Understock.com. Though Ken is retired, he is still very active. Ken reported the following financial information this year. Assume Ken files as a single taxpayer. Determine Ken's gross income and complete page 1 of Form 1040 for Ken.

tax forms

a) Ken won $1,200 in an illegal game of poker (the game was played in Utah, where gambling is illegal).

b) Ken sold 1,000 shares of stock for $32 a share. He inherited the stock two years ago. His tax basis (or investment) in the stock was $31 per share.

c) Ken received $25,000 from an annuity he purchased eight years ago. He purchased the annuity, to be paid annually for 20 years, for $210,000.

d) Ken received $13,000 in disability benefits for the year. He purchased the disability insurance policy last year.

e) Ken decided to go back to school to learn about European history. He received a $500 cash scholarship to attend. He used $300 to pay for his books and tuition, and he applied the rest toward his new car payment.

f) Ken's son, Mike, instructed his employer to make half of his final paycheck of the year payable to Ken as a gift from Mike to Ken. Ken received the check on December 30 in the amount of $1,100.

g) Ken received a $610 refund of the $3,600 in state income taxes his employer withheld from his pay last year. Ken claimed $6,350 in itemized deductions last year (the standard deduction for a single filer was $6,300).

h) Ken received $30,000 of interest from corporate bonds and money market accounts.

tax forms

77. Consider the following letter and answer Shady's question.

To my friendly student tax preparer:

Hello, my name is Shady Slim. I understand you are going to help me figure out my gross income for the year . . . whatever that means. It's been a busy year and I'm a busy man, so let me give you the lowdown on my life and you can do your thing.

I was unemployed at the beginning of the year and got $2,000 in unemployment compensation. I later got a job as a manager for Roca Cola. I earned $55,000 in base salary this year. My boss gave me a $5,000 Christmas bonus check on December 22. I decided to hold on to that check and not cash it until next year, so I won't have to pay taxes on it this year. Pretty smart, huh? My job's pretty cool. I get a lot of fringe benefits like a membership to the gym that costs $400 a year and all the Roca Cola I can drink, although I can't really drink a whole lot I figure $40 worth this year.

As part of my manager duties, I get to decide on certain things like contracts for the company. My good buddy, Eddie, runs a bottling company. I made sure that he won the bottling contract for Roca Cola for this year (even though his contract wasn't quite the best). Eddie bought me a Corvette this year for being such a good friend. The Corvette cost $50,000 and I'm sure he bought it for me out of the goodness of his heart. What a great guy!

Here's a bit of good luck for the year. Upon leaving my office one day, I found $8,000 lying in the street! Well, one person's bad luck is my good luck, right?

I like to gamble a lot. I won a $27,000 poker tournament in Las Vegas this year. I also won about $5,000 over the year playing the guys at our Friday night poker game. Can you believe that I didn't lose anything this year?

Speaking of the guys, one of them hit me with his car as we were leaving the game one night. He must have been pretty ticked that he lost! I broke my right leg and my left arm. I sued the guy and got $11,000 for my medical expenses, $3,000 to pay my psychotherapist for the emotional problems I had relating to the injuries (I got really depressed!), and I won $12,000 in punitive damages. That'll teach him that he's not so tough without his car!

Another bit of bad luck. My uncle Monty died this year. I really liked the guy, but the $200,000 inheritance I received from him made me feel a little better about the loss. I did the smart thing with the money and invested it in stocks and bonds and socked a little into my savings account. As a result, I received $600 in dividends from the stock, $200 in interest from the municipal bonds, and $300 in interest from my savings account.

My ex-wife, Alice, is still paying me alimony. She's a lawyer who divorced me a few years ago because I was "unethical" or something like that. Since she was making so much money and I was unemployed at the time, the judge ruled that she had to pay ME alimony. Isn't that something? She sent me $3,000 in alimony payments this year. She still kind of likes me, though. She sent me a check for $500 as a Christmas gift this year. I didn't get her anything, though.

So there you go. That's this year in a nutshell. Can you figure out my gross income and complete page 1 of Form 1040 for me? And since you're a student, this is free, right? Thanks, I owe you one! Let me know if I can get you a six-pack of Roca Cola or something.

tax forms

78. Diana and Ryan Workman were married on January 1 of last year. Diana has an eight-year-old son, Jorge, from her previous marriage. Ryan works as a computer programmer at Datafile Inc. (DI) earning a salary of $96,000. Diana is self-employed and runs a day care center. The Workmans reported the following financial information pertaining to their activities during the current year.

a) Ryan earned a $96,000 salary for the year.

b) Ryan borrowed $12,000 from DI to purchase a car. DI charged him 2 percent interest ($240) on the loan, which Ryan paid on December 31. DI would have charged Ryan $720 if interest had been calculated at the applicable federal interest rate.

c) Diana received $2,000 in alimony and $4,500 in child support payments from her former husband.

d) Diana won a $900 cash prize at her church-sponsored Bingo game.

e) The Workmans received $500 of interest from corporate bonds and $250 of interest from a municipal bond. Diana owned these bonds before she married Ryan.

f) The couple bought 50 shares of ABC Inc. stock for $40 per share on July 2. The stock was worth $47 a share on December 31. The stock paid a dividend of $1.00 per share on December 1.

g) Diana's father passed away on April 14. She inherited cash of $50,000 from her father and his baseball card collection, valued at $2,000. As the beneficiary of her father's life insurance policy, Diana also received $150,000.

h) The couple spent a weekend in Atlantic City in November and came home with gross gambling winnings of $1,200.

i) Ryan received $400 cash for reaching 10 years of continuous service at DI.

j) Ryan was hit and injured by a drunk driver while crossing a street at a crosswalk. He was unable to work for a month. He received $6,000 from his disability insurance. DI paid the premiums for Ryan, but it reported the amount of the premiums as compensation to Ryan on his year-end W-2.

k) The drunk driver who hit Ryan in part (j) was required to pay his $2,000 medical costs, $1,500 for the emotional trauma he suffered from the accident, and $5,000 for punitive damages.

l) For meeting his performance goals this year, Ryan was informed on December 27 that he would receive a $5,000 year-end bonus. DI (located in Houston, Texas) mailed Ryan's bonus check from its payroll processing center (Tampa, Florida) on December 28. Ryan didn't receive the check at his home until January 2.

m) Diana is a 10 percent owner of MNO Inc., a Subchapter S corporation. The company reported ordinary business income for the year of $92,000. Diana acquired the MNO stock two years ago.

n) Diana's day care business collected $35,000 in revenues. In addition, customers owed her $3,000 at year-end. During the year, Diana spent $5,500 for supplies, $1,500 for utilities, $15,000 for rent, and $500 for miscellaneous expenses. One customer gave her use of his vacation home for a week (worth $2,500) in exchange for Diana allowing his child to attend the day care center free of charge. Diana accounts for her business activities using the cash method of accounting.

o) Ryan's employer pays the couple's annual health insurance premiums of $5,500 for a qualified plan.

Required:

A) Assuming the Workmans file a joint tax return, determine their gross income.

B) Using your answer in part (a), complete page 1 of Form 1040 through line 22 for the Workmans.

C) Assuming the Workmans live in California, a community property state, and that Diana and Ryan file separately, what is Ryan's gross income?

D) Using your answer in part (c), complete page 1 of Form 1040 through line 22 for Ryan Workman.

ROGER | *CPA Review*

Sample CPA Exam questions from Roger CPA Review are available in Connect as support for the topics in this text. These Multiple Choice Questions and Task-Based Simulations include expert-written explanations and solutions, and provide a starting point for students to become familiar with the content and functionality of the actual CPA Exam.

chapter

6 Individual Deductions

Learning Objectives

Upon completing this chapter, you should be able to:

LO 6-1 Identify the common deductions necessary for calculating adjusted gross income (AGI).

LO 6-2 Describe the different types of itemized deductions available to individuals and compute itemized deductions.

LO 6-3 Explain the operation of the standard deduction, determine the deduction for personal and dependency exemptions, and compute taxable income.

© Image Source

Storyline Summary

Taxpayers:	Courtney Wilson, age 40 Courtney's mother, Dorothy "Gram" Weiss, age 70
Family description:	Courtney is divorced with a son, Deron, age 10, and a daughter, Ellen, age 20. Gram is currently residing with Courtney. Ellen is currently a full-time student.
Location:	Kansas City, Missouri
Employment status:	Courtney works as an architect for EWD. Gram is retired.
Filing status:	Courtney files as head-of-household. Gram files as a single taxpayer.
Current situation:	Courtney and Gram are trying to determine their allowable deductions and compute taxable income.

Now that Courtney has determined her gross income, she still must determine her deductions to compute taxable income. Fortunately, Courtney keeps detailed records of all the expenditures she believes to be deductible. Besides expenses associated with her weekend consulting work and rental property, Courtney incurred some significant costs moving from Cincinnati to Kansas City. She also paid self-employment taxes on her consulting income and paid tuition for Ellen to attend summer school. Courtney is confident most of these items are deductible, but she isn't quite sure about the tuition.

Based on her review of prior-year tax returns, Courtney has a pretty good handle on her itemized deductions. She incurred some extra medical expenses to treat a broken wrist from a mountain biking accident and had additional state income taxes withheld from her paycheck. Courtney paid real estate taxes for her personal residence and investment property and interest expense on loans secured by her new home. She also donated (cash and property) to her favorite charities. Courtney experienced losses when her purse was stolen and when she damaged her car in an accident. She isn't sure if these losses are deductible.

In a push to improve her job performance, Courtney incurred costs to attend motivational seminars and travel to other parts of the country to study different architectural designs. Despite the fact that she was trying to improve her job performance, EWD did not reimburse her for these costs.

Gram wasn't as busy as Courtney this year. Gram paid a penalty for cashing in her certificate of deposit early. She also paid some medical expenses and donated money to her local church. Gram is a little frustrated because she doesn't incur enough itemized deductions to exceed the standard deduction amount. Gram recently heard that she might be able to save taxes by "bunching" her itemized deductions into one year. She's hoping to learn a little bit more about this technique. In any event, Gram didn't pay any taxes during the year and she wants to learn how much she's going to owe. ■

In the previous chapter, we determined *gross income* for both Courtney and Gram. To compute their taxable income, however, we need to identify their deductions. As emphasized previously, taxpayers are not allowed to deduct expenditures unless there is a specific tax law authorizing the deductions. And as we learn in this chapter, Congress grants many deductions for taxpayers for a variety of reasons.

As we discussed in the Individual Income Tax Overview, Exemptions, and Filing Status chapter, deductions appear in one of two places in the individual income tax formula. Deductions "*for* AGI" (also called deductions "above the line") are subtracted directly from gross income.[1] Next, deductions "*from* AGI" (also called deductions "below the line" or "itemized" deductions) are subtracted directly *from* AGI, resulting in taxable income. Deductions *for* AGI are generally preferred over deductions *from* AGI because deductions above the line reduce taxable income dollar for dollar. In contrast, deductions *from* AGI sometimes have no effect on taxable income. Further, because many of the limitations on tax benefits for higher income taxpayers are based upon AGI, deductions *for* AGI often reduce these limitations, thereby increasing potential tax benefits. Thus, it's important to determine both the amount of the deduction and whether it's a deduction *for* AGI or *from* AGI. We begin our discussion of deductions by describing deductions *for* AGI, and we conclude by tackling itemized deductions, the standard deduction, and exemptions.

LO 6-1

DEDUCTIONS *FOR* AGI

Congress allows taxpayers to claim a variety of deductions *for* AGI.[2] To provide an overview, we select a cross section of deductions *for* AGI and classify them into three categories:

1. Deductions *directly* related to **business activities**.
2. Deductions *indirectly* related to business activities.
3. Deductions subsidizing specific activities.

We've organized our discussion around these categories to illustrate the variety of deductions *for* AGI and explain why Congress provides preferential treatment for certain deductions.

Deductions Directly Related to Business Activities

As a matter of equity, Congress allows taxpayers involved in business activities to deduct expenses incurred to generate business income. That is, because taxpayers include the revenue they receive from doing business in gross income, they should be allowed to deduct against gross income the expenses they incur to generate those revenues.

To begin, we must define "business activities" and, for reasons we discuss below, we must distinguish business activities from **investment activities.** In general, for tax

[1]Most, but not all, deductions *for* AGI appear on lines 23 through 35 on page 1 of Form 1040. The term "above the line" refers to the placement of deductions *for* AGI before the last line of the first page of Form 1040. This last line is the taxpayer's AGI.

[2]§62 identifies deductions *for* AGI.

purposes, activities are either *profit-motivated* or motivated by personal objectives. Profit-motivated activities are, in turn, classified as either (1) business activities or (2) investment activities. Business activities are sometimes referred to as a **trade or business,** and these activities require a relatively high level of involvement or effort. For example, if an individual is a full-time employee, the individual is in the business of being an employee. Self-employed individuals are also engaged in business activities. Unlike business activities, investment activities are profit-motivated activities that *don't* require a high degree of involvement or effort.[3] Instead, investment activities involve investing in property for appreciation or for income payments. An individual who occasionally buys land or stock in anticipation of appreciation or dividend payments would be engaged in an investment activity.

Example 6-1

Suppose that Courtney purchased a parcel of land for its appreciation potential. Would her ownership in the land be considered a business or investment activity?

Answer: Courtney's activity would most likely be considered an investment activity, because she acquired the land for its appreciation potential and she does not plan to exercise any special effort to develop the property or to become actively involved in other real estate speculation.

What if: Suppose that Courtney frequently buys and sells land or develops land to sell in small parcels to those wanting to build homes. Would Courtney's activity be considered a business or investment activity?

Answer: Courtney's activity would most likely be considered a business activity because she is actively involved in generating profits from the land by developing it rather than simply holding the land for appreciation.

The distinction between business and investment activities is critical for determining whether a deduction associated with the activity is above or below the line. With one exception, business expenses are deducted *for* AGI. The lone exception is unreimbursed employee business expenses, which are deductible as miscellaneous itemized deductions (*from* AGI deductions).[4] In contrast, investment expenses are deductible as itemized deductions, with one exception. Expenses associated with rental and royalty activities are deductible *for* AGI regardless of whether the activity qualifies as an investment or a business. Exhibit 6-1 summarizes the rules for classifying business and investment expenses as *for* and *from* AGI deductions.

EXHIBIT 6-1 Individual Business and Investment Expense Deductions *for* AGI and *from* AGI

	Deduction Type	
Activity Type	**Deduction *for* AGI**	**Deduction *from* AGI** (itemized deduction)
Business activities	Self-employed business expenses	Unreimbursed employee business expenses
Investment activities	Rental and royalty expenses	Other investment expenses

[3]§162 authorizes trade or business expense deductions, while §212 authorizes deductions for investment activities. The distinction between these activities is discussed in the Business Income, Deductions, and Accounting Methods chapter.

[4]For example, an employee may use her own automobile to make a business delivery for her employer. The expenses she incurs to make the delivery (cost of operating the automobile and parking) are business expenses that are deducted *from* AGI as miscellaneous itemized deductions.

Trade or Business Expenses Congress limits business deductions to expenses directly related to the business activity and those that are **ordinary and necessary** for the activity.[5] This means that deductible expenses must be appropriate and helpful for generating a profit. Although business deductions are one of the most common deductions *for* AGI, they are not readily visible on the front page of Form 1040. Instead, these deductions are reported with business revenues on Schedule C of Form 1040. Schedule C, presented in Exhibit 6-2, is essentially an income statement for the business that identifies typical ordinary and necessary business expenses. Taxpayers transfer the *net* income or loss from Schedule C to Form 1040 (page 1), line 12.

EXHIBIT 6-2 Parts I and II from Schedule C Profit or Loss from Business

Part I Income

1	Gross receipts or sales. See instructions for line 1 and check the box if this income was reported to you on Form W-2 and the "Statutory employee" box on that form was checked . . . . ▶ ☐	1	
2	Returns and allowances	2	
3	Subtract line 2 from line 1	3	
4	Cost of goods sold (from line 42)	4	
5	**Gross profit.** Subtract line 4 from line 3	5	
6	Other income, including federal and state gasoline or fuel tax credit or refund (see instructions)	6	
7	**Gross income.** Add lines 5 and 6 . . . ▶	7	

Part II Expenses. Enter expenses for business use of your home **only** on line 30.

8	Advertising	8		18	Office expense (see instructions)	18	
9	Car and truck expenses (see instructions)	9		19	Pension and profit-sharing plans	19	
				20	Rent or lease (see instructions):		
10	Commissions and fees	10		a	Vehicles, machinery, and equipment	20a	
11	Contract labor (see instructions)	11		b	Other business property	20b	
12	Depletion	12		21	Repairs and maintenance	21	
13	Depreciation and section 179 expense deduction (not included in Part III) (see instructions)	13		22	Supplies (not included in Part III)	22	
				23	Taxes and licenses	23	
				24	Travel, meals, and entertainment:		
14	Employee benefit programs (other than on line 19)	14		a	Travel	24a	
15	Insurance (other than health)	15		b	Deductible meals and entertainment (see instructions)	24b	
16	Interest:			25	Utilities	25	
a	Mortgage (paid to banks, etc.)	16a		26	Wages (less employment credits)	26	
b	Other	16b		27a	Other expenses (from line 48)	27a	
17	Legal and professional services	17		b	**Reserved for future use**	27b	

28	**Total expenses** before expenses for business use of home. Add lines 8 through 27a . . . ▶	28	
29	Tentative profit or (loss). Subtract line 28 from line 7	29	
30	Expenses for business use of your home. Do not report these expenses elsewhere. Attach Form 8829 unless using the simplified method (see instructions). **Simplified method filers only:** enter the total square footage of: (a) your home: ________ and (b) the part of your home used for business: ________. Use the Simplified Method Worksheet in the instructions to figure the amount to enter on line 30	30	
31	**Net profit or (loss).** Subtract line 30 from line 29. • If a profit, enter on both **Form 1040, line 12** (or **Form 1040NR, line 13**) and on **Schedule SE, line 2.** (If you checked the box on line 1, see instructions). Estates and trusts, enter on **Form 1041, line 3.** • If a loss, you **must** go to line 32.	31	
32	If you have a loss, check the box that describes your investment in this activity (see instructions). • If you checked 32a, enter the loss on both **Form 1040, line 12,** (or **Form 1040NR, line 13**) and on **Schedule SE, line 2.** (If you checked the box on line 1, see the line 31 instructions). Estates and trusts, enter on **Form 1041, line 3.** • If you checked 32b, you **must** attach **Form 6198.** Your loss may be limited.	32a ☐ All investment is at risk. 32b ☐ Some investment is not at risk.	

For Paperwork Reduction Act Notice, see the separate instructions. Cat. No. 11334P **Schedule C (Form 1040) 2016**

Example 6-2

Besides being employed by EWD, Courtney is also a self-employed consultant (a business activity). This year her consulting activity generated $19,500 of revenue and incurred $1,500 in expenses (primarily travel and transportation expenses). How does she report the revenue and deductions from the activity?

Answer: Courtney reports the $19,500 of revenue and deducts the $1,500 of business expenses *for* AGI on her Schedule C. Her net income of $18,000 from her consulting activities is included on the front page (line 12) of her individual tax return.

[5]§162. In the Business Income, Deductions, and Accounting Methods chapter, we address the requirements for deductible business expenses in detail.

Rental and Royalty Expenses Taxpayers are allowed to deduct their expenses associated with generating rental or royalty income *for* AGI.[6] Similar to business expenses, rental and royalty expenses do not appear directly on the front page of Form 1040. Instead, rental and royalty deductions are reported with rental and royalty revenues on Schedule E of Form 1040.[7] Schedule E, presented in Exhibit 6-3, is essentially an income statement for the taxpayer's rental or royalty activities. Taxpayers transfer the *net* income or loss from Schedule E to Form 1040 (page 1), line 17.

Rental and royalty endeavors are most commonly considered to be investment activities, but like trade or business expenses, rental and royalty deductions are claimed above the line.[8] Perhaps rental and royalty expenses are deductible *for* AGI because Congress believed that these activities usually require more taxpayer involvement than other types of investment activities. Despite this preferential treatment, the deductibility of rental losses (where expenses exceed income) is subject to limitations (basis, at-risk, and passive loss rules). We discuss these limitations in the Investments chapter when we discuss similar limitations that apply to investments in flow-through entities.

EXHIBIT 6-3 Page 1 of Schedule E Rental or Royalty Income

Income:	Properties:		A	B	C
3	Rents received	3			
4	Royalties received	4			
Expenses:					
5	Advertising	5			
6	Auto and travel (see instructions)	6			
7	Cleaning and maintenance	7			
8	Commissions	8			
9	Insurance	9			
10	Legal and other professional fees	10			
11	Management fees	11			
12	Mortgage interest paid to banks, etc. (see instructions)	12			
13	Other interest	13			
14	Repairs	14			
15	Supplies	15			
16	Taxes	16			
17	Utilities	17			
18	Depreciation expense or depletion	18			
19	Other (list) ►	19			
20	Total expenses. Add lines 5 through 19	20			
21	Subtract line 20 from line 3 (rents) and/or 4 (royalties). If result is a (loss), see instructions to find out if you must file **Form 6198**	21			
22	Deductible rental real estate loss after limitation, if any, on **Form 8582** (see instructions)	22	( )	( )	( )
23a	Total of all amounts reported on line 3 for all rental properties		23a		
b	Total of all amounts reported on line 4 for all royalty properties		23b		
c	Total of all amounts reported on line 12 for all properties		23c		
d	Total of all amounts reported on line 18 for all properties		23d		
e	Total of all amounts reported on line 20 for all properties		23e		
24	**Income.** Add positive amounts shown on line 21. **Do not** include any losses			24	
25	**Losses.** Add royalty losses from line 21 and rental real estate losses from line 22. Enter total losses here			25	( )
26	**Total rental real estate and royalty income or (loss).** Combine lines 24 and 25. Enter the result here. If Parts II, III, IV, and line 40 on page 2 do not apply to you, also enter this amount on Form 1040, line 17, or Form 1040NR, line 18. Otherwise, include this amount in the total on line 41 on page 2			26	

For Paperwork Reduction Act Notice, see the separate instructions. Cat. No. 11344L **Schedule E (Form 1040) 2016**

[6]§212(a)(4).

[7]Rental income and expenses for renting personal property (e.g., equipment, furniture, etc.) instead of real property is generally reported on Schedule C (not Schedule E). If the rental of personal property is not considered a trade or business, the rental income and expenses are reported on lines 21 and 36, respectively, of Form 1040.

[8]Royalties are received for allowing others to use property or rights to property. For example, royalties are paid for allowing others to use or sell copyrighted material, such as books or plays, or to extract natural resources from property. The amount of the royalty is often a percentage of total revenues derived from the property or rights to property.

Example 6-3

Courtney owns a condominium that she rents to tenants. This year she received $14,000 in rental revenue and incurred $9,000 of expenses associated with the rental, including management fees, maintenance, and depreciation. How does she report the revenue and expenses for tax purposes?

Answer: Courtney reports the $14,000 of rental receipts and deducts the $9,000 of rental expenses *for* AGI on Schedule E. The net rental income of $5,000 is reported on the front page (line 17) of her individual tax return.

Losses As we discuss in more detail in the Property Dispositions chapter, taxpayers disposing of business assets at a loss are allowed to deduct the losses *for* AGI. Also, individual taxpayers selling investment (capital) assets at a loss are allowed to deduct the "capital" losses against other capital gains. If the capital losses exceed the capital gains, they can deduct up to $3,000 as a net capital loss in a particular year. Losses in excess of the $3,000 limit are carried forward indefinitely to subsequent years when they are deductible subject to the same limitations.

Flow-Through Entities Income from flow-through entities such as partnerships, LLCs, and S corporations passes through to the owners of those entities and is reported on Schedule E of the tax returns of the owners. Similarly, any expenses and losses incurred by the entity pass through to the entity owners, who typically treat them as deductions *for* AGI, subject to certain restrictions (basis, at-risk, and passive loss rules) that we discuss in the Investments chapter.

Deductions Indirectly Related to Business Activities

Taxpayers can incur expenses in activities that are not directly related to making money but that they would not have incurred if they were not involved in a business activity. Taxpayers are allowed to deduct several of these expenses that are indirectly related to business activities as deductions *for* AGI. We describe several of these deductions below.

Moving Expenses The cost of moving personal possessions is not a direct cost of doing business or being employed. Nonetheless, individuals qualify for a moving expense deduction if they move *and* change their principal place of work. Specifically, individuals can deduct moving expenses as deductions *for* AGI if they meet two tests: (1) a distance test and (2) a time test associated with the move.[9]

To satisfy the distance test, the distance from the taxpayer's old residence to the new place of work must be at least 50 miles more than the distance from the old residence to the old place of work. In other words, if the taxpayer were staying in her old home, the new place of work must increase her commute by at least 50 miles, thereby justifying a move to a new residence. To satisfy the time test, the taxpayer must either be employed full-time for 39 of the first 52 weeks after the move or be self-employed for 78 of the first 104 weeks after the move. A taxpayer can deduct moving expenses on her return if she expects to meet the time test but has not yet done so at year-end. If the taxpayer later fails

[9]§217. Moving expenses are deducted on Form 3903.

to meet the time test, she must either amend her prior return to eliminate the moving expense deduction or include the previous moving expense deduction as other income on her return in the year the time test was not met.

Individuals need not change employers if they meet both tests. Indeed, taxpayers can qualify for a moving expense deduction by beginning their first job, by beginning a job after a prolonged absence from the workforce, or by changing locations with the same employer. In addition, a taxpayer's reasons for moving may be entirely personal, such as wanting to move to a milder climate; business-related, such as wanting to change jobs or start a new business; or some of both.

Example 6-4

Before moving to Kansas City, Courtney lived in Cincinnati, Ohio, where she commuted 10 miles to her place of work. The distance from Courtney's home in Cincinnati to EWD in Kansas City, her new place of work, is 580 miles. Can Courtney deduct the expenses of moving her residence to Kansas City?

Answer: Yes. Courtney meets both the distance and the time tests because 580 miles is more than 60 miles (her original 10-mile commute from her former residence to her former place of work, plus 50 miles), and because she worked for EWD for the requisite 39 weeks during her first 52 weeks after her move (she worked from mid-January through December 31).

What if: Suppose that Courtney started a new job at an office just outside of Cincinnati and moved into a new residence. The distance from Courtney's former residence to her former place of work was 12 miles. The distance from Courtney's former residence to her new place of work is 55 miles. Does Courtney meet the distance test for moving expenses?

Answer: No, because if she had stayed in her former residence her commute would have increased by only 43 miles. To qualify, the commute from her former residence to her new work must be at least 50 miles longer than her commute from her former residence to her former place of work. Note that the location of her new residence is irrelevant to the distance test.

What if: Suppose that Courtney started a new job at an office just outside of Cincinnati and moved into a new residence. If the distance from Courtney's former residence to her former place of work was 12 miles, and the distance from her former residence to her new work place is 80 miles, does Courtney meet the distance test for moving expenses?

Answer: Yes, the commute from her former residence to her new job is 68 miles longer than the commute from her former residence to her old job.

Deductible moving expenses are limited to reasonable expenses associated with moving personal possessions and traveling to the new residence, including transportation and lodging. Taxpayers are allowed to deduct a mileage rate in lieu of the actual costs of driving their personal automobiles during the move. In 2017, taxpayers are allowed to deduct 17 cents a mile for driving their personal automobiles during a move. Taxpayers may also deduct the cost of moving their personal belongings and the belongings of members of their households. Taxpayers are *not* allowed to deduct costs such as meals during the move or costs associated with house-hunting trips. Taxpayers who are reimbursed by their employers for actual moving expenses exclude the reimbursement from income but do not deduct the reimbursed expenses. However, taxpayers who receive a flat amount as a moving allowance from their employers (i.e., without a requirement to document actual moving expenses to the employer) are required to include the allowance in gross income and can deduct their actual moving expenses *for* AGI.

THE KEY FACTS

Moving Expenses

- Deductible *for* AGI for individuals who pass a mileage test and a time test.
- Mileage test: New job site must extend existing commute by at least 50 miles.
- Time test: Taxpayer must be employed at least 39 of 52 weeks or be self-employed for 78 of the 104 weeks following the move.

Example 6-5

Courtney drove 691 miles in her move from Cincinnati to Kansas City and incurred the following expenses related to the move:

Description	Amount
Moving company (personal belongings)	$5,000
Lodging (one night en route)	179
Meals en route	75
House-hunting trip	520

What amount can Courtney deduct as moving expenses?

Answer: Courtney can deduct $5,296 computed as follows:

Description	Deduction
Transportation (17¢ per mile times 691 miles)	$ 117
Moving company (personal belongings)	5,000
Lodging (one night en route)	179
Total deduction	**$5,296**

The meals and house-hunting trip are not deductible.

What if: Suppose that EWD agreed to reimburse Courtney for moving expenses up to a maximum of $2,000. What amount would Courtney deduct for moving expenses?

Answer: $3,296. Courtney would deduct $3,296 in moving expenses ($5,296 minus $2,000 reimbursement). She would not include the reimbursement in income and would not deduct the $2,000 of expenses for which she was reimbursed.

Health Insurance Deduction by Self-Employed Taxpayers The cost of health insurance is essentially a personal expense. However, *employers* often pay a portion of health insurance premiums for employees as a qualified fringe benefit. Employers are allowed to deduct health insurance premiums as compensation expense while employees are allowed to *exclude* these premiums from gross income. In contrast to employees, the health insurance fringe benefit does not apply to self-employed taxpayers because they are not "employees." To provide equitable treatment, Congress allows self-employed taxpayers to claim personal health insurance premiums for the taxpayer, the taxpayer's spouse, the taxpayer's dependents, and the taxpayer's children under age 27 (regardless of whether or not the child is a dependent of the taxpayer) as deductions *for* AGI, but only to the extent of the self-employment income derived from the specific trade or business.[10]

This deduction is intended to help self-employed taxpayers who must pay their own insurance premiums. Consequently, self-employed taxpayers are *not* allowed to deduct health care insurance premiums if the taxpayer is *eligible* to participate in an employer-provided health plan. This restriction applies regardless of whether the health plan is sponsored by either an employer of the taxpayer or an employer of the taxpayer's spouse, and it is irrelevant whether the taxpayer actually participates in the plan.[11]

[10]§162(l). As we'll explain shortly, health insurance premiums also qualify as itemized deductions as medical expenses, but itemizing these deductions may not produce any tax benefits. To the extent that self-employed taxpayers do not have sufficient self-employment income to deduct all of their health insurance premiums as a *for* AGI deduction, they may deduct the remaining premiums as an itemized deduction. Finally, subject to certain restrictions, self-employed taxpayers who purchase health insurance through an exchange, have household incomes below 400% of the poverty line, and are not eligible for affordable coverage through an employer health plan that provides at least 60% of the expected costs for covered services can receive a premium tax credit under §36B. Any premiums offset by the tax credit cannot be deducted as either a *for* AGI or itemized deduction.

[11]§162(l)(2)(B).

Self-Employment Tax Deduction Employees and employers each pay Social Security and Medicare tax on employee salaries. Employers deduct the Social Security and Medicare taxes they pay on employee salaries. In contrast, because self-employed individuals do not have an employer, these individuals are required to pay self-employment tax. This tax represents both the employee's *and* the employer's share of the Social Security and Medicare taxes. Unfortunately for the self-employed, the self-employment tax is *not* considered a business expense. To put self-employed individuals on somewhat equal footing with other employers who are allowed to deduct the *employer's* share of the Social Security and Medicare taxes, self-employed taxpayers are allowed to deduct the employer portion of the self-employment tax they pay.

Example 6-6

As we indicated in Example 6-2, Courtney reported $18,000 of net income from her self-employed consulting activities. She paid $482 in self-employment taxes on this income, with $241 representing the employer portion of the self-employment tax.[12] What amount of self-employment tax can she deduct this year?

Answer: $241 (the employer portion of the self-employment tax).

Penalty for Early Withdrawal of Savings This provision allows a deduction *for* AGI for any interest income an individual forfeits to a bank as a penalty for prematurely withdrawing a certificate of deposit or similar deposit. This deduction reduces the taxpayer's net interest income to the amount she actually received. Otherwise, taxpayers would be required to report the full amount of interest income as taxable income and could deduct only the forfeited interest as an investment-expense miscellaneous itemized deduction. As we discuss below, investment expenses deducted as miscellaneous itemized deductions are subject to limitations that substantially reduce their tax benefits.

Example 6-7

Gram invested $100,000 in a three-year certificate of deposit (CD). On December 31, she decided to cash out the certificate of deposit after holding it for less than a year. She receives the $4,100 of interest income the CD had generated up to the withdrawal date, less a $410 early withdrawal penalty. How will Gram report the interest and early withdrawal for tax purposes?

Answer: Gram reports $4,100 as interest income this year and deducts the $410 early withdrawal penalty as a deduction *for* AGI.

Deductions Subsidizing Specific Activities

To address specific policy objectives, Congress provides that certain expenditures are deductible *for* AGI. For example, alimony payments are deductible *for* AGI to maintain equity and contributions to retirement savings are deductible *for* AGI to encourage savings.[13] Further, Congress created two important deductions *for* AGI to encourage and subsidize higher education. Taxpayers are allowed to deduct *for* AGI, subject to certain limitations, (1) interest expense on **qualified educational loans** and (2) **qualified educational expenses.**[14] As we discuss throughout the text, Congress

[12]In this case, Courtney uses the following equation to determine her total self-employment tax: $18,000 × .9235 × .029 = $482 (Courtney's business income is subject to the Medicare tax but not the Social Security tax due to the level of her salary). Of the total self-employment tax, the employer portion is calculated as $18,000 × .9235 × .0145 = $241. We discuss how to compute the self-employment tax in detail in the Individual Income Tax Computation and Tax Credits chapter.

[13]See the Gross Income and Exclusions chapter for a detailed discussion of alimony and the Retirement Savings and Deferred Compensation chapter for a detailed discussion of the tax consequences of retirement savings.

[14]See §221 and §222.

THE KEY FACTS

Interest on Education Loans

- Up to $2,500 of interest on education loans is deductible *for* AGI.
- A loan qualifies as an education loan if the proceeds are used to fund qualified education.
- The interest deduction is phased out for taxpayers with AGI exceeding $65,000 ($135,000 married filing jointly).

has also created a number of related provisions, including education tax credits, to encourage and subsidize higher education.

Deduction for Interest on Qualified Education Loans Qualified education loans are loans whose proceeds are used to pay qualified education expenses.[15] Qualified education expenses encompass expenses paid for the education of the taxpayer, the taxpayer's spouse, or a taxpayer's dependent to attend a postsecondary institution of higher education.[16] These expenses include tuition and fees, books and expenses required for enrollment, room and board, and other necessary supplies and expenses, including travel.

The deduction for interest expense on qualified education loans is the amount of interest paid up to $2,500. However, the deduction is reduced (phased out) for taxpayers depending on the taxpayer's filing status and modified AGI. Modified AGI for this purpose is AGI *before* deducting interest expense on the qualified education loans and *before* deducting qualified education expenses (discussed below). Married individuals who file separately are not allowed to deduct this expense under any circumstance. The deduction limitations for other taxpayers are summarized in Exhibit 6-4.

EXHIBIT 6-4 **Summary of Limitations on Deduction of Interest on Education Loans**

Panel A: AGI Limitations

Modified AGI Level	Deduction
Not over $65,000 ($135,000 for married filing jointly)	Amount paid up to $2,500
Above $65,000 ($135,000 for married filing jointly) but below $80,000 ($165,000 for married filing jointly)	Amount paid up to $2,500 reduced by the phase-out amount. The phase-out amount is the amount paid up to $2,500 times the phase-out percentage (see Panel B for the phase-out percentage computation).
Equal to or above $80,000 ($165,000 for married filing jointly)	Zero

Panel B: Phase-Out Percentage*

Filing Status	Phase-Out Percentage
Single or head of household	(Modified AGI – $65,000)/$15,000
Married filing jointly	(Modified AGI – $135,000)/$30,000

*Married taxpayers filing separately are ineligible for the deduction.

Example 6-8

What if: Assume that Courtney's brother Jason paid interest on a qualified education loan that he used to pay the tuition and fees for his three daughters to attend State University. In 2017, Jason was married and filed a joint return, paid $2,000 of interest expense on the loan, and reported modified AGI of $147,000. What amount of interest expense on the education loan is Jason allowed to deduct as a *for* AGI deduction?

[15]Home equity loans cannot qualify as education loans regardless of how the loan proceeds are spent.

[16]Postsecondary education includes courses at a university, college, or vocational school, including internship programs leading to a degree or certificate. Qualifying costs claimed as deductions *for* AGI cannot be reimbursed by scholarships or Coverdell education savings accounts and are also ineligible for American opportunity and lifetime learning credit purposes.

Answer: $1,200, computed as follows:

Description	Amount	Explanation
(1) Modified AGI	$147,000	AGI before higher education deductions
(2) Amount of interest paid up to $2,500	2,000	Lesser of amount paid ($2,000) or $2,500
(3) Phase-out (reduction) percentage	40%	[(1) − $135,000]/30,000)
(4) Phase-out amount (reduction in maximum)	800	(2) × (3)
Deductible interest expense	**$ 1,200**	(2) − (4)

Deduction for Qualified Education Expenses This deduction subsidizes tuition payments for higher education. For purposes of this deduction, qualified education expenses are limited to the tuition and fees required for enrollment at a postsecondary institution of higher education. Thus, the definition of qualifying expenses is more restrictive for the qualified education expense deduction than it is for the education loan interest expense deduction. However, similar to the education interest expense deduction, the amount of the maximum education expense deduction depends on filing status and level of modified AGI. For purposes of the qualified education expense deduction, modified AGI is AGI *after* deducting the education loan interest expense but *before* deducting qualified education expenses. Just as with the qualified education loan interest deduction, married individuals filing separately are ineligible for the qualified education expense deduction. The rules for determining the allowable education expense deduction for taxpayers who qualify for the deduction are summarized in Exhibit 6-5.[17]

EXHIBIT 6-5 Summary of 2016 Limitations on Qualified Education Expenses

Modified AGI Level	Deduction
Not over $65,000 ($130,000 for married filing jointly)	Amount paid up to $4,000
Above $65,000 ($130,000 for married filing jointly) but less than or equal to $80,000 ($160,000)	Lesser of amount paid or $2,000
Above 80,000 ($160,000 for married filing jointly)	Zero

A taxpayer generally may only deduct the qualified education expenses that he or she pays. To deduct a dependent's education expense, the taxpayer must actually pay the expense and claim the student as a dependent. If a student pays his or her own education expenses and is eligible to be claimed as another taxpayer's dependent, no taxpayer (including the dependent) may deduct the education expense. In contrast, if another taxpayer pays a student's education expenses and the student is not considered the taxpayer's dependent, the payment of the student's education expense is considered a gift and the student can deduct the expenses.

There are two important differences between the AGI limits on the interest on education loans deduction (summarized in Exhibit 6-4) and the AGI limits on the educational expense deduction (summarized in Exhibit 6-5). First, the definition of modified AGI for qualified education expenses in Exhibit 6-5 includes the deduction for interest on education loans. Second, the interest expense on education loans is phased out gradually over a range of AGI but the deduction for qualified education expenses is phased out in specific AGI increments (the phase-out applies in steps).

[17]At press time, the deduction for qualified education expenses is scheduled to expire after 2016.

Example 6-9

Courtney paid $2,100 of tuition for Ellen to attend the University of Missouri–Kansas City during the summer. How much of this payment can Courtney deduct as a qualifying education expense?

Answer: None. The cost of the tuition is a qualified education expense, but Courtney's modified AGI exceeds $80,000. (Courtney files as a head of household.) Hence, Courtney is not allowed to deduct any of the cost of the tuition she paid for Ellen.

What if: Assume the same facts except that Courtney is married filing jointly and her modified AGI is $57,000. What amount can Courtney deduct as a qualifying education expense in this situation?

Answer: $2,100. She can deduct the full amount of the expenditure (limited to $4,000) because she is married filing jointly and her modified AGI is less than $130,000.

What if: Assume the original facts except that Courtney's modified AGI is $77,000. How much of the $2,100 tuition for Ellen would Courtney be allowed to deduct as a *for* AGI qualified education expense?

Answer: $2,000. Because Courtney's AGI is greater than $65,000 but not greater than $80,000 (she files as head of household), her deduction is the lesser of (1) her actual qualified education expenditures and (2) $2,000. Since Courtney's actual education expenditures were $2,100, her deduction is $2,000.

THE KEY FACTS

Education Expenses

- Up to $4,000 of qualified education expenses can be deducted *for* AGI.
- Qualified education expenses include tuition and related costs for postsecondary or higher education.
- The deduction is reduced for taxpayers with modified AGI over $65,000 ($130,000 married filing jointly) and eliminated for taxpayers with modified AGI exceeding $80,000 ($160,000 married filing jointly).

Because there are several education-related tax incentives, individuals can sometimes select among different tax benefits. For example, certain education expenses that qualify as deductions *for* AGI may also qualify for an education tax credit (see the Individual Income Tax Computation and Tax Credits chapter) or employee business expenses (deductible as miscellaneous itemized deductions, discussed later in the chapter). Likewise, as shown in the Gross Income and Exclusions chapter, up to $5,250 of education expenses paid by an employer's educational assistance program may be excluded from an employee's gross income (but not deducted or claimed as a credit by the employee). Typically, a single expenditure *cannot* generate multiple tax benefits. Consequently, individuals should select and apply to the expenses the tax provision that generates the most benefit.

Summary: Deductions *for* AGI

Business expenses and rental and royalty expenses are two of the most important deductions *for* AGI. There are other important deductions *for* AGI that are indirectly related to business or provided to subsidize certain activities. After we have determined the deductions *for* AGI, we can compute AGI. Exhibits 6-6 and 6-7 summarize the computation of AGI for Courtney and Gram. Exhibit 6-8 shows Courtney's AGI calculation as presented on the front page of her Form 1040.

EXHIBIT 6-6 Courtney's Adjusted Gross Income

Description	Amount	Reference
Gross income for current year	$ 198,037	Exhibit 5-4 and related discussion
Deductions *for* AGI:		
Business expenses	(1,500)	Example 6-2
Rental expenses	(9,000)	Example 6-3
Moving expenses	(5,296)	Example 6-5
Employer-portion of self-employment taxes	(241)	Example 6-6
Adjusted gross income	**$182,000**	

EXHIBIT 6-7 Gram's Adjusted Gross Income

Description	Amount	Reference
Gross income for current year	$ 16,000	Exhibit 5-6
Deduction *for* AGI:		
Penalty for early withdrawal of savings	(410)	Example 6-7
Adjusted gross income	**$15,590**	

EXHIBIT 6-8 Courtney's AGI Computation on Form 1040, Page 1

Income	7	Wages, salaries, tips, etc. Attach Form(s) W-2			7	142,800
	8a	**Taxable** interest. Attach Schedule B if required			8a	617
Attach Form(s) W-2 here. Also attach Forms W-2G and 1099-R if tax was withheld.	b	**Tax-exempt** interest. **Do not** include on line 8a	8b	500		
	9a	Ordinary dividends. Attach Schedule B if required			9a	700
	b	Qualified dividends	9b	700		
	10	Taxable refunds, credits, or offsets of state and local income taxes			10	420
	11	Alimony received			11	20,000
	12	Business income or (loss). Attach Schedule C or C-EZ			12	18,000
	13	Capital gain or (loss). Attach Schedule D if required. If not required, check here ▶ ☐			13	
If you did not get a W-2, see instructions.	14	Other gains or (losses). Attach Form 4797			14	
	15a	IRA distributions	15a	b Taxable amount	15b	
	16a	Pensions and annuities	16a	b Taxable amount	16b	
	17	Rental real estate, royalties, partnerships, S corporations, trusts, etc. Attach Schedule E			17	5,000
	18	Farm income or (loss). Attach Schedule F			18	
	19	Unemployment compensation			19	
	20a	Social security benefits	20a	b Taxable amount	20b	
	21	Other income. List type and amount			21	
	22	Combine the amounts in the far right column for lines 7 through 21. This is your **total income** ▶			22	187,537
Adjusted Gross Income	23	Educator expenses	23			
	24	Certain business expenses of reservists, performing artists, and fee-basis government officials. Attach Form 2106 or 2106-EZ	24			
	25	Health savings account deduction. Attach Form 8889	25			
	26	Moving expenses. Attach Form 3903	26	5,296		
	27	Deductible part of self-employment tax. Attach Schedule SE	27	241		
	28	Self-employed SEP, SIMPLE, and qualified plans	28			
	29	Self-employed health insurance deduction	29			
	30	Penalty on early withdrawal of savings	30			
	31a	Alimony paid b Recipient's SSN ▶	31a			
	32	IRA deduction	32			
	33	Student loan interest deduction	33			
	34	Tuition and fees. Attach Form 8917	34			
	35	Domestic production activities deduction. Attach Form 8903	35			
	36	Add lines 23 through 35			36	5,537
	37	Subtract line 36 from line 22. This is your **adjusted gross income** ▶			37	182,000

For Disclosure, Privacy Act, and Paperwork Reduction Act Notice, see separate instructions. Cat. No. 11320B Form **1040** (2016)

Once we have determined AGI, we calculate taxable income by identifying deductions *from* AGI. These deductions consist of (1) the greater of itemized deductions or the standard deduction and (2) personal and dependency exemption deductions. We address itemized deductions next.

DEDUCTIONS *FROM* AGI: ITEMIZED DEDUCTIONS

LO 6-2

There are a variety of itemized deductions, a few of which relate to profit-motivated activities (employee business expenses and investment expenses that are unrelated to rental or royalty activities). Many itemized deductions are personal in nature but are allowed to subsidize desirable activities such as home ownership and charitable giving. Other itemized deductions, such as medical expenses and casualty losses, provide relief for taxpayers whose ability to pay taxes has been involuntarily reduced. We discuss itemized deductions in the order they appear on the individual tax return, Form 1040, Schedule A.

Medical Expenses

The medical expense deduction is designed to provide relief for taxpayers whose ability to pay taxes is seriously hindered by health-related circumstances. Qualifying medical expenses include any payments for the care, prevention, diagnosis, or cure of injury, disease, or bodily function that are not reimbursed by health insurance or are not paid for through a "flexible spending account."[18] Taxpayers may also deduct medical expenses incurred to treat their spouses and their dependents.[19] Common medical expenses include

- Prescription medication, insulin, and medical aids such as eyeglasses, contact lenses, and wheelchairs. Over-the-counter medicines are generally not deductible.

[18]Taxpayers participating in flexible spending accounts are allowed to direct that a fixed amount of their salary be placed in an account to pay for medical expenses. The salary paid into these accounts is excluded from gross income and used to pay for medical expenses. See the Compensation chapter.

[19]For the purpose of deducting medical expenses, a dependent need not meet the gross income test [§213(a)], and a child of divorced parents is considered a dependent of both parents [§213(d)(5)]. We discuss the general requirements for dependency in the Individual Income Tax Overview, Exemptions, and Filing Status chapter.

- Payments to medical care *providers* such as doctors, dentists, and nurses and medical care *facilities* such as hospitals.
- Transportation for medical purposes.
- Long-term care facilities.
- Health insurance premiums (if not deducted *for* AGI by self-employed taxpayers) and insurance for long-term care services.[20,21]

Example 6-10

In April, Courtney broke her wrist in a mountain biking accident. She paid $2,000 for a visit to the hospital emergency room and follow-up visits with her doctor. While she recuperated, Courtney paid $300 for prescription medicine and $700 to a therapist for rehabilitation. Courtney's insurance reimbursed her $1,840 for these expenses. What is the amount of Courtney's qualifying medical expenses?

Answer: $1,160, computed as follows:

Description	Deduction
Emergency room and doctor visits	$ 2,000
Prescription medication	300
Physical therapy	700
Total qualifying medical expenses	$ 3,000
Less insurance reimbursement	−1,840
Qualifying medical expenses from the accident	**$1,160**

Medical expenses for cosmetic surgery or other similar procedures are not deductible unless the surgery or procedure is necessary to ameliorate a deformity arising from, or directly related to, a congenital abnormality, a personal injury resulting from an accident or trauma, or a disfiguring disease.[22]

TAXES IN THE REAL WORLD Are Discretionary Medical Expenses Deductible?

While cosmetic surgery is generally not deductible, discretionary medical costs may be deducted where the procedure affects the structure or function of the body. Take, for example, procedures that facilitate pregnancy by overcoming infertility. In IRS Letter Ruling 200318017, the IRS ruled that egg donor fees and expenses related to obtaining a willing donor, paid by a taxpayer who could not conceive using her own eggs, qualified as deductible medical expenses because they were incurred in preparation of the taxpayer's medical procedure (the implantation of a donated egg). Deductible expenses included the donor's fee for her time and expense in following the procedures to ensure successful egg retrieval, the agency's fee for procuring the donor and coordinating the transaction, expenses for medical and psychological testing and assistance of the donor before and after the procedure, and legal fees for preparing a contract between the taxpayer and the donor.

What about the same type of expenses paid by a single male to father a child through a surrogate? Are those expenses deductible? No, because in that situation, the expenses are not related to an underlying medical condition or defect of the taxpayer nor are they affecting any structure or function of his body. See *William Magdalin*, TC Memo 2008-293.

[20]This includes the annual cost of Medicare and prescription insurance withheld from the Social Security recipient's benefits checks.

[21]The portion of any premiums for health insurance purchased through an exchange and offset by a premium tax credit under §36B is not deductible as an itemized deduction.

[22]§213(d)(9)(A).

Transportation and Travel for Medical Purposes Taxpayers traveling for the primary purpose of receiving essential and deductible medical care may deduct the cost of lodging while away from home overnight (with certain restrictions) and transportation.[23] Taxpayers using personal automobiles for medical transportation purposes may deduct a standard mileage allowance in lieu of actual costs. For 2017, the mileage rate is 17 cents a mile.

Example 6-11

Gram drove Courtney, *in Courtney's car,* 110 miles back and forth from the doctor's office and the physical therapist's facility during the period Courtney was being treated for her broken wrist. What is the amount of Courtney's qualifying medical expense for her trips to the doctor's office?

Answer: $19 (110 × $0.17, rounded).

Hospitals and Long-Term Care Facilities Taxpayers may deduct the cost of meals and lodging at hospitals. However, the cost of meals and lodging at other types of facilities such as nursing homes are deductible only when the principal purpose for the stay is medical care rather than convenience.[24] Of course, taxpayers may deduct the costs of actual medical care whether the care is provided at hospitals or other long-term care facilities.

Example 6-12

Gram considered moving into a long-term care facility before she decided she would move in with Courtney. The facility was not primarily for medical care and would have cost Gram $36,000 a year. During discussions with facility administrators, Gram learned that typically 20 percent of the total cost for the facility is allocable to medical care. If Gram were to stay in the facility for an entire year, what amount of the long-term care costs would qualify as a medical expense for Gram?

Answer: $7,200 ($36,000 × 20% allocable to medical care).

Medical Expense Deduction Limitation The deduction for medical expenses is limited to the amount of unreimbursed qualifying medical expenses paid during the year (no matter when the services were provided) *reduced* by 10 percent of the taxpayer's AGI. If a taxpayer or his or her spouse is age 65 or older at the end of the tax year, the 10 percent AGI floor is reduced to 7.5 percent of AGI through 2016. This restriction is called a **floor limitation** because it eliminates any deduction for amounts below the floor. The purpose of a floor limitation is to restrict a deduction to taxpayers with substantial qualifying expenses. Because this floor limitation is set at a high percentage of AGI, unreimbursed medical expenses rarely produce tax benefits, especially for high income taxpayers.

[23]The cost of travel for and essential to medical care, including lodging (with certain limitations) is also deductible if the expense is not extravagant and the travel has no significant element of personal pleasure. However, under §213(d)(2) the deduction for the cost of lodging is limited to $50 per night per individual.

[24]Taxpayers may deduct the cost of long-term care facilities if they are chronically ill under a prescribed plan of care. A taxpayer is deemed to be chronically ill, generally, if she or he cannot perform at least two daily living tasks (eating, bathing, dressing, toileting, transferring, continence) for 90 days or more. §7702B. Taxpayers may also deduct long-term care insurance premiums, which are limited annually based on the age of the taxpayer.

Example 6-13

This year Courtney incurred $2,400 in unreimbursed qualifying medical expenses (including the $1,160 of qualifying medical expenses associated with the accident [Example 6-10] and the $19 transportation deduction for mileage [Example 6-11]). Given that Courtney's AGI is $182,000, what is the amount of Courtney's itemized medical expense deduction?

Answer: $0 computed as follows:

Description	Expense
Total unreimbursed qualifying medical expenses	$ 2,400
Minus: 10% of AGI ($182,000 × 10%)	(18,200)
Medical expense itemized deduction	**$ 0**

What if: What amount of medical expenses would Courtney be allowed to deduct if her AGI was $20,000?

Answer: $400, computed as follows:

Description	Expense
Total unreimbursed qualifying medical expenses	$ 2,400
Minus: 10% of AGI ($20,000 × 10%)	(2,000)
Medical expense itemized deduction	**$ 400**

Taxes

Individuals may deduct as itemized deductions payments made during the year for the following taxes:

- State, local, and foreign *income* taxes, including state and local taxes paid during the year through employer withholding, estimated tax payments, and overpayments on the prior year return that the taxpayer applies to the current year (the taxpayer asks the state to keep the overpayment rather than refund it).
- Real estate taxes on property held for personal or investment purposes.
- Personal property taxes that are assessed on the *value* of the specific property.[25]

Taxpayers may elect to deduct state and local sales taxes *instead* of deducting state and local income taxes. This election is particularly advantageous for taxpayers in states that don't have an individual state income tax.[26]

Example 6-14

During the year, Courtney paid $6,700 of state income taxes through withholding from her paycheck. She also paid $2,700 of real estate taxes on her personal residence and $980 of real estate taxes on an investment property she owns in Oklahoma. Finally, Courtney paid $180 as a registration fee for her automobile (the fee is based on the year the automobile was manufactured, not its value). What amount of these payments can Courtney deduct as itemized deductions?

[25] §164.

[26] The deduction can be based upon either the amount paid or the amount published in the IRS tables (IRS Publication 600) based upon the state of residence, income, and number of exemptions. The states with no income tax are Alaska, Florida, Nevada, South Dakota, Texas, Washington, and Wyoming. Tennessee and New Hampshire have no state income tax on wages, but do impose a tax on unearned income.

Answer: $10,380 ($6,700 state taxes + $2,700 real estate taxes on residence + $980 real estate taxes on investment property). Courtney is not allowed to deduct the registration fee for her car because the fee is not based on the value of the automobile.

What if: Suppose that on April 1, 2017, Courtney filed her 2016 state tax return and was due a refund from the state in the amount of $420. However, Courtney elected to have the state keep the overpayment and apply it to her 2017 tax payments. What amount of state income taxes is Courtney allowed to deduct as an itemized deduction in 2017?

Answer: $7,120 ($6,700 withholding + $420 overpayment applied to 2017). The treatment of the overpayment is the same as if Courtney had received the refund in 2017 and then remitted it to the state as payment of 2017 taxes. Because she paid the tax in 2017, she is allowed to deduct the tax in 2017. Recall that under the tax benefit rule (see the Gross Income and Exclusions chapter), Courtney was required to include the $420 in her 2017 gross income.

Interest

There are two itemized deductions for interest expense.[27] First, subject to limitations described in more detail in the Tax Consequences of Home Ownership chapter, individuals can deduct interest paid on acquisition indebtedness and home-equity indebtedness secured by a qualified residence (the taxpayer's principal residence and one other residence).[28] Acquisition indebtedness is any debt secured by a qualified residence that is incurred in acquiring, constructing, or substantially improving the residence.[29] Home-equity indebtedness is any other debt secured by the taxpayer's qualified residence. Two rules limit the mortgage interest deduction: (1) Taxpayers may only deduct mortgage interest on up to $1,000,000 of acquisition indebtedness and (2) The amount of qualified home-equity indebtedness is limited to the *lesser* of (a) the fair market value of the qualified residence(s) in excess of the acquisition debt related to the residence(s) (determined when the home-equity loan is executed) and (b) $100,000 ($50,000 for married filing separately). In combination, these limitations allow taxpayers to deduct interest on up to $100,000 of home-equity debt (no matter what the taxpayer does with the proceeds from the home-equity loan) plus interest on up to $1,000,000 acquisition debt.[30]

As we discuss in more detail in the Investments chapter, individuals can also deduct interest paid on loans used to purchase investment assets such as stocks, bonds, or land (investment interest expense). The deduction of investment interest is limited to a taxpayer's net investment income (investment income minus investment expenses). Any investment interest in excess of the net investment income limitation carries forward to the subsequent year. Taxpayers are not allowed to deduct interest on personal credit card debt or on loans to acquire (and secured by) personal-use automobiles.

[27]Interest paid on loans where the proceeds are used in a trade or business is fully deductible as a business expense deduction *for* AGI.

[28]In the Individual Income Tax Computation and Tax Credits chapter, we note that interest expense on home-equity loans not used to purchase or substantially improve the home is not deductible for AMT purposes.

[29]Subject to rules discussed in the Tax Consequences of Home Ownership chapter, points paid on indebtedness incurred in acquiring a home are also generally deductible as mortgage interest expense in the year the loan originates and points to refinance a home mortgage are typically amortized and deducted over the life of the loan (but see research memo in the Tax Compliance, the IRS, and Tax Authorities chapter for an exception).

[30]Taxpayers can also deduct premiums paid or accrued on mortgage insurance (insurance premiums paid by the borrower to protect the lender against the borrower defaulting on the loan) as qualified residence interest expense. At press time, the deduction for mortgage insurance premiums is scheduled to expire after 2016.

Example 6-15

Courtney acquired her home in Kansas City in January of this year for $300,000 (also its value throughout the year). She purchased it by paying $40,000 as a down payment and borrowing $260,000 from a credit union. Her home is the collateral for the loan. During the year, Courtney paid $15,800 in interest on the loan. How much of this interest may Courtney deduct?

Answer: $15,800. Because Courtney's home mortgage is secured by her home, she is allowed to deduct the interest expense on the home as an itemized deduction.

What if: Suppose Courtney paid $3,000 in interest this year on a $60,000 home-equity loan. When Courtney secured the home-equity loan her house was worth $450,000 and her acquisition indebtedness was $250,000. How much of the $3,000 interest is deductible?

Answer: $3,000. Because the $60,000 home-equity loan does not exceed the lesser of (a) the fair market value of the residence in excess of the acquisition debt ($450,000 − $250,000 = $200,000) or (b) $100,000, Courtney may deduct the $3,000 interest paid.

What if: Suppose Courtney paid $6,000 in interest this year on a $120,000 home-equity loan (the average balance for the year). When Courtney secured the home-equity loan her house was worth $450,000 and her acquisition indebtedness was $250,000. How much of the $6,000 interest is deductible?

Answer: $5,000. Courtney is limited to deducting interest on $100,000 of the home-equity debt, which is the lesser of (a) the fair market value of the residence in excess of the acquisition debt ($450,000 − $250,000 = $200,000) or (b) $100,000. The deductible interest on the home-equity debt is calculated as: $6,000 interest paid × ($100,000 home-equity limit/$120,000 home-equity debt) = $5,000.

What if: Suppose that Courtney borrowed $26,000 to purchase a new car (the loan was secured by the car). Would she be allowed to deduct the interest on the loan?

Answer: No, the loan was not used to purchase a personal residence or investment assets.

Charitable Contributions

Congress encourages donations to charities by allowing taxpayers to deduct contributions of money and other property to *qualified* domestic charitable organizations. Qualifying charitable organizations include organizations that engage in educational, religious, scientific, governmental, and other public activities.[31] Political and campaign contributions are not deductible even though they arguably indirectly support the government (contributions to which are generally deductible).

Example 6-16

This year Courtney donated $1,700 to the Red Cross. She also gave $200 in cash to various homeless people she met on the streets during the year. What amount of these donations is Courtney allowed to deduct as a charitable contribution?

Answer: $1,700. Because the Red Cross is a public charity recognized by the IRS, Courtney may deduct her $1,700 charitable contribution to it as an itemized deduction. However, despite Courtney's charitable intent, her donations to the homeless are not deductible as charitable contributions because individuals do not qualify as charitable organizations.

What if: Suppose that instead of transferring cash to homeless people on the streets, Courtney donated $200 cash to a local food bank that is listed in the IRS Exempt Organizations Select Check as a qualified charity. The food bank provides meals to those in need. Would Courtney be allowed to deduct this contribution?

Answer: Yes, because the food bank is a qualified charity.

[31]§170(c). The IRS Exempt Organizations Select Check (http://www.irs.gov/Charities-&-Non-Profits/Exempt-Organizations-Select-Check) lists the organizations that the IRS has determined to be qualified charities.

The *amount* of the charitable contribution deduction depends on whether the taxpayer contributes money or other property to the charity. Note that in virtually all circumstances, donations are only deductible if the contribution is substantiated by written records.[32]

Contributions of Money Cash contributions are deductible in the year paid, including donations of cash or by check, electronic funds transfers, credit card charges, and payroll deductions.[33] Taxpayers are also considered as making monetary contributions for the cost of transportation and travel for charitable purposes if there is no significant element of pleasure or entertainment in the travel. When taxpayers use their personal vehicles for charitable transportation purposes, they may deduct, as a cash contribution, a standard mileage allowance for each mile driven (14 cents a mile in 2017). While taxpayers are allowed to deduct their transportation costs and other out-of-pocket costs of providing services for charities, they are not allowed to deduct the value of the services they provide for charities.

Example 6-17

Once a month, Courtney does volunteer work at a Goodwill Industries outlet about 20 miles from her home. Altogether, Courtney traveled 500 miles during the year driving to and from the Goodwill outlet. Courtney has determined that the services she provided during the year are reasonably valued at $1,500. What amount is Courtney allowed to deduct for her volunteer work with Goodwill Industries?

Answer: $70. Courtney is *not* allowed to deduct the value of the services she provides to Goodwill. However, she is allowed to deduct the $70 cost of her transportation to and from the Goodwill outlet (500 miles × 14 cents per mile).

Taxpayers receiving goods or services from a charity in exchange for a contribution may deduct only the amount of the contribution *in excess of the fair market value of the goods or services they receive* in exchange for their contribution.[34]

Contributions of Property Other Than Money When a taxpayer donates *property* to a charity, the *amount* the taxpayer is allowed to deduct depends on whether the property is **capital gain property** or **ordinary income property.**

Capital gain property. In general, taxpayers are allowed to deduct the *fair market value* of capital gain property on the date of the donation. Capital gain property is any

[32]For example, to deduct monetary donations, taxpayers must keep a bank record or a written communication from the charity showing the name of the charity and the date and amount of the contribution. In addition, to deduct charitable contributions for cash or noncash contributions of $250 or more, a taxpayer must receive a written acknowledgment from the charity that shows the amount of cash and a description of any property contributed. The acknowledgment must also state whether the donee organization provided any goods or services to the donor for the contribution and if so, either include a description and estimate of the value of the goods or services provided by the donee organization or, if applicable, a statement that the goods or services provided by the donee organization consist entirely of intangible religious benefits. See Publication 526 for more information.

[33]When individual taxpayers mail a contribution, they are allowed to deduct the contribution when they place the payment in the mail. When they pay via credit card, they are allowed to deduct the contribution on the day of the charge. Rev. Rul. 78-38, 1978-1 CB 67.

[34]Reg. §1.170A-1(h). To help with this determination, a charity that provides goods or services in return for a contribution of more than $75 must provide contributors with a written statement estimating the value of goods and services that the charity has provided to the donor.

appreciated asset that would have generated a *long-term* capital gain if the taxpayer had sold the property for its fair market value instead of contributing the asset to charity. To qualify as long-term, the taxpayer must have held the asset for more than a year. Capital assets include the following assets:

- Investment assets (stocks, bonds, land held for investment, paintings, etc.).
- Business assets (to the extent that gain on the sale of the business asset would *not* have been considered ordinary income).[35]
- Personal-use assets.

Contributing capital gain property is a particularly tax-efficient way to make charitable contributions, because taxpayers are allowed to deduct the fair market value of the property, and they are *not* required to include the appreciation on the asset in gross income.

Example 6-18

In December of the current year, Courtney donated 100 shares of stock in JBD Corp. to her church, a qualified charity. Courtney purchased the stock several years ago for $2,600, but the shares were worth $10,600 at the time of the donation. What is the amount of Courtney's charitable deduction for donating the stock?

Answer: $10,600. Because the stock is an appreciated investment asset held for more than a year, it qualifies as capital gain property. Hence, Courtney is allowed to deduct the $10,600 fair market value of the stock, and she is *not* required to recognize any of the $8,000 realized gain ($10,600 − $2,600).

Certain contributions of capital gain property do not qualify for a fair market value deduction. The deduction for capital gain property that is *tangible personal property* is limited to the *adjusted basis* of the property if the charity uses the property for a purpose that is *unrelated* to its charitable purpose.[36] That is, this restriction applies to capital gain property that is (1) tangible, (2) personal property (not realty), and (3) unrelated to the charity's operations. The third requirement does not apply if, at the time of the donation, the taxpayer reasonably anticipates that the charity will put the property to a related use.

Example 6-19

What if: Suppose that Courtney donated a religious-themed painting to her church. Courtney purchased the painting several years ago for $2,600, but the painting was worth $10,600 at the time of the donation. When Courtney contributed the painting, she reasonably expected the church to hang the painting in the church chapel. What would be the amount of Courtney's charitable contribution deduction?

Answer: $10,600. Because Courtney reasonably expected the church to use the painting in a manner related to its tax-exempt purpose, Courtney is allowed to deduct the full fair market value of the painting without recognizing the $8,000 realized gain.

[35]These assets are considered to be §1231(b) assets. We discuss the tax treatment of dispositions of business assets in the Property Dispositions chapter.

[36]Reg. §1.170A-4(b)(2). The taxpayer's deduction for donating capital gain property is also limited to basis if the taxpayer contributes capital gain property other than publicly traded stock to a private nonoperating foundation. There are also other exceptions in which capital gain property might not otherwise qualify for deduction at value, such as the subsequent sales of donated property by the charity. These exceptions are beyond the scope of this text.

What if: Suppose that Courtney was told at the time she donated the painting that the church intended to sell it and use the cash to help fund expansion of the church building. What would be Courtney's charitable contribution deduction?

Answer: $2,600, the adjusted basis of the property. Because the church expects to sell it, the painting is being used for a purpose unrelated to the charitable purpose of the church. Thus, Courtney may deduct only the tax basis of the painting.

What if: Suppose that Courtney donated stock to her church ($10,600 current fair market value, originally purchased several years ago for $2,600) and the church informed her that it intended to immediately sell the stock. What would be the amount of Courtney's charitable contribution deduction?

Answer: $10,600. Stock is intangible property, not tangible personal property. Hence, Courtney would deduct the fair market value of the stock.

Ordinary income property. Taxpayers contributing ordinary income property can deduct only the *lesser* of (1) the property's fair market value or (2) the property's adjusted basis. Ordinary income property consists of all assets other than capital gain property. That is, ordinary income property is property that if sold would generate income taxed at ordinary rates. This includes the following types of assets:

- Assets the taxpayer has held for a year or less.
- Inventory the taxpayer sells in a trade or business.
- Business assets held for more than a year to the extent the taxpayer would recognize ordinary income under the depreciation recapture rules if the taxpayer had sold the property.[37]
- Assets, including investment assets and personal-use assets, with a value *less than* the taxpayer's basis in the assets (assets that have declined in value).

Example 6-20

Before her move from Cincinnati, Courtney decided to donate her excess possessions to Goodwill Industries. Courtney estimated that she paid over $900 for these items, including clothing, a table, and a couch. However, although the items were in excellent condition, they were worth only $160. What amount can Courtney deduct for her donation of these items?

Answer: $160. Because Courtney's possessions have declined in value, they are considered to be ordinary income property. Consequently, Courtney may deduct the lesser of (1) the fair market value of $160 or (2) her tax basis in the property of $900.

Charitable Contribution Deduction Limitations The amount of a taxpayer's charitable contribution deduction for the year is limited to a **ceiling** or maximum deduction. The ceiling depends upon the type of property the taxpayer donates and the nature of the charity receiving the donation; donations to public charities (charities that are publicly supported such as churches and schools) and **private operating foundations** (privately sponsored foundations that actually fund and conduct charitable activities) are subject to less stringent restrictions than other charities. In general, cash and property donations to public charities and private operating foundations are limited to 50 percent of the taxpayer's AGI. Deductions for contributions of capital gain property to public charities and private operating foundations are generally limited to 30 percent of the taxpayer's AGI. Deductions for cash and property contributions to **private nonoperating foundations** (privately sponsored foundations that disburse funds to other charities, such as the Bill and Melinda Gates Foundation) are limited to 30 percent of the taxpayer's AGI. Finally, deductions for contributions of

[37]We discuss depreciation recapture in the Property Dispositions chapter.

capital gain property to private nonoperating foundations are limited to 20 percent of the taxpayer's AGI. Exhibit 6-9 summarizes the charitable contribution limitations for individual taxpayers.

When taxpayers make contributions that are subject to different percentage limitations, they apply the AGI limitations in the following sequence:

Step 1: Determine the limitation for the 50 percent contributions.

Step 2: Apply the limitations to the 30 percent contributions. The 30 percent contribution limit is the *lesser* of (a) AGI × 30% or (b) AGI × 50% minus the contributions subject to the 50 percent limit.

Step 3: Apply the limitations to the 20 percent contributions. The 20 percent contribution limit is the *lesser* of (a) AGI × 20%, (b) AGI × 30% minus contributions subject to 30 percent limit, or (c) AGI × 50% minus the contributions subject to 50 percent and the contributions subject to the 30 percent limit.

EXHIBIT 6-9 Summary of Charitable Contribution Limitation Rules

Contribution Type	Public Charity and Private Operating Foundation	Private Nonoperating Foundation
Cash:		
Amount	Cash amount	Cash amount
AGI limit	50%	30%
Capital gain property:		
Amount	FMV	Basis*
AGI limit	30%	20%
Ordinary income property:		
Amount	Lesser of Basis or FMV	Lesser of Basis or FMV
AGI limit	50%	30%

*FMV if the stock is publicly traded [§170(e)(5)].

When a taxpayer's contributions exceed the AGI ceiling limitation for the year, the excess contribution is treated as though it were made in the subsequent tax year and is subject to the same AGI limitations in the next year. The excess contribution can be carried forward for five years before it expires. If a charitable contribution deduction is carried forward, the current year contributions must first be considered when applying the AGI percentage limitations. However, because the ceiling limitations are fairly generous, taxpayers exceed the ceiling limitations only in unusual circumstances.

Example 6-21

This year Courtney made the following contributions to qualified charities:

Organization	Amount	Type	AGI Limitation	Reference
Red Cross	$ 1,700	Cash	50%	Example 6-16
Goodwill Industries	70	Cash-mileage	50	Example 6-17
Goodwill Industries	160	Ordinary income property	50	Example 6-20
Church	10,600	Capital gain property	30	Example 6-18
Total contributions	**$12,530**			

After applying the AGI limitations, how much of the $12,530 in contributions is Courtney allowed to deduct?

Answer: $12,530, computed as follows:

Description	Amount	Explanation
(1) AGI	$182,000	Exhibit 6-6
(2) 50% contributions	1,930	($1,700 + 70 + 160)
(3) 50% AGI contribution limit	91,000	(1) × 50%
(4) Allowable 50% deductions	**1,930**	Lesser of (2) or (3)
(5) 30% contributions	10,600	
(6) 30% AGI contribution limit	54,600	(1) × 30%
(7) Remaining 50% AGI limitation	89,070	(3) – (4)
(8) Allowable 30% deductions	**10,600**	Least of (5), (6), or (7)
Deductible charitable contributions	**$ 12,530**	(4) + (8)

What if: Suppose that Courtney's AGI was $30,000. After applying the AGI limitations, how much of the $12,530 in contributions would Courtney be allowed to deduct?

Answer: $10,930, computed as follows:

Description	Amount	Explanation
(1) AGI	$ 30,000	
(2) 50% contributions	1,930	
(3) 50% AGI contribution limit	15,000	(1) × 50%
(4) Allowable 50% deductions	**1,930**	Lesser of (2) and (3)
(5) 30% contributions	10,600	
(6) 30% AGI contribution limit	9,000	(1) × 30%
(7) Remaining 50% AGI limitation	13,070	(3) – (4)
(8) Allowable 30% deductions	**9,000**	Least of (5), (6), or (7)
Deductible charitable contributions	**$10,930**	(4) + (8)

Courtney would not be allowed to deduct this year $1,600 of her $10,600 capital gain property contribution to her church. However, she will carry forward the $1,600 to next year (and up to four years after that, if necessary) and treat it as though she made a $1,600 contribution next year subject to the 30 percent of AGI limitation.

ETHICS

Sabrina loves the latest fashions, but she is also very charitable. Every year she donates her previous year's clothing to Goodwill to make room in her closet for this year's fashions. Sabrina estimates the value of her donation to be approximately $6,000. Sabrina recently learned that because her donation exceeds $5,000, she must support her donation with an appraisal and a signed statement by the appraiser on Form 8283. Sabrina decides to claim a charitable deduction of $4,900 to avoid the appraisal requirement. What do you think of Sabrina's decision? Do you think nationally that there is an abnormally large number of charitable contributions valued just under $5,000?

Casualty and Theft Losses on Personal-Use Assets

Individuals cannot deduct losses they realize when they sell or dispose of assets used for personal purposes (personal-use assets as opposed to business or investment assets). However, individuals *are* allowed to deduct casualty and theft losses realized on personal-use assets.[38] A **casualty loss** is defined as a loss arising from a *sudden, unexpected,* or *unusual* event such as a "fire, storm, or shipwreck" or loss from theft.[39] Taxpayers may deduct casualty losses in the year the casualty occurs or in the year the theft of an asset is discovered.

Tax Loss from Casualties Congress allows deductions for unreimbursed casualty and theft losses because these losses may substantially reduce a taxpayer's ability to pay taxes. However, limitations on the deduction generally ensure that taxpayers receive a tax benefit from such losses only when the losses are relatively large. The *amount* of the tax loss from any *specific casualty event* (including theft) is the *lesser* of (1) the decline in value of the property caused by the casualty or (2) the taxpayer's tax basis in the damaged or stolen asset. The loss is reduced by any reimbursements the individual is eligible to receive, such as insurance reimbursements. Likewise, any deductible loss reduces the taxpayer's basis in the underlying asset.

Example 6-22

In June, Courtney had a bad day at a nearby lake. Her purse containing $200 in cash was stolen, and she wrecked her car on the way home. Courtney purchased her purse for $150 and it was worth $125 at the time of the theft ($325 in total value was stolen). Courtney purchased her car earlier in the year for $25,000 and had to pay $2,000 to have it repaired. Courtney's insurance company reimbursed her $1,400 for the repairs. What is the amount of Courtney's casualty tax loss before considering deductibility limitations?

Answer: $925 ($325 theft + $600 accident). The theft and the automobile accident are considered to be two separate casualty events generating two different casualty losses. The amount of each casualty loss, before considering deductibility limitations, is computed as follows:

	Theft	Accident
Fair market value (FMV) before casualty	$ 325	
FMV after the casualty	−0	
(1) Decline in FMV (cost to repair)	325	$ 2,000
(2) Tax basis in property before casualty	350	25,000
Loss before reimbursement [lesser of (1) or (2)]	325	2,000
Insurance reimbursement	−0	−1,400
Unreimbursed casualty losses	**$325**	**$ 600**

Casualty Loss Deduction Floor Limitations Casualty losses must exceed two separate floor limitations to qualify as itemized deductions. The first floor is $100 for *each* casualty event during the year. This floor eliminates deductions for small losses. The second floor limitation is 10 percent of AGI, and it applies to the sum of all casualty losses for the year (after applying the $100 floor). In other words, the itemized deduction is the aggregate amount of casualty losses that exceeds 10 percent of AGI.

[38]§165. As we discuss in more detail in the Business Income, Deductions, and Accounting Methods chapter, businesses may deduct casualty and theft losses of business property as a deduction *for* AGI. Further, casualty or theft losses on investment assets are deductible as a miscellaneous itemized deduction not subject to the 2 percent of AGI floor.

[39]§165(c)(3). See also IRS Publication No. 547.

Example 6-23

Courtney's total casualty loss before applying the deduction limitations is $925. What amount of the $925 loss is Courtney allowed to deduct after applying the two floor limitations?

Answer: $0, computed as follows:

	Theft	Accident	Total
Losses before limitations	$ 325	$600	
Less $100 per casualty floor	−100	−100	
Casualty loss before AGI limit	$ 225	$500	$ 725
Less 10% of $182,000 AGI (Exhibit 6-6)			−18,200
Casualty loss deduction after AGI limit			**$ 0**

What if: Suppose that Courtney's automobile was worth $22,000, and that it was completely destroyed in the accident. What would be Courtney's casualty loss deduction if she received only $3,100 of insurance reimbursement for her loss?

Answer: $825, computed as follows:

	Theft	Accident	Total
Fair market value (FMV) before casualty	$325	$22,000	
FMV after the casualty	0	0	
(1) Decline in FMV (cost to repair)	$325	$22,000	
(2) Tax basis in property before casualty	$350	$25,000	
Loss before reimbursement [lesser of (1) or (2)]	$325	$22,000	
Less Insurance reimbursement	−0	−3,100	
Less $100 per casualty floor	−100	−100	
Unreimbursed casualty losses	$225	$18,800	$19,025
Less 10% of $182,000 AGI (Exhibit 6-6)			−18,200
Casualty loss deduction after AGI limit			**$ 825**

TAXES IN THE REAL WORLD "The Trilogy of the Rings"

In order to qualify for a casualty loss deduction, a taxpayer's personal loss must be sudden or unexpected. Taxpayers and the IRS sometimes disagree about what is a casualty. Consider the following three case summaries (sometimes called the "Trilogy of the Rings") and, for each case, see whether you can determine whether the taxpayer or the IRS was victorious.

Case 1

Nancy Carpenter cleaned her wedding ring by placing it in some ammonia near the kitchen sink. Nancy's husband, William, later emptied the ammonia into the drain along with the ring while doing the dishes. He then turned on the garbage disposal, destroying the ring [*William H. Carpenter,* decided by the Tax Court in 1966, 25 TCM 1186].

Case 2

John lovingly helped his wife Agnes from the car and started to shut the door. Agnes, upon realizing she had left something on the seat, reached her hand back toward the car only to have the door shut directly on her engagement ring. The setting of the ring broke on impact and the diamond was flung into the leaf-covered driveway as she retracted her hand. Despite all their efforts, John and Agnes never found the stone [*John P. White,* decided by the Tax Court in 1967, 48 TC 430].

Case 3

Mr. and Mrs. Keenan spent the night at a hotel. Mr. Keenan, who was suffering from a stuffy nose, used tissues he had placed near his bed throughout the night. During the night

(continued on page 6-26)

Mrs. Keenan removed her rings and placed them within a tissue at the bedside. Mr. Keenan awoke before his wife the following morning, and he gathered the tissues, including the ring, and flushed them down the toilet [*Keenan v. Bowers*, decided in 1950 by the South Carolina District Court, 50-2 USTC ¶9444].

So, what do you think?

The taxpayers won Case 1 and Case 2 because the losses were deemed to be "sudden and unexpected" in nature. However, the taxpayer lost Case 3 because the loss was due to a "chain of events on the parts of Mrs. Keenan and Mr. Keenan." Thus, the loss was not considered to be sudden in nature.

Miscellaneous Itemized Deductions Subject to AGI Floor

There are a variety of deductions that address specific objectives but do not fit easily into any category. Congress called these deductions **miscellaneous itemized deductions** and subjected most of these deductions to an AGI floor (only amounts over the floor are deductible). Miscellaneous itemized deductions subject to the floor limitation include employee business expenses, investment expenses, and certain other expenses. These miscellaneous deductions are summed together and are deductible only to the extent that their sum *exceeds* 2 percent of the taxpayer's AGI.

Employee Business Expenses While most business expenses are typically deductible as deductions for AGI, employee business expenses are deductible as miscellaneous itemized deductions. Expenses that qualify include those that are appropriate and helpful for the employee's work such as the cost of professional dues, uniforms (unless suitable as normal attire), union dues, and subscriptions to publications related to employment.

Example 6-24

Courtney subscribes to several architectural publications at an annual cost of $410. She finds these publications helpful, and it is certainly appropriate that an architect read current publications to keep up with new trends. Her employer does not reimburse Courtney for the cost of the subscriptions. What amount, if any, qualifies as a deductible employee business expense?

Answer: All $410 qualifies as a deductible employee business expense because the expense is appropriate and helpful to Courtney's employment.

Several types of employee expenses are restricted. For example, the costs of job hunting qualify if the job is in the employee's current trade or business, but not for the individual's first job. In addition, the cost of education qualifies if it serves to maintain or improve the employee's skill in the business, but not if the education is *required* to qualify for a new business or profession.[40] Thus, a high school teacher would not be able to deduct the cost of attending law school because a law degree would qualify him for a different profession.

Example 6-25

During the year, Courtney paid $1,529 to attend motivational seminars sponsored by a continuing education provider. Courtney has found these seminars helpful, and her employer has encouraged Courtney to attend. How much of the cost of the seminars qualifies as a deductible employee business expense?

Answer: All $1,529. The cost qualifies as an employee business expense because the courses are appropriate and helpful and do not qualify Courtney for a new business.

[40]If a taxpayer is self-employed (instead of an employee), the cost of education that maintains or improves his or her skills (but is not required for a new business or profession) is deductible on Schedule C (not on Schedule A as a miscellaneous itemized deduction).

TAXES IN THE REAL WORLD Is The Cost of an MBA Deductible?

Is the cost of an MBA deductible? That is a very good question with differing answers depending on the taxpayer's specific facts. The nature of an MBA degree lends itself to vigorous disputes as to whether the degree qualifies a taxpayer to engage in a new trade or business. On the one hand, an MBA degree is typically not a foundational requirement to practice in a profession. On the other hand, the knowledge and skills obtained in an MBA program may be stepping stones to opportunities that otherwise may have been out of reach to the taxpayer. As a result, the determination of whether MBA expenditures are deductible is fact-intensive. From a purely objective standpoint, an MBA degree surely qualifies its recipient for a new trade or business somewhere and someplace. The courts, however, have not focused on this fact. Instead, the courts have focused on the relationship of the MBA curriculum to the taxpayer's duties and responsibilities in his or her profession *before* and *after* he or she receives the degree. Thus, in the typical situation where students enter an MBA program to change career paths, the deductibility of the education is not likely to pass muster. For a taxpayer working in the same profession before and after the MBA degree (the more typical situation for an executive MBA program), the result is much more favorable.

Source: Matthew A. Melone, "Tax Court Upholds Deduction for MBA Tuition," *Practical Tax Strategies*, March 2010.

Travel and transportation. The cost of travel and transportation associated with the employee's work responsibilities may also qualify as miscellaneous itemized deductions. The cost of travel is deductible if the primary purpose of the trip is business. However, the cost of **commuting**—traveling from a residence to the place of business—is personal and never deductible.[41] When employees drive their personal automobiles for business purposes, they may deduct a standard mileage rate in lieu of deducting actual costs.[42] In 2017, the standard business mileage rate is 53.5 cents per mile. When employees travel on business trips long enough to be away from home overnight, meals and lodging also qualify as employee business expenses. Although meals and lodging are deductible employee business expenses, employees are allowed to deduct only half the cost of the meals. When the travel has both business and personal aspects, the deductibility of transportation costs depends on the primary purpose of the trip. If the primary purpose is business, the transportation costs to arrive at the location are fully deductible. If the primary purpose is personal, the transportation costs to arrive at the location are not deductible. For travel with both business and personal aspects, the meals (50 percent), lodging, transportation while at the location, and incidental expenses are deductible for the business portion of the trip (that is, for the business days of the trip).

Example 6-26

Because Courtney is extremely motivated to reach her potential as an architect (the seminars are doing wonders), she spent a week in September, at her own expense, driving her personal car to several large cities to study different architectural designs. During the trip, she drove a total of

(continued on page 6-28)

[41]Costs of commuting to and from a temporary place of work are deductible and costs of commuting from a first job to a second job are deductible. Employees may take *temporary* business trips that last for months. For these trips, the costs of the travel, including meals and lodging, are deductible for the duration of the trip. However, because trips in excess of one year are deemed to be *permanent,* the cost of travel on indefinite trips is *not* deductible.

[42]If an employee chooses to deduct actual automobile costs instead, she would deduct the automobile depreciation or lease payments (see the Property Acquisition and Cost Recovery chapter for applicable depreciation limits), gas, oil, repairs, license, and insurance attributable to business use. Expenses are allocated to business use based on the proportion of business miles to total miles driven for the year. Once a taxpayer chooses the actual cost method, she cannot switch to using the standard business mileage rate.

2,134 miles, spent $838 on lodging, and paid $500 for meals. What amount can Courtney deduct as unreimbursed employee business expenses before considering the 2 percent of AGI floor?

Answer: $2,230, computed as follows:

Description	Expense	Calculation
Transportation	$ 1,142	2,134 miles × 53.5 cents
Lodging	838	
Meals	250	$500 × 50%
Total employee business expense from trip	**$2,230**	

Employee expense reimbursements. Many employees are reimbursed for their business expenses by their employers. As a general rule, employees *include* reimbursements in gross income and *deduct* employee business expenses as miscellaneous itemized deductions. However, if an employee is required to submit documentation supporting expenses to receive reimbursement and the employer reimburses only legitimate business expenses, then the employer's reimbursement plan qualifies as an **accountable plan.** Under an accountable plan (which is the most common method for reimbursement) employees *exclude* expense reimbursements from gross income and do *not* deduct the reimbursed expenses. If the expenses exceed the reimbursements, the excess (unreimbursed) portion of each expense is deductible as an employee business expense. Thus, miscellaneous itemized deductions for employee business expenses are commonly referred to as deductions for *unreimbursed* employee business expenses.

Example 6-27

In November, Courtney went on a business trip to Los Angeles to meet with a prospective client and spent $1,700 on business travel including meals and lodging. EWD reimbursed Courtney for the entire $1,700 cost of the trip under an accountable plan. What amount can Courtney deduct?

Answer: $0. Because EWD's reimbursement is made under an accountable plan, Courtney ignores the reimbursement and the expenses for tax purposes; the reimbursement and expenses completely offset each other.

What if: Suppose that EWD provided Courtney with a flat amount of $2,000 to cover her expenses for the trip and did not require her to account for expenditures. How would Courtney treat the reimbursement and the expenses for tax purposes?

Answer: Courtney would include the $2,000 in gross income and claim the $1,700 from the trip *from* AGI as an employee business expense, miscellaneous itemized deduction subject to the 2 percent of AGI floor (and 50 percent meals limitation). The reimbursement was not made under an accountable plan because Courtney was not required to substantiate her expenses.

Investment Expenses As previously explained, investment expenses are itemized deductions. These expenses are classified as miscellaneous itemized deductions and include expenditures necessary for the production or collection of income, or for the management, conservation, or maintenance of property held for the production of income.[43] Common investment expenses include:

- Expenses associated with investment income or property.
- Investment advisory fees.
- Safe-deposit box fees.
- Subscriptions to investment-related publications.

[43]§212. As we discussed earlier in the chapter, rental and royalty expenses are the only investment expenses that qualify as a deduction *for* AGI.

Tax Preparation Fees Ordinary and necessary expenses incurred in connection with determining tax obligations imposed by federal, state, municipal, or foreign authorities are also deductible as miscellaneous itemized deductions subject to the 2 percent of AGI floor.[44] While the most common tax preparation fees are the costs of preparing taxpayers' tax returns, taxpayers may also deduct other related expenses such as the cost of property appraisals for tax purposes and the cost of contesting tax liabilities.

Example 6-28

In 2017, Courtney paid Quick Taxes Inc. $650 to prepare her 2016 income tax return. What amount of this expenditure can Courtney deduct before considering the 2 percent of AGI floor?

Answer: $650. The entire amount qualifies as a miscellaneous itemized deduction for 2017.

Hobby Losses As stated previously, individuals engaged in *business* activities are allowed to deduct their business expenses as deductions for AGI. However, taxpayers may engage in certain activities for primarily personal enjoyment but these activities may also generate revenue. For tax purposes, this type of activity is considered a **hobby** rather than a business. Hobby expenses are deductible only to the extent of the revenue generated by the hobby. Sometimes referred to as the *hobby loss limitation,* this limit is less taxpayer-friendly for a hobby than the limits on business expenses. Thus, it's important to determine whether an activity should be considered a business or a hobby for tax purposes. This determination hinges upon whether the taxpayer is engaged in the activity *primarily* to make a profit or *primarily* for personal enjoyment.

To help make this subjective determination, the regulations provide a list of the following factors to consider:[45]

- The manner in which the taxpayer carries on the activity.
- The expertise of the taxpayer or his advisers.
- The time and effort expended by the taxpayer in carrying on the activity.
- The expectation that assets used in the activity may appreciate in value.
- The success of the taxpayer in carrying on other, similar activities.
- The taxpayer's history of income or losses with respect to the activity.
- The amount of occasional profits, if any.
- The financial status of the taxpayer.
- The elements of personal pleasure or recreation.

One of the most important factors is the taxpayer's history of income or loss in the activity. In fact, the tax law explicitly presumes that an activity is a business if it generates a profit in three of five consecutive years.[46] This presumption is difficult for the IRS to overcome in disputes with taxpayers.

If an activity is determined to be a hobby, the taxpayer must *include* the revenue from the activity in gross income and may deduct the expenses, to the extent of the gross income from the activity, as itemized deductions (mortgage interest, real estate taxes, and *miscellaneous itemized deductions*). When hobby expenses exceed revenue, the expenses must be deducted in a particular sequence. Taxpayers first deduct expenses that

[44]§212.

[45]See Reg. §1.183-2.

[46]For activities involving breeding, training, or racing horses, the taxpayer need show a profit in only two of seven years for the activity to be presumed to be a business.

are deductible anyway, such as mortgage interest or property taxes. Second, taxpayers deduct all other hobby expenses except depreciation expense (deducted as miscellaneous itemized deductions). Finally, they deduct depreciation expense (also deducted as a miscellaneous itemized deduction). As discussed below, miscellaneous itemized deductions are deductible only to the extent that they exceed 2 percent of AGI. Thus, the revenue from the activity increases the taxpayer's AGI (and taxable income) dollar for dollar. However, the hobby deductions may or may not decrease taxable income, depending on whether and the extent to which the taxpayer's itemized deductions exceed her standard deduction and her miscellaneous itemized deductions exceed the 2 percent of AGI floor.

Example 6-29

Courtney's cousin, Phil T. Thrill, played golf at Arizona State University. He turned pro and tried to qualify for the PGA tour when he graduated from college. Unfortunately, he couldn't support his family playing golf and is currently employed as a high school physical education instructor. Every summer, Phil plays in several local and a few regional professional golf tournaments. His only source of revenue from golf is the prize money he wins in these tournaments. Phil has managed to earn prize money in excess of his expenses in only one of the previous five years. This year Phil received golf revenues of $3,200 and incurred golf-related expenses of $8,800, consisting of tournament entry fees, equipment, food, transportation, clothing, and lodging. For tax purposes, are Phil's golf activities considered to be a business or a hobby? If Phil's golfing activities are determined to be a *hobby*, how does Phil account for his revenues and expenses for tax purposes?

Answer: It could go either way. We need more facts regarding his golf activities to make a more clear determination. See *Donald C. Kimbrough*, TC Memo 1988-185, for an example in which the Tax Court ruled in a somewhat similar setting that the golfer was engaged in a business. Nonetheless, because Phil has only generated golf revenue in excess of expenses in one of the past five years, the activity is not presumed to be a business activity. To qualify as a business, Phil would have to convince the IRS that he is primarily engaging in golf activities to make a profit rather than for personal enjoyment. If the activity is determined to be a hobby, Phil includes the $3,200 of revenue in gross income as miscellaneous income. He is allowed to deduct $3,200 of his expenses as miscellaneous itemized deductions subject to the 2 percent floor (the deduction is limited to gross income from the activity).

What if: Suppose that Phil's golfing activities are determined to be a hobby and (1) his AGI is $70,000 before considering the effects of his golfing activity, (2) he has itemized deductions of $10,000 that are unrelated to the golf activity, (3) the applicable standard deduction is $6,350, and (4) he has no miscellaneous itemized deductions other than his golfing expenses. What is the effect of his golfing activities on his AGI and taxable income this year?

Answer: The golfing activities will increase Phil's AGI by $3,200 and his taxable income by $1,464 because the full amount of the revenue is included in gross income but his expense deductions are limited. Phil's AGI and taxable income are computed as follows:

Description	Amounts without Hobby	Amounts with Hobby	Explanation
(1) AGI before activity	$70,000	$70,000	
(2) Golf revenue (increase in AGI)		3,200	
(3) AGI after activity	70,000	73,200	(1) + (2)
(4) Golf expenses	0	8,800	
(5) Golf expenses after revenue limit	0	3,200	Lesser of (2) or (4)
(6) 2% of AGI floor	0	1,464	(3) × 2%
(7) Deductible golf expenses (as miscellaneous itemized deduction)	0	1,736	(5) − (6)
(8) Other itemized deductions	10,000	10,000	
(9) Total itemized deductions	10,000	11,736	(7) + (8)
(10) Taxable income (ignoring exemptions)	60,000	61,464	(3) − (9)
Increase in taxable income		**$ 1,464**	Difference in line (10)

What if: Suppose the same preceding facts, except that Phil does not have the $10,000 of itemized deductions unrelated to the golf activity. What is the effect of his golfing activities on his AGI and taxable income this year?

Answer: The golfing activities will increase Phil's AGI and taxable income by $3,200 because the full amount of the revenue is included in gross income but none of his expense deductions are deductible because his itemized deductions (including the $1,736 of golf expenses that exceed 2 percent of AGI) do not exceed the standard deduction. Thus, the $3,200 golf revenue increases his AGI and taxable income, but he gets no tax deduction for his related expenses because his itemized deductions do not exceed the standard deduction.

Limitation on Miscellaneous Itemized Deductions (2 Percent of AGI Floor) To apply the 2 percent floor limit and determine the miscellaneous itemized deduction, the sum of all deductions subject to the 2 percent floor limitation is reduced by 2 percent of AGI. If the 2 percent floor equals or exceeds the sum of miscellaneous itemized deductions, the deductions do not increase the taxpayer's itemized deductions (they don't provide any tax benefit). The 2 percent floor limitation makes it likely that most taxpayers will receive limited, if any, tax benefit from the deductions subject to the floor.

Example 6-30

What amount is Courtney's deduction for miscellaneous itemized deductions that are subject to the 2 percent floor?

Answer: $1,179, computed as follows:

Description	Amount	Reference
Subscriptions to publications	$ 410	Example 6-24
Educational costs	1,529	Example 6-25
Business trip to observe architecture	2,230	Example 6-26
Tax preparation fees	650	Example 6-28
Total deductions subject to 2% floor	$ 4,819	
2% of AGI floor (182,000 × 2%)	−3,640	Exhibit 6-6
Total miscellaneous itemized deductions	**$1,179**	

Courtney incurred a total of $4,819 of miscellaneous itemized deductions, but she can deduct only $1,179 of them due to the 2 percent of AGI restriction.

THE KEY FACTS

Miscellaneous Itemized Deductions

- Employee business expenses not reimbursed by an accountable plan.
- Investment expenses (if not in a rental or royalty activity).
- Tax preparation fees and allowable hobby expenses.
- Total miscellaneous itemized deductions are subject to a 2 percent of AGI floor limit.

Miscellaneous Itemized Deductions *Not* Subject to AGI Floor

Several deductions are considered to be miscellaneous itemized deductions but are not subject to the 2 percent of AGI floor. Perhaps because gambling includes a significant element of personal enjoyment (losers may think otherwise), individuals include all gambling winnings for the year in gross income but may also deduct gambling losses *to the extent of gambling winnings* for the year.[47] The deductible gambling losses are miscellaneous itemized deductions; therefore, *losses don't*

[47]§165(d).

directly offset winnings.[48] However, unlike other miscellaneous itemized deductions, gambling losses are *not* subject to the 2 percent of AGI floor. Casualty and theft losses on property held for investment and the unrecovered cost of a life annuity (the taxpayer died before recovering the full cost of the annuity) also qualify as miscellaneous itemized deductions not subject to the AGI floor.

Phase-Out of Itemized Deductions

In addition to limits on specific deductions, the amount of a taxpayer's *total* itemized deductions *other than* medical expenses, casualty losses, investment *interest* expense, and gambling losses is subject to a phase-out. That is, when AGI exceeds a certain threshold, itemized deductions are reduced. In 2017, the threshold begins at $313,800 for married taxpayers filing jointly, $287,650 for heads of household, $261,500 for single taxpayers, and $156,900 for married taxpayers filing separately. We provide the computation details of the phase-out in Appendix A to this chapter.

Summary of Itemized Deductions

This part of the chapter examined the various itemized deductions (deductions *from* AGI). We found that both medical expense and casualty loss deductions are designed to reduce the tax burden on individuals whose ability to pay has been involuntarily impaired, but because of large floor limitations these itemized deductions are unlikely to produce tax benefits. Most miscellaneous itemized deductions, including unreimbursed employee business expenses and investment expenses (excluding rental and royalty expenses), are likewise hampered by a relatively large floor limitation.

Example 6-31

Given Courtney's current year AGI of $182,000, what is the amount of her total itemized deductions she may claim on her tax return?

Answer: Courtney's itemized deductions for the year are $39,889, calculated as follows:

Description	Amount	Reference
Taxes	$10,380	Example 6-14
Interest on loans secured by residence	15,800	Example 6-15
Charitable contributions	12,530	Example 6-21
Miscellaneous itemized deductions	+1,179	Example 6-30
Total itemized deductions*	**$39,889**	

*Because Courtney's AGI of $182,000 is below the phase-out threshold of $287,650 for taxpayers filing as a head of household, none of her itemized deductions are phased-out.

Exhibit 6-10 presents Courtney's itemized deductions on Form 1040, Schedule A.

[48] If gambling is deemed to be a business activity (see *Linda M. Myers*, TC Summary Opinion 2007-194), then the taxpayer reports gambling winnings and losses on Schedule C (not as a miscellaneous itemized deduction). However, gambling losses remain only deductible to the extent of gambling winnings.

EXHIBIT 6-10 Courtney's Form 1040, Schedule A

SCHEDULE A (Form 1040)

Department of the Treasury Internal Revenue Service (99)

Itemized Deductions

▶ Information about Schedule A and its separate instructions is at *www.irs.gov/schedulea*.
▶ Attach to Form 1040.

OMB No. 1545-0074

2016

Attachment Sequence No. 07

Name(s) shown on Form 1040: Courtney Wilson

Your social security number: 123-45-6789

Section	Line	Description	Box	Amount	Line	Total
Medical and Dental Expenses		**Caution:** Do not include expenses reimbursed or paid by others.				
	1	Medical and dental expenses (see instructions)	1	2,400		
	2	Enter amount from Form 1040, line 38 — 2: 182,000				
	3	Multiply line 2 by 10% (0.10). But if either you or your spouse was born before January 2, 1952, multiply line 2 by 7.5% (0.075) instead	3	18,200		
	4	Subtract line 3 from line 1. If line 3 is more than line 1, enter -0-			4	0
Taxes You Paid	5	State and local **(check only one box):**				
		a ☑ Income taxes, **or** b ☐ General sales taxes	5	6,700		
	6	Real estate taxes (see instructions)	6	3,680		
	7	Personal property taxes	7			
	8	Other taxes. List type and amount ▶	8			
	9	Add lines 5 through 8			9	10,380
Interest You Paid	10	Home mortgage interest and points reported to you on Form 1098	10	15,800		
Note: Your mortgage interest deduction may be limited (see instructions).	11	Home mortgage interest not reported to you on Form 1098. If paid to the person from whom you bought the home, see instructions and show that person's name, identifying no., and address ▶	11			
	12	Points not reported to you on Form 1098. See instructions for special rules	12			
	13	Mortgage insurance premiums (see instructions)	13			
	14	Investment interest. Attach Form 4952 if required. (See instructions.)	14			
	15	Add lines 10 through 14			15	15,800
Gifts to Charity	16	Gifts by cash or check. If you made any gift of $250 or more, see instructions	16	1,770		
If you made a gift and got a benefit for it, see instructions.	17	Other than by cash or check. If any gift of $250 or more, see instructions. You **must** attach Form 8283 if over $500	17	10,760		
	18	Carryover from prior year	18			
	19	Add lines 16 through 18			19	12,530
Casualty and Theft Losses	20	Casualty or theft loss(es). Attach Form 4684. (See instructions.)			20	
Job Expenses and Certain Miscellaneous Deductions	21	Unreimbursed employee expenses—job travel, union dues, job education, etc. Attach Form 2106 or 2106-EZ if required. (See instructions.) ▶	21	3,759		
	22	Tax preparation fees	22	650		
	23	Other expenses—investment, safe deposit box, etc. List type and amount ▶ Subscriptions to Business Publications	23	410		
	24	Add lines 21 through 23	24	4,819		
	25	Enter amount from Form 1040, line 38 — 25: 182,000				
	26	Multiply line 25 by 2% (0.02)	26	3,640		
	27	Subtract line 26 from line 24. If line 26 is more than line 24, enter -0-			27	1,179
Other Miscellaneous Deductions	28	Other—from list in instructions. List type and amount ▶			28	
Total Itemized Deductions	29	Is Form 1040, line 38, over $155,650? ☐ **No.** Your deduction is not limited. Add the amounts in the far right column for lines 4 through 28. Also, enter this amount on Form 1040, line 40. ☑ **Yes.** Your deduction may be limited. See the Itemized Deductions Worksheet in the instructions to figure the amount to enter.			29	39,889
	30	If you elect to itemize deductions even though they are less than your standard deduction, check here ▶ ☐				

For Paperwork Reduction Act Notice, see Form 1040 instructions. Cat. No. 17145C **Schedule A (Form 1040) 2016**

LO 6-3

THE STANDARD DEDUCTION AND EXEMPTIONS

Standard Deduction

The **standard deduction** is a flat amount that most individuals can elect to deduct *instead* of deducting their itemized deductions (if any). That is, taxpayers generally deduct *the greater of their standard deduction or their itemized deductions.*

The amount of the standard deduction varies according to the taxpayer's filing status, age, and eyesight. The basic standard deduction is greater for married taxpayers filing jointly and those supporting a family (head of household) than it is for married taxpayers filing separately and unmarried taxpayers not supporting a family. Taxpayers who are at least 65 years of age on the last day of the year or blind are entitled to additional standard deduction amounts above and beyond their basic standard deduction.[49] Exhibit 6-11 summarizes the standard deduction amounts.[50]

EXHIBIT 6-11 Standard Deduction Amounts*

2016 Amounts		
Filing Status	**Basic Standard Deduction**	**Additional Standard Deduction for Age and/or Blindness at End of Year**
Married filing jointly	$12,600	$1,250
Head of household	9,300	1,550
Single	6,300	1,550
Married filing separately	6,300	1,250

2017 Amounts		
Filing Status	**Basic Standard Deduction**	**Additional Standard Deduction for Age and/or Blindness at End of Year**
Married filing jointly	$12,700	$1,250
Head of household	9,350	1,550
Single	6,350	1,550
Married filing separately	6,350	1,250

*For individuals claimed as a dependent on another return, the 2017 standard deduction is the greater of (1) $1,050 or (2) $350 plus earned income not to exceed the standard deduction amount of those who are not dependents.

For 2017, the additional standard deduction for either age and/or blindness is $1,250 for married taxpayers and $1,550 for taxpayers who are not married. Thus, a blind individual who is 65 years old and single is entitled to a standard deduction of $9,450 ($6,350 + $1,550 + $1,550). A married couple filing a joint return with one spouse over age 65 and one spouse considered legally blind is entitled to a standard deduction of $15,200 ($12,700 + $1,250 + $1,250). Finally, for an individual who is eligible to be claimed as a dependent on another's return, the standard deduction is the greater of (1) $1,050 or (2) $350 plus the individual's earned income limited to the regular standard deduction. The additional standard deduction amounts for age and blindness, if any, are not impacted by the preceding limitation for eligible dependents.

[49]Taxpayers are considered 65 on the day before their 65th birthday. Taxpayers are considered to be blind if they have a certified statement from their eye doctor or registered optometrist that their corrected vision of their better eye is no better than 20/200 or their field of vision is 20 degrees or less.

[50]The standard deduction amount is indexed for inflation.

Example 6-32

What is Courtney's standard deduction for the year?

Answer: $9,350. Because Courtney is unmarried at the end of the year and she maintains a household for more than six months for Deron and Ellen, who both qualify as her dependents (as qualifying children), Courtney's filing status is head of household, which allows her to claim a standard deduction of $9,350.

Given that Courtney's itemized deductions are $39,889, will Courtney deduct her itemized deductions or her standard deduction?

Answer: She will deduct her itemized deductions because they exceed her standard deduction.

What if: Suppose that Courtney's 10-year-old son, Deron, earned $600 this summer by mowing lawns for neighbors. If Courtney claims a dependency exemption for Deron, what amount of standard deduction can Deron claim on his individual return?

Answer: Deron will claim a minimum standard deduction of $1,050 because he is claimed as a dependent on Courtney's return. Hence, Deron will not pay any income tax because his taxable income is reduced to zero by the standard deduction.[51]

What if: Would there be any difference in the amount of the standard deduction if Deron earned $2,100?

Answer: Because of the amount of his earnings, Deron would claim a standard deduction in the amount of his earned income plus $350. Hence, Deron would claim a standard deduction of $2,450 and he would not pay any income tax.[52]

What if: Suppose that Deron earned $8,600?

Answer: Again, Deron would claim a standard deduction in the amount of his earned income plus $350. However, Deron's standard deduction is limited to $6,350, the maximum allowable standard deduction for a taxpayer filing single and claimed as a dependent on another's return. Hence, Deron would report taxable income of $2,250.

From the government's standpoint, the standard deduction serves two purposes. First, to help taxpayers with lower income, it automatically provides a minimum amount of income that is not subject to taxation. Second, it eliminates the need for the IRS to verify and audit itemized deductions for those taxpayers who choose to deduct the standard deduction. From the taxpayers' perspective, the standard deduction allows them to avoid taxation on a portion of their income, and for those not planning to itemize deductions, it eliminates the need to substantiate and collect information about them. The standard deduction, however, is a double-edged sword. While it reduces taxes by offsetting income with an automatic deduction, it eliminates the tax benefits of itemized deductions up to the amount of the standard deduction. This is a very important point to consider when evaluating the tax benefits of itemized deductions.

Example 6-33

In Example 6-31, we determined that Courtney is entitled to deduct $39,889 of itemized deductions this year. How much do Courtney's itemized deductions reduce her taxable income relative to a situation in which she has $0 itemized deductions?

Answer: $30,539. Because Courtney files as a head of household, she would have been able to deduct $9,350 as a standard deduction even if she had not incurred *any* itemized deductions. Consequently, her itemized deductions reduce her taxable income by only $30,539 ($39,889 − $9,350) beyond what her taxable income would have been if she did not itemize deductions.

[51]Deron will need to file a tax return because his self-employment income exceeds $400 and, as explained in the Individual Income Tax Computation and Tax Credits chapter, he will likely owe self-employment tax.

[52]As mentioned previously, Deron will need to file a tax return because his self-employment income exceeds $400 and, as explained in the Individual Income Tax Computation and Tax Credits chapter, he will likely owe self-employment taxes.

Bunching Itemized Deductions Some taxpayers may deduct the standard deduction every year because their itemized deductions always fall just short of the standard deduction amount and thus never produce any tax benefit. They may gain some tax benefit from their itemized deductions by implementing a simple tax planning strategy called **bunching itemized deductions.** The basic strategy consists of shifting itemized deductions into one year such that the amount of itemized deductions exceeds the standard deduction for the year, and then deducting the standard deduction in the next year (or vice versa).

Because individuals are cash-method taxpayers, they may shift certain itemized deductions by accelerating payment into the current year. For example, a taxpayer could make charitable contributions at the end of December rather than at the beginning of January in the following year. Taxpayers' ability to shift itemized deductions is limited because the timing of these payments is not completely discretionary. For example, real estate taxes have due dates, state taxes are generally paid throughout the year via withholding, and employees may incur and be required to pay business expenses throughout the year. However, taxpayers who annually make a certain amount of charitable contributions, for example, may consider lumping contributions for two years into one year and not contributing in the next year.[53]

Example 6-34

What if: Gram is 70 years old and files as a single taxpayer. Last year Gram paid deductible medical expenses (after the AGI floor limitation) of $4,000. She also contributed $3,000 to her local church. Last year her total itemized deductions were $7,000 ($4,000 medical + 3,000 charitable). Assuming Gram has similar expenditures this year, what amount of additional deductions would Gram have been able to deduct last year if she had bunched her deductions by making her 2016 and 2017 charitable contributions in 2017?

Answer: $2,100, computed as follows:

	No Bunching		Bunching	
	2016	**2017**	**2016**	**2017**
(1) Standard deduction*	$7,850	$7,900	$7,850	$ 7,900
(2) Itemized deductions	7,000	7,000	4,000	10,000
Greater of (1) and (2)	$7,850	$7,900	$7,850	$10,000
Total deductions (combined years)	$15,750 ($7,850 + $7,900)		$17,850 ($7,850 + $10,000)	
Deductions gained through bunching	**$2,100 ($17,850 bunching deductions – $15,750 nonbunching deductions)**			

*For 2016, her standard deduction is the $6,300 standard deduction for single taxpayers plus an additional $1,550 standard deduction amount for age. For 2017, her standard deduction is the $6,350 standard deduction for single taxpayers plus an additional $1,550 standard deduction amount for age. (See Exhibit 6-11.)

Deduction for Personal and Dependency Exemptions

As we learned in the Individual Income Tax Overview, Exemptions, and Filing Status chapter, taxpayers are generally allowed to deduct $4,050 in 2017 for each **personal** and **dependency exemption.** In general, then, a taxpayer's *from* AGI deduction for personal and dependency exemptions is $4,050 multiplied by the number of the taxpayer's **exemptions.** However, just as with itemized deductions, a taxpayer's total exemption deduction is phased out based on AGI for relatively high income taxpayers. The AGI threshold for the beginning of the phase-out and the AGI for the maximum phase-out depends on the taxpayer's filing status. The amounts for 2017 are presented in Exhibit 6-12. We discuss the computational details of the phase-out in Appendix B to this chapter.

[53]Of course, as we discussed in the Tax Planning Strategies and Related Limitations chapter, taxpayers adopting this strategy must also consider the time value of money for the contribution amounts they pay in advance to determine whether a tax planning strategy designed to save taxes makes economic sense.

EXHIBIT 6-12 **Maximum Phase-Out Range for Personal and Dependency Exemptions for 2017**

Filing Status	Threshold	AGI Maximum Phase-Out
Married filing jointly	$313,800	$436,301
Head of household	287,650	410,151
Single	261,500	384,001
Married filing separately	156,900	218,151

Example 6-35

This year, Courtney is allowed to claim a personal exemption for herself and dependency exemptions for her daughter Ellen and her son Deron. Courtney's filing status is head of household. What amount is Courtney allowed to deduct for her personal and dependency exemptions?

Answer: $12,150 ($4,050 × 3). Because Courtney's AGI is $182,000 and she files as a head of household, her AGI is below the $287,650 threshold for the exemption phase-out. Thus, she is allowed to deduct her full exemption amounts without phase-out.

Taxable Income Summary

We now have enough information to calculate Courtney's and Gram's taxable income. Exhibit 6-13 shows Courtney's taxable income calculation and Exhibit 6-14 illustrates how this information would be displayed on page 2 of Courtney's Form 1040.

Exhibit 6-15 provides Gram's taxable income calculation.

EXHIBIT 6-13 **Courtney's Taxable Income**

Description	Amount	Reference
AGI	$182,000	Exhibit 6-6
Less: Greater of (1) itemized deductions ($39,889) or (2) standard deduction ($9,350)	(39,889)	Example 6-31
Less: Personal and dependency exemptions	(12,150)	Example 6-35
Taxable income	$129,961	

EXHIBIT 6-14 **Courtney's Taxable Income Computation as Presented on Form 1040, Page 2**

Form 1040 (2016) Page **2**

Tax and Credits	38	Amount from line 37 (adjusted gross income)	38	182,000
	39a	Check if: ☐ **You** were born before January 2, 1952, ☐ Blind. ☐ **Spouse** was born before January 2, 1952, ☐ Blind. } **Total boxes checked ▶ 39a** ☐		
	b	If your spouse itemizes on a separate return or you were a dual-status alien, check here ▶ **39b** ☐		
Standard Deduction for—	40	**Itemized deductions** (from Schedule A) **or** your **standard deduction** (see left margin)	40	39,889
	41	Subtract line 40 from line 38	41	142,111
• People who check any box on line	42	**Exemptions.** If line 38 is $155,650 or less, multiply $4,050 by the number on line 6d. Otherwise, see instructions	42	12,150
	43	**Taxable income.** Subtract line 42 from line 41. If line 42 is more than line 41, enter -0-	43	129,961

EXHIBIT 6-15 **Gram's Taxable Income**

Description	Amount	Reference
(1) AGI	$15,590	Exhibit 6-7
(2) Greater of (a) itemized deductions ($7,000) or (b) standard deduction ($7,900)	(7,900)	Example 6-34
(3) Personal and dependency exemptions	(4,050)	One exemption
Taxable income	$ 3,640	(1) + (2) + (3)

Note that because Gram's gross income of $16,000 (Exhibit 5-6) is more than the sum of her basic standard deduction amount plus her personal and dependency exemption ($7,900 + $4,050 = $11,950), she is required to file a tax return.

CONCLUSION

We started this chapter with Courtney's and Gram's gross incomes. In this chapter, we first identified the duo's separate deductions *for* AGI and computed their AGI. We then determined their *from* AGI deductions. Courtney deducted her itemized deductions because they exceeded her standard deduction. Gram, on the other hand, deducted her standard deduction. Finally, Courtney deducted three exemptions: a personal exemption for herself and dependency exemptions for each of her two children, Deron and Ellen. Gram deducted one personal exemption for herself. By subtracting their *from* AGI deductions from their AGI, we determined taxable income for both Courtney and Gram. With this knowledge, we proceed to the next two chapters and address issues relating to investments and determining the amount of tax Courtney and Gram are required to pay on their taxable income.

Appendix A Calculation of Itemized Deduction Phase-Out for 2017

The amount of the itemized deduction phase-out for 2017 is the lesser of:

1. 3 percent × [AGI minus $313,800 ($287,650 for heads of household, $261,500 for single taxpayers, and $156,900 for married taxpayers filing separately)] or
2. 80 percent of the total itemized deductions subject to phase-out.

Example 6-1A

What if: Suppose Courtney's AGI is $320,000. What is the amount of total itemized deductions she may claim on her tax return after computing the itemized deduction phase-out?

Answer: Courtney's itemized deductions for the year are $38,918, calculated as follows:

Description	Amount	Reference
Taxes	$10,380	Example 6-14
Interest on loans secured by residence	15,800	Example 6-15
Charitable contributions	12,530	Example 6-21
Miscellaneous itemized deductions	1,179	Example 6-30
Total itemized deductions subject to phase-out	$39,889	
Less phase-out of itemized deductions	−971	See calculation below.
Total itemized deductions	$38,918	

Calculation of the phase-out:

Lesser of

(1) 3 percent × (AGI minus $287,650) = 3 percent × ($320,000 − $287,650) = $971 (rounded) or
(2) 80 percent of the total itemized deductions subject to phase-out ($39,889) = $31,911

Appendix B Personal Exemption Phase-Out Computation for 2017

The process of determining the amount of the phase-out involves the following five steps:

Step 1: Subtract the taxpayer's AGI from the AGI threshold based on the taxpayer's filing status. If the threshold equals or exceeds the taxpayer's AGI, the taxpayer deducts her full personal and dependency exemption.

Step 2: Divide the excess AGI (the amount from Step 1) by 2,500. If the result is not a whole number (i.e., the excess AGI is not evenly divisible by 2,500), round *up* to the next whole number. (For married filing separate taxpayers, replace the 2,500 amount with 1,250.)

Step 3: Multiply the outcome of Step 2 by 2 percent, but limit the product to 100 percent.

Step 4: Multiply the percentage determined in Step 3 by the taxpayer's total personal and dependency exemptions (i.e., number of personal and dependency exemptions times $4,050 in 2017). The product is the amount of personal and dependency exemption that is phased-out (i.e., the taxpayer is *not* allowed to deduct this amount).

Step 5: Subtract the Step 4 result from the taxpayer's total personal and dependency exemptions that would be deductible without any phase-out (i.e., number of personal and dependency exemptions times $4,050 in 2017).

Example 6-1B

What if: Suppose that Courtney's AGI is $343,150 and her personal and dependency exemptions total $12,150 ($4,050 × 3). What amount of personal and dependency exemptions will she be allowed to deduct with the phase-out?

Answer: $6,561, computed as follows:

	Amount	Explanation
Step 1:	$55,500	$343,150 – $287,650 (Excess AGI).
Step 2:	23	Divide $55,500 by 2,500 and round up to nearest whole number $55,500/2,500 = 22.2 = 23 (rounded).
Step 3:	46%	Multiply the amount in Step 2 by 2% (i.e., 23 × 2%).
Step 4:	$ 5,589	Multiply the Step 3 result by the total exemption amount (i.e., $12,150 × 46%). This is the amount of the phase-out.
Step 5:	$ 6,561	Subtract the Step 4 result from the total exemption amount (i.e., $12,150 – $5,589). This is the deductible exemption amount.

Summary

Identify the common deductions necessary for calculating adjusted gross income (AGI). LO 6-1

- Deductions *for* AGI may be categorized into those that are directly or indirectly business-related and those that address specific policy issues.
- The business-related deductions *for* AGI include business expenses, rent and royalty expenses, self-employment taxes, moving expenses, medical and health insurance by self-employed taxpayers, and forfeited interest.
- Other common deductions *for* AGI include the deductions for alimony, interest on student loans, qualified education expenses, and early withdrawal penalties.

LO 6-2 Describe the different types of itemized deductions available to individuals and compute itemized deductions.

- The medical expense and casualty loss deductions are designed to provide tax benefits to needy individuals but both are subject to significant floor limitations.
- The itemized deduction for interest is limited to interest related to a personal residence and investment interest, and the latter is limited by net investment income.
- The deduction for charitable contributions extends to contributions of money and property to qualifying charities. The charitable deduction is subject to ceiling limitations, which are more restrictive for donations of property.
- The deduction for taxes includes state income and property taxes. Sales taxes can be deducted in lieu of deducting state and local income taxes.
- Employee business expenses and investment expenses (except rental and royalty expenses) are miscellaneous itemized deductions subject to a 2 percent of AGI floor limitation.

LO 6-3 Explain the operation of the standard deduction, determine the deduction for personal and dependency exemptions, and compute taxable income.

- Itemized deductions do not produce any tax benefit unless the total itemized deductions exceed the standard deduction.
- Certain itemized deductions are subject to a phase-out for high income taxpayers.
- Personal exemptions are allowed for the taxpayer and spouse (if married filing jointly).
- Personal and dependency exemptions are subject to a phase-out for high income taxpayers.

KEY TERMS

accountable plan (6-28)
bunching itemized deductions (6-36)
business activities (6-2)
capital gain property (6-19)
casualty loss (6-24)
ceiling (6-21)
commuting (6-27)
dependency exemption (6-36)
exemption (6-36)
floor limitation (6-15)
hobby (6-29)
investment activities (6-2)
miscellaneous itemized deductions (6-26)
ordinary and necessary (6-4)
ordinary income property (6-19)
personal exemption (6-36)
private nonoperating foundations (6-21)
private operating foundations (6-21)
qualified educational expenses (6-9)
qualified educational loans (6-9)
standard deduction (6-34)
trade or business (6-3)

DISCUSSION QUESTIONS

Discussion Questions are available in Connect®.

LO 6-1 1. It has been suggested that tax policy favors deductions *for* AGI compared to itemized deductions. Describe two ways in which deductions *for* AGI are treated more favorably than itemized deductions.

LO 6-1 2. How is a business activity distinguished from an investment activity? Why is this distinction important for the purpose of calculating federal income taxes?

LO 6-1 3. Describe how a business element is reflected in the requirements to deduct moving expenses and how Congress limited this deduction to substantial moves.

LO 6-1 4. Explain why Congress allows self-employed taxpayers to deduct the cost of health insurance above the line (*for* AGI) when employees can only itemize this cost as a medical expense. Would a self-employed taxpayer ever prefer to claim health insurance premiums as an itemized deduction rather than a deduction *for* AGI? Explain.

5. Explain why Congress allows self-employed taxpayers to deduct the employer portion of their self-employment tax. LO 6-1
6. Using the Internal Revenue Code, describe two deductions *for* AGI that are not discussed in this chapter. LO 6-1 research
7. Explain why Congress allows taxpayers to deduct interest forfeited as a penalty on the premature withdrawal from a certificate of deposit. LO 6-1
8. Describe the mechanical limitation on the deduction for interest on qualified educational loans. LO 6-1
9. Explain why the medical expense and casualty loss provisions are sometimes referred to as "wherewithal" deductions and how this rationale is reflected in the limits on these deductions. LO 6-2
10. Describe the type of medical expenditures that qualify for the medical expense deduction. Does the cost of meals consumed while hospitalized qualify for the deduction? Do over-the-counter drugs and medicines qualify for the deduction? LO 6-2
11. Under what circumstances can a taxpayer deduct medical expenses paid for a member of his family? Does it matter if the family member reports significant amounts of gross income and cannot be claimed as a dependent? LO 6-2
12. What types of taxes qualify to be deducted as itemized deductions? Would a vehicle registration fee qualify as a deductible tax? LO 6-2
13. Compare and contrast the limits on the deduction of interest on home acquisition indebtedness versus home equity loans. Are these limits consistent with horizontal equity? Explain. LO 6-2
14. Explain the argument that the deductions for charitable contributions and home mortgage interest represent indirect subsidies for these activities. LO 6-2
15. Cash donations to charity are subject to a number of very specific substantiation requirements. Describe these requirements and how charitable gifts can be substantiated. Describe the substantiation requirements for property donations. LO 6-2 research
16. Describe the conditions in which a donation of property to a charity will result in a charitable contribution deduction of fair market value and when it will result in a deduction of the tax basis of the property. LO 6-2
17. Describe the type of event that qualifies as a casualty for tax purposes. LO 6-2
18. A casualty loss from the complete destruction of a personal asset is limited to the lesser of fair market value or the property's adjusted basis. Explain the rationale for this rule as opposed to just allowing a deduction for the basis of the asset. LO 6-2
19. This week Jim's residence was heavily damaged by a storm system that spread destruction throughout the region. While Jim's property insurance covers some of the damage, there is a significant amount of uninsured loss. The governor of Jim's state has requested that the president declare the region a federal disaster area and provide federal disaster assistance. Explain to Jim the income tax implications of such a declaration and any associated tax planning possibilities. LO 6-2 research
20. Describe the types of expenses that constitute miscellaneous itemized deductions and explain why these expenses rarely produce any tax benefits. LO 6-2
21. Explain why the cost of commuting from home to work is not deductible as a business expense. LO 6-2
22. When is the cost of education deductible as an employee business expense? LO 6-2
23. How might the reimbursement of a portion of an employee expense influence the deductibility of the expense for the employee? LO 6-2

LO 6-2 24. Explain why an employee should be concerned about whether his employer reimburses business expenses using an "accountable" plan.

LO 6-2 25. Jake is a retired jockey who takes monthly trips to Las Vegas to gamble on horse races. Jake also trains racehorses part time at his Louisville ranch. So far this year, Jake has won almost $47,500 during his trips to Las Vegas while spending $27,250 on travel expenses and incurring $62,400 of gambling losses. Jake also received $60,000 in revenue from his training activities and he incurred $72,000 of associated costs. Explain how Jake's gambling winnings and related costs will be treated for tax purposes. Describe the factors that will influence how Jake's ranch expenses are treated for tax purposes.

LO 6-2 research 26. Frank paid $3,700 in fees for an accountant to tabulate business information (Frank operates as a self-employed contractor and files a Schedule C). The accountant also spent time tabulating Frank's income from his investments and determining Frank's personal itemized deductions. Explain to Frank whether or not he can deduct the $3,700 as a business expense or as an itemized deduction, and provide a citation to an authority that supports your conclusion.

LO 6-2 27. Contrast ceiling and floor limitations, and give an example of each.

LO 6-2 28. Identify which itemized deductions are subject to floor limitations, ceiling limitations, or some combination of these limits.

LO 6-3 29. Describe the tax benefits from "bunching" itemized deductions in one year. Describe the characteristics of the taxpayers who are most likely to benefit from using bunching and explain why this is so.

LO 6-3 30. Explain how the standard deduction is rationalized and why the standard deduction might be viewed as a floor limit on itemized deductions.

LO 6-3 31. Explain how the calculation of the standard deduction limits the ability to shift income to a dependent.

LO 6-3 32. Explain why the overall phase-out of itemized deductions has been described as a "haircut" of itemized deductions. Explain whether it is possible for taxpayers to lose all their itemized deductions under the phase-out rules.

LO 6-3 33. Describe the mechanism for phasing out exemptions. Can a taxpayer lose the benefit of all of her personal and dependency exemptions?

LO 6-3 research 34. Determine whether a taxpayer can change his or her election to itemize deductions once a return is filed. (*Hint:* Read about itemization under Reg. §1.63-1.)

LO 6-3 research 35. Determine whether a taxpayer who is claimed as a dependent on another return is entitled to an addition to the standard deduction for age or blindness. (*Hint:* Read the calculation of the standard deduction under IRC §63.)

PROBLEMS

Select problems are available in Connect®. connect

LO 6-1 36. Clem is married and is a skilled carpenter. Clem's wife, Wanda, works part-time as a substitute grade school teacher. Determine the amount of Clem's expenses that are deductible *for* AGI this year (if any) under the following independent circumstances:

a) Clem is self-employed and this year he incurred $525 in expenses for tools and supplies related to his job. Since neither were covered by a qualified health plan, Wanda paid health insurance premiums of $3,600 to provide coverage for herself and Clem (not through an exchange).

b) Clem and Wanda own a garage downtown that they rent to a local business for storage. This year they incurred expenses of $1,250 in utilities and $780 in depreciation.

c) Clem paid self-employment tax of $15,300 (the employer portion is $7,650), and Wanda had $3,000 of Social Security taxes withheld from her pay.

d) Clem paid $45 to rent a safe deposit box to store his coin collection. Clem has collected coins intermittently since he was a boy, and he expects to sell his collection when he retires.

37. Clyde currently commutes 55 miles to work in the city. He is considering a new assignment in the suburbs on the other side of the city that would increase his commute considerably. He would like to accept the assignment, but he thinks it might require that he move to the other side of the city. Determine if Clyde's move qualifies for a moving expense deduction and calculate the amount (if any) under the following circumstances: LO 6-1

a) Clyde estimates that unless he moves across town, his new commute would be almost 70 miles. He also estimates the costs of a move as follows:

Lodging while searching for an apartment	$ 126
Transportation—auto (100 miles @ 17 cents/mile)	17
Mover's fee (furniture and possessions)	1,500
Meals while en route	35

b) Same as part (a), except Clyde estimates that unless he moves across town, his new commute would be almost 115 miles.

c) Same as part (a), except Clyde's new commute would be almost 150 miles and the movers intend to impose a $450 surcharge on the moving fee for the additional distance.

38. Smithers is a self-employed individual who earns $30,000 per year in self-employment income. Smithers pays $2,200 in annual health insurance premiums (not through an exchange) for his own medical care. In each of the following situations, determine the amount of the deductible health insurance premium for Smithers before any AGI limitation. LO 6-1

a) Smithers is single and the self-employment income is his only source of income.

b) Smithers is single, but besides being self-employed, Smithers is also employed part-time by SF Power Corporation. This year Smithers elected not to participate in SF's health plan.

c) Smithers is self-employed and he is also married. Smithers's spouse, Samantha, is employed full-time by SF Power Corporation and is covered by SF's health plan. Smithers is not eligible to participate in SF's health plan.

d) Smithers is self-employed and he is also married. Smithers's spouse, Samantha, is employed full-time by SF Power Corporation and is covered by SF's health plan. Smithers elected not to participate in SF's health plan.

39. Hardaway earned $100,000 of compensation this year. He also paid (or had paid for him) $3,000 of health insurance (not through an exchange). What is Hardaway's AGI in each of the following situations? (Ignore the effects of Social Security and self-employment taxes.) LO 6-1

a) Hardaway is an employee and his employer paid Hardaway's $3,000 of health insurance for him as a nontaxable fringe benefit. Consequently, Hardaway received $97,000 of taxable compensation and $3,000 of nontaxable compensation.

b) Hardaway is a self-employed taxpayer, and he paid $3,000 of health insurance himself. He is not eligible to participate in an employer-sponsored plan.

LO 6-1 tax forms

40. Betty operates a beauty salon as a sole proprietorship. Betty also owns and rents an apartment building. This year Betty had the following income and expenses. Determine Betty's AGI and complete page 1 of Form 1040 for Betty. You may assume that Betty will owe $2,502 in self-employment tax on her salon income.

Interest income	$11,255
Salon sales and revenue	86,360
Salaries paid to beauticians	45,250
Beauty salon supplies	23,400
Alimony paid to her ex-husband, Rocky	6,000
Rental revenue from apartment building	31,220
Depreciation on apartment building	12,900
Real estate taxes paid on apartment building	11,100
Real estate taxes paid on personal residence	6,241
Contributions to charity	4,237

LO 6-1

41. Lionel is an unmarried law student at State University Law School, a qualified educational institution. This year Lionel borrowed $24,000 from County Bank and paid interest of $1,440. Lionel used the loan proceeds to pay his law school tuition. Calculate the amounts Lionel can deduct for higher education expenses and interest on higher education loans under the following circumstances (assume the 2016 rules apply for purposes of the qualified education deduction):

a) Lionel's AGI before deducting interest on higher education loans is $50,000.

b) Lionel's AGI before deducting interest on higher education loans is $74,000.

c) Lionel's AGI before deducting interest on higher education loans is $90,000.

LO 6-1 planning

42. This year Jack intends to file a married-joint return with two dependents. Jack received $167,500 of salary and paid $5,000 of interest on loans used to pay qualified tuition costs for his dependent daughter, Deb. This year Jack has also paid qualified moving expenses of $4,300 and $24,000 of alimony.

a) What is Jack's adjusted gross income? Assume that Jack will opt to treat tax items in a manner to minimize his AGI.

b) Suppose that Jack also reported income of $8,800 from a half share of profits from a partnership. Disregard any potential self-employment taxes on this income. What AGI would Jack report under these circumstances? Again, assume that Jack will opt to treat tax items in a manner to minimize his AGI.

LO 6-1 LO 6-2

43. In each of the following independent cases, indicate the amount (1) deductible *for* AGI, (2) deductible *from* AGI, and (3) deductible neither *for* nor *from* AGI before considering income limitations or the standard deduction.

a) Ted paid $50 rent on a safety deposit box at the bank. In this box he kept the few shares of stock that he owned.

b) Tyler paid $85 for minor repairs to the fence at a rental house he owned.

c) Timmy paid $545 for health insurance premiums this year (not through an exchange and not with pretax dollars). Timmy is employed full-time and his employer paid the remaining premiums as a qualified fringe benefit.

d) Tess paid $1,150 of state income taxes on her consulting income.

44. In each of the following independent cases, indicate the amount (1) deductible *for* AGI, (2) deductible *from* AGI, and (3) deductible neither *for* nor *from* AGI before considering income limitations or the standard deduction. LO 6-1 LO 6-2
   a) Fran spent $90 for uniforms for use on her job. Her employer reimbursed her for $75 of this amount under an accountable plan (and did not report the reimbursement as wages).
   b) Timothy, a plumber employed by ACE Plumbing, spent $65 for small tools to be used on his job, but he was not reimbursed by ACE.
   c) Jake is a perfume salesperson. Because of his high pay, he receives no allowance or reimbursement from his employer for advertising expenses even though his position requires him to advertise frequently. During the year, he spent $2,200 on legitimate business advertisements.
   d) Trey is a self-employed special-duty nurse. He spent $120 for uniforms.
   e) Mary, a professor at a community college, spent $340 for magazine subscriptions. The magazines were helpful for her research activities, but she was not reimbursed for the expenditures.
   f) Wayne lost $325 on the bets he made at the race track, but he won $57 playing slot machines.

45. Ted is a successful attorney, but when he turned 50 years old he decided to retire from his law practice and become a professional golfer. Ted has been a very successful amateur golfer, so beginning this year, Ted began competing in professional golf tournaments. At year-end, Ted reported the following expenses associated with competing in 15 professional events: LO 6-2

Transportation from his home to various tournaments	$25,000
Lodging for the 15 weeks on the road	18,200
Meals while traveling and during golf tournaments	5,200
Entry fees	7,500
Lessons from various golf teachers	12,500
Golf supplies (balls, tees, etc.)	783
Total expenses	$69,183

   a) Suppose that Ted reports $175,000 in gross income from his pension and various investments. Describe the various considerations that will dictate the extent to which Ted can deduct the expenses associated with professional golf.
   b) Calculate Ted's deduction for golf expenses assuming that the IRS and the courts are convinced that Ted engages in competitive golf primarily for enjoyment rather than the expectation of making a profit. Assume Ted wins $10,000 this year and his AGI is $185,000 (including the golf revenues).

46. Penny, a full-time biochemist, loves stock car racing. To feed her passion, she bought a used dirt-track car and has started entering some local dirt-track races. The prize money is pretty small ($1,000 for the winner), but she really is not in it for the money. Penny reported the following income and expenses from her nights at the track: LO 6-2

Prize money	$2,500
Expenses:	
Transportation from her home to the races	1,000
Depreciation on the dirt-track car	4,000
Entry fees	3,500
Oil, gas, supplies, repairs for the dirt-track car	2,050

Calculate Penny's deduction for the racing expenses assuming that the racing activity is a hobby. Also assume Penny's AGI is $97,500 *before* considering the prize money.

LO 6-2

47. Simpson is a single individual who is employed full-time by Duff Corporation. This year Simpson reports AGI of $50,000 and has incurred the following medical expenses:

Dentist charges	$ 900
Physician charges	1,800
Optical charges	500
Cost of eyeglasses	300
Hospital charges	2,100
Prescription drugs	250
Over-the-counter drugs	450
Medical insurance premiums (not through an exchange)	775

a) Calculate the amount of medical expenses that will be included with Simpson's itemized deductions after any applicable limitations.

b) Suppose that Simpson was reimbursed for $250 of the physician's charges and $1,200 for the hospital costs. Calculate the amount of medical expenses that will be included with Simpson's itemized deductions after any applicable limitations.

LO 6-2 research

48. This year Tim is age 45 and is considering enrolling in an insurance program that provides for long-term care insurance. He is curious about whether the insurance premiums are deductible as a medical expense and, if so, what the maximum amount is that can be deducted in any year.

LO 6-2 research

49. Doctor Bones prescribed physical therapy in a pool to treat Jack's broken back. In response to this advice (and for no other reason), Jack built a swimming pool in his backyard and strictly limited use of the pool to physical therapy. Jack paid $25,000 to build the pool, but he wondered if this amount could be deducted as a medical expense. Determine if a capital expenditure such as the cost of a swimming pool qualifies for the medical expense deduction.

LO 6-1 LO 6-2

50. Charles has AGI of $50,000 and has made the following payments related to (1) land he inherited from his deceased aunt and (2) a personal vacation taken last year. Calculate the amount of taxes Charles may include in his itemized deductions for the year under the following circumstances:

State inheritance tax on the land	$1,200
County real estate tax on the land	1,500
School district tax on the land	690
City special assessment on the land (replacing curbs and gutters)	700
State tax on airline tickets (paid on vacation)	125
Local hotel tax (paid during vacation)	195

a) Suppose that Charles holds the land for appreciation.

b) Suppose that Charles holds the land for rent.

c) Suppose that Charles holds the land for appreciation and that the vacation was actually a business trip.

LO 6-2

51. Dan has AGI of $50,000 and paid the following taxes during this tax year. Calculate how much Dan can deduct for taxes as an itemized deduction this year.

State income tax withholding	$1,400
State income tax estimated payments	750
Federal income tax withholding	3,000
Social Security tax withheld from wages	2,100
State excise tax on liquor	400
Automobile license (based on the car's weight)	300
State sales tax paid	475

52. Tim is a single, cash-method taxpayer with one personal exemption and an AGI of $50,000. In April of this year, Tim paid $1,020 with his state income tax return for the previous year. During the year, Tim had $5,400 of state income tax and $18,250 of federal income tax withheld from his salary. In addition, Tim made estimated payments of $1,360 and $1,900 of state and federal income taxes, respectively. Finally, Tim expects to receive a refund of $500 for state income taxes when he files his state tax return for this year in April next year. What is the amount of taxes that Tim can deduct as an itemized deduction? LO 6-1 LO 6-2

53. This year Randy paid $28,000 of interest. (Randy borrowed $450,000 to buy his residence, which is currently worth $500,000.) Randy also paid $2,500 of interest on his car loan and $4,200 of margin interest to his stockbroker (investment interest expense). How much of this interest expense can Randy deduct as an itemized deduction under the following circumstances? LO 6-2
    a) Randy received $2,200 of interest this year and no other investment income or expenses. His AGI is $75,000.
    b) Randy had no investment income this year, and his AGI is $75,000.

54. This year, Major Healy paid $40,000 of interest on a mortgage on his home (Major Healy borrowed $800,000 to buy the residence; $900,000 original purchase price and value at purchase; $1,000,000 current worth), $6,000 of interest on a $120,000 home equity loan on his home (loan proceeds were used to buy antique cars), and $10,000 of interest on a mortgage on his vacation home (loan of $200,000; home purchased for $500,000). Major Healy's AGI is $220,000. LO 6-2
    a) How much interest expense can Major Healy deduct as an itemized deduction?
    b) Assume the original facts, except that Major Healy's home had a fair market value of $1,000,000 when he purchased the home and took out the home equity debt, but now the home is worth $500,000. How much interest expense can Major Healy deduct as an itemized deduction?

55. Ray Ray made the following contributions this year. LO 6-2

Charity	Property	Cost	FMV
Athens Academy School	Cash	$ 5,000	$ 5,000
United Way	Cash	4,000	4,000
American Heart Association	Antique painting	15,000	75,000
First Methodist Church	Coca-Cola stock	12,000	20,000

Determine the maximum amount of charitable deduction for each of these contributions *ignoring* the AGI ceiling on charitable contributions and assuming that the American Heart Association plans to sell the antique painting to fund its operations. Ray Ray has owned the painting and Coca-Cola stock since 1990.

56. Calvin reviewed his canceled checks and receipts this year for charitable contributions. He has owned the IBM stock and painting since 2005. LO 6-2

Donee	Item	Cost	FMV
Hobbs Medical Center	IBM stock	$5,000	$22,000
State Museum	Painting	5,000	3,000
A needy family	Food and clothes	400	250
United Way	Cash	8,000	8,000

Calculate Calvin's charitable contribution deduction and carryover (if any) under the following circumstances.

a) Calvin's AGI is $100,000.

b) Calvin's AGI is $100,000 but the State Museum told Calvin that it plans to sell the painting.

c) Calvin's AGI is $50,000.

d) Calvin's AGI is $100,000 and Hobbs is a private nonoperating foundation.

e) Calvin's AGI is $100,000 but the painting is worth $10,000.

LO 6-2

57. In addition to cash contributions to charity, Dean decided to donate shares of stock and a portrait painted during the earlier part of the last century. Dean purchased the stock and portrait many years ago as investments. Dean reported the following recipients:

Charity	Property	Cost	FMV
State University	Cash	$15,000	$15,000
Red Cross	Cash	14,500	14,500
State History Museum	Painting	5,000	82,000
City Medical Center	Dell stock	28,000	17,000

a) Determine the maximum amount of charitable deduction for each of these contributions *ignoring* the AGI ceiling on charitable contributions.

b) Assume that Dean's AGI this year is $150,000. Determine Dean's itemized deduction for his charitable contributions this year and any carryover.

c) Assume that Dean's AGI this year is $240,000. Determine Dean's itemized deduction for his charitable contributions this year and any carryover.

d) Suppose Dean is a dealer in antique paintings and had held the painting for sale before the contribution. What is Dean's charitable contribution deduction for the painting in this situation (ignoring AGI limitations)?

e) Suppose that Dean's objective with the donation to the museum was to finance expansion of the historical collection. Hence, Dean was not surprised when the museum announced the sale of the painting because of its limited historical value. What is Dean's charitable contribution deduction for the painting in this situation (ignoring AGI limitations)?

LO 6-2

58. Tim suffered greatly this year. In January a freak storm damaged his sailboat and in July Tim's motorcycle was stolen from his vacation home. Tim originally paid $27,000 for the boat, but he was able to repair the damage for $6,200. Tim paid $15,500 for the motorcycle, but it was worth $17,000 before it was stolen. Insurance reimbursed $1,000 for the boat repairs and the cycle was uninsured.

a) Calculate Tim's deductible casualty loss if his AGI is $50,000.

b) Calculate Tim's deductible casualty loss if his AGI is $150,000.

c) How would you answer (a) if Tim received an additional $65,000 in interest from municipal bonds this year?

LO 6-2
planning

59. Trevor is a single individual who is a cash-method calendar-year taxpayer. For each of the next two years (year 1 and year 2), Trevor expects to report AGI of $80,000, contribute $3,500 to charity, and pay $2,500 in state income taxes.

a) Estimate Trevor's taxable income for year 1 and year 2 using the 2017 amounts for the standard deduction and personal exemption for both years.

b) Now assume that Trevor combines his anticipated charitable contributions for the next two years and makes the combined contribution in December of year 1. Estimate Trevor's taxable income for each of the next two years using the 2017 amounts for the standard deduction and personal exemption. Reconcile the total taxable income to your solution to part (a).

c) Trevor plans to purchase a residence next year, and he estimates that additional property taxes and residential interest will each cost $4,000 annually ($8,000 in total annually). Estimate Trevor's taxable income for each of the next two years (year 1 and year 2) using the 2017 amounts for the standard deduction and personal exemption and also assuming Trevor makes the charitable contribution of $3,500 and state tax payments of $2,500 in each year.

d) Assume that Trevor makes the charitable contribution for year 2 and pays the real estate taxes for year 2 in December of year 1. Estimate Trevor's taxable income for year 1 and year 2 using the 2017 amounts for the standard deduction and personal exemption. Reconcile the total taxable income to your solution to part (c).

e) Explain the conditions in which the bunching strategy in part (d) will generate tax savings for Trevor.

60. Baker paid $775 for the preparation of his tax return and incurred $375 of employee business expenses, of which $60 was reimbursed by his employer through an accountable plan. Baker also paid a $100 fee for investment advice. Calculate the amount of these expenses that Baker is able to deduct assuming he itemizes his deductions in each of the following situations: LO 6-2

a) Baker's AGI is $50,000.

b) Baker's AGI is $100,000.

61. Simon lost $5,000 gambling this year on a trip to Las Vegas. In addition, he paid $2,000 to his broker for managing his $200,000 portfolio and $1,500 to his accountant for preparing his tax return. In addition, Simon incurred $2,500 in transportation costs commuting back and forth from his home to his employer's office, which were not reimbursed. Calculate the amount of these expenses that Simon is able to deduct, assuming he itemizes his deductions, in each of the following situations: LO 6-2

a) Simon's AGI is $40,000.

b) Simon's AGI is $200,000.

62. Zack is employed as a full-time airport security guard. This year Zack's employer transferred him from Dallas to Houston. At year-end, Zack discovered a number of unreimbursed expenses related to his employment in Dallas prior to his move to Houston. Identify which expenses are deductible and whether the deductions are *for* or *from* AGI. LO 6-2

Cost of bus transportation from his home to the airport	$ 150
Subscription to *Journal of Security Guards*	52
Lunch with colleagues	195
Cost of self-defense course at local community center	500
Cost of lunch with supervisor during evaluations	383
Total	$1,280

63. Stephanie is 12 years old and often assists neighbors on weekends by babysitting their children. Calculate the 2017 standard deduction Stephanie will claim under the following independent circumstances (assume that Stephanie's parents will claim her as a dependent). LO 6-3

a) Stephanie reported $850 of earnings from her babysitting.

b) Stephanie reported $1,500 of earnings from her babysitting.

c) Stephanie reported $8,000 of earnings from her babysitting.

LO 6-1 LO 6-2 LO 6-3 research

64. Tammy teaches elementary school history for the Metro School District. In 2017 she incurred the following expenses associated with her job:

Noncredit correspondence course on history	$ 900
Teaching cases for classroom use	1,800
Tuition for university graduate course in physics	1,200
Transportation between school and home	750
Photocopying class materials	100
Transportation from school to extracurricular activities	110
Cost of lunches eaten during study halls	540

Tammy receives a base salary of $45,000 and a $200 salary supplement to help her cover expenses associated with her school extracurricular activities.

a) Identify the amount and type (*for* AGI or *from* AGI) of deductible expenses (assume the 2016 rules apply for purposes of the qualified education expense deduction).

b) Calculate Tammy's AGI and taxable income for 2017 assuming she files single with one personal exemption (assume the 2016 rules apply for purposes of the qualified education expense deduction).

LO 6-3

65. In 2017, Jeff, who is single, is entitled to the following deductions before phase-outs:

State income taxes	$7,850
Real estate taxes	1,900
Home mortgage interest	8,200
Charitable contributions	1,700

a) Assume that Jeff's AGI is $280,000. Calculate Jeff's itemized deductions after considering the overall phase-out of itemized deductions.

b) Suppose that Jeff's AGI increases to $1,280,000. Calculate Jeff's itemized deductions after considering the overall phase-out of itemized deductions.

LO 6-3

66. Jim files as head of household and has three dependent children. Calculate his deductible total personal and dependency exemptions under the following independent conditions:

a) Jim has AGI of $150,000.

b) Jim has AGI of $305,100.

c) Jim has AGI of $450,000.

COMPREHENSIVE PROBLEMS

Select problems are available in Connect®. connect

67. This year Evan graduated from college and took a job as a deliveryman in the city. Evan was paid a salary of $68,500 and he received $700 in hourly pay for part-time work over the weekends. Evan summarized his expenses below:

Cost of moving his possessions to the city (125 miles away)	$1,200
Interest paid on accumulated student loans	2,800
Cost of purchasing a delivery uniform	1,400
Contribution to State University deliveryman program	1,300

Calculate Evan's AGI and taxable income if he files single with one personal exemption. Assume that interest payments were initially required on Evan's student loans this year.

68. Read the following letter and help Shady Slim with his tax situation. Please assume that his gross income is $172,900 (which consists only of salary) for purposes of this problem.

tax forms

December 31, 2017

To the friendly student tax preparer:

Hi, it's Shady Slim again. I just got back from my 55th birthday party, and I'm told that you need some more information from me in order to complete my tax return. I'm an open book! I'll tell you whatever I think you need to know.

Let me tell you a few more things about my life. As you may recall, I am divorced from my wife, Alice. I know that it's unusual, but I have custody of my son, Shady, Jr. The judge owed me a few favors and I really love the kid. He lives with me full-time and my wife gets him every other weekend. I pay the vast majority of my son's expenses. I think Alice should have to pay some child support, but she doesn't have to pay a dime. The judge didn't owe me that much, I guess.

I had to move this year after getting my job at Roca Cola. We moved on February 3 of this year, and I worked my job at Roca Cola for the rest of the year. I still live in the same state, but I moved 500 miles away from my old house. I left a little bit early to go on a house-hunting trip that cost me a total of $450. I hired a moving company to move our stuff at a cost of $2,300, and I drove Junior in my car. Junior and I got a hotel room along the way that cost us $65 (I love Super 8!). We spent $35 on meals on the way to our new home. Oh yeah, I took Junior to a movie on the way and that cost $20.

Can you believe I'm still paying off my student loans, even after 15 years? I paid a total of $900 in interest on my old student loans this year.

Remember when I told you about that guy that hit me with his car? I had a bunch of medical expenses that were not reimbursed by the lawsuit or by my insurance. I incurred a total of $20,000 in medical expenses, and I was only reimbursed for $11,000. Good thing I can write off medical expenses, right?

I contributed a lot of money to charity this year (and have receipt documentation for all contributions). I'm such a nice guy! I gave $1,000 in cash to the March of Dimes. I contributed some of my old furniture to the church. It was some good stuff! I contributed a red velvet couch and my old recliner. The furniture is considered vintage and is worth $5,000 today (the appraiser surprised me!), even though I only paid $1,000 for it back in the day. When I contributed the furniture, the pastor said he didn't like the fabric and was going to sell the furniture to pay for some more pews in the church. Oh well, some people just have no taste, right? Roca Cola had a charity drive for the United Way this year and I contributed $90. Turns out, I don't even miss it, because Roca Cola takes it right off my paycheck every month . . . $15 a month starting in July. My pay stub verifies that I contributed the $90 to the United Way. Oh, one other bit of charity from me this year. An old buddy of mine was down on his luck. He lost his job and his house. I gave him $500 to help him out.

I paid a lot of money in interest this year. I paid a total of $950 in personal credit card interest. I also paid $13,000 in interest on my home mortgage. I also paid $2,000 in real estate taxes for my new house.

A few other things I want to tell you about this year. Someone broke into my house and stole my kid's brand new bicycle and my set of golf clubs. The total loss from theft was $900. I paid $125 in union dues this year. I had to pay $1,200 for new suits for my job. Roca Cola requires its managers to wear suits every day on the job. I spent a total of $1,300 to pay for gas to commute to my job this year.

Oh, this is pretty cool. I've always wanted to be a firefighter. I spent $1,400 in tuition to go to the local firefighter's school. I did this because someone told me that I can deduct the tuition as an itemized deduction, so the money would be coming back to me.

That should be all the information you need right now. Please calculate my taxable income and complete pages 1 and 2 of Form 1040 (through taxable income, line 43) and Schedule A. You're still doing this for free, right?

69. Jeremy and Alyssa Johnson have been married for five years and do not have any children. Jeremy was married previously and has one child from the prior marriage. He is self-employed and operates his own computer repair store. For the first two months of the year, Alyssa worked for Office Depot as an employee. In March, Alyssa accepted a new job with Super Toys Inc. (ST), where she worked for the remainder of the year. This year, the Johnsons received $255,000 of gross income. Determine the Johnsons' AGI given the following information (assume the 2016 rules apply for purposes of the qualified education expense deduction):
   a) Expenses associated with Jeremy's store include $40,000 in salary (and employment taxes) to employees, $45,000 of supplies, and $18,000 in rent and other administrative expenses.
   b) As a salesperson, Alyssa incurred $2,000 in travel expenses related to her employment that were not reimbursed by her employer.
   c) The Johnsons own a piece of raw land held as an investment. They paid $500 of real property taxes on the property and they incurred $200 of expenses in travel costs to see the property and to evaluate other similar potential investment properties.
   d) The Johnsons own a rental home. They incurred $8,500 of expenses associated with the property.
   e) The Johnsons' home was only five miles from the Office Depot store where Alyssa worked in January and February. The ST store was 60 miles from their home, so the Johnsons decided to move to make the commute easier for Alyssa. The Johnsons' new home was only 10 miles from the ST store. However, their new home was 50 miles from their former residence. The Johnsons paid a moving company $2,002 to move their possessions to the new location. They also drove the 50 miles to their new residence. They stopped along the way for lunch and spent $60 eating at Denny's. None of the moving expenses were reimbursed by ST.
   f) Jeremy paid $4,500 for health insurance coverage for himself (not through an exchange). Alyssa was covered by health plans provided by her employer, but Jeremy is not eligible for the plan until next year.
   g) Jeremy paid $2,500 in self-employment taxes ($1,250 represents the employer portion of the self-employment taxes).
   h) Jeremy paid $5,000 in alimony and $3,000 in child support from his prior marriage.
   i) Alyssa paid $3,100 of tuition and fees to attend night classes at a local university. The Johnsons would like to deduct as much of this expenditure as possible rather than claim a credit.
   j) The Johnsons donated $2,000 to their favorite charity.

tax forms

70. Shauna Coleman is single. She is employed as an architectural designer for Streamline Design (SD). Shauna wanted to determine her taxable income for this year. She correctly calculated her AGI. However, she wasn't sure how to compute the rest of her taxable income. She provided the following information with hopes that you could use it to determine her taxable income.
   a) Shauna paid $4,680 for medical expenses for care from a broken ankle. Also, Shauna's boyfriend, Blake, drove Shauna (in her car) a total of 115 miles to the doctor's office so she could receive care for her broken ankle.
   b) Shauna paid a total of $3,400 in health insurance premiums during the year (not through an exchange). SD did not reimburse any of this expense. Besides the

health insurance premiums and the medical expenses for her broken ankle, Shauna had Lasik eye surgery last year and she paid $3,000 for the surgery (she received no insurance reimbursement). She also incurred $450 of other medical expenses for the year.

c) SD withheld $1,800 of state income tax, $7,495 of Social Security tax, and $14,500 of federal income tax from Shauna's paychecks throughout the year.

d) In 2017, Shauna was due a refund of $250 for overpaying her 2016 state taxes. On her 2016 state tax return that she filed in April 2017, she applied the overpayment toward her 2017 state tax liability. She estimated that her state tax liability for 2017 will be $2,300.

e) Shauna paid $3,200 of property taxes on her personal residence. She also paid $500 to the developer of her subdivision, because he had to replace the sidewalk in certain areas of the subdivision.

f) Shauna paid a $200 property tax based on the state's estimate of the value of her car.

g) Shauna has a home mortgage loan in the amount of $220,000 that she secured when she purchased her home. The home is worth about $400,000. Shauna paid interest of $12,300 on the loan this year.

h) Shauna made several charitable contributions throughout the year. She contributed stock in ZYX Corp. to the Red Cross. On the date of the contribution, the fair market value of the donated shares was $1,000 and her basis in the shares was $400. Shauna originally bought the ZYX Corp. stock in 2008. Shauna also contributed $300 cash to State University and religious artifacts she has held for several years to her church. The artifacts were valued at $500 and Shauna's basis in the items was $300. Shauna had every reason to believe the church would keep them on display indefinitely. Shauna also drove 200 miles doing church-related errands for her minister. Finally, Shauna contributed $1,200 of services to her church last year.

i) Shauna's car was totaled in a wreck in January. The car was worth $14,000 and her cost basis in the car was $16,000. The car was a complete loss. Shauna received $2,000 in insurance reimbursements for the loss.

j) Shauna paid $300 for architectural design publications, $100 for continuing education courses to keep her up to date on the latest design technology, and $200 for professional dues to maintain her status in a professional designer's organization.

k) Shauna paid $250 in investment advisory fees and another $150 to have her tax return prepared (that is, she paid $150 in 2017 to have her 2016 tax return prepared).

l) Shauna is involved in horse racing as a hobby. During the year, she won $2,500 in prize money and incurred $10,000 in expenses. She has never had a profitable year with her horse-racing activities, so she acknowledges that this is a hobby for federal income tax purposes.

m) Shauna sustained $2,000 in gambling losses over the year (mostly horse-racing bets) and only had $200 in winnings.

Required

A) Determine Shauna's taxable income and complete page 2 of Form 1040 (through taxable income, line 43) and Schedule A assuming her AGI is $107,000.

B) Determine Shauna's taxable income and complete page 2 of Form 1040 (through taxable income, line 43) and Schedule A assuming her AGI is $207,000.

71. Joe and Jessie are married and have one dependent child, Lizzie. Lizzie is currently in college at State University. Joe works as a design engineer for a manufacturing firm while Jessie runs a craft business from their home. Jessie's craft business

consists of making craft items for sale at craft shows that are held periodically at various locations. Jessie spends considerable time and effort on her craft business and it has been consistently profitable over the years. Joe and Jessie own a home and pay interest on their home loan (balance of $220,000) and a personal loan to pay for Lizzie's college expenses (balance of $35,000). Neither Joe nor Jessie is blind or over age 65, and they plan to file as married joint. Based on their estimates, determine Joe and Jessie's AGI and taxable income for the year and complete pages 1 and 2 of Form 1040 (through taxable income, line 43) and Schedule A. Assume that the 2016 rules apply for purposes of the qualified education expense deduction and the employer portion of the self-employment tax on Jessie's income is $808. Joe and Jessie have summarized the income and expenses they expect to report this year as follows:

Income:	
Joe's salary	$124,100
Jessie's craft sales	18,400
Interest from certificate of deposit	1,650
Interest from Treasury bond funds	727
Interest from municipal bond funds	920
Expenditures:	
Federal income tax withheld from Joe's wages	$13,700
State income tax withheld from Joe's wages	6,400
Social Security tax withheld from Joe's wages	7,482
Real estate taxes on residence	6,200
Automobile licenses (based on weight)	310
State sales tax paid	1,150
Home mortgage interest	14,000
Interest on Masterdebt credit card	2,300
Medical expenses (unreimbursed)	1,690
Joe's employee expenses (unreimbursed)	2,400
Cost of Jessie's craft supplies	4,260
Postage for mailing crafts	145
Travel and lodging for craft shows	2,230
Meals during craft shows	670
Self-employment tax on Jessie's craft income	1,615
College tuition paid for Lizzie	5,780
Interest on loans to pay Lizzie's tuition	3,200
Lizzie's room and board at college	12,620
Cash contributions to the Red Cross	525

ROGER | CPA Review

Sample CPA Exam questions from Roger CPA Review are available in Connect as support for the topics in this text. These Multiple Choice Questions and Task-Based Simulations include expert-written explanations and solutions, and provide a starting point for students to become familiar with the content and functionality of the actual CPA Exam.

chapter

7 Investments

Learning Objectives

Upon completing this chapter, you should be able to:

LO 7-1 Explain how interest income and dividend income are taxed.

LO 7-2 Compute the tax consequences associated with the disposition of capital assets, including the netting process for calculating gains and losses.

LO 7-3 Calculate the deduction for portfolio investment-related expenses, including investment expenses and investment interest expense.

LO 7-4 Understand the distinction between portfolio investments and passive investments and apply tax-basis, at-risk, and passive activity loss limits to losses from passive investments.

© Image Source

Storyline Summary

Taxpayers:	Courtney Wilson, age 40 Courtney's uncle, Jeb Landers, age 65
Family description:	Courtney is divorced with a son, Deron, age 10, and a daughter, Ellen, age 20. Jeb is single.
Location:	Kansas City, Missouri
Employment status:	Courtney works as an architect for EWD. Her salary is $118,000. Jeb is recently retired.
Current situation:	Courtney is deciding how to invest her inheritance. Jeb is concerned about the tax effects of selling investment assets.

Courtney has settled into her new Kansas City location and is now focusing on her investment portfolio. When her father, "Gramps," passed away last December, he left Courtney an inheritance of $100,000 with the stipulation that she "invest it to financially benefit her family." After considerable thought, Courtney decided to invest the inheritance to accomplish two financial goals. First, she wants to save for her son Deron's college education. She figures that if she immediately invests $50,000 of the inheritance for his college education, she should have a significant sum accumulated when Deron starts college in eight years. Second, she decided that she will immediately invest the remaining $50,000 for five years and use the accumulation to make a significant down payment on a vacation home in Park City, Utah, a town she fell in love with during a college ski trip. Courtney is concerned about how different investment choices will be taxed and how this might affect her ability to meet her financial goals.

Courtney's Uncle Jeb, who is single, has sold several investments during the year with the hope that he could use the proceeds to fulfill his lifelong dream of owning a sailboat. He is uncertain about how much tax he will owe after selling the assets. ■

THE KEY FACTS

Investments Overview

- After-tax rate of return of investment depends on
  - Before-tax rate of return.
  - When investment income and gains are taxed.
    - Taxed annually
    - Tax deferred
    - Tax-exempt
  - When investment losses are deducted.
    - Deduction annually
    - Deduction deferred
  - Rate at which investment income or gains/expenses or losses are taxed/deducted.
    - Ordinary tax rates
    - Preferential tax rates
    - Zero tax rate

INVESTMENTS OVERVIEW

Investors are attracted to certain investments according to their investment philosophy and their appetite for risk, among other things. Some prefer investments that provide a consistent income stream. Others prefer investments that have significant appreciation potential but provide no current cash flows. These investment attributes affect the before-tax returns on investments. However, taxes are levied on **investment income,** and thus, it would be unwise to make an investment without considering the tax cost. For example, it is possible that two investments with identical before-tax rates of return will generate different after-tax rates of return because the investments are taxed differently. Indeed, it is possible that an investment with a lower before-tax rate of return compared to an alternative investment will have a higher after-tax rate of return because income from the investment is taxed at a later date or taxed at a lower rate than the alternative investment.

Two key tax characteristics that affect after-tax returns from investments are (1) the timing of tax payments or tax benefits and (2) the rate at which investment income or gains are taxed or deductible expenses or losses generate tax savings. Not surprisingly, these variables are directly related to the timing and conversion tax planning strategies introduced in the Tax Planning Strategies and Related Limitations chapter.

Income from **portfolio investments** (investments producing **dividends,** interest, royalties, annuities, or capital gains) may be taxed at ordinary rates, preferential rates, or may be exempt from taxation. Further, depending on the type of investment, tax on income from a portfolio investment may be imposed annually or may be deferred until the taxpayer sells the investment. Losses from portfolio investments are deferred until the investment is sold and are typically subject to limitations.

In contrast to portfolio investments, **passive investments** generate **operating income** and **operating losses.** Operating income is always taxed annually at ordinary rates while operating losses are either deducted annually at ordinary rates or deferred and deducted later at ordinary rates depending on the investor's circumstances. Losses from passive investments are also subject to limitations.

This chapter explores several common portfolio and passive investments, discusses important tax and nontax considerations relevant for those investments, and compares investment returns on an after-tax basis.

LO 7-1

PORTFOLIO INCOME: INTEREST AND DIVIDENDS

THE KEY FACTS

Interest and Dividend Income

- Interest
  - Interest is taxed at ordinary rates.
  - Cash interest payments are taxed annually.
  - Accrued market discount is taxed at sale or maturity.
  - Savings bonds are taxed at sale or maturity.
  - Original issue discount is taxed annually.

(continued)

Taxpayers who desire current cash flows from their investments may choose investments that generate interest or regular dividends. Investments generating interest income include **certificates of deposit (CDs),** savings accounts, corporate **bonds,** and governmental bonds. Investments generating dividend income include direct equity investments in corporate stocks or investments in **mutual funds** that invest in corporate stock.[1] Although all of these investments generate current cash flows, they differ significantly in terms of their economic and tax consequences.

By lending money to banks, governmental entities, or corporations, investors essentially become debt holders. As such, they are legally entitled to receive periodic interest payments *and* to recover the amount of principal loaned (in the case of bonds, principal is the **maturity value** or **face value** of the bonds). Interest payments and the time and manner of repayment of the loan principal are defined either contractually for CDs and savings accounts or by bond covenants for loans made either to governments or corporations. In contrast, investors who purchase stocks become shareholders (also called equity holders) of a corporation. As shareholders, they are entitled to receive

[1]Mutual funds are portfolios of investment assets managed by professional money managers. Generally, the income earned by mutual funds flows through to the owners of mutual fund shares who pay the resulting taxes due. The nature of the assets held by the mutual fund determines the character of the income.

dividends if the company declares dividends and to *indirectly* share in either the future appreciation or depreciation in the value of a corporation through stock ownership. Unlike debt holders, shareholders are not legally entitled to receive dividend payments or to recover their initial investment. Thus, from an investor's perspective, debt tends to be less risky than equity.

For tax purposes, individual investors typically are taxed on both interest and dividend income when they receive it. However, interest income is taxed at ordinary rates while dividend income is generally taxed at lower capital gains rates.

- Dividends
  - Dividends are taxed annually.
  - Qualified dividends are taxed at preferential rates.

Interest

In general, taxpayers recognize interest income from investments when they receive the interest payments.[2] Taxpayers investing in savings accounts, money market accounts, CDs, and most bonds receive interest payments based on a stated annual rate of return at yearly or more frequent intervals.

Special rules apply for determining the timing and amount of interest from bonds when there is a **bond discount** (bonds are issued at an amount below the maturity value) or a **bond premium** (bonds are issued at an amount above the maturity value). Below we discuss these rules as they apply to corporate, U.S. Treasury bonds, and **U.S. savings bonds.**

Corporate and U.S. Treasury Bonds Both corporations and the U.S. Treasury raise money from debt markets by issuing bonds.[3] Corporate bonds, **Treasury bonds,** and **Treasury notes** are issued at maturity value, at a discount, or at a premium, depending on prevailing interest rates.[4] Treasury bonds and Treasury notes pay a stated rate of interest semiannually.[5] However, corporate bonds may pay interest at a stated "coupon" rate or they may not provide any periodic interest payments. Corporate bonds that do not pay periodic interest are called **zero-coupon bonds.** Overall, the consequences of holding corporate or Treasury bonds are very similar. The two primary differences are that (1) interest from Treasury bonds is exempt from *state* taxation while interest from corporate bonds is not and (2) Treasury bonds always pay interest periodically while corporate bonds may or may not. The tax rules for determining the timing and amount of interest income from corporate and U.S. Treasury bonds are as follows:

- Taxpayers include the actual interest payments they receive in gross income.
- If the bond was issued at a discount, special **original issue discount (OID)** rules apply. Taxpayers are required to amortize the discount and include the amount of the current year **amortization** in gross income in addition to any interest payments the taxpayer actually receives.[6] In the case of corporate zero-coupon bonds, this means taxpayers must report and pay taxes on income related to the bonds even though they did not receive *any* payments from the bonds. Bond issuers or brokers are responsible for calculating the yearly amortization of the original issue discount and providing this information to investors using Form 1099-OID.

[2]Interest income is reported on Part I of Schedule B filed with taxpayers' Form 1040.

[3]Investors in corporate bonds assume more risk than investors in Treasury securities because they are relying on the creditworthiness of the corporation issuing the bonds. To compensate bondholders for this additional risk, corporate bonds usually yield higher before-tax rates of return than Treasury securities.

[4]The bonds are issued at a discount (premium) if the market interest rate is higher (lower) than the stated rate on the bonds.

[5]Treasury notes and bonds differ in terms of their maturities. Treasury notes are issued with 2-, 5-, and 10-year maturities. In contrast, Treasury bonds are issued with maturities greater than 10 years. From this point forward, we use the term Treasury bonds to refer to both Treasury notes and Treasury bonds.

[6]§1272. Original issue discount is amortized semiannually under the constant yield method, which is consistent with the approach used to amortize bond discount under GAAP.

- If the bond was issued at a premium, taxpayers may *elect* to amortize the premium.[7] Taxpayers or their advisers are responsible for determining the yearly amortization of bond premium if the election to amortize the premium has been made. The amount of the current year amortization offsets a portion of the actual interest payments that taxpayers must include in gross income. The original tax basis of the bond includes the premium and is reduced by any amortization of bond premium over the life of the bond.
- If the bond is purchased in the secondary bond market at a discount, the taxpayer treats some of or all of the **market discount** as interest income *when she sells the bond or the bond matures.*[8] If the bond is sold prior to **maturity,** a ratable amount of the market discount (based on the number of days the bond is held over the number of days until maturity when the bond is purchased), called the **accrued market discount,** is treated as interest income on the date of sale.[9] If the bond is held to maturity, the entire bond discount is treated as interest income at maturity.
- If the bond is purchased in the secondary bond market at a premium, the premium is treated exactly like original issue bond premiums. As a result, the taxpayer may elect to amortize the **market premium** to reduce the annual interest income received from the bond. Otherwise, the premium remains as part of the tax basis of the bond and affects the capital gain or loss the taxpayer recognizes when the taxpayer sells or redeems the bond.

U.S. Savings Bonds U.S. savings bonds such as Series EE or Series I bonds are issued at either face value or at a discount. These bonds do not pay periodic interest; rather, interest accumulates over the term of the bonds and is paid when investors redeem them at maturity or earlier.[10] That is, the amount of interest income taxpayers recognize *when they redeem* the bonds is the excess of the bond proceeds over the taxpayer's **basis** (purchase price) in the bonds. Taxpayers may elect to include the increase in the bond redemption value in income each year, but this is generally not advisable because it accelerates the income from the bond without providing any cash to pay the taxes.[11] Finally, interest from Series EE and Series I bonds may be excluded from gross income to the extent the bond proceeds are used to pay qualifying educational expenses. However, this exclusion benefit is subject to phase-out based on the taxpayer's AGI.

Example 7-1

What if: *Assume* that Courtney was deciding whether to invest the $50,000 earmarked for the Park City vacation home in (1) Series EE savings bonds that mature in exactly five years, (2) original issue AMD Corporation *zero-coupon* bonds that mature in exactly five years, or (3) U.S. Treasury bonds that pay $46,250 at maturity in five years trading in the secondary bond market with a stated annual interest rate of 10 percent. Further, assume that all bonds yield 8 percent annual before-tax returns compounded semiannually. At the end of the first year, (1) the redemption value of the EE savings bonds would be $54,080, or (2) Courtney would receive a Form 1099-OID from AMD reporting $4,080 of

[7]§171. Like an original issue discount, a bond premium is amortized semiannually under the constant yield method—the same method used to amortize bond premiums under GAAP. Unlike premiums on taxable bonds, premiums on tax-exempt bonds must always be amortized.

[8]§1276(a). Under §1278(b)(1), taxpayers may elect to include the amortization of market discount in their income annually. However, this election accelerates the recognition of income from the market discount and is therefore usually not advisable.

[9]§1276(b).

[10]Series EE savings bonds are issued at a discount and Series I savings bonds are issued at maturity value. EE bonds provide a constant rate of return while Series I bonds provide a return that is indexed for inflation and thus increases over time.

[11]§454(a). Investors that make this election report the annual increase in the redemption value of their savings bonds using savings bond redemption tables published by the Treasury Department.

OID amortization for the year, or (3) she would receive two semiannual interest payments of $2,312.50 from the Treasury bonds. Under the general rules, how much interest income from each bond would Courtney report at the end of the first year?

Answer: $0 from the Series EE savings bonds, $4,080 from the AMD bonds, and $4,625 (two semiannual payments of $2,312.50) from the Treasury bonds. Note, however, that Courtney could *elect* to include the $4,080 increase in redemption value of the Series EE bonds in interest income even though she did not receive any interest payments on the bonds (probably not optimal). She also could *elect* to amortize $637.50 of the $3,750 premium ($50,000 purchase price less the $46,250 maturity value) on the Treasury bonds to offset the $4,625 in actual interest payments she received on the bonds (probably a good idea). The calculations required to amortize the premium on the Treasury bonds for the first year are reflected in the following table:

Semiannual Period	(A) Adjusted Basis of Bonds at Beginning of Semiannual Period	(B) Interest Received and Reported ($46,250 × 10% × .5)	(C) Interest Earned (A) × 8% × .5	Premium Amortization (B) − (C)
1	$50,000.00	$2,312.50	$2,000.00	$312.50
2	49,687.50	2,312.50	1,987.50	325.00
Yearly Total		4,625.00	3,987.50	637.50

Intuitively, would Courtney be better or worse off purchasing the Series EE savings bonds rather than a corporate bond to save for the Park City home?

Answer: She would be better off in two respects. First, she wouldn't have to pay state income taxes on the interest earned from the savings bonds. Second, she would be able to defer paying taxes on the accumulated interest from the savings bonds until the savings bonds are cashed in at maturity. This would increase the after-tax returns from the savings bonds relative to a corporate bond.

Intuitively, would Courtney be better or worse off purchasing the AMD zero-coupon bonds rather than a corporate bond to save for the Park City home?

Answer: She would be worse off because she would have to pay taxes currently from the OID amortization on the AMD bonds without receiving any cash flow from the bonds to pay the taxes due. This would reduce the after-tax returns from the AMD bonds relative to a corporate bond.

Example 7-2

What if: Assume that on January 1, Courtney used the $50,000 earmarked for the Park City vacation home to purchase AMD zero-coupon bonds in the *secondary bond market* almost immediately after they were originally issued. If the bonds mature in exactly five years and have a maturity value of $74,000, how much interest income will Courtney report at the end of the first year and in the year the bonds mature?

Answer: $0 in the first year and $24,000 in the year the bonds mature. Because the AMD zero-coupon bonds were not purchased at original issue, the entire $24,000 market discount on the bonds will be reported as interest income when the bonds mature. Thus, Courtney will not report any income related to the AMD bonds until the year the bonds mature.

What if: Assume the same facts as above, except Courtney purchased U.S. Series EE bonds instead of AMD zero-coupon bonds to fund the Park City vacation home in five years. How much interest income will she report at the end of the first year and in the year the bonds mature?

Answer: $0 in the first year and $24,000 in the year the EE savings bonds mature; exactly the same outcome as the investment in the AMD zero-coupon bonds.

As our discussion suggests, for certain types of investments such as savings accounts, money market accounts, and CDs, computing the annual taxable interest income is relatively straightforward. However, for investments in bonds, the process is much more involved. Exhibit 7-1 summarizes the general rule and exceptions for the timing of interest payments and related tax payments.

EXHIBIT 7-1 Timing of Interest Payments and Taxes

General Rule	Exception	Exception
Interest Received Annually and Taxed Annually	**Interest Received at Sale or Maturity and Taxed at Sale or Maturity**	**Interest Received at Sale or Maturity but Taxed Annually**
• Savings accounts • CDs • Money market accounts • Bond interest payments actually received in the year	• Accrued market discount on bonds • Interest earned on U.S. savings bonds	• Original issue discount (OID) on corporate and Treasury bonds

Dividends

Historically, dividends received by investors have been taxed at the same rate as interest income; however, in 2003 Congress changed the law for dividends to mitigate the so-called "double tax" on dividend income.[12] Consistent with the general rule for taxing interest income, dividend payments (including reinvested dividends) are taxed annually.[13] However, as we discuss in the Individual Income Tax Computation and Tax Credits chapter, **qualified dividends** are taxed at a preferential rate: 0, 15, or 20 percent, depending on the rate at which the dividends would be taxed if they were ordinary income.[14] Qualified dividends are those paid by domestic or certain qualified foreign corporations provided investors hold the dividend-paying stock for *more than* 60 days during the 121-day period that begins 60 days before the **ex-dividend date** (the first day on which the purchaser of the stock would not be entitled to receive a declared dividend on the stock).[15] Exhibit 7-2 illustrates the 121-day period surrounding the ex-dividend date. Nonqualified dividends are not eligible for the reduced rate and are therefore taxed at ordinary rates. Corporations report the amounts of the dividends and indicate whether the dividends are potentially eligible for the preferential rate when they send Form 1099-DIV to shareholders after year-end. However, shareholders ultimately must determine if they qualify for the preferential rate by confirming they held the stock for the required number of days around the ex-dividend date.

EXHIBIT 7-2 Holding Period for Qualified Dividends

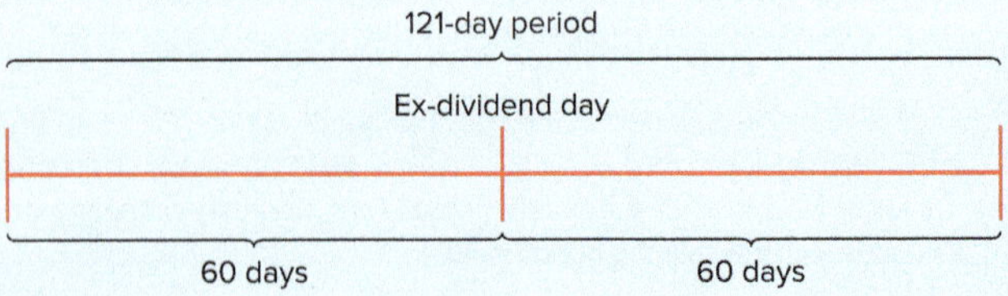

[12]Because corporations pay income taxes, dividends are taxed once at the corporate level, when the income used to pay dividends is earned by the corporation, and a second time when dividends are received by investors.

[13]Dividends are reported on Part II of Schedule B filed with taxpayers' Form 1040.

[14]Qualified dividends that would have been taxed at 10 or 15 percent if they were ordinary income are taxed at 0 percent, qualified dividends that would have been taxed at 39.6 percent as ordinary income are taxed at 20 percent, and all other qualified dividends are taxed at 15 percent.

[15]Qualified foreign corporations are those incorporated in a U.S. possession (e.g., Puerto Rico, U.S. Virgin Islands), those eligible for the benefits of a comprehensive income tax treaty with the United States, or those whose shares are readily traded on an established U.S. securities market.

Example 7-3

What if: Assume Courtney decides to purchase dividend-paying stocks to achieve her financial objectives. She invests $50,000 in Xerox stock, which she intends to hold for five years and then sell to fund the Park City home down payment. She invests another $50,000 in Coca-Cola stock, which she intends to hold for eight years and then sell to fund her son's education. How much dividend income will Courtney report at the end of the first year if the dividend payments provide an 8 percent return on her investments?[16]

Answer: Courtney will report $4,000 ($50,000 × .08) of dividend income from the Xerox stock for the first year of her investment and $4,000 ($50,000 × .08) of dividend income from the Coca-Cola stock for a total of $8,000 of dividend income.

What if: Assume Courtney's ordinary marginal tax rate is 30 percent. How much tax will Courtney owe on her dividend income if the dividends are nonqualified?

Answer: Courtney will owe $2,400 ($8,000 × 30%) of tax if the dividends are nonqualified because the income will be taxed at her ordinary income tax rate.

What if: What amount of tax will Courtney owe if the dividends are qualified?

Answer: Courtney will owe $1,200 ($8,000 × 15%) of tax if the dividends are qualified because qualified dividends are taxed at preferential rates. Courtney's dividends are taxed at 15 percent because her ordinary tax rate is more than 15 percent but less than 39.6 percent.

Because dividend income is taxed generally at lower rates than interest income, it appears that taxpayers seeking current cash flows from their investments should favor dividend-paying investments over interest-paying investments. This raises the question of why anyone would ever prefer investments paying interest over those paying dividends. Remember, though, that savvy investors also should consider nontax factors such as before-tax rates of return, risk, and liquidity needs when choosing among alternative investments. These fundamental differences explain why investors may continue to seek out interest income in spite of the associated tax disadvantages.

PORTFOLIO INCOME: CAPITAL GAINS AND LOSSES

LO 7-2

Investors who don't need annual cash flows from their investments may prefer to invest in assets with the expectation that the investments will appreciate in value over time, providing cash at some point in the future when they sell the assets. Investors also may be willing to assume greater risk in exchange for greater returns than those provided by interest or dividend-paying investments. For example, they might purchase raw land, fine art, rare coins, precious gems or metals, growth stocks (stock in corporations that reinvest their earnings to grow the company as opposed to distributing earnings to shareholders in the form of dividends), mutual fund shares, or even vintage automobiles. Purchasing any such asset is not without risk. Indeed, investments held solely for appreciation potential *may* actually decline in value.

When taxpayers buy and hold assets with appreciation potential, they typically are investing in **capital assets.** As we discussed in the Individual Income Tax Overview, Exemptions, and Filing Status chapter, capital assets are typically investment-type assets and personal-use assets.[17] Thus, artwork, corporate stock, bonds, your personal residence, and even your iPhone are capital assets.

[16]Annual returns from dividend-paying stocks are typically lower than the return from taxable bonds. However, it is assumed here that the returns are equal for the sake of comparability.

[17]§1221 defines capital assets in the negative. This code section excludes inventory, depreciable property or real property used in a trade or business, certain self-created intangibles, accounts or notes receivable, U.S. government publications, certain commodities, derivative financial instruments, certain hedging transactions, and supplies from the definition of a capital asset.

While it may be enjoyable to view collectible fine art in your home or watch a stock portfolio grow in value on quarterly brokerage statements, from a tax perspective the real advantages of investing in capital assets are (1) gains are deferred for tax purposes until the taxpayer sells or otherwise disposes of the assets[18] and (2) gains generally are taxed at preferential rates relative to ordinary income.[19] Why the favorable treatment? One reason is that taxpayers may not have the wherewithal (cash) to pay the tax on their gains until they sell the investment. Another is that the preferential tax rate provides an incentive for taxpayers to invest in assets that may stimulate the economy. Investors can capture these tax benefits when they sell capital assets at a gain. However, when they sell capital assets at a loss, their ability to deduct the loss may be limited.

When a taxpayer sells a capital asset for more than its **tax basis,** the taxpayer recognizes a capital gain; if a taxpayer sells a capital asset for less than its tax basis, the taxpayer recognizes a capital loss (to the extent the loss is deductible).[20] The amount realized or selling price of a capital asset includes the cash and fair market value of other property received, less broker's fees and other selling costs. The basis of any asset, including a capital asset, is generally the taxpayer's "cost" of acquiring the asset, including the initial purchase price and other costs incurred to purchase or improve the asset.[21] Thus, the tax basis of corporate stock purchased from a stockbroker includes the cost of the stock and any additional brokerage fees paid by the taxpayer to acquire the stock. Also, the tax basis in a personal residence includes the initial purchase price plus the cost of subsequent improvements to the home.

TAXES IN THE REAL WORLD Creative Genius

The tax code defines capital assets by listing assets that are *not* capital assets in §1221. Listed among the assets not to be treated as capital are copyrights and literary, musical, and artistic compositions. This placed those who create intangible products on par with those who produce tangible products because §1221 also defines inventory as not a capital asset. Back in 2005, Congress passed temporary legislation (later made permanent in 2006) that permits musicians to treat the sale of their creative works as the sale of capital assets. In 2011, the IRS issued final regulations on making this election. As a result of making this election, a composer who sells copyrighted material will pay tax on any gain at the lower capital gains tax rates.

Source: Federal Tax Updates on Checkpoint Newsstand tab, February 7, 2011.

Because a taxpayer cannot accurately compute the gain or loss on the sale of a capital asset without knowing its basis, it is important for taxpayers to maintain accurate records to track their basis in capital assets. This process is relatively

[18]Similarly, interest related to the market discount on bonds and the original issue discount on U.S. EE savings bonds accumulates free of tax until the bonds mature or are sold. However, ordinary rather than capital gains rates apply when the tax must finally be paid.

[19]Mutual funds that generate current income by regularly selling capital assets or by holding income-producing securities are an exception to this general rule. However, tax-efficient mutual funds that only buy and hold growth stocks are treated more like other capital assets for tax purposes (capital gains are deferred until mutual fund shares are sold).

[20]As discussed below, losses on personal assets are not deductible for tax purposes.

[21]For stocks acquired on or after January 1, 2011, brokers are required to report to the IRS the tax basis of securities their customers sell. Starting January 1, 2012, brokers are required to report cost basis information for sales associated with shares of mutual funds and dividend reinvestment plans that were purchased on or after January 1, 2012. Finally, for all other securities not previously mentioned, starting for sales after January 1, 2013, cost basis information must be reported if the securities were purchased on or after January 1, 2013.

straightforward for unique assets such as a taxpayer's personal residence or individual jewels in a taxpayer's jewelry collection. However, capital assets such as shares of stock are much more homogeneous and difficult to track. For example, a taxpayer may purchase blocks of stock in a given corporation at different times over a period of several years, paying a different price per share for each block of stock acquired. When the taxpayer sells shares of this stock in subsequent years, what basis does she use to compute gain or loss? By default, taxpayers are required to use the **first-in, first-out (FIFO) method** of determining the basis of the shares they sell.[22] However, if they (or their broker) track the basis of their stock, taxpayers can sell (or instruct their broker to sell) specific shares using the **specific identification method** to determine the basis of the shares they sell. Taxpayers using the specific identification method can choose to sell their high-basis stock first, minimizing their gains or increasing their losses on stock dispositions.

Example 7-4

After Courtney's car broke down, she decided to buy a new one. To fund the down payment, she sold 200 shares of Cisco stock at the current market price of $40 per share for a total amount realized of $8,000. Courtney held the following blocks of Cisco stock at the time of the sale:

Cisco Corporation Stock Ownership

Holding Period	(1) Cost per Share	(2) Shares	(1) × (2) Basis	Basis of 200 Shares Sold	Explanation
5 years	$25	250	$6,250	$5,000	FIFO basis ($25 × 200)
2 years	$32	250	$8,000	$6,400	Specific ID basis ($32 × 200)

How much capital gain will Courtney recognize if she uses the FIFO method of computing the basis in the Cisco shares sold?

Answer: $3,000. $8,000 amount realized ($40 × 200) minus $5,000 FIFO basis ($25 × 200). As indicated in the table above, under the FIFO (oldest first) method, they are treated as though she sold the stock held for five years.

What if: How much capital gain will Courtney recognize if they use the specific identification method of computing the basis in the shares sold to minimize the taxable gain on the sale?

Answer: $1,600. $8,000 amount realized ($40 × 200) minus $6,400 ($32 × 200). To minimize her gain on the sale under the specific identification method, Courtney would choose to sell the 200 shares with the highest basis. As indicated in the table above, the shares with the higher basis are those acquired and held two years for $32 per share.

Note in the above example that Courtney receives $8,000 from the stock sale ($40 per share × 200 shares sold) regardless of the method she uses to compute the basis of the shares she sells. The difference between the FIFO and specific identification methods lies in the amount of taxable gain on the *current* sale. Over time, as taxpayers sell all of their stock, both methods will ultimately allow taxpayers to fully recover their cost in the investments. However, applying the specific identification method will result in lower capital gains taxes currently and thereby minimize the present value of the taxes paid on stock sales.

[22] Reg. §1.1012-1(c)(1).

Types of Capital Gains and Losses

Taxpayers selling capital assets that they hold for a year or less recognize **short-term capital gains or losses.**[23] Alternatively, taxpayers selling capital assets they hold for more than a year recognize **long-term capital gains or losses.** Short-term capital gains are taxed at ordinary rather than preferential rates. In contrast, long-term capital gains are taxed at preferential rates. However, not all long-term capital gains are created equal. Just like dividends, most long-term capital gains are taxed at either 0 percent, 15 percent, or 20 percent, depending on the rate at which the gains would be taxed if they were ordinary income. Long-term capital gains that would be taxed at 10 or 15 percent as ordinary income are taxed at 0 percent; gains that would be taxed at 39.6 percent as ordinary income are taxed at 20 percent; and other long-term capital gains are taxed at 15 percent. However, certain long-term capital gains are taxed at a maximum rate of 25 percent **(unrecaptured §1250 gain)** and others are taxed at a maximum 28 percent rate **(collectibles** and **qualified small business stock)** for tax policy reasons.

25 Percent Gains When individuals sell depreciable real property held more than one year at a gain, a portion (or even all) of the gain may be taxed at a maximum rate of 25 percent (the unrecaptured §1250 gain portion) and a portion may be taxed as a 0/15/20 percent gain. In the Property Dispositions chapter, we discuss the details of how to compute the amount of 25 percent gain and the amount of 0/15/20 percent gain when an individual sells depreciable real property; however, we include a brief discussion in this chapter because the amount of 25 percent gain affects the capital gain and loss netting process we discuss in this chapter.

Example 7-5

What if: Assume Jeb Landers (single), Courtney's uncle, recently sold a rental home for $160,000. He originally acquired the home many years ago for $100,000, and he has fully depreciated it for tax purposes. Assume that $100,000 of the gain (the unrecaptured §1250 gain portion) is taxed at a maximum rate of 25 percent. If Jeb's marginal ordinary tax rate is 35 percent, what tax does he owe on the gain if he did not sell any other property during the year?

Answer: $34,000. Because Jeb's tax basis in the home is $0 (he has fully depreciated it), his gain on the sale is $160,000. Jeb owes 25 percent tax on the $100,000, resulting in $25,000 of tax on this portion of the gain ($100,000 × 25%). The remaining $60,000 of gain is taxed at 15 percent, so he owes $9,000 of tax on this portion ($60,000 × 15%). In total, he owes $34,000 of tax on the gain ($25,000 + $9,000).

What if: Suppose Jeb's marginal ordinary tax rate is 39.6 percent rather than 35 percent. What tax does he owe on the gain?

Answer: $37,000. The $100,000 is taxed at 25 percent for a tax of $25,000. The remaining $60,000 of gain is taxed at 20 percent because it would have been taxed at 39.6 percent if it were ordinary income. Consequently, he owes $12,000 of tax on this portion ($60,000 × 20%). In total, Jeb owes $37,000 of tax on the gain ($25,000 + $12,000).

28 Percent Gains Gains from two types of capital assets are taxable at a maximum 28 percent rate. The first type, collectibles, consists of works of art, any rug or antique, any metal or gem, any stamp or coin, any alcoholic beverage, or other similar items held

[23]Nonbusiness bad debt is treated as a short-term capital loss no matter how long the debt was outstanding before it became worthless. Whether a bad debt is considered to be a business bad debt for individuals depends on the facts and circumstances. In general, if the taxpayer experiencing the loss is in the business of loaning money, the bad debt should be considered to be business bad debt; otherwise, the bad debt will likely be considered nonbusiness bad debt.

for more than one year.[24] The second type is qualified small business stock held for *more than five years*.[25] In general, §1202 defines qualified small business stock as stock received at *original issue* from a C corporation with a gross tax basis in its assets both before and after the issuance of no more than $50,000,000 and with at least 80 percent of the value of its assets used in the active conduct of certain qualified trades or businesses. Under this definition, many investors and employees who hold stock in closely held corporations are likely to hold qualified small business stock. When taxpayers sell qualified small business stock after holding it for more than five years, they may exclude a portion of the gain on the sale from regular taxation. The excluded portion depends on the date the taxpayer acquired the stock.

EXHIBIT 7-3 Exclusion for §1202 Stock Held More Than Five Years

Acquisition Date	Exclusion	Effective Capital Gains Tax Rate
After September 27, 2010, and before January 1, 2014	100%	0%
After February 17, 2009, and before September 28, 2010	75	7
After August 10, 1993, and before February 18, 2009	50	14

The capital gain not excluded from income is taxed at 28 percent. For example, using the minimum exclusion percentage of 50 percent, the effective capital gains tax rate is 14 percent.[26]

Example 7-6

What if: Assume that Jeb sold his stock in Gangbusters Inc., a qualified small business stock, for $200,000 on December 12, 2016. He acquired the stock on November 8, 2010, and his basis in the stock is $50,000. How much tax will he owe on the sale if his ordinary marginal rate is 35 percent?

Answer: $0. Because Jeb held the qualified small business stock for more than five years and because he acquired the stock when the exclusion percentage was 100 percent, he will exclude the entire $150,000 gain from income.

What if: Assume instead that Jeb sold his Gangbusters stock on December 12, 2016, but had acquired the stock on February 17, 2013. How much tax will he owe on the sale?

Answer: $22,500. Because Jeb didn't hold the stock for more than five years, he must recognize all $150,000 of long-term capital gain. This gain is taxed at 15 percent, yielding a total tax due of $22,500.

Exhibit 7-4 presents the maximum tax rates applicable to capital gains.

[24] §408(m).

[25] §1(h)(7).

[26] The maximum exclusion is the greater of $10,000,000 ($5,000,000 for married taxpayers filing separately) or 10 times the adjusted basis of the stock [see §1202(b)(1)]. The Protecting Americans from Tax Hikes Act of 2015 (PATH Act) made permanent the exclusion of 100 percent of the gain on the sale or exchange of qualified small business stock acquired after September 27, 2010, and held for more than five years. The PATH Act also permanently extended the rule that eliminates the 100 percent excluded gain as a preference item for AMT purposes. Lastly, the excluded gain is not subject to the 3.8 percent net investment income tax imposed on capital gains (and other investment income) on high-income taxpayers.

EXHIBIT 7-4 Classification of Capital Gains by Maximum Applicable Tax Rates

Short-Term or Long-Term	Type	Maximum Rate
Short-term	All	39.6%*
Long-term	Collectibles	28*
Held > 5 years	Qualified small business stock	14%**
Long-term	Unrecaptured §1250 gain from depreciable realty	25*
Long-term	All remaining capital (and §1231 gains) gain not included elsewhere	20†,‡

*Lower rates will apply when the taxpayer's ordinary rate is less than the rates reflected in this exhibit.

**The maximum rate of 15% applies when the lowest exclusion percentage of 50% is in effect.

†This gain is taxed at 0 percent to the extent it would have been taxed at a rate of 15 percent or less if it were ordinary income, taxed at 20 percent to the extent it would have been taxed at 39.6 percent as ordinary income, and taxed at 15 percent otherwise.

‡High income taxpayers may also be subject to an additional 3.8% net investment income tax on capital gains.

Netting Process for Gains and Losses To this point, our discussion of applicable tax rates for capital gains hasn't considered situations in which taxpayers recognize both capital gains and capital losses in the same year. To determine the appropriate tax treatment for the capital gains and losses recognized during the year, the taxpayer must complete a netting process. This netting process can be complex when taxpayers recognize capital losses and long-term capital gains subject to different maximum tax rates. In essence, the netting process separates capital gains and losses into short-term and three different long-term categories (based on the maximum rate applicable to the long-term gains). Although the process is complex, the underlying intuition is to have taxpayers net all long-term capital gains and losses together allowing long-term losses to offset the highest rate long-term gains first. Then, taxpayers use **net long-term capital losses** to offset short-term gains or **net short-term capital losses** to offset long-term gains.

After completing the netting process, taxpayers must calculate the tax consequences of the resulting outcomes. Net short-term capital gains are taxed at the same rate as ordinary income. Net long-term capital gains are taxed at a maximum of 28 percent if from the collectible and §1202 category, a maximum of 25 percent if from the unrecaptured §1250 gain category, or 0/15/20 percent for all other long-term capital gains. In the 0/15/20 percent category, net long-term gains are taxed at 20 percent to the extent the gains would have been taxed at 39.6 percent if they were ordinary income; at 15 percent to the extent the gains would have been taxed between 15 and 39.6 percent if they were ordinary income; and at 0 percent to the extent they would have been taxed at a rate of 15 percent or lower if they were ordinary income.

Taxpayers can deduct up to $3,000 ($1,500 if married filing separately) of net capital losses against ordinary income. Net capital losses in excess of $3,000 ($1,500 if married filing separately) retain their short- or long-term character and are carried forward and treated as though they were incurred in the subsequent year. Short-term losses are applied first to reduce ordinary income when the taxpayer recognizes both short- and long-term net capital losses. Capital loss carryovers for individuals never expire.

The following provides a step-by-step guide to the capital gains and losses netting process.

Step 1: Net all short-term capital gains and short-term capital losses, including any short-term capital loss carried forward from the prior year. A net positive amount is a **net short-term capital gain.** A net negative amount is a **net short-term capital loss.** If there are no long-term capital gains or losses, the netting process is complete. Otherwise, continue to step 2.

Step 2: Separate long-term capital gains and losses into three rate groups (28 percent, 25 percent, and 0/15/20 percent). Place any net long-term capital loss carried over from the prior year into the 28 percent rate group. Sum the gains and losses within each group. The outcome will be a net 28 percent gain or loss, a 25 percent gain (there are no 25 percent losses), and/or a net 0/15/20 percent gain or loss. Proceed to step 3.

Step 3: (A) If none of the long-term rate groups from step 2 nets to a gain, transfer the net loss (if any) in the 0/15/20 percent rate group to the 28 percent rate group, combine it with the loss in that group (if any), and proceed to step 4.

(B) If none of the long-term rate groups from step 2 nets to a loss, proceed to step 6.

(C) Combining net gains and losses in long-term rate groups:

1. If step 2 results in net losses in both the 28 percent and 0/15/20 percent rate groups, combine the net losses and then apply them to offset gains in the 25 percent rate group. If the losses exceed the gain, the result is a net long-term capital loss. Proceed to step 4. If the gain exceeds the losses, the result is a net long-term capital gain. Proceed to step 6.
2. If the step 2 outcomes include a net loss in the 28 percent rate group and net gains in the other rate groups, apply the net loss from the 28 percent rate group to the gain in the 25 percent rate group until the 25 percent rate group gain is reduced to zero. Then offset any remaining 28 percent rate group loss against the net gain in the 0/15/20 percent rate group. If the net loss from the 28 percent rate group exceeds the net gains from the other rate groups, the net loss is a net long-term capital loss. Proceed to step 4. If gain remains in the 25 percent and/or 0/15/20 percent rate groups after applying the loss, the result is a net long-term capital gain. Proceed to step 6.
3. If the amounts from step 2 include a net loss in the 0/15/20 percent rate group and net gains in the 28 percent and/or the 25 percent rate groups, apply the net loss from the 0/15/20 percent rate group to the net gain in the 28 percent rate group until the net gain is reduced to zero. Then offset any remaining loss against the gain in the 25 percent rate group. If the net loss from the 0/15/20 percent rate group exceeds the net gains from the other rate groups, the net loss is a net long-term capital loss. Proceed to step 4. If gain remains in the 28 percent and/or 25 percent rate groups after applying the loss, the result is a net long-term capital gain. Proceed to step 6.

Step 4: If there is no net short-term capital gain or loss from step 1, the netting process is complete; apply the net capital loss deduction limitations as described previously and ignore the remaining steps. If the result from step 1 is a net short-term capital loss *and* the result from step 3 is a net long-term capital loss, the netting process is complete: Apply the net capital loss deduction limitations described previously and ignore the remaining steps. Otherwise, continue on to step 5.

Step 5: If step 1 produces a net short-term capital gain *and* step 3 produces a net long-term capital loss, sum the net short-term capital gain and the net long-term capital loss.

(a) If the outcome is a net loss, the netting process is complete. Apply the net capital loss deduction limitations described previously.

(b) If the outcome is a net gain, the net gain is treated the same as a net short-term capital gain and is taxed at ordinary rates. The netting process is complete.

Step 6: If there is no net short-term capital gain or loss from step 1, the netting process is complete. The tax on the net long-term capital gain remaining in each long-term group is determined as described in the next section. If the step 1 outcome is a net short-term capital gain, skip to step 7. If the step 1 outcome is a net short-term capital loss *and* step 3 results in a net gain in any (or all) of the long-term rate groups, first use the short-term capital loss to offset the gain in the 28 percent rate group (if any), then the gain in the 25 percent rate group (if any), and finally the gain in 0/15/20 percent rate group (if any).

(a) If the net short-term capital loss exceeds all gains in the long-term rate groups, the netting process is complete. Apply the net capital loss deduction limitations described previously.

(b) If the net short-term capital loss does not offset all of the gain in any (or all) of the long-term rate groups, the netting process is complete. The result is a **net capital gain.** The tax on the gain remaining in each long-term group is determined as described in the next section.

Step 7: If step 1 produces a net short-term capital gain *and* step 3 produces a net long-term capital gain(s), the netting process is complete. The tax on the remaining gains is determined as described in the next section.

Example 7-7

Jeb Landers has recently retired and now wants to pursue his life-long dream of owning a sailboat. To come up with the necessary cash, he sells the following investments:

Stock	Market Value	Basis	Capital Gain/Loss	Scenario 1 Type	Scenario 2 Type
A	$40,000	$ 5,000	$ 35,000	Long	Short
B	20,000	30,000	(10,000)	Long	Short
C	20,000	12,000	8,000	Short	Long
D	17,000	28,000	(11,000)	Short	Long

What is the amount and nature of Jeb's capital gains and losses (Scenario 1)?

Answer: $22,000 net capital gain (treated as long-term capital gain), computed as follows:

Step 1: Net short-term gains and short-term losses. The $8,000 short-term gain on stock C is netted against the $11,000 short-term loss on stock D, yielding a net short-term capital loss of $3,000.

Step 2: Separate long-term gains and losses into rate groups and sum within the groups. Both long-term transactions are 0/15/20 percent types. The $35,000 long-term gain on stock A is netted against the $10,000 long-term loss on stock B, producing a gain of $25,000.

Step 3: 3(A) does not apply. 3(B) applies and requires skipping to step 6.

Step 4: Not required.

Step 5: Not required.

Step 6: Combine the net long-term capital gain of $25,000 with the net short-term capital loss of $3,000. This step results in a net capital gain of $22,000. The netting process is complete.

What if: Consider the original facts, except that Scenario 2 dictates the long- and short-term capital gains. What is the amount and character of Jeb's net gain (or loss) on the sale of the shares in this situation?

Answer: $22,000 net short-term capital gain, computed as follows:

Step 1: The gain from stock A would first be netted with the loss from stock B to produce a $25,000 net short-term capital gain [$35,000 + ($10,000)].

Step 2: The loss from stock D and the gain from stock C are both 0/15/20 percent types and are combined to provide a $3,000 loss [($11,000) + $8,000].

Step 3: 3(A) applies as the loss from step 2 is the only long-term amount and we proceed to step 4.

Step 4: Continue to step 5.

Step 5: 5(b) applies. The results from step 1 and step 2 are netted to reach a $22,000 net short-term capital gain [$25,000 + ($3,000)].

Example 7-7 included long-term capital gains and losses only in the 0/15/20 percent group. Example 7-8 shows the netting process when taxpayers also sell long-term capital assets and recognize gains subject to the 25 percent and/or 28 percent capital gains rates.

Example 7-8

What if: Assume that in addition to selling stocks, Jeb sold gold coins and a rental home as follows:

Capital Asset	Market Value	Tax Basis	Capital Gain/Loss	Scenario 1 Type
A stock	$ 40,000	$ 5,000	$ 35,000	Long 0/15/20%
B stock	20,000	30,000	(10,000)	Long 0/15/20%
C stock	20,000	12,000	8,000	Short
D stock	17,000	28,000	(11,000)	Short
Gold coins	4,000	3,000	1,000	Long 28%
Rental home	200,000	80,000	120,000	Long 25% and 0/15/20%*
Overall gain			$143,000	

*$50,000 of the gain is 25 percent gain and the remaining $70,000 is 0/15/20 percent gain.

Assuming Jeb did not sell any other capital assets during the year, he recognizes an overall capital gain of $143,000. What is (are) the maximum tax rate(s) applicable to this gain?

Answer: $95,000 of gain is subject to a 0/15/20 percent maximum rate and $48,000 of gain is subject to a 25 percent rate, computed as follows:

Step 1: $3,000 net short-term capital loss [$8,000 + ($11,000)].

Step 2: Stock A and Stock B are placed in the 0/15/20 percent group, the gold coins are placed in the 28 percent group, $50,000 of the gain from the sale of the rental home is placed in the 25 percent group, and the remaining $70,000 gain from the rental home is placed in the 0/15/20 percent group. The sum of the gains and losses in each group results in a net 28 percent gain of $1,000, a 25 percent gain of $50,000, and a net $95,000 gain in the 0/15/20 percent group.

Step 3: 3(A) does not apply. 3(B) applies because all of the long-term rate groups have a net gain from step 2. We proceed to step 6.

Step 4: Not required.

Step 5: Not required.

Step 6: Move the $3,000 loss from step 1 into the 28 percent group to offset the $1,000 gain. Next, move the remaining $2,000 loss [$1,000 gain on gold + ($3,000) short-term loss from step 1] into the 25 percent group to offset the $50,000 gain. The netting process is complete at this point because the net short-term capital loss does not offset all of the gains in the long-term rate groups (step 6[b]) and only gains remain in the long-term rate groups.

Step 7: Not required.

(continued on page 7-16)

THE KEY FACTS

25 Percent and 28 Percent Rate Capital Gains

- Certain gains from the sale of depreciable real property held long-term are taxed at a maximum rate of 25 percent (unrecaptured §1250 gain).
- Gains from collectibles and from qualified small business stock not held for five years are taxed at a maximum rate of 28 percent.
- When taxpayers have 25 percent or 28 percent rate capital gains, the netting process requires that losses be applied to higher rate groups before lower rate groups.
- When taxable income without long-term capital gains would be taxed in the 28 percent or higher ordinary income rate bracket, the capital gains in each rate group are simply taxed according to the capital gains rate applicable to each group. Otherwise applicable capital gains rates must be adjusted to reflect their inclusion in lower ordinary income rate brackets.

Jeb's netting process is reflected in the following table:

Description	Short-Term	Long-Term 28%	Long-Term 25%	Long-Term 0/15/20%
Stock C	$8,000			
Stock D	(11,000)			
Step 1:	(3,000)			
Coins		$1,000		
Unrecaptured §1250 Gain			$50,000	
Remaining Gain from Rental Property				$70,000
Stock A				35,000
Stock B				(10,000)
Step 2:		$1,000	$50,000	$95,000
Step 6:	(3,000) →	(3,000)		
		(2,000) →	(2,000)	
			$48,000	
Summary			$48,000	$95,000
Applicable Rate			25%	0/15/20%

Reporting capital gains and losses When taxpayers sell capital assets, they report the details of their sales on Form 8949 (dates of sale and purchase are additional items provided on Form 8949). After listing their sales on Form 8949, taxpayers then use Schedule D to summarize the sales and apply the basic capital gains netting process. Exhibits 7-5 and 7-6 illustrate how Jeb would report his stock sales in Example 7-7, Scenario 1.

Calculating Tax Liability on Net Capital Gains So, we've learned how to determine the *maximum* tax rates applicable to different types of capital gains. How do we go about actually calculating the effect these gains have on the taxpayer's tax liability? Follow these basic guidelines:

- If the long-term capital gains would have been taxed at a rate of 39.6 percent if they were ordinary income, the gain is taxed at the maximum rate for their group (0/15/20 percent, 25 percent, or 28 percent).
- To the extent the long-term capital gains would have been taxed at a rate of 15 percent or lower if they were ordinary income, the 0/15/20 percent gains are taxed at 0 percent, and the 25 percent and 28 percent gains are taxed at the taxpayer's ordinary rate.
- For other situations, use the following steps to determine the tax on the gains:[27]

Step 1: Fill up the 10, 15, 25, 28, 35, and 39.6 percent tax rate brackets with taxable income, exclusive of long-term capital gains subject to preferential rates.

Step 2: Next, if there is any remaining space in the 10 or 15 percent brackets, add any 25 percent rate capital gains to these brackets to the extent room remains in either of these brackets after step 1. Twenty-five percent rate capital gains included in these brackets are taxed at the ordinary rates applicable to these brackets.

[27]§1(h).

EXHIBIT 7-5 Jeb's Form 8949

Form **8949**

Department of the Treasury
Internal Revenue Service

Sales and Other Dispositions of Capital Assets

▶ Information about Form 8949 and its separate instructions is at *www.irs.gov/form8949.*

▶ File with your Schedule D to list your transactions for lines 1b, 2, 3, 8b, 9, and 10 of Schedule D.

OMB No. 1545-0074
2016
Attachment Sequence No. 12A

Name(s) shown on return: Jeb Landers | **Social security number or taxpayer identification number**

Before you check Box A, B, or C below, see whether you received any Form(s) 1099-B or substitute statement(s) from your broker. A substitute statement will have the same information as Form 1099-B. Either will show whether your basis (usually your cost) was reported to the IRS by your broker and may even tell you which box to check.

Part I **Short-Term.** Transactions involving capital assets you held 1 year or less are short term. For long-term transactions, see page 2.

Note: You may aggregate all short-term transactions reported on Form(s) 1099-B showing basis was reported to the IRS and for which no adjustments or codes are required. Enter the totals directly on Schedule D, line 1a; you aren't required to report these transactions on Form 8949 (see instructions).

You *must* check Box A, B, *or* C below. Check only one box. If more than one box applies for your short-term transactions, complete a separate Form 8949, page 1, for each applicable box. If you have more short-term transactions than will fit on this page for one or more of the boxes, complete as many forms with the same box checked as you need.

☑ **(A)** Short-term transactions reported on Form(s) 1099-B showing basis was reported to the IRS (see **Note** above)
☐ **(B)** Short-term transactions reported on Form(s) 1099-B showing basis **wasn't** reported to the IRS
☐ **(C)** Short-term transactions not reported to you on Form 1099-B

1 (a) Description of property (Example: 100 sh. XYZ Co.)	(b) Date acquired (Mo., day, yr.)	(c) Date sold or disposed of (Mo., day, yr.)	(d) Proceeds (sales price) (see instructions)	(e) Cost or other basis. See the **Note** below and see *Column (e)* in the separate instructions	Adjustment, if any, to gain or loss. If you enter an amount in column (g), enter a code in column (f). **See the separate instructions.** (f) Code(s) from instructions	(g) Amount of adjustment	(h) **Gain or (loss).** Subtract column (e) from column (d) and combine the result with column (g)
Stock C	3/01/16	11/15/16	20,000	12,000			8,000
Stock D	2/02/16	6/09/16	17,000	28,000			(11,000)
2 Totals. Add the amounts in columns (d), (e), (g), and (h) (subtract negative amounts). Enter each total here and include on your Schedule D, **line 1b** (if **Box A** above is checked), **line 2** (if **Box B** above is checked), or **line 3** (if **Box C** above is checked) ▶			37,000	40,000			(3,000)

Note: If you checked Box A above but the basis reported to the IRS was incorrect, enter in column (e) the basis as reported to the IRS, and enter an adjustment in column (g) to correct the basis. See *Column (g)* in the separate instructions for how to figure the amount of the adjustment.

For Paperwork Reduction Act Notice, see your tax return instructions. Cat. No. 37768Z Form **8949** (2016)

EXHIBIT 7-5 Jeb's Form 8949 (*continued*)

Form 8949 (2016) Attachment Sequence No. **12A** Page **2**

Name(s) shown on return. Name and SSN or taxpayer identification no. not required if shown on other side | **Social security number or taxpayer identification number**

Jeb Landers

Before you check Box D, E, or F below, see whether you received any Form(s) 1099-B or substitute statement(s) from your broker. A substitute statement will have the same information as Form 1099-B. Either will show whether your basis (usually your cost) was reported to the IRS by your broker and may even tell you which box to check.

Part II **Long-Term.** Transactions involving capital assets you held more than 1 year are long term. For short-term transactions, see page 1.

Note: You may aggregate all long-term transactions reported on Form(s) 1099-B showing basis was reported to the IRS and for which no adjustments or codes are required. Enter the totals directly on Schedule D, line 8a; you aren't required to report these transactions on Form 8949 (see instructions).

You *must* check Box D, E, *or* F below. Check only one box. If more than one box applies for your long-term transactions, complete a separate Form 8949, page 2, for each applicable box. If you have more long-term transactions than will fit on this page for one or more of the boxes, complete as many forms with the same box checked as you need.

☑ **(D)** Long-term transactions reported on Form(s) 1099-B showing basis was reported to the IRS (see **Note** above)

☐ **(E)** Long-term transactions reported on Form(s) 1099-B showing basis **wasn't** reported to the IRS

☐ **(F)** Long-term transactions not reported to you on Form 1099-B

1 (a) Description of property (Example: 100 sh. XYZ Co.)	(b) Date acquired (Mo., day, yr.)	(c) Date sold or disposed of (Mo., day, yr.)	(d) Proceeds (sales price) (see instructions)	(e) Cost or other basis. See the **Note** below and see *Column (e)* in the separate instructions	Adjustment, if any, to gain or loss. If you enter an amount in column (g), enter a code in column (f). **See the separate instructions.** (f) Code(s) from instructions	(g) Amount of adjustment	(h) **Gain or (loss).** Subtract column (e) from column (d) and combine the result with column (g)
Stock A	11/07/13	3/06/16	40,000	5,000			35,000
Stock B	7/09/12	9/01/16	20,000	30,000			(10,000)
2 Totals. Add the amounts in columns (d), (e), (g), and (h) (subtract negative amounts). Enter each total here and include on your Schedule D, **line 8b** (if **Box D** above is checked), **line 9** (if **Box E** above is checked), or **line 10** (if **Box F** above is checked) ▶			60,000	35,000			25,000

Note: If you checked Box D above but the basis reported to the IRS was incorrect, enter in column (e) the basis as reported to the IRS, and enter an adjustment in column (g) to correct the basis. See *Column (g)* in the separate instructions for how to figure the amount of the adjustment.

Form **8949** (2016)

EXHIBIT 7-6 Jeb's Schedule D

SCHEDULE D (Form 1040)

Department of the Treasury
Internal Revenue Service (99)

Capital Gains and Losses

▶ Attach to Form 1040 or Form 1040NR.
▶ Information about Schedule D and its separate instructions is at *www.irs.gov/scheduled*.
▶ Use Form 8949 to list your transactions for lines 1b, 2, 3, 8b, 9, and 10.

OMB No. 1545-0074
2016
Attachment Sequence No. 12

Name(s) shown on return: Jeb Landers

Your social security number

Part I **Short-Term Capital Gains and Losses—Assets Held One Year or Less**

See instructions for how to figure the amounts to enter on the lines below. This form may be easier to complete if you round off cents to whole dollars.	(d) Proceeds (sales price)	(e) Cost (or other basis)	(g) Adjustments to gain or loss from Form(s) 8949, Part I, line 2, column (g)	(h) Gain or (loss) Subtract column (e) from column (d) and combine the result with column (g)
1a Totals for all short-term transactions reported on Form 1099-B for which basis was reported to the IRS and for which you have no adjustments (see instructions). However, if you choose to report all these transactions on Form 8949, leave this line blank and go to line 1b .	37,000	40,000		(3,000)
1b Totals for all transactions reported on Form(s) 8949 with **Box A** checked				
2 Totals for all transactions reported on Form(s) 8949 with **Box B** checked				
3 Totals for all transactions reported on Form(s) 8949 with **Box C** checked				

4 Short-term gain from Form 6252 and short-term gain or (loss) from Forms 4684, 6781, and 8824 .	4	
5 Net short-term gain or (loss) from partnerships, S corporations, estates, and trusts from Schedule(s) K-1	5	
6 Short-term capital loss carryover. Enter the amount, if any, from line 8 of your **Capital Loss Carryover Worksheet** in the instructions	6	( )
7 **Net short-term capital gain or (loss).** Combine lines 1a through 6 in column (h). If you have any long-term capital gains or losses, go to Part II below. Otherwise, go to Part III on the back	7	(3,000)

Part II **Long-Term Capital Gains and Losses—Assets Held More Than One Year**

See instructions for how to figure the amounts to enter on the lines below. This form may be easier to complete if you round off cents to whole dollars.	(d) Proceeds (sales price)	(e) Cost (or other basis)	(g) Adjustments to gain or loss from Form(s) 8949, Part II, line 2, column (g)	(h) Gain or (loss) Subtract column (e) from column (d) and combine the result with column (g)
8a Totals for all long-term transactions reported on Form 1099-B for which basis was reported to the IRS and for which you have no adjustments (see instructions). However, if you choose to report all these transactions on Form 8949, leave this line blank and go to line 8b .	60,000	35,000		25,000
8b Totals for all transactions reported on Form(s) 8949 with **Box D** checked				
9 Totals for all transactions reported on Form(s) 8949 with **Box E** checked				
10 Totals for all transactions reported on Form(s) 8949 with **Box F** checked.				

11 Gain from Form 4797, Part I; long-term gain from Forms 2439 and 6252; and long-term gain or (loss) from Forms 4684, 6781, and 8824	11	
12 Net long-term gain or (loss) from partnerships, S corporations, estates, and trusts from Schedule(s) K-1	12	
13 Capital gain distributions. See the instructions	13	
14 Long-term capital loss carryover. Enter the amount, if any, from line 13 of your **Capital Loss Carryover Worksheet** in the instructions	14	( )
15 **Net long-term capital gain or (loss).** Combine lines 8a through 14 in column (h). Then go to Part III on the back .	15	25,000

For Paperwork Reduction Act Notice, see your tax return instructions. Cat. No. 11338H **Schedule D (Form 1040) 2016**

Step 3: Next, if there is any remaining space in the 10 or 15 percent brackets, add any 28 percent rate capital gains to these brackets to the extent room remains in either of these brackets after step 2. Twenty-eight percent rate capital gains included in these brackets are taxed at the ordinary rates applicable to these brackets.

Step 4: Next, add any 0/15/20 percent rate capital gains to either the 10 percent or 15 percent brackets to the extent room remains in either of these brackets after step 3. Any 0/15/20 percent rate capital gains included in these brackets are taxed at 0 percent.

Step 5: Add any remaining 0/15/20 percent rate capital gains (those not taxed in Step 4) to the 25, 28, 33, 35, and 39.6 percent brackets. The 0/15/20 percent rate capital gains included in brackets below 39.6 percent are taxed at 15 percent. The 0/15/20 percent rate capital gains included in the 39.6 percent bracket are taxed at 20 percent.

Step 6: Any remaining 25 percent rate capital gains (those not taxed in step 2) are taxed at 25 percent. Any remaining 28 percent rate capital gains are taxed at 28 percent. (This means that 28 percent rate capital gains that would have been taxed at 25 percent if they were ordinary income are taxed at the higher 28 percent rate. If, however, a taxpayer's tax liability would be lower using the regular tax rates for all ordinary income and capital gains [which is possible but not typical], the taxpayer would simply owe tax based on the regular tax rates.)

Example 7-9

What if: Let's return to the facts of the previous example where Jeb recognized a $48,000 25 percent net capital gain and a $95,000 0/15/20 percent net capital gain. Also, assume that Jeb's taxable income before considering the net capital gains is $10,000. Jeb's filing status is single. What is Jeb's gross tax liability for the year?

Answer: $24,488.75, computed as follows:

Amount and Type of Income	Applicable Rate	Tax	Explanation
$9,325; ordinary	10%	$ 932.50	$9,325 × 10%. The first $9,325 of Jeb's $10,000 of ordinary income is taxed at 10 percent (see single tax rate schedule for this and other computations).
$675	15	101.25	$675 × 15%. Jeb's remaining $675 of ordinary income ($10,000 − $9,325) is taxed at 15 percent.
$27,950; 25 percent rate capital gains	15	4,192.50	$27,950 × 15%. The end of the 15 percent bracket is $37,950 minus $10,000 ($9,325 + $675) already taxed.
$20,050; 25 percent rate capital gains	25	5,012.50	$20,050 × 25%. $48,000 total 25% gain minus $27,950 25 percent gain already taxed at 15 percent.
$95,000; 15 percent rate capital gains	15	14,250.00	$95,000 × 15%. All of the 15 percent gain would have been taxed at a rate higher than 15 percent but less than 39.6%, so it is all taxed at 15 percent.
Gross tax liability		**$24,488.75**	

What if: Suppose Jeb's 0/15/20 percent capital gain was $400,000 rather than $95,000. What is Jeb's gross tax liability for the year?

Answer: $72,218.75, computed as follows:

Amount and Type of Income	Applicable Rate	Tax	Explanation
$9,325; ordinary	10%	$ 932.50	$9,325 × 10%. The first $9,325 of Jeb's $10,000 of ordinary income is taxed at 10 percent (see single tax rate schedule for this and other computations).
$675	15	101.25	$675 × 15%. Jeb's remaining $725 of ordinary income ($10,000 – $9,275) is taxed at 15 percent.
$27,950; 25 percent rate capital gains	15	4,192.50	$27,950 × 15%. The end of the 15 percent bracket is $37,950 minus $10,000 ($9,325 + $675) already taxed.
$20,050; 25 percent rate capital gains	25	5,012.50	$20,050 × 25%. $48,000 total 25 percent gain minus $27,950 25 percent gain already taxed at 15 percent.
$360,400; 0/15/20 percent rate capital gains	15	54,060.00	$360,400 × 15%. $360,400 represents the 0/15/20 percent gain that would have been taxed at 25, 28, 33, or 35 percent if it were ordinary. This gain is taxed at 15 percent.
$39,600; 0/15/20 percent rate capital gains	20	7,920.00	$39,600 × 20%. The remaining 0/15/20 percent gain that would have been taxed at 39.6 percent had it been ordinary is taxed at the maximum 20 percent.
Gross tax liability		**$72,218.75**	

Limitations on Capital Losses

We've previously discussed the general rule that taxpayers may deduct capital losses against capital gains in the netting process and that individual taxpayers may deduct up to $3,000 ($1,500 if married filing separately) of net capital losses against ordinary income in a given year. This general rule, however, is subject to certain exceptions as described below.

Losses on the Sale of Personal-Use Assets As previously described, personal-use assets fall within the category of capital assets. When taxpayers sell personal-use assets, what are the tax consequences? Consider an engaged taxpayer who calls off the wedding plans. After getting the ring back from his former fiancée, the taxpayer sells the engagement ring for more than its purchase price. Does he recognize a taxable gain? Absolutely—the gain from the sale of a personal-use asset is taxable even though it was not purchased for its appreciation potential. The tax rate on the gain depends on the amount of time between the date the taxpayer purchased the ring and the date he sold it and on the netting process involving the seller's other capital gains and losses during the year. What if a taxpayer sold her car for less than she paid for it? Does she get to deduct the capital loss? Unfortunately, no—losses on the sale of personal-use assets are *not* deductible, and therefore never become part of the netting process.

Capital Losses on Sales to Related Parties When taxpayers sell capital assets at a loss to related parties, they are not able to deduct the loss.[28] As we described in detail in the Property Dispositions chapter, the related party acquiring the asset may eventually be allowed to deduct all, a portion, or none of the disallowed loss on a subsequent sale.

Wash Sales Consider the case of a taxpayer attempting to do some tax planning near the end of the year: She has invested in the stock of several corporations; some of these investments have appreciated while others have declined in value. The taxpayer wants to capture the tax benefit of the stock losses in the current year to offset ordinary income (up to $3,000) or to offset other capital gains she has already recognized during the year. However, she can't deduct the losses until she sells the stock. Why might this be a problem? If the taxpayer believes that the stocks with unrealized losses are likely to appreciate in the near future, she may prefer *not* to sell those stocks but rather to keep them in her investment portfolio. What might this taxpayer do to deduct the losses while continuing to hold the investment in the stocks? For one, she might be tempted to sell the stocks and then immediately buy them back. Or, she might buy more of the same stock and then sell the stock she originally held to recognize the losses. With this strategy, she hopes to realize (and then recognize or deduct) the losses and, at the end of the day, still hold the stocks in her investment portfolio.

Although this might sound like a great plan, certain **wash sale** tax rules prevent this strategy from accomplishing the taxpayer's objective. A wash sale occurs when an investor sells or trades stock or securities at a loss *and* within 30 days *either before or after* the day of sale buys substantially identical stocks or securities.[29] Because the day of sale is included, the 30 days before and after period creates a 61-day window during which the wash sale provisions may apply.[30] When the wash sale provisions apply to a sale of stock, realized losses are not recognized; instead, the amount of *the unrecognized loss is added to the basis of the newly acquired stock.* Congress created this rule to prevent taxpayers from accelerating losses on securities that have declined in value without actually altering their investment in the securities. The 61-day period ensures that taxpayers cannot deduct losses from stock sales without exposing themselves to the risk that the stock they sold will subsequently increase in value.

Example 7-10

What if: Suppose Courtney owns 100 shares of Cisco stock that she purchased in June 2015 for $50 a share. On December 21, 2017, Courtney sells the shares for $40 a share to generate cash for the holidays. This sale generates a capital loss of $1,000 [$4,000 sale proceeds (100 × $40) – $5,000 tax basis ($50 × 100)]. Later, however, Courtney decides that Cisco might be a good long-term investment. On January 3, 2018 (13 days later), Courtney purchases 100 shares of Cisco stock for $41 a share ($4,100). Does Courtney realize a short- term or a long-term capital loss on the December 21 sale?

Answer: Long-term capital loss. She held the stock for more than one year (June 2015 to December 2017) before selling.

How much of the realized $1,000 long-term capital loss can Courtney recognize or deduct on her 2017 tax return?

[28]§267(a).

[29]Substantially identical stocks or securities include contracts or options to buy substantially identical securities. However, corporate bonds and preferred stock are not generally considered substantially identical to common stock of the same corporation.

[30]§1091.

Answer: Zero. Because Courtney sold the stock at a loss and purchased the same stock within the 61-day period centered on the date of sale (30 days before December 21, and 30 days after December 21), the wash sale rules disallow the loss in 2017. Had Courtney waited another 18 days to repurchase the Cisco shares, she could have avoided the wash sale rules. In that case, under the general rules for capital loss deductibility, Courtney *would* be able to deduct the $1,000 capital loss from the sale against her ordinary income on her 2017 income tax return.

What tax basis will Courtney have in the Cisco stock she purchased (or repurchased) on January 3, 2018?

Answer: $5,100. Under the wash sale rules, Courtney adds the $1,000 disallowed loss to the basis of the stock she purchased on January 3. Thus, she now owns 100 shares of Cisco stock with a $5,100 basis in the shares, which is $1,000 more than she paid for it.

What if: How much of the $1,000 realized loss would Courtney have recognized if she had only purchased 40 shares of Cisco stock instead of 100 shares on January 3, 2018?

Answer: $600. The wash sale rules disallow the loss to the extent taxpayers acquire other shares in the 61-day window. In this situation, Courtney only acquired 40 percent (40 of 100) of the shares she sold at a loss within the window. Consequently, she must disallow 40 percent, or $400, of the loss, and she is allowed to deduct the remaining $600 loss.

THE KEY FACTS

Capital Gains and Losses

- Tax on the appreciation of capital assets is deferred until the asset is sold.
  - The longer the holding period, the greater the after-tax rate of return for a given before-tax rate of return.
- Tracking the basis of stock sold.
  - FIFO method is the default.
  - Specific identification is allowed.
- Capital gains and losses.
  - Long-term capital gain if the asset is held more than a year before sold; short-term otherwise.
  - Net long-term capital gains are taxed at the maximum 0/15/20 percent rate.
  - ($3,000) net capital loss is deductible annually against ordinary income.
  - Losses on personal-use assets are not deductible.
  - Losses on wash sales are not deductible but are added to the basis of new shares acquired.
- Basic tax planning strategies.
  - Hold capital assets for more than a year before selling.
  - Sell loss capital assets to offset gains.

ETHICS

In December, T. D. Weber evaluated his stock portfolio and found that his DLW Inc. common stock had declined in value since T. D. purchased it. He strategizes to sell the DLW stock on December 15. However, T. D. figures that he'd like to retain an interest in the company. So, knowing that he needs to avoid the wash sale rules, when he sells the common stock on December 15th he simultaneously purchases an equivalent amount of preferred stock in DLW Inc. On January 17 of the next year, T. D. sells the preferred stock and repurchases DLW common stock. What do you think of his strategy?

Balancing Tax Planning Strategies for Capital Assets with Other Goals

When taxpayers invest in capital assets and hold the assets for more than a year, they receive at least two benefits. First, they are able to defer recognizing gains on the assets until they sell them—the longer the deferral period, the lower the present value of the capital gains tax when taxpayers ultimately sell the assets. Second, they pay taxes on the gains at preferential rates. These tax advantages provide taxpayers with a greater after-tax rate of return on these investments than they would obtain from less tax-favored assets that earn equivalent before-tax rates of return. Investors who quickly sell investments pay taxes on gains at higher, ordinary rates and incur significantly greater transaction costs. Nevertheless, taxpayers should balance the tax benefits available for holding assets with the risk that the asset values will have declined by the time they want to sell the assets.

Example 7-11

What if: Assume Courtney decides to purchase Intel stock for $100,000. She plans to hold half of the shares for five years to purchase the Park City home and hold the other half for 8 years to pay for Deron's education. If the Intel stock grows at a constant 8 percent before-tax rate and does not pay any dividends, how much cash will Courtney accumulate after taxes for the Park City home?

(continued on page 7-24)

Answer: $69,946, computed as follows:

Description	Amount	Explanation
1. Proceeds from sale	$ 73,466	[$50,000 × (1 + .08)^5]
2. Basis in fund shares	50,000	This is the nondeductible investment in the shares.
3. Gain realized on sale	$ 23,466	(1) − (2)
4. Tax rate on gain	× 15%	Low rate for long-term capital gain.*
5. Tax on gain	$ 3,520	(3) × (4)
After-tax cash for Park City home	**$69,946**	(1) − (5)

*Assumes Courtney doesn't have any capital losses.

How much cash will Courtney accumulate after taxes for Deron's education?

Answer: $86,165, computed as follows:

Description	Amount	Explanation
1. Proceeds from sale	$ 92,547	[$50,000 × (1 + .08)^8]
2. Basis in fund shares	50,000	This is the nondeductible investment in the shares.
3. Gain realized on sale	$ 42,547	(1) − (2)
4. Tax rate on gain	× 15%	Low rate for long-term capital gain.*
5. Tax on gain	$ 6,382	(3) × (4)
After-tax cash for education goal	**$86,165**	(1) − (5)

*Assumes Courtney doesn't have capital losses.

When investing in capital assets, taxpayers run the risk that some of their investments may decline in value. Thus, a productive strategy for managing investments in capital assets is to sell investments with built-in losses. This strategy is commonly referred to as "loss harvesting." By selectively selling loss assets, taxpayers can reduce their taxes by deducting up to $3,000 against their ordinary income and by reducing the amount of capital gains that would otherwise be subject to tax during the year. This is particularly beneficial for taxpayers who have short-term capital gains that will be taxed at higher ordinary rates absent offsetting capital losses. Note, however, that taxpayers should not sell investments to gain tax benefits if they believe that the potential economic benefit of holding the investment outweighs the tax benefits of selling the stock. Also, keep in mind that capital losses on stock sales may not be deductible due to the wash sale rules discussed above.

TAXES IN THE REAL WORLD Turning Losses into Gains

Many investors have seen their investments plummet in value in recent years due to the economic downturn. However, financial advisers remind us that even in the midst of such seemingly bad news, there is good news. The tax code allows individuals to reduce or eliminate tax on their current gains using these losses, which in turn raises overall returns. Using capital losses to offset capital gains (or even up to $3,000 of ordinary income) is a term investment advisers call *tax-loss harvesting.* Tax advisers encourage investors to take advantage of the available capital loss offset and many investors do. For example, New York's billionaire mayor, Michael Bloomberg, disclosed that he would declare no net capital gains on his 2010 tax return. So, how much can loss harvesting improve your returns? Investment advisers have differing predictions but claim that loss harvesting can add up to 2 percentage points over a 10-year period. Pretty good considering that the Standard & Poor's 500 stock index's annualized total return for the period has been under 2 percent.

Source: The Wall Street Journal, Laura Saunders, August 20, 2011.

PORTFOLIO INCOME SUMMARY

As we've discussed the tax consequences of various investments up to this point in the chapter, we have proceeded from the least tax-advantaged (taxed annually at ordinary rates) to the most tax-advantaged (capital gains). By moving along this continuum from investments taxed annually at ordinary rates (corporate bonds[31]) to investments taxed annually at capital gains rates (dividend-paying stock), investors are in essence employing the conversion planning strategy referred to repeatedly throughout this text. As taxpayers move from dividend-paying stock to growth stock, which provides tax deferral in addition to preferential tax rates, taxpayers combine the conversion strategy with the basic strategy of shifting income from one time period to another.

In this chapter and elsewhere in this text, we emphasize that tax planning must not be done in a vacuum without considering all relevant parties and taxpayers' economic and personal objectives. Because investments typically are not designed to accommodate the specific needs of each individual investor, considering the other party in the deal is not as relevant when investing as it is in other transactions. However, it is vital that investors carefully balance the tax characteristics of their investment options with the other attributes of their investment options, such as risk and liquidity.

PORTFOLIO INVESTMENT EXPENSES

LO 7-3

Now that we've discussed how *income* from various forms of investments is taxed, let's explore the deductibility of expenses taxpayers incur to acquire or maintain their investments. We first discuss tax consequences associated with **investment expenses,** and we conclude by discussing the deductibility of **investment interest expense.** Even though the names of these two deductions sound very similar, investment expenses and investment interest expense are two different deductions with different deductibility limitations. So, when you are reading about an investment-related expense, pay careful attention to whether the expense is an *investment expense* or an *investment interest expense*. Exhibit 7-7 provides a description of these expenses and the limitations on the deductibility of the expenses.

EXHIBIT 7-7 Summary of Investment-Related Expenses

Item	Investment Expense	Investment *Interest* Expense
Description	Expenses (other than interest) incurred to generate investment income	Interest expense on loans used to acquire investments.
Deduction type	Miscellaneous itemized deduction (subject to 2 percent of AGI floor).	Interest expense itemized deduction.
Deduction limitations	Deductible only when investment expenses and other miscellaneous itemized deductions exceed 2 percent of AGI floor.	Deduction limited to taxpayer's net investment income for the year. Net investment income is gross investment income reduced by *deductible investment expenses.*
Nondeductible amounts due to limitations	Deduct it in the year incurred or lose it.	Carry over indefinitely.

Investment Expenses

Just as taxpayers can deduct ordinary and necessary business expenditures when conducting business activities, individual taxpayers are allowed to deduct ordinary and necessary expenses they incur in investment activities to produce or collect income and for expenses

[31]We refer here to corporate bonds issued or acquired at face value.

THE KEY FACTS

Investment-Related Expenses

- Investment expenses deducted as miscellaneous itemized deductions are subject to the 2 percent of AGI floor.
  - Expenses other than interest incurred to generate investment income.
  - No carryover of amounts not currently deductible.

they pay or incur to manage property held for producing income—such as safe deposit box rental fees, attorney and accounting fees that are necessary to produce investment income, and expenses for investment advice, among other things.[32]

The arrangement makes sense if you think about it: The government taxes investment income, so it is willing to allow taxpayers to deduct expenses they incur to generate investment income. Conversely, to the extent taxpayers incur expenses to produce tax-exempt income, such as municipal bond interest, they are not allowed to deduct the related expenses.[33] For example, a taxpayer who keeps a fully taxable corporate bond in a safe deposit box would be allowed an investment expense deduction for the cost of renting the box, but one who keeps a tax-exempt municipal bond in a safe deposit box would not.

The bad news here for taxpayers is that investment expenses are treated as miscellaneous itemized deductions subject to the 2 percent of AGI floor.[34] Thus, taxpayers with investment expenses will only realize tax benefits from these expenses if they itemize deductions *and* their total miscellaneous itemized deductions (fees for investment advice, tax return preparation fees, an employee's job-related magazine subscriptions, and other unreimbursed employee business expenses—see the Individual Deductions chapter)—including investment expenses—exceed 2 percent of their AGI. Consequently, it is likely that taxpayers with taxable investments and investment expenses will receive little tax benefit, if any, from the expenses.

Example 7-12

What if: Suppose Courtney met with a financial planner who advised her about her investment decisions. Courtney paid the adviser $500 for her services. Also, during the year Courtney paid a CPA $250 to prepare her tax return. Courtney had no other miscellaneous itemized deductions for the year. Does Courtney gain any tax benefit from the $500 she paid to the financial planner (her AGI is $162,000)?

Answer: No. The $500 payment is a deductible investment expense for Courtney. However, to receive any tax benefit from the payment, her total miscellaneous itemized deductions must exceed 2 percent of her AGI. The computation for her deductible investment expense is as follows:

Description	Amount
Investment expenses	$ 500
Tax return preparation fees	250
Total miscellaneous itemized deductions	750
Less: 2 percent of AGI ($162,000 × 2%)	3,240
Miscellaneous itemized deductions over 2 percent of AGI floor	0

Because her miscellaneous itemized deductions are less than 2 percent of her AGI, Courtney does not gain any tax benefit from the $500 investment expense (it does not reduce taxable income).

In fact, Courtney could have paid another $2,490 of investment expenses before she would have exceeded the 2 percent of AGI threshold and received any tax benefit from the payment ($3,240 − $750).

Investment Interest Expense

When taxpayers borrow money to acquire investments, the interest expense they pay on the loan is investment interest expense. For example, if you borrow funds to buy stock, any interest you pay on the loan would be considered investment interest expense.

[32]IRC §212. Rental expenses are also deductible under §212 as we discuss in the Individual Deductions chapter.

[33]§265.

[34]See the Individual Deductions chapter for a discussion of the tax treatment of miscellaneous itemized deductions. Also note that as we discussed in that chapter, investment expenses from rental and royalty-related activities are deductible as *for* AGI and not as itemized deductions.

Investment interest expense may be deductible as an itemized deduction.[35] Unlike investment expenses, the investment interest expense deduction is *not* a miscellaneous itemized deduction subject to the 2 percent of AGI floor. It is, however, subject to a different limitation. A taxpayer's investment interest expense deduction for the year is limited to the taxpayer's **net investment income** for the year.[36]

Net Investment Income Net investment income is gross investment income reduced by *deductible* investment expenses. Deductible investment expenses are investment expenses that actually reduce taxable income *after* applying the 2 percent of AGI floor.[37] Gross investment income includes interest, annuity, and royalty income not derived in the ordinary course of a trade or business. It also includes net *short*-term capital gains, and nonqualified dividends. However, investment income generally does not include net long-term capital gains and qualified dividends because this income is taxed at a preferential rate.

Example 7-13

What if: Suppose that during the year, Courtney recognized the following income from investments: $3,000 of qualified dividends and $500 of taxable interest. What is Courtney's gross investment income?

Answer: $500. The taxable interest is included, and the qualified dividends are excluded because they are taxed at a preferential rate.

What is Courtney's *net* investment income?

Answer: $500. Recall that net investment income is gross investment income minus deductible (taxable income reducing) investment expenses. In Example 7-12, we found that Courtney's deductible investment expenses were $0. Thus, her net investment income is $500 ($500 – $0).

Taxpayers may deduct their investment interest expense up to the amount of their net investment income. Any investment interest expense in excess of net investment income is carried over and treated as though it was incurred in the next year when it is subject to the same limitations. The carryover amount never expires. That is, taxpayers can carry over the excess investment interest expense until they generate sufficient net investment income to deduct it.

Example 7-14

What if: Continuing with Example 7-13, suppose that in July of this year, Courtney purchased a parcel of undeveloped land as an investment for $120,000. She made a $20,000 down payment and financed the remaining $100,000 with a loan from her local credit union. The interest rate on the loan was 9 percent, payable annually. During the year, Courtney paid $4,500 in interest expense on the loan. Because the loan was used to purchase an investment, the interest expense is investment interest expense. What amount of this investment interest expense is Courtney allowed to deduct this year?

Answer: $500. Although she incurred $4,500 of investment interest expense, her deduction for the current year is limited to her $500 net investment income (see Example 7-13). The $4,000 of investment interest expense that is not deductible this year is carried forward until Courtney generates enough net investment income to deduct it.

[35]§163.

[36]The investment interest expense limitation is calculated on Form 4952. Note that taxpayers can avoid the limitations on investment interest expense by acquiring the investment assets with funds from a qualified home equity loan. As we discuss in the Tax Consequences of Home Ownership chapter, interest on home equity loans is generally fully deductible.

[37]When taxpayers have both investment expenses and other miscellaneous itemized deductions subject to the 2 percent of AGI floor, deductible amounts in excess of the 2 percent of AGI floor are considered to first come from investment expenses up to the total amount of investment expenses and then from other miscellaneous itemized deductions.

Congress allows taxpayers to *elect to include* preferentially taxed income in investment income if they are willing to subject this income to tax at the ordinary (not preferential) tax rates. Taxpayers who make this election benefit from increasing their net investment income and thus increasing their current year investment interest expense deduction. However, this additional deduction comes at a price because they must subject their net long-term capital gains and qualified dividends included in investment income to ordinary tax rates.[38]

Example 7-15

THE KEY FACTS

Investment-Related Expenses

- Investment *interest* expense.
  - Itemized deduction not subject to the 2 percent of AGI floor.
  - Interest expense on loans used to purchase taxable investments.
  - Deductible to the extent of net investment income.
  - Net investment income is gross investment income minus deductible investment expenses.
  - Investment income includes interest, annuity, and other investment-type income not taxed at the preferential rate (long-term capital gains and qualified dividends).
  - Taxpayers can elect to include long-term capital gains and dividends in investment income but must tax them at the ordinary (not the preferential) rate.
  - Investment interest expense not deducted carries forward indefinitely.

In Examples 7-13 and 7-14, we discovered that Courtney paid $4,500 of investment interest expense during the year but was only able to deduct $500 of the interest expense because her net investment income was only $500. However, as indicated in Example 7-13, Courtney also received $3,000 of qualified dividends that were *excluded* from the net investment income computation. Courtney may elect to increase her investment income by the amount of the qualified dividends (and increase her investment interest expense deduction), but by doing so, she must subject the qualified dividends to her ordinary tax rate (30 percent) instead of the preferential rate (15 percent). Thus, Courtney is faced with a choice of whether to include the $3,000 dividend in investment income and tax it at ordinary rates (Alternative 1) or exclude it from investment income and tax it at preferential rates (Alternative 2). How much more investment interest expense is she allowed to deduct under Alternative 1 than Alternative 2?

Answer: $3,000 more under Alternative 1, computed as follows:

Alternative 1: *Include the $3,000 dividends in investment income.*

Description	Amount	Explanation
1. Increase in net investment income	$3,000	Elect to include dividends in net investment income.
2. Increase in investment interest expense deduction	**3,000**	Investment interest expense deduction increased from $500 to $3,500.
3. Tax benefit from additional deduction	900	(2) × 30%
4. Tax cost of taxing dividends at ordinary rate	450	(1) × (30% − 15%)
5. Current savings from election to include dividends in net investment income	450	(3) − (4)
Investment interest expense carryforward	$1,000	$4,500 total − $3,500 deducted

Alternative 2: *Exclude the $3,000 dividends from investment income.*

Description	Amount	Explanation
Forgone tax benefit available *this year* under Alternative 1	$ 450	Under Alternative 2, Courtney doesn't receive the tax savings available under Alternative 1.
1. Increase in investment interest expense carryforward	3,000	Investment interest expense not deducted under Alternative 2.
Total investment interest expense carryforward	$4,000	(1) + $1,000 investment interest expense carryforward under Alternative 1.

Whether or not it makes sense to elect to include net long-term capital gains and qualified dividends in investment income depends on the taxpayers' circumstances and their personal preferences. As we see in Example 7-15, Courtney could save $450 this

[38]Note that the election is not an all-or-nothing proposition. Taxpayers can elect to include all or only a portion of their net long-term capital gains and qualifying dividends in investment income. However, the amount they include in investment income is subject to tax at ordinary tax rates.

year by electing to include this income in investment income. However, by doing so, she is forgoing $3,000 of investment interest expense carryforward ($4,000 − $1,000) that would be available to offset ordinary income in future years.

Net Investment Income Tax

A net investment income tax is imposed on net investment income. The tax imposed is 3.8 percent of the lesser of (a) net investment income or (b) the excess of modified adjusted gross income over $250,000 for married-joint filers and surviving spouses, $125,000 for married separate filers, and $200,000 for other taxpayers. Modified adjusted gross income equals adjusted gross income increased by income excluded under the foreign-earned income exclusion less any disallowed deductions associated with the foreign-earned income exclusion. The tax is calculated and reported on Form 8960. Additional details and examples of the tax are provided in the Individual Income Tax Computation and Tax Credits chapter.

PASSIVE ACTIVITY INCOME AND LOSSES

LO 7-4

Thus far we have discussed how taxpayers may invest in business- and income-producing activities and earn various forms of income that are taxed as *portfolio income.* For example, taxpayers acquiring stock in a **C corporation** that files tax returns and pays taxes or taxpayers purchasing bonds issued by a taxable corporation are taxed on the portfolio income these investments generate in the form of dividends and interest. On the other hand, a taxpayer may invest directly in an income-producing enterprise by purchasing rental property or by forming a business as a sole proprietor. Similarly, a taxpayer could invest in a partial interest in a trade or business or rental activity by acquiring an ownership interest in a **flow-through entity** that doesn't pay taxes such as a partnership, limited liability company (taxed as a partnership), or an S corporation (taxed similar to a partnership by shareholders' election). No matter whether an investor makes a direct investment in rental property or in a sole proprietorship or makes an indirect investment in a business or rental activity through a partnership, limited liability company, or S corporation, the *actual operating income or loss* from these investments flows through to the taxpayer as it is earned and is treated as ordinary income or ordinary loss. If trade or business or rental activities (held either directly or indirectly through flow-through entities) generate ordinary operating income, taxpayers report it on their tax returns and it is taxed at ordinary rates. However, if these activities generate operating losses, the operating losses must clear three hurdles to be deductible currently. The three loss limits are the tax-basis, at-risk, and passive loss limits.

The tax-basis hurdle limits a taxpayer's deductible operating losses to the taxpayer's tax basis in the business or rental activity. This limitation is very similar to loss limitations that apply when a taxpayer sells an investment asset such as corporate stock or another similar capital asset. Recall that the formula for determining gain or loss on an exchange is the amount realized less the taxpayer's adjusted basis in the property. If a taxpayer were to sell an asset for nothing, the loss would be the amount of her tax basis in the property, but no more.

Obviously, in order to apply the tax-basis loss limitation, we must first determine the taxpayer's tax basis in the activity. Very generally speaking, the tax basis is the taxpayer's investment in the activity adjusted for certain items (namely, income, debt, and investments). The adjustments are beyond the scope of this chapter; however, tax basis is discussed in later chapters relating to flow-through entities.

When a loss from a business or business-related activity clears the tax-basis hurdle, it next must clear an **at-risk** hurdle on its journey toward deductibility.[39] The at-risk rules are meant to limit the ability of investors to deduct "artificial" ordinary losses produced

[39]§465.

with certain types of debt. These rules serve to limit ordinary losses to a taxpayer's economic risk in an activity. Generally, a taxpayer is considered to be "at risk" in an activity to the extent of any cash personally contributed to the activity and certain other adjustments similar (but not identical) to those for tax basis.[40] Because the computation of tax basis and at-risk amount are so similar, a taxpayer's tax basis and her at-risk amount in the activity are frequently the same so that when she clears the tax-basis hurdle for deducting a loss, she also clears the at-risk hurdle. If the at-risk amount does differ from the tax basis, the at-risk amount will be less than the tax basis. Losses that do not clear the at-risk hurdle are suspended until the taxpayer generates more at-risk amounts to absorb the loss or until the activity is sold, when they may offset the seller's gain from the disposition of the activity.

Example 7-16

What if: Assume that instead of investing solely in assets that generate portfolio income, Courtney used $10,000 of the inheritance from "Gramps" to acquire a 5 percent interest in a limited partnership (a flow-through entity) called Color Comfort Sheets (CCS). Courtney's share of CCS's loss for the year is $15,000. What amount of this loss is Courtney allowed to deduct after applying the tax basis and at-risk limitations?

Answer: $10,000. Since Courtney's tax basis and at-risk amount in her CCS interest are both $10,000 (the amount of cash invested), the tax-basis and at-risk amount limitations result in the same limitation. Thus, Courtney may deduct $10,000 of the $15,000 loss before considering the passive activity loss limits discussed below.

Even when a taxpayer has sufficient tax basis and sufficient amounts at risk to absorb a loss from a business-related activity, the loss may still be limited by the passive activity loss rules. Prior to 1986, investors were able to use ordinary losses from certain passive activities to offset portfolio income (interest, dividends, and capital gains), salary income, and self-employment income, including income from other trades or businesses they were actively involved in managing. During this time, a **tax shelter** industry thrived by marketing investments to wealthy investors designed primarily to generate ordinary losses that could be used to shield other income from tax. To combat this practice, Congress introduced the passive activity loss rules.[41] Specifically, these rules limit the ability of investors in certain passive activities involving interests in trades or businesses and in rental property, including real estate, to use their ordinary losses from these activities currently to reduce taxable income from other sources.[42] The passive activity loss rules are applied to any losses remaining *after* applying the tax-basis and at-risk loss limits.

Passive Activity Definition

The **passive activity loss (PAL) rules** define a passive activity as "any activity which involves the conduct of a trade or business, and in which the taxpayer does not materially participate." According to the tax code, participants in rental activities, including rental real estate, and limited partners in partnerships are generally deemed to be passive participants, and participants in all other trade or business activities are passive unless their

[40]A detailed discussion of these adjustments is beyond the scope of this chapter.

[41]§469.

[42]Before passage of the passive activity loss rules, the "at-risk rules" in §465 were adopted in an attempt to limit the ability of investors to deduct "artificial" ordinary losses. Given the similarity of the at-risk and tax-basis computations, especially for real estate investments, the at-risk rules were not entirely successful at accomplishing this objective. The passive activity loss rules were adopted as a backstop to the at-risk rules and both sets of rules may potentially apply to a given activity.

involvement in an activity is "regular, continuous, and substantial." Clearly, these terms are quite subjective and difficult to apply. Fortunately, regulations provide more certainty in this area by listing seven separate tests for material participation.[43] An individual, other than a limited partner, can be classified as a material participant in an activity by meeting any one of the seven tests in Exhibit 7-8. Therefore, investors who purchase rental property or an interest in a trade or business without intending to be involved in the management of the trade or business are classified as passive participants, and these activities are classified as passive activities with respect to them.

EXHIBIT 7-8 Tests for Material Participation

Individuals are generally considered material participants for the activity if they meet any *one* of these tests:

1. The individual participates in the activity more than 500 hours during the year.
2. The individual's activity constitutes substantially all of the participation in such activity by all individuals, including nonowners.
3. The individual participates more than 100 hours during the year, and the individual's participation is not less than any other individual's participation in the activity.
4. The activity qualifies as a "significant participation activity" (more than 100 hours spent during the year) and the aggregate of all "significant participation activities" is greater than 500 hours for the year.
5. The individual materially participated in the activity for any 5 of the preceding 10 taxable years.
6. The individual materially participated for any three preceding years in any personal service activity (personal services in health, law, accounting, architecture, etc.).
7. Taking into account all the facts and circumstances, the individual participates on a regular, continuous, and substantial basis during the year.

Income and Loss Categories

Under the passive activity loss rules, each item of a taxpayer's income or loss for the year is placed in one of three categories. Losses from *the passive category* cannot offset income from other categories. The three different categories are as follows (see Exhibit 7-9):

1. *Passive activity income or loss*—income or loss from an activity in which the taxpayer is not a material participant.

EXHIBIT 7-9 Income and Loss Categories

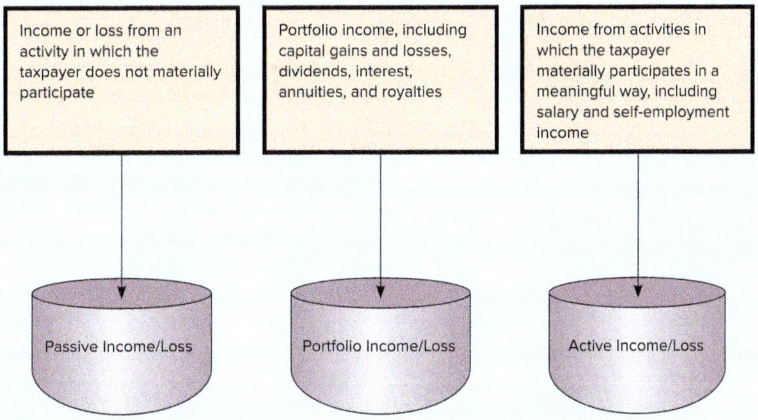

[43]§1.469-5T.

2. *Portfolio income*—income from investments including capital gains and losses, dividends, interest, annuities, and royalties.
3. *Active business income*—income from sources in which the taxpayer is a material participant. For individuals, this includes salary and self-employment income. Thus, an individual with income in this category is no longer an investor with respect to this source of income given that we define investors in this chapter as individuals with portfolio and/or passive income and losses.

The impact of segregating taxpayers' income in these categories is to limit their ability to apply passive activity losses against income in the other two categories. In effect, passive activity losses are suspended and remain in the passive income or loss category until the taxpayer generates passive income, either from the passive activity producing the loss or from some other passive activity, or until the taxpayer sells the entire activity that generated the passive loss in a taxable transaction. On the sale, current and suspended passive losses from the activity are first applied to reduce gain from the sale of the activity, then to reduce net passive income from other passive activities, and then to reduce nonpassive income.[44]

Example 7-17

What if: Let's return to the facts in the previous example where Courtney's share of CCS loss is $15,000, her tax basis in her CCS interest is $10,000, and her at-risk amount in the activity is also $10,000. Further assume that Courtney received $170,000 in combined salary, $4,000 of taxable interest income from corporate bonds, $3,000 of dividends, and $5,000 of long-term capital gains. Finally, assume that Courtney also owns a rental condominium that generated $8,000 of net income. How would each of these income or loss items be allocated among the passive, portfolio, and active income and loss categories?

Answer: Courtney's $10,000 loss from CCS remaining after applying the tax-basis and at-risk loss limits is placed in the passive category because, as a limited partner, Courtney did not materially participate in the activity. Further, her $8,000 of net income from her rental property is included in the passive category because rental activities are generally considered to be passive. The $4,000 of taxable interest income, $3,000 of dividends, and $5,000 of long-term capital gains are all included in the portfolio income category. Finally, the $170,000 of salary is included in the active income category.

What if: What is Courtney's AGI for the year assuming, other than the items described above, no other items affect her AGI?

Answer: $182,000, computed as follows:

Description	Amount	Explanation
1. Active income	$170,000	Salary
2. Portfolio income	12,000	Interest of $4,000; dividends of $3,000; $5,000 of long-term capital gains.
3. Passive income	0	$10,000 passive loss that clears tax-basis and at-risk hurdles and $8,000 of passive income. However, the passive loss clearing the basis and at-risk hurdles is deductible only to the extent of passive income. The suspended passive loss is ($2,000).
AGI	$182,000	(1) + (2) + (3)

What if: Assume the facts above and that at the beginning of next year Courtney sells her limited partnership interest for $12,000. If Courtney's tax basis on the date of sale is $0, what effect does the sale have on her AGI?

THE KEY FACTS

Passive Activities

- Ordinary losses from flow-though entities and other enterprises will be classified as passive if the taxpayer is not a material participant.
- Losses from limited partnerships and from rental activities, including rental real estate, are generally deemed to be passive losses.
- Passive loss rules limit losses from passive activities to passive income from other sources.
  - Active business income such as salary and self-employment income is not passive income.
  - Investment-type income such as interest and dividends is portfolio income, not passive income.

(continued)

[44]§469(g).

Answer: $10,000 increase in AGI, computed as follows:

Description	Amount	Explanation
1. Capital gain	$12,000	Gain recognized = $12,000 − $0 tax basis
2. Ordinary loss	0	The ($5,000) loss that was suspended at the basis level is not deductible on the sale. This loss expires unused. There was no loss suspended at the at-risk level or it would have been deductible on the sale.
3. Ordinary loss	(2,000)	This is the loss that was suspended at the passive loss level last year.
Increase in AGI	$10,000	(1) + (2) + (3)

- Passive losses in excess of passive income are suspended and deductible against passive income in the future or when the taxpayer sells the passive activity generating the loss.
- Income from passive activities is subject to the net investment income tax.

Rental Real Estate Exception to the Passive Activity Loss Rules

Tax laws are renowned for exceptions to rules and, not surprisingly, the general rule that passive activity losses cannot be used to offset nonpassive types of income is subject to a few important exceptions. The one we choose to discuss here applies to lower-to-middle income individuals with rental real estate.[45] A taxpayer who is an **active participant in a rental activity** may be allowed to deduct up to $25,000 of the rental loss against other types of income. To be considered an active participant, the taxpayer must (1) own at least 10 percent of the rental property and (2) participate in the process of making management decisions such as approving new tenants, deciding on rental terms, and approving repairs and capital expenditures.

Consistent with a number of tax benefits, the exception amount for active owners is phased out as adjusted gross income increases. The $25,000 maximum exception amount is phased out by 50 cents for every dollar the taxpayer's adjusted gross income (before considering the rental loss) exceeds $100,000. Consequently, the entire $25,000 deduction is phased out when the taxpayer's adjusted gross income reaches $150,000.

THE KEY FACTS

Rental Real Estate Losses

- Rental real estate exception to passive loss rules.
  - Applies to active participants in rental property.
  - Deduct up to $25,000 of rental real estate loss against ordinary income.
  - $25,000 maximum deduction phased out by 50 cents for every dollar of AGI over $100,000 (excluding the rental loss deduction).
  - Fully phased out at $150,000 of AGI.

Example 7-18

What if: Assume that Jeb Landers, Courtney's uncle, owns and rents a condominium. Jeb is involved in approving new tenants for the rental home and in managing its maintenance. During the year, he reported a net loss of $5,000 from the rental activity, and he had sufficient tax-basis and at-risk amounts to absorb the loss. Further, his only sources of income during the year were $126,000 of salary and $22,000 of long-term capital gains. Given Jeb's $5,000 loss from his rental home, how much of the loss could he deduct currently and what would be his passive loss carryforward?

Answer: Jeb's rental loss deductible in the current year is $1,000, and his passive loss carryforward is $4,000. Because Jeb meets the definition of an "active participant" and has adjusted gross income of less than $150,000, before considering his rental loss, he may deduct a portion of the loss against his other income. His $1,000 deduction is computed as follows:

Description	Amount	Explanation
1. Maximum deduction available before phase-out	$25,000	
2. Phase-out of maximum deduction	24,000	[($148,000 − 100,000) × .5]
3. Maximum deduction in current year	$ 1,000	(1) − (2)
4. Rental loss in current year	5,000	
5. Rental loss deductible in current year	**1,000**	Lesser of (3) or (4)
Passive loss carryforward	**$ 4,000**	(4) − (3)

(continued on page 7-34)

[45]§469(b)(7) provides another important exception to the general rule that all real estate activities are passive. To overcome this presumption, taxpayers must spend more than half their time working in real estate trades or businesses and for more than 750 hours during the year. This exception benefits individuals that spend a substantial amount of time in activities like real estate development and construction.

What if: Assume that Jeb's salary for the year had been $50,000 and he reported $22,000 from the sale of his stock. How much of his rental loss could he deduct currently?

Answer: Because Jeb's adjusted gross income would only be $72,000 under this scenario, he could deduct his entire $5,000 rental loss during the year.

Net Investment Income Tax on Net Passive Income

Earlier in this chapter we noted that taxpayers with modified AGI over certain thresholds are required to pay a 3.8 percent tax on their net investment income (in addition to the income tax). In calculating net investment income for this tax, taxpayers must include their net passive income.

Example 7-19

What if: Suppose Courtney has income from her salary of $170,000. Assume that in addition to this income, Courtney also owns 50 percent of an S corporation in which she does not materially participate. The S corporation is profitable and generates $100,000 of flow-through income to her this year. How much net investment income tax will Courtney owe?

Answer: $2,660, calculated as follows:

Description	Amount	Explanation
1. Net investment income	$100,000	Income from passive investment
2. Modified AGI	270,000	$170,000 salaries + $100,000 LLC income
3. Modified AGI threshold	200,000	
4. Excess modified AGI above threshold	70,000	(2) − (3)
5. Net investment income tax base	70,000	Lesser of (1) or (4)
Net investment income tax	**2,660**	(5) × 3.8%

What if: Assume that Courtney spends 525 hours participating in the activity during the year. How much net investment income tax will she owe?

Answer: $0. Because Courtney materially participates in the S corporation, the flow-through income is no longer passive income and she will not be subject to the net investment income tax.

CONCLUSION

Investors and their advisers face numerous tax rules that apply to investment income and expenses. Understanding these rules is important, not only to comply with the tax law, but also to make wise investment choices. Investments differ in terms of their potential for implementing the conversion and shifting tax planning strategies. Failing to consider these strategies when investing will lead to less than optimal results. By carefully weighing nontax investment objectives along with the tax characteristics of different investment options, informed investors will be better equipped to select investments appropriate for them.

Summary

Explain how interest income and dividend income are taxed. **LO 7-1**

- Investors seeking current income invest in interest-bearing securities or dividend-paying stocks.
- Interest income received from certificates of deposit, U.S. Treasury securities, corporate bonds, and other similar investments is typically taxed annually at ordinary rates.
- Accrued market discount on bonds and interest earned on U.S. savings bonds is taxed at sale or maturity, while original issue discount on bonds is taxed annually.
- Bond premiums increase the tax basis of bonds and affect the amount of capital gains or losses investors report.
- Taxpayers may elect to amortize bond premiums to reduce the amount of annual interest reported on bonds purchased at a premium.
- Dividend income, like interest income, is taxed annually when it is received. However, most dividend income currently is taxed at preferential capital gains rates.

Compute the tax consequences associated with the disposition of capital assets, including the netting process for calculating gains and losses. **LO 7-2**

- When taxpayers sell stock, they may determine the basis of the stock using the specific identification method or the FIFO method.
- Capital assets held for more than one year generate long-term capital gains or losses on sale or disposition. Other capital assets generate short-term capital gains or losses on sale or disposition.
- Generally, net long-term capital gains in excess of net short-term losses are taxed at either a 0, 15, or 20 percent tax rate depending on the taxpayers' income.
- Unrecaptured §1250 gain is taxed at a maximum 25 percent rate, and gains from collectibles and §1202 stock are taxed at a maximum 28 percent rate.
- Up to $3,000 of net capital losses are deductible against ordinary income for the year.
- A taxpayer's capital gains and losses for the year are reported on Schedule D of Form 1040.
- Wash sale provisions prevent taxpayers from selling stock at a loss, deducting the loss, and replacing the stock sold with the same stock or substantially identical securities within 30 days either before or after the day of sale.
- Losses on the disposition of property held for personal use are not deductible.
- Because of the deferral of the capital gains tax, after-tax returns from capital assets will increase as an investor's investment horizon increases.

Calculate the deduction for portfolio investment-related expenses, including investment expenses and investment interest expense. **LO 7-3**

- Investment expenses are miscellaneous itemized deductions subject to the 2 percent of AGI floor.
- Investment interest expense is deductible to the extent of net investment income.
- Net investment income is investment income minus deductible investment expenses.
- Net long-term capital gains and qualified dividends are not included in investment income unless the taxpayer elects to tax them as ordinary income.

Understand the distinction between portfolio investments and passive investments and apply tax-basis, at-risk, and passive activity loss limits to losses from passive investments. **LO 7-4**

- A taxpayer's share of operating losses from flow-through entities and other trade or business activities are deductible to the extent they clear the tax-basis, at-risk, and passive activity loss hurdles.
- A taxpayer's ordinary losses from flow-through entities and other trade or business activities may be classified as passive if the taxpayer's involvement is not regular, continuous, and substantial.
- A taxpayer's operating losses from rental activities are, with limited exceptions, deemed to be passive regardless of taxpayer's activity level.

- A taxpayer's passive losses from an activity are limited to passive income from all other sources until disposition of the activity. On disposition, current and prior passive losses from an activity can be used without limitation.
- A rental real estate exception allows taxpayers to deduct up to $25,000 of operating losses from rental real estate annually provided they are actively involved in managing the rental real estate and have adjusted gross income of less than $150,000.

KEY TERMS

accrued market discount (7-4)
active participant in a rental activity (7-33)
amortization (7-3)
at-risk amount (7-29)
basis (7-4)
bond (7-2)
bond discount (7-3)
bond premium (7-3)
C corporation (7-29)
capital asset (7-7)
certificate of deposit (CD) (7-2)
collectibles (7-10)
dividend (7-2)
ex-dividend date (7-6)
face value (7-2)
first-in, first-out (FIFO) method (7-9)
flow-through entities (7-29)
investment expenses (7-25)
investment income (7-2)
investment interest expense (7-25)
long-term capital gains or losses (7-10)
market discount (7-4)
market premium (7-4)
maturity (7-4)
maturity value (7-2)
mutual fund (7-2)
net capital gain (7-14)
net investment income (7-27)
net long-term capital gain (7-12)
net long-term capital loss (7-12)
net short-term capital gain (7-12)
net short-term capital loss (7-12)
operating income (7-2)
operating loss (7-2)
original issue discount (OID) (7-3)
passive activity loss (PAL) rules (7-30)
passive investments (7-2)
portfolio investments (7-2)
qualified dividends (7-6)
qualified small business stock (7-10)
short-term capital gains or losses (7-10)
specific identification method (7-9)
tax basis (7-8)
tax shelter (7-30)
Treasury bond (7-3)
Treasury note (7-3)
unrecaptured §1250 gain (7-10)
U.S. savings bonds (7-3)
wash sale (7-22)
zero-coupon bonds (7-3)

DISCUSSION QUESTIONS

Discussion Questions are available in Connect®. connect

LO 7-1 1. Describe how interest income and dividend income are taxed. What are the similarities and differences in their tax treatment?

LO 7-1 2. What is the underlying policy rationale for the current tax rules applicable to interest income and dividend income?

LO 7-1 3. Compare and contrast the tax treatment of interest from a Treasury bond and qualified dividends from corporate stock.

LO 7-1 4. How are Treasury notes and Treasury bonds treated for federal and state income tax purposes?

LO 7-1 5. Why would taxpayers generally prefer the tax treatment of market discount to the treatment of original issue discount on corporate bonds?

LO 7-1 6. In what ways are U.S. savings bonds treated more favorably for tax purposes than corporate bonds?

research LO 7-1 7. When should investors consider making an election to amortize the market discount on a bond into income annually? [*Hint:* See §1278(b).]

planning LO 7-1 8. Why might investors purchase interest-paying securities rather than dividend-paying stocks?

LO 7-1 9. Compare and contrast the tax treatment of dividend-paying stocks and growth stocks.

LO 7-2 10. What is the definition of a capital asset? Give three examples of capital assets.

LO 7-2 11. Why does the tax law allow a taxpayer to defer gains accrued on a capital asset until the taxpayer actually sells the asset?

12. Why does the tax law provide preferential rates on certain capital gains? LO 7-2
13. What is the deciding factor in determining whether a capital gain is a short-term or long-term capital gain? LO 7-2
14. What methods may taxpayers use to determine the adjusted basis of stock they have sold? LO 7-2
15. What tax rate applies to net short-term capital gains? LO 7-2
16. What limitations are placed on the deductibility of capital losses for individual taxpayers? LO 7-2
17. What happens to capital losses that are not deductible in the current year? LO 7-2
18. Are all long-term capital gains taxable at the same maximum rate? If not, what rates may apply to long-term capital gains? LO 7-2
19. This year, David, a taxpayer in the highest tax rate bracket, has the option to purchase either stock in a Fortune 500 company or qualified small business stock in his friend's corporation. All else being equal, which of the two will he prefer from a tax perspective if he intends to hold the stock for six years? Which would he prefer if he only plans to hold the stock for two years? LO 7-2 planning
20. What is a "wash sale"? What is the purpose of the wash sale tax rules? LO 7-2
21. Nick does not use his car for business purposes. If he sells his car for less than he paid for it, does he get to deduct the loss for tax purposes? Why or why not? LO 7-2
22. Describe three basic tax planning strategies available to taxpayers investing in capital assets. LO 7-2
23. Clark owns stock in BCS Corporation that he purchased in January of the current year. The stock has appreciated significantly during the year. It is now December of the current year, and Clark is deciding whether or not he should sell the stock. What tax and nontax factors should Clark consider before making the decision on whether to sell the stock now? LO 7-2 planning
24. Are dividends and capital gains considered to be investment income for purposes of determining the amount of a taxpayer's deductible investment interest expense for the year? LO 7-3
25. How is the amount of net investment income determined for a taxpayer with investment expenses and other noninvestment miscellaneous itemized deductions? LO 7-3
26. What limitations are placed on the deductibility of investment interest expense? What happens to investment interest expense that is not deductible because of the limitations? LO 7-3
27. When taxpayers borrow money to buy municipal bonds, are they allowed to deduct interest expense on the loan? Why or why not? LO 7-3
28. What types of losses may potentially be characterized as passive losses? LO 7-3
29. What are the implications of treating losses as passive? LO 7-4
30. What tests are applied to determine if losses should be characterized as passive? LO 7-4
31. All else being equal, would a taxpayer with passive losses prefer to have wage income or passive income? LO 7-4 planning

PROBLEMS

Select problems are available in Connect®.

32. Matt recently deposited $20,000 in a savings account paying a guaranteed interest rate of 4 percent for the next 10 years. If Matt expects his marginal tax rate to be 20 percent for the next 10 years, how much interest will he earn after-tax for the first year of his investment? How much interest will he earn after-tax for the second year of his investment if he withdraws enough cash every year to pay the tax on the interest he earns? How much will he have in the account after 4 years? How much will he have in the account after 7 years? LO 7-1

LO 7-1 33. Dana intends to invest $30,000 in either a Treasury bond or a corporate bond. The Treasury bond yields 5 percent before tax and the corporate bond yields 6 percent before tax. Assuming Dana's federal marginal rate is 25 percent and her marginal state rate is 5 percent, which of the two options should she choose? If she were to move to another state where her marginal state rate would be 10 percent, would her choice be any different? Assume that Dana itemizes deductions.

LO 7-1 34. At the beginning of his current tax year, David invests $12,000 in original issue U.S. Treasury bonds with a $10,000 face value that mature in exactly 10 years. David receives $700 in interest ($350 every six months) from the Treasury bonds during the current year, and the yield to maturity on the bonds is 5 percent.

a) How much interest income will he report this year if he elects to amortize the bond premium?

b) How much interest will he report this year if he does not elect to amortize the bond premium?

LO 7-1 35. Seth invested $20,000 in Series EE savings bonds on April 1. By December 31, the published redemption value of the bonds had increased to $20,700. How much interest income will Seth report from the savings bonds in the current year absent any special election?

LO 7-1 36. At the beginning of her current tax year, Angela purchased a zero-coupon corporate bond at original issue for $30,000 with a yield to maturity of 6 percent. Given that she will not actually receive any interest payments until the bond matures in 10 years, how much interest income will she report this year assuming semiannual compounding of interest?

LO 7-1 37. At the beginning of his current tax year, Eric bought a corporate bond with a maturity value of $50,000 from the secondary market for $45,000. The bond has a stated annual interest rate of 5 percent payable on June 30 and December 31, and it matures in five years on December 31. Absent any special tax elections, how much interest income will Eric report from the bond this year and in the year the bond matures?

LO 7-1 38. Hayley recently invested $50,000 in a public utility stock paying a 3 percent annual dividend. If Hayley reinvests the annual dividend she receives net of any taxes owed on the dividend, how much will her investment be worth in four years if the dividends paid are qualified dividends? (Hayley's marginal income tax rate is 28 percent.) What will her investment be worth in four years if the dividends are nonqualified?

LO 7-1 planning 39. Five years ago, Kate purchased a dividend-paying stock for $10,000. For all five years, the stock paid an annual dividend of 4 percent before tax and Kate's marginal tax rate was 25 percent. Every year Kate reinvested her after-tax dividends in the same stock. For the first two years of her investment, the dividends qualified for the 15 percent capital gains rate; however, for the last three years the 15 percent dividend rate was repealed and dividends were taxed at ordinary rates.

a) What is the current value (at the beginning of year 6) of Kate's investment assuming the stock has not appreciated in value?

b) What will Kate's investment be worth three years from now (at the beginning of year 9) assuming her marginal tax rate increases to 35 percent for the next three years?

LO 7-2 40. John bought 1,000 shares of Intel stock on October 18, 2014, for $30 per share plus a $750 commission he paid to his broker. On December 12, 2017, he sells the shares for $42.50 per share. He also incurs a $1,000 fee for this transaction.

a) What is John's adjusted basis in the 1,000 shares of Intel stock?

b) What amount does John realize when he sells the 1,000 shares?

c) What is the gain/loss for John on the sale of his Intel stock? What is the character of the gain/loss?

41. Dahlia is in the 28 percent tax rate bracket and has purchased the following shares of Microsoft common stock over the years: LO 7-2

Date Purchased	Shares	Basis
7/10/2007	400	$12,000
4/20/2008	300	10,750
1/29/2009	500	12,230
11/02/2011	250	7,300

If Dahlia sells 800 shares of Microsoft for $40,000 on December 20, 2017, what is her capital gain or loss in each of the following assumptions?

a) She uses the FIFO method.

b) She uses the specific identification method and she wants to minimize her current year capital gain.

42. Karyn loaned $20,000 to her co-worker to begin a new business several years ago. If her co-worker declares bankruptcy on June 22 of the current year, is Karyn allowed to deduct the bad debt loss this year? If she can deduct the loss, what is the character of the loss? LO 7-2

43. Sue has 5,000 shares of Sony stock that have an adjusted basis of $27,500. She sold the 5,000 shares of stock for cash of $10,000, and she also received a piece of land as part of the proceeds. The land was valued at $20,000 and had an adjusted basis to the buyer of $12,000. What is Sue's gain or loss on the sale of 5,000 shares of Sony stock? LO 7-2 research

44. Matt and Meg Comer are married. They do not have any children. Matt works as a history professor at a local university and earns a salary of $64,000. Meg works part-time at the same university. She earns $21,000 a year. The couple does not itemize deductions. Other than salary, the Comers' only other source of income is from the disposition of various capital assets (mostly stocks). LO 7-2

a) What is the Comers' tax liability for 2017 if they report the following capital gains and losses for the year?

Short-term capital gains	$ 9,000
Short-term capital losses	(2,000)
Long-term capital gains	15,000
Long-term capital losses	(6,000)

b) What is the Comers' tax liability for 2017 if they report the following capital gains and losses for the year?

Short-term capital gains	$ 1,500
Short-term capital losses	0
Long-term capital gains	13,000
Long-term capital losses	(10,000)

45. Grayson is in the 25 percent tax rate bracket and has sold the following stocks in 2017: LO 7-2

	Date Purchased	Basis	Date Sold	Amount Realized
Stock A	1/23/1993	$ 7,250	7/22/2017	$ 4,500
Stock B	4/10/2017	14,000	9/13/2017	17,500
Stock C	8/23/2015	10,750	10/12/2017	15,300
Stock D	5/19/2007	5,230	10/12/2017	12,400
Stock E	8/20/2017	7,300	11/14/2017	3,500

a) What is Grayson's net short-term capital gain or loss from these transactions?

b) What is Grayson's net long-term gain or loss from these transactions?

c) What is Grayson's overall net gain or loss from these transactions?

d) What amount of the gain, if any, is subject to the preferential rate for certain capital gains?

LO 7-2 46. George bought the following amounts of Stock A over the years:

	Date Purchased	Number of Shares	Adjusted Basis
Stock A	11/21/1991	1,000	$24,000
Stock A	3/18/1997	500	9,000
Stock A	5/22/2006	750	27,000

On October 12, 2017, he sold 1,200 of his shares of Stock A for $38 per share.

a) How much gain/loss will George have to recognize if he uses the FIFO method of accounting for the shares sold?

b) How much gain/loss will George have to recognize if he specifically identifies the shares to be sold by telling his broker to sell all 750 shares from the 5/22/2006 purchase and 450 shares from the 11/21/1991 purchase?

LO 7-2 47. During the current year, Ron and Anne sold the following assets:

Capital Asset	Market Value	Tax Basis	Holding Period
L stock	$ 50,000	$41,000	> 1 year
M stock	28,000	39,000	> 1 year
N stock	30,000	22,000	< 1 year
O stock	26,000	33,000	< 1 year
Antiques	7,000	4,000	> 1 year
Rental home	300,000*	90,000	> 1 year

*$30,000 of the gain is 25 percent gain (from accumulated depreciation on the property).

a) Given that Ron and Anne have taxable income of only $20,000 (all ordinary) before considering the tax effect of their asset sales, what is their gross tax liability for 2017 assuming they file a joint return?

b) Given that Ron and Anne have taxable income of $400,000 (all ordinary) before considering the tax effect of their asset sales, what is their gross tax liability for 2017 assuming they file a joint return?

LO 7-2 48. In 2017, Tom and Amanda Jackson (married filing jointly) have $200,000 of taxable income before considering the following events:

a) On May 12, 2017, they sold a painting (art) for $110,000 that was inherited from Grandma on July 23, 2015. The fair market value on the date of Grandma's death was $90,000 and Grandma's adjusted basis of the painting was $25,000.

b) They applied a long-term capital loss carryover from 2016 of $10,000.

c) They recognized a $12,000 loss on the 11/1/2017 sale of bonds (acquired on 5/12/2007).

d) They recognized a $4,000 gain on the 12/12/2017 sale of IBM stock (acquired on 2/5/2017).

e) They recognized a $17,000 gain on the 10/17/2017 sale of rental property (the only §1231 transaction) of which $8,000 is reportable as gain subject to the 25 percent maximum rate and the remaining $9,000 is subject to the 0/15/20 percent maximum rates (the property was acquired on 8/2/2011).

f) They recognized a $12,000 loss on the 12/20/2017 sale of bonds (acquired on 1/18/2017).

g) They recognized a $7,000 gain on the 6/27/2017 sale of BH stock (acquired on 7/30/2008).

h) They recognized an $11,000 loss on the 6/13/2017 sale of QuikCo stock (acquired on 3/20/2010).

i) They received $500 of qualified dividends on 7/15/2017.

Complete the required capital gains netting procedures and calculate the Jacksons' 2017 tax liability.

49. For 2017, Sherri has a short-term loss of $2,500 and a long-term loss of $4,750. LO 7-2

a) How much loss can Sherri deduct in 2017?

b) How much loss will Sherri carry over to 2018, and what is the character of the loss carryover?

50. Three years ago, Adrian purchased 100 shares of stock in X Corp. for $10,000. On December 30 of year 4, Adrian sells the 100 shares for $6,000. LO 7-2

a) Assuming Adrian has no other capital gains or losses, how much of the loss is Adrian able to deduct on her year 4 tax return?

b) Assume the same facts as in part (a), except that on January 20 of year 5, Adrian purchases 100 shares of X Corp. stock for $6,000. How much loss from the sale on December 30 of year 4 is deductible on Adrian's year 4 tax return? What basis does Adrian take in the stock purchased on January 20 of ear 5?

51. Christopher sold 100 shares of Cisco stock for $5,500 in the current year. He purchased the shares several years ago for $2,200. Assuming his ordinary income tax rate is 28 percent, and he has no other capital gains or losses, how much tax will he pay on this gain? LO 7-2

52. Christina, who is single, purchased 100 shares of Apple Inc. stock several years ago for $3,500. During her year-end tax planning, she decided to sell 50 shares of Apple for $1,500 on December 30. However, two weeks later, Apple introduced its latest iPhone, and she decided that she should buy the 50 shares (cost of $1,600) of Apple back before prices skyrocket. LO 7-2

a) What is Christina's deductible loss on the sale of 50 shares? What is her basis in the 50 new shares?

b) Assume the same facts, except that Christina repurchased only 25 shares for $800. What is Christina's deductible loss on the sale of 50 shares? What is her basis in the 25 new shares?

53. Arden purchased 300 shares of AMC common stock several years ago for $1,500. On April 30, Arden sold the shares of AMC common for $500 and then purchased 250 shares of AMC preferred stock two days later for $700. The AMC preferred stock is not convertible into AMC common stock. What is Arden's deductible loss from the sale of the 300 shares of AMC common stock? LO 7-2 research

54. Shaun bought 300 shares of Dental Equipment Inc. several years ago for $10,000. Currently the stock is worth $8,000. Shaun's marginal tax rate this year is 25 percent, and he has no other capital gains or losses. Shaun expects to have a marginal rate of 30 percent next year, but he also expects to have a long-term capital gain of $10,000. To minimize taxes, should Shaun sell the stock on December 31 of this year or January 1 of next year (ignore the time value of money)? LO 7-2 planning

55. Becky recently discovered some high-tech cooking technology that has advantages over microwave and traditional ovens. She received a patent on the technology that gives her exclusive rights to the technology for 20 years. Becky would prefer to LO 7-2 research

retain the patent, but she doesn't want to deal with the manufacturing and marketing of the technology. She was able to reach a compromise. A little over a year after she secured the patent, Becky signed a contract with DEF Company giving DEF control to manufacture and market the technology. In exchange, Becky is to receive a royalty based on the sales of the technology. For tax purposes, Becky is not sure how to treat her arrangement with DEF. If the exchange with DEF is treated as a sale, she will recognize long-term capital gain because the patent is a capital asset held for more than a year. If the exchange is not treated as a sale, Becky will recognize ordinary income as she receives the royalties. (*Hint:* See IRC §1235 and http://www.aicpa.org/publications/taxadviser/2013/december/pages/kelley_dec2013.aspx.)

a) Is it possible for Becky to treat the exchange with DEF as a sale even though she never relinquishes actual title of the patent? If so, what requirements must she meet to treat the contract as a sale for tax purposes?

b) Does your answer to the question above change if Becky's contract with DEF gives DEF Company control over the income from the patent for the next 10 years of the patent's remaining 19-year life?

LO 7-3

56. Zach and Melissa Nieland file a joint tax return, and they itemize deductions. Assume their marginal tax rate on ordinary income is 25 percent. The Nielands incur $2,000 in miscellaneous itemized deductions, excluding investment expenses. They also incur $1,000 in noninterest investment expenses during the year. What tax savings do they receive from the investment expenses under the following assumptions:

a) Their AGI is $90,000.

b) Their AGI is $130,000.

LO 7-3

57. Mickey and Jenny Porter file a joint tax return, and they itemize deductions. The Porters incur $2,000 in employment-related miscellaneous itemized deductions. They also incur $3,000 of investment interest expense during the year. The Porters' income for the year consists of $150,000 in salary and $2,500 of interest income.

a) What is the amount of the Porters' investment interest expense deduction for the year?

b) What would their investment interest expense deduction be if they also had a ($2,000) long-term capital loss?

LO 7-3 planning

58. On January 1 of year 1, Nick and Rachel Sutton purchased a parcel of undeveloped land as an investment. The purchase price of the land was $150,000. They paid for the property by making a down payment of $50,000 and borrowing $100,000 from the bank at an interest rate of 6 percent per year. At the end of the first year, the Suttons paid $6,000 of interest to the bank. During year 1, the Suttons' only source of income was salary. On December 31 of year 2, the Suttons paid $6,000 of interest to the bank and sold the land for $210,000. They used $100,000 of the sale proceeds to pay off the $100,000 loan. The Suttons itemize deductions and are subject to a marginal ordinary income tax rate of 35 percent.

a) Should the Suttons treat the capital gain from the land sale as investment income in year 2 in order to minimize their year 2 tax bill? If so, how much could the Suttons save?

b) How much does this cost or save them in year 2?

LO 7-3 research

59. George recently received a great stock tip from his friend, Mason. George didn't have any cash on hand to invest, so he decided to take out a $20,000 loan to facilitate the stock acquisition. The loan terms are 8 percent interest with interest-only payments due each year for five years. At the end of the five-year

period the entire loan principal is due. When George closed on the loan on April 1, 2017, he decided to invest $16,000 in stock and to use the remaining $4,000 to purchase a four-wheel recreation vehicle. George is unsure how he will treat the interest paid on the $20,000 loan. In 2017, George paid $1,200 interest expense on the loan. For tax purposes, how should he treat the 2017 interest expense? (*Hint:* Visit www.irs.gov and consider IRS Publication 550.)

60. Larry recently invested $20,000 (tax basis) in purchasing a limited partnership interest. His at-risk amount is also $20,000. In addition, Larry's share of the limited partnership loss for the year is $2,000, his share of income from a different limited partnership is $1,000, and he has $3,000 of dividend income from the stock he owns. How much of Larry's $2,000 loss from the limited partnership can he deduct in the current year? LO 7-4

61. Rubio recently invested $20,000 (tax basis) in purchasing a limited partnership interest. His at-risk amount is $15,000. In addition, Rubio's share of the limited partnership loss for the year is $22,000, his share of income from a different limited partnership is $5,000, and he has $40,000 in wage income and $10,000 in long-term capital gains. LO 7-4
   a) How much of Rubio's $22,000 loss is allowed considering only the tax-basis loss limitations?
   b) How much of the loss from part (a) is allowed under the at-risk limitations?
   c) How much of Rubio's $22,000 loss from the limited partnership can he deduct in the current year considering all limitations?

62. Molly Grey (single) acquired a 30 percent limited partnership interest in Beau Geste LLP several years ago for $48,000. At the beginning of year 1, Molly has tax basis and an at-risk amount of $20,000. In year 1, Beau Geste incurs a loss of $180,000 and does not make any distributions to the partners. LO 7-4
   - In year 1, Molly's AGI (excluding any income or loss from Beau Geste) is $60,000. This includes $10,000 of passive income from other passive activities.
   - In year 2, Beau Geste earns income of $30,000. In addition, Molly contributes an additional $30,000 to Beau Geste during year 2. Molly's AGI in year 2 is $63,000 (excluding any income or loss from Beau Geste). This amount includes $8,000 in income from her other passive investments.

   a) Based on the above information, determine the following amounts:
      - At-risk amount at the end of year 1.
      - At-risk amount at the end of year 2.
      - Losses allowed under the at-risk rules in year 2.
      - Total suspended passive losses at the end of year 1.
      - Total suspended at-risk losses at the end of year 2.
      - Deductible losses in year 1.
      - Year 2 AGI after considering Beau Geste events.

   b) Briefly describe actions Molly Grey could undertake in year 2 to utilize any suspended passive losses from year 1.

63. Anwer owns a rental home and is involved in maintaining it and approving renters. During the year he has a net loss of $8,000 from renting the home. His other sources of income during the year are a salary of $111,000 and $34,000 of long-term capital gains. How much of Anwer's $8,000 rental loss can he deduct currently if he has no sources of passive income? LO 7-4

COMPREHENSIVE PROBLEMS

Select problems are available in Connect®.

tax forms

64. During 2017, your clients, Mr. and Mrs. Howell, owned the following investment assets:

Investment Assets	Date Acquired	Purchase Price	Broker's Commission Paid at Time of Purchase
300 shares of IBM common	11/22/14	$ 10,350	$ 100
200 shares of IBM common	4/3/15	43,250	300
3,000 shares of Apple preferred	12/12/15	147,000	1,300
2,100 shares of Cisco common	8/14/16	52,500	550
420 shares of Vanguard mutual fund	3/2/17	14,700	No load fund*

*No commissions are charged when no load mutual funds are bought and sold.

Because of the downturn in the stock market, Mr. and Mrs. Howell decided to sell most of their stocks and the mutual fund in 2017 and to reinvest in municipal bonds. The following investment assets were sold in 2017:

Investment Assets	Date Sold	Sale Price	Broker's Commission Paid at Time of Sale
300 shares of IBM common	5/6	$ 13,700	$ 100
3,000 shares of Apple preferred	10/5	221,400	2,000
2,100 shares of Cisco common	8/15	63,250	650
451 Shares of Vanguard mutual fund	12/21	15,700	No load fund*

*No commissions are charged when no load mutual funds are bought and sold.

The Howells' broker issued them a Form 1099-B showing the sales proceeds net of the commissions paid. For example, the IBM sales proceeds were reported as $13,600 on the Form 1099-B they received.

In addition to the sales reflected in the table above, the Howells provided you with the following additional information concerning 2017:

- The Howells received a Form 1099-B from the Vanguard mutual fund reporting a $900 long-term capital gain distribution. This distribution was reinvested in 31 additional Vanguard mutual fund shares on 6/30/2017.
- In 2012, Mrs. Howell loaned $6,000 to a friend who was starting a new multilevel marketing company called LD3. The friend declared bankruptcy in 2017, and Mrs. Howell has been notified she will not be receiving any repayment of the loan.
- The Howells have a $2,300 short-term capital loss carryover and a $4,800 long-term capital loss carryover from prior years.
- The Howells did not instruct their broker to sell any particular lot of IBM stock.
- The Howells earned $3,000 in municipal bond interest, $3,000 in interest from corporate bonds, and $4,000 in qualified dividends.
- Assume the Howells have $130,000 of wage income during the year.

a) Go to the IRS website (www.irs.gov) and download the most current version of Form 8949 and Schedule D. Use Form 8949 and page 1 of Schedule D to compute net long-term and short-term capital gains. Then, compute the Howells' tax liability for the year (ignoring the alternative minimum tax and any phase-out provisions) assuming they file a joint return, they have no dependents, they don't make any special tax elections, and their itemized deductions total $25,000. Assume that asset bases are reported to the IRS.

b) Are there any tax planning recommendations related to the stock sales that you should have shared with the Howells before their decision to sell?

c) Assume the Howells' short-term capital loss carryover from prior years is $82,300 rather than $2,300 as indicated above. If this is the case, how much short-term and long-term capital loss carryover remains to be carried beyond 2017 to future tax years?

ROGER | *CPA Review*

Sample CPA Exam questions from Roger CPA Review are available in Connect as support for the topics in this text. These Multiple Choice Questions and Task-Based Simulations include expert-written explanations and solutions, and provide a starting point for students to become familiar with the content and functionality of the actual CPA Exam.

chapter 8

Individual Income Tax Computation and Tax Credits

Learning Objectives

Upon completing this chapter, you should be able to:

LO 8-1 Determine a taxpayer's regular tax liability and identify tax issues associated with the process.

LO 8-2 Compute a taxpayer's alternative minimum tax liability and describe the tax characteristics of taxpayers most likely to owe the alternative minimum tax.

LO 8-3 Calculate a taxpayer's employment and self-employment taxes payable and explain tax considerations relating to whether a taxpayer is considered to be an employee or a self-employed independent contractor.

LO 8-4 Describe the different general types of tax credits, identify specific tax credits, and compute a taxpayer's allowable child tax credit, child and dependent care credit, American opportunity credit, lifetime learning credit, and earned income credit.

LO 8-5 Explain taxpayer filing and tax payment requirements and describe in general terms how to compute a taxpayer's underpayment, late filing, and late payment penalties.

© Image Source

Storyline Summary

Taxpayers:	Courtney Wilson, age 40, Courtney's mother Dorothy "Gram" Weiss, age 70
Family description:	Courtney is divorced with a son, Deron, age 10, and a daughter, Ellen, age 20. Gram is currently residing with Courtney.
Location:	Kansas City, Missouri
Employment status:	Courtney works as an architect for EWD. Gram is retired.
Filing status:	Courtney is head of household. Gram is single.
Current situation:	Courtney and Gram have computed their taxable income. Now they are trying to determine their tax liability, tax refund or additional taxes due, and whether they owe any payment-related penalties.

Courtney has already determined her taxable income. Now she's working on computing her tax liability. She knows she owes a significant amount of regular income tax on her employment and business activities. However, she's not sure how to compute the tax on the qualified dividends she received from General Electric. Courtney is worried that she may be subject to the alternative minimum tax this year because she's heard that an increasing number of taxpayers in her income range must pay the tax. Finally, Courtney knows she owes some self-employment taxes on her business income. Courtney would like to determine whether she is eligible to claim any tax credits such as the child tax credit for her two children and education credits because she paid for a portion of her daughter Ellen's tuition at the University of Missouri–Kansas City this year. Courtney is hoping that she has paid enough in taxes during the year to avoid underpayment penalties. She's planning on filing her tax return and paying her taxes on time.

Gram's tax situation is much more straightforward. She needs to determine the regular income tax on her taxable income. Her income is so low she knows she need not worry about the alternative minimum tax, and she believes she doesn't owe any self-employment tax. Gram didn't prepay any taxes this year, so she is concerned that she might be required to pay an underpayment penalty. She also expects to file her tax return and pay her taxes by the looming due date.

to be continued . . .

In prior chapters we've learned how to compute taxable income for taxpayers such as Courtney and Gram. This chapter describes how to determine a taxpayer's tax liability for the year. We discover that the process is not as easy as simply applying taxable income to the applicable tax rate schedule or tax table. Taxpayers may generate taxable income that is taxed at rates not provided in the tax rate schedules or tax tables. We will learn that they may also be required to pay taxes in addition to the regular income tax. We also describe tax credits taxpayers may use to reduce their gross taxes payable. We conclude the chapter by describing taxpayer filing requirements and identifying certain penalties taxpayers may be required to pay when they underpay or are late paying their taxes. We start our coverage by explaining how to compute one's regular tax liability.

LO 8-1

REGULAR FEDERAL INCOME TAX COMPUTATION

When taxpayers have determined their taxable income, they are ready to compute their gross tax from a series of progressive tax rates called a **tax rate schedule.**

Tax Rate Schedules

Congress has constructed four different tax rate schedules for individuals. The applicable tax rate schedule is determined by the taxpayer's filing status, which we discussed in depth in the Individual Income Tax Overview, Exemptions, and Filing Status chapter. Recall that a taxpayer's filing status is one of the following:

1. Married filing jointly.
2. Qualifying widow or widower, also referred to as surviving spouse.
3. Married filing separately.
4. Head of household.
5. Single.

As we described in the An Introduction to Tax chapter, a tax rate schedule is composed of several ranges of income taxed at different (increasing) rates. Each separate range of income subject to a different tax rate is referred to as a **tax bracket.** While each filing status has its own tax rate schedule (married filing jointly and qualifying widow or widower use the same rate schedule), all tax rate schedules consist of tax brackets taxed at 10 percent, 15 percent, 25 percent, 28 percent, 33 percent, 35 percent, and 39.6 percent. However, the width or range of income within each bracket varies by filing status. In general, the tax brackets are widest and higher levels of income are taxed at the lowest rates for the married filing jointly filing status, followed by the head of household filing status, single filing status, and finally, the married filing separately filing status.

The tax rate schedule for each filing status is provided in Appendix D. Notice that the married filing separately schedule is the same as the married filing jointly schedule except that the taxable income levels listed in the schedule are exactly one-half the taxable income levels for married filing jointly.

Example 8-1

As we determined in the Individual Deductions chapter, Courtney files under the head of household filing status and her 2017 taxable income is $129,961 (see Exhibit 6-14).

What if: For now, let's *assume* that all of Courtney's income is taxed as ordinary income. That is, assume that none of her income is taxed at a preferential rate (some is, but we'll address this in a bit). What is the tax on her taxable income?

Answer: $26,743. Using the head of household tax rate schedule, her taxable income falls in the 25 percent marginal tax rate bracket, in between $50,800 and $131,200, so her tax is computed as follows:

Description	Amount	Explanation
(1) Base tax	$ 6,952.50	From head of household tax rate schedule for taxpayer with taxable income in 25% bracket.
(2) Income taxed at marginal tax rate	79,161	$129,961 – 50,800 from head of household tax rate schedule.
(3) Marginal tax rate	25%	From head of household tax rate schedule.
(4) Tax on income at marginal tax rate	19,790.25	(2) × (3)
Tax on taxable income	**$26,743**	(1) + (4), rounded

Example 8-2

As we determined in the Individual Deductions chapter, Gram files under the single filing status. In the Individual Deductions chapter we calculated her 2017 taxable income to be $3,640 (see Exhibit 6-15). None of her income is taxed at a preferential rate. What is the tax on her taxable income using the tax rate schedules?

Answer: $364 ($3,640 × 10%)

For administrative convenience and to prevent low- and middle-income taxpayers from making mathematical errors using a tax rate schedule, the IRS provides **tax tables** that present the gross tax for various amounts of taxable income under $100,000 and filing status (it's impractical to provide a table for essentially unlimited amounts of income). Taxpayers with taxable income less than $100,000 generally must use the tax tables to determine their tax liability.[1]

Because the tax tables generate nearly the same tax as calculated from the tax rate schedule, we use the tax rate schedules throughout this chapter.

Marriage Penalty or Benefit

An interesting artifact of the tax rate schedules is that they can impose what some refer to as a **marriage penalty,** but they may actually produce a **marriage benefit.** A marriage penalty (benefit) occurs when, for a given level of income, a married couple has a greater (lesser) tax liability when they use the married filing jointly tax rate schedule to determine the tax on their joint income than they would have owed (in total) if each spouse would have used the single tax rate schedule to compute the tax on each spouse's individual income. Exhibit 8-1 explores the marriage penalty in a scenario in which both spouses earn income and another in which only one spouse earns income. As the exhibit illustrates, the marriage penalty applies to couples with two wage earners, but a marriage benefit applies to couples with single breadwinners.

Exceptions to the Basic Tax Computation

In certain circumstances, taxpayers cannot completely determine their final tax liability from their tax rate schedule or tax table. Taxpayers must perform additional computations to determine their tax liability (1) when they recognize long-term capital gains or receive dividends that are taxed at preferential (lower) rates, (2) when they receive investment income subject to the net investment income tax, or (3) when the taxpayer is a child and the child's unearned income is taxed at her parent's **marginal tax rate.** We describe these additional computations in detail below.

[1]Exceptions to this requirement include taxpayers subject to the kiddie tax, with qualified dividends or capital gains, or claiming the foreign-earned income exclusion. You may view the tax tables in the instructions for Form 1040 located at www.irs.gov/.

EXHIBIT 8-1 2017 Marriage Penalty (Benefit): Two-Income vs. Single-Income Married Couple*

Married Couple	Taxable Income	Tax If Filing Jointly (1)	Tax If Filing Single† (2)	Marriage Penalty (Benefit) (1) − (2)
Scenario 1: *Two wage earners*				
Wife	$100,000		$20,981.75	
Husband	100,000		$20,981.75	
Combined	$200,000	$42,884.50	$41,963.50	$921
Scenario 2: *One wage earner*				
Wife	$200,000		$49,399.25	
Husband	0		0	
Combined	$200,000	$42,884.50	$49,399.25	($6,514.75)

*This analysis assumes the taxpayers do not owe any alternative minimum tax (discussed below).

†Married couples do not actually have the option of filing as single. If they choose not to file jointly they must file as married filing separately.

Preferential Tax Rates for Capital Gains and Dividends As we described in detail in the Investments chapter, certain capital gains and certain dividends are taxed at a lower or **preferential tax rate** relative to other types of income. In general, the preferential tax rate is 0 percent, 15 percent, or 20 percent. The preferential tax rate is 0 percent *to the extent* the income would have been taxed in the 10 percent or 15 percent tax rate bracket if it were ordinary income, 20 percent to the extent the income would have been taxed in the 39.6 percent tax rate bracket if it were ordinary income, and 15 percent for all other taxpayers.[2] The tax rate tables and tax rate schedules allow taxpayers to compute their tax on ordinary but not **preferentially taxed income.** This is true even though preferentially taxed income is included in adjusted gross income (AGI) and in taxable income. Taxpayers with income subject to the preferential rate (long-term capital gains and qualified dividends) can use the following three-step process to determine their tax liability.

Step 1: Split taxable income into the portion that is subject to the preferential rate and the portion taxed at the ordinary rates.

Step 2: Compute the tax separately on each type of income. Note that the income that is not taxed at the preferential rate is taxed at the ordinary tax rates using the tax rate schedule for the taxpayer's filing status.

Step 3: Add the tax on the income subject to the preferential tax rates and the tax on the income subject to the ordinary rates. This is the taxpayer's regular tax liability.

Example 8-3

Courtney's taxable income of $129,961 includes $700 of qualified dividends from GE (Exhibit 5-4). What is her tax liability on her taxable income?

Answer: $26,673, computed at head of household rates as follows:

Description	Amount	Explanation
(1) Taxable income	$129,961	Exhibit 6-14
(2) Preferentially taxed income	700	Exhibit 5-4
(3) Income taxed at ordinary rates	$129,261	(1) − (2)

[2]As we discovered in the Investments chapter, some types of income may be taxed at a preferential rate of 28 percent or 25 percent. In addition, as we discuss later in this chapter, dividends and capital gains for higher income taxpayers are subject to the 3.8% net investment income tax.

Description	Amount	Explanation
(4) Tax on income taxed at ordinary rates	26,567.75	[$6,952.50 + (129,261 – 50,800) × 25%]
(5) Tax on preferentially taxed income	105	(2) × 15% [Note that if (2) were ordinary income it would have been taxed at 25 percent.]
Tax on taxable income	**$26,673**	(4) + (5), rounded

In this example, what is Courtney's tax savings from having the dividends taxed at the preferential rate rather than the ordinary rate?

Answer: $70. $700 × (25% – 15%). This is the amount of the dividend times the difference in the ordinary and preferential tax rate.

What if: Assume that Courtney's taxable income is $454,550, including $15,000 of qualified dividends taxed at the preferential rate. What would be Courtney's tax liability under these circumstances?

Answer: $127,950, computed using the head of household tax rate schedule as follows:

Description	Amount	Explanation
(1) Taxable income	$ 454,550	
(2) Preferentially taxed income	15,000	
(3) Income taxed at ordinary rates	439,550	(1) – (2)
(4) Tax on income at ordinary tax rates	125,200	$117,202.50 + [($439,550 – $416,700) × 35%] (See tax rate schedule for head of household.)
(5) Tax on preferentially taxed income	2,750	[($5,000 × 15%) + ($10,000 × 20%)]*
Tax	**$127,950**	(4) + (5)

*Courtney had $15,000 of preferentially taxed income. If this income was ordinary income, $5,000 would have been taxed at 35 percent [$444,550 (end of 35 percent bracket) – $439,550 (ordinary taxable income)] and the remaining $10,000 would have been taxed at 39.6 percent [$454,550 (total taxable income) – $444,550 (end of 35 percent bracket)]. Consequently, $5,000 of the preferential income is taxed at 15 percent and the remaining $10,000 is taxed at 20 percent.

Net Investment Income Tax Higher-income taxpayers are required to pay a 3.8 percent tax on **net investment income.** For purposes of the **net investment income tax,** net investment income equals the sum of:

1. Gross income from interest, dividends, annuities, royalties, and rents (unless these items are derived in a trade or business to which the net investment income tax does not apply).
2. Income from a trade or business that is a passive activity or a trade or business of trading financial instruments or commodities.
3. Net gain from disposing of property (other than property held in a trade or business in which the net investment income tax does not apply).[3]
4. Less the allowable deductions that are allocable to items 1, 2, and 3.

Tax-exempt interest, veterans' benefits, excluded gain from the sale of a principal residence, distributions from qualified retirement plans, and any amounts subject to self-employment tax are not subject to the net investment income tax.

The tax imposed is 3.8 percent of the lesser of (1) net investment income or (2) the excess of modified adjusted gross income over $250,000 for married joint filers and surviving spouses, $125,000 for married separate filers, and $200,000 for other taxpayers.

[3]However, the income, gain, or loss attributable to invested working capital of a trade or business is subject to the net investment income tax. §1411(c)(3).

Modified adjusted gross income equals adjusted gross income increased by income excluded under the foreign-earned income exclusion less any disallowed deductions associated with the foreign-earned income exclusion.[4]

Example 8-4

Courtney's AGI (and modified AGI) is $182,000, and her investment income consists of $617 of taxable interest, $700 of dividends, and $5,000 of rental income. How much net investment income tax will Courtney owe?

Answer: $0. Because Courtney's modified AGI ($182,000) is less than the $200,000 threshold for the net investment income tax for a taxpayer filing as head of household, she will not be subject to the tax.

What if: Assume that Courtney's AGI (and modified AGI) is $225,000. How much net investment income tax will Courtney owe?

Answer: $240, calculated as follows:

Description	Amount	Explanation
(1) Net investment income	$ 6,317	$617 interest + $700 dividends + $5,000 rental income
(2) Modified AGI	225,000	
(3) Modified AGI threshold	200,000	
(4) Excess modified AGI above threshold	25,000	(2) − (3)
(5) Net investment income tax base	6,317	Lesser of (1) or (4)
Net investment income tax	**240**	(5) × 3.8%

Kiddie Tax Parents can reduce their family's income tax bill by shifting income that would otherwise be taxed at their higher tax rates to their children whose income is taxed at lower rates. However, as we described in the Gross Income and Exclusions chapter, under the assignment of income doctrine, taxpayers cannot simply assign or transfer income to other parties. Earned income, or income from services or labor, is taxed to the person who earns it. Thus, it's difficult for a parent to shift *earned* income to a child. However, unearned income or income from property such as dividends from stocks or interest from bonds is taxed to the *owner* of the property. Thus, a parent can shift unearned income to a child by transferring actual ownership of the income-producing property to the child. By transferring ownership, the parent runs the risk that the child will sell the asset or use it in a way unintended by the parent. However, this risk is relatively small for parents transferring property ownership to younger children.

The tax laws reduce parents' ability to shift unearned income to children through the so-called **kiddie tax.** The kiddie tax provisions apply (or potentially apply) to a child if (1) the child is under 18 years old at year-end, (2) the child is 18 at year-end but her earned income does *not* exceed half of her support, or (3) the child is over age 18 but under age 24 at year-end, is a full-time student during the year, and her earned income does not exceed half of her support (excluding scholarships).[5] The kiddie tax does not apply to a child filing a joint tax return or to a child without living parents.

In general terms, if the kiddie tax applies, children must pay tax on a certain amount of their unearned income (their **net unearned income,** discussed below) at their parents' marginal tax rate rather than at their own marginal tax rate, unless the parents' marginal tax rate on the income (the preferential tax rate if the income is long-term capital gain or qualified dividends) would be lower than the child's marginal tax rate.[6] When the parents

[4]Taxpayers compute the net investment income tax using Form 8960.

[5]§1(g)(2)(A).

[6]§1(g).

of the child are not married, this provision applies to the custodial parent.[7] That is, the kiddie tax will never allow children to pay less tax than they would have been required to pay without the kiddie tax provision.

The kiddie tax base is the child's net unearned income. Net unearned income is the *lesser* of (1) the child's gross *unearned income* minus $2,100[8] or (2) the child's taxable income (the child is not taxed on more than her taxable income).[9] Consequently, the kiddie tax does not apply unless the child has *unearned* income in *excess* of $2,100.[10] Thus the kiddie tax significantly limits, but does not eliminate, the tax benefit gained by a family unit when parents transfer income-producing assets to children.

Example 8-5

What if: Suppose that during 2017, Deron received $1,100 in interest from the IBM bond, and he received another $2,200 in interest income from a money market account that his parents have been contributing to over the years. Is Deron potentially subject to the kiddie tax?

Answer: Yes, Deron is younger than 18 years old at the end of the year and his net unearned income exceeds $2,100.

What is Deron's taxable income and corresponding tax liability?

Answer: $2,250 taxable income and $405 tax liability, calculated as follows:

Description	Amount	Explanation
(1) Gross income/AGI	$ 3,300	$1,100 interest from IBM bond + $2,200 interest. All unearned income.
(2) Standard deduction	1,050	Minimum for taxpayer claimed as a dependent on another return (no earned income, so must use minimum). See the Individual Deductions chapter.
(3) Personal exemption	0	Claimed as a dependent on Courtney's return.
(4) Taxable income	**$2,250**	(1) – (2) – (3)
(5) Gross unearned income minus $2,100	1,200	(1) – 2,100
(6) Net unearned income	$ 1,200	Lesser of (4) or (5)
(7) Courtney's ordinary marginal rate	25%	See Example 8-3 (Use Courtney's rate because she is the custodial parent.)
(8) Kiddie tax	$ 300	(6) × (7) (Deron's income taxed at Courtney's marginal rate.)
(9) Taxable income taxed at Deron's rate	1,050	(4) – (6)
(10) Tax on taxable income using Deron's tax rates	$ 105	(9) × 10% (See single filing status, $1,050 taxable income.)
Deron's total tax liability	**$ 405**	(8) + (10)

What if: Assume Deron's only source of income is qualified dividends of $2,200 (unearned income). What is his taxable income and tax liability?

(continued on page 8-8)

THE KEY FACTS

Tax Rates

- Regular tax rates
  - Schedule depends on filing status.
  - Progressive tax rate schedules with tax rates ranging from 10 percent to 39.6 percent.
  - Marriage penalty (benefit) occurs because dual-earning spouses pay more (less) combined tax than if they each filed single.
- Preferential tax rates
  - Net long-term capital gains and qualified dividends generally taxed at 0 percent, 15 percent, or 20 percent.
- Net investment income tax
  - 3.8 percent tax on lesser of (a) net investment income or (b) excess of modified AGI over applicable threshold based on filing status.
- Kiddie tax
  - Unearned income in excess of $2,100 is taxed at parent's marginal tax rate if child is (1) under age 18, (2) 18 but earned income does not exceed one-half of support, or (3) over 18 and under 24, full-time student, and earned income does not exceed one-half of support.

[7]§1(g)(5).

[8]The $2,100 consists of $1,050 of the child's standard deduction (even if the child is entitled to a larger standard deduction) plus an *extra* $1,050. See the Individual Deductions chapter for a discussion of the standard deduction for the dependent of another taxpayer. If the child itemizes deductions, then the calculation becomes more complex and is beyond the scope of this text.

[9]§1(g)(4).

[10]Under §1(g)(7), subject to certain requirements, parents may elect to include their child's unearned income on their own tax return (on Form 8814).

Answer: Taxable income is $1,150; tax liability is $15, computed as follows:

Description	Amount	Explanation
(1) Gross income/(AGI)	$ 2,200	Qualified dividends, all unearned income.
(2) Minimum standard	1,050	Minimum for taxpayer claimed as a dependent deduction on another return (all unearned income, so must use minimum). See the Individual Deductions chapter.
(3) Personal exemption	0	Claimed as a dependent on Courtney's return.
(4) Taxable income	**$1,150**	(1) – (2) – (3)
(5) Gross unearned income minus $2,100	100	(1) – $2,100
(6) Net unearned income	$ 100	Lesser of (4) or (5)

Description	Amount	Explanation
(7) Courtney's marginal tax rate on qualified dividend income	15%	See Example 8-3. (Her marginal rate on ordinary income is 25%, so her marginal rate on preferentially taxed income is 15%.)
(8) Kiddie tax	$ 15	(6) × (7) (Deron's income taxed at Courtney's marginal rate on the dividend income.)
(9) Taxable income taxed at Deron's rate	1,050	(4) – (6)
(10) Tax on taxable income using Deron's tax rates	$ 0	(9) × 0% (Deron's marginal rate on the dividend would be 10% if it were ordinary income, so he qualifies for 0% rate on dividend.)
Deron's total tax liability	**$ 15**	(8) + (10)

As we've just described, all individual taxpayers must pay federal income taxes on their federal taxable income. However, taxpayers may be liable for other federal taxes in addition to the regular tax liability. Many taxpayers are also required to pay the alternative minimum tax, and some working taxpayers are required to pay employment or self-employment taxes. We delve into these additional taxes below.

LO 8-2

ALTERNATIVE MINIMUM TAX

Each year, a number of taxpayers are required to pay the **alternative minimum tax (AMT)** in *addition to* their *regular* tax liability. The **alternative minimum tax system** was implemented in 1986 (earlier variations date back to the late 1960s) to ensure that taxpayers generating income pay some *minimum* amount of income tax each year. The tax was originally targeted at higher-income taxpayers who were benefiting from or were perceived by the public to be benefiting from the *excessive* use (more than Congress intended) of tax preference items such as exclusions, deferrals, and deductions to reduce or even eliminate their tax liabilities. However, as currently structured, the tax forces many taxpayers who don't fit this description to pay the tax.

In general terms, the alternative minimum tax is a tax on an *alternative* tax base meant to more closely reflect economic income than the regular income tax base. Thus the **alternative minimum tax (AMT) base** is more inclusive (or more broadly defined) than is the regular income tax base. To compute their AMT, taxpayers first compute their regular income tax liability. Then, they compute the AMT base and multiply the base by the applicable alternative tax rate.[11] They must pay the AMT only when the tax on the AMT base exceeds their regular tax liability.

[11]The rate of the alternative minimum tax (AMT) was set below that of the income tax with the objective of avoiding the perception that the AMT was an additional assessment.

Alternative Minimum Tax Formula

Regular taxable income is the starting point for determining the alternative minimum tax. As the AMT formula in Exhibit 8-2 illustrates, taxpayers make several "plus" and "minus" adjustments to regular taxable income to compute alternative minimum taxable income (AMTI). They then arrive at the AMT base by subtracting an AMT exemption from AMTI. Taxpayers multiply the AMT base by the AMT rate to determine their **tentative minimum tax.** Finally, to determine their alternative minimum tax, taxpayers subtract their regular tax liability from the tentative minimum tax. The alternative minimum tax is the *excess* of the tentative minimum tax over the regular tax. If the regular tax liability equals or exceeds the tentative minimum tax, taxpayers need not pay any AMT. Individual taxpayers compute their AMT on Form 6251 (see Exhibit 8-3).

Alternative Minimum Taxable Income (AMTI) In order to compute alternative minimum taxable income (AMTI), taxpayers make several **alternative minimum tax adjustments** to regular taxable income. Many of these are plus adjustments that are added to regular taxable income to reach AMTI and some are minus adjustments that are subtracted from regular taxable income to determine AMTI. Consequently, these adjustments tend to expand the regular income tax base to more closely reflect economic income.

Exemptions, standard deduction, and itemized deduction phase-out. Taxpayers first add back to regular taxable income the amount of personal and dependency exemptions they actually deducted, after considering phase-outs, in determining their regular taxable income. The exemption deduction is added back because it does not represent an actual economic outflow. Next, taxpayers add back the standard deduction amount, but only *if they deducted it* in determining taxable income. Again, just like exemptions, taxpayers add back the standard deduction because it is a deduction that does not reflect an actual economic outflow from the taxpayer.[12] Finally, taxpayers *subtract* the amount of itemized deductions they incurred but did not deduct because the deductions were phased-out or reduced for regular tax purposes (see discussion in the Individual Deductions chapter). The phase-out is subtracted because it represents an economic outflow that did not reduce taxable income.

EXHIBIT 8-2 Formula for Computing the Alternative Minimum Tax

	Regular Taxable Income
Plus:	Personal exemptions and standard deduction if taxpayer deducted the standard deduction in computing regular taxable income
Minus:	Phase-out of itemized deductions for regular tax purposes (if applicable)
Plus or Minus:	Other adjustments*
	Alternative minimum taxable income
Minus:	AMT exemption amount (if any)
Equals:	Tax base for AMT
Times:	AMT rate
Equals:	Tentative minimum tax
Minus:	Regular tax
Equals:	Alternative minimum tax

*Technically, some of these adjustments are referred to as preference items and some are referred to as adjustments. We refer to all of these items as adjustments for simplicity's sake.

[12]The AMT add back of personal and dependency exemptions and the standard deduction is accomplished on Form 6251 by beginning with taxable income before personal and dependency exemptions (and before the standard deduction if the taxpayer does not itemize).

EXHIBIT 8-3 2016 Form 6251 (Page 1 of 2)

Form **6251**

Department of the Treasury
Internal Revenue Service (99)

Alternative Minimum Tax—Individuals

▶ Information about Form 6251 and its separate instructions is at *www.irs.gov/form6251.*
▶ Attach to Form 1040 or Form 1040NR.

OMB No. 1545-0074
2016
Attachment Sequence No. 32

Name(s) shown on Form 1040 or Form 1040NR | **Your social security number**

Part I **Alternative Minimum Taxable Income** (See instructions for how to complete each line.)

1	If filing Schedule A (Form 1040), enter the amount from Form 1040, line 41, and go to line 2. Otherwise, enter the amount from Form 1040, line 38, and go to line 7. (If less than zero, enter as a negative amount.)	1	
2	Medical and dental. If you or your spouse was 65 or older, enter the **smaller** of Schedule A (Form 1040), line 4, **or** 2.5% (0.025) of Form 1040, line 38. If zero or less, enter -0-	2	
3	Taxes from Schedule A (Form 1040), line 9	3	
4	Enter the home mortgage interest adjustment, if any, from line 6 of the worksheet in the instructions for this line	4	
5	Miscellaneous deductions from Schedule A (Form 1040), line 27	5	
6	If Form 1040, line 38, is $155,650 or less, enter -0-. Otherwise, see instructions	6	( )
7	Tax refund from Form 1040, line 10 or line 21	7	( )
8	Investment interest expense (difference between regular tax and AMT)	8	
9	Depletion (difference between regular tax and AMT)	9	
10	Net operating loss deduction from Form 1040, line 21. Enter as a positive amount	10	
11	Alternative tax net operating loss deduction	11	( )
12	Interest from specified private activity bonds exempt from the regular tax	12	
13	Qualified small business stock, see instructions	13	
14	Exercise of incentive stock options (excess of AMT income over regular tax income)	14	
15	Estates and trusts (amount from Schedule K-1 (Form 1041), box 12, code A)	15	
16	Electing large partnerships (amount from Schedule K-1 (Form 1065-B), box 6)	16	
17	Disposition of property (difference between AMT and regular tax gain or loss)	17	
18	Depreciation on assets placed in service after 1986 (difference between regular tax and AMT)	18	
19	Passive activities (difference between AMT and regular tax income or loss)	19	
20	Loss limitations (difference between AMT and regular tax income or loss)	20	
21	Circulation costs (difference between regular tax and AMT)	21	
22	Long-term contracts (difference between AMT and regular tax income)	22	
23	Mining costs (difference between regular tax and AMT)	23	
24	Research and experimental costs (difference between regular tax and AMT)	24	
25	Income from certain installment sales before January 1, 1987	25	( )
26	Intangible drilling costs preference	26	
27	Other adjustments, including income-based related adjustments	27	
28	**Alternative minimum taxable income.** Combine lines 1 through 27. (If married filing separately and line 28 is more than $247,450, see instructions.)	28	

Part II **Alternative Minimum Tax (AMT)**

29 Exemption. (If you were under age 24 at the end of 2016, see instructions.)

IF your filing status is . . .	**AND line 28 is not over . . .**	**THEN enter on line 29 . . .**
Single or head of household	$119,700	$53,900
Married filing jointly or qualifying widow(er)	159,700	83,800
Married filing separately	79,850	41,900

If line 28 is **over** the amount shown above for your filing status, see instructions. — **29**

30	Subtract line 29 from line 28. If more than zero, go to line 31. If zero or less, enter -0- here and on lines 31, 33, and 35, and go to line 34	30	
31	• If you are filing Form 2555 or 2555-EZ, see instructions for the amount to enter. • If you reported capital gain distributions directly on Form 1040, line 13; you reported qualified dividends on Form 1040, line 9b; **or** you had a gain on both lines 15 and 16 of Schedule D (Form 1040) (as refigured for the AMT, if necessary), complete Part III on the back and enter the amount from line 64 here. • **All others:** If line 30 is $186,300 or less ($93,150 or less if married filing separately), multiply line 30 by 26% (0.26). Otherwise, multiply line 30 by 28% (0.28) and subtract $3,726 ($1,863 if married filing separately) from the result.	31	
32	Alternative minimum tax foreign tax credit (see instructions)	32	
33	Tentative minimum tax. Subtract line 32 from line 31	33	
34	Add Form 1040, line 44 (minus any tax from Form 4972), and Form 1040, line 46. Subtract from the result any foreign tax credit from Form 1040, line 48. If you used Schedule J to figure your tax on Form 1040, line 44, refigure that tax without using Schedule J before completing this line (see instructions)	34	
35	**AMT.** Subtract line 34 from line 33. If zero or less, enter -0-. Enter here and on Form 1040, line 45	35	

For Paperwork Reduction Act Notice, see your tax return instructions. Cat. No. 13600G Form **6251** (2016)

Example 8-6

Courtney started the process of determining whether she owed any AMT by adjusting her regular taxable income for her exemptions. What is Courtney's AMTI before other adjustments?

Answer: $142,111, computed as follows:

Description	Amount	Explanation
(1) Taxable income	$ 129,961	Exhibit 6-14
(2) Exemptions	12,150	Exhibit 6-14
AMTI before other adjustments	**$142,111**	(1) + (2)

Other adjustments. Taxpayers are required to make several other adjustments to compute AMTI. Exhibit 8-4 describes the most common of these adjustments.

EXHIBIT 8-4 Common AMT Adjustments

Adjustment	Description
Plus adjustments:	
Tax-exempt interest from private activity bonds	Taxpayers must add back interest income that was excluded for regular tax purposes if the bonds were used to fund private activities (privately owned baseball stadium or private business subsidies) and not for the public good (build or repair public roads). However, taxpayers do not add back interest income from private activity bonds if the bonds were issued in either 2009 or 2010.
Real property and personal property taxes deducted as itemized deductions	Deductible for regular tax purposes, but not for AMT purposes.
State income or sales taxes	Deductible for regular tax purposes, but not for AMT purposes.
Home-equity interest expense	This is *not deductible* for AMT purposes if the proceeds from the loan are used for *purposes other than to acquire or substantially improve the home.*
Miscellaneous itemized deductions (subject to the 2 percent floor) in excess of the 2 percent floor	Deductible for regular tax purposes but not for AMT purposes.
Plus or Minus adjustment:	
Depreciation	Taxpayers must compute their depreciation expense for AMT purposes. For certain types of assets, the regular tax method is more accelerated than the AMT method. In any event, if the regular tax depreciation exceeds the AMT depreciation, this is a plus adjustment. If the AMT depreciation exceeds the regular tax depreciation, this is a minus adjustment.
Minus adjustments:	
State income tax refunds included in regular taxable income	Because state income taxes paid are not deductible for AMT purposes, refunds are not taxable (they do not increase the AMT base).
Gain or loss on sale of depreciable assets	Due to differences in regular tax and AMT depreciation methods, taxpayers may have a different adjusted basis (cost minus accumulated depreciation) for regular tax and for AMT purposes. Thus, they may have a different gain or loss for regular tax purposes than they do for AMT purposes. If regular tax gain exceeds AMT gain, this is a minus adjustment. Because AMT accumulated depreciation will never exceed regular tax accumulated depreciation, this would never be a plus adjustment.

As Exhibit 8-4 indicates, several itemized deductions are not deductible for AMT purposes. The major itemized deductions that are deductible for both regular tax and AMT purposes using the *same limitations* are:

- Casualty and theft losses.
- Charitable contributions.
- Home mortgage interest expenses.
- Gambling losses.

Deductions that are deductible for regular tax and AMT purposes but have *different limitations* are:

- Medical expenses [10 percent of AGI floor for AMT purposes rather than 7.5 percent for regular tax purposes if the taxpayer (or his or her spouse) is age 65 or older].[13] Note that for regular tax and AMT purposes, all other taxpayers have a 10 percent AGI floor for medical expenses.
- Home-equity interest (interest is not deductible for AMT purposes unless loan proceeds are used to acquire or substantially improve the home).
- Investment interest expense (interest income that is tax exempt for regular tax purposes but included in the AMT base is included in investment income for determining the AMT investment interest expense deduction).

Example 8-7

Courtney continued to work on her AMT computation by determining the other adjustments she needs to make to determine her alternative minimum taxable income (AMTI). What is Courtney's AMTI?

Answer: $153,750, computed as follows:

Description	Amount	Explanation
(1) AMTI before other adjustments	$ 142,111	Example 8-6
Plus adjustments:		
(2) Tax-exempt interest on Cincinnati bond used to pay for renovations to major league baseball stadium (Private activity bond: issued in 2005)	500	Example 5-22
(3) Real estate property taxes	3,680	Example 6-14
(4) State income taxes	6,700	Example 6-14
(5) Miscellaneous itemized deductions in excess of 2 percent floor	1,179	Example 6-30
Minus adjustments:		
(6) State income tax refund	(420)	Example 5-3
Alternative minimum taxable income	**$153,750**	Sum of (1) through (6)

AMT Exemption To help ensure that low-income taxpayers aren't required to pay the alternative minimum tax, Congress allows taxpayers to deduct an **alternative minimum tax (AMT) exemption** amount to determine their alternative minimum tax base.[14] The amount of the exemption depends on the taxpayer's filing status. The exemption is phased out (reduced) by 25 cents for every dollar the AMTI exceeds the threshold amount. Exhibit 8-5 identifies, by filing status, the base exemption amount, the phase-out threshold, and the range of AMTI over which the exemption is phased out for 2017.

[13]At press time, the 7.5 percent of AGI floor for taxpayers age 65 or older is scheduled to increase to 10 percent of AGI for years after 2016.

[14]Similar to exemption and standard deduction amounts, the AMT exemption is indexed for inflation. The phase-out threshold amounts are also indexed annually for inflation.

EXHIBIT 8-5 2017 AMT Exemptions

Filing Status	Exemption	Phase-Out Begins at This Level of AMTI	Phase-Out Complete for This Level of AMTI
Married filing jointly	$84,500	$160,900	$498,900
Married filing separately	42,250	80,450	249,450
Head of household and single	54,300	120,700	337,900

Example 8-8

What is Courtney's AMT base?

Answer: $107,713 computed by subtracting her allowable exemption amount from her AMTI as follows:

Description	Amount	Explanation
(1) AMTI	$ 153,750	Example 8-7
(2) Full AMT exemption (head of household)	54,300	Exhibit 8-5
(3) Exemption phase-out threshold	120,700	
(4) AMTI in excess of exemption phase-out threshold	33,050	(1) – (3)
(5) Exemption phase-out percentage	25%	
(6) Exemption phase-out amount	8,263	(4) × (5), rounded
(7) Deductible exemption amount	46,037	(2) – (6)
AMT base	**$107,713**	(1) – (7)

Tentative Minimum Tax and AMT Computation Taxpayers compute the tentative minimum tax by multiplying the AMT base by the applicable AMT rates. The 2017 AMT rate schedule consists of just two regular brackets, as follows:

- 26 percent on the first $187,800 (indexed for inflation annually) of AMT base for all taxpayers other than married taxpayers filing separately ($93,900, indexed for inflation annually, for married taxpayers filing separately).
- 28 percent on AMT base in excess of $187,800 (indexed for inflation annually) for all taxpayers other than married taxpayers filing separately ($93,900, indexed for inflation annually, for married taxpayers filing separately).

However, for AMT purposes long-term capital gains and dividends are taxed at the same preferential rate as they were taxed for regular tax purposes (generally 0 percent, 15 percent, or 20 percent).

Example 8-9

Courtney's AMT base is $107,713. However, Courtney also received $700 in dividends that are included in the base but are subject to a tax rate of 15 percent even under the AMT system. The remaining $107,013 ($107,713 – $700) is taxed at the normal AMT rates. What is Courtney's tentative minimum tax?

Answer: $27,928, computed as follows:

Description	Amount	Explanation
(1) AMT base	$107,713	Example 8-8
(2) Dividends taxed at preferential rate	700	Example 8-3
(3) Tax rate applicable to dividends	15%	
(4) Tax on dividends	105	(2) × (3)
(5) AMT base taxed at regular AMT rates	107,013	(1) – (2)
(6) Regular AMT tax rate	26%	For AMT base below $187,800.
(7) Tax on AMT base taxed at regular AMT rates	27,823	(5) × (6), rounded
Tentative minimum tax	**$ 27,928**	(4) + (7)

Taxpayers subtract their regular tax liability from their tentative minimum tax to determine their AMT.[15] If the taxpayer's regular tax liability is equal to or exceeds the tentative minimum tax liability, the taxpayer does not owe any AMT.

Example 8-10

What is Courtney's alternative minimum tax liability?

Answer: $1,255, computed as follows:

Description	Amount	Reference
(1) Tentative minimum tax	$27,928	Example 8-9
(2) Regular tax liability	26,673	Example 8-3
Alternative minimum tax	**$ 1,255**	(1) – (2) ($0 if negative)

Courtney owes alternative minimum tax because her regular tax liability exceeds her tentative minimum tax.

THE KEY FACTS

Alternative Minimum Tax (AMT)

- Implemented to ensure taxpayers pay some minimum level of income tax.
- AMT base
  - More broad than regular income tax base.
  - No deductions for exemptions, standard deduction, state income taxes, property taxes, and others.
- AMT exemption amounts for 2017
  - $84,500 married filing jointly.
  - $42,250 married filing separately.
  - $54,300 other.
  - Phased out by 25 cents for each dollar of AMTI over threshold.
- AMT rates
  - 26 percent on first $187,800 of AMT base.
  - 28 percent on AMT base in excess of $187,800.
  - Net long-term capital gains and qualified dividends taxed at same preferential rates used for regular tax purposes.
- AMT is the excess of tentative minimum tax (tax on AMT base) over regular tax liability.

In some situations, taxpayers who pay the AMT are entitled to a **minimum tax credit** to use when the regular tax exceeds the tentative minimum tax. They can use the credit to offset regular tax but not below the tentative minimum tax for that year.[16]

General AMT Planning Strategies Based on the nature of the adjustments we've explained, it's clear that the taxpayers who tend to get hit the hardest by AMT are taxpayers who (1) have many dependents, (2) live in a high-income-tax state (they deduct state taxes for regular tax purposes but not AMT purposes), (3) pay high real estate or other property taxes, and/or (4) have relatively high capital gains (the capital gains increase AMTI, which reduces the exemption amount and thus exposes more income to the AMT). In certain circumstances, taxpayers can implement tax planning strategies to mitigate the impact of the AMT. For example, consistent with the tax rate timing strategy we discussed in the Tax Planning Strategies and Related Limitations chapter, taxpayers who pay AMT at 26 percent (or 28 percent) one year and expect to pay regular tax at 35 percent in the next year may want to consider accelerating income into the AMT year to ensure that it is taxed at a lower rate than it would be in a regular tax year. In any event, taxpayers who either pay or may pay the AMT should consider their tax situation to determine whether and how to use timing tax planning strategies to reduce their combined tax burden (regular tax and AMT) given their circumstances.

LO 8-3

EMPLOYMENT AND SELF-EMPLOYMENT TAXES

As we discussed in the An Introduction to Tax chapter, employees and self-employed taxpayers must pay employment (or self-employment) taxes known as FICA taxes.[17] The FICA tax consists of a Social Security and a Medicare component that are payable by both employees and employers. The **Social Security tax** is intended to provide basic

[15]As might be expected, self-employment taxes and the 3.8 percent net investment income tax are not considered as part of a taxpayer's regular tax liability in determining whether a taxpayer owes AMT.

[16]The credit applies only when the taxpayer has positive adjustments that will reverse and become negative adjustments in the future. For example, depreciation, gain or loss on asset sales, and incentive stock option bargain element adjustments (see the Compensation chapter) fall into this category. Due to the nature of her adjustments, Courtney does not qualify for the minimum tax credit.

[17]FICA stands for Federal Insurance Contributions Act.

pension coverage for the retired and disabled. The **Medicare tax** helps pay medical costs for qualifying individuals. Because Social Security and Medicare taxes are paid by working taxpayers but received by retired taxpayers, Social Security and Medicare taxes represent intergenerational transfers. The Social Security tax rate is 12.4 percent on the tax base (limited to $127,200 in 2017). The Medicare tax rate is 2.9 percent on the tax base up to $200,000 ($125,000 for married filing separately; $250,000 for married filing jointly) and 3.8 percent on the tax base in excess of $200,000 ($125,000 for married filing separately; $250,000 for married filing jointly). The party responsible for paying the tax and the tax base depends on whether the taxpayer is an employee or whether the taxpayer is self-employed.

THE KEY FACTS

Employee FICA Tax

- Social Security tax
  - 6.2 percent rate on wage base.
  - 2017 wage base limit is $127,200.
- Medicare tax
  - 1.45 percent rate on wage base up to $200,000 ($125,000 for married filing separately; $250,000 for married filing jointly) and 2.35 percent rate on excess wage base.
  - Wage base unlimited.

Employee FICA Taxes Payable

Both employees and employers have to pay **FICA taxes** on employee salary, wages, and other compensation paid by employers. The Social Security tax rate for employees is 6.2 percent of their salary or wages (wage base limited to $127,200 in 2017). The Medicare tax rate for employees is 1.45 percent on salary or wages up to $200,000 ($125,000 for married filing separate; $250,000 of combined salary or wages for married filing joint) and 2.35 percent on salary or wages in excess of $200,000 ($125,000 for married filing separate; $250,000 of combined salary or wages for married filing joint). Employers withhold the employees' FICA tax liabilities from the employees' paychecks for both the Social Security tax and the Medicare tax. For the Medicare tax, employers are required to withhold the tax at a rate of 1.45 percent on salary or wages up to $200,000 and at a rate of 2.35 percent for any salary or wages above $200,000, irrespective of the taxpayer's filing status (e.g., single, married filing separate, married filing joint, or head of household).[18] Taxpayers use Form 8959 to determine their liability for the .9 percent additional Medicare tax and report all of the .9 percent additional Medicare tax withheld as a tax payment on Form 1040 (line 62).

Employers must also pay their portion of the Social Security tax (6.2 percent of employee salary or wages) and Medicare tax (1.45 percent of employee salary or wages, regardless of the amount of salary or wages). In contrast to employees, employers are not subject to the .9 percent additional Medicare tax on employee salary or wages.

Example 8-11

While she was attending school full-time, Ellen received $15,000 in wages working part-time for an off-campus employer during 2017. How much in FICA taxes should Ellen's employer have withheld from her paychecks during the year?

Answer: $1,148, computed as follows:

Description	Amount	Reference
(1) Wages	$15,000	
(2) Social Security tax rate	6.2%	
(3) Social Security tax	930	(1) × (2)
(4) Medicare tax rate	1.45%	
(5) Medicare tax	218	(1) × (4)
FICA taxes withheld	**$ 1,148**	(3) + (5)

[18]To avoid potential underpayment penalty, taxpayers can request additional income tax withholding or make estimated tax payments to pay any Medicare tax that otherwise would have been owed upon filing their tax return.

Example 8-12

During 2017, Courtney received a total of $142,800 in employee compensation from EWD. Recall that the compensation consisted of $118,000 in wages, $4,800 performance bonus, $6,000 discount for architectural design services, $4,000 compensation for a below-market loan, and $10,000 forgiveness of debt (see Exhibit 5-4). What is her FICA tax liability on this income?

Answer: $9,957, computed as follows:

Description	Amount	Reference
(1) Compensation subject to FICA tax	$142,800	
(2) Social Security tax base limit for 2017	127,200	
(3) Compensation subject to Social Security tax	127,200	Lesser of (1) or (2)
(4) Social Security tax rate	6.2%	
(5) Social Security tax	7,886	(3) × (4)
(6) Medicare tax rate on compensation up to $200,000	1.45%	
(7) Medicare tax	2,071	(1) × (6)
FICA taxes	**$ 9,957**	(5) + (7)

What amount of FICA taxes for the year must EWD pay on Courtney's behalf?

Answer: $9,957, which includes $7,886 of Social Security tax ($127,200 × 6.2%) and $2,071 of Medicare tax ($142,800 × 1.45%).

What if: Courtney received a total of $220,000 in employee compensation. What is her FICA tax liability on this income?

Answer: $11,256, computed as follows:

Description	Amount	Reference
(1) Compensation subject to FICA tax	$220,000	
(2) Social Security tax base limit for 2017	127,200	
(3) Compensation subject to Social Security tax	127,200	Lesser of (1) or (2)
(4) Social Security tax rate	6.2%	
(5) Social Security tax	7,886	(3) × (4)
(6) Medicare tax rate on compensation up to $200,000	1.45%	
(7) Compensation subject to 1.45% Medicare tax	200,000	Lesser of (1) or $200,000
(8) Medicare tax rate on compensation in excess of $200,000	2.35%	
(9) Compensation subject to 2.35% Medicare tax	20,000	Greater of [(1) – $200,000] or $0
(10) Medicare tax	3,370	[(6) × (7)] + [(8) × (9)]
FICA taxes	**11,256**	(5) + (10)

What amount of FICA taxes for the year must EWD pay on Courtney's behalf?

Answer: $11,076, which includes $7,886 of Social Security tax ($127,200 × 6.2%) and $3,190 of Medicare tax ($220,000 × 1.45%).

Employees who work for multiple employers within a calendar year may receive aggregate compensation that exceeds the Social Security wage base. Because each employer is required to withhold Social Security taxes on the employee's wages until the employee has reached the wage base limit *with that employer,* the employee may end up paying Social Security tax in *excess* of the required maximum. Similar to situations in which excess Medicare tax has been withheld, the IRS treats the excess Social Security tax paid through withholding as an additional federal income tax payment (or credit) on Page 2 of

Form 1040 (line 71). The government refunds the excess withholding to the employee through either lower taxes payable with the tax return or a greater tax refund. Employers, on the other hand, are *not* able to recover excess Social Security taxes paid on behalf of their employees.

Example 8-13

What if: Suppose that Courtney worked for her former employer Landmark Architects Inc. (LA), in Cincinnati for two weeks in January 2017 before moving to Kansas City. During those two weeks, Courtney would have earned $4,000 in salary. LA would have withheld $306 in FICA taxes from her final paycheck consisting of $248 of Social Security taxes ($4,000 × 6.2%) and $58 of Medicare taxes ($4,000 × 1.45%). How much excess Social Security tax would have been withheld from Courtney's combined salaries from LA and EWD during 2017?

Answer: $248 ($4,000 wages earned with LA × 6.2% Social Security rate). Due to the $127,200 Social Security tax wage base for the year, Courtney's Social Security tax liability is limited to $7,886 ($127,200 × 6.2%). However, through employer withholding, she would have paid a total of $8,134 in Social Security taxes, consisting of $248 withheld by LA ($4,000 × 6.2%) and $7,886 withheld by EWD ($127,200 × 6.2%). Thus, given these facts, Courtney's *excess* Social Security tax withheld was $248 ($8,134 – $7,886). Courtney would get this amount back from the government through either lower taxes payable with her tax return or a greater tax refund.

Self-Employment Taxes

While employees share their FICA (Social Security and Medicare) tax burden with employers, self-employed taxpayers must pay the *entire* FICA tax burden on their self-employment earnings.[19] Just as it is with FICA taxes for employees, self-employment taxes consist of both Social Security and Medicare taxes. Because their FICA taxes are based on their self-employment earnings, FICA taxes for self-employed taxpayers are referred to as **self-employment taxes.** Just as it is with employees, the base for the Social Security component of the self-employment tax is limited to $127,200. The base for the Medicare portion of the self-employment tax is unlimited. Taxpayers use Schedule SE to determine their Social Security tax and 2.9 percent Medicare tax on self-employment earnings and Form 8959 to determine the .9 percent additional Medicare tax on self-employment earnings. Although applied to self-employment earnings, the .9 percent additional Medicare tax is *not* considered technically a part of the self-employment tax. The process for determining the taxpayer's self-employment taxes (and .9 percent additional Medicare tax) payable requires the following steps:

Step 1: Compute the amount of the taxpayer's net income from self-employment activities that is subject to self-employment taxes. (This is generally the taxpayer's net income from **Schedule C** of Form 1040. Schedule C reports the taxpayers self-employment-related income and expenses.)

Step 2: Multiply the amount from Step (1) by 92.35 percent. The product is called **net earnings from self-employment.** Because self-employed taxpayers are responsible for paying the *entire* amount of their FICA taxes, they are allowed an implicit deduction for the 7.65 percent "employer's portion" of the taxes, leaving 92.35 percent (100% – 7.65%) of the full amount subject to self-employment taxes. Note that the 7.65 percent consists of the 6.2 percent Social Security tax and 1.45 percent Medicare tax. Net earnings from

[19]As we discussed in the Gross Income and Exclusions and Individual Deductions chapters, self-employed taxpayers report their self-employment earnings on Schedule C of Form 1040. Individuals who are partners in partnerships and who are actively involved in the partnerships' business activities may be required to pay self-employment taxes on the income they are allocated from the partnerships. They would report these earnings on Schedule E of Form 1040.

self-employment is the base for the self-employment tax. If net earnings from self-employment is less than $400, the taxpayer is not subject to self-employment tax (but the taxpayer is still subject to income tax on the earnings).

Step 3: Compute the Social Security tax. The Social Security tax component of the self-employment tax equals 12.4 percent [the combined Social Security tax rate for employer and employee (6.2% + 6.2% = 12.4%)] multiplied by the lesser of (a) the taxpayer's net earnings from self-employment (from Step 2) or (b) $127,200 (the maximum tax base for the Social Security tax).

Step 4: Compute the Medicare tax. The Medicare tax component of the self-employment tax equals 2.9 percent [the combined Medicare tax rate for employer and employee (1.45% + 1.45% = 2.9%)] multiplied by the net earnings from self-employment (from Step 2).

Step 5: Compute the .9 percent additional Medicare tax. The .9 percent additional Medicare tax due on net self-employment earnings equals .9 percent multiplied by the greater of (1) zero or (2) net earnings from self-employment (from Step 2) less $200,000 ($125,000 for married filing separately; $250,000 for married filing jointly). The .9 percent additional Medicare tax is considered an "employee" tax (and not a "self-employment" tax).

Note that as we discussed in the Individual Deductions chapter, taxpayers are allowed to deduct the employer portion of their self-employment taxes as a *for* AGI deduction. For years prior to 2011, the employer and employee portions of self-employment tax were equal. Since 2011, the employer and employee portions potentially vary based on the level of self-employment earnings. Nonetheless, the employer portion is simple to calculate if you know the Social Security and Medicare tax rates that apply to employers.

Example 8-14

What if: Assume that Courtney's only income for the year is her $18,000 in net self-employment income from her weekend consulting business. What amount of self-employment taxes and .9 percent additional Medicare tax would Courtney be required to pay on this income?

Answer: $2,543 self-employment taxes and $0 of .9 percent additional Medicare tax, computed as follows:

Step 1: $18,000 of net self-employment income subject to self-employment taxes.

Step 2: $18,000 × .9235 = $16,623. This is net earnings from self-employment.

Step 3: $16,623 × 12.4% = $2,061. This is Courtney's Social Security tax payable for her self-employment income.

Step 4: $16,623 × 2.9% = $482. This is Courtney's Medicare tax payable for her self-employment income.

Step 5: $0. Since Courtney's net earnings from self-employment do not exceed $200,000, she is not subject to the .9 percent additional Medicare tax.

Total $2,543 self-employment taxes [sum of steps (3) and (4)] and $0 of .9 percent additional Medicare tax [step (5)].

Under these circumstances, Courtney would be able to deduct $1,272 as a *for* AGI deduction for the employer portion of self-employment taxes she paid [i.e., $16,623 × (6.2% + 1.45%)].

When a taxpayer receives *both* employee compensation and self-employment earnings in the same year, the calculation of Social Security and Medicare taxes is a bit more complicated. For the Social Security tax component, the taxpayer's *total earnings* subject to the Social Security tax are capped at $127,200. In these situations, the taxpayer's Social Security tax liability on the employee compensation is determined as if the employee had no self-employment income. The taxpayer then computes her Social Security tax on her net self-employment earnings. This ordering is favorable for taxpayers because it allows them to use up all or a portion of the Social Security wage base limit with their employee income (taxed at 6.2 percent) before they determine the Social Security tax on their net earnings from self-employment (taxed at 12.4 percent). Consequently, if an employee's wages exceed the Social Security tax wage base limitation, she is not required to pay any Social Security tax on her self-employment earnings.

Likewise, the Medicare tax calculation is more complicated when (1) the taxpayer receives both employee compensation and self-employment earnings or (2) the taxpayer files married jointly with a spouse receiving employee compensation or net self-employment earnings. Specifically, while the employer portion of the Medicare tax is 1.45 percent regardless of the level of net self-employment earnings, the employee portion of the Medicare tax varies based on the combined amount of employee compensation and net self-employment earnings for the taxpayer (or the taxpayer and his or her spouse, if they file married jointly). For taxpayers not filing married jointly, the employee portion of the Medicare tax rate is 1.45 percent on the taxpayer's salary or wages and net self-employment earnings up to $200,000 ($125,000 for married filing separately) and 2.35 percent on salary or wages and net self-employment earnings in excess of $200,000 ($125,000 for married filing separately). For married filing jointly taxpayers, the employee portion of the Medicare tax rate is 1.45 percent on the taxpayer's and his or her spouse's salary or wages and net self-employment earnings up to $250,000 and 2.35 percent on the taxpayer's and his or her spouse's salary or wages and net self-employment earnings in excess of $250,000.

The calculation of the taxpayer's Social Security and Medicare taxes on self-employment earnings in these settings can be determined as follows:[20]

Social Security Tax:

Step 1: Determine the limit on the Social Security portion of the self-employment tax base by subtracting the employee compensation from the Social Security wage base ($127,200 in 2017) (not below $0).

Step 2: Determine the net earnings from self-employment (self-employment earnings times 92.35 percent).

Step 3: Multiply the lesser of Steps (1) and (2) by 12.4 percent. This is the amount of Social Security taxes due on the self-employment income.

Medicare Tax:

Step 4: Multiply the amount from Step (2) by 2.9 percent, the combined Medicare tax rate for employer and employee.

.9 Percent Additional Medicare Tax:

Step 5: Add the amount from Step (2) and the taxpayer's compensation. If married filing jointly, also add the spouse's compensation and net earnings from self-employment (spouse's self-employment earnings times 92.35 percent).

Step 6: Multiply the greater of [(a) zero or (b) the amount from Step (5) minus $200,000 ($125,000 for married filing separately; $250,000 for married filing jointly)] by .9 percent.

Step 7: Take the amount from Step 6 and subtract the amount of the .9 percent additional Medicare tax withheld by the taxpayer's employer (and his or her spouse's employer if married filing jointly). This is the .9 percent additional Medicare tax due on the self-employment income.

[20]If net earnings from self-employment is less than $400, the taxpayer is not subject to self-employment tax (but the taxpayer is still subject to income tax on the earnings).

Example 8-15

In 2017, Courtney received $142,800 in taxable compensation from EWD (see Example 8-12) and $18,000 in self-employment income from her weekend consulting activities (see Example 6-2). What are Courtney's *self-employment taxes* and .9 percent additional Medicare tax payable on her $18,000 of income from self-employment? Assume that Courtney's employer correctly withheld $7,614 of Social Security tax and $1,781 of Medicare tax.

Answer: $482 of self-employment taxes and $0 of .9 percent additional Medicare tax, computed as follows:

Description	Amount	Explanation
(1) Social Security wage base limit less employee compensation subject to Social Security tax	$ 0	$127,200 – $127,200, limited to $0
(2) Net earnings from self-employment	16,623	$18,000 × 92.35%
(3) Social Security portion of self-employment tax	0	[Lesser of Step (1) or (2)] × 12.4%
(4) Medicare tax	482	Step (2) × 2.9%
(5) Sum of taxpayer's compensation and net earnings from self-employment	159,423	$142,800 + Step (2)
(6) [Greater of (a) zero or (b) the amount from Step (5) minus $200,000] × 0.9%	0	0 × 0.9%
(7) Step (6) less any .9 percent additional Medicare tax withheld by Courtney's employer	0	0 – 0
(8) Steps (3) + (4) + (7)	482	0 + 482 + 0. [$482 of self-employment taxes (3) + (4) and $0 of .9 percent additional Medicare tax]

As we reported in the Individual Deductions chapter, Courtney is entitled to a $241 *for* AGI deduction for the employer portion of the $482 self-employment taxes she incurred during the year ($16,623 × 1.45% employer portion of the Medicare tax rate = $241).

Example 8-16

What if: Let's change the facts and assume that Courtney received $100,000 of taxable compensation from EWD in 2017, and she received $180,000 in self-employment income from her weekend consulting activities. What amount of self-employment taxes and .9 percent additional Medicare tax is Courtney required to pay on her $180,000 of business income? Assume that Courtney's employer correctly withheld $6,200 of Social Security tax, $1,450 of Medicare tax, and $0 of .9 percent additional Medicare tax.

Answer: $8,194 of self-employment taxes and $596 of .9 percent additional Medicare tax, computed as follows:

Description	Amount	Explanation
(1) Social Security wage base limit less employee compensation subject to Social Security tax	$ 27,200	$127,200 – $100,000, limited to $0
(2) Net earnings from self-employment	166,230	$180,000 × 92.35%
(3) Social Security portion of self-employment tax	3,373	[Lesser of Step (1) or (2)] × 12.4%
(4) Medicare tax	4,821	Step (2) × 2.9%

Description	Amount	Explanation
(5) Sum of taxpayer's compensation and net earnings from self-employment	266,230	$100,000 + Step (2)
(6) [Greater of (a) zero or (b) the amount from Step (5) minus $200,000] × 0.9%	596	66,230 × 0.9%
(7) Step (6) less any .9 percent additional Medicare tax withheld by Courtney's employer	596	596 – 0
(8) Steps (3) + (4) + (7)	8,790	3,373 + 4,821 + 596. [$8,194 of self-employment taxes (3) + (4) and $596 of .9 percent additional Medicare tax]

What if: Now let's assume that Courtney is married and files jointly. Assume that Courtney received $100,000 of taxable compensation from EWD in 2017 and $180,000 in self-employment income from her weekend consulting activities. In addition, her husband received $75,000 of taxable compensation from his employer. What amount of self-employment taxes and .9 percent additional Medicare tax is Courtney required to pay on her $180,000 of business income? Assume that Courtney's employer correctly withheld $6,200 of Social Security tax, $1,450 of Medicare tax, and $0 of .9 percent additional Medicare tax and that her husband's employer correctly withheld $4,650 of Social Security tax, $1,088 of Medicare tax, and $0 of .9 percent additional Medicare tax.

Answer: $8,194 of self-employment taxes and $821 of .9 percent additional Medicare tax, computed as follows:

Description	Amount	Explanation
(1) Social Security wage base limit less employee compensation subject to Social Security tax	$ 27,200	$127,200 – $100,000, limited to $0
(2) Net earnings from self-employment	166,230	$180,000 × 92.35%
(3) Social Security portion of self-employment tax	3,373	[Lesser of Step (1) or (2)] × 12.4%
(4) Medicare tax	4,821	Step (2) × 2.9%
(5) Sum of taxpayer's and spouse's compensation and net earnings from self-employment	341,230	$100,000 + $75,000 + Step (2)
(6) [Greater of (a) zero or (b) the amount from Step (5) minus $250,000] × 0.9%	821	91,230 × 0.9%
(7) Step (6) less any .9 percent additional Medicare tax withheld by Courtney's employer and her husband's employer	821	821 – 0
(8) Steps (3) + (4) + (7)	9,015	3,373 + 4,821 + 821. [$8,194 of self-employment taxes (3) + (4) and $821 of .9 percent additional Medicare tax]

Unlike employees, whose employers withhold tax throughout the year on their behalf, self-employed taxpayers must satisfy their self-employment tax obligations through periodic, usually quarterly, estimated tax payments. Taxpayers who are employed and self-employed (an employee with a business on the side, like Courtney) may have their employers withhold enough taxes to cover both their income, self-employment, and .9 percent additional Medicare tax obligations. Any self-employment or .9 percent additional Medicare taxes not paid through these mechanisms must be paid with the self-employed taxpayer's individual tax return.

continued from page 8-1...

Courtney was enjoying her work with EWD but she also really liked her weekend consulting work. A couple of months ago, after Courtney had played an integral part in completing a successful project, Courtney's boss jokingly mentioned that, if Courtney ever decided to leave EWD to work for herself as a full-time consultant, EWD would love to hire her back for contract work. This caused Courtney to start thinking about the possibilities of starting her own consulting business. She's always had some interest in working for herself, but she is not at a point in her life where she can take significant financial risks even if it might mean a more satisfying career. Courtney knew that before making such a move she would need to seriously consider the nontax issues associated with self-employment and she would need to learn more about the tax consequences of working as an independent contractor. She was particularly interested in the tax consequences of working for EWD as an independent contractor (contract worker) relative to working for EWD as an employee. ■

Employee vs. Self-Employed (Independent Contractor)

Determining whether an individual is taxed as an **employee** or as an **independent contractor** can be straightforward or quite complex, depending on the specific arrangement between the parties. In its published guidance, the IRS stipulates that an employer/employee relationship exists when the party for whom services are performed has the right to direct or control the individual performing services.[21] To assist taxpayers in deciding whether the party receiving services has the requisite amount of control over the individual providing services, the IRS has published a list of 20 factors to consider.[22] A few of the factors suggesting independent contractor rather than employee status include the contractor's ability to:

1. Set her own working hours.
2. Work part-time.
3. Work for more than one firm.
4. Realize either a profit or a loss from the activities.
5. Perform work somewhere other than on an employer's premises.
6. Work without frequent oversight.

When these factors are absent, individuals are more likely to be classified as employees. Rather than simply summing the number of factors in favor of independent contractor status and those in favor of employee status, however, taxpayers and their advisers should use the factors as guides in determining the overall substance of the contractual relationship.

Whether a taxpayer is classified as an employee or as an independent contractor (self-employed) has both tax and nontax consequences to the employer and the taxpayer. The best classification for the taxpayer is situation-specific.

Employee vs. Independent Contractor Comparison The two primary *tax* differences between independent contractors and employees relate to (1) the amount of their FICA taxes payable and (2) the deductibility of their business expenses.[23] However, there are several nontax factors to consider as well. In the previous section, we detailed how to

[21]IRS Publication 1779. Independent Contractor or Employee brochure.

[22]Rev. Rul. 87-41, 1987-1 CB 296.

[23]Also, independent contractors generally receive a Form 1099 from each client reporting the gross income they received from the client during the year. Employees receive Form W-2 reporting the compensation the employee received from the employer during the year.

determine the FICA taxes payable for employees and independent contractors (self-employed taxpayers). In terms of the deductibility of business expenses, as we discussed in the Individual Deductions chapter, *employees* who incur unreimbursed business expenses relating to their employment can deduct these expenses as miscellaneous itemized deductions subject to a 2 percent of AGI floor. This floor means, in many cases, that employees receive little or no tax benefit for their employee business expenses. In contrast, as we also described in the Individual Deductions chapter, self-employed independent contractors are able to deduct expenses relating to their business activities as *for* AGI deductions, which they can deduct without restriction. While these factors appear to favor independent contractor status over employee status, note that employees generally don't incur many unreimbursed expenses relating to their employment. Thus, even though independent contractors may be able to deduct more expenses than employees, they typically incur more costs in doing business.

When taxpayers are classified as independent contractors rather than employees, they are not eligible for nontaxable fringe benefits available to employees, such as health care insurance, retirement plan benefits, and other fringe benefits provided to employees. Further, independent contractors are responsible for paying their estimated tax liability throughout the year through estimated tax payments because the employer does not withhold taxes from an independent contractor's pay. However, as we mentioned above, taxpayers are allowed to deduct the employer portion of the self-employment taxes they pay.

From the employer's perspective, it is generally less costly to hire an independent contractor than an employee because the employer need not provide these benefits and the employer need not withhold or pay any FICA taxes on behalf of an independent contractor. As a result, an employer may be willing to offer an apparently higher level of taxable compensation to an independent contractor than a similarly situated employee. However, after considering all relevant factors, the taxpayer may do better receiving less compensation as an employee than slightly higher compensation as an independent contractor.

ETHICS

Sudipta is an accounting major who works during the day and takes classes in the evening. He was excited to finally land his first accounting job doing the books for a local dry cleaners. In his new job, Sudipta works 30 hours a week at the dry cleaners' main office. His excitement quickly dampened when he realized that his new employer was not withholding any income taxes or FICA taxes from his paycheck. Apparently, Sudipta's employer is treating him as an independent contractor. Sudipta likes his job, loves the money that he is earning, but recognizes that he should be treated as an employee instead of an independent contractor. What would you do if you were Sudipta?

Example 8-17

What if: Let's compare Courtney's compensation as an employee with EWD to her compensation if she were to work for EWD as an independent contractor. *Assume* that Courtney works an average of 40 hours per week for 50 weeks per year to earn a salary of $100,000; in addition she receives fringe benefits including a 5 percent contribution to her retirement plan, life insurance coverage, and health insurance coverage. Would Courtney be "made whole" in terms of her hourly rate if EWD agreed to pay her $55 an hour for her contract work (10 percent more than her hourly rate as an employee)?

Answer: Not very likely. As an independent contractor, Courtney must pay more costly self-employment taxes (at nearly twice the rate of employment taxes) under the new arrangement. In addition, she will be ineligible for the nontaxable fringe benefits (retirement plan contributions, life insurance, and health coverage) she was receiving as an employee and will not receive as a contractor.

THE KEY FACTS

Employee vs. Independent Contractor

- Employees
  - Less control over how, when, and where to perform duties.
  - Pay 6.2 percent Social Security tax subject to limit.

(continued)

- Pay Medicare tax from 1.45 percent to 2.35 percent.
- Independent contractors
  - More control over how, when, and where to perform duties.
  - Report income and expenses on Form 1040, Schedule C.
  - Pay 12.4 percent Social Security tax subject to limit.
  - Pay Medicare tax from 2.9 percent to 3.8 percent.
  - Self-employment tax base is 92.35 percent of net self-employment income.
  - Deduct the employer portion of self-employment taxes paid *for* AGI.

We've described how to calculate a taxpayer's regular tax liability, alternative minimum tax liability, and self-employment tax liability. These tax liabilities sum to a taxpayer's gross tax liability. While Gram's gross tax is simply her regular income tax liability of $364 (see Example 8-2), Courtney's gross tax includes other taxes. Courtney's gross tax liability is calculated in Exhibit 8-6.

EXHIBIT 8-6 Courtney's Gross Tax

Description	Amount	Explanation
(1) Regular federal income tax	$26,673	Example 8-3
(2) Alternative minimum tax	1,255	Example 8-10
(3) Self-employment tax	482	Example 8-15
Gross tax	$28,410	(1) + (2) + (3)

Taxpayers reduce their gross tax by tax credits and tax prepayments (withholding and estimated tax payments) for the year. As indicated in Exhibit 8-7, if the gross tax exceeds the tax credits and prepayments, the taxpayer owes additional taxes when she files her tax return. In contrast, if the prepayments exceed the gross tax after applying tax credits, the taxpayer is entitled to a tax refund. We next explore available tax credits and conclude the chapter by dealing with taxpayer prepayments.

EXHIBIT 8-7 Formula for Computing Net Tax Due or Refund

Gross tax
Minus: Tax credits
Minus: Prepayments
Net tax due (refund)

LO 8-4

TAX CREDITS

Congress provides a considerable number of credits for taxpayers. **Tax credits** reduce a taxpayer's *tax liability* dollar for dollar. In contrast, deductions reduce *taxable income* dollar for dollar, but the tax savings deductions generated depend on the taxpayer's marginal tax rate. Because tax credits generate tax savings *independent of* a taxpayer's marginal tax rate, they are a popular tax policy tool for avoiding the perception that tax benefits for certain tax policies are distributed disproportionately to taxpayers with higher incomes and corresponding higher marginal tax rates. Further, tax credits are powerful tax policy tools because they directly affect taxes due. By using tax credits, policy makers can adjust the magnitude of the tax effects of tax policy without changing tax rates.

Tax credits may be either nonrefundable or refundable. A **nonrefundable credit** may reduce a taxpayer's gross tax liability to zero, but if the amount of the credit exceeds the amount of the taxpayer's gross tax liability, the credit in excess of the gross tax liability is not refunded to the taxpayer and expires without ever providing tax benefits (unless the unused credit can be carried over to a different year). Refundable credits in excess of a taxpayer's gross tax liability are refunded to the taxpayer.

Tax credits are generally classified into one of three categories: nonrefundable personal, refundable personal, or business credits, depending on the nature of the credit. The primary exception to this general rule is the foreign tax credit. The foreign tax credit is a hybrid between personal and business credits because, like nonrefundable personal credits, it reduces the taxpayer's liability before business credits but, like business credits, unused foreign tax credits can be carried over to use in other years.

Nonrefundable Personal Credits

Congress provides many nonrefundable personal tax credits to generate tax relief for certain groups of individuals. For example, the child tax credit (partially refundable) provides tax relief for taxpayers who provide a home for dependent children and the child and dependent care credit provides tax relief for taxpayers who incur expenses to care for their children and other dependents in order to work. The American opportunity credit (partially refundable) and the lifetime learning credit help taxpayers pay for the cost of higher education. Because the child tax credit, the child and dependent care credit, and the American opportunity and lifetime learning credits are some of the most common nonrefundable personal credits, we discuss them in detail.

THE KEY FACTS

Child Tax Credit

- Taxpayers may claim a $1,000 credit for each qualifying child under age 17.
- Credit is phased out for taxpayers with AGI above threshold.
  - Lose $50 for every $1,000 or portion thereof that AGI exceeds threshold.

Child Tax Credit Taxpayers may claim a $1,000 **child tax credit** for *each qualifying child* (same definition for dependency exemption purposes—see §152(c) and the Individual Income Tax Overview, Exemptions, and Filing Status chapter) who is under age 17 at the end of the year and who is claimed as their dependent.[24] The credit is subject to phase-out based on the taxpayer's AGI. The phase-out threshold depends on the taxpayer's filing status and is provided in Exhibit 8-8.

EXHIBIT 8-8 Child Tax Credit Phase-Out Threshold

Filing Status	Phase-Out Threshold
Married filing jointly	$110,000
Married filing separately	55,000
Head of household and single	75,000

The total amount of the credit ($1,000 × number of qualifying children) is phased out, but not below zero, by $50 for each $1,000 *or portion thereof* by which the taxpayer's AGI exceeds the applicable threshold. Taxpayers can determine their allowable child tax credit after the phase-out by using the following four steps:

Step 1: Determine the excess AGI by subtracting the threshold amount (see Exhibit 8-8) from the taxpayer's AGI.

Step 2: Divide the excess AGI from step (1) by 1,000 and round up to the next whole number.

Step 3: Multiply the amount from step (2) by $50. This is the amount of the total credit that is phased out or disallowed.

Step 4: Subtract the amount from step (3) from the total credit before phase-out (limited to $0) to determine the allowable child tax credit.

Because the phase-out is based upon a fixed amount ($50) rather than a percentage, the phase-out range varies according to the amount of credit claimed.[25]

[24]§24(a).

[25]The child tax credit is partially refundable. The refundable portion of the credit is the lesser of (1) the taxpayer's earned income in excess of $3,000 times 15 percent, or (2) the amount of the unclaimed portion of the otherwise nonrefundable credit. Thus, if a taxpayer has enough tax liability to absorb the nonrefundable portion of the credit, the refundable portion is reduced to zero. The computation is modified for taxpayers with three or more qualifying children. See IRS Publication 972 for more information relating to the child tax credit.

Example 8-18

Both Ellen and Deron are Courtney's qualifying children. Courtney may claim a child tax credit for Deron but she may *not* claim a child tax credit for Ellen because Ellen is not under age 17 at the end of the year. What amount of child tax credit is Courtney allowed to claim for Deron after accounting for the credit phase-out?

Answer: $0. Because Courtney's AGI of $182,000 exceeds the $75,000 AGI phase-out threshold, she must determine her credit after the phase-out. Her phase-out is computed as follows:

1. $182,000 AGI (Exhibit 6-6) – $75,000 head of household threshold (Exhibit 8-8) = $107,000.
2. $107,000 excess AGI divided by 1,000 = 107 (if her AGI was $107,001, this would be 108).
3. 107 × $50 = $5,350. This is the amount of the phase-out.
4. $1,000 allowable credit minus $5,350 = $0 (limited to $0).

Courtney is *not able to claim any child tax credit* because the entire amount is phased out.

What if: How much child tax credit would Courtney be able to claim after the phase-out if she had claimed six qualifying children under the age of 17 as dependents?

Answer: $650. Her total child tax credit before phase-outs would be $6,000 ($1,000 × 6). Assuming the same AGI of $182,000, she would be required to phase out $5,350 of the credit. Consequently, she would still be able to reduce her taxes by the $650 portion of the credit that was not phased out ($6,000 – $5,350).

Child and Dependent Care Credit The child and dependent care credit is a tax subsidy to help taxpayers pay the cost of providing care for their dependents to allow taxpayers to work or look for work. The amount of the credit is based on the amount of the taxpayer's expenditures to provide care for one or more qualifying persons. A qualifying person includes (1) a dependent under the age of 13, and (2) a dependent or spouse who is physically or mentally incapable of caring for herself or himself and who lives in the taxpayer's home for more than half the year.

The amount of expenditures eligible for the credit is the *least* of the following three amounts:

1. The total amount of dependent care expenditures for the year.
2. $3,000 for one qualifying person or $6,000 for two or more qualifying persons.
3. The taxpayer's earned income including wage, salary, or other taxable employee compensation, or net earnings from self-employment. Married taxpayers must file a joint tax return and the amount of earned income for purposes of the dependent care credit limitation is the earned income of the lesser-earning spouse.[26]

Expenditures for care qualify whether the care is provided outside or within the home. But, expenditures for care do *not* qualify if the caregiver is a dependent relative or child of the taxpayer.[27] The amount of the credit is calculated by multiplying qualifying expenditures by the appropriate credit percentage. The credit percentage is based upon the taxpayer's AGI level and begins at 35 percent for taxpayers with AGI of $15,000 or less. The minimum dependent care credit is 20 percent for taxpayers with AGI over $43,000. Exhibit 8-9 provides the dependent care credit percentage for different levels of AGI.

THE KEY FACTS

Child and Dependent Care Credit

- Designed to help taxpayers who work or seek work when they must provide care for dependents.
- Nonrefundable.
- Based on maximum qualifying expenditures multiplied by the rate based on AGI.
  - Maximum expenditures are $3,000 for one qualifying person or $6,000 for two or more qualifying persons.
  - Rate is 35 percent for the lowest AGI taxpayers and 20 percent for the highest.

[26]If the lesser-earning spouse cannot work due to a disability or is a full-time student, the lesser-earning spouse is *deemed* to have earned $250 a month if the couple is computing the credit for one qualifying person or $500 a month if the couple is computing the credit for more than one qualifying person.

[27]§21(e)(6). Also, the regulations indicate that the costs of summer school and tutoring programs are indistinguishable from general education and, therefore, do not qualify for the credit [See Reg. §1.21-1(b)].

EXHIBIT 8-9 Child and Dependent Care Credit Percentage

If AGI is over	but not over	then the percentage is
$ 0	15,000	35%
15,000	17,000	34
17,000	19,000	33
19,000	21,000	32
21,000	23,000	31
23,000	25,000	30
25,000	27,000	29
27,000	29,000	28
29,000	31,000	27
31,000	33,000	26
33,000	35,000	25
35,000	37,000	24
37,000	39,000	23
39,000	41,000	22
41,000	43,000	21
43,000	No limit	20

Example 8-19

What if: Suppose that this year, Courtney paid a neighbor $3,200 to care for her 10-year-old son, Deron, so Courtney could work. Would Courtney be allowed to claim the child and dependent care credit for the expenditures she made for Deron's care?

Answer: Yes. (1) Courtney paid for Deron's care to allow her to work, and (2) Deron is a qualifying person for purposes of the credit because (a) he is Courtney's dependent and (b) he is under 13 years of age at the end of the year.

What amount of child and dependent care credit, if any, would Courtney be allowed to claim for the $3,200 she spent to provide Deron's care given her AGI is $182,000?

Answer: $600, computed as follows:

Description	Amount	Explanation
(1) Dependent care expenditures	$ 3,200	
(2) Limit on qualifying expenditures for one dependent	3,000	
(3) Courtney's earned income	160,800	$142,800 compensation from EWD + $18,000 business income (see Example 8-15)
(4) Expenditures eligible for credit	3,000	Least of (1), (2), and (3)
(5) Credit percentage rate	20%	AGI over $43,000 (see Exhibit 8-9)
Dependent care credit	**$ 600**	(4) × (5)

What if: If Courtney's AGI (and her earned income) were only $31,500, what would be her child and dependent care credit?

Answer: $780, computed as follows:

Description	Amount	Explanation
(1) Dependent care expenditures	$ 3,200	
(2) Limit on qualifying expenditures for one dependent	3,000	
(3) Courtney's earned income	31,500	
(4) Expenditures eligible for credit	3,000	Least of (1), (2), and (3)
(5) Credit percentage rate	26%	AGI between $31,000 and $33,000 (see Exhibit 8-9)
Dependent care credit	**$ 780**	(4) × (5)

Education Credits Congress provides the American opportunity credit (AOC) (formerly called the Hope scholarship credit) and the lifetime learning credit to encourage taxpayers and their dependents to obtain higher education by reducing the costs of the education. In contrast to the payment rules discussed in the Individual Deductions chapter for the deduction for Qualified Education Expense, taxpayers may claim credits for eligible expenditures made for themselves, their dependents, and third parties on behalf of the taxpayers' dependents.[28] If a student is claimed as a dependent of another taxpayer, only that taxpayer may claim the education credits (even if the dependent or another third party actually pays the education expenses).[29] Married taxpayers filing separate returns are not eligible for the AOC or the lifetime learning credit.

The AOC is available for students in their *first four years* of postsecondary (post high school) education. To qualify, students must be enrolled in a qualified postsecondary educational institution at least half time.[30] The amount of the credit is 100 percent of the first $2,000 of eligible expenses paid by the taxpayer (or another person) plus 25 percent of the next $2,000 of eligible expenses paid by the taxpayer (or another person). Thus, the maximum AOC for eligible expenses paid for any one person is $2,500 [$2,000 + (25% × $2,000)]. To be eligible for the 2017 credit, taxpayers must pay the eligible expenses in 2017 for any academic period beginning in 2017 or in the first three months of 2018.[31] Eligible expenses for the AOC include tuition, fees, and course materials (cost of books and other materials) needed for courses of instruction at an eligible educational institution.[32] The AOC is applied on a *per student* basis. Consequently, a taxpayer with three eligible dependents can claim a maximum AOC of $2,500 for *each* dependent. The AOC is subject to phase-out based on the taxpayer's AGI. The credit is phased out pro rata for taxpayers with AGI between $80,000 and $90,000 ($160,000 – $180,000 for married taxpayers filing jointly).[33] Forty percent of a taxpayer's allowable AOC is refundable.[34]

Example 8-20

Courtney paid $2,000 of tuition and $300 for books for Ellen to attend the University of Missouri–Kansas City during the summer at the end of her freshman year. What is the maximum American opportunity credit (AOC) (before phase-out) Courtney may claim for these expenses?

Answer: $2,075. Because the cost of tuition and books is an eligible expense Courtney may claim a maximum AOC before phase-out of $2,075 [($2,000 × 100%) + ($2,300 – $2,000) × 25%].

How much AOC is Courtney allowed to claim on her 2017 tax return (how much can she claim after applying the phase-out)?

Answer: $0. Because Courtney's AGI exceeds the head of household limit of $90,000, she is not allowed to claim any AOC.

THE KEY FACTS

Education Credits

- American opportunity credit
  - Qualifying expenses include tuition for a qualifying student incurred during the first four years at a qualifying institution of higher education.
  - Maximum credit of $2,500 per student calculated as percentage of maximum of $4,000 qualifying expenses.

(continued)

[28]§25A(g)(3).

[29]If a third party pays the education expenses of a student claimed as a dependent by another taxpayer, the dependent is deemed to have paid the education expenses and the taxpayer claiming the student as a dependent is allowed to claim the credit for the expenses.

[30]§25A(b). Generally, eligible institutions are those eligible to participate in the federal student loan program [§25A(f)(2)].

[31]Reg. §1.25A-3(e).

[32]§25A(i)(3). Eligible expenses for both the AOC and the lifetime learning credit must be reduced by scholarships received to pay for these expenses or other amounts received as reimbursements for the expenses (Pell grants, employer-sponsored reimbursement plans, Educational IRAs, 529 plans, and the like). The cost of room and board or other personal expenses do not qualify as eligible expenses for either the AOC or the lifetime learning credit.

[33]§25A(i)(4).

[34]§25A(i)(5). The refundability of the tax credit is not applicable to a taxpayer that is a child subject to the "kiddie tax" rules—i.e., a child (a) who does not file a joint return, (b) has at least one living parent, and who is either (1) under 18 years old at year-end, (2) 18 at year-end with earned income that does not exceed half of her support, or (3) over age 18 but under age 24 at year-end, is a full-time student during the year, and has earned income that does not exceed half of her support.

What if: How much AOC would Courtney have been allowed to claim on her 2017 tax return if she were married and filed a joint return with her husband (assuming the couple's AGI is $162,000)?

Answer: $1,867, computed as follows:

Description	Amount	Explanation
(1) AOC before phase-out	$ 2,075	
(2) AGI	162,000	
(3) Phase-out threshold	160,000	
(4) Excess AGI	2,000	(2) − (3)
(5) Phase-out range for taxpayer filing for married filing jointly	20,000	$180,000 − $160,000
(6) Phase-out percentage	10%	(4)/(5)
(7) Phase-out amount	208	(1) × (6)
AOC after phase-out	**$ 1,867**	(1) − (7)

What if: Suppose Courtney could claim a $1,867 AOC in 2017 (after phase-out). How much of this credit would be refundable?

Answer: $747 ($1,867 × 40%).

- Subject to phase-out for taxpayers with AGI in excess of $80,000 ($160,000 married filing jointly).
- Lifetime learning credit
  - Qualifying expenses include costs at a qualifying institution associated with acquiring or improving job skills.
  - Maximum credit of $2,000 per taxpayer calculated as percentage of maximum of $10,000 in annual expenses.
  - Subject to phase-out for taxpayers with AGI in excess of $56,000 ($112,000 married filing jointly).

The lifetime learning credit is a nonrefundable credit that applies to the cost of tuition and fees (but generally not books) for any course of instruction to acquire or improve a taxpayer's job skills.[35] This includes the cost of professional or graduate school tuition (expenses are not limited to those incurred in the first four years of postsecondary education). The credit is equal to 20 percent of eligible expenses up to an annual maximum of $10,000 of eligible expenses (maximum of $2,000). The credit for a year is based on the amount paid during that year for an academic period beginning in that year or the first three months of the following year. In contrast to the American opportunity credit, the lifetime learning credit limit applies to the taxpayer (a married couple filing a joint return may claim only $2,000 of lifetime learning credit). Thus, a taxpayer with multiple eligible dependents can claim a maximum lifetime learning credit of only $2,000. Finally, the credit is phased out pro rata for taxpayers with AGI between $56,000 and $66,000 ($112,000 and $132,000 for married taxpayers filing jointly).[36]

Example 8-21

Courtney paid $1,550 to attend a class at the local university to help her improve her job skills. Courtney could elect to claim the lifetime learning credit for these expenses instead of deducting them as miscellaneous itemized deductions. If Courtney decided to claim a credit for these expenditures, what would be her lifetime learning credit (before phase-out)?

Answer: $310 ($1,550 × 20%)

How much lifetime learning credit is Courtney allowed to claim on her 2017 tax return (how much can she claim after applying the phase-out)?

Answer: $0. Because Courtney's AGI exceeds the head of household limit of $66,000 she is not allowed to claim any lifetime learning credit.

For expenses that qualify for both the AOC and lifetime learning credit (tuition and fees during the first four years of postsecondary education), taxpayers may choose which

[35]§25A(f)(1).

[36]§25A(d).

credit to use, but they may not claim both credits for the same student in the same year. In addition, taxpayers may choose to *either* (1) deduct qualifying education expenses of an individual as a *for* AGI deduction (see discussion of this *for* AGI deduction in the Individual Deductions chapter) or claim an education credit for the individual's expenses.[37] However, if a taxpayer claims *any* educational credit for an individual's educational expenditures, the taxpayer may not claim *any for* AGI deduction for that individual's qualifying expenditures (and vice versa).[38]

Example 8-22

What if: Suppose Courtney paid $5,000 of tuition for Ellen to attend the University of Missouri–Kansas City during the summer at the end of her freshman year. Further assume that Courtney's AGI is $45,000, so her education credits are not subject to phase-out. Courtney would be allowed to claim the maximum AOC of $2,500 on the first $4,000 of the qualifying educational expenditures. Assuming Courtney used $4,000 of the educational expenses to claim the maximum AOC, would she be allowed to deduct (or claim the lifetime credit on) the remaining $1,000 of tuition costs ($5,000 total expenses – $4,000 maximum AOC expenses)? Assume the 2016 rules apply for purposes of the qualified education expense deduction.

Answer: No. If Courtney claims any AOC for Ellen's expenditures, she is not allowed to deduct or claim a lifetime learning credit for Ellen's expenditures (even for the expenses not used in computing the AOC).

What if: Assume that both Ellen and Deron were in their first year of college and that Courtney paid tuition for both Ellen and Deron. Further, assume that Courtney's AGI is below the phase-out threshold. Is Courtney allowed to claim an AOC for Ellen's expenses and also claim a *for* AGI educational expense deduction for Deron's expenses?

Answer: Yes. Courtney may claim an AOC or a deduction for Ellen's expenses, and she may claim an AOC or a deduction for Deron's expenses.

Example 8-23

What if: Assume that Courtney paid $8,000 tuition for Ellen to attend graduate school at the University of Missouri–Kansas City (assume this is her fifth year at the university and that Ellen still qualifies as Courtney's dependent). Further assume that Courtney's AGI is $61,000, so her potential lifetime learning credit for Ellen would be phased out by 50 percent (assume Courtney did not claim the credit for herself). Before phase-out, Courtney would be allowed to claim a $1,600 lifetime learning credit ($8,000 tuition × 20% credit percentage). After the phase-out, however, Courtney would be able to claim an $800 lifetime learning credit ($1,600 full credit × 1–50% phase-out percentage). If Courtney claims the $800 lifetime learning credit for Ellen's tuition, is she allowed to claim any *for* AGI deduction for Ellen's tuition since half of the lifetime learning credit is phased out based on Courtney's AGI? Assume the 2016 rules apply for purposes of the qualified education expense deduction.

Answer: No. As we discussed above, if Courtney claims *any* lifetime learning credit for Ellen's expenditures, she is not allowed to deduct any *for* AGI deduction for Ellen's expenditures (even the portion of the expenses that provided no tax benefit because the credit was partially phased out).

What if: Assume the same facts as above and that Courtney's marginal tax rate is 15%. Would Courtney be better off claiming an $800 lifetime learning credit or a $4,000 *for* AGI qualified education expense deduction for the cost of Ellen's tuition?

Answer: The $800 lifetime learning credit. The credit saves Courtney $800 while the qualified education expense deduction would save her $600 ($4,000 × 15%).

[37]At press time, the deduction for qualified education expenses is scheduled to expire after 2016.
[38]§222(c)(2)(A).

Refundable Personal Credits

Several personal credits are refundable, the most common of which is the earned income credit, which we discuss in this chapter.

Earned Income Credit The **earned income credit** is a refundable credit that is designed to help offset the effect of employment taxes on compensation paid to low-income taxpayers and to encourage lower-income taxpayers to seek employment. Because it is refundable (if the credit exceeds the tax after considering nonrefundable credits the taxpayer receives a refund for the excess), it is sometimes referred to as a *negative income tax*. The credit is available for qualified individuals who have earned income for the year.[39] Qualified individuals generally include (1) any individual who has at least one qualifying child (same definition of qualifying child for dependent purposes—see the Individual Income Tax Overview, Exemptions, and Filing Status chapter) or (2) any individual who does not have a qualifying child for the taxable year, but who lives in the United States for more than half the year, is at least 25 years old but younger than 65 years old at the end of the year, and is not a dependent of another taxpayer. Earned income includes wages, salaries, tips, and other employee compensation included in gross income and net earnings from self-employment. Taxpayers with investment income such as interest, dividends, and capital gains in excess of $3,450 are ineligible for the credit.[40]

The amount of the credit depends on the taxpayer's filing status, the number of the taxpayer's qualifying children who live in the home for more than half of the year, and the amount of the taxpayer's earned income. To be eligible for the credit, married taxpayers must file a joint tax return. The credit is computed by multiplying the appropriate credit percentage times the taxpayer's earned income up to a maximum amount. The credit percentage depends upon the number of qualifying children in the home and is subject to a phase-out based upon AGI (or earned income if greater). As summarized in Exhibit 8-10, the earned income credit increases as taxpayers receive earned income up to the maximum amount of earned income eligible for the credit. However, as taxpayers earn more income, the credit begins to phase out and is completely eliminated once taxpayers' earned income reaches established levels.

EXHIBIT 8-10 **2017 Earned Income Credit Table**

Qualifying Children	(1) Maximum Earned Income Eligible for Credit	(2) Credit %	(3) Maximum Credit (1) × (2)	(4) Credit Phase-Out for AGI (or earned income if greater) Over This Amount	(5) Phase-Out Percentage	No Credit When AGI (or earned income if greater) Equals or Exceeds This Amount (4) + [(3)/(5)]
			Married taxpayers filing joint returns			
0	$ 6,670	7.65%	$ 510	$13,930	7.65%	$20,600
1	10,000	34	3,400	23,930	15.98	45,207
2	14,040	40	5,616	23,930	21.06	50,597
3+	14,040	45	6,318	23,930	21.06	53,930
			All taxpayers *except* married taxpayers filing joint returns			
0	$ 6,670	7.65%	$ 510	$ 8,340	7.65%	$15,010
1	10,000	34	3,400	18,340	15.98	39,617
2	14,040	40	5,616	18,340	21.06	45,007
3+	14,040	45	6,318	18,340	21.06	48,340

[39] §32.
[40] §32(i).

Example 8-24

Courtney's earned income for the year is $160,800 (Example 8-19) and her AGI is $182,000 (Exhibit 6-6). Deron and Ellen both qualify as Courtney's qualifying children. What amount of earned income credit is Courtney entitled to claim on her 2017 tax return?

Answer: $0. Courtney's AGI (which is greater than her earned income) exceeds the $45,007 limit for unmarried taxpayers with two or more qualifying children. Consequently, Courtney is not allowed to claim any earned income credit.

What if: Assume that Courtney's only source of income for the year was $30,000 in salary. Also assume Courtney's AGI for the year was $30,000. What would be Courtney's earned income credit in these circumstances?

Answer: $3,160, computed as follows:

Description	Amount	Explanation
(1) Earned income	$30,000	
(2) Maximum earned income eligible for earned income credit for taxpayers filing as head of household with two qualifying children	14,040	Exhibit 8-10
(3) Earned income eligible for credit	14,040	Lesser of (1) and (2)
(4) Earned income credit percentage for taxpayer with two qualifying children	40%	
(5) Earned income credit before phase-out	5,616	(3) × (4)
(6) Phase-out threshold begins at this level of AGI (or earned income if greater)	18,340	See Exhibit 8-10 for head of household filing status and two qualifying children.
(7) Greater of (a) AGI or (b) earned income, less the phase-out threshold	11,660	(1) – (6) In this example, AGI equals earned income.
(8) Phase-out percentage	21.06%	See Exhibit 8-10
(9) Credit phase-out amount	2,456	(7) × (8), rounded
Earned income credit after phase-out	**$ 3,160**	(5) – (9)

TAXES IN THE REAL WORLD Taking a Bite Out of Earned Income Tax Credit Abuse

The IRS has special reporting requirements (Form 8867) for tax professionals filing tax returns that include an earned income tax credit. Form 8867, the Paid Preparer's Earned Income Credit Checklist, is intended to ensure that tax professionals use appropriate due diligence in determining the amount of, and a taxpayer's eligibility for, the earned income tax credit.

Why the extra concern with the earned income tax credit? Because the earned income tax credit is a refundable tax credit, the potential for abuse (fraudulent claim) is quite high. Only paid tax preparers are required to complete the form, and failure to do so could result in a $500 penalty for each failure. See Form 8867 and IRC Sec. 6695(g).

Other Refundable Personal Credits Other refundable personal tax credits include a portion of the child tax credit (discussed above), excess FICA withholdings (see discussion above under FICA taxes), and taxes withheld on wages and estimated tax payments. We address withholdings and estimated taxes below when we discuss tax prepayments.

Business Tax Credits

Business tax credits are designed to provide incentives for taxpayers to hire certain types of individuals or to participate in certain business activities. For example, Congress provides the employment tax credit to encourage businesses to hire certain unemployed individuals, and it provides the research and development credit to encourage businesses to expend funds to develop new technology. Business tax credits are *nonrefundable* credits. However, when business credits other than the foreign tax credit (discussed below), exceed the taxpayer's gross tax for the year, the credits are carried *back* one year and forward 20 years to use in years when the taxpayer has sufficient gross tax liability to use the credits.

Why discuss business credits in an individual tax chapter? We discuss business credits here because self-employed individuals may qualify for these credits. Also, individuals may be allocated business credits from flow-through entities (partnerships, LLCs, and S corporations). Finally, individuals working as employees overseas or receiving dividends from investments in foreign securities may qualify for the foreign tax credit.

Foreign Tax Credit

U.S. citizens must pay U.S. tax on their worldwide income. However, when they generate some or all of their income in other countries, they generally are required to pay income taxes to the foreign country where they earned their income. Without some form of tax relief, taxpayers earning income overseas would be double-taxed on this income. When taxpayers pay income taxes to foreign countries, for U.S. tax purposes, they may treat the payment in one of three ways: (1) as we discussed in the Gross Income and Exclusions chapter when we introduced the foreign-earned income exclusion, taxpayers may exclude the foreign-earned income from U.S. taxation (in which case they would *not* deduct or receive a credit for any foreign taxes paid); (2) taxpayers may include the foreign income in their gross income and deduct the foreign taxes paid as itemized deductions; or (3) taxpayers may include foreign income in gross income and claim a foreign tax credit for the foreign taxes paid. Here, we discuss the foreign tax credit.

The foreign tax credit helps reduce the double tax taxpayers may pay when they pay income taxes on foreign-earned income to the United States and to foreign countries. Taxpayers are allowed to claim a foreign tax credit, against their U.S. tax liability, for the income taxes they pay to foreign countries.[41] In certain situations, taxpayers may not be able to claim the full amount of foreign tax paid as a credit. This restriction may apply when the taxpayer's effective foreign tax rate is higher than the effective U.S. tax rate on the foreign earnings. Taxpayers generally benefit from claiming credits rather than deductions for foreign taxes paid because credits reduce their liabilities dollar for dollar. However, in circumstances when the foreign tax credit is restricted (see above), taxpayers may benefit by claiming deductions for the taxes paid instead of credits.

As we discussed above, the foreign tax credit may be limited in circumstances where a taxpayer's effective foreign tax rate exceeds her U.S. tax rate. In addition, as a nonrefundable credit, it may only reduce the taxpayer's tax liability to zero. When the use of a foreign tax credit is limited, taxpayers may carry back their unused credits one year and carry forward the credits up to 10 years.[42]

[41]§904.

[42]See IRS Publication 514 "Foreign Tax Credit for Individuals" for more information about the foreign tax credit.

Tax Credit Summary

Exhibit 8-11 identifies several tax credits and for each credit identifies the credit type, notes the IRC section allowing the credit, and describes the credit.

EXHIBIT 8-11 Summary of Selected Tax Credits

Credit	Type of Credit	IRC	Description
Child and dependent care credit	Nonrefundable personal	§21	Credit for taxpayers who pay dependent care expenses due to their employment activities.
Credit for elderly and disabled	Nonrefundable personal	§22	Credit for elderly low-income taxpayers who retire because of a disability.
Adoption expense credit	Nonrefundable personal	§23	Credit for qualified adoption-related expenses.
Child tax credit	Nonrefundable and refundable personal	§24	Credit for providing home for dependent children under the age of 17.
American opportunity credit	Nonrefundable and refundable personal	§25A	Credit for higher education expenses for the first four years of postsecondary education.
Lifetime learning credit	Nonrefundable personal	§25A	Credit for higher education expenses.
Saver's credit	Nonrefundable personal	§25B	Credit for contributing to qualified retirement plans.
Residential energy	Nonrefundable personal	§25D	Credit for qualified expenditures for solar electric property, solar water heating property, fuel cell property, wind energy property, and qualified geothermal heat pump property.
Earned income credit	Refundable personal	§32	Credit to encourage low-income taxpayers to work.
Premium tax credit	Refundable personal	§36B	Credit for health insurance purchased through an exchange for individuals and families with household incomes between 100% and 400% of the poverty line.
Credit for increasing research activities	Business	§41	Credit to encourage research and development.
Employer-provided child care credit	Business	§45F	Credit for providing child care for employees.
Small employer health insurance credit	Business	§45R	Credit to encourage employer-provided health insurance.
Rehabilitation credit	Business	§47	Credit for expenditures to renovate or restore older business buildings.
Energy credit	Business	§48	Credit for businesses that invest in energy conservation measures.
Work opportunity credit	Business	§51	Credit for hiring certain qualified veterans.
Foreign tax credit	Hybrid business and personal	§904	Credit to reduce effects of double taxation of foreign income.

Credit Application Sequence

As we've discussed, credits are applied against a taxpayer's gross tax. However, we still must describe what happens when the taxpayer's allowable credits exceed the taxpayer's gross tax. To set up this discussion, it is important to understand that nonrefundable personal credits and business credits may be used to reduce a taxpayer's gross tax to zero, but not below zero.[43] In contrast, by definition, a refundable credit may reduce a taxpayer's gross tax below zero. This excess refundable credit generates a tax refund for the taxpayer.

When a nonrefundable personal credit exceeds the taxpayer's gross tax, it reduces the gross tax to zero, but the excess credit (credit in excess of the taxpayer's gross tax) disappears. That is, the taxpayer may *not* carry over any excess nonrefundable personal credits to use in other years. However, when a business credit or foreign tax credit exceeds the gross tax, it reduces the taxpayer's gross tax to zero, but the excess credit may be carried forward or back to be used in other years when the taxpayer has sufficient gross tax to use the credit (subject to certain time restrictions discussed above).

Because the tax treatment of excess credits depends on the type of credit, it is important to identify the sequence in which taxpayers apply the credits when they have more than one type of credit for the year. When taxpayers have multiple credit types in the same year, they apply the credits against their gross tax in the following order: (1) nonrefundable personal credits, (2) business credits, and (3) refundable credits. This sequence maximizes the chances that taxpayers will receive full benefit for their tax credits.

Because, as we discuss above, the foreign tax credit is a hybrid credit subject to a unique set of application rules, we exclude it from our general discussion on applying credits. Exhibit 8-12 summarizes the order in which the credits are applied against gross tax and indicates the tax treatment of any excess credits.

EXHIBIT 8-12 **Credit Application**

Credit Type	Order Applied	Excess Credit
Nonrefundable personal	First	Lost
Business	Second	Carryback and carryover
Refundable personal	Last	Refunded

Example 8-25

What if: As we describe in Example 8-2, Gram's gross tax liability is $364. For illustrative purposes, let's *assume* that Gram is entitled to an $800 nonrefundable personal tax credit, a $700 business tax credit, and a $600 refundable personal tax credit. What is the amount of Gram's refund or taxes due?

Answer: $600 refund. Gram would apply these credits as follows:

Description	Amount	Treatment of Excess Credit
Gross tax liability	$ 364	Example 8-2
Nonrefundable personal credits	(364)	$436 ($800 – $364) excess credit expires unused
Business credits	0	$700 carried back one year or forward 20 years (10 years for foreign tax credit)
Refundable personal credits	**(600)**	Generates $600 tax refund to Gram

TAXPAYER PREPAYMENTS AND FILING REQUIREMENTS

LO 8-5

Even after determining their tax liabilities, taxpayers must still file a tax return and pay any additional tax due or receive a refund. When taxpayers don't pay enough taxes during the year or when they are late filing their tax return or paying their taxes due, they may be subject to certain penalties.

[43]In general, nonrefundable personal credits can offset a taxpayer's regular tax and AMT (§26) but not self-employment tax. The limitation on business credits is more complex. We limit our discussion here to basic concepts. See §38(c) for the detailed limitations.

Prepayments

The income tax must be paid on a *pay-as-you-go* basis. This means that the tax must be prepaid via **withholding** from salary or through periodic **estimated tax payments** during the tax year. Employees pay tax through withholding, and self-employed taxpayers generally pay taxes through estimated tax payments. Employers are required to withhold taxes from an employee's wages based upon the employee's marital status, exemptions, and estimated annual pay. Wages include both cash and noncash remuneration for services, and employers remit withholdings to the government on behalf of employees. At the end of the year employers report the amounts withheld to each employee via Form W-2. Estimated tax payments are required only if withholdings are insufficient to meet the taxpayer's tax liability. For calendar-year taxpayers, estimated tax payments are due on April 15, June 15, and September 15 of the current year and January 15 of the following year. If the due date falls on a Saturday, Sunday, or holiday, it is automatically extended to the next day that is not a Saturday, Sunday, or holiday.

Example 8-26

Courtney's gross tax liability for the year, including federal income tax, alternative minimum tax, and self-employment taxes, is $28,410 (see Exhibit 8-6). However, because she had only $24,410 withheld from her paycheck by EWD, she underpaid $4,000 for the year ($28,410 – $24,410). Because Courtney did not pay her full tax liability, she is potentially subject to underpayment penalties discussed below. If she had been aware that her withholding would be insufficient, she could have increased her withholding at any time during the year (even in her December paycheck) or made estimated tax payments of $1,000 on April 17, June 15, and September 15 in 2017 and January 16, 2018 ($4,000/4).

What if: If Courtney was self-employed (instead of employed by EWD) and thus had no tax withholdings by an employer, she would be *required* to pay quarterly estimated tax payments. In this scenario, she would need to pay $7,102.50 ($28,410/4 = $7,102.50) by April 17, June 15, and September 15 of 2017 and $7,102.50 by January 16, 2018, to cover her gross tax liability of $28,410.

Underpayment Penalties When taxpayers like Courtney fall behind on their tax prepayments, they may be subject to an **underpayment penalty.**[44] Taxpayers with unpredictable income streams may be particularly susceptible to this penalty because it is difficult for them to accurately estimate their tax liability for the year. To help taxpayers who may not be able to predict their earnings for the year and to provide some margin of error for those who can, the tax laws provide some **safe-harbor provisions.** Under these provisions taxpayers can avoid underpayment penalties if their withholdings and estimated tax payments equal or exceed one of the following two safe harbors: (1) 90 percent of their *current tax liability* or (2) 100 percent of their *previous year tax liability* (110 percent for individuals with AGI greater than $150,000).

These two safe harbors determine on a quarterly basis the minimum tax prepayments that a taxpayer must have made to avoid the underpayment penalty. The first safe harbor requires that a taxpayer must have paid at least 22.5 percent (90 percent/4 = 22.5 percent) of the *current*-year liability via withholdings or estimated tax payments by April 15 to avoid the underpayment penalty for the first quarter. Similarly by June 15, September 15, and January 15, the taxpayer must have paid 45 percent (22.5 percent × 2), 67.5 percent (22.5 percent × 3), and 90 percent (22.5 percent × 4), respectively, of the current-year liability via withholding or estimated tax payments to avoid the underpayment penalty in the second,

[44]§6654.

third, and fourth quarters.[45] In determining taxpayers' prepayments for a quarter, tax withholdings are generally treated as though they are withheld evenly throughout the year. In contrast, estimated tax payments are credited to the taxpayer's account when they are remitted.

Example 8-27

Because all of Courtney's prepayments were made through withholding by EWD, the payments are treated as though they were made evenly throughout the year. What are Courtney's actual and required withholdings under the 90 percent safe-harbor provision throughout the year?

Answer: See the following table:

Dates	(1) Actual Withholding	(2) Required Withholding	(1) – (2) Over- (Under-) Withheld
April 17, 2017	$6,103 ($24,410 × .25)	$6,392 ($28,410 × .9 × .25)	($289)
June 15, 2017	$12,205 ($24,410 × .50)	$12,785 ($28,410 × .9 × .50)	(580)
September 15, 2017	$18,308 ($24,410 × .75)	$19,177 ($28,410 × .9 × .75)	(869)
January 16, 2018	$24,410	$25,569 ($28,410 × .9 × 1)	(1,159)

It looks like Courtney is underwithheld in each quarter.

The second safe harbor requires that by April 15, June 15, September 15, and January 15, the taxpayer must have paid 25 percent, 50 percent (25 percent × 2), 75 percent (25 percent × 3), and 100 percent (25 percent × 4), respectively, of the *previous* year tax liability (110 percent of the previous year tax liability for individuals with AGI greater than $150,000) via withholding or estimated tax payments to avoid the underpayment penalty in the first, second, third, and fourth quarters.

If the taxpayer does not satisfy either of the safe-harbor provisions, the taxpayer can compute the underpayment penalty owed using Form 2210. The underpayment penalty is determined by multiplying the **federal short-term interest rate** plus 3 percentage points by the amount of tax underpayment per quarter. For purposes of this computation, the quarterly tax underpayment is the difference between the taxpayer's quarterly withholding and estimated tax payments and the required minimum tax payment under the first or second safe harbor (whichever is less). If the taxpayer does not complete Form 2210 and remit the underpayment penalty with the taxpayer's tax return, the IRS will compute and assess the penalty for the taxpayer.

Example 8-28

In the previous example, we discovered that Courtney was underwithheld in each quarter based on the first (90 percent of current year) safe-harbor provision. Assuming Courtney was underwithheld by even more under the second (100 percent of prior year) safe-harbor provision, she is required to pay an underpayment penalty based on the underpayments determined using the first safe-harbor provision. Assuming the federal short-term rate is 5 percent, what is Courtney's underpayment penalty for 2017?

(continued on page 8-38)

[45]As an alternative method of estimating safe harbor, (1) taxpayers can compute 90 percent of the current liability using the seasonal method. This method allows taxpayers to estimate 90 percent of their current tax liability by annualizing their taxable income earned through the month prior to the payment date (e.g., through March for April 15, May for June 15, and August for September 15). Taxpayers with uneven taxable income throughout the year with smaller taxable income earlier in the year benefit from this method.

Answer: $59, computed as follows:

Description	First Quarter	Second Quarter	Third Quarter	Fourth Quarter
Underpayment	$289	$580	$869	$1,159
Times: Federal rate + 3% (5% + 3%)	× 8%	× 8%	× 8%	× 8%
	$ 23	$ 46	$ 70	$ 93
Times one quarter of a year[46]	× 25%	× 25%	× 25%	× 25%
Underpayment penalty per quarter	$ 6	$ 12	$ 18	$ 23

That's a lot of work to figure out a $59 penalty: (6 + 12 + 18 + 23 = $59)

As a matter of administrative convenience, taxpayers who either (1) had no tax liability in the previous year or (2) whose tax payable after subtracting their withholding amounts (but not estimated payments) is less than $1,000 are not subject to underpayment penalties.

Example 8-29

Gram's tax liability for the year is $364 (Example 8-2), but she did not have any taxes withheld during the year, and she did not make any estimated tax payments. What is Gram's underpayment penalty?

Answer: $0. Because Gram's $364 tax payable after subtracting her withholding amounts ($364 tax – $0 withholding) is less than $1,000, she is not subject to an underpayment penalty.

THE KEY FACTS

Taxpayer Prepayments and Underpayment Penalties

- Taxpayers prepay their tax via withholding from salary or through periodic estimated tax payments during the tax year.
- Estimated tax payments are required only if withholdings are insufficient to meet the taxpayer's tax liability.
- For calendar-year taxpayers, estimated tax payments are due on April 15, June 15, and September 15 of the current year and January 15 of the following year.
- Taxpayers can avoid an underpayment penalty if their withholdings and estimated tax payments equal or exceed one of two safe harbors.
- The underpayment penalty is determined by multiplying the federal short-term interest rate plus 3 percentage points by the amount of tax underpayment per quarter.

Filing Requirements

Individual taxpayers are required to file a tax return only if their *gross income* exceeds certain thresholds, which vary based on the taxpayer's filing status and age. However, a taxpayer may prefer to file a tax return even when she is not required to do so. For example, a taxpayer with gross income less than the threshold may want to file a tax return to receive a refund of income taxes withheld. In general, the thresholds are simply the applicable standard deduction amount for the different filing statuses plus the personal exemption amount (twice the personal exemption amount of married taxpayers filing jointly).[47]

Individual tax returns are due on April 15 for calendar-year individuals (the fifteenth day of the fourth month following year-end). If the due date falls on a Saturday, Sunday, or holiday, it is automatically extended to the next day that is not a Saturday, Sunday, or holiday. Taxpayers unable to file a tax return by the original due date can request (by that same deadline) a six-month extension to file, which is granted automatically by the IRS. The extension gives the taxpayer additional time to file the tax return, but does *not* extend the due date for paying the tax.

Late Filing Penalty The tax law imposes a penalty on taxpayers that do not file a tax return by the required date (the original due date plus extension).[48] The penalty equals

[46]Form 2210 actually computes the penalty per quarter based on the number of days in the quarter divided by the number of days in the year. For simplicity, we assume this ratio is per quarter.

[47]§6012. Filing requirements for individuals who are dependents of other taxpayers are subject to special rules that consider the individual's unearned income, earned income, and gross income. See IRS Publication 17 "Your Federal Income Tax."

[48]§6651.

5 percent of the amount of tax owed for each month (or fraction thereof) that the tax return is late, with a maximum penalty of 25 percent. For fraudulent failure to file, the penalty is 15 percent of the amount of tax owed per month with a maximum penalty of 75 percent. If the taxpayer owes no tax as of the due date of the tax return (plus extension), the tax law does not impose a **late filing penalty.**

Late Payment Penalty An extension allows the taxpayer to delay filing a tax return but does *not* extend the due date for tax payments. If a taxpayer fails to pay the entire balance of tax owed by the original due date of the tax return, the tax law imposes a **late payment penalty** from the due date of the return until the taxpayer pays the tax.[49] The late payment penalty equals .5 percent of the amount of tax owed for each month (or fraction thereof) that the tax is not paid.

The *combined* maximum penalty that may be imposed for late payment and late filing (nonfraudulent) is 5 percent per month (25 percent in total). For late payment and filing due to fraud, the combined maximum penalty for late payment and late filing is 15 percent per month (75 percent in total).

Example 8-30

Courtney filed her tax return on April 10 and included a check with the return for $4,059 made payable to the United States Treasury. The $4,059 consisted of her underpaid tax liability of $4,000 (Example 8-26) and her $59 underpayment penalty (Example 8-28).

What if: If Courtney had waited until May 1 to file her return and pay her taxes, what late filing and late payment penalties would she owe?

Answer: Her combined *late filing penalty* and *late payment penalty* would be $200 ($4,000 late payment × 5 percent × 1 month or portion thereof—the combined penalty is limited to 5 percent per month).

TAX SUMMARY

Courtney's and Gram's net taxes due, including an underpayment penalty for Courtney, are provided in Exhibits 8-13 and 8-15, respectively. Exhibit 8-14 illustrates how this information would be presented on Courtney's tax return by providing Courtney's Form 1040, page 2.

THE KEY FACTS

Filing Requirements and Filing-Related Penalties

- Filing requirements vary based on the taxpayer's filing status, age, and gross income.
- Individual tax returns are due on April 15 for calendar-year individuals.
- Taxpayers unable to file a tax return by the original due date can request a six-month extension to file.
- The tax law imposes penalties on taxpayers who do not file a tax return (by the original due date plus extension) or pay the tax owed (by the original due date).

EXHIBIT 8-13 Courtney's Net Tax Payable

Description	Amount	Reference
(1) Regular federal income tax	$ 26,673	Example 8-3
(2) Alternative minimum tax	1,255	Example 8-10
(3) Self-employment tax	482	Example 8-15
(4) Gross tax	$ 28,410	(1) + (2) + (3)
(5) Tax credits	0	Examples 8-18, 8-20, 8-21, and 8-24
(6) Prepayments	($24,410)	Example 8-26
(7) Underpayment penalties	59	Example 8-28
Tax and penalties due with tax return	$ 4,059	

[49]§6651. As we discussed in the Tax Compliance, the IRS, and Tax Authorities chapter, the tax law also assesses interest on any tax underpayments until the tax is paid (§6601).

EXHIBIT 8-14 Courtney's Net Tax Payable (as presented on her Form 1040, page 2)

Form 1040 (2016) Page 2

Section	Line	Description			Line	Amount
Tax and Credits	38	Amount from line 37 (adjusted gross income)			38	182,000
	39a	Check if: ☐ **You** were born before January 2, 1952, ☐ Blind. ☐ **Spouse** was born before January 2, 1952, ☐ Blind. **Total boxes checked ▶ 39a**				
	b	If your spouse itemizes on a separate return or you were a dual-status alien, check here▶ 39b☐				
Standard Deduction for—	40	**Itemized deductions** (from Schedule A) **or** your **standard deduction** (see left margin)			40	39,889
• People who check any box on line 39a or 39b **or** who can be claimed as a dependent, see instructions.	41	Subtract line 40 from line 38			41	142,111
• All others:	42	**Exemptions.** If line 38 is $155,650 or less, multiply $4,050 by the number on line 6d. Otherwise, see instructions			42	12,150
Single or Married filing separately, $6,300	43	**Taxable income.** Subtract line 42 from line 41. If line 42 is more than line 41, enter -0-			43	129,961
Married filing jointly or Qualifying widow(er), $12,600	44	**Tax** (see instructions). Check if any from: **a** ☐ Form(s) 8814 **b** ☐ Form 4972 **c** ☐			44	26,673
Head of household, $9,300	45	**Alternative minimum tax** (see instructions). Attach Form 6251			45	1,255
	46	Excess advance premium tax credit repayment. Attach Form 8962			46	
	47	Add lines 44, 45, and 46 ▶			47	27,928
	48	Foreign tax credit. Attach Form 1116 if required	48			
	49	Credit for child and dependent care expenses. Attach Form 2441	49			
	50	Education credits from Form 8863, line 19	50			
	51	Retirement savings contributions credit. Attach Form 8880	51			
	52	Child tax credit. Attach Schedule 8812, if required	52			
	53	Residential energy credits. Attach Form 5695	53			
	54	Other credits from Form: **a** ☐ 3800 **b** ☐ 8801 **c** ☐	54			
	55	Add lines 48 through 54. These are your **total credits**			55	
	56	Subtract line 55 from line 47. If line 55 is more than line 47, enter -0- ▶			56	27,928
Other Taxes	57	Self-employment tax. Attach Schedule SE			57	482
	58	Unreported social security and Medicare tax from Form: **a** ☐ 4137 **b** ☐ 8919			58	
	59	Additional tax on IRAs, other qualified retirement plans, etc. Attach Form 5329 if required			59	
	60a	Household employment taxes from Schedule H			60a	
	b	First-time homebuyer credit repayment. Attach Form 5405 if required			60b	
	61	Health care: individual responsibility (see instructions) Full-year coverage ☐			61	
	62	Taxes from: **a** ☐ Form 8959 **b** ☐ Form 8960 **c** ☐ Instructions; enter code(s)			62	
	63	Add lines 56 through 62. This is your **total tax** ▶			63	28,410
Payments	64	Federal income tax withheld from Forms W-2 and 1099	64	24,410		
	65	2016 estimated tax payments and amount applied from 2015 return	65			
If you have a qualifying child, attach Schedule EIC.	66a	**Earned income credit (EIC)**	66a			
	b	Nontaxable combat pay election 66b				
	67	Additional child tax credit. Attach Schedule 8812	67			
	68	American opportunity credit from Form 8863, line 8	68			
	69	Net premium tax credit. Attach Form 8962	69			
	70	Amount paid with request for extension to file	70			
	71	Excess social security and tier 1 RRTA tax withheld	71			
	72	Credit for federal tax on fuels. Attach Form 4136	72			
	73	Credits from Form: **a** ☐ 2439 **b** ☐ Reserved **c** ☐ 8885 **d** ☐	73			
	74	Add lines 64, 65, 66a, and 67 through 73. These are your **total payments** ▶			74	24,410
Refund	75	If line 74 is more than line 63, subtract line 63 from line 74. This is the amount you **overpaid**			75	
	76a	Amount of line 75 you want **refunded to you.** If Form 8888 is attached, check here ▶☐			76a	
Direct deposit? See instructions.	▶ b	Routing number ▶ c Type: ☐ Checking ☐ Savings				
	▶ d	Account number				
	77	Amount of line 75 you want **applied to your 2017 estimated tax** ▶	77			
Amount You Owe	78	**Amount you owe.** Subtract line 74 from line 63. For details on how to pay, see instructions ▶			78	4,059
	79	Estimated tax penalty (see instructions)	79	59		

Third Party Designee Do you want to allow another person to discuss this return with the IRS (see instructions)? ☐ **Yes.** Complete below. ☐ **No**
Designee's name ▶ Phone no. ▶ Personal identification number (PIN) ▶

Sign Here Under penalties of perjury, I declare that I have examined this return and accompanying schedules and statements, and to the best of my knowledge and belief, they are true, correct, and accurately list all amounts and sources of income I received during the tax year. Declaration of preparer (other than taxpayer) is based on all information of which preparer has any knowledge.
Joint return? See instructions. Keep a copy for your records.
Your signature | Date | Your occupation | Daytime phone number
Spouse's signature. If a joint return, **both** must sign. | Date | Spouse's occupation | If the IRS sent you an Identity Protection PIN, enter it here (see inst.)

Paid Preparer Use Only Print/Type preparer's name | Preparer's signature | Date | Check ☐ if self-employed | PTIN
Firm's name ▶ | Firm's EIN ▶
Firm's address ▶ | Phone no.

www.irs.gov/form1040 Form **1040** (2016)

EXHIBIT 8-15 Gram's Tax Payable

Description	Amount	Reference
(1) Gross tax	$364	Example 8-2
(2) Alternative minimum tax	0	
(3) Self-employment tax	0	
(4) Gross tax	$364	(1) + (2) + (3)
(5) Tax credits	0	
(6) Prepayments	0	
(7) Penalties	0	
Tax due with return	$364	(4) − (5) − (6) − (7)

CONCLUSION

This chapter reviewed the process for determining an individual's gross and net tax liability. We discovered that taxpayers may be required to pay regular federal income tax, alternative minimum tax, and employment-related tax. Taxpayers are able to offset their gross tax liability dollar for dollar with various types of tax credits and by the amount of tax they prepay during the year. Taxpayers must pay additional taxes with their tax return or they may receive a refund when they file their tax return depending on their gross tax liability and their available tax credits and tax prepayments. The previous chapters have covered the basic individual tax formula. The next three chapters address issues relevant for taxpayers involved in business activities.

Summary

Determine a taxpayer's regular tax liability and identify tax issues associated with the process. **LO 8-1**

- Individual income is taxed using progressive tax rate schedules with rates ranging from 10 percent to 39.6 percent.
- Marginal tax rates depend on filing status and amount of taxable income.
- Progressive tax rate schedules may lead to either a marriage penalty or a marriage benefit for married taxpayers.
- Long-term capital gains and qualified dividends are taxed at either 0 percent, 15 percent, or 20 percent, depending on the amount of taxable income.
- A 3.8 percent tax is levied on net investment income for higher-income taxpayers.
- Strategies to shift investment income from parents to children are limited by the "kiddie tax" whereby children's investment income is taxed at the parents' marginal tax rate.

Compute a taxpayer's alternative minimum tax liability and describe the tax characteristics of taxpayers most likely to owe the alternative minimum tax. **LO 8-2**

- The AMT was designed to ensure that higher-income taxpayers pay some minimum level of income tax.
- The AMT base is broader than the regular income tax base. The AMT base is designed to more closely reflect economic income, as opposed to regular taxable income.
- The starting point for calculating AMT is regular taxable income. To compute AMTI, taxpayers add back items not deductible for AMT purposes. In some cases, taxpayers may subtract items not includable in AMTI and items deductible for AMT but not for regular tax purposes. Taxpayers then subtract the allowable AMT exemption to generate the AMT base. They then apply the AMT rates and compare the product (the tentative minimum tax) to their regular tax liability. They owe AMT if the tentative minimum tax exceeds the regular tax liability.
- The AMT exemption depends on the taxpayer's filing status and is subject to phase-out of 25 cents for each dollar of AMTI over the specific thresholds based on filing status.
- The 2017 AMT tax rates are 26 percent up to $187,800 of AMT base ($93,900 of AMT base for married taxpayers filing separately) and 28 percent thereafter. However, long-term capital gains and qualified dividends are subject to the same preferential rate at which they are taxed for regular tax purposes.
- The amount of the AMT is the excess of the tentative minimum tax over the taxpayer's regular tax liability.

Calculate a taxpayer's employment and self-employment taxes payable and explain tax considerations relating to whether a taxpayer is considered to be an employee or a self-employed independent contractor. **LO 8-3**

- Employees' wages are subject to FICA tax. The Social Security component is 6.2 percent and the Medicare component ranges from 1.45 percent to 2.35 percent for employees. For employers, the Social Security component is 6.2 percent and the Medicare component is 1.45 percent. The Social Security tax applies to the first $127,200 of salary or wages in 2017. The wage base on the Medicare tax is unlimited.

- Self-employed taxpayers pay self-employment tax on their net self-employment income (92.35 percent of their net Schedule C income). They pay Social Security tax of 12.4 percent and Medicare tax of 2.9 percent to 3.8 percent on their net self-employment income. The Social Security tax applies to the first $127,200 of net Schedule C income in 2017. The base for the Medicare tax is unlimited.
- The determination as to whether to treat a worker as an independent contractor or as an employee for tax purposes is a subjective test based in large part on the extent of control the worker has over things such as the nature, timing, and location of work performed.
- Independent contractors are able to deduct ordinary and necessary business expenses as *for* AGI deductions. Employees incurring unreimbursed business expenses must deduct the items as miscellaneous itemized deductions subject to the 2 percent of AGI floor.
- Independent contractors may deduct the employer portion of their self-employment taxes paid during the year. Employees may not deduct their FICA taxes.
- Independent contractors are required to pay self-employment tax, which represents the employer and employee portions of FICA taxes. Further, independent contractors must pay estimated taxes on their income because the employer does not withhold taxes from the independent contractor's paychecks.
- Hiring independent contractors is generally less costly for employers than is hiring employees. Employers do not pay FICA taxes, withhold taxes, or provide fringe benefits for independent contractors.

LO 8-4 Describe the different general types of tax credits, identify specific tax credits, and compute a taxpayer's allowable child tax credit, child and dependent care credit, American opportunity credit, lifetime learning credit, and earned income credit.

- Tax credits are generally classified into one of three categories: business, nonrefundable personal, or refundable personal credits.
- Nonrefundable personal tax credits provide tax relief to specified groups of individuals.
- The child tax credit is a $1,000 credit for low-income taxpayers who provide a home for dependent children under the age of 17.
- The child and dependent care credit is provided to help taxpayers pay the cost of providing care for their dependents and allow taxpayers to work or to look for work.
- The American opportunity credit provides a credit for a percentage of the costs of the first four years of a student's college education. Forty percent of the credit is refundable.
- The lifetime learning credit provides a credit for a percentage of the costs for instruction in a postsecondary degree program or the costs to acquire or improve a taxpayer's job skills.
- Nonrefundable credits are first used to reduce a taxpayer's gross tax but cannot reduce the gross tax below zero. Any excess credit is lost unless it is allowed to be carried to a different tax year.
- The earned income credit is refundable but subject to a very complex calculation.
- Business credits reduce the tax after applying nonrefundable credits. Any credit in excess of the remaining tax is generally allowed to be carried over or back to be used in other years.
- Refundable credits are the last credit applied to the tax after applying nonrefundable and business credits. Any refundable credit in excess of the remaining tax is treated as an overpayment and refunded to the taxpayer.

LO 8-5 Explain taxpayer filing and tax payment requirements and describe in general terms how to compute a taxpayer's underpayment, late filing, and late payment penalties.

- The income tax must be prepaid via withholding from salary or through periodic estimated tax payments during the tax year. Estimated tax payments are required only if withholdings are insufficient to meet the taxpayer's tax liability. For calendar-year taxpayers, estimated tax payments are due on April 15, June 15, and September 15 of the current year and January 15 of the following year.

- Taxpayers can avoid an underpayment penalty if their withholdings and estimated tax payments equal or exceed one of two safe harbors: (1) 90 percent of current-year tax or (2) 100 percent of previous year tax (110 percent if AGI exceeds $150,000). If the taxpayer does not satisfy either of the safe-harbor provisions, the underpayment penalty is determined by multiplying the federal short-term interest rate plus 3 percentage points by the amount of tax underpayment per quarter.
- Individual taxpayers are required to file a tax return only if their *gross income* exceeds certain thresholds, which vary based on the taxpayer's filing status, age, and gross income.
- Individual tax returns are due on April 15 for calendar-year individuals. Taxpayers unable to file a tax return by the original due date can request a six-month extension to file.
- The tax law imposes penalties on taxpayers that do not file a tax return (by the original due date plus extension) or pay the tax owed (by the original due date). The failure-to-file penalty equals 5 percent of the amount of tax owed for each month (or fraction thereof) that the tax return is late with a maximum penalty of 25 percent. The late payment penalty equals .5 percent of the amount of tax owed for each month (or fraction thereof) that the tax is not paid. The combined maximum penalty that may be imposed for late filing and late payment is 5 percent per month (25 percent in total). The late filing and late payment penalties are higher if fraud is involved.

KEY TERMS

alternative minimum tax (AMT) (8-8)
alternative minimum tax adjustments (8-9)
alternative minimum tax (AMT) base (8-8)
alternative minimum tax (AMT) exemption (8-12)
alternative minimum tax system (8-8)
business tax credits (8-33)
child tax credits (8-25)
earned income credit (8-31)
employee (8-22)
estimated tax payments (8-36)
federal short-term interest rate (8-37)
FICA taxes (8-15)
independent contractor (8-22)
kiddie tax (8-6)
late filing penalty (8-39)
late payment penalty (8-39)
marginal tax rate (8-3)
marriage benefit (8-3)
marriage penalty (8-3)
Medicare tax (8-15)
minimum tax credit (8-14)
net earnings from self-employment (8-17)
net investment income tax (8-5)
net unearned income (8-6)
nonrefundable credit (8-24)
preferential tax rate (8-4)
preferentially taxed income (8-4)
safe-harbor provisions (8-36)
Schedule C (8-17)
self-employment taxes (8-17)
Social Security tax (8-14)
tax bracket (8-2)
tax credits (8-24)
tax rate schedule (8-2)
tax tables (8-3)
tentative minimum tax (8-9)
underpayment penalty (8-36)
withholding (8-36)

DISCUSSION QUESTIONS

Discussion Questions are available in Connect®.

1. What is a tax bracket? What is the relationship between filing status and the width of the tax brackets in the tax rate schedule? LO 8-1
2. In 2017, for a taxpayer with $50,000 of taxable income, without doing any actual computations, which filing status do you expect to provide the lowest tax liability? Which filing status provides the highest tax liability? LO 8-1
3. What is the tax marriage penalty and when does it apply? Under what circumstances would a couple experience a tax marriage benefit? LO 8-1
4. Once they've computed their taxable income, how do taxpayers determine their regular tax liability? What additional steps must taxpayers take to compute their tax liability when they have preferentially taxed income? LO 8-1

LO 8-1 research
5. Are there circumstances in which preferentially taxed income (long-term capital gains and qualified dividends) is taxed at the same rate as ordinary income? Explain.

LO 8-1
6. Augustana received $10,000 of qualified dividends this year. Under what circumstances would all $10,000 be taxed at the same rate? Under what circumstances might the entire $10,000 of income not be taxed at the same rate?

LO 8-1
7. What is the difference between earned and unearned income?

LO 8-1
8. Does the kiddie tax eliminate the tax benefits gained by a family when parents transfer income-producing assets to children? Explain.

LO 8-1
9. Does the kiddie tax apply to all children no matter their age? Explain.

LO 8-1
10. What is the kiddie tax and on whose tax return is the kiddie tax liability reported? Explain.

LO 8-1
11. Lauren is 17 years old. She reports earned income of $3,000 and unearned income of $2,200. Is it likely that she is subject to the kiddie tax? Explain.

LO 8-2
12. In very general terms, how is the alternative minimum tax system different from the regular income tax system? How is it similar?

LO 8-2
13. Describe, in general terms, why Congress implemented the AMT.

LO 8-2
14. Do taxpayers always add back the standard deduction when computing alternative minimum taxable income? Explain.

LO 8-2
15. The starting point for computing alternative minimum taxable income is regular taxable income. What are some of the plus adjustments, plus or minus adjustments, and minus adjustments to regular taxable income to compute alternative minimum taxable income?

LO 8-2
16. Describe what the AMT exemption is and who is and isn't allowed to deduct the exemption. How is it similar to the standard deduction and how is it dissimilar?

LO 8-1 LO 8-2
17. How do the AMT tax rates compare to the regular income tax rates?

LO 8-2
18. Is it possible for a taxpayer who pays AMT to have a marginal tax rate higher than the stated AMT rate? Explain.

LO 8-2
19. What is the difference between the tentative minimum tax and the AMT?

LO 8-2 planning
20. Lee is single and runs his own business. He uses the cash method of accounting to determine his business income. Near the end of the year, Lee performed work that he needs to bill a client for. The value of his services is $5,000. Lee figures that if he immediately takes the time to put the bill together and send it out, the client will pay him before year-end. However, if he doesn't send out the bill for one week, he won't receive the client's payment until the beginning of next year. Lee expects that he will owe AMT this year and that his AMT base will be around $200,000 before counting any of the additional business income. Further, Lee anticipates that he will not owe AMT next year. He anticipates his regular taxable income next year will be in the $200,000 range. Would you advise Lee to immediately bill his client or to wait? What factors would you consider in making your recommendation?

LO 8-3
21. Are an employee's entire wages subject to the FICA tax? Explain.

LO 8-3
22. Bobbie works as an employee for Altron Corp. for the first half of the year and for Betel Inc. for the rest of the year. She is relatively well paid. What FICA tax issues

is she likely to encounter? What FICA tax issues do Altron Corp. and Betel Inc. need to consider?

23. Compare and contrast an employee's FICA tax payment responsibilities with those of a self-employed taxpayer. LO 8-3

24. When a taxpayer works as an employee and as a self-employed independent contractor during the year, how does the taxpayer determine her employment and self-employment taxes payable? LO 8-3

25. What are the primary factors to consider when deciding whether a worker should be considered an employee or a self-employed taxpayer for tax purposes? LO 8-3

26. How do the tax consequences of being an employee differ from those of being self-employed? LO 8-3

27. Mike wanted to work for a CPA firm but he also wanted to work on his father's farm in Montana. Because the CPA firm wanted Mike to be happy, they offered to let him work for them as an independent contractor during the fall and winter and let him return to Montana to work for his father during the spring and summer. He was very excited to hear that they were also going to give him a 5 percent higher "salary" for the six months he would be working for the firm over what he would have made over the same six-month period if he worked full-time as an employee (i.e., an increase from $30,000 to $31,500). Should Mike be excited about his 5 percent raise? Why or why not? What counteroffer could Mike reasonably suggest? LO 8-3 planning

28. How are tax credits and tax deductions similar? How are they dissimilar? LO 8-4

29. What are the three types of tax credits? Explain why it is important to distinguish between the different types of tax credits. LO 8-4

30. Explain why there is such a large number and variety of tax credits. LO 8-4

31. What is the difference between a refundable and nonrefundable tax credit? LO 8-4

32. Is the child tax credit a refundable or nonrefundable credit? Explain. LO 8-4

33. Diane has a job working three-quarter time. She hired her mother to take care of her two small children so Diane could work. Do Diane's child care payments to her mother qualify for the child and dependent care credit? Explain. LO 8-4

34. The amount of the child and dependent care credit is based on the amount of the taxpayer's expenditures to provide care for one or more qualifying persons. Who is considered to be a qualifying person for this purpose? LO 8-4

35. Compare and contrast the lifetime learning credit with the American opportunity credit. LO 8-4

36. Jennie's grandfather paid her tuition this fall to State University (an eligible educational institution). Jennie is claimed as a dependent by her parents, but she also files her own tax return. Can Jennie claim an education credit for the tuition paid by her grandfather? What difference would it make, if any, if Jennie did not qualify as a dependent of her parents (or anyone else)? LO 8-4 research

37. Why is the earned income credit referred to as a negative income tax? LO 8-4

38. Under what circumstances can a college student qualify for the earned income credit? LO 8-4

39. How are business credits similar to personal credits? How are they dissimilar? LO 8-4

40. Is the foreign tax credit a personal credit or a business credit? Explain. LO 8-4

LO 8-4 41. When a U.S. taxpayer pays income taxes to a foreign government, what options does the taxpayer have when determining how to treat the expenditure on her U.S. individual income tax return?

LO 8-4 42. Describe the order in which different types of tax credits are applied to reduce a taxpayer's tax liability.

LO 8-5 43. Describe the two methods that taxpayers use to prepay their taxes.

LO 8-5 44. What are the consequences of a taxpayer underpaying his or her tax liability throughout the year? Explain the safe-harbor provisions that may apply in this situation.

LO 8-5 45. Describe how the underpayment penalty is calculated.

LO 8-5 46. What determines if a taxpayer is required to file a tax return? If a taxpayer is not required to file a tax return, does this mean that the taxpayer should not file a tax return?

LO 8-5 47. What is the due date for individual tax returns? What extensions are available?

LO 8-5 48. Describe the consequences for failure to file a tax return and late payment of taxes owed.

PROBLEMS

Select problems are available in Connect®. connect

LO 8-1 49. Whitney received $75,000 of taxable income in 2017. All of the income was salary from her employer. What is her income tax liability in each of the following alternative situations?

a) She files under the single filing status.

b) She files a joint tax return with her spouse. Together their taxable income is $75,000.

c) She is married but files a separate tax return. Her taxable income is $75,000.

d) She files as a head of household.

LO 8-1 50. In 2017, Lisa and Fred, a married couple, had taxable income of $300,000. If they were to file separate tax returns, Lisa would have reported taxable income of $125,000 and Fred would have reported taxable income of $175,000. What is the couple's marriage penalty or benefit?

LO 8-1 51. In 2017, Jasmine and Thomas, a married couple, had taxable income of $150,000. If they were to file separate tax returns, Jasmine would have reported taxable income of $140,000 and Thomas would have reported taxable income of $10,000. What is the couple's marriage penalty or benefit?

LO 8-1 52. Lacy is a single taxpayer. In 2017, her taxable income is $40,000. What is her tax liability in each of the following alternative situations?

a) All of her income is salary from her employer.

b) Her $40,000 of taxable income includes $1,000 of qualified dividends.

c) Her $40,000 of taxable income includes $5,000 of qualified dividends.

LO 8-1 53. Henrich is a single taxpayer. In 2017, his taxable income is $425,000. What is his income tax and net investment income tax liability in each of the following alternative scenarios?

a) All of his income is salary from his employer.

b) His $425,000 of taxable income includes $2,000 of long-term capital gain that is taxed at preferential rates.

c) His $425,000 of taxable income includes $55,000 of long-term capital gain that is taxed at preferential rates.

d) Henrich has $195,000 of taxable income, which includes $50,000 of long-term capital gain that is taxed at preferential rates. Assume his modified AGI is $210,000.

54. In 2017, Sheryl is claimed as a dependent on her parents' tax return. Her parents' ordinary income marginal tax rate is 35 percent. Sheryl did not provide more than half her own support. What is Sheryl's tax liability for the year in each of the following alternative circumstances? LO 8-1

a) She received $7,000 from a part-time job. This was her only source of income. She is 16 years old at year-end.

b) She received $7,000 of interest income from corporate bonds she received several years ago. This is her only source of income. She is 16 years old at year-end.

c) She received $7,000 of interest income from corporate bonds she received several years ago. This is her only source of income. She is 20 years old at year-end and is a full-time student.

d) She received $7,000 of qualified dividend income. This is her only source of income. She is 16 years old at year-end.

55. In 2017, Carson is claimed as a dependent on his parents' tax return. His parents' ordinary income marginal tax rate is 28 percent. Carson's parents provided most of his support. What is Carson's tax liability for the year in each of the following alternative circumstances? LO 8-1

a) Carson is 17 years old at year-end and earned $12,000 from his summer job and part-time job after school. This was his only source of income.

b) Carson is 23 years old at year-end. He is a full-time student and earned $12,000 from his summer internship and part-time job. He also received $5,000 of qualified dividend income.

56. Brooklyn files as a head of household for 2017 and claims a total of three exemptions (3 × $4,050 = $12,150). She claimed the standard deduction of $9,350 for regular tax purposes. Her regular taxable income was $80,000. What is Brooklyn's AMTI? LO 8-2

57. Sylvester files as a single taxpayer during 2017 and claims one personal exemption. He itemizes deductions for regular tax purposes. He paid charitable contributions of $7,000, real estate taxes of $1,000, state income taxes of $4,000, and interest on a home-equity loan of $2,000. Sylvester's regular taxable income is $100,000. LO 8-2

a) What is Sylvester's AMTI if he used the home-equity proceeds to purchase a car?

b) What is Sylvester's AMTI if he used the home-equity loan proceeds to build a new garage next to his home?

58. In 2017, Nadia has $100,000 of regular taxable income. She itemizes her deductions as follows: real property taxes of $1,500, state income taxes of $2,000, and mortgage interest expense of $10,000 (not a home-equity loan). In addition, she receives tax-exempt interest of $1,000 from a municipal bond (issued in 2006) that was used to fund a new business building for a (formerly) out-of-state employer. Finally, she received a state tax refund of $300 from the prior year. LO 8-2 tax forms

a) What is Nadia's AMTI this year if she deducted $15,000 of itemized deductions last year and did not owe any AMT last year? Complete Form 6251 (through line 28) for Nadia.

b) What is Nadia's AMTI this year if she deducted the standard deduction last year and did not owe any AMT last year? Complete Form 6251 (through line 28) for Nadia.

LO 8-2 tax forms

59. In 2017, Sven is single and has $120,000 of regular taxable income. He itemizes his deductions as follows: real property tax of $2,000, state income tax of $4,000, mortgage interest expense of $15,000 (not a home-equity loan). He also paid $2,000 in tax preparation fees and has a positive AMT depreciation adjustment of $500. What is Sven's alternative minimum taxable income (AMTI)? Complete Form 6251 (through line 28) for Sven.

LO 8-2

60. Olga is married and files a joint tax return with her husband. What amount of AMT exemption may she deduct under each of the following alternative circumstances?
   a) Her AMTI is $90,000.
   b) Her AMTI is $180,000.
   c) Her AMTI is $500,000.

LO 8-2

61. Corbett's AMTI is $130,000. What is his AMT exemption under the following alternative circumstances?
   a) He is married and files a joint return.
   b) He is married and files a separate return.
   c) His filing status is single.
   d) His filing status is head of household.

LO 8-2

62. In 2017, Juanita is married and files a joint tax return with her husband. What is her tentative minimum tax in each of the following alternative circumstances?
   a) Her AMT base is $100,000, all ordinary income.
   b) Her AMT base is $250,000, all ordinary income.
   c) Her AMT base is $100,000, which includes $10,000 of qualified dividends.
   d) Her AMT base is $250,000, which includes $10,000 of qualified dividends.

LO 8-2

63. Steve's tentative minimum tax for 2017 is $15,000. What is his AMT if
   a) His regular tax is $10,000?
   b) His regular tax is $20,000?

LO 8-2 tax forms

64. In 2017, Janet and Ray are married filing jointly. They have five dependent children under 18 years of age. Janet and Ray's taxable income is $140,000, and they itemize their deductions as follows: real property taxes of $5,000, state income taxes of $9,000, and mortgage interest expense of $15,000 (not a home-equity loan). What is Janet and Ray's AMT? Complete Form 6251 for Janet and Ray.

LO 8-2 tax forms

65. In 2017, Deon and NeNe are married filing jointly. They have three dependent children under 18 years of age. Deon and NeNe's AGI is $813,800, their taxable income is $722,750, and they itemize their deductions as follows: real property taxes of $10,000, state income taxes of $40,000, miscellaneous itemized deductions of $4,000 (subject to but in excess of 2 percent AGI floor), charitable contributions of $11,050, and mortgage interest expense of $41,000 ($11,000 of which is attributable to a home-equity loan used to buy a new car). What is Deon and NeNe's AMT? Complete Form 6251 for Deon and NeNe.

LO 8-3

66. Brooke, a single taxpayer, works for Company A for all of 2017, earning a salary of $50,000.
   a) What is her FICA tax obligation for the year?

b) Assume Brooke works for Company A for half of 2017, earning $50,000 in salary, and she works for Company B for the second half of 2017, earning $90,000 in salary. What is Brooke's FICA tax obligation for the year?

67. Rasheed works for Company A, earning $350,000 in salary during 2017. Assuming he is single and has no other sources of income, what amount of FICA tax will Rasheed pay for the year? LO 8-3

68. Alice is single and self-employed in 2017. Her net business profit on her Schedule C for the year is $140,000. What is her self-employment tax liability and .9 percent additional Medicare tax liability for 2017? LO 8-3

69. Kyle, a single taxpayer, worked as a free-lance software engineer for the first three months of 2017. During that time, he earned $44,000 of self-employment income. On April 1, 2017, Kyle took a job as a full-time software engineer with one of his former clients, Hoogle Inc. From April through the end of the year, Kyle earned $178,000 in salary. What amount of FICA taxes (self-employment and employment related) does Kyle owe for the year? LO 8-3

70. Eva received $60,000 in compensation payments from JAZZ Corp. during 2017. Eva incurred $5,000 in business expenses relating to her work for JAZZ Corp. JAZZ did not reimburse Eva for any of these expenses. Eva is single and she deducts a standard deduction of $6,350 and a personal exemption of $4,050. Based on these facts answer the following questions: LO 8-3

a) Assume that Eva is considered to be an *employee*. What amount of FICA taxes is she required to pay for the year?

b) Assume that Eva is considered to be an *employee*. What is her regular income tax liability for the year?

c) Assume that Eva is considered to be a *self-employed contractor*. What is her self-employment tax liability and .9 percent additional Medicare tax liability for the year?

d) Assume that Eva is considered to be a *self-employed contractor*. What is her regular tax liability for the year?

71. Terry Hutchison worked as a self-employed lawyer until two years ago when he retired. He used the cash method of accounting in his business for tax purposes. Five years ago, Terry represented his client ABC corporation in an antitrust lawsuit against XYZ corporation. During that year, Terry paid self-employment taxes on all of his income. ABC won the lawsuit but Terry and ABC could not agree on the amount of his earnings. Finally, this year, the issue got resolved and ABC paid Terry $90,000 for the services he provided five years ago. Terry plans to include the payment in his gross income, but because he spends most of his time playing golf and absolutely no time working on legal matters, he does not intend to pay self-employment taxes on the income. Is Terry subject to self-employment taxes on this income? LO 8-3 research

72. Trey claims a dependency exemption for both of his daughters, ages 14 and 17, at year-end. Trey files a joint return with his wife. What amount of child credit will Trey be able to claim for his daughters under each of the following alternative situations? LO 8-4

a) His AGI is $100,000.

b) His AGI is $120,000.

c) His AGI is $122,100, and his daughters are ages 10 and 12.

73. Julie paid a day care center to watch her two-year-old son while she worked as a computer programmer for a local start-up company. What amount of child and dependent care credit can Julie claim in each of the following alternative scenarios? LO 8-4

a) Julie paid $2,000 to the day care center and her AGI is $50,000 (all salary).

b) Julie paid $5,000 to the day care center and her AGI is $50,000 (all salary).
c) Julie paid $4,000 to the day care center and her AGI is $25,000 (all salary).
d) Julie paid $2,000 to the day care center and her AGI is $14,000 (all salary).
e) Julie paid $4,000 to the day care center and her AGI is $14,000 ($2,000 salary and $12,000 unearned income).

LO 8-4

74. In 2017, Elaine paid $2,800 of tuition and $600 for books for her dependent son to attend State University this past fall as a freshman. Elaine files a joint return with her husband. What is the maximum American opportunity credit that Elaine can claim for the tuition payment and books in each of the following alternative situations?
a) Elaine's AGI is $80,000.
b) Elaine's AGI is $168,000.
c) Elaine's AGI is $184,000.

LO 8-4
planning

75. In 2017, Laureen is currently single. She paid $2,800 of qualified tuition and related expenses for each of her twin daughters Sheri and Meri to attend State University as freshmen ($2,800 each for a total of $5,600). Sheri and Meri qualify as Laureen's dependents. Laureen also paid $1,900 for her son Ryan's (also Laureen's dependent) tuition and related expenses to attend his junior year at State University. Finally, Laureen paid $1,200 for herself to attend seminars at a community college to help her improve her job skills. What is the maximum amount of education credits Laureen can claim for these expenditures in each of the following alternative scenarios? Assume the 2016 rules apply for purposes of the qualified education expense deduction.
a) Laureen's AGI is $45,000. If Laureen claims education credits for her three children and herself, how much credit is she allowed to claim in total?
If she claims education credits for her children, how much of her children's tuition costs that do not generate credits may she deduct as *for* AGI expenses?
b) Laureen's AGI is $95,000. What options does Laureen have for deducting her continuing education costs to the extent the costs don't generate a credit?
c) Laureen's AGI is $45,000 and Laureen paid $12,000 (not $1,900) for Ryan to attend graduate school (i.e, his fifth year not his junior year).

LO 8-4

76. In 2017, Amanda and Jaxon Stuart have a daughter who is 1 year old. The Stuarts are full-time students and they are both 23 years old. Their only sources of income are gains from stock they held for three years before selling and wages from part-time jobs. What is their earned income credit in the following alternative scenarios if they file jointly?
a) Their AGI is $15,000, consisting of $5,000 of capital gains and $10,000 of wages.
b) Their AGI is $15,000, consisting of $10,000 of lottery winnings (unearned income) and $5,000 of wages.
c) Their AGI is $25,000, consisting of $20,000 of wages and $5,000 of lottery winnings (unearned income).
d) Their AGI is $25,000, consisting of $5,000 of wages and $20,000 of lottery winnings (unearned income).
e) Their AGI is $10,000, consisting of $10,000 of lottery winnings (unearned income).

77. In 2017, Zach is single with no dependents. He is not claimed as a dependent on another's return. All of his income is from salary and he does not have any *for* AGI deductions. What is his earned income credit in the following alternative scenarios? LO 8-4
    a) Zach is 29 years old and his AGI is $5,000.
    b) Zach is 29 years old and his AGI is $10,000.
    c) Zach is 29 years old and his AGI is $19,000.
    d) Zach is 24 years old and his AGI is $5,000.

78. This year Luke has calculated his gross tax liability at $1,800. Luke is entitled to a $2,400 nonrefundable personal tax credit, a $1,500 business tax credit, and a $600 refundable personal tax credit. In addition, Luke has had $2,300 of income taxes withheld from his salary. What is Luke's net tax due or refund? LO 8-4

79. This year Lloyd, a single taxpayer, estimates that his tax liability will be $10,000. Last year, his total tax liability was $15,000. He estimates that his tax withholding from his employer will be $7,800. LO 8-5 planning
    a) Is Lloyd required to increase his withholding or make estimated tax payments this year to avoid the underpayment penalty? If so, how much?
    b) Assuming Lloyd does not make any additional payments, what is the amount of his underpayment penalty? Assume the federal short-term rate is 5 percent.

80. This year, Paula and Simon (married filing jointly) estimate that their tax liability will be $200,000. Last year, their total tax liability was $170,000. They estimate that their tax withholding from their employers will be $175,000. Are Paula and Simon required to increase their withholdings or make estimated tax payments this year to avoid the underpayment penalty? If so, how much? LO 8-5 planning

81. This year, Santhosh, a single taxpayer, estimates that his tax liability will be $100,000. Last year, his total tax liability was $15,000. He estimates that his tax withholding from his employer will be $35,000. Is Santhosh required to increase his withholding or make estimated tax payments this year to avoid the underpayment penalty? If so, how much? LO 8-5 planning

82. For the following taxpayers, determine if they are required to file a tax return in 2017. LO 8-5
    a) Ricko, single taxpayer, with gross income of $12,000.
    b) Fantasia, head of household, with gross income of $17,500.
    c) Ken and Barbie, married taxpayers with no dependents, with gross income of $12,000.
    d) Dorothy and Rudolf, married taxpayers, both age 68, with gross income of $19,000.
    e) Janyce, single taxpayer, age 73, with gross income of $12,500.

83. For the following taxpayers, determine the due date of their tax returns. LO 8-5
    a) Jerome, a single taxpayer, is not requesting an extension this year. Assume the due date falls on a Tuesday.
    b) Lashaunda, a single taxpayer, requests an extension this year. Assume the extended due date falls on a Wednesday.
    c) Barney and Betty, married taxpayers, do not request an extension this year. Assume the due date falls on a Sunday.
    d) Fred and Wilma, married taxpayers, request an extension this year. Assume the extended date falls on a Saturday.

LO 8-5

planning

84. Determine the amount of the late filing and late payment penalties that apply for the following taxpayers.
    a) Jolene filed her tax return by its original due date but did not pay the $2,000 in taxes she owed with the return until one and a half months later.
    b) Oscar filed his tax return and paid his $3,000 tax liability seven months late.
    c) Wilfred, attempting to evade his taxes, did not file a tax return or pay his $10,000 in taxes for several years.

COMPREHENSIVE PROBLEMS

Select problems are available in Connect®.

85. In 2017, Jack and Diane Heart are married with two children, ages 10 and 12. Jack works full-time and earns an annual salary of $80,000, while Diane works as a substitute teacher and earns approximately $25,000 per year. Jack and Diane expect to file jointly and do not itemize their deductions. In the fall of this year, Diane was offered a full-time teaching position that would pay her an additional $20,000.
    a) Calculate the marginal tax rate on the additional income, *excluding employment taxes,* to help Jack and Diane evaluate the offer.
    b) Calculate the marginal tax rate on the additional income, *including employment taxes,* to help Jack and Diane evaluate the offer.
    c) Calculate the marginal tax rate on the additional income, *including self-employment taxes,* if Diane earned an additional $20,000 as a self-employed contractor ($20,000 self-employment income in addition to the $25,000 as an employee).

planning

86. Matt and Carrie are married, have two children, and file a joint return. Their daughter Katie is 19 years old and is a full-time student at State University. During 2017, she completed her freshman year and one semester as a sophomore. Katie's expenses while she was away at school during the year were as follows:

Tuition	$5,000
Class fees	300
Books	500
Room and board	4,500

Katie received a half-tuition scholarship that paid for $2,500 of her tuition costs. Katie's parents paid the rest of these expenses. Matt and Carrie are able to claim Katie as a dependent on their tax return.

Matt and Carrie's 23-year-old son Todd also attended graduate school (fifth year of college) full time at a nearby college. Todd's expenses while away at school were as follows:

Tuition	$3,000
Class fees	0
Books	250
Room and board	4,000

Matt and Carrie paid for Todd's tuition, books, and room and board.

Since Matt and Carrie still benefit from claiming Todd as a dependent on their tax return, they decided to provide Todd with additional financial assistance by making the payments on Todd's outstanding student loans. Besides paying off some of the loan principal, Matt and Carrie paid a total of $900 of interest on the loan.

This year Carrie decided to take some classes at the local community college to help improve her skills as a schoolteacher. The community college is considered to be a qualifying postsecondary institution of higher education. Carrie spent a total of $1,300 on tuition for the classes, and she was not reimbursed by her employer. Matt and Carrie's AGI for 2017 before any education-related tax deductions is $121,000 and their taxable income before considering any education-related tax benefits is $80,000. Matt and Carrie incurred $500 of miscellaneous itemized deductions subject to the 2 percent floor not counting any education-related expenses.

Required:

Determine the mix of tax benefits that maximize tax savings for Matt and Carrie. Assume the 2016 rules apply for purposes of the qualified education expense deduction. Their options for credits for each student are as follows:

a) They may claim either a credit or a qualified education deduction for Katie's expenses.
b) They may claim either a credit or a qualified education deduction for Todd.
c) They may claim (1) a credit or (2) a qualified education deduction for Carrie. They may deduct any amount not included in (1) or (2) as a miscellaneous itemized deduction subject to the 2 percent of AGI floor.

Remember to apply any applicable limits or phase-outs in your computations.

87. Reba Dixon is a fifth-grade schoolteacher who earned a salary of $38,000 in 2017. She is 45 years old and has been divorced for four years. She receives $1,200 of alimony payments each month from her former husband. Reba also rents out a small apartment building. This year Reba received $30,000 of rental payments from tenants and she incurred $19,500 of expenses associated with the rental. **tax forms**

Reba and her daughter Heather (20 years old at the end of the year) moved to Georgia in January of this year. Reba provides more than one-half of Heather's support. They had been living in Colorado for the past 15 years, but ever since her divorce, Reba has been wanting to move back to Georgia to be closer to her family. Luckily, last December, a teaching position opened up and Reba and Heather decided to make the move. Reba paid a moving company $2,010 to move their personal belongings, and she and Heather spent two days driving the 1,426 miles to Georgia. During the trip, Reba paid $200 for lodging and $85 for meals. Reba's mother was so excited to have her daughter and granddaughter move back to Georgia that she gave Reba $3,000 to help out with the moving costs.

Reba rented a home in Georgia. Heather decided to continue living at home with her mom, but she started attending school full-time in January at a nearby university. She was awarded a $3,000 partial tuition scholarship this year, and Reba helped out by paying the remaining $500 tuition cost. If possible, Reba thought it would be best to claim the education credit for these expenses.

Reba wasn't sure if she would have enough items to help her benefit from itemizing on her tax return. However, she kept track of several expenses this year that she thought might qualify if she was able to itemize. Reba paid $2,800 in state income taxes and $6,500 in charitable contributions during the year. She also paid the following medical-related expenses for her and Heather:

Insurance premiums	$4,795
Medical care expenses	1,100
Prescription medicine	350
Nonprescription medicine	100
New contact lenses for Heather	200

Shortly after the move, Reba got distracted while driving and she ran into a street sign. The accident caused $900 in damage to the car and gave her whiplash. Because the repairs were less than her insurance deductible, she paid the entire cost of the repairs. Reba wasn't able to work for two months after the accident. Fortunately, she received $2,000 from her disability insurance. Her employer, the Central Georgia School District, paid 60 percent of the premiums on the policy as a nontaxable fringe benefit and Reba paid the remaining 40 percent portion.

A few years ago, Reba acquired several investments with her portion of the divorce settlement. This year she reported the following income from her investments: $2,200 of interest income from corporate bonds and $1,500 interest income from City of Denver municipal bonds. Overall, Reba's stock portfolio appreciated by $12,000 but she did not sell any of her stocks.

Heather reported $3,200 of interest income from corporate bonds she received as gifts from her father over the last several years. This was Heather's only source of income for the year.

Reba had $10,000 of federal income taxes withheld by her employer. Heather made $500 of estimated tax payments during the year. Reba did not make any estimated payments. Reba had qualifying insurance for purposes of the Affordable Care Act (ACA).

Required:

Determine Reba's federal income taxes due or taxes payable for the current year. Complete pages 1 and 2 of Form 1040 for Reba.

a) Is Reba allowed to file as a head of household or single?

b) Determine the amount of FICA taxes Reba was required to pay on her salary.

c) Determine Heather's federal income taxes due or payable.

tax forms

88. John and Sandy Ferguson got married eight years ago and have a seven-year-old daughter Samantha. In 2017, John worked as a computer technician at a local university earning a salary of $52,000, and Sandy worked part-time as a receptionist for a law firm earning a salary of $29,000. John also does some Web design work on the side and reported revenues of $4,000 and associated expenses of $750. The Fergusons received $800 in qualified dividends and a $200 refund of their state income taxes. The Fergusons always itemize their deductions and their itemized deductions were well over the standard deduction amount last year. The Fergusons had qualifying insurance for purposes of the Affordable Care Act (ACA).

The Fergusons reported making the following payments during the year:

- State income taxes of $4,400. Federal tax withholding of $4,000.
- Alimony payments to John's former wife of $10,000.
- Child support payments for John's child with his former wife of $4,100.
- $3,200 of real property taxes.
- Sandy was reimbursed $600 for employee business expenses she incurred. She was required to provide documentation for her expenses to her employer.

- In addition to the $750 of Web design expenses, John attended a conference to improve his skills associated with his Web design work. His trip was for three days and he incurred the following expenses: airfare $370, total taxi fares for trip $180, meals $80, and conference fee of $200.
- $3,600 to Kid Care day care center for Samantha's care while John and Sandy worked.
- $14,000 interest on their home mortgage.
- $3,000 interest on a $40,000 home-equity loan. They used the loan to pay for a family vacation and new car.
- $6,000 cash charitable contributions to qualified charities.
- Donation of used furniture to Goodwill. The furniture had a fair market value of $400 and cost $2,000.

Required:

What is the Fergusons' 2017 federal income taxes payable or refund, including any self-employment tax and AMT, if applicable? Complete pages 1 and 2 of Form 1040 and Form 6251 for John and Sandy.

ROGER | *CPA Review*

Sample CPA Exam questions from Roger CPA Review are available in Connect as support for the topics in this text. These Multiple Choice Questions and Task-Based Simulations include expert-written explanations and solutions, and provide a starting point for students to become familiar with the content and functionality of the actual CPA Exam.

chapter

12 Compensation

Learning Objectives

Upon completing this chapter, you should be able to:

LO 12-1 Discuss and explain the tax implications of compensation in the form of salary and wages from the employee's and employer's perspectives.

LO 12-2 Describe and distinguish the tax implications of various forms of equity-based compensation from the employee's and employer's perspectives.

LO 12-3 Compare and contrast taxable and nontaxable fringe benefits and explain the employee and employer tax consequences associated with fringe benefits.

© Alija/iStock/Getty Images

Storyline Summary

Taxpayers:	Julie and Ethan Clark
Location:	San Diego, California
Employment status:	Julie—mid-level executive for Premier Computer Corporation (PCC); current salary $240,000 Ethan—mechanical engineer; current salary $70,000
Filing status:	Married filing jointly
Dependents:	Two children
Marginal ordinary tax rate:	40 percent
Current situation:	Julie is considering an offer for the vice president of marketing position with Technology Products Inc (TPI).

Julie and Ethan Clark and their two children have been settled into their life in San Diego, California, for some time. Julie has decided her career is at a crossroads. On the one hand, her employment as a mid-level executive for Premier Computer Corporation (PCC) is going well, but the work is not as challenging as it used to be. She suspects that, given her skills and abilities, she could put her career on the fast track with the right opportunity, engaging in more fulfilling work and gaining a significant increase in compensation.

Julie was sitting at her desk contemplating her career when she received yet another call from a corporate headhunter. While she usually quickly dismisses such calls, this time her interest and curiosity were piqued and she gave her full attention. He asked if she had any interest in a vice president of marketing position with a publicly traded company located nearby. After the headhunter answered a few of her questions, Julie gave him the go-ahead to set up an interview.

A couple of weeks later, Julie had been through two rounds of interviews for the marketing VP position when she received a call informing her that she was the one Technology Products Inc. (TPI) wanted for the job and that an offer letter with the details was on its way. The letter indicated TPI was offering a $280,000 salary (a significant increase from her current salary). TPI was also offering her a choice of certain types of equity-based compensation and some attractive fringe benefits. While excited by the letter, Julie knew she needed to learn more about the equity-based compensation alternatives and the other forms of compensation TPI was offering before she could adequately evaluate the offer and reach her decision.

to be continued . . .

As TPI's letter to Julie illustrates, employers are able to offer many different forms of compensation to employees. They can also pay some compensation now and defer some to the future. Each type of compensation has unique tax and nontax consequences.

This chapter addresses the tax and nontax consequences of *current* compensation packages from both the employee's and the employer's perspective. The next chapter addresses *future* or *deferred* compensation.

LO 12-1

SALARY AND WAGES

Current compensation paid to **employees** in the form of **salary** and **wages,** usually paid in cash, has tax consequences to both employees and employers. Below, we address the tax (and nontax) considerations of salary and wages from the employee's perspective, followed by the employer's perspective.

Employee Considerations for Salary and Wages

Employees receiving salary generally earn a fixed amount of compensation for the year no matter how many hours they work. In addition, salaried employees may be eligible for bonuses based on satisfying certain criteria. In contrast, employees receiving wages generally get paid by the hour. Salary, bonus, and wages are taxed to employees as ordinary income. Employees generally report income from salary and wages as they receive it.[1] As we discussed in detail in the Individual Income Tax Computation and Tax Credits chapter, employees must pay **FICA taxes** on their wages.[2] FICA tax consists of both a Social Security and a Medicare component.

At the end of each year, employees receive a **Form W-2** (see Exhibit 12-1) from their employers summarizing their salary or wage compensation and the various withholding amounts made during the year.[3] Employees simply report their wages on Page 1, line 7, of the 1040 federal tax return and report their federal income taxes withheld on line 64 of Page 2. Self-employed taxpayers receive a Form 1099 indicating the compensation they received, which they report on Schedule C.

THE KEY FACTS

Employment-Related Forms

- **Form W-2**
  - Summarizes an employee's taxable salary and wages.
  - Provides annual federal and state withholding information.
  - Generated by employer on an annual basis.
- **Form W-4**
  - Supplies an employee's withholding information to employer.
  - Generated by employee.
  - Numbers reported on form remain constant unless employee makes changes.
- **Form 1099**
  - Summarizes an independent contractor's or nonemployee's taxable compensation.
  - Generated by person or entity paying the compensation.

Tax Withholding When employees begin employment with a firm, they complete a **Form W-4** to supply the information the firm needs in order to withhold the correct amount of tax from each paycheck. Specifically, employees use Form W-4 to indicate (1) whether to withhold at the single rate or at the lower married rate, (2) the number of withholding allowances the employee chooses to claim (the more withholding allowances claimed, the less the withholding amount), and (3) whether the employee wants an additional amount of tax withheld each period above the amount based on the number of allowances claimed.

Employer Considerations for Salary and Wages

Storyline Summary

Taxpayer:	TPI Corporation
Location:	San Diego, California
Ownership:	Publicly traded corporation
Industry:	Manufacturer of high-technology products
CEO:	Daniel Hewitt
Marginal tax rate:	35 percent
Current Situation:	Recruiting Julie Clark for VP of marketing position

[1]Reg. §1.451-1(a).

[2]FICA stands for Federal Insurance Contributions Act.

[3]Compensation received by taxpayers who are self-employed is not considered to be salary and wages.

EXHIBIT 12-1 **Form W-2***

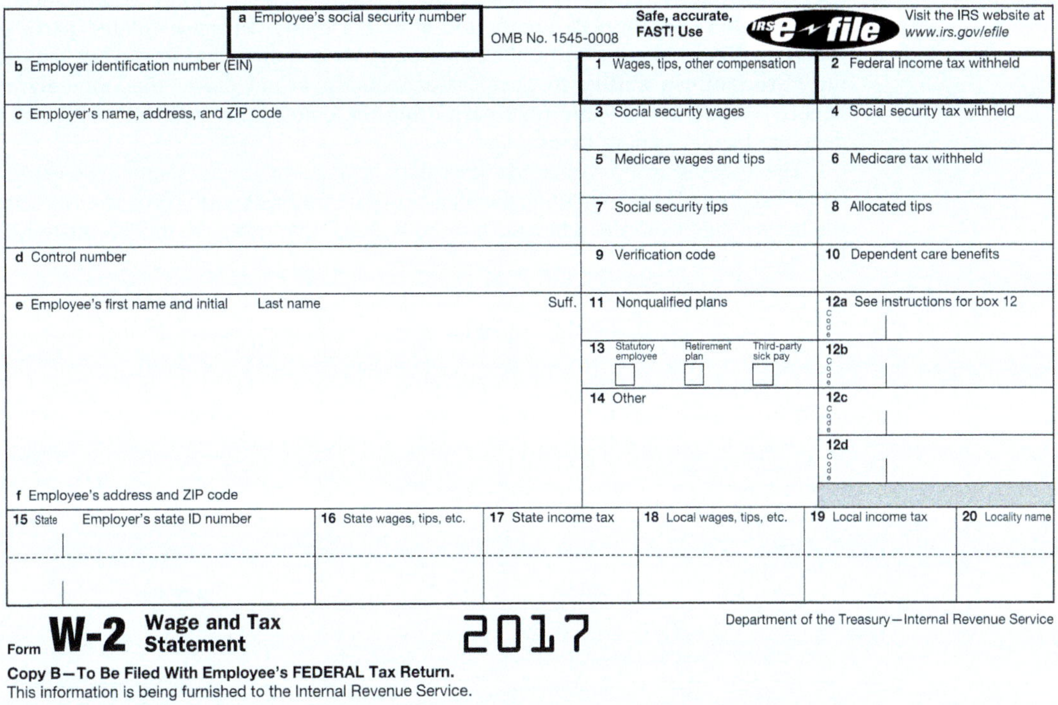
a Employee's social security number
OMB No. 1545-0008
Safe, accurate, FAST! Use IRS e-file
Visit the IRS website at www.irs.gov/efile
b Employer identification number (EIN)
1 Wages, tips, other compensation
2 Federal income tax withheld
c Employer's name, address, and ZIP code
3 Social security wages
4 Social security tax withheld
5 Medicare wages and tips
6 Medicare tax withheld
7 Social security tips
8 Allocated tips
d Control number
9 Verification code
10 Dependent care benefits
e Employee's first name and initial Last name Suff.
11 Nonqualified plans
12a See instructions for box 12
13 Statutory employee Retirement plan Third-party sick pay
12b
14 Other
12c
12d
f Employee's address and ZIP code
15 State Employer's state ID number
16 State wages, tips, etc.
17 State income tax
18 Local wages, tips, etc.
19 Local income tax
20 Locality name
Form W-2 Wage and Tax Statement 2017
Department of the Treasury—Internal Revenue Service
Copy B—To Be Filed With Employee's FEDERAL Tax Return.
This information is being furnished to the Internal Revenue Service.

*The 2018 Form W-2 was unavailable at press time. Please visit the IRS website (www.irs.gov) for the final 2018 form.

Deductibility of Salary Payments Employers computing taxable income under the cash method of accounting generally deduct salary and wages when they pay the employee.[4] Employers computing taxable income under the accrual method generally deduct wages payable to employees as the employees earn the wages.[5] This general rule holds even in situations when the employer accrues compensation expense in one year but actually pays the employee in the subsequent year, as long as the company makes the payment within 2½ months after the employer's year-end. If the employer pays the employee more than 2½ months after the employer's year-end, the wages are considered deferred compensation and are not deductible by the employer until the employee recognizes the salary as income (receives payment).[6] Because most employers pay regular salary and wages to employees each month (or more frequently), the 2½-month rule is likely to be more of an issue for accrued compensation, such as one-time year-end bonuses, than it is for normal wages.

In situations when the employer and employee are "related" parties, special rules apply. In this context, the definition of related parties includes an employee/shareholder who owns more than 50 percent of the value of the employer corporation.[7] When the corporation and employee/shareholder are related parties, a

THE KEY FACTS

Compensation Deductibility for Accrual-Basis Taxpayers

- Compensation expense accrued at end of year *is* deductible in year accrued if
  - Paid to an *unrelated* party within 2½ months of year-end.
- Compensation expense accrued at end of year *is not* deductible when paid if
  - Paid to *related* party owning > 50 percent of corporate employer.

[4]Reg. §1.461-1(a)(1).

[5]Reg. §1.461-1(a)(2). See the Business Income, Deductions, and Accounting Methods chapter for a detailed discussion of the cash and accrual accounting methods.

[6]Reg. §1.404(b)-1T(A-2). We discuss tax issues and consequences relating to deferred compensation in the Retirement Savings and Deferred Compensation chapter.

[7]See §267(b) for the complete definition of "related" parties.

corporation is not allowed to deduct the compensation expense until the employee/shareholder (related party) includes the payment in income.[8] Therefore, for an accrual-method company paying compensation, such as wages or a bonus, to a related employee, the 2½-month rule does not apply. Because related parties are theoretically considered to be the same taxpayer to some extent, the tax laws limit the corporation's ability to accelerate deductions and enjoy the immediate tax benefits, while at the same time permitting the employee a deferral of income and delaying the payment of taxes.

The after-tax cost of providing this salary is generally much less than the before-tax cost.[9] The formula for computing the after-tax cost of the salary (the cost after subtracting the tax savings from the deduction), or any deductible expense, for that matter, is as follows:

Deductible expenditure × (1 − Marginal tax rate)

Example 12-1

What are PCC's before-tax and after-tax costs of paying Julie a $240,000 salary? (Note that PCC's marginal tax rate is 35 percent.)

Answer: $240,000 before taxes and $156,000 after taxes, computed as follows:

Description	Amount	Explanation
Before tax cost of salary:		
(1) **Compensation**	**$240,000**	
(2) (1 − Marginal tax rate)	× 65%	(1 − 35%)
After-tax cost of salary	**$156,000**	(1) × (2)

TAXES IN THE REAL WORLD Are CEOs Rewarded for Tax Dodging?

In 2011, the Institute for Policy Studies reported that 25 U.S. companies paid their CEOs more than they paid the U.S. government in taxes. The list of companies included: International Paper, General Electric, Verizon, Boeing, and Ford Motor Company. On average, the companies reported $1.6 billion in profits and $16.7 million in executive compensation. In total, the companies also reported 556 subsidiaries located in tax havens, $12.6 million in campaign contributions, and $129 million in lobbying expenditures (campaign contributions and lobbying expenditures are nondeductible for tax). On average, these CEOs were paid $5.9 million more than the average of CEOs comprising the S&P 500.

Limits on salary deductibility. Employers are generally allowed to deduct reasonable compensation paid to employees.[10] Determining whether compensation is reasonable in amount is a **facts and circumstances test** that involves considering the duties of the employee, the complexities of the business, and the amount of salary compared with the

[8]§267(a)(2).

[9]As discussed in the Individual Income Tax Computation and Tax Credits chapter, employers are required to pay FICA taxes on employees' compensation. Employers may also be required to pay other expenses based on employee wages such as workers' compensation insurance.

[10]As we discussed in the Business Income, Deductions, and Accounting Methods chapter, all business expenses (not just compensation) must be reasonable in amount to be fully deductible.

income of the business, among other things. The amount of salary in excess of the amount considered reasonable is not deductible. The reasonable compensation limit typically applies to closely held businesses where the employee is also an owner of the company or the employee is a relative of the business owner. For publicly traded corporations, another limitation applies that is generally more restrictive than the reasonableness limitation: §162(m) of the Internal Revenue Code.

Responding to a growing public perception that executives of publicly traded corporations were being overpaid at the expense of shareholders and that the government was subsidizing (paying a part of) the excess by allowing corporations to deduct the high salaries, in 1993 Congress enacted §162(m) of the Internal Revenue Code.[11] This provision limits the deduction for compensation paid by publicly traded corporations to covered employees to $1 million per year. Covered employees include the principal executive officer (CEO) and the next three highest paid officers (not including the principal financial officer [CFO]).[12] However, certain exceptions allow companies to pay and deduct compensation in excess of the $1 million limit. For example, the limit does not apply to compensation based on (1) performance (this is the most significant of the exceptions in terms of dollars and frequency of application), (2) commissions, (3) contributions to qualified retirement plans, or (4) other tax-free benefits.

While most publicly traded corporations are aware of and are sensitive to the limitation, they may take different approaches in dealing with it. For example, as described in the excerpt from its 2016 proxy statement (see Exhibit 12-2), Callaway Golf attempts to maximize its compensation deduction, yet it acknowledges that there are situations when, in order to achieve its nontax goals, it may provide compensation to executives that is not deductible.

THE KEY FACTS

Limits on Salary Deductibility of Publicly Traded Corporations

- $1,000,000 maximum annual compensation deduction per person.
  - Limit applies to CEO and three other highest compensated officers (not including the CFO).
  - Does not apply to performance-based compensation.

EXHIBIT 12-2 Excerpt from Callaway Golf's 2016 Proxy Statement

The tax deductibility of compensation should be maximized where appropriate.
In designing and approving the Company's executive compensation plans, the Compensation Committee considers the effect of all applicable tax regulations, including Section 162(m) of the Internal Revenue Code of 1986, as amended (the "Code"), which generally disallows a tax deduction to public corporations for nonqualifying compensation in excess of $1.0 million paid to the chief executive officer or certain of the Company's other executive officers. Although maximizing the tax deductibility of compensation is an important consideration, the Compensation Committee may from time to time approve compensation that does not qualify for deductibility where it is appropriate to do so in light of other compelling interests or objectives. In addition, because of ambiguities and uncertainties as to the application and interpretation of Section 162(m) and related regulations, and the fact that such regulations and interpretations may change from time to time (with potentially retroactive effect), no assurance can be given that compensation intended to satisfy the requirements for deductibility under Section 162(m) will in fact do so.

In contrast, State Street Corporation takes a slightly different approach. As indicated in the following excerpt from its 2016 proxy statement (see Exhibit 12-3), State Street caps its salaries at $1 million. Apparently, the firm wants to make sure salaries paid to executives are fully deductible.

[11]Daniel Nelson, "Section 162(m) Revisited," *Tax Notes Today,* January 10, 2005, pp. 8–22.

[12]Notice 2007-49. Section 162(m) defines "covered employees" as the CEO and the four most highly compensated officers (as of the end of the year). In providing this definition, Section 162(m) references and relies on executive compensation rules provided in the Securities Exchange Act of 1934. In September of 2006, the SEC modified the executive compensation disclosure rules referenced in Section 162(m). Nevertheless, Section 162(m) has not been updated to reflect this change. To resolve the inconsistency in the definition of "covered employee" between the language in Section 162(m) and the modified executive compensation rules, the IRS issued Notice 2007-49.

EXHIBIT 12-3 **Excerpt from State Street Corporation's 2016 Proxy Statement**

Tax Deductibility of Executive Compensation

Section 162(m) of the U.S. Internal Revenue Code, or Section 162(m), generally limits to $1 million the U.S. federal income tax deductibility of compensation paid in one year to any one of a group of specified employees, including our Named Executive Officers (other than our Chief Financial Officer). Performance-based compensation is not subject to the limits on deductibility of Section 162(m), provided such compensation meets specified requirements, including shareholder approval of material terms of compensation. The Compensation Committee considers tax deductibility in making compensation decisions, to the extent deductibility is reasonably practicable and consistent with our other compensation objectives. . . . The Compensation Committee believes, however, that shareholder interests are best served by not restricting its discretion and flexibility.

The difference in philosophy between Callaway and State Street may be driven by nontax considerations. To be deductible, compensation to executives in excess of $1 million generally must be performance-based. This means that the executives bear the risk that they won't receive the additional compensation if certain performance benchmarks, like stock-price targets, aren't met. Some companies may decide they don't want their executives to shoulder this risk, so they pay them salaries in excess of the deductible amount to guarantee a certain level of compensation. Companies may also decide to cap executive salaries at $1 million just to avoid the public perception that they are being fiscally irresponsible by paying more than the deductibility limits.

Example 12-2

Several years ago, TPI was actively searching for a new CEO. The board of directors eventually chose Daniel Hewitt. During negotiations, Daniel indicated he wanted a $2 million salary (Option 1) in addition to the equity-based compensation the board was offering. While this level of salary could be considered reasonable, the board of directors was concerned about the $1 million limitation on deductible salary, so the board offered an alternative proposal. Under this proposal, TPI would pay Daniel a $1 million salary and offer him an additional $1.2 million bonus, contingent on achieving realistic financial performance goals for TPI (Option 2). Confident he could meet the financial goals, Daniel accepted the offer. Assuming the performance goals are met, what is TPI's after-tax cost of providing the current-year compensation under Option 1 and Option 2?

Answer: $1,650,000 under Option 1 and $1,430,000 under Option 2, computed as follows:

	Option 1 ($2,000,000 salary $0 bonus)	**Option 2** ($1,000,000 salary $1,200,000 bonus)	**Explanation**
Before-tax cost:			
(1) Total compensation	$ 2,000,000	$ 2,200,000	Salary + bonus
(2) Deductible amount	$ 1,000,000	$ 2,200,000	Option 1: $1M salary not deductible
(3) Marginal tax rate	× 35%	× 35%	
(4) Tax savings from compensation deduction	$ 350,000	$ 770,000	(2) × (3)
After-tax cost	**$1,650,000**	**$1,430,000**	(1) − (4)

Assuming the performance goals are met, both parties benefit from the arrangement. Daniel prefers Option 2 because it provides him with $200,000 more of before-tax compensation ($2.2M − $2M). TPI also prefers Option 2 because it costs $220,000 less after taxes than Option 1 ($1,650,000 − $1,430,000). Of course, Daniel is the one who must bear the risk of the contingent compensation in Option 2, so he must consider this risk before accepting the offer.

As this example illustrates, the $1 million deduction limitation can have a considerable impact on the after-tax cost of providing compensation to corporate executives. However, employers frequently utilize the options described above to craft offers that meet the needs of both parties.

EQUITY-BASED COMPENSATION

LO 12-2

continued from page 12-1 . . .

As she read TPI's offer letter more carefully, Julie discovered that on the first day of January following her acceptance of the offer, she would be granted 10,000 shares of restricted stock, 50 incentive stock options (ISOs), and 200 nonqualified stock options (NQOs). Each stock option would give her the right to purchase 100 shares of stock (50 ISOs allows up to 5,000 shares and 200 NQOs allows up to 20,000 shares) at a fixed price equal to the market value of TPI stock on the date of grant. As she read on, Julie noticed that she would not be able to exercise either type of stock option (i.e., purchase TPI stock for the exercise price stated in the options) until the options vest (the options become hers when they vest), which would be two years from the grant date. Further, Julie understood that, after the restricted stock vests (one year from the grant date on January 1), she will be free to do what she wants with it. The last detail Julie noticed when reading this part of the offer letter was that both types of options expire 10 years from the grant date. She understands this to mean that if she does not exercise her options sometime before their expiration date, she will lose them.

Although it is obvious to Julie that the value of the options and restricted stock will increase as the share price of TPI increases from the current share price of $5 per share, she remains unsure about the terminology used in this section of the letter. She realizes she needs to know more about the economic and tax implications of stock options and restricted stock before making her decision.

to be continued . . .

Equity-based compensation such as stock options and restricted stock provides risks and potential rewards not available with other forms of compensation. If the employer's stock price increases after it grants options and restricted stock, employees can be rewarded handsomely. On the other hand, if employer stock prices don't increase, the value of restricted stock will be limited and stock options will expire worthless.

THE KEY FACTS

Equity-Based Compensation

- Stock options
  - Allow employees to purchase stock at a discount.
- Restricted stock
  - Form of compensation that provides actual stock ownership to employees after restrictions lapse.

Employers use equity-based compensation, in part, to motivate their employees to take ownership in their companies. When employees hold employer options and stock, their compensation is more directly tied to the fortunes of their employer and its shareholders—that is, employees' compensation increases in tandem with their employer's stock price. This philosophy is reflected in an excerpt from Adobe's 2016 proxy statement presented in Exhibit 12-4.

EXHIBIT 12-4 Excerpt from Adobe's 2016 Proxy Statement

Goals of Equity Compensation

We use equity compensation to motivate and reward strong corporate performance and to retain valued executive officers. We also use equity incentive awards as a means to attract and recruit qualified executives. We believe that equity awards serve to align the interests of our Named Executive Officers (NEOs) with those of our stockholders by rewarding them for stock price growth. By having a significant percentage of our NEOs' target tax deductible compensation payable in the form of multi-year equity and, thus, subject to higher risk and longer vesting than cash compensation, our NEOs are motivated to take actions that will benefit Adobe and its stockholders in the long term.

In addition to its motivational effects, equity-based compensation has traditionally brought employers cash flow benefits as well. How? Unless employers purchase their own stock in a market transaction to satisfy option exercises and stock grants, there are no cash outflows associated with this form of compensation. In fact, employers actually *receive* cash from their employees in the amount of the exercise price on the options exercised. There are a couple of downsides to this benefit, however. First, employers experience the opportunity cost of selling shares at a discounted price to employees rather than selling the shares at fair market value on the open market. Second, because employers must issue new shares to satisfy option exercises and stock grants, the total number of shares outstanding increases, and therefore, earnings per share are diluted, which is a detriment to existing shareholders. The only way for employers to mitigate this problem without increasing earnings is to use their cash reserves to acquire their own shares to satisfy the options exercise.[13] However, from a cash-flow perspective, this is no different than paying cash compensation.

THE KEY FACTS

Stock Option Terminology

- *Incentive stock options* satisfy certain tax code requirements to provide favorable tax treatment to employees.
- *Nonqualified stock options* are any options that don't meet the requirements for being classified as incentive stock options.
- The *grant date* is the date employees are initially allocated stock options.
- The *exercise date* is the date that employees purchase stock using their options.
- The *exercise price* (or strike price) is the amount paid to acquire shares with stock options.
- The *bargain element* is the difference between the fair market value of stock and the exercise price on the exercise date.
- The *vesting date* is the time when stock options granted can be exercised.

Stock Options

As a form of equity-based compensation, stock options have two important characteristics: (1) employees must use cash to purchase the employer's stock once they are allowed to exercise the options and (2) employees often never exercise options when share prices are depressed. When stock options **vest,** employees are legally entitled to buy or exercise employer stock at a stipulated price, referred to as the **exercise price** or **strike price.** Options may be exercised anytime between the vesting date and the expiration date of the options.[14] If the share price does not go above the exercise price at some point during this

[13]Because earnings per share is calculated by dividing earnings by the number of shares of stock outstanding, for a given level of earnings, earnings per share could even increase when new shares are issued to satisfy option exercises if earnings increase by an amount that more than offsets the effect of issuing new shares into the market.

[14]Vesting dates are frequently specified as future calendar dates or they may be triggered when certain events occur (i.e., predefined performance objectives are met, or the company has been sold).

EXHIBIT 12-5 Sample Timeline for Incentive and Nonqualified Options

The economic and tax consequences of Julie's initial stock option award will depend on the future share price of TPI, on the time Julie decides to exercise her options, and on the time Julie decides to sell the shares received from the option exercise. The stock option examples in this chapter initially draw from the timeline below for the necessary assumptions regarding these key variables.

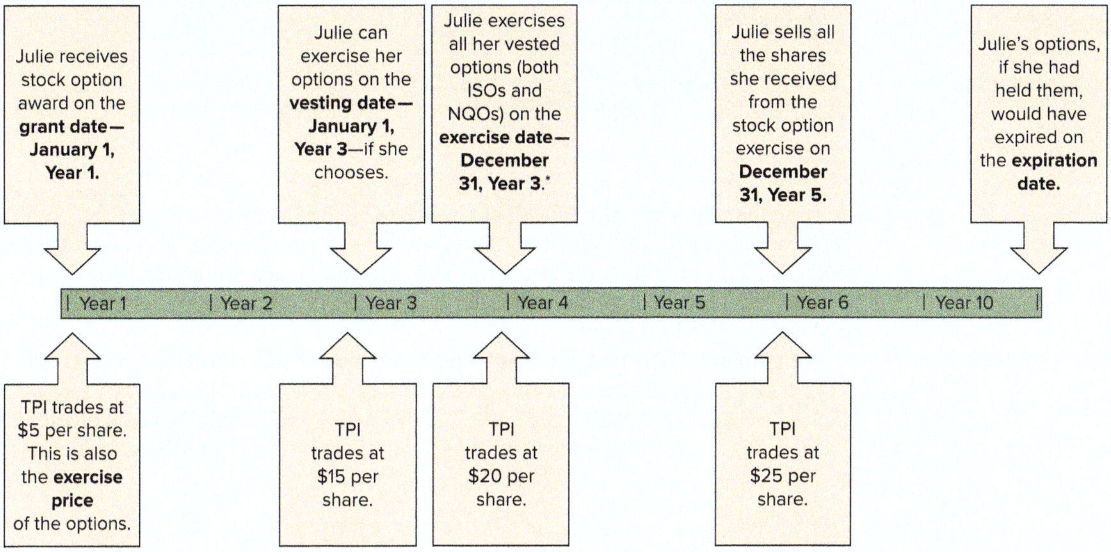

*Julie will acquire 5,000 shares of TPI (50 ISOs × 100 shares per ISO) with ISOs and 20,000 shares of TPI (200 NQOs × 100 shares per NQO) with NQOs. In total, Julie will acquire 25,000 shares of TPI.

TPI will receive $125,000 from Julie when she exercises her options if it issues new shares to cover the option exercise. If new shares are issued, however, TPI's earnings per share will drop relative to what it would have been had the new shares not been issued. If, to avoid dilution of its earnings per share, TPI purchases its own shares from the market instead of issuing new shares, it would pay $500,000 (25,000 shares purchased × $20 per share) resulting in total cash outflows of $375,000 net of the $125,000 Julie paid in to exercise her options.

interval, employees will not exercise their options and the options will expire without providing them any benefit.

As suggested in Exhibit 12-5, the future value of stock option awards will depend on the exercise price, the company's future share price, the exercise date of the options, and the timing for selling the shares received from the **option exercise.**

Example 12-3

Given the assumptions in the stock option timeline shown in Exhibit 12-5 (above), how much will it cost Julie to exercise all of her options at the end of year 3 (before taxes), and how much will she have if she were to immediately sell the acquired shares (before taxes)?[15]

(continued on page 12-10)

[15]According to the facts presented in Exhibit 12-5, Julie could have exercised her options as early as the vesting date for her options at the end of year 2. We assume she waits one year to exercise her options to better illustrate the implications of deferring the option exercise beyond the vesting date. In reality, it is quite common for employees to exercise their stock options on the vesting date.

Answer: $125,000 cost to exercise; $375,000 remaining after sale before taxes, calculated as follows:

Description	Amount	Explanation
(1) Shares acquired	25,000	(20,000 NQOs and 5,000 ISOs)
(2) Exercise price	$ 5	Exhibit 12-5
(3) **Cash needed to exercise**	**$125,000**	(1) × (2)
(4) Market price	$ 20	Exhibit 12-5
(5) Market value of shares	$ 500,000	(1) × (4)
Net proceeds upon sale	**$375,000**	(5) − (3)

If, in the prior example, Julie didn't have enough cash on hand to cover the $125,000 cost of exercising the options, she could simultaneously exercise the options and sell the stock, using $125,000 of the proceeds from the stock sale to pay for exercising the options. This so-called **cashless exercise** is typically facilitated using the services of an employer-provided stockbroker.

An employee who uses options to purchase shares experiences an increase in net worth equal to the difference between the exercise price and the market value of the acquired shares on the date of exercise. This difference is called the **bargain element.** In Example 12-3, the bargain element is $15 per share and the total bargain element is $375,000 (25,000 shares × $15 per share).

Example 12-4

What if: What is Julie's economic loss from her stock options if the TPI shares fall to $3 per share and remain there after the options are granted?

Answer: Zero. If TPI's stock price never increases above the $5 per share exercise price before the expiration date of the options, Julie will not exercise her options to purchase TPI shares, and those options will expire worthless.

Employee Considerations for Stock Options Stock options are classified for tax purposes as either **nonqualified stock options (NQOs)** or **incentive stock options (ISOs).** They differ in terms of when and how the bargain element is taxed. To appreciate these differences, it's important to understand what happens on the **grant date,** the **vesting date,** the **exercise date,** and the date the shares are ultimately sold.

For either type of option, employees experience no tax consequences on the grant date and vesting date. However, when they exercise *nonqualified* stock options, employees report ordinary income equal to the total bargain element on the shares of stock acquired (as if they were sold)—whether they hold the shares or sell them immediately.[16] A taxpayer's basis in nonqualified stock options acquired is the fair market value on the date of exercise. Thus the basis includes the exercise price plus the ordinary income the taxpayer recognizes on the exercise (the bargain element). In contrast, when *incentive* stock options are exercised, employees don't report any income for regular tax purposes (as long as they don't immediately sell

[16]The bargain element income is reflected on an employee's Form W-2 and the applicable income and payroll taxes are withheld.

their shares). Their basis in shares acquired with ISOs is the exercise price. The holding period for stock shares acquired with NQOs and ISOs begins on the exercise date.

When taxpayers exercise incentive stock options, the bargain element is added to their alternative minimum taxable income. This increases the likelihood that taxpayers exercising incentive stock options will be required to pay the alternative minimum tax—this is almost always true if the bargain element is large. We discuss the alternative minimum tax in the Individual Income Tax Computation and Tax Credits chapter.

Example 12-5

On the date Julie exercises her options (Example 12-3), she acquires 20,000 shares of TPI with NQOs (200 NQOs × 100 shares per NQO) and 5,000 shares with ISOs (50 ISOs × 100 shares per ISO). Given that the bargain element for each share she purchased is $15, how much income will Julie report on the day she exercises the options?

Answer: $300,000 ordinary income from the NQOs, calculated below, and $0 for the ISOs (she must include the bargain element of $75,000 on the 5,000 ISOs in her AMT calculation).

Description	Amount	Explanation
(1) Shares acquired with NQOs	20,000	
(2) Market price per share	$ 20	Exhibit 12-5
(3) Exercise price	5	Exhibit 12-5
(4) Bargain element per share	$ 15	(2) − (3)
Bargain element (ordinary income)	**$300,000**	(1) × (4)

What is Julie's basis in the 20,000 shares she acquired with NQOs?

Answer: $400,000. [$100,000 (20,000 shares × $5 per share exercise price) + $300,000 (bargain element taxed as ordinary income).]

What is Julie's basis in the 5,000 shares she acquired through ISOs?

Answer: $25,000 is the regular tax basis (5,000 shares acquired × $5 per share exercise price). $100,000 is the AMT basis ($25,000 regular tax basis + the $75,000 bargain element).

Once they've exercised their stock options, employees face different choices depending on the type of option. Employees who purchase stock with NQOs and retain the stock are in the same position for tax purposes as any other investor: Their basis in the stock is the fair market value on the date they exercised the options (this is the exercise price of the stock plus the bargain element), and any *future* appreciation or depreciation of the stock will be treated for tax purposes as either short-term or long-term capital gain(s) or loss(es) depending on the holding period, which begins on the date of exercise. Moreover, employees using NQOs to purchase employer stock are also in the same economic position as any other investor in that the value of the stock is subject to investment risk (the risk that the value of the stock will go down). To avoid overweighting their investment portfolios with a single stock, employees exercising NQOs often immediately sell all or a significant portion of the shares acquired on the exercise date, a practice referred to as a cashless exercise or **same-day sale.**[17]

[17]In addition to limiting investment risk, employees also engage in same-day sales to cover all or a portion of the exercise price associated with the options exercised, to pay the taxes triggered when nonqualified options are exercised, and to fund planned purchases.

Example 12-6

THE KEY FACTS

Nonqualified Stock Options (NQOs)

- No tax consequences on grant date.
- On exercise date, bargain element is treated as ordinary (compensation) income to employee.
  - Employee holds stock with holding period beginning on date of exercise.
- Employers deduct bargain element as compensation expense on exercise date.

What if: Suppose that five years after Julie exercised her NQOs and acquired 20,000 TPI shares with a basis of $20 per share, she sold all of the shares for $25 per share. What is the amount and character of the gain she will recognize on the sale?

Answer: $100,000 long-term capital gain, calculated as follows:

Description	Amount	Explanation
(1) Amount realized (sale proceeds)	$ 500,000	(20,000 × $25)
(2) Tax basis	400,000	Example 12-5
Long-term capital gain recognized	**$100,000**	(1) − (2)

What if: Suppose Julie sold the shares for $25 per share six months after she exercised them. What is the character of the $100,000 gain she recognized on the sale?

Answer: Short-term capital gain because she held the shares for one year or less before selling.

Employees who acquire shares through the exercise of ISOs also have an additional tax benefit: If they hold such shares *for at least two years after the grant date and one year after the exercise date,* they will not be taxed until they sell the stock.[18] When they sell, employees will treat the difference between the sale proceeds and the tax basis (the exercise price) as a long-term capital gain in the year of disposition. Thus, employees prefer ISOs to NQOs.

Example 12-7

What if: Suppose that five years after Julie exercised her ISOs and acquired 5,000 TPI shares with a basis of $5 per share, she sold all of the shares for $25 per share. What is the amount and character of the gain she will recognize on the sale?

Answer: Julie will recognize a $100,000 long-term capital gain, calculated as follows:

Description	Amount	Explanation
(1) Amount realized	$ 125,000	(5,000 × $25)
(2) Tax basis	25,000	Example 12-5
Long-term capital gain recognized	**$100,000**	(1) − (2)

If the two-year and one-year requirements are not met, the premature sale of stock is classified as a **disqualifying disposition,** and the bargain element is taxed at the time of sale *as if* the option had been an NQO. Thus, when holders of ISOs execute same-day sales, they forgo the benefit of taxing the bargain element at lower capital gains rates—but they do so in order to eliminate the investment risk they would otherwise have to bear if they attempted to satisfy the two-year-from-grant-date and one-year-from-exercise holding period requirements.

Example 12-8

What if: Assume that Julie exercised her ISOs and executed a same-day sale of the 5,000 shares on the vesting date (January 1, year 3) when the share price was $15. What is the amount and character of income she will recognize on these transactions?

[18]§422(a)(1).

Answer: $50,000 ordinary income, as calculated below. Because Julie's sale is a disqualifying disposition, the transactions are recast as though she exercised nonqualified options.

Description	Amount	Explanation
(1) Shares acquired with ISOs that were disqualified (became NQOs)	5,000	
(2) Market price per share	$ 15	
(3) Exercise price	5	Exhibit 12-5
(4) Bargain element per share	$ 10	(2) – (3)
Bargain element (ordinary income)	**$50,000**	(1) × (4)

THE KEY FACTS

Incentive Stock Options (ISOs)

- No tax consequences on grant date.
- No regular tax consequences on exercise date if employee holds stock for two years from grant date and one year from exercise date.
  - If holding requirements are not met (if there is a disqualifying disposition), option becomes an NQO.
- For AMT, the bargain element is taxed on the exercise date.
- When employee sells stock, employee recognizes long-term capital gain on difference between selling price and exercise price.
- No deduction for employers unless employee doesn't meet holding requirements.

TAXES IN THE REAL WORLD Stock Options

Sometimes, stock option compensation is the icing on the cake. Other times, options are the entire cake. According to Oracle Corporation's 2016 proxy statement, it paid founder and CEO Larry Ellison an annual salary of $1 in cash ($1 is not a misprint) and stock options worth almost $22 million and option awards worth over $18 million. No need to pay taxes on the compensation now; once the shares vest, Mr. Ellison can choose when to exercise the shares and, consequently, time his tax payments as well.

Source: Oracle Corporation 2016 Proxy Statement.

Employer Considerations for Stock Options As is true for employees, an employer's tax treatment of stock options depends on whether the options are NQOs or ISOs.

Nonqualified options. With NQOs, employers deduct the bargain element that employees recognize as income when the employees exercise the NQOs. From the employer's perspective, no other date is relevant for tax purposes.

Example 12-9

What if: Suppose that in year 3, Julie exercises NQOs to acquire 20,000 shares of TPI, and she reports $300,000 of ordinary income for the bargain element of the exercise (see Example 12-5). How much compensation expense for Julie's stock option exercise can TPI deduct in year 3?

Answer: $300,000. TPI can deduct the bargain element of Julie's exercise.

Note that this tax deduction is not tied to a cash payment. Thus, unless employers purchase their own shares to satisfy their employees' stock option exercises, they'll be entitled to a tax deduction without incurring any cash outflow.

Another important tax benefit associated with NQOs derives from the fact that income from NQOs is usually viewed as performance-based compensation. As a result, employers frequently use these options to circumvent the $1,000,000 deduction limitation imposed by §162(m). In fact, the stock option income of key executives at publicly traded companies usually dwarfs their cash salaries.

Incentive stock options. Employers typically don't view incentive stock options as favorably as NQOs, because (1) ISOs don't provide them with the same tax benefits (no tax deduction) and (2) the IRS regulatory requirements for ISOs can be cumbersome. That is, as long as the employee doesn't sell the stock in a disqualifying disposition, the employer does not get a tax deduction for ISOs. For this reason, employers with high marginal tax rates may lose significant tax benefits by issuing ISOs rather than NQOs. On the other hand, start-up companies or employers with net operating losses may actually benefit by issuing ISOs instead of NQOs. Due to their low or nonexistent marginal tax rates, companies in this position may not lose tax benefits by granting ISOs; however, because of the potential tax benefits ISOs provide to their employees relative to NQOs, they may be able to persuade their employees to accept relatively fewer ISOs.

ETHICS

Many companies use stock options as a form of equity compensation—to motivate executives and key employees. Some stock option issuers have either backdated and/or repriced stock options. Backdating is an illegal practice where a company, after-the-fact, chooses a date (timed retroactively) where the stock price was at its lowest point in order to maximize executive compensation. Stock option repricing is used when stock options are underwater (the market price is below the strike price). Repricing simply resets the strike price to a price below the current market price. While backdating options is illegal and obviously unethical, what do you think about the practice of repricing stock options?

Accounting issues. Historically, a major reason that companies used stock options to compensate their employees was the favorable accounting treatment stock options were afforded. Before 2006, companies were not required to reflect stock options as an expense in their financial statements. Thus, before 2006, companies that used stock options in lieu of cash salaries typically reported higher earnings than equally situated firms that were not heavy users of stock options. To increase the comparability of financial statements as well as to ensure that the true cost of stock options would be reflected in the financial statements, the Financial Accounting Standards Board (FASB) mandated the expensing of stock options for financial accounting purposes for years beginning on or after January 1, 2006.[19] Firms must measure the economic value of options on the grant date and then amortize this cost on a straight-line basis over the vesting period of the options.[20]

Example 12-10

What if: Assume that an accounting employee benefits specialist calculated the economic value of Julie's stock option grant (NQOs and ISOs) to be $32,000. Also assume that Julie's options vest 50 percent in year 1 (the year of the grant) and 50 percent in year 2. What compensation expense for book purposes would TPI report for Julie's stock options in year 1 and year 2?

Answer: $16,000 ($32,000 × 50%) in year 1 and $16,000 in year 2.

THE KEY FACTS

Stock Option Expense: GAAP vs. Tax

- For tax purposes, employers deduct the bargain element of NQOs on the exercise date but receive no tax deduction for ISOs unless they become disqualified.
- For GAAP purposes, employers expense the estimated value of the option pro rata over the vesting period.

As you probably realize by now, the tax rules governing the treatment of stock options differ markedly from generally accepted accounting principles in terms of both the amount and the timing of the stock option expense. To compare the tax and book treatment, we present TPI's book expense and tax deduction resulting from its stock option grant to Julie (given prior assumptions) in Exhibit 12-6.

The tremendous difference between the book and tax numbers presented in Exhibit 12-6 is driven by the increase in TPI's share price, from $5 on the date of

[19]Accounting Standards Codification (ASC) 718, Stock Compensation.

[20]Although the exercise price of compensatory stock options typically equals the stock price on the date of grant, compensatory options are, nevertheless, economically valuable on the grant date. They have economic value because the stock price may eventually exceed the exercise price before the options expire. To determine economic value, firms typically use either the Black-Scholes option pricing model or the binomial option pricing model.

EXHIBIT 12-6 **TPI's Tax Deductions and Book Expense from Stock Option Grant to Julie**

	Tax Deduction if Stock Price Increases	Tax Deduction if Stock Price Decreases	Book Expense
Year 1	$ 0	$0	$16,000
Year 2	0	0	16,000
Year 3	300,000	0*	0

*There would be no exercise because the exercise price exceeds the stock price.

grant to $20 on the date of exercise. The economic valuation of the stock options used to determine the book expense did not anticipate the extent of the stock appreciation before exercise.

Restricted Stock

Like stock options described above, **restricted stock** can't be sold or otherwise treated as owned by employees until they legally have the right to sell the shares on the vesting date. However, unlike the stock acquired through options exercises, employees receive restricted stock on the vesting date *without having to pay for it,* after which they can either sell it immediately or retain it.

As indicated in the timeline in Exhibit 12-7, the initial value of an employee's restricted stock award depends on the share price of the stock on the vesting date.

EXHIBIT 12-7 **Sample Timeline for Restricted Stock**

If Julie doesn't make any special tax elections, the economic and tax consequences of Julie's initial restricted stock award will depend on the future share price of TPI, on the vesting date of the restricted stock. The restricted stock examples in this chapter initially draw from the timeline below for the necessary assumptions regarding these key variables.

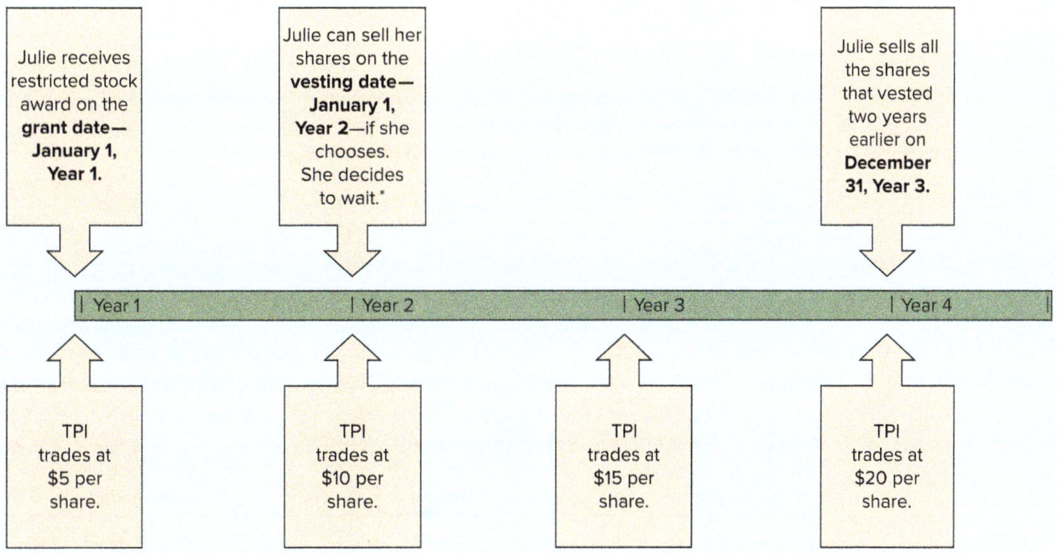

*As stipulated in her offer letter, Julie will receive 10,000 shares of TPI stock when the restrictions lapse on the vesting date (January 1 of year 2).

Example 12-11

Given the assumptions regarding the restricted stock in Exhibit 12-7, by how much would Julie's wealth increase on the vesting date?

Answer: Julie's wealth would increase by $100,000 (10,000 shares × $10 per share).

What if: Assuming that the stock decreased to $3 per share on the vesting date, by how much would Julie's wealth increase or decrease on the vesting date?

Answer: $30,000 increase ($3 × 10,000). Until the vesting date, Julie was not entitled to any economic benefit from the restricted stock. On the vesting date, however, she is entitled to stock valued at $30,000. Thus, the vesting of Julie's restricted stock increases her wealth even if the stock price decreases between the grant date and vesting date (unlike options, which would be worthless).

THE KEY FACTS

Restricted Stock *without* §83(b) Election

- No tax consequences on grant date.
- Employee recognizes ordinary income on fair market value of stock on vesting date.
- Holding period for stock begins on vesting date.
- Employer deducts fair market value of stock on vesting date.

Employee Considerations for Restricted Stock Restricted stock is taxed like NQOs with two important distinctions: While employees receiving NQOs are taxed at ordinary rates on the bargain element of the shares when they exercise their options, employees receiving restricted stock are taxed on the *full fair market value* of the shares *on the date the restricted stock vests.* They are taxed on the fair market value of the stock because they are entitled to receive the stock without any payment requirements (contrast this with the exercise price paid for stock options). Any subsequent appreciation in the value of the stock is taxed as either long-term or short-term capital gain(s) or loss(es) when the taxpayer sells the stock, depending on the holding period and future movement of the stock price. The employee's holding period for the stock begins on the vesting date.

Example 12-12

Assume that the restricted stock vests in year 2 when the market price is $10 (see Exhibit 12-7). What is the amount and character of the income Julie recognizes in year 2?

Answer: $100,000 ordinary income (10,000 shares × $10 per share).

Assume the same facts as above and that Julie sells the shares in year 4 when the market price is $20. What is the amount and character of the income she will recognize on the sale?

Answer: $100,000 long-term capital gain, calculated as follows:

Description	Amount	Explanation
(1) Amount realized	$200,000	10,000 shares × $20 per share
(2) Tax basis	100,000	Gain recognized on vesting date
Long-term capital gain	**$100,000**	(1) – (2)

What if: Assume the original facts except that Julie sells the shares in year 4 and the market price is now $4. What is the amount and character of the gain or loss she recognizes on the sale?

Answer: $60,000 long-term capital loss, calculated as follows:

Description	Amount	Explanation
(1) Amount realized	$ 40,000	10,000 shares × $4 per share
(2) Adjusted basis	100,000	Gain recognized on vesting date
Long-term capital loss	**($60,000)**	(1) – (2)

§83(b) election. The tax laws allow employees who receive restricted stock to make a tax election that can significantly change the tax consequences by treating the stock nearly the same as vested stock. Up until 30 days after the grant date, employees can make what is known as an **§83(b) election;** once made, however, this election is irrevocable. If the employee makes the §83(b) election, the value of the restricted stock is taxed on the grant date rather than the date on which the stock vests. The effect of the election is to accelerate the tax on the market value of the restricted shares—which, you'll recall from the Tax Planning Strategies and Related Limitations chapter, is usually not desirable from a tax planning perspective. However, if the employee expects the share price to increase after the grant date, making the election converts subsequent stock value appreciation from ordinary income into long-term capital gain (which, assuming the shares are held for more than one year after the grant date, results in a preferential tax rate when the taxpayer sells the shares). Without the §83(b) election, the employee reports no income when the shares are granted but is taxed on their fair market value at ordinary rates when the stock vests. With the §83(b) election, the employee simply pays tax at ordinary rates on the market value of the shares at the grant date.

THE KEY FACTS

Restricted Stock *with* Section §83(b) Election

- On grant date, employee recognizes market value of stock as ordinary income.
- Employee takes fair market value basis in stock.
- Holding period for stock begins on grant date.
- If employee never vests, no deduction for basis in stock.
- Employer deducts value of stock on grant date.

Example 12-13

What if: How much tax on the restricted stock will Julie pay in year 1 if she does not make an §83(b) election?

Answer: $0. The stock has not vested yet so she has no income.

What if: How much tax on the restricted stock will Julie pay in year 1 if she makes an §83(b) election?

Answer: $20,000 [$50,000 ordinary income (10,000 shares × $5 per share) × 40 percent marginal ordinary tax rate].

What if: How much tax will Julie pay in year 2 on the restricted stock (the year the restricted stock vests) if she *does not* make an §83(b) election in year 1 (the stock is trading at $10 a share on the vesting date)?

Answer: $40,000 [$100,000 ordinary income (10,000 shares × $10 per share) × 40 percent marginal ordinary tax rate].

What if: How much tax will Julie pay in year 2 on the restricted stock if she makes the §83(b) election in year 1?

Answer: $0. With the §83(b) election, Julie treated the stock as though it vested in year 1, not year 2, so she does not have a taxable event in year 2 when the stock actually vests.

What if: How much tax will Julie pay in year 4 on the restricted stock when she sells the stock for $20 a share (on December 31) if she *does not* make the §83(b) election in year 1?

Answer: $20,000 {[$200,000 (10,000 × $20) – $100,000 tax basis (fair market value on vesting date in year 2)] × 20 percent long-term capital gains rate}.

What if: How much tax would Julie pay in year 4 on the restricted stock when she sells the stock for $20 a share (on December 31) if she made the §83(b) election in year 1?

Answer: $30,000 {[$200,000 (10,000 × $20) – $50,000 tax basis (fair market value in year 1 when made §83(b) election)] × 20 percent long-term capital gains rate}.

Given the analyses above, what amount of taxes would Julie save by making the §83(b) election (ignore time value of money)?

(continued on page 12-18)

Answer: $10,000 ($50,000 with election; $60,000 without), computed as follows:

Taxes Payable		
Description	**With Election**	**Without Election**
Year 1 taxes on ordinary income	$ 20,000	$ 0
Year 2 taxes on ordinary income	0	40,000
Year 4 taxes on long-term capital gains	30,000	20,000
Total taxes	**$50,000**	**$60,000**

Note that Julie reduces her taxable income because the election allowed her to convert $50,000 in income from ordinary income taxed at 40 percent into long-term capital gain taxed at 20 percent.

Also note that this computation overstates to some degree the benefits of making the §83(b) election because it ignores the time value of money. In order to have a greater portion of her gains taxed at the preferential capital gain rates, Julie gave up some tax deferral when she accelerated $50,000 of income from year 4 into year 1.

Employees making the §83(b) election essentially trade off some additional current tax now in order to convert ordinary income into a long-term capital gain later. Accordingly, the §83(b) election is advisable when the potential for growth in the stock value is high and the amount of additional current tax is manageable. If an employee makes an §83(b) election and then forfeits the stock for any reason, the employee cannot deduct the loss on the forfeiture.[21] Thus, the risk of making the election is that if the employee forfeits the stock, tax would have been paid on value never received.

Employer Considerations for Restricted Stock Like the tax treatment of NQOs, the employer's deduction for restricted stock equals the amount of ordinary income reported by its employees. The timing of the deduction is determined by the employee's decision regarding the §83(b) election. If the employee makes an §83(b) election, the employer claims the deduction in the year the restricted stock is granted. Otherwise, the employer claims a deduction when the restrictions lapse. Some employers believe that restricted stock is a superior form of compensation to stock options. See Apple Inc.'s 2016 proxy statement in Exhibit 12-8.

EXHIBIT 12-8 Excerpt from Apple Inc.'s 2016 Proxy Statement

The Role of Long-Term Equity Awards

Emphasis on restricted stock units (RSUs). The Company has traditionally believed that long-term equity awards in the form of RSUs are the most effective way to attract and retain a talented executive team and align executives' interests with those of shareholders. Accordingly, the Company's executive compensation program in recent years has been weighted considerably toward long-term equity awards rather than cash compensation. The Company believes RSUs create incentives for performance and further align executives' interests with those of shareholders because an RSU's value increases or decreases in conjunction with the Company's stock price. As explained in more detail above, the Company is committed to including performance criteria in a portion of the equity awards it grants to executive officers in the future. At Mr. Cook's request, the Compensation Committee began this initiative in 2013 by amending his 2011 RSU award to include performance-based vesting conditions.

The accounting treatment for restricted stock is similar to the accounting treatment for stock options.[22] If restricted stock grants vest over time, the value of restricted stock on the *date of grant* is expensed pro rata over the vesting period.

[21]Reg. §1.83-2(a).

[22]ASC 718.

Example 12-14

What if: Given the assumptions in Exhibit 12-7, what amount can TPI deduct for tax purposes in year 1 and in year 2 assuming Julie *does not* make an §83(b) election?

Answer: $0 in year 1 and $100,000 in year 2 (10,000 shares of restricted stock vested × $10 per share market price at vesting date).

What if: What amount can TPI deduct in year 1 and in year 2 if Julie *does* make an §83(b) election?

Answer: $50,000 in year 1 (10,000 shares of restricted stock awarded × $5 per share market price on the grant date) and $0 in year 2.

What is TPI's compensation expense for financial accounting purposes for Julie's restricted stock in year 1 and in year 2?

Answer: $50,000 book expense in year 1. Because the value of Julie's restricted stock award on the date of grant is $50,000, TPI expenses the award on its books over the vesting period, which in this case is just one year (it has a one-year vesting period).

Equity-Based Compensation Summary

To summarize our discussion of the tax treatment of equity-based compensation, Exhibit 12-9 highlights the general tax treatment of NQOs, ISOs, and restricted stock on a per share basis from both employee and employer perspectives given an arbitrary time series of share prices. In addition to future share prices, the exhibit assumes options are exercisable for the share price on the grant date.

THE KEY FACTS

Restricted Stock Expense: GAAP vs. Tax

- For tax purposes, employers deduct the market value of stock when the employee recognizes income.
- For GAAP purposes, employers deduct the grant date value over the vesting period.

EXHIBIT 12-9 Reportable Income and Deductions from Equity-Based Compensation (for given time frame and stock prices)

	Party Affected	NQOs	ISOs	Restricted Stock
Grant date–year 1 Stock (exercise) price = $1/share	Employee	No effect	No effect	No effect
	Employer	No effect	No effect	No effect
Vesting date–year 4 Stock price = $6/share	Employee	No effect	No effect	$6/share ordinary income
	Employer	No effect	No effect	$6/share ordinary deduction
Exercise date for options–year 6 Stock price = $11/share	Employee	$10/share ordinary income	No effect*	N/A
	Employer	$10/share ordinary deduction	No effect	N/A
Sale date–year 8 Stock price = $16/share	Employee	$5/share LT capital gain	$15/share LT capital gain	$10/share Capital gain
	Employer	No effect	No effect	No effect

*$10 per share is included in alternative minimum taxable income.

FRINGE BENEFITS

LO 12-3

continued from page 12-7. . .

The final section of TPI's offer letter indicated Julie would receive fringe benefits in the form of health and dental insurance (value of $18,000), $750,000 of group-term life insurance, a biennial $30,000 automobile allowance, monthly parking, and a flexible spending account for medical expenses. ■

Employees generally receive most of their compensation in the form of cash salary or wages. However, employers often provide noncash benefits to employees in addition to their cash compensation. These **fringe benefits** range from the common (health insurance) to the exotic (use of a corporate aircraft). As a general rule, because fringe benefits are employee compensation, they are taxable to the employee on receipt. In fact, fringe benefits are specifically mentioned in the definition of gross income. As we indicated in the Gross Income and Exclusions chapter, IRC §61(a) indicates that, "gross income means all income from whatever source derived, including . . . (1) Compensation for services, including fees, commissions, *fringe benefits,* and similar items" (emphasis added). This definition of income notwithstanding, the tax laws specifically *exclude* certain fringe benefits from an employee's gross income. Thus, some fringe benefits are taxable and others are not.

THE KEY FACTS

Taxable Fringe Benefits

- Employees recognize compensation income on all benefits received unless specifically excluded by tax laws.
- Employees treat benefits received like taxable cash compensation.
- Employer deducts cost and pays employer's share of FICA taxes on benefit.

Taxable Fringe Benefits

Taxable fringe benefits are fringe benefits not specifically excluded from gross income. Congress views many of the taxable fringe benefits as luxuries and chooses not to subsidize them. Taxable fringe benefits include such things as below-market interest rate loans (see discussion in the Gross Income and Exclusions chapter), gym memberships, season tickets to the local NBA team, an automobile allowance for a personal automobile, or anything else not specifically excluded by the tax laws. Employers generally provide taxable fringe benefits to executives and higher-salaried employees rather than to the rank-and-file employees.

Employee Considerations for Taxable Fringe Benefits From an employee's perspective, taxable fringe benefits are treated just like cash. Employees recognize ordinary compensation income when they receive taxable benefits and, just as they do with salary, pay FICA taxes on the value of the benefit. As a result, taxable fringe benefits cost employees the amount of tax they must pay on the benefits.

Example 12-15

Julie's offer includes a biennial auto allowance of up to $30,000. That is, every other year, TPI will reimburse Julie for an automobile purchase up to $30,000. TPI provides this benefit to executives that interact with the public on a regular basis. Julie purchases a Toyota 4Runner with a retail price of $35,000. What tax is Julie required to pay if she uses the allowance to apply toward the purchase? What is Julie's after-tax cost of the automobile if her marginal tax rate is 40 percent (ignoring FICA taxes)?

Answer: $12,000 in income taxes and $17,000 after-tax cost, computed as follows:

Description	Amount	Explanation
(1) Fair market value of Toyota	$35,000	
(2) Automobile allowance	30,000	Taxable fringe benefit
(3) Julie's additional cost	5,000	(1) − (2)
(4) Income tax on allowance	12,000	(2) × 40%
Total after-tax cost	**$17,000**	(3) + (4)

From Julie's perspective, this is a pretty good deal—particularly if she was willing to pay the market price for the car.

Employees may prefer a taxable benefit to an equivalent amount of cash when they benefit from employer-provided quantity or group discounts associated with the benefit. For example, many companies provide (pay premiums for) **group-term life insurance** as a fringe benefit, in part, because they can purchase the insurance at a lower rate than employees could individually. However, employees must recognize a certain amount of gross income when employers pay life insurance premiums for employee policies with a death benefit in excess of $50,000.[23] Consequently, a portion of the group-term life insurance benefit is taxable and a portion is nontaxable. In these circumstances, the employer determines the employee's taxable amount using a table provided in the Treasury Regulations. An excerpt of this table is provided in Exhibit 12-10.[24] To compute the annual taxable benefit, taxpayers use the following steps:

Step 1: Subtract $50,000 from the death benefit of their employer-provided group-term life insurance policy.

Step 2: Divide the Step 1 result by $1,000.

Step 3: Multiply the result from Step 2 by the cost per $1,000 of protection for one month from the table (Exhibit 12-10) based on the taxpayer's age.

Step 4: Multiply the outcome of Step 3 by the number of months the benefit was received during the taxable year.

EXHIBIT 12-10 Uniform Premiums for $1,000 of Group-Term Life Insurance Protection

5-Year Age Bracket	Cost per $1,000 of Protection for One Month
Under 25	$0.05
25 to 29	.06
30 to 34	.08
35 to 39	.09
40 to 44	.10
45 to 49	.15
50 to 54	.23
55 to 59	.43
60 to 64	.66
65 to 69	1.27
70 and above	2.06

Example 12-16

Julie's offer from TPI includes $750,000 of group-term life insurance. TPI's cost to provide Julie the insurance is $500 per year. If Julie were to purchase the insurance herself she would pay $2,000 per year. Assume that Julie is 37 years old. Based on the Treasury's table (see Exhibit 12-10), the monthly premium per $1,000 of insurance is $.09. What is Julie's taxable compensation from receiving the group-term life insurance benefit? What does this benefit cost Julie (ignoring FICA taxes)?

(continued on page 12-22)

[23] §79.

[24] Reg. §1.79-3(d)(2) provides an age-based table and instructions to calculate the employee's includable amount.

Answer: $756 of taxable compensation and $302 cost to Julie (all taxes), calculated as follows. Julie's cost is the income and Medicare taxes she must pay on the compensation.

Group-Term Life Insurance Description	Amount	Explanation
(1) Insurance coverage	$750,000	Provided by employer
(2) Excluded coverage	(50,000)	Nontaxable portion
(3) Taxable benefit	$700,000	(1) + (2) (Step 1)
(4) Divide by 1,000	1,000	Divide by 1,000 (Step 2)
(5) Result of Step 2	700	(3)/(4)
(6) Monthly cost per $1,000	× 0.09	Taxable portion per $1,000 (from Exhibit 12-10)
(7) Monthly benefit	$ 63	(5) × (6), (Step 3)
(8) Months	× 12	Annualize monthly taxable amount
(9) Annual taxable benefit	**$ 756**	(7) × (8) (Step 4)
Income taxes	**$ 302**	(9) × 40%

Note that Julie's income is not based on TPI's actual cost ($500) of providing the policy.

Taxpayers receiving taxable fringe benefits may experience some financial strain because they must pay the tax on the benefits. Frequently, when corporations provide taxable fringe benefits to senior executives, they also provide the executives enough cash to cover the taxes so the benefit(s) costs the executive nothing.[25] This is commonly referred to as a *gross-up*. For example, GE's 2015 proxy statement reveals that it made payments of $1,048,864 to John G. Rice, its vice chairman, and indicates that the additional cash is for "Expatriate Tax Benefits."[26] Employees can choose to forgo a benefit if they prefer not to pay taxes on it.

Employer Considerations for Taxable Fringe Benefits Like employees, employers treat taxable fringe benefits just like cash compensation. That is, the employer has an outlay for the cost of the benefit and deducts its *cost* of the benefit, not the *value* of the benefit to the employee.[27] As we mention above, employers are often able to purchase fringe benefits at a lower cost than individual employees can. For example, employers may receive a group discount for purchasing life insurance, automobiles, financial or tax planning services, or accident insurance.

Example 12-17

In Example 12-16, TPI provided Julie with $750,000 of group-term life insurance. Its cost of providing the entire $750,000 of coverage is $500 per year. If Julie were to purchase the policy herself, it would cost her $2,000 per year. Assuming TPI's marginal tax rate is 35 percent, what is TPI's after-tax cost of the partially taxable group-term life insurance benefit it provided to Julie?

[25]Companies generally choose a formula to determine how much cash (gross-up) they need to pay the employee in addition to the taxable benefit to ensure the benefit costs the employee nothing.

[26]This amount represents the tax gross-up payments made on behalf of Mr. Heintzelman in connection with his nonpermanent relocation, at the company's request, to Florence, Italy, consistent with the company's policy for all employees.

[27]The employer also has an outlay for the cost of the employer's share of FICA taxes on the taxable portion of benefits it provides to employees and receives a deduction for the FICA taxes paid.

Answer: TPI's after-tax cost of the benefit provided is $325, calculated as follows:

Description	Amount	Explanation
(1) Cost of policy	$ 500	
(2) Income tax benefit	(175)	(1) × 35%
Total after-tax cost	**$325**	(1) + (2)

Finally, employers may discriminate between employees when providing taxable benefits. That is, they can select which employees receive the taxable benefits and which do not. Not surprisingly, the more highly compensated employees tend to receive these benefits. For example, as described in an excerpt from Walmart's 2016 proxy statement in Exhibit 12-11, Walmart's perquisite and supplemental benefits provide certain officers with use of the company aircraft and home security systems. Walmart is unlikely to offer these same benefits to its hourly sales associates.

EXHIBIT 12-11 Excerpt from Walmart's 2016 Proxy Statement

What perquisites and other benefits do our NEOs receive?

Our NEOs receive a limited number of perquisites and supplemental benefits. We cover the cost of annual physical examinations for our NEOs and provide each NEO with personal use of our aircraft for a limited number of hours each year. Our NEOs also receive company-paid life and accidental death and dismemberment insurance. Additionally, our NEOs are entitled to benefits available to officers generally, such as participation in the Deferred Compensation Matching Plan, and benefits available to Associates generally, including a Walmart discount card, a limited 15 percent match of purchases of Shares through our Associate Stock Purchase Plan, participation in our 401(k) Plan, medical benefits, and foreign business travel insurance. We provide these perquisites and supplemental benefits to attract talented executives to our company and to retain our current executives, and we believe their limited cost is outweighed by the benefits to our company.

TAXES IN THE REAL WORLD Fringe Benefits

Google Takes Off

At Alphabet (Google's parent), the company's stock price isn't the only thing that has taken off; its executive usage of aircraft paid for by the company has as well. According to two excerpts from Alphabet's 2016 Proxy Statement, this amount exceeds $1 million:

In 2015, we paid for personal security for Eric and incremental costs related to the personal use of non-commercial aircraft for Eric, Sundar, Ruth, and Omid. Pursuant to our Non-Commercial Aircraft Policy, named executive officers and their guests may use company aircraft with appropriate approvals and pay tax on any associated imputed income.

Corporate Use of Personal Aircraft

Eric E. Schmidt beneficially owns 100% of one aircraft and 33% of another aircraft, both of which are used by Eric and our other executive officers from time to time for business trips. The reimbursement rate for use of these aircraft is $7,500 per hour. Our Board of Directors approved this hourly reimbursement rate based upon a competitive analysis of comparable chartered aircraft rates that showed that the reimbursement rate is at or below market rates for the charter of similar aircraft. In 2015, we used these aircraft for business-related travel services for certain of our executive officers, including Eric, and we reimbursed Eric approximately $396,000. Due to the fact that the $7,500 hourly rate paid for the use of these aircraft is less than the actual operational costs incurred by Eric as owner of these aircraft, Eric does not profit from the use of these aircraft.

Nontaxable Fringe Benefits

For policy reasons, Congress specifically excludes certain fringe benefits, such as health insurance, from employees' gross income to encourage employers to provide the benefits.[28] We refer to excluded benefits as **nontaxable fringe benefits.** Other nontaxable fringe benefits enable taxpayers to become or stay employed, including meals or lodging for the convenience of the employer, educational assistance, dependent-care benefits, moving expense benefits, and transportation-related benefits. Finally, some benefits are excluded for simplicity's sake, such as no-additional-cost services, qualified employee discounts, and *de minimis* (small) fringe benefits. Exhibit 12-12 provides a partial list of nontaxable fringe benefits, and in the text that follows, we discuss these benefits in more detail.

EXHIBIT 12-12 Common Forms of Nontaxable Fringe Benefits

Benefit	Description
Group-term life insurance (§79)	Employer-paid premiums on up to $50,000 group-term life insurance policy are excluded from employees' income.
Health benefits (§§105–106)	Employer-paid premiums covering health, medical, and dental insurance and the benefits provided through the insurance.
Meals or lodging for the convenience of the employer (§119)*	Meals provided on employer's premises and lodging provided by the employer as a condition of employment.
Employee educational assistance (§127)	Up to $5,250 exclusion for tuition, books, and fees. See IRS Publication 970, *Tax Benefits for Education.*
Dependent care benefits (§129)	Up to $5,000 exclusion for cost of providing care for a dependent who is under 13 years old or a dependent who is disabled.
No-additional-cost services [§132(a)(1)]	Benefits that don't cost the employer a material amount.
Qualified employee discounts [§132(a)(2)]	Reduced prices on employer's product within certain limits.
Working condition fringe benefits [§132(a)(3)]*	A benefit provided by an employer that would be deductible as an ordinary and necessary business expense by the employee if the employee rather than the employer paid the expense.
De minimis fringe benefits [§132(a)(4)]*	Relatively small and infrequently provided benefits.
Qualified transportation fringe benefits [§132(a)(5)]*	Mass transit passes up to monthly limit of $255, qualified parking up to monthly limit of $255, or use of company-owned carpool vehicles (vans).
Qualified moving expense reimbursement [§132(a)(6)]*	Reimbursement for allowable moving expenses, such as moving household goods and travel.
Cafeteria plans (§125)	A plan where employees can choose from among various nontaxable fringe benefits or cash. Taxable to the extent employees receive cash.

*Employer may discriminate in providing this benefit.

Group-Term Life Insurance As we mentioned in the taxable benefits section, employees may exclude from income the employer-provided benefit for the first $50,000 of group-term life insurance.[29] Any remaining group-term life insurance benefit is taxable

[28] The nontaxable fringe benefits are listed with "items specifically excluded from gross income" in §§101–140 of the Internal Revenue Code. Employers are generally prohibited from discriminating among employees with respect to nontaxable fringe benefits (they cannot offer them only to executives). This chapter indicates whether or not discrimination for a particular benefit is allowed. However, the discrimination rules are complex and vary from benefit to benefit in ways too numerous to explain in detail in this text.

[29] §79.

(see Example 12-16). An employer may not discriminate between employees in providing nontaxable group-term life insurance benefits.

Health and Accident Insurance and Benefits When employers pay for **health and accident insurance** for an employee and the employee's spouse and dependents, the employee excludes the benefit from her gross income.[30] For example, if TPI pays health premiums of $18,000 for Julie and her family, Julie is not required to include this $18,000 fringe benefit in her gross income.[31] Further, when employees receive cash reimbursements for medical care, they can exclude the reimbursement from gross income.[32] For example, if TPI reimburses Julie for $450 of medical co-payments she makes during the year, Julie excludes the $450 from gross income. Generally, employers may not discriminate between employees when providing health and accident insurance benefits.[33]

TAXES IN THE REAL WORLD Free Lunch

Apple, Google, and Facebook are famous for their cafeterias, which have been chronicled in *Bon Appetit* and other foodie magazines. These cafeterias are light years ahead of the dorm cafeteria you ate in as a college freshman. And better yet, they are either free or almost free for employees. However, the secret is out—and now the IRS is questioning whether these benefits are taxable or nontaxable. To be considered nontaxable, the benefit has to be provided "for the convenience of the employer" rather than as a way to attract and compensate employees. These companies are arguing that without these cafeterias employees will be away from the company premises more and lose the opportunity to talk together, both of which are detrimental to the employer. The IRS has made this issue an administrative priority; that could be bad news for those companies that have relied on such perks to lure the best and brightest employees. The result may also cost the companies and employees back taxes in the future.

Meals and Lodging for the Convenience of the Employer The value of certain meals and lodging the employer provides to an employee may be excluded from an employee's gross income if the benefit meets two criteria: (1) the meals and lodging are provided on the employer's business premises to the employee (and the employee's spouse and dependents, if any) and (2) the meals and lodging are provided for the convenience of the employer.[34] For example, employers may provide meals at their place of business so employees can continue working efficiently without taking time off to go out to eat. Accounting firms frequently provide meals to tax professionals working late during tax season. Employers are allowed to deduct the full cost of meals provided to employees for the convenience of the employer. That is, the cost is not subject to the 50 percent deductibility limitation on meals we discussed in the Business Income, Deductions, and Accounting Methods chapter.[35] Employers may generally discriminate between employees in providing **for the convenience of the employer benefits.**

Example 12-18

What if: Assume that last year Julie purchased 25 meals, at a cost of $500, on evenings when she worked late. Julie turned in expense reports and receipts for the meals totaling $500, which PCC reimbursed. What is the amount Julie must include in income?

Answer: Julie will not include the value of any of the overtime meals in income because they were provided for PCC's convenience.

[30]§106.

[31]If Julie were to purchase the health insurance with after-tax dollars the equivalent would be $30,000 [$18,000/(1 – .4 marginal tax rate)].

[32]§105(b). Although, reimbursement in excess of costs is included in income.

[33]However, employers may exclude part-time employees from participation.

[34]§119(a)(1).

[35]§274(n).

In some situations, employers may provide lodging for employees and require employees to live on the business premises as a condition of their employment. In these cases, employees may exclude the value of the lodging from gross income.[36] For example, an employer may require an apartment complex manager to live in an apartment in the complex (free of charge) so the employee can respond to tenant needs, provide security, and handle emergencies. The apartment manager can exclude the value of the lodging from gross income.

Employee Educational Assistance Employees can exclude from income up to $5,250 of employee **educational assistance benefits** covering tuition, books, and fees.[37] Amounts received in excess of this limit are taxed as compensation to the employee. (See IRS Publication 970 for details related to education benefits.) This includes amounts employers provide for employee undergraduate- or graduate-level courses or for courses that lead to a professional degree. Amounts excluded from income cannot qualify for educational deductions or credits (such as the American opportunity and lifetime learning credits).

Dependent Care Benefits Employees can exclude up to $5,000 for benefits paid or reimbursed by employers for caring for children under age 13 or dependents or spouses who are physically or mentally unable to care for themselves.[38] Excluded amounts do not qualify for the child and dependent care credit (see the Individual Income Tax Computations and Tax Credits chapter).

No-Additional-Cost Services Employees can exclude the value of **no-additional-cost services.** These are any services employers provide to employees in the ordinary course of business that generate no substantial costs to the employer (including opportunity costs).[39] For example, airline companies can provide employees with free flight benefits on a space-available basis, hoteliers can allow employees to use vacant hotel rooms, and telephone companies can provide free basic phone service to their employees—all without the employees recognizing gross income. Exhibit 12-13 describes no-cost benefits that airline companies like JetBlue provide to their employees.[40]

EXHIBIT 12-13 Flight Benefits

JetBlue, like most other airlines, offers the following flight benefits to employees:

- It's our favorite perk! JetBlue crewmembers enjoy the benefit of free standby travel on JetBlue, as well as reduced-rate standby travel on some other airlines.

Example 12-19

What if: Assume that Julie's current employer, PCC, has a division that provides wireless Internet service and virus protection software. Because PCC has such a large contract with a national provider, its contract has sufficient bandwidth to allow employees to use the service without incurring additional cost. The market value of the services is $1,080 per year. What amount of this benefit must Julie include in her gross income?

Answer: $0. Julie may exclude the value of the wireless Internet from her income because it qualifies as a no-additional-cost service under §132.

[36]§119(a)(2).

[37]§127(a)(2). The discrimination and eligibility rules are provided in §127(b)(2).

[38]§129.

[39]§132(a)(1).

[40]See http://www.jetblue.com/work-here/benefits.aspx

Qualified Employee Discounts Employers frequently allow employees to purchase their goods and services at a discount. Employees may exclude **qualified employee discounts** from income as long as they don't acquire *goods* at a discount greater than the average gross profit percentage for the employer's goods.[41] Employees may also exclude qualified employee discounts on *services* as long as the discount is not more than 20 percent of the price of the services that are offered to customers. This can be a fairly significant nontaxable benefit to employees, particularly for higher priced products. For example, Ford Motor Company could allow employees a substantial discount on its Ford, Lincoln, and Mercury brand cars. Exhibit 12-14 presents an excerpt from the IBM website describing the IBM employee product purchase plan, which allows employees to acquire home appliances at a significant discount.

EXHIBIT 12-14 Excerpt from IBM's Website

Employee Purchase Program

Up to 25% off PCs for IBMers, friends & family. Free extended warranties & ground shipping!

See www-304.ibm.com/shop/americas/content/home/store_eppus/en_US/epplogin.html

From a nontax perspective, employers can use this qualified fringe benefit to entice and retain employees who would otherwise purchase the employer's brand or product.

Example 12-20

What if: Assume that Julie's current employer, PCC, allows all employees to purchase computers (both laptops and desktops) from its retail stores at a discount. Julie purchased two computers during the current year: a laptop for $1,600 (retails for $2,100, with a cost to PCC of $1,500) and a desktop for $1,300 (retails for $1,800, with a cost of $1,250). Julie saved $500 ($2,100 − $1,600) on the laptop and $500 ($1,800 − $1,300) on the desktop. Assume that PCC's average gross profit percentage is 25 percent. What amount of the savings must Julie include in her gross income?

Answer: Julie must include $50 in her gross income. The $50 of income is from the desktop because the employee discount of $500 ($1,800 retail price less the $1,300 purchase price) exceeds the $450 discount allowed ($1,800 retail price x 25% average gross profit percentage). The $500 savings on the laptop may be excluded from her income because the savings are less than the $525 ($2,100 x 25%) qualified employee discount under §132.

What if: Suppose that the laptop Julie purchased for $1,600 has a cost of $1,700 (instead of $1,500 as stated above). What amount of the tax savings on the laptop must Julie include in her gross income?

Answer: Zero for the laptop, because Julie's employee discount of $500 is still less than the allowable qualified employee discount of $525 ($2,100 x 25%). The qualified discount is tied to PCC's gross profit percentage, not the purchase price of a specific item.

What if: Assume that Julie's current employer, PCC, allows all employees to receive one free computer each year. Julie selected the laptop (retails for $2,100, with a cost to PCC of $1,500) as her free computer. What amount must PCC include in Julie's gross income?

Answer: $1,575. Julie's cost of the computer ($0) is $1,575 less than PCC's sales price ($2,100) less its gross profit percentage $525 ($2,100 x 25%). Therefore, she must include $1,575 in income. Employee discounts only qualify as a qualified employee discount under §132 to the extent they don't exceed the employer's gross profit percentage.

[41]§132(a)(2).

Working Condition Fringe Benefits Employees may exclude from income any benefit or reimbursement of a benefit provided by an employer that would be deductible as an ordinary and necessary expense by the employee if the employee rather than the employer paid the expense (or the employer did not reimburse the employee). For example, if a company or firm reimburses its employees for professional licensing costs or dues (e.g., CPA or bar fees or AICPA dues), the reimbursement may be excluded from an employee's income.[42] Additionally, telephones or computers provided to employees for business use may be excluded. Employers may discriminate between employees with respect to **working condition fringe benefits.**

Example 12-21

What if: Assume that Julie's employer reimburses executives for business-related continuing education courses as well as travel costs related to such education. Julie attended a certificate (nondegree program) course at the University of Chicago this year. Her costs were as follows: $2,500 for the course, $600 for airfare, $800 for hotels, and $200 for books and course materials. PCC reimbursed Julie for the entire $4,100 ($2,500 + $600 + $800 + $200). What amount of the reimbursement must Julie include in her gross income?

Answer: $0. The reimbursement qualifies as a working condition fringe benefit under §132.

What if: Assume that Ethan's employer allows all of its engineers to take home products for consumer testing and evaluation. For example, Ethan is currently designing a new disc brake system for mountain bikes. So Ethan is allowed to check out up to three mountain bikes at a time to see how various different brake systems work. The annual rental value of products Ethan uses is $2,500. What amount of the annual rental value must Ethan include in his gross income?

Answer: $0. The value of the consumer testing products is an excludable working condition fringe benefit under §132.

***De Minimis* Fringe Benefits** Employees can also exclude from income occasional or incidental ***de minimis* fringe benefits** (very small).[43] These typically include occasional personal use of a copy machine, company-sponsored picnics, noncash traditional holiday gifts (Thanksgiving turkey or Christmas ham), and occasional tickets to sporting or theatrical events. Employers are allowed to discriminate between employees when providing *de minimis* fringe benefits. Who do you think gets to use a company's NBA tickets—the new employee or the boss?

Qualified Transportation Fringe Benefits Employees may exclude from income the value of certain transportation benefits they receive from employers, whether employers pay for these benefits directly or reimburse employees for the transportation costs.[44] These **qualified transportation fringe benefits** eligible for exclusion include the value of company-owned carpool vehicles for commuting to and from work, the cost of mass transit passes, and the cost of qualified parking near the workplace. In 2016, the maximum exclusion for the carpool vehicle and mass transit pass is $255 per month and the maximum exclusion for the qualified parking benefit is also up to $255 per month.

Qualified Moving Expense Reimbursement Employees receiving payments (or reimbursements) from employers for **qualified moving expense reimbursements** may exclude the payments from gross income to the extent that they do not deduct the moving expenses.[45] As we discussed in the Individual Deductions chapter, qualified moving

[42]Employees can exclude reimbursements from their income if they properly document their expenses through expense reports, mileage logs, and receipts.

[43]§132(a)(4).

[44]§132(f)(1).

[45]§132(a)(6).

expenses include the cost of moving household items and travel, including lodging, for the employee and dependents as long as the employee's move meets certain distance and length of employment tests. Employees are, however, taxed on payments they receive from employers for house-hunting trips, temporary housing allowances, and reimbursements for expenses related to the sale of their prior residence.

Cafeteria Plans and Flexible Spending Accounts (FSAs) Employers choose the benefits they make available to employees. Some employers offer a standard package of benefits that employees can either take or leave. Standard benefits typically include health and dental insurance for the employee and family, dependent care benefits, and group-term life insurance for the employee. However, a standard benefit plan is not optimal for all employees because each employee has individual needs. So how can employers tailor their benefits to the needs of employees? The answer is cafeteria plans and flexible spending accounts.

Under a **cafeteria plan,** employers determine the total cost of benefits they are willing to provide for each employee. Each employee then either chooses (or buys) benefits up to the determined amount from a menu of nontaxable fringe benefits or may receive a cash equivalent in lieu of forgone benefits.[46] However, cash received from a cafeteria plan is taxable compensation to employees. Cafeteria plans are popular because each employee may desire different types of nontaxable fringe benefits. For example, if an employer provides $3,000 of dependent care benefits to every employee, the benefits would be worthless to employees without dependents. Through a cafeteria plan, employees can select the benefits best suited to their needs. For example, instead of selecting dependent care benefits, an employee with no dependents could choose any combination of nontaxable benefits such as dental insurance, educational benefits, or cash if none of the benefits are desirable.

Employers can also offer **flexible spending accounts (FSAs),** which allow employees to set aside a portion of their before-tax salary for payment of either health and/or dependent-care benefits. These plans allow employees to set aside either employee contributions (on a before-tax basis) or employer contributions (a leftover cafeteria plan amount) to pay for medical-related expenses (such as co-payments and prescriptions) or dependent care. The Patient Protection and Affordable Care Act reduces the limit for medical-related expenses to $2,600 in 2016. Generally, amounts placed in flexible spending accounts must be used for qualifying benefits during the FSA plan year (which is often the calendar year). However, employers may allow employees to use the remaining balance from one year within the first two and a half months of the next FSA plan year.[47] Any remaining balance is forfeited by the employee.

THE KEY FACTS

Nontaxable Fringe Benefits

- Specifically identified in the Code.
- Employee excludes benefit from taxable income.
- Employer deducts cost when benefit is paid.

Employee and Employer Considerations for Nontaxable Fringe Benefits

Nontaxable fringe benefits are very attractive to employees because their after-tax cost of these benefits is zero.[48] They do not pay for the benefits and they are not taxed on the value of the benefits they receive. In contrast to taxable fringe benefits, nontaxable fringe benefits cannot, with a few exceptions noted above, be provided on a discriminatory basis (i.e., provided to some employees and not others). Employers deduct the cost of providing the benefits, which (thanks to group or quantity discounts) can be

[46]§125.

[47]Employers can elect to allow employees to use funds set aside for one year until March 15 of the following year under Notice 2005-42. If employers don't make the election, employees must use their account balance by December 31 of the current year or they lose it after year-end.

[48]Furthermore, there are nontax reasons for employees to value nontaxable benefits, such as the fact that many employer-provided group health insurance plans allow for preexisting health conditions, whereas employees may not be able to obtain health insurance plans that cover preexisting health conditions on their own.

considerably lower than the cost to the employee of purchasing the benefit(s) separately. IRS publication 15-B "Employer's Tax Guide to Fringe Benefits" (available at www.IRS.gov) provides tax guidance for employers providing fringe benefits.

Tax Planning with Fringe Benefits

The fact that employees can exclude nontaxable fringe benefits from gross income, while employers can deduct the cost of providing them (just as they deduct the cost of taxable fringe benefits), gives rise to compensation-related tax-planning opportunities that may benefit both employee and employer.

Example 12-22

TPI proposed to reimburse Julie $200 a month for her parking costs. What amount of this reimbursement would be a nontaxable qualified transportation fringe benefit to Julie?

Answer: All $2,400. Julie can exclude up to $255 per month ($3,060 per year) as a qualified transportation fringe benefit.

What if: Assume that TPI will not reimburse Julie's parking costs unless Julie is willing to accept a reduction in salary. Assuming Julie is subject to a 40 percent marginal tax rate, how much salary should Julie be willing to forgo to receive the $2,400 of nontaxable parking benefits?

Answer: $4,000, computed as follows:

Description	Amount	Explanation
(1) Annual fringe benefit	$ 2,400	
(2) Marginal ordinary tax rate	40%	
Before-tax compensation required to pay for annual fringe benefit	**$4,000**	(1)/[1 − (2)]

Example 12-23

What if: Assume that instead of a parking benefit, TPI will pay Julie $4,000 of salary that she can then use to pay for her parking. What is TPI's after-tax cost of paying $4,000 of salary to Julie assuming its marginal tax rate is 35 percent?

Answer: $2,600, calculated as follows:

Description	Amount	Explanation
(1) Taxable salary paid	$ 4,000	
(2) Income tax benefit	(1,400)	(1) × 35%
Total after-tax cost of salary	**$2,600**	(1) + (2)

What if: Assume that TPI will provide Julie $2,400 of qualified transportation fringe benefits in the form of parking. What will be its after-tax cost of paying the $2,400 nontaxable fringe benefit to Julie assuming its marginal tax rate is 35 percent?

Answer: $1,560, calculated as follows:

Description	Amount	Explanation
(1) Nontaxable fringe benefit paid	$ 2,400	
(2) Income tax benefit	(840)	(1) × 35%
Total after-tax cost of nontaxable benefit	**$1,560**	(1) + (2)

Can an employer and an employee work together to implement the conversion tax planning strategy to make both the employee and the employer better off by substituting desired nontaxable fringe benefits for taxable salary in the compensation package? The answer is yes!

Example 12-24

What if: As shown in Example 12-22, Julie is indifferent between receiving (1) $4,000 in salary or (2) $2,400 in nontaxable parking benefits. Consequently, if TPI paid Julie $2,400 in nontaxable benefits and any amount of additional salary, she would be better off than she would be by receiving no parking and $4,000 in salary. As shown in Example 12-23, TPI would be better off after taxes by providing Julie with (1) $2,400 in nontaxable benefits (cost of $1,560) rather than (2) salary of $4,000 (after-tax cost of $2,600). What amount of salary could TPI provide in addition to the $2,400 of nontaxable benefits to make it indifferent between providing the parking and the additional salary or providing salary of $4,000?

Answer: $1,600 additional salary, calculated as follows:

Description	Amount	Explanation
(1) After-tax cost of salary	$2,600	Example 12-23
(2) After-tax cost of fringe benefit	1,560	Example 12-23
(3) After-tax cost of additional salary	$1,040	(1) − (2)
(4) After-tax cost percentage	65%	(1 − .35)
Additional before-tax salary	**$1,600**	(3)/(4)

To summarize, if TPI pays Julie's parking costs and provides her with additional salary of any amount below $1,600, it will be better off than it would be by not providing the parking and paying her $4,000 in salary. Julie is better off if TPI pays her parking and gives her any additional salary than she is if it doesn't pay her parking but pays her $4,000 of salary.

Fringe Benefits Summary

Fringe benefits, both taxable and nontaxable, can make up a significant portion of an employee's compensation. Fringe benefits are taxable unless the tax laws specifically exclude them from gross income. Taxable fringe benefits usually represent a luxury perk, while nontaxable fringe benefits are generally excluded for public policy reasons. At this point, you should be able to distinguish between taxable and nontaxable fringe benefits. Exhibit 12-15 presents an excerpt from Disney Company's 2016 proxy statement. Read through the excerpt and see if you can determine which of the benefits received by Mr. Iger are taxable and which are nontaxable.

Mr. Iger's taxable benefits include the personal air travel, security, wellness-related purposes, reimbursement for financial consulting, and perhaps part of the group-term life insurance. Mr. Iger's nontaxable benefits include theme park access (a no-additional-cost service), merchandise discounts (qualified employee discount), occasional sporting events (*de minimis* fringe benefit), educational expense reimbursements, health insurance, and group-term life insurance (some of this coverage may be taxable).

Recall the fringe benefits included in Julie's offer letter: health and dental insurance (valued at $18,000), $750,000 of group-term life insurance, a biennial $30,000 automobile allowance, and a flexible spending account (no amounts given—assume she elects $1,500). She also received an annual parking benefit of $2,400 (Example 12-22). Which benefits are taxable and which are nontaxable? Exhibit 12-16 summarizes how each of these benefits is classified for tax purposes, Julie's after-tax benefit, and TPI's after-tax cost.

EXHIBIT 12-15 **Excerpt from Disney Company's 2016 Proxy Statement Dealing with Fringe Benefits**

The following table identifies the incremental cost of each perquisite or personal benefit that exceeded the greater of $25,000 or 10% of the total amount of perquisites and personal benefits for a named executive officer in fiscal 2015.

Fiscal 2015 Perquisites and Personal Benefits

Executive	Year	Personal Air Travel	Security	Other	Total
Robert A. Iger	2015	$277,489	$683,245	$49,550	$1,010,284

The incremental cost to the Company of the items specified above was determined as follows:

- Personal air travel: the actual catering costs, landing and ramp fees, fuel costs and lodging costs incurred by flight crew plus a per hour charge based on the average hourly maintenance costs for the aircraft during the year for flights that were purely personal in nature, and a pro rata portion of catering costs where personal guests accompanied a named executive officer on flights that were business in nature. Where a personal flight coincided with the repositioning of an aircraft following a business flight, only the incremental costs of the flight compared to an immediate repositioning of the aircraft are included. As noted on pages 22 to 23, above, Mr. Iger is required for security reasons to use corporate aircraft for all of his personal travel.
- Security: the actual costs incurred by the Company for providing security equipment and services.

The "Other" column in the table above includes, to the extent a named executive officer elected to receive any of these benefits, the incremental cost to the Company of the vehicle benefit, personal air travel or security services where the cost to the Company was less than $25,000, reimbursement of up to $1,000 per calendar year for wellness-related purposes such as fitness, nutrition and stress management, and reimbursement of expenses for financial consulting. With respect to Mr. Iger, the "Other" column also includes legal fees incurred in connection with the renegotiation of his employment agreement.

The named executive officers also were eligible to receive the other benefits described in the Compensation Discussion and Analysis under the discussion of "Benefits and Perquisites" in the "Compensation Program Elements" section, which involved no incremental cost to the Company or are offered through group life, health or medical reimbursement plans that are available generally to all of the Company's salaried employees.

EXHIBIT 12-16 **Summary of Julie's Nonsalary Benefits from TPI**

Benefit	Nontaxable Fringe	Taxable Fringe	Employee After-Tax Benefit	Employer After-Tax Cost
Auto allowance		X	**$18,000** ($30,000 − $12,000) (Example 12-15)	**$19,500** [$30,000 × (1 − .35)]
Health and dental insurance	X		**$18,000** [$18,000 × (1 − .0)]	**$11,700** [$18,000 × (1 − .35)]
Flexible spending account	X		**$1,500** [$1,500 × (1 − .0)]	**$975** [$1,500 × (1 − .35)]
Parking reimbursement	X		**$2,400** [$2,400 × (1 − .0)] (Example 12-22)	**$1,560** [$2,400 × (1 − .35)] (Example 12-23)
Group-term life insurance	X	X	**$1,698** ($2,000 − $302)* (Examples 12-16, 17)	**$325** [$500 × (1 − .35)] (Example 12-17)
Total			**$41,598**	**$34,060**

*This is the fair market value of the benefit less the actual taxes payable by Julie.

CONCLUSION

Individuals and employers routinely make choices involving compensation issues. As they do so, they must understand how alternative forms of compensation are taxed. In this chapter, we have discussed the tax compliance and planning implications associated with common types of payment including salary and wages, equity-based compensation (such as stock options and restricted stock), and taxable and nontaxable fringe benefits from both employee and employer perspectives. Throughout, we have emphasized that both tax and nontax issues must be considered in the broader context of compensation planning. Armed with the information provided in this chapter, future employees and employers can approach the compensation decisions they will undoubtedly face with more confidence and insight.

Summary

Discuss and explain the tax implications of compensation in the form of salary and wages from the employee's and employer's perspectives. LO 12-1

- Employees are taxed on salary at ordinary income rates.
- Employees use Form W-4 to supply their employer with withholding information. Employees can use the W-4 to manage withholding throughout the year because withholding is treated as though it is withheld evenly throughout the year for estimated tax purposes.
- Cash-method employers deduct wages when paid. Accrual-method employers deduct wages when accrued as long as the wages are paid within 2½ months of year-end. If paid after 2½ months of year-end, wages are deductible when the employee recognizes the income (when paid). When an employer accrues wages to a related-party employee (more than 50 percent ownership), the wages are not deductible until the employee recognizes the income (when paid).
- Employers' after-tax cost of wages is the cost of the wages minus the tax benefit of the deduction for the wages.
- For publicly traded corporations, the tax deduction for nonperformance-based compensation paid to the CEO and the three other most highly compensated officers, not including the CFO, is limited to $1,000,000 per year per individual.

Describe and distinguish the tax implications of various forms of equity-based compensation from the employee's and employer's perspectives. LO 12-2

- Stock options and restricted stock are common forms of equity-based compensation. Although both reward employees for increases in the stock price of their employers, there are fundamental economic differences between them.
- Stock options are treated as either nonqualified stock options (NQOs) or incentive stock options (ISOs) for tax purposes.
- Employees recognize ordinary income equal to the bargain element on NQOs when they are exercised. Employers are able to deduct the bargain element when NQOs are exercised. Any appreciation in the value of shares subsequent to the exercise of NQOs is treated as capital gain by employees when the shares are sold.
- If certain holding period requirements are met, employees exercising ISOs don't recognize any income until the shares received from the exercised options are sold. When the shares are sold, the difference between the exercise price and the share price is long-term capital gain (assuming appreciation). Employers are not permitted a deduction for ISOs.
- Generally, employees prefer ISOs and employers prefer NQOs because of differences in the way the two types of options are taxed.
- Employers treat stock options differently for book and tax purposes.

- Employees recognize ordinary income from restricted stock equal to the fair market value of the stock on the vesting date. Employers receive a corresponding tax deduction.
- Employees may elect to recognize taxable income from restricted stock on the date it is received rather than on the vesting date if they make an §83(b) election. Although this election accelerates the recognition of income, it gives the employee the ability to convert ordinary income from further appreciation into a capital gain.

LO 12-3 Compare and contrast taxable and nontaxable fringe benefits and explain the employee and employer tax consequences associated with fringe benefits.

- Fringe benefits are taxable to the employee unless the Code specifically excludes the benefit from gross income. Taxable fringe benefits are generally luxury perks, such as corporate air travel and security.
- Nontaxable fringe benefits include up to $50,000 of group-term life insurance, health benefits, meals and lodging for the convenience of the employer, educational assistance, dependent care benefits, qualified employee discounts, and qualified transportation benefits (among others).

KEY TERMS

bargain element (12-10)
cafeteria plan (12-29)
cashless exercise (12-10)
***de minimis* fringe benefit (12-28)**
disqualifying disposition (12-12)
educational assistance benefit (12-26)
employee (12-2)
exercise date (12-10)
exercise price (12-8)
facts and circumstances test (12-4)
FICA taxes (12-2)
flexible spending account (FSA) (12-29)
for the convenience of the employer benefits (12-25)
Form W-2 (12-2)
Form W-4 (12-2)
fringe benefits (12-20)
grant date (12-10)
group-term life insurance (12-21)
health and accident insurance (12-25)
incentive stock option (ISO) (12-10)
no-additional-cost services (12-26)
nonqualified stock option (NQO) (12-10)
nontaxable fringe benefit (12-24)
option exercise (12-9)
qualified employee discount (12-27)
qualified moving expense reimbursement (12-28)
qualified transportation fringe benefit (12-28)
restricted stock (12-15)
salary (12-2)
same-day sale (12-11)
§83(b) election (12-17)
strike price (12-8)
taxable fringe benefit (12-20)
vest (12-8)
vesting date (12-10)
wages (12-2)
working condition fringe benefit (12-28)

DISCUSSION QUESTIONS

Discussion Questions are available in Connect®. connect

LO 12-1 1. Nicole and Braxton are each 50 percent shareholders of NB Corporation. Nicole is also an employee of the corporation. NB is a calendar-year taxpayer and uses the accrual method of accounting. The corporation pays its employees monthly on the first day of the month after the salary is earned by the employees. What issues must NB consider with respect to the deductibility of the wages it pays to Nicole if Nicole is Braxton's sister? What issues arise if Nicole and Braxton are unrelated?

LO 12-1 2. Holding all else equal, does an employer with a higher marginal tax rate or lower marginal tax rate have a lower after-tax cost of paying a particular employee's salary? Explain.

LO 12-1 3. What are nontax reasons for why a corporation may choose to cap its executives' salaries at $1 million?

4. What are tax reasons why a corporation may choose to cap its executives' salaries at $1 million? LO 12-1
5. Lea is a highly paid executive with MCC Inc., a publicly traded corporation. What are the circumstances under which MCC will be able to deduct more than $1 million of compensation paid to Lea during the year? LO 12-1
6. From an *employee* perspective, how are ISOs treated differently than NQOs for tax purposes? In general, for a given number of options, which type of stock option should employees prefer? LO 12-2
7. From an *employer* perspective, how are ISOs treated differently than NQOs for tax purposes? In general, for a given number of options, which type of stock option should employers prefer? LO 12-2
8. Why do employers use stock options in addition to salary to compensate their employees? For employers, are stock options treated more favorably than salary for tax purposes? Explain. LO 12-2
9. What is a "disqualifying disposition" of ISOs, and how does it affect employees who have exercised ISOs? LO 12-2
10. Compare and contrast how employers record book and tax expense for stock options. LO 12-2
11. How is the tax treatment of restricted stock different from that of NQOs? How is it similar? LO 12-2
12. Matt just started work with Boom Zoom Inc., a manufacturer of credit-card-sized devices for storing and playing back music. Due to the popularity of its devices, analysts expect Boom Zoom's stock price to increase dramatically. In addition to his salary, Matt received Boom Zoom restricted stock. How will Matt's restricted stock be treated for tax purposes? Should Matt consider making the §83(b) election? What are the factors he should consider in making this decision? From a tax perspective, would this election help or hurt Boom Zoom? LO 12-2
13. What risks do employees making an §83(b) election on a restricted stock grant assume? LO 12-2
14. Explain the differences and similarities between fringe benefits and salary as forms of compensation. LO 12-3
15. When an employer provides group-term life insurance to an employee, what are the tax consequences for the employee? What are the tax consequences for the employer? LO 12-3
16. Compare and contrast the employer's tax consequences of providing taxable versus nontaxable fringe benefits. LO 12-3
17. Mike is working his way through college and trying to make ends meet. Tara, a friend, is graduating soon and tells Mike about a really great job opportunity. She is the onsite manager for an apartment complex catering to students. The job entails working in the office for about 10 hours a week, collecting rent each month, and answering after-hours emergency calls. The owner of the apartment complex requires the manager to live onsite as a condition of employment. The pay is $10 per hour, plus a rent-free apartment (worth about $500 per month). Tara then tells him the best part: the rent-free apartment is tax-free. Knowing that you are a tax student, Mike asks you if the rent-free apartment is really tax-free or if Tara is mistaken. Explain to Mike whether the compensation for the apartment is really a nontaxable fringe benefit. LO 12-3
18. Assume that your friend has accepted a position working as an accountant for a large automaker. As a signing bonus, the employer provides the traditional cash incentive but also provides the employee with a vehicle not to exceed a retail price of $25,000. Explain to your friend whether the value of the vehicle is included, excluded, or partially included in the employee's gross income. LO 12-3

LO 12-3 19. Explain why an employee might accept a lower salary to receive a nontaxable fringe benefit. Why might an employee not accept a lower salary to receive a nontaxable fringe benefit?

LO 12-3 20. Describe a cafeteria plan and discuss why an employer would provide a cafeteria plan for its employees.

LO 12-3 21. Explain why Congress allows employees to receive certain fringe benefits tax-free but others are taxable.

LO 12-3 22. Explain the policy reason for including the value of a country club membership provided to an executive as a taxable fringe benefit.

LO 12-3 23. Describe the circumstances in which an employee may not value a nontaxable fringe benefit.

PROBLEMS

Select problems are available in Connect®.

LO 12-1 24. North Inc. is a calendar-year C corporation, accrual-basis taxpayer. At the end of year 1, North accrued and deducted the following bonuses for certain employees for financial accounting purposes.

- $7,500 for Lisa Tanaka, a 30 percent shareholder.
- $10,000 for Jared Zabaski, a 35 percent shareholder.
- $12,500 for Helen Talanian, a 20 percent shareholder.
- $5,000 for Steve Nielson, a 0 percent shareholder.

Unless stated otherwise, assume these shareholders are unrelated.
How much of the accrued bonuses can North Inc. deduct in year 1 under the following alternative scenarios?

a) North paid the bonuses to the employees on March 1 of year 2.
b) North paid the bonuses to the employees on April 1 of year 2.
c) North paid the bonuses to employees on March 1 of year 2 and Lisa and Jared are related to each other, so they are treated as owning each other's stock in North.
d) North paid the bonuses to employees on March 1 of year 2 and Lisa and Helen are related to each other, so they are treated as owning each other's stock in North.

LO 12-1 25. Jorgensen High Tech Inc. is a calendar-year, accrual-method taxpayer. At the end of year 1, Jorgensen accrued and deducted the following bonuses for certain employees for financial accounting purposes.

- $40,000 for Ken.
- $30,000 for Jayne.
- $20,000 for Jill.
- $10,000 for Justin.

How much of the accrued bonuses can Jorgensen deduct in year 1 under the following alternative scenarios?

a) Jorgensen paid the bonuses to the employees on March 1 of year 2.
b) Jorgensen paid the bonuses to the employees on April 1 of year 2.
c) Jorgensen paid the bonuses to employees on March 1 of year 2, and there is a requirement that the employee remain employed with Jorgensen on the payment date to receive the bonus.

d) Jorgensen paid the bonuses to employees on March 1 of year 2, and there is a requirement that the employee remain employed with Jorgensen on the payment date to receive the bonus; if not, the forfeited bonus is reallocated to the other employees.

26. Lynette is the CEO of publicly traded TTT Corporation and earns a salary of $200,000 in the current year. Assume TTT has a 35 percent marginal tax rate. What is TTT Corporation's after-tax cost of paying Lynette's salary? LO 12-1

27. Marcus is the CEO of publicly traded ABC Corporation and earns a salary of $1,500,000. Assume ABC has a 35 percent marginal tax rate. LO 12-1

a) What is ABC's after-tax cost of paying Marcus's salary?

b) Now assume that Marcus, in addition to the $1.5 million salary, earns a performance-based bonus of $500,000. What is ABC's after-tax cost of paying Marcus's salary?

28. Ramon has finally arrived. He has interviewed for the CEO position with MMM Corporation. They have presented him with two alternative compensation offers. Alternative 1 is for a straight salary of $2,500,000. Option 2 is for a salary of $1,000,000 and performance-based compensation of up to $2,000,000. Assume that Ramon has a marginal tax rate of 40 percent and MMM has a marginal tax rate of 35 percent. Answer the questions under each of the following alternative scenarios. LO 12-1 planning

a) If Ramon is 100 percent certain he can meet the qualifications for the full performance-based compensation, which offer should he choose?

b) If Ramon believes there is only a 20 percent chance that he can meet the performance-based requirements, which offer should he choose (assume he is risk neutral)?

c) What is MMM's after-tax cost of providing Ramon with Option 1?

d) What is MMM's expected after-tax cost of providing Ramon with Option 2 if it believes there is a 40 percent chance Ramon will qualify for the performance-based compensation?

29. Cammie received 100 NQOs (each option provides a right to purchase 10 shares of MNL stock for $10 per share) at the time she started working for MNL Corporation (5/1/Y1) four years ago when MNL's stock price was $8 per share. Now (8/15/Y5) that MNL's stock price is $40 per share, she intends to exercise all of her options. After acquiring the 1,000 MNL shares with her options, she held the shares for over one year (10/1/Y6) and sold them at $60 per share. LO 12-2 tax forms

a) What are Cammie's taxes due on the grant date (5/1/Y1), exercise date (8/15/Y5), and sale date (10/1/Y6), assuming her ordinary marginal rate is 30 percent and her long-term capital gains rate is 15 percent?

b) What are MNL Corporation's tax savings on grant date (5/1/Y6), exercise date (8/15/Y5), and sale date (10/1/Y6), assuming its marginal tax rate is 35 percent?

c) Complete Cammie's Form 8949 and Schedule D for the year of sale. Also assume that the sale transaction of the MNL Corporation stock was not reported to Cammie on a Form 1099-B.

30. Yost received 300 NQOs (each option gives Yost the right to purchase 10 shares of Cutter Corporation stock for $15 per share) at the time he started working for Cutter Corporation three years ago. Cutter's stock price was $15 per share. Yost exercises all of his options when the share price is $26 per share. Two years after acquiring the shares, he sold them at $47 per share. LO 12-2 planning

a) What are Yost's taxes due on the grant date, exercise date, and sale date, assuming his ordinary marginal rate is 35 percent and his long-term capital gains rate is 15 percent?

b) What are Cutter Corporation's tax consequences (amount of deduction and tax savings from deduction) on the grant date, the exercise date, and the date Yost sells the shares, assuming its marginal tax rate is 25 percent?

c) Assume that Yost is "cash poor" and needs to engage in a same-day sale in order to buy his shares. Due to his belief that the stock price is going to increase significantly, he wants to maintain as many shares as possible. How many shares must he sell in order to cover his purchase price and taxes payable on the exercise?

d) Assume that Yost's options were exercisable at $20 and expired after five years. If the stock only reached $18 dollars during its high point during the five-year period, what are Yost's tax consequences on the grant date, the exercise date, and the date the shares are sold, assuming his ordinary marginal rate is 35 percent and his long-term capital gains rate is 15 percent?

LO 12-2

31. Haven received 200 NQOs (each option gives him the right to purchase 20 shares of Barlow Corporation stock for $7 per share) at the time he started working for Barlow Corporation three years ago when its stock price was $7 per share. Now that Barlow's share price is $50 per share, he intends to exercise all of his options. After acquiring the 4,000 Barlow shares with his options, he intends to hold the shares for more than one year and then sell the shares when the price reaches $75 per share.

a) What are Haven's taxes due on the grant date, exercise date, and sale date, assuming his ordinary marginal rate is 30 percent and his long-term capital gains rate is 15 percent?

b) What are the cash flow effects for Barlow Corporation resulting from Haven's option exercise if Barlow's marginal tax rate is 35 percent?

LO 12-2

32. Mark received 10 ISOs (each option gives him the right to purchase 10 shares of Hendricks Corporation stock for $5 per share) at the time he started working for Hendricks Corporation five years ago when Hendricks's stock price was $5 per share. Now that Hendricks's share price is $35 per share, Mark intends to exercise all options and hold all of his shares for more than one year. Assume that more than a year after exercise, Mark sells the stock for $35 a share.

a) What are Mark's taxes due on the grant date, the exercise date, and the date he sells the shares, assuming his ordinary marginal rate is 30 percent and his long-term capital gains rate is 15 percent?

b) What are Hendricks's tax consequences on the grant date, the exercise date, and the date Mark sells the shares, assuming its marginal tax rate is 25 percent?

LO 12-2

33. Antonio received 40 ISOs (each option gives him the right to purchase 20 shares of Zorro stock for $3 per share) at the time he started working for Zorro Corporation six years ago. Zorro's stock price was $3 per share at the time. Now that Zorro's stock price is $50 per share, Antonio intends to exercise all of his options and immediately sell all the shares he receives from the options exercise.

a) What are Antonio's taxes due on the grant date, the exercise date, and the date the shares are sold, assuming his ordinary marginal rate is 30 percent and his long-term capital gains rate is 15 percent?

b) What are Zorro's tax consequences on the grant date, the exercise date, and the date Antonio sells the shares, assuming its marginal tax rate is 25 percent?

c) What are the cash flow effects of these transactions to Antonio, assuming his ordinary marginal rate is 25 percent and his long-term capital gains rate is 15 percent?

d) What are the cash flow effects to Zorro Corporation resulting from Antonio's option exercise if Zorro's marginal tax rate is 35 percent?

34. Harmer Inc. is now a successful company. In the early days (before it became profitable), it issued ISOs to its employees. Now Harmer is trying to decide whether to issue NQOs or ISOs to its employees. Initially, Harmer would like to give each employee 20 options (each option allows the employee to acquire one share of Harmer stock). For purposes of this problem, assume that the options are exercised in three years (*three years from now*) and that the underlying stock is sold in five years (*five years from now*). Assume that taxes are paid at the same time the income generating the tax is recognized. Also assume the following facts: LO 12-2 planning

- The after-tax discount rate for both Harmer Inc. and its employees is 10 percent.
- The corporate tax rate is 35 percent.
- The personal (employee) ordinary income rate is 40 percent.
- The personal (employee) long-term capital gains rate is 20 percent.
- The exercise price of the options is $7.
- The market price of Harmer at date of grant is $5.
- The market price of Harmer at date of exercise is $25.
- The market price of Harmer at date of sale is $35.

Answer the following questions:

a) Considering these facts, which type of option plan, NQO or ISO, should Harmer Inc. prefer? Explain.

b) Assuming Harmer issues NQOs, what is Harmer's tax benefit from the options for each employee in the year each employee exercises the NQOs?

c) Assuming Harmer issues ISOs, what is the tax benefit to Harmer in the year the ISOs are exercised?

d) Which type of option plan should Harmer's employees prefer?

e) What is the present value of each employee's after-tax cash flows from year 1 through year 5 if the employees receive ISOs?

f) What is the present value of each employee's after-tax cash flows from year 1 through year 5 if the employees receive NQOs?

g) How many NQOs would Harmer have to grant to keep its employees indifferent between NQOs and 20 ISOs?

35. On January 1, year 1, Dave received 1,000 shares of restricted stock from his employer, RRK Corporation. On that date, the stock price was $7 per share. Dave's restricted shares will vest at the end of year 2. He intends to hold the shares until the end of year 4 when he intends to sell them to help fund the purchase of a new home. Dave predicts the share price of RRK will be $30 per share when his shares vest and will be $40 per share when he sells them. LO 12-2

a) If Dave's stock price predictions are correct, what are the taxes due on these transactions to Dave if his ordinary marginal rate is 30 percent and his long-term capital gains rate is 15 percent?

b) If Dave's stock price predictions are correct, what are the tax consequences of these transactions to RRK if its marginal rate is 35 percent?

36. On January 1, year 1, Dave received 1,000 shares of restricted stock from his employer, RRK Corporation. On that date, the stock price was $7 per share. On receiving the restricted stock, Dave made the §83(b) election. Dave's restricted shares will vest at the end of year 2. He intends to hold the shares until the end of year 4 when he intends to sell them to help fund the purchase of a new home. Dave predicts the share price of RRK will be $30 per share when his shares vest and will be $40 per LO 12-2

share when he sells them. Assume that Dave's price predictions are correct and answer the following questions:

a) What are Dave's taxes due if his ordinary marginal rate is 30 percent and his long-term capital gains rate is 15 percent?

b) What are the tax consequences of these transactions to RRK if its marginal rate is 35 percent?

LO 12-2

37. On January 1, year 1, Jessica received 10,000 shares of restricted stock from her employer, Rocket Corporation. On that date, the stock price was $10 per share. On receiving the restricted stock, Jessica made the §83(b) election. Jessica's restricted shares will all vest at the end of year 4. After the shares vest, she intends to sell them immediately to fund an around-the-world cruise. Unfortunately, Jessica decided that she couldn't wait four years and she quit her job to start her cruise on January 1, year 3.

a) What are Jessica's taxes due in year 1 assuming her marginal tax rate is 33 percent and her long-term capital gains rate is 15 percent?

b) What are Jessica's taxes due in year 3 assuming her marginal tax rate is 33 percent and her long-term capital gains rate is 15 percent?

LO 12-2

38. On May 1, year 1, Anna received 5,000 shares of restricted stock from her employer, Jarbal Corporation. On that date, the stock price was $5 per share. On receiving the restricted stock, Anna made the §83(b) election. Anna's restricted shares will all vest on May 1, year 3. After the shares vest, she intends to sell them immediately to purchase a condo. True to her plan, Anna sold the shares immediately after they were vested.

a) What is Anna's ordinary income in year 1?

b) What is Anna's gain or loss in year 3 if the stock is valued at $1 per share on the day the shares vest?

c) What is Anna's gain or loss in year 3 if the stock is valued at $9 per share on the day the shares vest?

d) What is Anna's gain or loss in year 3 if the stock is valued at $5 per share on the day the shares vest?

LO 12-2
planning

39. On January 1, year 1, Tyra started working for Hatch Corporation. New employees must choose immediately between receiving 7 NQOs (each NQO provides the right to purchase for $5 per share 10 shares of Hatch stock) or 50 restricted shares. Hatch's stock price is $5 on Tyra's start date. Either form of equity-based compensation will vest in two years. Tyra believes that the stock will be worth $15 per share in two years and $25 in four years when she will sell the stock. Tyra's marginal tax rate is 30 percent and her long-term capital gains rate is 15 percent. Assuming that Tyra's price predictions are correct, answer the following questions (ignore present value, use nominal dollars):

a) What are the cash-flow effects to Tyra in the year she receives the options, in the year the options vest and she exercises the options, and in the year she sells the stock if she chooses the NQOs?

b) What are the cash-flow effects to Tyra in the year she receives the restricted stock, in the year the stock vests, and in the year she sells the stock if Tyra chooses the restricted stock?

c) What are the cash-flow effects to Tyra in the year she receives the restricted stock, in the year the stock vests, and in the year she sells the stock if she makes an §83(b) election?

d) What recommendation would you give Tyra? Explain.

40. Nicole's employer, Poe Corporation, provides her with an automobile allowance of $20,000 every other year. Her marginal tax rate is 30 percent. Poe Corporation has a marginal tax rate of 35 percent. Answer the following questions relating to this fringe benefit. LO 12-3
   a) What is Nicole's after-tax benefit if she receives the allowance this year?
   b) What is Poe's after-tax cost of providing the auto allowance?

41. Bills Corporation runs a defense contracting business that requires security clearance. To prevent unauthorized access to its materials, Bills requires its security personnel to be on duty except for a 15-minute break every two hours. Since the nearest restaurants are a 25-minute round trip, Bills provides free lunches to its security personnel. Bills has never included the value of these meals in its employees' compensation. Bills is currently under audit, and the IRS agent wants to deny Bills a deduction for past meals. The agent also wants Bills to begin including the value of the meals in employee compensation starting with the current year. As Bills's tax adviser, provide a recommendation on whether to appeal the agent's decision. (*Hint:* See *Boyd Gaming Corp.*, CA-9, 99-1 USTC ¶50,530 (Acq.), 177 F3d 1096.) LO 12-3 research

42. Lars Osberg, a single taxpayer with a 35 percent marginal tax rate, desires health insurance. The health insurance would cost Lars $8,500 to purchase if he pays for it himself through the health exchange (Lars's AGI is too high to receive any tax deduction for the insurance as a medical expense). Volvo, Lars's employer, has a 40 percent marginal tax rate. Answer the following questions about this benefit. LO 12-3 planning
   a) What is the maximum amount of before-tax salary Lars would give up to receive health insurance from Volvo?
   b) What would be the after-tax cost to Volvo to provide Lars with health insurance if it could purchase the insurance through its group plan for $5,000?
   c) Assume that Volvo could purchase the insurance for $5,000. Lars is interested in getting health insurance and he is willing to receive a lower salary in exchange for the health insurance. What is the least amount by which Volvo would be willing to reduce Lars's salary while agreeing to pay his health insurance?
   d) Will Volvo and Lars be able to reach an agreement by which Volvo will provide Lars with health insurance?

43. Seiko's current salary is $85,000. Her marginal tax rate is 30 percent and she fancies European sports cars. She purchases a new auto each year. Seiko is currently a manager for an office equipment company. Her friend, knowing of her interest in sports cars, tells her about a manager position at the local BMW and Porsche dealer. The new position pays only $75,000 per year, but it allows employees to purchase one new car per year at a discount of $15,000. This discount qualifies as a nontaxable fringe benefit. In an effort to keep Seiko as an employee, her current employer offers her a $10,000 raise. Answer the following questions about this analysis. LO 12-3 planning
   a) Assuming it has a 35 percent marginal tax rate, what is the annual after-tax cost to her current employer (the office equipment company) if it provides Seiko with the $10,000 increase in salary?
   b) Financially, which offer is better for Seiko on an after-tax basis and by how much? (Assume that Seiko is going to purchase the new car whether she switches jobs or not.)
   c) What salary would Seiko need to receive from her current employer to make her financially indifferent (after taxes) between receiving additional salary from her current employer and accepting a position at the auto dealership?

LO 12-1 LO 12-3 44. JDD Corporation provides the following benefits to its employee, Ahmed (age 47):

Salary	$300,000
Health insurance	10,000
Dental insurance	2,000
Life insurance	3,000
Dependent care	5,000
Professional dues	500
Personal use of company jet	200,000

The life insurance is a group-term life insurance policy that provides $200,000 of coverage for Ahmed. Assuming Ahmed is subject to a marginal tax rate of 30 percent, what is his after-tax benefit of receiving each of these benefits?

LO 12-3 45. Gray's employer is now offering group-term life insurance. The company will provide each employee with $100,000 of group-term life insurance. It costs Gray's employer $300 to provide this amount of insurance to Gray each year. Assuming that Gray is 52 years old, determine the monthly premium that Gray must include in gross income as a result of receiving the group-term life benefit.

LO 12-3 46. Brady graduated from SUNY–New Paltz with his bachelor's degree recently. He works for Makarov & Company CPAs. The firm pays his tuition ($10,000 per year) for him so that he can receive his Master of Science in Taxation, which will qualify him to sit for the CPA exam. How much of the $10,000 tuition benefit does Brady need to include in gross income?

LO 12-3 47. Meg works for Freedom Airlines in the accounts payable department. Meg and all other employees receive free flight benefits (for the employee, family, and 10 free buddy passes for friends per year) as part of its employee benefits package. If Meg uses 30 flights with a value of $12,350 this year, how much must she include in her compensation this year?

LO 12-3 research 48. Sharmilla works for Shasta Lumber, a local lumber supplier. The company annually provides each employee with a Shasta Lumber shirt so that employees look branded and advertise for the business while wearing the shirts. Are Shasta's employees required to include the value of the shirts in income?

LO 12-3 research 49. LaMont works for a company in downtown Chicago. The firm encourages employees to use public transportation (to save the environment) by providing them with transit passes at a cost of $260 per month.

a) If LaMont receives one pass (worth $260) each month, how much of this benefit must he include in his gross income each year?

b) If the company provides each employee with $260 per month in parking benefits, how much of the parking benefit must LaMont include in his gross income each year?

LO 12-3 50. Jasmine works in Washington, D.C. She accepts a new position with her current firm in Los Angeles. Her employer provides the following moving benefits:

- Temporary housing for one month—$3,000.
- Transportation for her household goods—$4,500.
- Flight and hotel for a house-hunting trip—$1,750.
- Flights to Los Angeles for her and her family—$2,000.

What amount of these benefits must Jasmine include in her gross income?

LO 12-3 51. Jarvie loves to bike. In fact, he has always turned down better-paying jobs to work in bicycle shops where he gets an employee discount. At Jarvie's current shop, Bad Dog Cycles, each employee is allowed to purchase four bicycles a year at a discount. Bad Dog has an average gross profit percentage on bicycles of 25 percent. During the current year, Jarvie bought the following bikes:

Description	Retail Price	Cost	Employee Price
Specialized road bike	$3,200	$2,000	$2,240
Rocky Mountain mountain bike	3,800	3,200	3,040
Trek road bike	2,700	2,000	1,890
Yeti mountain bike	3,500	2,500	2,800

a) What amount is Jarvie required to include in taxable income from these purchases?
b) What amount of deductions is Bad Dog allowed to claim from these transactions?

52. Matt works for Fresh Corporation. Fresh offers a cafeteria plan that allows each employee to receive $15,000 worth of benefits each year. The menu of benefits is as follows: LO 12-1 LO 12-3

Benefit	Cost
Health insurance—single	$ 5,000
Health insurance—with spouse	$ 8,000
Health insurance—with spouse and dependents	$11,000
Dental and vision	$ 1,500
Dependent care—any specified amount up to $5,000	Variable
Adoption benefits—any specified amount up to $5,000	Variable
Educational benefits—any specified amount (no limit)	Variable
Cash—any specified amount up to $15,000 plan benefit	Variable
401(k)—any specified amount up to $10,000	Variable

For each of the following independent circumstances, determine the amount of income Matt must recognize and the amount of deduction Fresh may claim:

a) Matt selects the single health insurance and places $10,000 in his 401(k).
b) Matt selects the single health insurance, is reimbursed $5,000 for MBA tuition, and takes the remainder in cash.
c) Matt selects the single health insurance and is reimbursed for MBA tuition of $10,000.
d) Matt gets married and selects the health insurance with spouse and takes the rest in cash to help pay for the wedding.
e) Matt elects to take all cash.

COMPREHENSIVE PROBLEMS

Select problems are available with Connect®. connect

53. Pratt is ready to graduate and leave College Park. His future employer (Ferndale Corp.) offers the following four compensation packages from which Pratt may choose. Pratt will start working for Ferndale on January 1, year 1. tax forms

Benefit Description	Option 1	Option 2	Option 3	Option 4
Salary	$60,000	$50,000	$45,000	$45,000
Health insurance	No coverage	5,000	5,000	5,000
Restricted stock	0	0	1,000 shares	0
NQOs	0	0	0	100 options

Assume that the restricted stock is 1,000 shares that trade at $5 per share on the grant date (January 1, year 1) and are expected to be worth $10 per share on the vesting date at the end of year 1. Each NQO allows the employee to purchase 10 shares at a $5 strike price). The stock trades at $5 per share on the grant date (January 1, year 1) and is expected to be worth $10 per share on the vesting date at the end of year 1. Also assume that Pratt spends on average $3,000 on health-related costs that would be covered by insurance if he had coverage. Assume that Pratt's marginal tax rate is 35 percent. Assume that Pratt spends $3,000 in after-tax dollars for health expenses when he doesn't have health insurance coverage (treat this as an outflow), and that there is no effect when he has health insurance coverage. (Ignore FICA taxes and time value of money considerations).

a) What is the after-tax value of each compensation package for year 1?

b) If Pratt's sole consideration is maximizing after-tax value for year 1, which scheme should he select?

c) Assuming Pratt chooses Option 3 and sells the stock on the vesting date (on the last day of year 1), complete Pratt's Schedule D for the sale of the restricted stock.

54. Santini's new contract for 2017 indicates the following compensation and benefits:

Benefit Description	Amount
Salary	$130,000
Health insurance	9,000
Restricted stock grant	2,500
Bonus	5,000
Hawaii trip	4,000
Group-term life insurance	1,600
Parking ($285 per month)	3,420

Santini is 54 years old at the end of 2017. He is single and has no dependents. Assume that the employer matches $1 for $1 for the first $6,000 that the employee contributes to his 401(k) during the year. The restricted stock grant is 500 shares granted when the market price was $5 per share. Assume that the stock vests on December 31, 2017, and that the market price on that date is $7.50 per share. Also assume that Santini is willing to make any elections to reduce equity-based compensation taxes. The Hawaii trip was given to him as the outstanding salesperson for 2016. The group-term life policy gives him $150,000 of coverage. Assume that Santini does not itemize deductions for the year. Determine Santini's taxable income and income tax liability for 2017.

planning 55. Sylvana is given a job offer with two alternative compensation packages to choose from. The first package offers her $250,000 annual salary with no qualified fringe benefits. The second package offers $235,000 annual salary plus health and life insurance benefits. If Sylvana were required to purchase the health and life insurance benefits herself, she would need to pay $10,000 annually after taxes. Assume her marginal tax rate is 33 percent.

a) Which compensation package should she choose and by how much would she benefit in after-tax dollars by choosing this package?

b) Assume the second package offers $240,000 plus benefits instead of $235,000 plus benefits. Which compensation package should she choose and by how much would she benefit in after-tax dollars by choosing this package?

planning 56. In the current year, Jill, age 35, received a job offer with two alternative compensation packages to choose from. The first package offers her $90,000 annual salary with no qualified fringe benefits, requires her to pay $3,500 a year for parking, and she purchases life insurance at a cost of $1,000. The second package offers $80,000 annual salary, employer-provided health insurance, annual free parking (worth $310 per month), $200,000 of life insurance (purchasing on her own would have been $1,000 annually), and free flight benefits (she estimates that it will save her $5,000 per year). If Jill chooses the first package, she would purchase the health and life insurance benefits herself at a cost of $1,000 annually after taxes and spend another $5,000 in flights while traveling. Assume her marginal tax rate is 28 percent.

a) Which compensation package should she choose, and by how much would she benefit in after-tax dollars by choosing this compensation package instead of the alternative package?

b) Assume the first package offers $100,000 salary instead of $90,000 salary and the other benefits and costs are the same. Which compensation package should she choose, and by how much would she benefit in after-tax dollars by choosing this package?

ROGER | *CPA Review*

Sample CPA Exam questions from Roger CPA Review are available in Connect as support for the topics in this text. These Multiple Choice Questions and Task-Based Simulations include expert-written explanations and solutions, and provide a starting point for students to become familiar with the content and functionality of the actual CPA Exam.

chapter 13

Retirement Savings and Deferred Compensation

Learning Objectives

Upon completing this chapter, you should be able to:

LO 13-1 Describe the tax and nontax aspects of employer-provided defined benefit plans from both the employer's and the employee's perspective.

LO 13-2 Explain and determine the tax consequences associated with employer-provided defined contribution plans, including traditional 401(k) and Roth 401(k) plans.

LO 13-3 Describe the tax implications of deferred compensation from both the employer's and the employee's perspective.

LO 13-4 Determine the tax consequences of traditional and Roth IRAs (individual retirement accounts) and explain the differences between them.

LO 13-5 Describe retirement savings options available to self-employed taxpayers and compute the limitations for deductible contributions to retirement accounts for self-employed taxpayers.

LO 13-6 Compute the saver's credit.

© Paul Bradbury/age fotostock

Storyline Summary

Taxpayer:	Tina Hillman
Location:	Chicago, Illinois
Employment status:	Graduating student about to begin career in the tax department of Corporate Business Associates
Starting salary:	$60,000 per year
Filing status:	Single
Dependents:	None
Marginal tax rate:	Current year 15 percent, next year 25 percent
Taxpayer:	Lisa Whitlark
Location:	Chicago, Illinois
Employment status:	Recently promoted to chief financial officer (CFO) for Corporate Business Associates
Salary:	$400,000
Filing status:	Married, filing jointly
Marginal tax rate:	33 percent
Dependents:	Spouse and three children
Taxpayer:	Dave Allan
Location:	Chicago, Illinois
Employment status:	Recently retired as CFO for Corporate Business Associates after 20 years of employment with the company
Salary at retirement:	$490,000
Retirement benefits:	Participant in Corporate Business Associates's defined benefit plan, 401(k) plan, and nonqualified deferred compensation plan
Filing status:	Married filing jointly
Dependents:	Spouse
Marginal tax rate:	35 percent for current year
Taxpayer:	Corporate Business Associates (CBA)
Location:	Chicago, Illinois
Marginal tax rate:	35 percent
Status:	Publicly traded corporation

Tina Hillman

Tina Hillman has just completed her last exam, finally fulfilling the requirements for a bachelor's degree in accounting. It is the end of June and she will finally have some time to vacation and see her family before September when she will start her professional career working in the tax department of Corporate Business Associates (CBA). While Tina is looking forward to the time off, she is also eager to start making money instead of just spending it. She had a great experience during her internship at CBA last year. She had some challenging but enjoyable work assignments and she got along very well with the staff. Overall, she is excited about the work opportunities she will get at CBA.

Tina recently received an information packet on the benefits available to her as a CBA employee. The information indicated that Tina would be eligible to participate in CBA's 401(k) retirement plan on January 1 of next year. Tina plans on contributing to the plan as soon as she is eligible because CBA matches employee contributions to the plan such that for every dollar contributed by the employee (up to 4 percent of the employee's salary) CBA contributes 2 dollars. In the meantime, Tina wonders if she has any retirement savings options during the current year while waiting to become eligible to participate in CBA's plan.

Lisa Whitlark

Lisa Whitlark is finally getting used to her new responsibilities. She was recently promoted to the position of chief financial officer (CFO) for CBA. Lisa threw her name into the ring a few months ago when CBA announced that Dave Allan, the former CFO, would be retiring. Lisa had been working as CBA's tax director for the last 10 years. As a top executive of the company, Lisa is now eligible to participate in CBA's nonqualified deferred compensation program. She didn't have this option as a tax director. Lisa knows she should consider both tax and nontax factors when deciding whether and to what extent she will participate in the plan.

Dave Allan

Dave Allan couldn't believe that he was actually retiring at the end of this year. Looking back, his successful career had passed so quickly. At age 72, he is now ready to move on and spend time seeing the world with his wife. Dave's retirement plans are going to be quite expensive. Fortunately, he has accumulated substantial retirement benefits during his CBA career. Dave will be receiving retirement benefits from CBA's defined benefit plan, 401(k) plan, and nonqualified deferred compensation plan. He knows he has some choices about the timing and amounts of his distributions from these plans. Dave wants to be sure to evaluate both the tax and nontax considerations before making these decisions. ■

At different stages in their careers, taxpayers are likely to face issues similar to those confronting Tina, Lisa, and Dave. Saving for retirement is not always easy to do because it requires forgoing cash now in order to receive benefits at some point in the future. However, not saving for retirement can be a costly mistake because it's not likely that government-promised Social Security benefits alone will satisfy most taxpayers' retirement needs.[1] Many employers help employees save for retirement by sponsoring retirement plans on behalf of their employees. These plans may be "qualified" retirement plans or "nonqualified" deferred compensation plans. Qualified plans are subject to certain restrictions not applicable to nonqualified plans. Both qualified and nonqualified plans are useful tools through which employers can achieve various

[1]Under current law, the projected cost of Social Security generally increases faster than projected income because of the aging of the baby-boom generation, continuing low fertility since the baby-boom period, and increasing life expectancy. Social Security's total expenditures have exceeded noninterest income of its combined trust funds since 2010. The 2016 Social Security Trustees report projects that the Social Security Trust fund reserves will be depleted in 2034. See https://www.ssa.gov/oact/TR/2016/II_D_project.html#105057

compensation-related goals. In this chapter, we discuss the tax and nontax consequences of qualified retirement plans and nonqualified plans to both employers and employees, including issues relating to contributions to and distributions from these plans. We also discuss individually managed retirement savings plans available to certain individual taxpayers and qualified retirement plans available to self-employed taxpayers.

EMPLOYER-PROVIDED QUALIFIED PLANS

Traditional **qualified retirement plans** grew from a congressional concern that, if unregulated, employers might not adequately fund and protect employee pension benefits and that they might be tempted to provide lavish retirement plans to highly compensated employees such as executives and business owners to the detriment of rank-and-file employees. To address these concerns, Congress mandated that employer-provided plans only receive tax-favored qualified plan status if they meet certain requirements ensuring the plan does not discriminate against rank-and-file employees and if promised benefits are secure. Over the years, the rules addressing these issues have evolved, but the concept of a qualified plan eligible for favorable tax treatment remains the same.

Employer-provided qualified plans can be generally classified as **defined benefit plans** or **defined contribution plans.** As the name suggests, defined benefit plans spell out the specific benefit the employee will receive on retirement. In contrast, defined contribution plans specify the maximum annual contributions that employers and employees may contribute to the plan. While we explore both basic plan types below, we emphasize defined contribution plans because they are much more common than defined benefit plans.

DEFINED BENEFIT PLANS

LO 13-1

Defined benefit plans are traditional pension plans used by many older and more established companies and tax-exempt organizations. These plans provide standard retirement benefits to employees based on a fixed formula. The formula to determine the standard retirement benefit is usually a function of years of service and employees' compensation levels as they near retirement. For employees who retire in 2017, the maximum annual benefit an employee can receive is the *lesser* of (1) 100 percent of the average of the employee's three highest years of compensation or (2) $215,000.[2]

Example 13-1

CBA provides a defined benefit plan for its employees. The plan uses a fixed formula to determine employee benefits. The formula specifies a benefit of 2 percent for each year of service, up to a maximum of 50 percent (25 years of service), of the average of the employee's three highest years of salary. In 2017, Dave retires from CBA. On the date of retirement, Dave had been a CBA employee for 20 years. The average of his three highest years of salary was $450,000. What is Dave's annual benefit from the defined benefit plan?

Answer: $180,000 a year. The benefit is calculated by multiplying 40 percent (2 percent for each of his 20 years of service) by $450,000 (the average of his highest three years of salary).

What if: Assume the same facts except that the average of Dave's three highest years of salary was $600,000. What is the annual benefit he will receive from the plan?

Answer: $215,000. The lesser of (1) $240,000 ($600,000 × 40%) or (2) $215,000.

[2]§415(b)(1). The maximum benefit is adjusted annually for inflation.

THE KEY FACTS

Defined Benefit Plans

- Employer specifies benefit employee receives on retirement based on years of service and salary.
- The maximum annual benefit for employees who retire in 2017 is the lesser of (1) 100 percent of the average of the employee's three highest years of compensation or (2) $215,000.
- Employee must vest to receive benefits using at a minimum
  - 5-year cliff vesting schedule
  - 7-year graded vesting schedule

Vesting

We've discussed the idea that an employee's benefit is based on the number of years she works for an employer. When an employee works for an employer for only a short time before leaving, her benefit depends on her salary, the number of full years she worked for the employer, and the employer's vesting schedule. **Vesting** is the process of becoming legally entitled to a certain right or property. Thus, a taxpayer vests in retirement benefits (becomes legally entitled to the retirement benefits) as she meets certain requirements set forth by the employer. The most restrictive vesting requirements an employer can impose on a qualified defined benefit plan is either a five-year "cliff" or a seven-year graded vesting schedule.[3] Under the **cliff vesting** option, after a certain period of time, benefits vest all at once. With a **graded vesting** schedule, the employee's vested benefit increases each full year she works for the employer. Exhibit 13-1 features the five-year cliff and seven-year graded minimum vesting schedules for defined benefit plans.

EXHIBIT 13-1 Defined Benefit Plans Minimum Vesting Schedules*

Full Years of Service	5-Year Cliff	7-Year Graded
1	0%	0%
2	0	0
3	0	20
4	0	40
5	100	60
6	N/A	80
7	N/A	100

*Percent of employee benefit no longer subject to forfeiture.

Example 13-2

What if: CBA provides a defined benefit plan to its employees. Under the plan, employees earn a benefit equal to 2 percent of their average salary for every year of service, using their three highest years of compensation. CBA implements a seven-year graded vesting schedule as part of the plan. If Tina works for CBA for four years, earning annual salaries of $60,000, $65,000, $70,000, and $75,000, and then leaves to work for another employer, what annual benefit will she be entitled to receive (i.e., what is her vested benefit)?

Answer: $2,240, computed as follows:

Description	Amount	Explanation
(1) Average of three highest years of salary	$70,000	($65,000 + 70,000 + 75,000)/3
(2) Benefit percentage	× 8%	Four years of service × 2 percent per year
(3) Full annual benefit	$ 5,600	(1) × (2)
(4) Vesting percentage	× 40%	Four years of service on 7-year graded vesting schedule (see Exhibit 13-1)
Vested benefit	**$ 2,240**	(3) × (4) = Amount that she is allowed to keep

Tina would forfeit her unvested benefit of $3,360 ($5,600 − $2,240 vested benefit).

What if: Assume the same facts except that CBA uses a five-year cliff schedule. What would be Tina's vested benefit?

Answer: $0. She did not work for CBA for five years so her benefits in CBA's defined benefit plan do not vest.

[3]§411(a) specifies maximum vesting periods for employer contributions to qualified plans. Employers are allowed to adopt more generous vesting requirements such as immediate vesting if they choose.

Distributions

When their benefits have vested, employees are entitled to receive future distributions according to the provisions of the plan—these distributions are taxable as ordinary income in the year received.[4] Distributions from defined benefit plans (and defined contribution plans) are subject to early distribution requirements and to minimum distribution requirements. Distributions violating these requirements are penalized. However, because defined benefit plans typically don't permit payout arrangements that would trigger the early distribution or minimum distribution penalties, these penalties are of greater concern to participants in defined contribution plans. Consequently, we address these penalties in more detail when we discuss distributions from defined contribution plans.

Nontax Considerations

From a nontax perspective, a defined benefit plan imposes administrative burdens and risks on the employer sponsoring the plan. A significant amount of work is required to track employee benefits and to compute required contributions to the plan. Because defined benefit plans require employers to provide particular benefits to employees on retirement, the employer bears the investment risk associated with investments within the plan. Beyond the additional administrative costs and risk, defined benefit plans impose significant funding costs on employers relative to alternative retirement plans. Consequently, in recent years, many employers have begun replacing defined benefit plans with defined contribution plans.

THE KEY FACTS

Defined Benefit Plans

- Employer, not employee, bears investment risk of plan.
- Early and minimum distribution rules apply, but are usually not restrictive.

TAXES IN THE REAL WORLD Define Your Benefit and Deduct It While You're at It

Because defined benefit plans create significantly more administrative burdens and economic risks for employers than defined contribution plans, defined benefit plans are losing popularity with employers. However, self-employed taxpayers and taxpayers running family businesses may be able to use defined benefit plans to contribute significantly more to qualified retirement plans on behalf of themselves and working family members than they would be able to otherwise contribute to a defined contribution plan. Former Florida governor (and presidential candidate at the time he released his tax returns) Jeb Bush provides Exhibit A for this strategy. Mr. Bush released his tax returns in July 2015. His tax returns reported that he claimed deductions for payments to "pension and profit-sharing plans" that averaged $350,000 a year for the previous five years. Mr. Bush's (completely legal) defined benefit plan was set up for two people working for his consulting firm Jeb Bush & Associates LLC. Those in the know believe the plan likely covered Mr. Bush and his son, Jeb Bush Jr. The $350,000 annual contribution average is more than three times the contribution limit otherwise allowable to be made to a defined contribution plan. Why was he able to contribute so much more to a defined benefit plan than he could have contributed to a defined contribution plan? Under a defined benefit plan, the business is allowed to contribute as much as required to fund the expected benefit it must pay to the recipient. Because Mr. Bush started the plan when he was nearing retirement age, the business was allowed to contribute (and deduct) significantly more to fund Mr. Bush's retirement than if he had started the plan when he had a longer time-horizon to work before retirement. In contrast, contributions to defined contribution plans are limited to $60,000 per year (in 2017) for taxpayers who are at least 50 years of age (and $54,000 per year for those who are not), no matter when the taxpayer is planning to retire.

Based on: "Pension Plan Cut Jeb Bush's Taxes," by Mark Maremont, updated July 2, 2015, *The Wall Street Journal*, http://www.wsj.com/articles/jeb-bushs-pension-cut-his-taxes-1435858574.

[4]Distributions of both defined benefit plans and defined contribution plans are reported to taxpayers on Form 1099-R.

LO 13-2

DEFINED CONTRIBUTION PLANS

THE KEY FACTS

Traditional Defined Contribution Plans: Overview

- Employer specifies amount it will contribute to employee's retirement account, *not* the amount the employee will receive at retirement.
  - Employers typically match employee contributions.
- Employee chooses how funds are invested and bears market risk.

Defined contribution plans provide an alternative approach for employers to help employees save for retirement. While defined contribution plans and defined benefit plans have similar overall objectives, they are different in important ways. First, employers maintain separate accounts for *each* employee participating in a defined contribution plan. Second, defined contribution plans specify the up-front contributions the employer will make to the employee's separate account rather than specifying the ultimate benefit the employee will receive from the plan. Third, employees are often allowed to contribute to their own defined contribution plans, and in many instances they contribute more than their employers do. Finally, employees are generally free to choose how amounts in their retirement accounts are invested. If investments in the plan perform well, employees benefit; if the investments perform poorly, employees suffer the financial consequences. Thus, relative to defined benefit plans, defined contribution plans shift the funding responsibility and investment risk from the employer to the employee.

Employers may provide different types of defined contribution plans such as 401(k) plans (used by for-profit companies), 403(b) plans (used by nonprofit organizations, including educational institutions), 457 plans (used by government agencies), profit sharing plans, and money purchase pension plans.[5] Employers may even offer multiple defined contribution plans. Because of their popularity, we use 401(k) plans here to represent the general category of defined contribution plans. However, no matter what defined contribution plan(s) employers provide, employers must ensure that their plans meet certain requirements relating to annual contribution limits and vesting requirements. Also, to a greater extent than with defined benefit plans, *participants* in defined contribution plans should be careful to avoid the penalties associated with either early distributions or insufficient minimum distributions from these plans (discussed later in the chapter).

THE KEY FACTS

Traditional Defined Contribution Plans: Contribution Limits

- 2017 overall contribution limits for sum of employer and employee contributions.
  - Lesser of $54,000 ($60,000 for employees 50 years old by year-end) or 100 percent of employee's annual compensation.
- 2017 employee contribution limit to 401(k) plan:
  - $18,000 or
  - $24,000 for employees 50 years old by year-end.

Employer Matching

Employers, but not employees, typically contribute to certain defined contribution plan types such as profit-sharing plans (contributions may be made based on a fixed formula based on profits or may be at the employer's discretion) and money-purchase plans (contributions are a fixed percentage of the employee's compensation). In contrast, employees contribute to 401(k) type plans. Many employers also "match" employee contributions to these plans. When deciding whether to contribute to a 401(k) plan, employees should take into account the matching policies of their employers. For companies matching employee contributions, the match can range from a small percentage (25 cents on the dollar) to a multiple of the employee's contribution. A dollar-for-dollar match gives employees a 100 percent immediate return on their contributions. Therefore, whenever possible, employees should contribute enough to receive the full match from the employer because, subject to the the plan's vesting requirements, the match represents an immediate, no-risk return on the amount contributed.

Example 13-3

Tina's offer from CBA includes participation in its 401(k) plan effective the beginning of next year. The plan's formula provides that CBA will match employee contributions on a two-for-one basis up to employee contributions of 4 percent of the employee's annuaj salary. Next year when she's eligible, Tina will contribute 4 percent of her salary to the plan. Assuming a $60,000 salary for next year, how much will Tina contribute and how much will CBA contribute to Tina's 401(k) account?

Answer: Tina will contribute $2,400 ($60,000 × 4%) to her 401(k) account and CBA will contribute $4,800 ($2,400 × 2).

[5] 401(k), 403(b), and 457 plans reflect the Code sections describing the plans.

Contribution Limits

For 2017, the sum of employer *and* employee contributions to an employee's defined contribution account(s) is limited to the *lesser* of (1) \$54,000 (\$60,000 for employees who are at least 50 years of age by the end of the year) or (2) 100 percent of the employee's compensation for the year.[6] *Employee* contributions to an employee's 401(k) account are limited to \$18,000 (or \$24,000 for employees who reach age 50 by the end of the year).[7] While this limit applies only to employee contributions, the \$54,000 (or \$60,000) limit still applies to the sum of employer and employee contributions. For example, if an employee under age 50 contributes the maximum \$18,000 to her employer-sponsored 401(k) plan in 2017, the employer's contribution would be limited to \$36,000 (\$54,000 − \$18,000).[8] Because of this limit on employer contributions, highly compensated employees may not be able to receive the full employer match available to other employees.

Example 13-4

Before Dave retires at the end of 2017 he continues to contribute to his CBA-sponsored 401(k) account. CBA matches employee contributions on a two-for-one basis up to 4 percent of the employee's salary. Dave is 72 years old at the end of the year and he earned a salary of \$490,000 during the year. Dave contributed \$24,000 to his 401(k) account. How much would CBA contribute to Dave's 401(k) account?

Answer: \$36,000 [\$60,000 (Dave is 50+ years old) minus \$24,000 (Dave's contribution)]. Without the limitation, CBA would have contributed \$39,200 (\$490,000 × 4% × 2) to Dave's account.

What if: Assume Dave contributed \$23,000 to his 401(k) account. How much would CBA contribute to his account?

Answer: \$37,000. Note that this is a better deal for Dave because \$60,000 ends up in his account either way, but he funded \$23,000 of the contribution instead of \$24,000.

Vesting

When employees contribute to a defined contribution plan, they are fully vested in the accrued benefit from those contributions (employee contributions plus earnings on their contributions). However, employees vest in the accrued benefit from employer contributions (employer contributions plus earnings on the contributions) based on the plan's vesting schedule. When separate employee accounts are not maintained, the accrued benefit from employee contributions is determined by multiplying the total accrued benefit in the account by the ratio of employee contributions to total contributions (employee plus employer) to the account.[9] The accrued benefit from employer contributions is the difference between the total accrued benefit and the accrued benefit from employee contributions. The minimum vesting requirements for defined contribution plans are a bit more accelerated than the five-year cliff and seven-year graded vesting schedules applicable to defined benefit plans. For defined contribution plans, employers have

[6]§415(c)(1). The amount is indexed for inflation under §415(d)(1)(C). Note that the increase in the limit for taxpayers age 50 and older increases the amount the employee can contribute but does not affect the limit the employer can contribute.

[7]§402(g)(1). The amount is indexed for inflation under §402(g)(4).

[8]If an employee participates in more than one defined contribution plan, these limits apply to the total employee and employer contributions to all defined contribution plans. Thus, in a situation where the employee participates in more than one defined contribution plan, the contribution limits for any one defined contribution plan may be less than the overall contribution limits described here.

[9]§411(c).

the option of providing three-year cliff or six-year graded vesting. These minimum vesting schedules are presented in Exhibit 13-2.

EXHIBIT 13-2 Defined Contribution Plans Minimum Vesting Schedules*

Full Years of Service with Employer	3-Year Cliff	6-Year Graded
1	0%	0%
2	0	20
3	100	40
4	N/A	60
5	N/A	80
6	N/A	100

*Percent of employer contributions no longer subject to forfeiture.

Example 13-5

THE KEY FACTS

Traditional Defined Contribution Plans: Vesting and After-Tax Cost

- Employee must vest to be entitled to employer contributions (and earnings on those contributions) using:
  - 3-year cliff vesting schedule.
  - 6-year graded vesting schedule.
- Employee contributes before-tax amounts (contributions are deductible).
- After-tax cost is before-tax contribution minus tax savings from contribution.

What if: Suppose that in three and one-half years the balance in Tina's 401(k) account is $33,000. In total, Tina has contributed $9,000 to the account and CBA has contributed $18,000. Also assume that Tina is 40 percent vested in her accrued benefit from CBA contributions. What is Tina's vested benefit?

Answer: $19,800 [$11,000 accrued benefit from her contributions + $8,800, which is 40 percent of the $22,000 accrued benefit from CBA contributions]. Tina is fully vested in the $11,000 accrued benefit from her contributions ($33,000 total accrued benefit in account × $9,000 employee contributions/$27,000 total contributions to her account) and 40 percent vested in the $22,000 accrued benefit from CBA contributions ($33,000 total accrued benefit in account minus $11,000 accrued benefit from her contributions).

After-Tax Cost of Contributions to Traditional (non-Roth) Defined Contribution Plans

Employer-sponsored traditional defined contribution plans include all plans except Roth 401(k) plans (discussed below). Employees effectively deduct their contributions to traditional defined contribution plans, because contributions are removed from their taxable salary (they are, however, still subject to FICA taxes on funds contributed to defined contribution plans).[10] Consequently, the after-tax cost of a contribution to a traditional defined contribution plan is the contribution amount minus the tax savings generated by the deduction from the contribution.

Example 13-6

Tina contributed $2,400 to her CBA-sponsored traditional 401(k) account in her first full calendar year with CBA. Given Tina's marginal tax rate of 25 percent, what is the after-tax cost of her $2,400 contribution?

Answer: $1,800 computed as follows:

Description	Amount	Explanation
(1) Contribution amount	$2,400	Cost of contribution before tax savings
(2) Tax savings from contribution	(600)	$2,400 deduction × 25 percent marginal tax rate
After-tax cost of contribution	**$1,800**	(1) + (2)

[10]Employees pay the same FICA taxes no matter how much they contribute to defined contribution plans.

Distributions from Traditional Defined Contribution Plans

When employees receive distributions from traditional defined contribution plans, the distributions are taxed as ordinary income. However, when employees receive distributions (or take withdrawals) from traditional defined contribution plans either too early or too late, they must pay a penalty in addition to the ordinary income taxes they owe on the distributions. Generally, employees who receive distributions before they reach

- 59½ years of age or
- 55 years of age *and* have separated from service (retired or employment terminated by employer)

are subject to a 10 percent nondeductible penalty on the amount of the early distributions.

Example 13-7

What if: Assume that when she reaches 60 years of age, Lisa Whitlark retires from CBA and receives a $60,000 distribution from her traditional 401(k) account in the year she retires. Assuming her marginal ordinary tax rate is 33 percent, what amount of tax and penalty will Lisa pay on the distribution?

Answer: $19,800 taxes ($60,000 × 33%) + $0 penalty (she is over 59½ years of age on date of distribution).

What if: Assume that when Lisa is 57 years of age and still employed by CBA, she requests and receives a $60,000 distribution from her traditional 401(k) account. What amount of tax and penalty is Lisa required to pay on the distribution?

Answer: $19,800 taxes ($60,000 × 33%) + $6,000 penalty ($60,000 × 10%).

What if: Assume that Lisa's employment is terminated by CBA when she is 57 years old. In that same year, she requests and receives a $60,000 distribution from her traditional 401(k) account. What amount of tax and penalty is Lisa required to pay on the distribution?

Answer: $19,800 taxes ($60,000 × 33%) + $0 penalty (she is over 55 years of age and has separated from service with CBA).

Taxpayers who fail to receive a minimum distribution for (pertaining to) a particular year are also penalized. The year for which taxpayers must receive their *first* minimum distribution is the *later* of

- The year in which the employee reaches 70½ years of age.
- The year in which the employee retires.

Taxpayers must receive their first required minimum distribution no later than April 1 of the year after the year to which the distribution pertains.[11] Taxpayers generally must receive minimum distributions for subsequent years by the end of the years to which they pertain. Thus, a retired taxpayer who turns 70½ years of age in 2016 must receive a minimum distribution for 2017 by April 1, 2018. The same taxpayer must also receive a minimum distribution for 2018 by December 31, 2018.

The amount of the minimum required distribution for a particular year is the taxpayer's account balance at the end of the year *prior to* the year to which the distribution pertains multiplied by a percentage from an IRS Uniform Lifetime Table. The

THE KEY FACTS

Traditional Defined Contribution Plans: Distributions

- Taxed at ordinary rates.
- 10 percent penalty on early distributions:
  - Before 59½ years of age if not retired or
  - Before 55 years of age if retired.
- Minimum distribution requirements:
  - Must receive by April 1 of the later of (1) the year after the year in which taxpayer reaches 70½ years of age or (2) the year after the year in which the employee retires.
  - If retired employee waits until year after 70½ to begin receiving distributions, must receive two distributions in year of first distribution.
  - 50 percent penalty on excess of required minimum distribution amounts and amount actually distributed.

[11]The amount of the required minimum distribution *for the year* in which a retired employee turns 70½ is the same whether the employee receives the distribution in the year she turns 70½ or whether she defers receiving the distribution until the next year (no later than April 1).

percentage is based on the distribution period (in years), which depends on the taxpayer's age at the end of the year to which the distribution pertains. An abbreviated version of the table is presented in Exhibit 13-3.[12]

EXHIBIT 13-3 Abbreviated Uniform Lifetime Table

Age of Participant	Distribution Period	Applicable Percentage*
70	27.4	3.65%
71	26.5	3.77
72	25.6	3.91
73	24.7	4.05
74	23.8	4.20
75	22.9	4.37
76	22.0	4.54
77	21.2	4.72

*The applicable percentage is calculated by dividing 1 by the relevant distribution period.

Example 13-8

What if: Suppose that Dave retires from CBA in 2017 at age 72 (and he is still 72 at year-end). When must he receive his minimum distribution for 2017 from his traditional 401(k) account?

Answer: By April 1, 2018.

What if: Assuming Dave retires in 2017 and that his traditional 401(k) account balance on December 31, 2016, is $3,500,000, what is the amount of the minimum distribution Dave must receive by April 1, 2018?

Answer: $136,850 ($3,500,000 × 3.91%). The percentage from the IRS table for determining this minimum distribution is based on Dave's age at the end of 2017, which is 72 years old.

What if: Assuming Dave's traditional 401(k) account balance on December 31, 2017, is $3,700,000, what is the minimum distribution for 2018 Dave must receive sometime during 2018 (in addition to the $136,850 distribution by April 1)?

Answer: $149,850 ($3,700,000 × 4.05%) must be received by Dave in 2018.

The consequences for failing to receive timely minimum distributions from defined contribution plans are even more severe than receiving distributions too early. Taxpayers incur a 50 percent nondeductible penalty on the amount of a minimum distribution the employee should have received but did not (the penalty is payable as an additional tax for the calendar year containing the last day by which the amount is required to be distributed). For this reason, it is vital that payouts from defined contribution plans be monitored to avoid not only the 10 percent premature distribution penalty, but also the 50 percent penalty for failing to receive timely required minimum distributions.

Example 13-9

What if: In the previous example, we determined that Dave must receive a minimum distribution of $136,850 from his traditional 401(k) account by April 1, 2018. If Dave does not receive any distribution before April 1, 2018, what penalty will he be required to pay?

Answer: $68,425 ($136,850 × 50%). Dave will pay this penalty as an other tax on his 2018 tax return. This nondeductible penalty is a strong incentive to take the required minimum distributions or at least to take the penalty into consideration when developing a distribution plan.

[12]See Reg. §1.401(a)(9)-9 Q&A 2 to reference the full version of the table. The table provided in this exhibit applies in most circumstances.

What if: Assume that Dave received his first distribution from his traditional 401(k) account on March 1, 2018, in the amount of $100,000. But, he did not receive any other distributions before April 1, 2018. What penalty is Dave required to pay?

Answer: $18,425 [($136,850 – $100,000) × 50%]

In contrast to defined benefit plans, defined contribution plans often provide distribution options that could trigger the penalty for premature distributions for the uninformed or unwary. For example, an employee who retires (or is fired) and takes a lump-sum distribution from her defined contribution account in a year before the year in which she turns 55 will be subject to a 10 percent early distribution penalty on the entire amount of the distribution. Employees who receive such lump-sum distributions may avoid the 10 percent penalty by electing to "roll over" (deposit) the distributions into one of the individually managed retirement plans we discuss later in this chapter.

After-Tax Rates of Return for Traditional Defined Contribution Plans

For a given before-tax rate of return and a constant tax rate, the longer the taxpayer defers distributions from a traditional defined contribution plan, the greater the taxpayer's after-tax rate of return on the retirement account, because deferring the distribution reduces the present value of the taxes paid on the distribution. A taxpayer's after-tax rate of return also depends on the taxpayer's marginal tax rate at the time she contributes to the plan and at the time she receives distributions from the plan. All else being equal, the higher her marginal tax rate at the time she contributes to the plan, the higher the after-tax rate of return (the higher tax rate increases the tax savings from the deduction); likewise, the lower her marginal tax rate at the time she receives distributions from the plan, the higher the after-tax rate of return (the lower rate reduces the taxes from the distribution).

Of course, any employer contributions to an employee's account, such as CBA's two-for-one matching contributions to Tina's account, significantly increase the after-tax rate of return (and after-tax accumulation) because the contributions increase the employee's after-tax proceeds, but the employee's cost of these contributions is zero.

Exhibit 13-4 summarizes the tax aspects of defined benefit and defined contribution plans.

Roth 401(k) Plans

Employers that provide **traditional 401(k)** plans to employees may also provide **Roth 401(k)** plans. As we discuss below, employee tax consequences for Roth 401(k) plans differ from tax consequences of other traditional defined contribution plans.

When employers provide a Roth 401(k) plan, *employees* may elect to contribute to the Roth 401(k) *instead of or in addition to* contributing to a traditional 401(k) plan. However, *employer* contributions to an employee's 401(k) account must go to the employee's *traditional* 401(k) account rather than the employee's Roth 401(k) account. Consequently, the balance in an employee's Roth 401(k) account must consist of only the employee's contributions and the earnings on those contributions. Because employers providing Roth 401(k) plans to employees are not allowed to contribute to the Roth plans, these employers are required to maintain traditional 401(k) accounts for each employee participating in the Roth 401(k) plan.

In contrast to contributions to traditional 401(k) plans, employee contributions to Roth 401(k) accounts are *not* deductible and, therefore, do not produce any immediate tax

THE KEY FACTS

Roth 401(k) Defined Contribution Plans

- Employees but not employers may contribute.
  - Employers contribute to traditional 401(k).
- Contributions are not deductible.
- Same contribution limits as traditional 401(k) plans.

EXHIBIT 13-4 Defined Benefit Plan versus Defined Contribution Plan Summary

	Defined Benefit Plan	Defined Contribution Plan
Benefits	• Specifies benefit employee receives on retirement. • Maximum benefit in 2017 lesser of (1) 100 percent of average of highest three years' compensation or (2) $215,000.	• Specifies the amounts employer and employee contribute to the account. • Ultimate benefit depends on earnings on contributions.
Payout type	• Life annuity. • Lump sum distribution of the present value of standard benefit.	• Life annuity. • Lump sum. • Fixed number of years.
Funding requirements	• Employers fund increase in expected future liability each year.	• No funding requirement other than to make required contributions to employee accounts.
Employer's contributions tax deductible?	• Yes.	• Yes, but limited to 25 percent of aggregate employee annual compensation.
Employee's contributions tax deductible?	• No employee contributions.	• Yes, subject to limitations on the amount that can be contributed [$18,000 ($24,000 if 50 or older) maximum contribution to 401(k) plan in 2017].
Contribution limits	• Not applicable.	• In 2017, lesser of (1) $54,000 ($60,000 for taxpayers at least 50 years of age at end of year) and (2) 100 percent of the employee's compensation for year.
Other factors	• All employees paid from same account. • Heavy administrative burden. • Employers make investment choices and assume investment risk.	• Separate accounts for each employee. • Employees assume investment risk.
Vesting requirements	• 5-year cliff or • 7-year graded	• 3-year cliff or • 6-year graded • Employee contributions vest immediately.
Distributions	• Taxed as ordinary income. • No 10 percent penalty if either 59½ years of age or 55 years of age and retired. • Minimum distributions required by April 1 of year after the later of (1) year employee reaches 70½ or (2) year employee retires.	• Taxed as ordinary income (except Roth-type accounts). • No 10 percent penalty if either 59½ years of age or 55 years of age and retired. • Minimum distributions requirements same as for defined benefit plan.

savings for employees. Therefore, employees wanting to contribute a certain amount to a Roth 401(k) plan must earn more than that specified amount in order to have the desired contribution amount remaining *after* paying taxes on the amount they earn. For example, assume an employee with a 20 percent marginal tax rate wants to contribute $2,000 to a Roth 401(k) account. To earn the funds to make this contribution, the employee must earn $2,500 before taxes. The tax on the $2,500 of income is $500 ($2,500 × 20%). This leaves the taxpayer with $2,000 after taxes ($2,500 before taxes minus $500 in taxes) to contribute to the Roth 401(k) account.

Example 13-10

What if: Let's assume that CBA offers a Roth 401(k) plan in addition to its traditional 401(k) plan. In her first full calendar year of employment with CBA, Tina elects to contribute 4 percent of her $60,000 salary to CBA's Roth 401(k) plan instead of CBA's traditional 401(k) plan. What is Tina's after-tax cost of this $2,400 contribution (her marginal tax rate is 25 percent)?

Answer: $2,400. Her after-tax cost is her $2,400 contribution because the contribution does not generate any tax savings.

What is Tina's before-tax cost of the contribution? That is, how much did Tina need to earn before taxes to fund the $2,400 after-tax contribution?

Answer: $3,200. Because her marginal tax rate is 25 percent, she needs to earn $3,200 before taxes [$2,400/(1 − .25)] to have $2,400 to contribute to the Roth 401(k) after taxes [$3,200 × (1 − .25)]. When she contributes $2,400 *after taxes* to the Roth 401(k), she is contributing $3,200 *before taxes*.

THE KEY FACTS

Roth 401(k) Defined Contribution Plans

- Qualified distributions are not taxable.
  - Account open for five years.
  - Employee at least 59½ at time of distribution.
- Nonqualified distributions.
  - Distributions of account earnings are taxable and subject to 10 percent penalty if taxpayer is not either 59½ years of age or 55 years of age and retired.
  - Distributions of contributions are not taxed or penalized.
  - Distribution × ratio of contributions to account balance is nontaxable. The remainder of distribution is out of account earnings.
- After-tax return equals before-tax return.

While contributions to Roth 401(k) accounts are not deductible and, as a result, do not generate any current tax savings, *qualified* distributions from Roth 401(k) accounts are excluded from gross income. Because contributions to Roth 401(k) accounts are not deductible and qualified distributions from Roth 401(k) accounts are not taxable, the before-tax rate of return equals the after-tax rate of return on Roth 401(k) accounts. Note also that because qualified Roth 401(k) distributions are excluded from income, in contrast to traditional 401(k) distributions, they do not increase AGI and thus do not cause AGI-based tax benefit phase-outs (e.g., certain itemized deductions and tax credits) and they do not cause an increase in the taxation of the recipient's Social Security benefits (see the Gross Income and Exclusions chapter for a discussion of the taxation of Social Security benefits).

Example 13-11

What if: In the previous example, Tina contributed $2,400 to her Roth 401(k) account in her first calendar year on the job with CBA. Let's assume that Tina leaves this contribution in the account until she retires in 40 years at the age of 63, that her contribution earns an annual 8 percent before-tax rate of return, and that her marginal tax rate will be 30 percent when she receives the distribution. How much will Tina have accumulated after taxes if she withdraws the initial contribution and all the earnings on the contribution when she retires?

Answer: $52,139 ($2,400 × 1.08^{40}). Tina's after-tax rate of return on her $2,400 after-tax contribution is exactly 8 percent, the same as the before-tax rate of return. With a Roth 401(k) the after-tax rate of return should always equal the before-tax rate of return because the contributions are not deductible and distributions are not taxable.

Qualified distributions from Roth 401(k) accounts are those made after the employee's account has been open for five taxable years *and* the employee is at least 59½ years of age. All other distributions are nonqualified distributions. When a taxpayer receives a *non*qualified distribution from a Roth 401(k) account, the tax consequences of the distribution depend on the extent to which the distribution is from the account earnings and the extent to which it is from the employee's contributions to the account. Nonqualified distributions of account *earnings* are fully taxable. Nonqualified distributions of account earnings are also subject to a 10 percent early distribution penalty unless the taxpayer is either 59½ years of age at the time of the distribution or at least 55 years of age and retired at the time of the distribution. Nonqualified distributions of the taxpayer's account *contributions* are not subject to tax because the taxpayer did not deduct these amounts. If less than the entire balance in the plan is distributed, the nontaxable portion of the distribution is determined by multiplying the amount of the distribution by the ratio of account contributions to the total account balance. This formula is very similar to the formula described in the Gross Income and Exclusions chapter for determining the nontaxable portion of an annuity payment.

Example 13-12

What if: In the previous example, Tina contributed $2,400 to CBA's Roth 401(k) plan, her account generated an 8 percent before-tax rate of return, and she withdrew the entire balance 40 years after the contribution. Let's assume that at the end of year 6, Tina needs cash, so she withdraws $1,000 from the account when the account balance is $3,808 and her marginal tax rate is 28 percent. How much tax and penalty, if any, is Tina required to pay on this nonqualified distribution?

Answer: $104 tax and $37 penalty, computed as follows:

Description	Amount	Explanation
(1) Contribution to Roth 401(k) (nondeductible)	$2,400	Beginning of year 1
(2) Account balance end of year 6	3,808	$2,400 × 1.08^6$
(3) Nonqualified distribution end of year 6	1,000	
(4) Percentage of distribution that is not taxable	63.03%	(1)/(2)
(5) Nontaxable portion of distribution	630	(3) × (4)
(6) Taxable portion of distribution	370	(3) − (5)
(7) Marginal tax rate in year 6	28%	
(8) Regular income tax on distribution	**104**	**(6) × (7)**
(9) Penalty tax percentage for early distributions	10%	
(10) Penalty tax on early distribution	**37**	**(6) × (9)**
Total tax and penalty on early distribution	$ 141	(8) + (10)

Finally, it is important to note that the minimum distribution requirements applicable to traditional 401(k) accounts also apply to Roth 401(k) accounts.

Comparing Traditional Defined Contribution Plans and Roth 401(k) Plans

We've described and discussed the tax consequences associated with participating in traditional and Roth 401(k) plans. So which is better for employees? If given a choice, which type of 401(k) plan should you contribute to? While many factors should be considered in making this decision, perhaps the most important is the taxpayer's current marginal tax rate (the rate in the year of contributions) compared to the taxpayer's expected future marginal tax rate (the expected rate in the year of distributions). Taxpayers generally should prefer traditional 401(k) plans when their current marginal rate is higher (greater tax savings derived from deductions) than their expected future marginal rate (lower tax cost on income from distributions) and they should prefer Roth 401(k) plans when their current marginal rate is lower than their expected future tax rate. When future rates are higher than current rates, taxpayers should generally prefer Roth 401(k) plans because the forgone tax savings from a nondeductible contribution is smaller when the marginal tax rate is lower and the tax savings from excluding the distribution from income is greater when the marginal tax rate is higher. While current and expected future marginal tax rates are important to consider, other factors relevant to this decision include, among others, the uncertainty of future tax rates and the taxpayer's risk tolerance for this uncertainty and how a taxpayer reinvests the tax savings from contributions to traditional 401(k) plans. A detailed discussion of all factors relevant to this decision is beyond the scope of this text. Exhibit 13-5 summarizes and compares the tax consequences of traditional 401(k) plans and Roth 401(k) plans.

EXHIBIT 13-5 Traditional 401(k) Plan versus Roth 401(k) Plan Summary

	Traditional 401(k) Plans	Roth 401(k) Plans
Employer contributions allowed	• Yes.	• No.
Tax consequences to employer	• Contributions deductible when paid.	• Not applicable.
Tax consequences to employee	• Contributions are deductible.	• Contributions are not deductible.
Distributions	• Taxed as ordinary income. • No 10 percent penalty if the taxpayer is at least 59½ years of age or at least 55 years of age and retired at time of distribution. • If life annuity or joint and survivor annuity, no penalty even if not 55 years of age. • Minimum distributions required by April 1 of the later of (1) the year after the year in which the employee reaches 70½ or (2) the year after the year in which the employee retires. • Failure to meet minimum distribution timing and amount requirements triggers 50 percent penalty.	• Qualified distributions not taxed. • Qualified distributions when account is open for at least 5 years and employee has reached age 59½. • No 10 percent penalty on taxable part of nonqualified distribution if the taxpayer is at least 59½ years of age or at least 55 years of age and retired at time of distribution. • If life annuity or joint and survivor annuity, no penalty even if not 55 years of age. • Minimum distribution requirements and penalties are the same as for traditional 401(k) plans. • If nonqualified distribution, nontaxable percentage of distribution is the ratio of contributions to total account value.

NONQUALIFIED DEFERRED COMPENSATION PLANS

LO 13-3

So far, our discussion has emphasized the tax and nontax aspects of employer-provided *qualified* defined benefit and defined contribution plans. In addition to or perhaps in lieu of these types of qualified plans, employers may offer **nonqualified deferred compensation** plans to certain employees.

Nonqualified Plans versus Qualified Defined Contribution Plans

Deferred compensation plans permit employees to defer (or contribute) current salary in exchange for a future payment from the employer. From an employee's perspective, the tax consequences of contributions to and distributions from nonqualified plans are similar to the tax consequences of contributions to and distributions from qualified defined contribution plans. For example, just as with defined contribution plans, employee contributions to nonqualified deferred compensation (NQDC) plans reduce an employee's taxable income in the year of contribution.[13] Also, just as with qualified plans, employees are not taxed on the balance in their accounts until they receive distributions. Finally, like distributions from qualified plans, distributions from NQDC plans are taxed as ordinary income.

[13]Technically, employees participating in NQDC plans defer the receipt of current salary and employers credit the employee's account for the amount of the deferral. This has the same effect as if the employee had actually made a deductible contribution (*for* AGI) to her account, as an employee participating in a defined contribution plan would do.

Example 13-13

CBA provides a nonqualified deferred compensation plan under which executives may elect to defer up to 10 percent of their salary. Dave Allan has been participating in the plan by deferring a portion of his salary each year for the last 15 years. The balance in his deferred compensation account is currently $2,000,000. In keeping with a fixed payment schedule Dave elected under the plan, he receives a $50,000 distribution. What amount of tax must Dave pay on the distribution (recall that his marginal tax rate is 35 percent)?

Answer: $17,500 ($50,000 × .35).

For employers, NQDC plans are treated differently than qualified plans. For example, because nonqualified plans are not subject to the same restrictive requirements pertaining to qualified plans, employers may discriminate in terms of who they allow to participate in the plan. In fact, employers generally restrict participation in nonqualified plans to more highly compensated employees. Also, employers are not required to "fund" nonqualified plans. That is, employers are not required to formally set aside and accumulate funds specifically to pay the deferred compensation obligation when it comes due. Rather, employers typically retain funds deferred by employees under the plan, use the funds for business operations, and pay the deferred compensation out of their general funds when it becomes payable. Because employers retain, control, and generate income on funds deferred by employees under nonqualified plans, employers are allowed to *deduct only actual payments* of deferred compensation to employees. That is, employers cannot deduct the amount of deferred compensation they accrue each year. Thus, for tax purposes, an employer may not deduct the deferred compensation when an employee initially earns the compensation even though the employer becomes liable for the deferred compensation payment. In contrast, for financial accounting purposes, companies generally expense deferred compensation in the year employees earn it and record a corresponding deferred compensation liability.[14]

THE KEY FACTS

Nonqualified Deferred Compensation Plans

- Employees defer current income in exchange for future payment.
  - Employee is taxed when payment is received.
  - Employee generally selects deemed investment choices up front to determine return on deferral.
  - Just like traditional deferred compensation plans, after-tax rate of return depends on before-tax rate of return, marginal tax rate at time of deferral, and marginal tax rate at time of distribution.
  - Payment is not guaranteed. If employer doesn't pay, employee becomes unsecured creditor.

Employee Considerations

Should employees participate in nonqualified plans when given the chance? The decision obviously involves several considerations. First, employees must decide if the benefits they expect to receive from qualified retirement plans (or other sources) will be adequate to provide for their expected costs during retirement. Next, employees should consider whether they can afford to defer current salary. This may not be a significant concern for most eligible participants, however, because nonqualified plans are generally available only to highly compensated employees who likely may not have the liquidity concerns that lower-compensated employees may face. Also, employees should consider the expected after-tax rate of return on the deferred salary relative to what they could earn on the salary by receiving it currently and personally investing it.

Generally, larger employers allow employees participating in nonqualified plans to choose how their deferred compensation will be invested from among alternative investments provided under the plan (money market, various bond funds, and stock funds, among others). However, because employers *do not actually invest* compensation deferred under the plan on the employee's behalf, the employer credits the employee's account "as if" the employee's contributions had been invested in the employee's *deemed*

[14]Employers record additional expense and liability as earnings on the deferred compensation accumulate.

investment choices. The description of Coca-Cola Company's nonqualified retirement plan, presented in Exhibit 13-6, illustrates this concept.

EXHIBIT 13-6 Description of Nonqualified Retirement Plan
Excerpt from Coca-Cola Company's proxy statement

Deferred Compensation Plan. The Deferred Compensation Plan is a nonqualified and unfunded deferred compensation program offered to approximately 1,000 U.S. based Company employees in 2015. International service associates do not participate in the Deferred Compensation Plan. Eligible participants may defer up to 80% of base salary and up to 95% of their annual incentive. The Company has the benefit of full unrestricted use of all amounts deferred under the Deferred Compensation Plan until such amounts are required to be distributed to the plan participants. Gains and losses are credited based on the participant's election of a variety of deemed investment choices. The Company does not match any employee deferral or guarantee a return. Participants' accounts may or may not appreciate and may depreciate depending on the performance of their deemed investment choices. None of the deemed investment choices provide returns at above-market or preferential rates. All deferrals are paid out in cash upon distribution. Participants may schedule a distribution during employment or may opt to receive their balance after separation from service.

Just as with qualified defined contribution plans, other than Roth 401(k) plans, an employee's after-tax rate of return on deferred compensation depends on the employee's investment choices *and* on the employee's marginal tax rates at the time of the contribution and at the time of the distribution.

Example 13-14

As a new executive with CBA, Lisa Whitlark is eligible to participate in CBA's nonqualified deferred compensation plan. Recall that CBA provides an NQDC plan under which executives may elect to defer up to 10 percent of their salary. In her first year with CBA, Lisa elects to defer $40,000 of salary ($400,000 × 10%) under the plan. Because her current marginal income tax rate is 33 percent, she saves $13,200 in taxes by deferring the salary ($40,000 × 33%). Consequently, her after-tax cost of deferring the compensation is $26,800 ($40,000 − $13,200). She plans to receive a distribution from the nonqualified plan in 20 years when she expects her marginal tax rate to be 28 percent. Lisa selects a stock index fund as her "deemed" investment choice. She expects the fund to provide an 8 percent before-tax rate of return on her $40,000 deferral. What will Lisa receive after taxes from her $40,000 deferral?

Answer: $134,235 after-tax accumulation, computed as follows:

Description	Amount	Explanation
Contribution to plan	$ 40,000	Deferral of 10 percent of her current salary
Times future value factor	× 1.08^{20}	8 percent annual rate of return for 20 years
Future value of deferred compensation	186,438	Value of deferral/distribution 20 years after deferral
Minus: taxes payable on distribution	(52,203)	$186,438 value of account × 28 percent marginal tax rate
After-tax proceeds from distributions	**$134,235**	Value of account minus taxes payable on distribution

Deferring salary to a future period is potentially an effective tax planning technique, particularly when the employee anticipates her marginal tax rate will be lower in the year she will receive the deferred compensation than it is in the year she defers the salary. In fact, if employees had complete flexibility as to when they could receive distributions from deferred compensation plans, they would likely accelerate distributions from deferred compensation plans into years they knew with certainty would have relatively low marginal tax rates. This strategy is limited, however, by rules requiring employees to specify the timing of the future payments at the time they decide to participate in deferred compensation plans.[15]

Employees considering participating in nonqualified deferred compensation plans should also consider the potential financial risks of doing so. Recall that employers are not required to fund nonqualified plans. So, there's always the possibility that the employer may become bankrupt and not have the funds to pay the employee on the scheduled distribution dates. If the employer is not able to make the payments, the employee becomes an unsecured creditor of the company and may never receive the full compensation owed to her. Consequently, the employee should evaluate the financial stability of the company when deciding whether to defer compensation under the employer's plan.

THE KEY FACTS

Nonqualified Deferred Compensation Plans

- Employer promises to pay deferred compensation at some point in future.
  - Deduct when paid to employee.
  - Not required to fund obligation.
  - Use to accomplish compensation objectives like avoid $1M deductibility and to provide more deferred compensation to employees who are over contribution limits on qualified plans.
  - Employer's marginal tax rates at time of deferral relative to those at time of payment affect after-tax cost of providing deferred compensation relative to current compensation.

Employer Considerations

It's pretty clear that nonqualified plans can provide significant benefits to employees. How might employers benefit from providing nonqualified plans? First, employers may benefit if they are able to earn a better rate of return on the deferred compensation than the rate of return they are required to pay employees participating in the plan. In addition, employers can use nonqualified plans to achieve certain compensation objectives. For example, nonqualified plans could be a component of a compensation package a company may use to attract prospective executives. Also, because deferred compensation is not deductible until it is paid, deferred compensation plans provide a potentially effective way for employers to circumvent the $1 million salary deduction limitation for executives of publicly traded corporations imposed by the **§162(m) limitation** (see the Compensation chapter discussion of this limitation). That is, an employer may pay an executive $1 million of current compensation and defer compensation over $1 million to a future period. By doing this, the employer is able to deduct the full $1 million of salary and the entire amount of the deferred compensation as long as the employee has retired at the time the employer pays the deferred compensation. This is because the $1 million deductibility limitation on compensation does not apply if the executive is no longer employed by the company when the company pays the deferred compensation. However, if the executive is still an employee when the deferred compensation is paid, it is subject to the $1 million deduction limit.

Likewise, deferring compensation may be an important tax planning tool for employers in situations where their current marginal tax rates are low (employers currently experiencing net operating losses) and they expect their future marginal tax rates when deferred compensation is paid to be significantly higher (employers expect to return to profitability). In effect, deferring compensation into a year with a higher marginal tax rate increases the after-tax benefit of the compensation deduction, which reduces the after-tax cost of the compensation to the employer.

[15]§409A. These rules do provide, however, that specified payments from deferred compensation plans may commence while employees are still employed.

Exhibit 13-7 summarizes and compares qualified retirement plans and nonqualified deferred compensation plans.

EXHIBIT 13-7 Qualified Plans versus Nonqualified Plans Summary

	Qualified Plans	Nonqualified Plans
Types	• Defined benefit (Pension). • Defined contribution [401(k)].	• Deferred compensation.
Requirements	• May not discriminate against "rank and file" employees of the company. • Funding or contribution requirements. • Vesting requirements.	• May discriminate. • Generally provided to executives and highly compensated employees. • No formal funding requirements (employee is essentially an unsecured creditor). • No formal vesting requirements.
Tax consequences to employers	• Immediately deduct contributions to plan (amount funded).	• Employee contributions (or deferrals) are deductible.
Tax consequences to employees	• Employee contributions deductible unless to Roth-type account. • Earnings deferred until distributed to employee. • Employer contributions not immediately taxed. • Distributions from non-Roth plans treated as ordinary income.	• Taxed as ordinary income when received. • Earnings deferred until distributed to employee.

INDIVIDUALLY MANAGED QUALIFIED RETIREMENT PLANS

We've covered tax and nontax issues relating to both qualified and nonqualified employer-sponsored retirement savings plans. However, not all employers provide retirement savings plans, and when they do, some employees may not be eligible to participate, while others who are eligible may elect to not participate in these plans. The tax laws provide opportunities for these taxpayers to provide for their own retirement security through individually managed retirement plans. The **individual retirement account (IRA)** is the most common of the individually managed retirement plans. Other types of individually managed plans are available to self-employed taxpayers.

INDIVIDUAL RETIREMENT ACCOUNTS

LO 13-4

Taxpayers who meet certain eligibility requirements can contribute to **traditional IRAs,** to **Roth IRAs,** or to both. Just like traditional and Roth 401(k) plans, traditional IRAs and Roth IRAs have different tax characteristics. In fact, in most respects, the tax characteristics of traditional 401(k) plans mirror those of traditional IRAs and tax characteristics of Roth 401(k) plans mirror those of Roth IRA accounts. To minimize redundancy, we focus on the tax characteristics that differ between employer-sponsored 401(k) plans and self-managed IRAs.

Traditional IRAs

Contributions Deductible contributions to IRAs are *for* AGI deductions. The maximum deductible contribution for a taxpayer in 2017 depends on the taxpayer's age as follows:

- $5,500 deduction limit if the taxpayer is less than 50 years of age at year-end.[16,17]
- $6,500 deduction limit if the taxpayer is at least 50 years of age at year-end.[18]
- $0 deduction if the taxpayer is at least 70½ years of age at year-end.

The deductible contribution limit may be further restricted depending on the following factors:

- Whether the taxpayer is an active participant in an employer-sponsored retirement plan.
- The taxpayer's filing status.
- The amount of the taxpayer's earned income.
- The taxpayer's AGI.

Unmarried taxpayers not participating in an employer-sponsored retirement plan may deduct IRA contributions up to the *lesser* of

- $5,500 ($6,500 for taxpayers 50+ years of age).
- Earned income.

As we discuss in the Gross Income and Exclusions chapter, earned income generally includes income actually earned through the taxpayer's efforts, such as wages, salaries, tips, and other employee compensation, plus the amount of the taxpayer's net earnings from self-employment. Alimony income is also considered as earned income for this purpose.

THE KEY FACTS

Traditional IRAs

- 2017 deductible contribution limit:
  - Lesser of $5,500 or earned income.
  - Taxpayers over 50, lesser of $6,500 or earned income.
- If taxpayers participate in employer-provided plan:
  - For 2017, deduction limit phased out for single taxpayers with AGI between $62,000 and $72,000 and for married filing jointly taxpayers with AGI between $99,000 and $119,000.
  - Special rules if one spouse is covered by plan and the other is not.

Example 13-15

In the year she graduated from college, Tina earned $25,000. She earned $5,000 in salary working part-time while she was in school and she earned $20,000 in salary working for CBA from September through December. To get an early start saving for retirement, she contributed $5,000 to a *traditional* IRA (recall that Tina is not eligible to participate in CBA's 401(k) retirement plan until January of next year). How much of this contribution may Tina deduct?

Answer: $5,000. Because Tina is not participating in an employer-sponsored retirement plan during the current year, Tina may deduct the full $5,000 contribution as a *for* AGI deduction, reducing her AGI from $25,000 to $20,000.

For *unmarried taxpayers* who actively participate in an employer-sponsored retirement plan, the deduction limits are the same as for those who do not participate except that the maximum deduction is phased out based on the taxpayer's AGI as follows:

- No phase-out if AGI is equal to or less than $62,000.
- Proportional phase-out of full limit for AGI between $62,000 and $72,000 [The phase-out percentage is computed as follows: (AGI minus $62,000) divided by ($72,000 – $62,000). For example, if the AGI is $64,000, the taxpayer loses 20 percent of contribution limit].
- Full phase-out (no deduction) if AGI is equal to or greater than $72,000.

[16]Lump-sum distributions from qualified plans other than Roth 401(k)s received prior to retirement are frequently rolled over into traditional IRA accounts to avoid the 10 percent premature distribution penalty and current taxation. Rollover contributions are not subject to normal contribution limits for traditional IRAs.

[17]The IRA contribution limit is indexed for inflation.

[18]The $1,000 increase in the deduction limit for older taxpayers is granted to allow taxpayers nearing retirement age to "catch up" on contributions they may have not made in previous years.

Married taxpayers can make deductible contributions to separate IRAs (i.e., an IRA for each spouse), subject to limitations. If the married couple files jointly, before considering any AGI-based phase-out amounts (discussed below), the maximum deduction for the spouse with the *higher* amount of earned income is the same as it is for unmarried taxpayers [$5,500 ($6,500 if at least 50 years of age at year-end) or earned income if it is less]. However, the maximum deduction for the spouse with the *lesser* amount of earned income is limited to the lesser of

- $5,500 ($6,500 if this spouse is age 50+).
- Total earned income of both spouses reduced by deductible and nondeductible contributions to the higher-earning spouse's traditional IRA and by contributions to the higher-earning spouse's Roth IRA.[19]

The contribution to the lesser-earning spouse's IRA is called a **spousal IRA.** The money in the account belongs to the lesser-earning spouse no matter where the funds for the contribution came from.

If either spouse is an active participant in an employer's retirement plan, and the couple files jointly, the maximum deduction for each spouse is phased out based on the *couple's* AGI as follows:

- No phase-out if the couple's AGI is equal to or less than $99,000.
- Proportional phase-out of full limit for AGI between $99,000 and $119,000 (for example, if the taxpayer's AGI is $111,000, the taxpayer loses 60 percent of deductible contribution limit).
- Full phase-out (no deduction) if AGI is equal to or greater than $119,000.

If one spouse is an active participant in an employer's retirement plan and the other is not, and the couple files jointly, the deduction for the spouse who is not an active participant is phased out based on the couple's AGI as follows (the phase-out applies whether the spouse is the higher or lesser earning spouse):

- No phase-out if the couple's AGI is equal to or less than $186,000.
- Proportional phase-out of full limit for AGI between $186,000 and $196,000.
- Full phase-out (no deduction) if AGI is equal to or greater than $196,000.

Married taxpayers who file separately may also make deductible contributions to an IRA. The maximum deduction is the lesser of

- $5,500 ($6,500 if taxpayer is 50+).
- The taxpayer's earned income.

However, if either spouse is an active participant in an employer's retirement plan, and they file separately, then each spouse's deductible contribution (including the nonactive participant spouse) is phased out over the spouse's AGI as follows:

- No phase-out if the taxpayer's AGI is $0 (also no tax benefit of deducting).
- Proportional phase-out of full limit for AGI between $0 and $10,000.
- Full phase-out (no deduction) if AGI is equal to or greater than $10,000.

If the couple files separate tax returns and did not live with each other at any time during the year, both spouses will be treated as unmarried taxpayers for purposes of the IRA deduction limitations. Appendix A at the end of this chapter provides a flowchart for determining traditional IRA deduction limitations.

THE KEY FACTS

Traditional IRAs

- If taxpayer does not participate in employer-provided plan but spouse does
  - Deduction limit phased out for AGI between $186,000 and $196,000.
- Distribution taxed as ordinary income
  - If distribution before taxpayer is 59½, 10 percent penalty generally applies.

[19]§219(c).

Example 13-16

In her first full calendar year working for CBA, Tina earns $60,000. Because she contributes $2,400 of her salary to CBA's 401(k) plan, her AGI is $57,600 ($60,000 – $2,400). Tina would like to make the maximum deductible contribution to her IRA. Assuming the 2017 limitations apply, how much is she allowed to deduct?

Answer: $5,500. Because Tina is a participant in CBA's retirement plan, the $5,500 deduction limit is subject to phase-out. However, because Tina's AGI is less than the beginning of the phase-out threshold ($62,000), she is allowed to deduct the maximum contribution.

What if: Assume that in her first full calendar year working for CBA, Tina earns $66,000. Because she contributes $2,400 of her salary to CBA's 401(k) plan, her AGI is $63,600 ($66,000 – $2,400). Tina would like to make the maximum deductible contribution to her IRA. How much is she allowed to deduct?

Answer: $4,620. The deductible amount before considering AGI limitations is $5,500. However, because Tina is a participant in CBA's retirement plan, the $5,500 deduction limit is subject to phase-out. Because Tina's AGI is 16 percent of the way through the $62,000 – $72,000 phase-out range for a single taxpayer [($63,600 – $62,000)/($72,000 – $62,000)], the $5,500 deductible contribution limit is reduced by 16 percent, to $4,620 [$5,500 × (1 – .16)]. So, $4,620 is the maximum deductible contribution she can make to her traditional IRA.

What if: Assume that Tina is married and files a joint return with her spouse Steve. Tina participates in CBA's 401(k) plan and she receives $60,000 in salary from CBA for the year. Steve is a full-time student and is unemployed. The couple's AGI before considering IRA contributions is $60,000. What is Tina's maximum deductible IRA contribution for the year? What is Steve's maximum deductible IRA contribution for the year?

Answer: Tina's maximum deductible contribution for the year is $5,500. Because Tina is married, files a joint return, and reports AGI under $99,000 with her husband, her contribution is not phased out at all even though she is an active participant in CBA's retirement plan.

Steve's maximum deductible contribution for the year is also $5,500. Because Steve reports less earned income than Tina (in fact he doesn't report any earned income for the year), his deductible IRA contribution is limited to the lesser of (1) $5,500 or (2) $54,500 ($60,000 - $5,500), which is the couple's earned income minus Tina's deductible IRA contribution.

What if: Assume the same facts as the previous what-if example, except that Tina and Steve file separately. What is each spouse's maximum deductible IRA contribution for the year?

Answer: $0 for Tina and $0 for Steve. Tina is ineligible to make a deductible IRA contribution because her AGI of $60,000 exceeds the $10,000 phase-out limit and Steve may not make a deductible contribution to the IRA because he does not report any earned income.

Nondeductible Contributions For all taxpayers, to the extent the maximum deductible contribution is phased out based on AGI, taxpayers can still make *nondeductible* contributions of up to $5,500 per year ($6,500 for taxpayers who are at least 55 years of age at year-end). Taxpayers who have reached age 70½ by year-end are not allowed to contribute at all to an IRA. Earned income limitations (including the spousal IRA limits) that apply to deductible IRA contributions also apply to nondeductible contributions. That is, a taxpayer must have earned income in order to make nondeductible contributions to a traditional IRA (with the exception of a spouse who is contributing to a spousal IRA). The earnings on nondeductible contributions grow tax-free until the taxpayer receives distributions from the IRA. On distribution, the taxpayer is taxed on the earnings generated by the nondeductible contributions but not on the actual nondeductible contributions. When taxpayers take partial distributions from an IRA to which they have made deductible and nondeductible contributions, each distribution consists of a taxable and nontaxable component. The portion of the distribution that is nontaxable is the ratio of the nondeductible contributions to the total account balance at the time of the distribution.

This is exactly the same formula used in Example 13-12 to determine the nontaxable portion of nonqualified distributions from Roth 401(k) accounts and is similar to the formula described in the Gross Income and Exclusions chapter for determining the nontaxable portion of an annuity payment. Most taxpayers exceeding the deductibility limits on traditional IRAs would likely do better by contributing to a Roth IRA, if eligible, instead of making nondeductible contributions to traditional IRAs.

Taxpayers who are eligible to contribute to an IRA may contribute to the IRA up to the unextended tax return due date (generally, April 15 of the subsequent year). That is, as long as the taxpayer makes a contribution to the IRA by April 15 of year 2, the contribution counts as though it were made during year 1 (the prior calendar year).

Distributions Just as with traditional 401(k) plans, distributions from traditional IRAs are taxed as ordinary income to the taxpayer. Also, taxpayers withdrawing funds from traditional IRAs before reaching the age of 59½ are subject to a 10 percent early distribution penalty on the amount of the withdrawal. The IRA rules exempt certain distributions from the 10 percent penalty for early withdrawal. Among others, these distributions include proceeds distributed in the form of a life annuity (fixed payment each month or year over the taxpayer's life) and proceeds used for qualifying medical expenses, health insurance premiums for the owner, qualified higher education expenses, or first-time home purchases (limited to $10,000).[20] Taxpayers must receive their first required minimum distribution by April 1 of the year following the year in which the taxpayer reaches 70½ years of age. Because the distribution rules for traditional IRAs are so similar to the rules for traditional 401(k) accounts, taxpayers with traditional IRAs face virtually the same issues as participants in traditional 401(k) plans when planning for distributions. Thus, they should be careful to avoid the 10 percent penalty while at the same time taking similar steps to maximize the tax deferral on their traditional IRA account balances.

Roth IRAs

As an alternative to traditional IRAs, taxpayers meeting certain requirements can contribute to Roth IRAs. Contributions to Roth IRAs are *not* deductible and *qualifying* distributions from Roth IRAs are *not* taxable.

Contributions Roth IRAs are subject to the same annual contribution limits as traditional IRAs [the lesser of $5,500 ($6,500 if at least age 50 at year-end) or earned income]. Further, the same spousal IRA rules that apply to traditional IRAs apply to Roth IRA contributions. These limits apply to the sum of a taxpayer's contributions to deductible IRAs, nondeductible IRAs, and Roth IRAs.

Whether or not they participate in an employer-sponsored retirement plan, the Roth IRA contribution limitation phases out as follows:

Unmarried taxpayers

- No phase-out if the taxpayer's AGI is $118,000 or below.
- Proportional phase-out of full limit for AGI between $118,000 and $133,000.
- Full phase-out (no contribution) if AGI is $133,000 or higher.

Married taxpayers filing jointly

- No phase-out if the taxpayer's AGI is $186,000 or below.
- Proportional phase-out of full limit for AGI between $186,000 and $196,000.
- Full phase-out (no contribution) if AGI is $196,000 or higher.

Married taxpayers filing separately

- No phase-out if the taxpayer's AGI is $0.
- Proportional phase-out of full limit if taxpayer's AGI is between $0 and $10,000.
- Full phase-out (no contribution) if taxpayer's AGI is equal to or greater than $10,000.

Appendix B at the end of this chapter provides a flowchart for determining Roth IRA contribution limits.

THE KEY FACTS

Roth IRAs

- Contributions are not deductible.
- Same contribution limits as traditional IRAs but
  - For 2017, contribution phases out for AGI between $118,000 and $133,000 for unmarried taxpayers and between $186,000 and $196,000 for married filing jointly taxpayers.
- Qualified distributions are not taxable.
  - To qualify, account must be open for at least five years before distribution and distribution made after taxpayer reaches 59½ years of age (among others).
- Nonqualified distributions of account earnings
  - Taxed at ordinary rates and subject to 10 percent penalty if the taxpayer is not at least 59½ years of age at the time of the distribution.
- Distributions first come from contributions and then from account earnings.

[20]§72(t). A first-time homebuyer is someone who did not own a principal residence in the two years before acquiring the new home [see §72(t)(8)(D)].

Distributions *Qualified* distributions from Roth IRAs are not taxable. A qualified distribution is a distribution from funds or earnings from funds in a Roth IRA *if the distribution is at least five years after the taxpayer opened the Roth IRA*[21] and the distribution meets one of the following requirements:

- Distribution is made on or after the date the taxpayer reaches 59½ years of age,
- Distribution is made to a beneficiary (or to the estate of the taxpayer) on or after the death of the taxpayer,
- Distribution is attributable to the taxpayer being disabled, or
- Distribution is used to pay qualified acquisition costs for first-time homebuyers (limited to $10,000).[22]

All other distributions are considered to be *nonqualified* distributions.

Nonqualified distributions are not necessarily taxable, however. Because taxpayers do not deduct Roth IRA contributions, they are able to withdraw the contributions tax-free at any time. However, *nonqualified* distributions of the *earnings* of a Roth IRA are taxable as ordinary income. The distributed earnings are also subject to a 10 percent penalty unless the taxpayer is 59½ years of age at the time of the distribution.[23] Nonqualified distributions are deemed to come

- First from the taxpayer's contributions (nontaxable),
- Then from account earnings after the total contributions have been distributed (note that this is different than the equivalent rule for Roth 401(k) plans).

Thus, taxpayers can treat the Roth IRA as an emergency savings account to the extent of their contributions without incurring any penalties.

ETHICS

Ryan had just finished a finance class and had learned about the importance of the time value of money. With this knowledge, he wanted to start saving for retirement. Last year Ryan had a job and earned $2,000. After paying his expenses, he placed the remaining $500 in a savings account in the bank. This year, however, Ryan decided to focus on his studies so he did not earn any income. He paid his living expenses through student loans. At the end of the current year, Ryan contributed $400 to a Roth IRA. On his tax return for the year, Ryan reported $400 of self-employment income (even though he didn't earn any). Why did Ryan report this "phantom" income? What do you think of his strategy?

Example 13-17

What if: Assume that when Tina started working for CBA, she made a one-time contribution of $4,000 to a Roth IRA. Years later, she retired at the age of 65 when the value of her Roth account was $60,000. If Tina receives a $10,000 distribution from her Roth IRA, what amount of taxes (and penalty, if applicable) must she pay on the distribution (assume her ordinary marginal rate is 30 percent)?

Answer: $0 taxes and $0 penalty. Qualified Roth IRA distributions are not taxable.

What if: Assume the same facts as above, except that Tina received a $10,000 distribution when she was 57 years of age. What amount of taxes (and penalty, if applicable) is she required to pay on the distribution (assume a 30 percent ordinary marginal rate)?

Answer: $2,400 in total consisting of $1,800 in taxes ($6,000 earnings distributed × 30 percent marginal tax rate) and $600 penalty ($6,000 earnings × 10 percent penalty rate). Because Tina has not reached age 59½ at the time of the distribution, this is a nonqualified distribution. Consequently, she is

[21]The five-year period starts on January 1 of the year in which the contribution was made and ends on the last day of the fifth taxable year. See Reg §1.408A-6, Q&A2 and Q&A-5(b).

[22]§408A(d)(2).

[23]See §72(t)(2) for other exceptions to the penalty.

taxed on the $6,000 distribution of earnings ($10,000 distribution minus $4,000 contribution). She is penalized on the distribution of earnings because she is not 59½ years of age at the time of the distribution.

What if: Assume that when Tina was 62 years old, she opened a Roth IRA, contributing $4,000. Three years later, Tina withdrew the entire account balance of $5,000. What amount of taxes (and penalty, if applicable) must Tina pay on the distribution (assume her marginal tax rate is 30 percent)?

Answer: $300 of taxes ($1,000 earnings × 30 percent marginal tax rate) but $0 penalty. The distribution is a nonqualified distribution because Tina did not have the Roth IRA open for five years before receiving the distribution. Consequently, she must pay tax on the $1,000 earnings portion of the distribution ($5,000 − $4,000) but she is not penalized on the distribution because she was over 59½ years of age at the time of the distribution.

In contrast to taxpayers with traditional IRAs, taxpayers are *not* required to take minimum distributions from Roth IRAs. Thus, taxpayers can minimize distributions from Roth IRAs to maintain a source of tax-free income during their lifetime.

Rollover from Traditional to Roth IRA

Many taxpayers made contributions to traditional IRAs before Roth IRAs were available. Some taxpayers may have contributed to traditional IRAs and then later decided they should have contributed to Roth IRAs. The tax laws accommodate these taxpayers by allowing them to transfer funds from a traditional IRA (and other qualified defined contribution plans) to a Roth IRA.[24] This transfer of funds is called a **rollover.** When taxpayers do this, however, the entire amount taken out of the traditional IRA is taxed at ordinary rates but is not subject to the 10 percent penalty tax as long as the taxpayer contributes the *full amount* (before-tax) to a Roth IRA within 60 days of the withdrawal from the traditional IRA.[25]

Example 13-18

What if: Let's assume that in the year she graduated from college and began working for CBA, Tina made a fully deductible $4,000 contribution to a *traditional* IRA. Three years later, when her marginal tax rate is 25 percent, she rolls over the entire $5,000 account balance into a Roth IRA. What amount of taxes is she required to pay on the rollover?

Answer: $1,250 ($5,000 × 25%). The entire $5,000 transferred from the IRA to the Roth IRA is taxed at 25 percent but is not subject to the 10 percent early withdrawal penalty. Even though Tina pays $1,250 in taxes on the transfer, she is required to contribute $5,000 to the Roth IRA within 60 days from the time she withdraws the money from the traditional IRA.

What if: What are the tax consequences if Tina pays the $1,250 tax bill and contributes only $3,750 to the Roth IRA account?

Answer: She must pay a $125 penalty. The penalty is 10 percent of the $1,250 that she withdrew from the IRA and did not contribute to the Roth IRA ($5,000 − $3,750).

THE KEY FACTS

Roth IRAs

- Rollovers from traditional IRAs to Roth IRAs.
  - Amount withdrawn from traditional IRA is fully taxable but not penalized.
  - Must contribute full amount withdrawn to Roth IRA account within 60 days of withdrawal.
  - Amounts withdrawn but not contributed are subject to tax and 10 percent penalty.

Why would anyone be willing to pay taxes currently in order to avoid paying taxes later? Typically, a rollover from a traditional to a Roth IRA makes sense when a taxpayer's marginal tax rate is currently low (when the tax cost of the rollover is low) and expected to be significantly higher in the future (when the expected benefit of the rollover is high). Note that high-income taxpayers may not be allowed to contribute to Roth IRAs due to the AGI restrictions on contribution limits. However, because currently there is no AGI restriction on who may roll over funds from a traditional IRA (or other qualified

[24]See Notice 2009-75, 2009-39 IRB.

[25]§408(d)(3). Taxpayers who roll over funds from a traditional IRA (or other traditional retirement account) to a Roth IRA must wait at least five years from the date of the rollover to withdraw the funds from the rollover in order to avoid a 10 percent penalty on the distribution (§408(d)(3)(F)).

defined contribution plan) into a Roth IRA, high-income taxpayers who would like to fund a Roth IRA may do so through a rollover.[26]

Comparing Traditional and Roth IRAs

So, which type of IRA is better for taxpayers? The tax considerations are very similar to those we already discussed when we compared traditional and Roth 401(k) plans. In general, after-tax rates of return from traditional IRAs will exceed those from Roth IRAs when marginal tax rates decline. However, after-tax rates of return from Roth IRAs will exceed those from traditional IRAs when tax rates increase.

Unrelated to marginal tax rates, Roth IRAs have other advantages relative to traditional IRAs as follows:

- Taxpayers can contribute to Roth IRAs at any age. In contrast, taxpayers are not allowed to make deductible contributions to traditional IRAs once they have reached 70½ years of age.
- The minimum distribution requirements for traditional IRAs do not apply to Roth IRAs. This provision permits owners of Roth IRAs to use their accounts to generate tax-free returns long after retirement.
- Taxpayers can withdraw their Roth contributions tax-free at any time without paying tax or paying a penalty. Taxpayers who withdraw their traditional IRA contributions are taxed on the distribution and potentially penalized.

Exhibit 13-8 summarizes tax-related requirements for traditional and Roth IRAs.

EXHIBIT 13-8 Traditional IRA versus Roth IRA Summary

	Traditional IRA	Roth IRA
Contributions requirements	• Taxpayer must not be a participant in an employer-sponsored plan or, if participating in an employer-provided plan, must meet certain income thresholds. Those above the threshold will have deductible portion of contribution phased out.	• No deduction allowed for contributions. Must meet certain income requirements to be able to contribute to a Roth IRA.
Contributions	• Deductible unless taxpayer is a participant in an employer plan and has high AGI. • Nondeductible contributions allowed.	• Not deductible. • May not contribute if high AGI.
Maximum contribution	• Lesser of $5,500 per taxpayer ($6,500 for taxpayers over 50 years old) or earned income. • The contribution limits apply to the sum of contributions to traditional deductible IRAs, nondeductible IRAs, and Roth IRAs for the year. • For married couples filing jointly, contributions for the lesser earning spouse may not exceed the total earned income of both spouses reduced by deductible and nondeductible contributions to the other spouse's traditional IRA and by contributions to the other spouse's Roth IRA.	• Same as traditional IRA.
Contribution dates	• Can contribute up to unextended tax return due date, generally April 15.	• Same as traditional IRA.
Distributions	• Generally taxed as ordinary income. • If made before 59½, generally subject to 10 percent penalty. • If nondeductible contribution made, allocate distribution between taxable and nontaxable amounts similar to annuity rules. • Minimum distributions required by April 1 of the year after the year in which the taxpayer reaches 70½. • Failure to meet minimum distribution timing and amount requirements triggers 50 percent penalty.	• Qualified distributions are not taxed. • Generally, distributions are qualified after account has been open for five years and employee has reached the age of 59½. • Nonqualified distributions are not taxed to the extent of prior contributions. • Nonqualified distributions of earnings are subject to tax at ordinary rates and are also subject to a 10 percent penalty if the taxpayer is not at least 59½ years of age at the time of the distribution. • No minimum distribution requirements.

[26]§408A(c)(3).

TAXES IN THE REAL WORLD Roth or Traditional Retirement Savings Vehicle?

With increasing budgetary deficits and the government's increasing need for revenues, one can reasonably anticipate that future tax rates will exceed current tax rates. With increasing tax rates, taxpayers should favor Roth 401(k) plans and Roth IRAs over traditional retirement savings vehicles. Yet, less than 10 percent of employees who could contribute to Roth 401(k) plans choose to do so and more than 15 times more taxpayers use traditional IRAs than use Roth IRAs. Why are so many more taxpayers choosing traditional retirement savings options when Roth accounts may theoretically provide a greater after-tax sum at retirement? It could be that there are not a lot of taxpayers who expect their marginal tax rates to be higher at retirement than they are now, it could be that taxpayers prefer deductible retirement savings contributions for the current tax savings, or it could be that taxpayers believe that in the future Congress may change the tax laws so that distributions from Roth accounts will become taxable. A sound response to the tax law uncertainty would be to hedge your bets and include some retirement savings in traditional accounts and some in Roth accounts so that you can adapt to changing tax laws over time.

Source: Carolyn T. Geer, "Bad Math: Taxes Rise as Savings Fall," *The Wall Street Journal,* January 20, 2013.

SELF-EMPLOYED RETIREMENT ACCOUNTS

LO 13-5

We've discussed retirement savings opportunities available to employees. However, many taxpayers are self-employed small business owners who do not have access to employer-sponsored plans.[27] Moreover, individually managed retirement plans such as traditional and Roth IRAs are not particularly attractive to self-employed taxpayers due to the relatively low contribution limits on these plans. What retirement savings options, then, are available to the self-employed?

Congress has created a number of retirement savings plans targeted toward self-employed taxpayers. Two of the more popular plans for the self-employed are simplified employee pension (SEP) IRAs and individual (or "self-employed") 401(k) plans. These are defined contribution plans that generally work the same as employer-provided plans. That is, amounts set aside in these plans are deducted from income, earnings are free from tax until distributed, and distributions from the plans are fully taxable.[28] As we discuss below, these plans differ in terms of their annual contribution limits. They also have different nontax characteristics including their suitability for businesses with employees other than the owner and their administration costs. As you might expect, these factors come into play when self-employed small business owners choose a retirement plan.[29] We describe SEP IRAs and individual 401(k) plans below.[30]

THE KEY FACTS

Self-Employed Retirement Accounts

- Popular plans include SEP IRAs and individual 401(k)s.
- Similar to (non-Roth) qualified defined contribution plans.
  - Contributions are deductible and distributions are taxable.

Simplified Employee Pension (SEP) IRA

A simplified employee pension (SEP) can be administered through an individual retirement account (IRA) called a **SEP IRA.**[31] The owner of a sole proprietorship can make

[27]Because sole proprietorships with self-employment income are very common, we assume in our examples and explanations here that any self-employment income originates from a sole proprietorship. In some cases, however, partners and LLC members may also have self-employment income from a partnership or LLC.

[28]"Keogh" self-employed defined benefit plans are also an option. Generally, defined benefit plans are attractive to older, self-employed individuals with profitable businesses because they allow for greater deductible contributions. However, they are usually more costly to maintain than the defined contribution plans we mention here.

[29]Many investment firms provide comparisons to help taxpayers select self-employed retirement plans. One particularly good comparison is provided by Fidelity Investments at www.fidelity.com/retirement/small-business/compare-plans-chart.

[30]A Savings Incentive Match Plans for Employees (SIMPLE) IRA is another popular form of retirement plan for the self-employed. For those earning lower amounts of self-employment income, the contribution limits for a SIMPLE IRA are generally higher than contribution limits for SEP IRAs.

[31]§408(k).

annual contributions directly to her SEP IRA. For 2017, the annual contribution is limited to the *lesser* of

- $54,000.
- 20 percent of Schedule C net income after reducing Schedule C net income by the deduction for the employer's portion of self-employment taxes paid (50 percent of the self-employment taxes paid).[32]

Contributions can be made up to the extended due date of the tax return.[33]

Example 13-19

THE KEY FACTS

Self-Employed Retirement Accounts

- SEP IRA 2017 contribution limit.
  - Lesser of (1) $54,000 or (2) 20 percent of Schedule C net income (after reducing Schedule C net income by the deduction for the employer's portion of self-employment taxes paid).

What if: Dave (age 64) reports Schedule C net income of $40,000 during the current year. If he sets up a SEP IRA for himself, what is the maximum contribution he may make to the plan (assuming he has no other source of employee or self-employment income)?

Answer: $7,435, computed as follows:

Description	Amount	Explanation
(1) First limit on contribution	$54,000	
(2) Schedule C net income minus the self-employment tax deduction	37,174	$40,000 − ($40,000 × .9235 × 15.3% × 50%)
(3) Percentage for limitation based on (2)	20%	
(4) Second limit on contribution	7,435	(2) × (3)
Maximum contribution	**$ 7,435**	Lesser of (1) or (4)

What if: Assume Dave is 48 years old at the end of the year. What is his maximum deductible contribution?

Answer: $7,435. Dave's maximum deductible contribution for a SEP IRA does not depend on his age.

What if: Suppose Dave reports $310,000 of Schedule C net income rather than $40,000. What is his maximum deductible contribution to his SEP IRA account?

Answer: $54,000, the lesser of (1) $54,000 or (2) $59,592 {20% × [$310,000 − (((310,000 × .9235 − $127,200) × 2.9% × 50%) + ($127,200 × 15.3% × 50%))]}.

Nontax Considerations If a sole proprietor has hired employees, the sole proprietor *must* contribute to the employees' respective SEP IRAs based on their compensation. Because owners may view this requirement as being too favorable to employees, this plan is best suited for sole proprietors who do not have employees or for situations where owners are willing to provide generous benefits to their employees. From an administrative perspective, SEP IRAs are easy to set up and have relatively low administrative costs from year to year.

Individual 401(k) Plans

Individual 401(k) plans are strictly for sole proprietors (and the spouse of the sole proprietor) who do not have employees. Under this type of plan, for 2017, the sole proprietor can contribute the lesser of

- $54,000.
- 20 percent of Schedule C net income after reducing Schedule C net income by the deduction for the employer's portion of self-employment taxes paid (50 percent of self-employment taxes paid) (employer's contribution) plus an additional $18,000 (employee's contribution).

[32]The Individual Income Tax Computation and Tax Credits chapter addresses self-employment taxes in more detail. Also note that for SEP IRAs no catch-up contributions are allowed for taxpayers 50 years and older.

[33]§404(h). This is September 15 for a calendar-year taxpayer.

Further, if the sole proprietor is at least 50 years of age by the end of the tax year, she may contribute an *additional* $6,000 as a catch-up contribution. Thus, a self-employed taxpayer with sufficient self-employment earnings and who is at least 50 years of age at year-end could contribute up to $60,000 to an individual 401(k) for 2017 ($54,000 + $6,000).

Finally, even though the individual 401(k) contribution limits provide for taxpayers to contribute an additional $18,000 or $24,000 (this includes the additional $6,000 for taxpayers at least 50 years of age at year-end) relative to a SEP IRA, a taxpayer's individual 401(k) contributions for the year are not allowed to exceed the taxpayer's Schedule C net income minus the self-employment tax deduction. Consequently, a taxpayer with limited self-employment income may not be able to take advantage of the additional $18,000 ($24,000) of contributions that individual 401(k)s allow relative to SEP IRAs.

Example 13-20

What if: Suppose that Dave is 64 years old at the end of the year, reports $40,000 of Schedule C net income, and has no other sources of income. What is the maximum amount he can contribute to an individual 401(k) account?

Answer: $31,435, computed as follows:

Description	Amount	Explanation
(1) First limit on contribution	$ 54,000	
(2) Schedule C net income minus the self-employment tax deduction	37,174	$40,000 – ($40,000 × .9235 × 15.3% × 50%)
(3) Percentage for limitation based on (2)	20%	
(4) Limit on employer's contribution	7,435	(2) × (3)
(5) Limit on employee's contribution	18,000	
(6) Second limitation	25,435	(4) + (5)
(7) Maximum contribution before catch-up contribution	25,435	Lesser of (1) or (6)
(8) Catch-up contribution	6,000	Dave is 64 years old at year-end
Maximum contribution	**$31,435**	(7) + (8), not to exceed (2)

THE KEY FACTS

Self-Employed Retirement Accounts

- Individual 401(k) 2017 contribution limit.
  - Lesser of (1) $54,000 or (2) 20 percent of Schedule C net income (after reducing Schedule C net income by the deduction for the employer's portion of self-employment taxes paid) plus $18,000.
  - Taxpayers who are at least 50 years old at the end of the year may contribute an additional $6,000 per year (maximum of $60,000, if self-employment earnings are sufficient).
  - Contribution cannot exceed Schedule C net income minus self-employment tax deduction.

Example 13-21

What if: Assume Dave is 48 years old at the end of the year, reports $40,000 of Schedule C net income, and has no other sources of income. What is his maximum deductible contribution to his individual 401(k) account?

Answer: $25,435. This is the same as the amount he could contribute as a 64-year-old (see prior example), minus the $6,000 catch-up adjustment ($31,435 – $6,000).

What if: Assume the same facts as above except that Dave (age 64) earned $10,000 of Schedule C net income rather than $40,000. What is his maximum deductible contribution to his individual 401(k)?

(continued on page 13-30)

Answer: $9,294, computed as follows (Dave's contribution is limited to his Schedule C net income minus self-employment tax deduction):

Description	Amount	Explanation
(1) First limit on contribution	$54,000	
(2) Schedule C net income minus self-employment tax deduction	9,294	$10,000 − ($10,000 × .9235 × 15.3% × 50%)
(3) Percentage for limitation based on (2)	20%	
(4) Limit on employer's contribution	1,859	(2) × (3)
(5) Limit on employee's contribution	18,000	
(6) Second limitation	19,859	(4) + (5)
(7) Maximum contribution before catch-up contribution	19,859	Lesser of (1) or (6)
(8) Catch-up contribution	6,000	Dave is 64 years old at year-end
Maximum contribution	**$ 9,294**	(7) + (8), not to exceed (2)

Example 13-22

What if: Assume Dave (age 64) earned $400,000 of Schedule C net income. What is his maximum deductible contribution to his individual 401(k)?

Answer: $60,000, computed as follows:

Description	Amount	Explanation
(1) First limit on contribution	$ 54,000	
(2) Schedule C net income minus self-employment tax deduction	386,757	$400,000 − {[(400,000 × .9235 − 127,200) × 2.9% × 50%] + [127,200 × 15.3% × 50%]}
(3) Percentage for limitation based on (2)	20%	
(4) Limit on employer's contribution	77,351	(2) × (3)
(5) Limit on employee's contribution	18,000	
(6) Second limitation	95,351	(4) + (5)
(7) Maximum contribution before catch-up contribution	54,000	Lesser of (1) or (6)
(8) Catch-up contribution	6,000	Dave is 64 years old at year-end
Maximum contribution	**$ 60,000**	(7) + (8), not to exceed (2)

Nontax Considerations As we mentioned above, the individual 401(k) plan is not available for sole proprietors with employees, so providing benefits to employees under the plan is not a concern. However, the administrative burden of establishing, operating, and maintaining a 401(k) plan is potentially higher than it is for the other self-employed plans.

LO 13-6

SAVER'S CREDIT

To encourage middle- and low-income taxpayers to take advantage of the retirement savings opportunities discussed in this chapter, Congress provides an additional saver's credit for an individual's elective contribution of up to $2,000 to any of the qualified retirement plans discussed in this chapter, including employer-sponsored qualified plans, traditional and Roth IRA plans, and self-employed qualified plans. The credit is provided *in addition to* any deduction the taxpayer is allowed for contributing to a retirement account. It is calculated by multiplying the taxpayer's contribution, up to a maximum of $2,000, by the applicable percentage depending on the taxpayer's filing status and AGI. The credit is nonrefundable. Exhibit 13-9 provides the applicable percentages for 2017 according to a taxpayer's filing status and AGI.[34]

THE KEY FACTS

Saver's Credit

- Credit for taxpayers contributing to qualified plan.
- Credit is based on contributions up to $2,000, taxpayer's filing status, and AGI.
  - Phased out as AGI increases.
  - Maximum credit is $1,000.
  - Unavailable for married filing jointly taxpayers with AGI over $62,000, head of household taxpayers with AGI above $46,500, and all other taxpayers with AGI above $31,000.

EXHIBIT 13-9 **2017 Applicable Percentages for Saver's Credit by Filing Status and AGI**

Applicable Percentage	Joint Filers AGI	Heads of Household AGI	All Other Filers AGI
50%	0 to $37,000	0 to $27,750	0 to $18,500
20	$37,001 to $40,000	$27,751 to $30,000	$18,501 to $20,000
10	$40,001 to $62,000	$30,001 to $46,500	$20,001 to $31,000
No credit available	Above $62,000	Above $46,500	Above $31,000

In addition to restricting the credit to taxpayers with AGI below a certain threshold, the credit is also restricted to individuals who are 18 years of age or older, are not claimed as dependents by another taxpayer, and are not full-time students at a qualified educational organization during each of five calendar months of the taxpayer's tax year.[35] Although limited in scope, the saver's credit provides some tax benefits for those taxpayers who qualify.

Example 13-23

What if: Tina earned $24,000 during the year she began working for CBA. She earned $4,000 in salary working part-time while she was in school and $20,000 in salary working for CBA from September through December. To get an early start saving for retirement, assume she contributed $4,000 to a traditional IRA. Because Tina did not participate in an employer-sponsored retirement plan during the current year she may deduct the full $4,000 contribution as a *for* AGI deduction, reducing her AGI from $24,000 to $20,000. What amount of saver's credit, if any, is Tina allowed to claim, assuming she was a full-time student during four months of the year?

Answer: $400 ($2,000 × 20 percent applicable credit).

What if: What saver's credit may Tina claim if her AGI is $15,000?

Answer: $1,000 ($2,000 × 50 percent applicable credit).

CONCLUSION

The decisions that employees like Tina, Lisa, and Dave must deal with highlight the role that tax issues play in this important area. Employers, like their employees, must also pay careful attention to tax considerations when deciding on retirement savings vehicles to offer their employees. Further, as has been a recurring theme throughout this book, nontax issues play an equal, if not more important, role in the retirement savings decisions of both employees and employers.

[34]For this purpose, AGI is determined without considering the foreign-earned income exclusion provided for U.S. residents living abroad under §911.

[35]§152(f)(2).

Appendix A (Page 1) Traditional IRA Deduction Limitations

NOTE: For married couples, go through flowchart separately for each spouse.

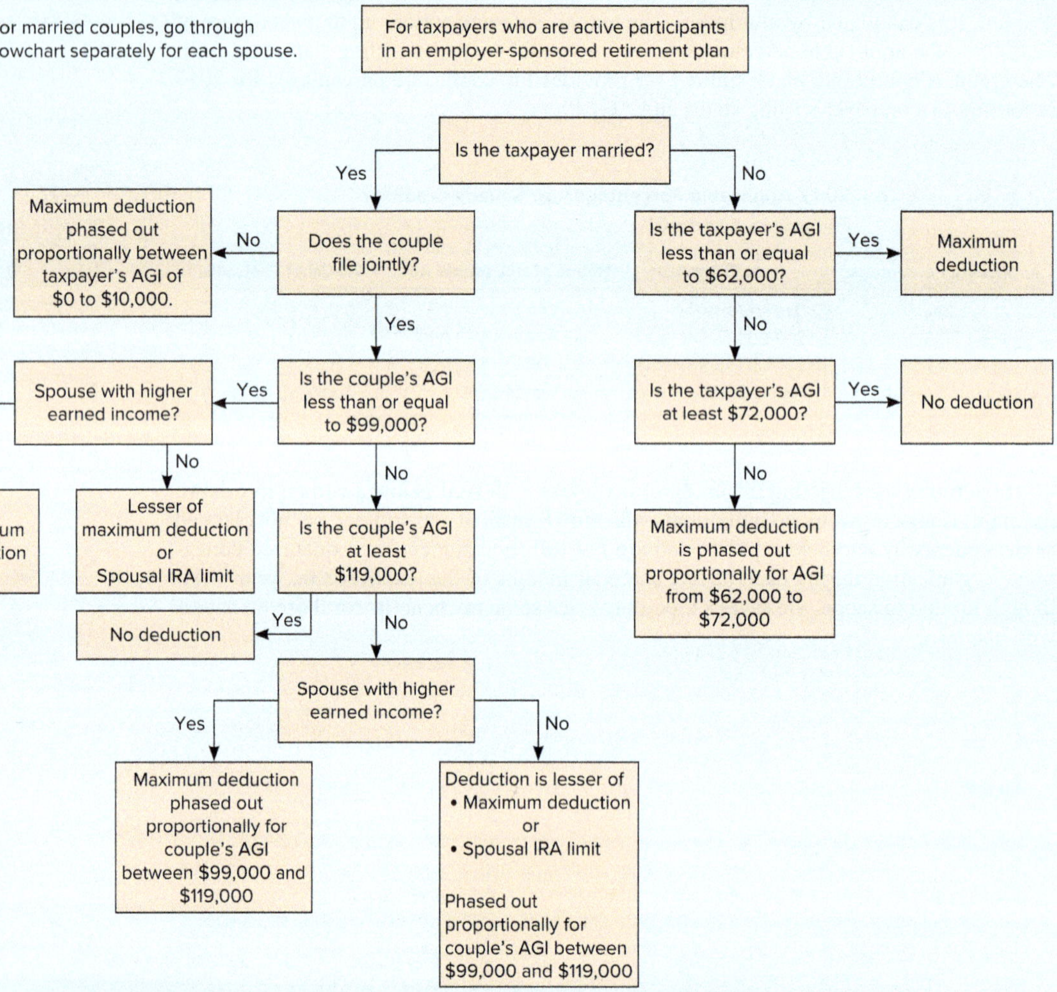

Spousal IRA Limit.
Total earned income of both spouses reduced by contributions to deductible IRAs, nondeductible IRA, and Roth IRA made by higher-earning spouse.

Maximum Deduction
Least of:
- $5,500 ($6,500 if at least age 50 at year-end)
- $0 if at least age 70½ at year-end
- Taxpayer's earned income for year

NOTE: The sum of the taxpayer's deductible IRA contributions, nondeductible IRA contributions, and Roth IRA contributions cannot exceed $5,500 (or $6,500 if the taxpayer is at least 50 years old at year-end).

(Page 2) Traditional IRA Deduction Limitations

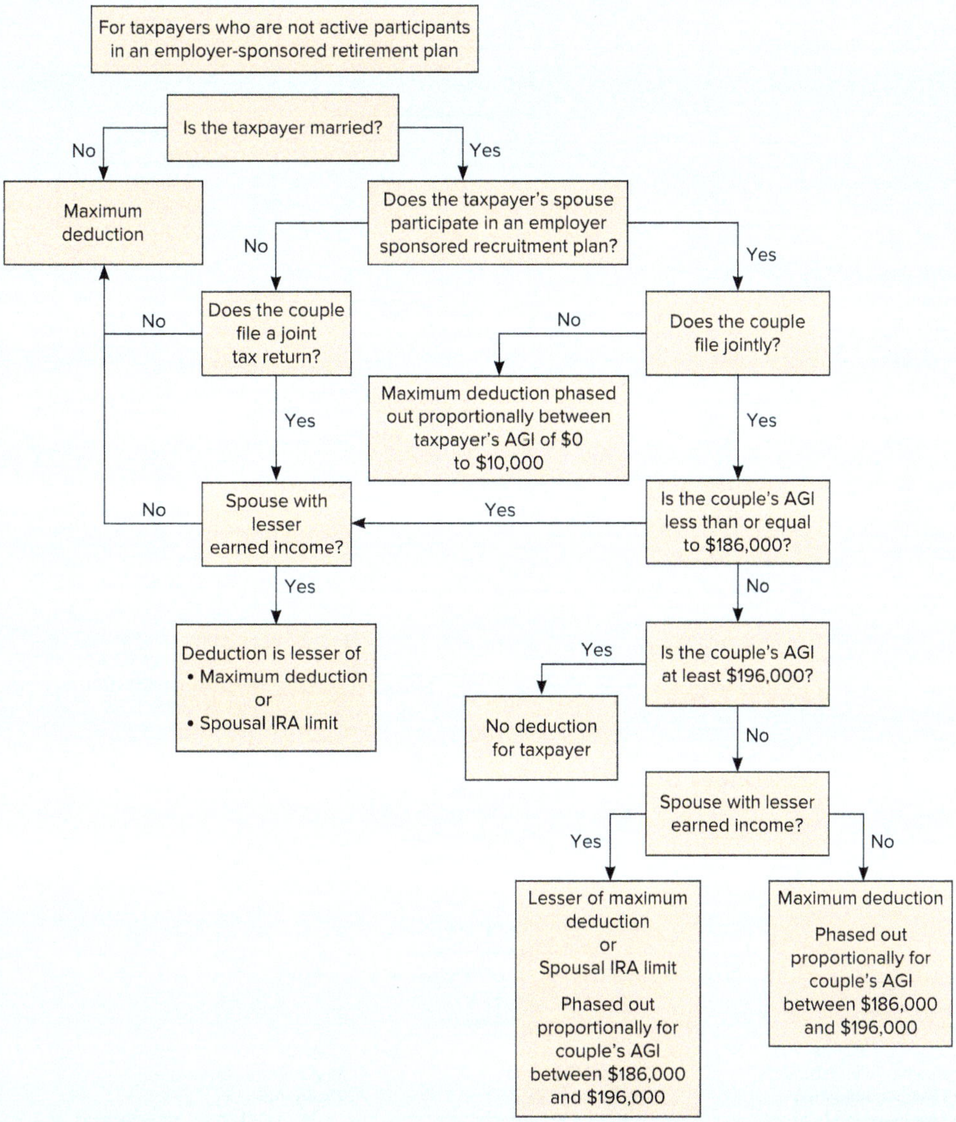

Spousal IRA Limit.
Total earned income of both spouses reduced by contributions to deductible IRAs, nondeductible IRA, and Roth IRA made by higher-earning spouse.

Maximum Deduction
Least of:
- $5,500 ($6,500 if at least age 50 at year-end)
- $0 if at least age 70½ at year-end
- Taxpayer's earned income for year

NOTE: The sum of the taxpayer's deductible IRA contributions, nondeductible IRA contributions, and Roth IRA contributions cannot exceed $5,500 (or $6,500 if the taxpayer is at least 50 years old at year-end).

Appendix B Roth IRA Contribution Limits

NOTE: For married couples, go through flowchart for each spouse separately.

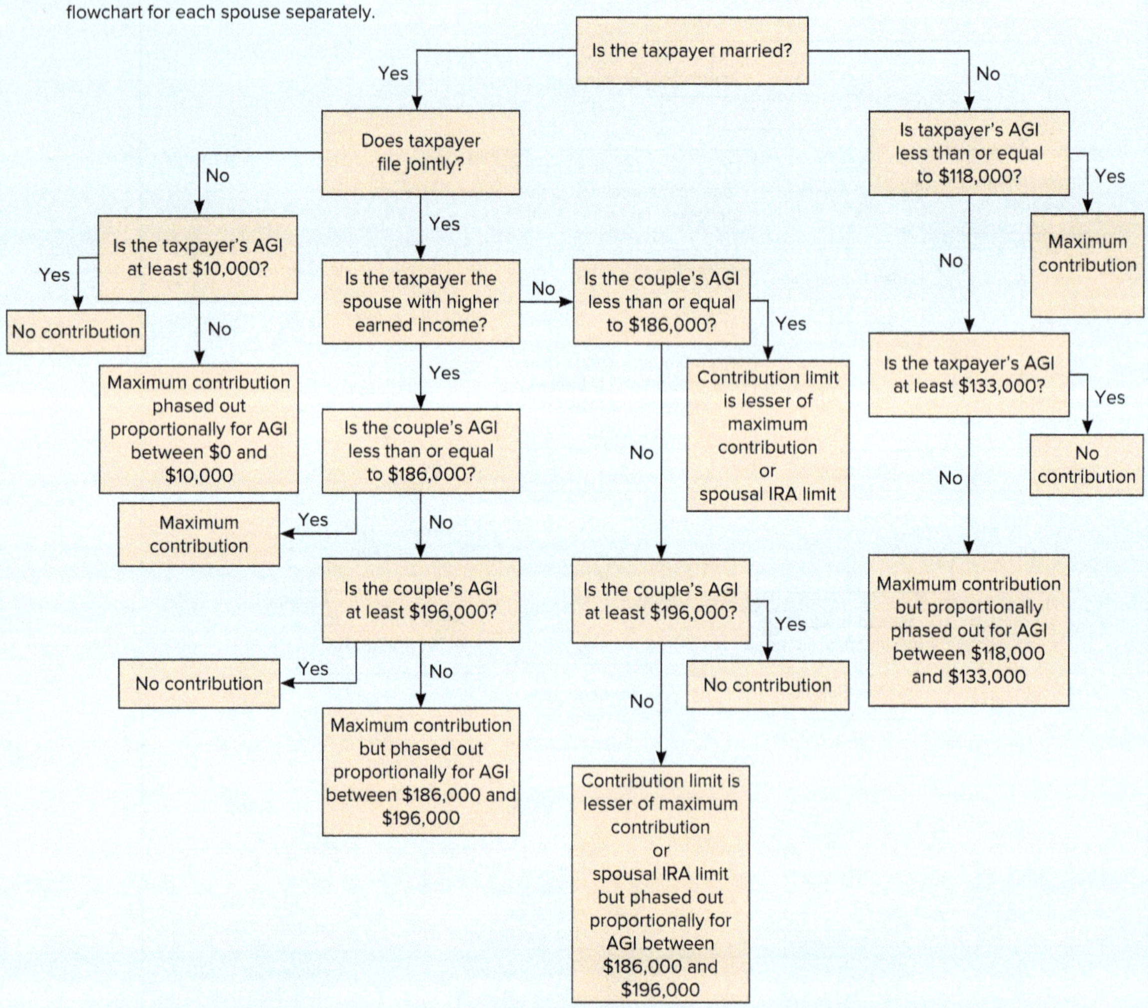

NOTE: The sum of the taxpayer's deductible IRA contributions, nondeductible IRA contributions and both IRA contributions cannot exceed $5,500 (or $6,500 if the taxpayer is at least 50 years old at year-end.)

Spousal IRA Limit
Total earned income of both spouses reduced by contributions to deductible IRA, nondeductible IRA, and Roth IRA.

Maximum Contribution
Lesser or
- $5,500 ($6,500 if the taxpayer is at least age 50 at year-end) and
- Taxpayer's earned income.

Summary

Describe the tax and nontax aspects of employer-provided defined benefit plans from both the employer's and the employee's perspective. LO 13-1

- Benefits are determined based on years of service and salary. The maximum annual benefit is capped and adjusted upward annually for inflation.
- Benefits vest over time using (at a minimum) either a five-year cliff or seven-year graded vesting schedule.
- Employers deduct cash contributions to fund the plan and employees treat cash distributions as ordinary income in the year received.
- Employers bear investment risk with defined benefit plans.
- Premature distribution and minimum distribution penalties don't typically apply to defined benefit distributions.
- Because of the high cost of funding and maintaining defined benefit plans, they are waning in popularity.

Explain and determine the tax consequences associated with employer-provided defined contribution plans, including traditional 401(k) and Roth 401(k) plans. LO 13-2

- Employers specify the amount they will contribute to defined contribution plans instead of the annual benefit. However, employers are not permitted to contribute to Roth 401(k) plans.
- Employees may contribute to either a traditional 401(k) or a Roth 401(k) account, and they determine how employer and employee contributions are invested. Employees bear investment risk with defined contribution plans.
- Annual employer and employee contributions are limited and maximum contribution amounts are adjusted annually for inflation.
- Employer contributions to traditional plans vest over time using (at a minimum) either a three-year cliff or six-year graded vesting schedule.
- Employers deduct their contributions to traditional defined contribution plans.
- Employee contributions to traditional defined contribution plans are excluded from their taxable wages on Form W-2. Employee contributions to Roth 401(k) plans are not excluded.
- Distributions from traditional 401(k) plans are taxable at ordinary rates and qualified distributions from Roth 401(k) plans are not taxable.
- Distributions from both traditional 401(k) and Roth 401(k) plans are subject to premature and minimum distribution penalties.
- After-tax rates of return from Roth 401(k) plans are generally superior to those from traditional 401(k) plans when marginal tax rates are increasing.

Describe the tax implications of deferred compensation from both the employer's and the employee's perspective. LO 13-3

- Employees elect to defer current salary in exchange for promised future payments from the employer.
- Because the employer's promise of future payment is unsecured, employees recognize ordinary income when future payments are received. Employers wait to deduct payments until cash is actually paid.
- The after-tax rate of return and costs from deferred compensation arrangements to employees and employers depend on the current and future marginal tax rates of both the employee and the employer.
- Deferred compensation can be used to overcome deductibility constraints imposed on salary and qualified pension plans.
- Employees bear more risk with deferred compensation relative to other forms of retirement savings because employees are unsecured creditors of their employers and because the investments upon which their compensation is based have risk.

LO 13-4 Determine the tax consequences of traditional and Roth IRAs (individual retirement accounts) and explain the differences between them.

- The same inflation-adjusted annual contribution limits apply to both traditional IRAs and Roth IRAs.
- The deduction for traditional IRA contributions is phased out for taxpayers covered by a retirement plan at work and with AGI above certain inflation-adjusted amounts. Special rules pertain for spouses not covered by an employer plan.
- The ability to contribute to a Roth IRA is phased out for individuals with AGI above certain inflation-adjusted amounts.
- Distributions from traditional IRAs are taxed at ordinary rates. A 10 percent premature distribution penalty generally applies to distributions from traditional IRAs received before age 59½.
- Distributions from Roth IRAs received after a Roth IRA account has been open for at least five years and after the recipient reaches age 59½ are not taxable. The earnings component of any distributions not meeting these requirements is generally taxable and subject to the 10 percent premature distribution penalty.
- Taxpayers generally prefer Roth IRAs to traditional IRAs when they expect their marginal tax rates to increase.

LO 13-5 Describe retirement savings options available to self-employed taxpayers and compute the limitations for deductible contributions to retirement accounts for self-employed taxpayers.

- Self-employed individuals may set up their own qualified pension plans such as SEP IRAs and individual 401(k) plans.
- Contribution limits generally parallel those for employer-sponsored plans, allowing self-employed individuals to have the same access to qualified plans that employees have.
- Self-employed individuals with employees may have to incur the cost of covering their employees when they establish a qualified retirement plan.

LO 13-6 Compute the saver's credit.

- Individuals may receive up to a $1,000 tax credit for contributions they make to IRAs and employer-sponsored qualified plans.
- The amount of the credit is a function of the taxpayer's filing status and AGI.

KEY TERMS

cliff vesting (13-4)
defined benefit plans (13-3)
defined contribution plans (13-3)
graded vesting (13-4)
individual retirement account (IRA) (13-19)
nonqualified deferred compensation (13-15)
qualified retirement plans (13-3)
rollover (13-25)
Roth 401(k) (13-11)
Roth IRA (13-19)
§162(m) limitation (13-18)
SEP IRA (13-27)
spousal IRA (13-21)
traditional 401(k) (13-11)
traditional IRA (13-19)
vesting (13-4)

DISCUSSION QUESTIONS

Discussion Questions are available in Connect®.

1. LO 13-1 LO 13-2 How are defined benefit plans different from defined contribution plans? How are they similar?
2. LO 13-1 Describe how an employee's benefit under a defined benefit plan is computed.
3. LO 13-1 LO 13-2 What does it mean to vest in a defined benefit or defined contribution plan?
4. LO 13-1 LO 13-2 Compare and contrast the minimum vesting requirements for defined benefit plans and defined contribution plans.
5. LO 13-1 LO 13-2 What are the nontax advantages and disadvantages of defined benefit plans relative to defined contribution plans?

6. Describe the maximum annual benefit that taxpayers may receive under defined benefit plans. LO 13-1
7. Describe the distribution or payout options available to taxpayers participating in qualified defined benefit plans. How are defined benefit plan distributions to recipients taxed? LO 13-1
8. Describe the minimum distribution requirements for defined benefit plans. Are these requirements typically an item of concern for taxpayers? LO 13-1 LO 13-2
9. Compare and contrast the employer's responsibilities for providing a defined benefit plan to employees relative to providing a defined contribution plan. LO 13-1 LO 13-2
10. Describe how an employee's benefit under a defined contribution plan is determined. LO 13-2
11. Is there a limit to how much an employer and/or employee may contribute to an employee's defined contribution account(s) for the year? If so, describe the limit. LO 13-2
12. Cami (age 52 and married) was recently laid off as part of her employer's reduction in force program. Cami's annual AGI was usually around $50,000. Shortly after Cami's employment was terminated, her employer distributed the balance of her employer-sponsored 401(k) account to her. What could Cami do to avoid being assessed the 10 percent early distribution penalty? LO 13-2
13. When may employees begin to receive defined contribution plan distributions without penalty? LO 13-2
14. Describe the circumstances under which distributions from defined contribution plans are penalized. What are the penalties? LO 13-2
15. Brady Corporation has a profit-sharing plan that allocates 10 percent of all after-tax income to employees. The profit sharing is allocated to individual employees based on relative employee compensation. The profit-sharing contributions vest to employees under a six-year graded plan. If an employee terminates his or her employment before fully vesting, the plan allocates the forfeited amounts among the remaining participants according to their account balances. Is this forfeiture allocation policy discriminatory, and will it cause the plan to lose its qualified status? Use Rev. Rul. 81-10 to help formulate your answer. LO 13-2 research
16. What does it mean if an employer "matches" employee contributions to 401(k) plans? LO 13-2
17. What nontax factor(s) should an employee consider when deciding whether and to what extent to participate in an employer's 401(k) plan? LO 13-2 planning
18. What are the differences between a traditional 401(k) and a Roth 401(k) plan? LO 13-2
19. Can employers match employee contributions to Roth 401(k) plans? Explain. LO 13-2
20. Describe the annual limitation on employer and employee contributions to traditional 401(k) and Roth 401(k) plans. LO 13-2
21. When a company is limited by the tax laws in the amount it can contribute to an employee's 401(k) plan, what will it generally do to make the employee whole? Is this likely an issue for rank-and-file employees? Why or why not? LO 13-2 LO 13-3
22. From a tax perspective, how would taxpayers determine whether they should contribute to a traditional 401(k) or a Roth 401(k)? LO 13-2 planning
23. Could a taxpayer contributing to a traditional 401(k) plan earn an after-tax return *greater* than the before-tax return? Explain. LO 13-2
24. Explain the *tax* similarities and differences between qualified defined contribution plans and nonqualified deferred compensation plans from an *employer's* perspective. LO 13-2 LO 13-3
25. Explain the *tax* similarities and differences between qualified defined contribution plans and nonqualified deferred compensation plans from an *employee's* perspective. LO 13-2 LO 13-3

LO 13-2 LO 13-3 26. Explain the *nontax* similarities and differences between qualified defined contribution plans and nonqualified deferred compensation plans from an *employer's* perspective.

LO 13-2 LO 13-3 27. Explain the *nontax* similarities and differences between qualified defined contribution plans and nonqualified deferred compensation plans from an *employee's* perspective.

LO 13-3 planning 28. From a *tax* perspective, what issues does an employee need to consider in deciding whether to defer compensation under a nonqualified deferred compensation plan or to receive it immediately?

LO 13-3 planning 29. From a *nontax* perspective, what issues does an employee need to consider in deciding whether to defer compensation under a nonqualified deferred compensation plan or to receive it immediately?

LO 13-3 30. What are reasons why companies provide nonqualified deferred compensation plans for certain employees?

planning LO 13-2 31. How can companies use deferred compensation to avoid the §162(m) limitation on salary deductibility?

LO 13-3 32. Are companies allowed to decide who can and cannot participate in nonqualified deferred compensation plans? Briefly explain.

LO 13-1 LO 13-2 LO 13-3 33. How might the ultimate benefits to an employee who participates in a qualified retirement plan of a company differ from the ultimate benefits to an employee who participates in a nonqualified deferred compensation plan of the company if the company experiences bankruptcy before the employee is scheduled to receive the benefits?

LO 13-4 34. What are the primary tax differences between traditional IRAs and Roth IRAs?

planning LO 13-4 35. Describe the circumstances in which it would be more favorable for a taxpayer to contribute to a traditional IRA rather than a Roth IRA and vice versa.

LO 13-4 36. What are the requirements for a taxpayer to make a deductible contribution to a traditional IRA? Why do the tax laws impose these restrictions?

LO 13-4 37. What is the limitation on a deductible IRA contribution for 2017?

LO 13-4 38. Compare the minimum distribution requirements for traditional IRAs to those of Roth IRAs.

LO 13-4 39. How are qualified distributions from Roth IRAs taxed? How are nonqualified distributions taxed?

LO 13-4 40. Explain when a taxpayer will be subject to the 10 percent penalty when receiving distributions from a Roth IRA.

LO 13-4 41. Is a taxpayer who contributed to a traditional IRA able to transfer or "roll over" the money into a Roth IRA? If yes, explain the tax consequences of the transfer.

LO 13-4 42. Assume a taxpayer makes a nondeductible contribution to a traditional IRA. How does the taxpayer determine the taxability of distributions from the IRA on reaching retirement?

LO 13-4 43. When a taxpayer takes a nonqualified distribution from a Roth IRA, is the entire amount of the distribution treated as taxable income?

LO 13-5 44. What types of retirement plans are available to self-employed taxpayers?

LO 13-5 45. Compare and contrast the annual limitations on deductible contributions for self-employed taxpayers to SEP IRAs and individual 401(k) accounts.

planning LO 13-5 46. What are the nontax considerations for self-employed taxpayers deciding whether to set up a SEP IRA or an individual 401(k)?

LO 13-6 47. What is the saver's credit and who is eligible to receive it?

LO 13-6 48. What is the maximum saver's credit available to taxpayers? What taxpayer characteristics are relevant to the determination?

LO 13-6 49. How is the saver's credit computed?

PROBLEMS

Select problems are available in Connect®.

50. Javier recently graduated and started his career with DNL Inc. DNL provides a defined benefit plan to all employees. According to the terms of the plan, for each full year of service working for the employer, employees receive a benefit of 1.5 percent of their average salary over their highest three years of compensation from the company. Employees may accrue only 30 years of benefit under the plan (45 percent). Determine Javier's annual benefit on retirement, before taxes, under each of the following scenarios: LO 13-1
    a) Javier works for DNL for three years and three months before he leaves for another job. Javier's annual salary was $55,000, $65,000, $70,000, and $72,000 for years 1, 2, 3, and 4, respectively. DNL uses a five-year cliff vesting schedule.
    b) Javier works for DNL for three years and three months before he leaves for another job. Javier's annual salary was $55,000, $65,000, $70,000, and $72,000 for years 1, 2, 3, and 4, respectively. DNL uses a seven-year graded vesting schedule.
    c) Javier works for DNL for six years and three months before he leaves for another job. Javier's annual salary was $75,000, $85,000, $90,000, and $95,000 for years 4, 5, 6, and 7, respectively. DNL uses a five-year cliff vesting schedule.
    d) Javier works for DNL for six years and three months before he leaves for another job. Javier's annual salary was $75,000, $85,000, $90,000, and $95,000 for years 4, 5, 6, and 7, respectively. DNL uses a seven-year graded vesting schedule.
    e) Javier works for DNL for 32 years and three months before retiring. Javier's annual salary was $175,000, $185,000, $190,000, and $195,000 (note that he didn't work for the entire year in the year he retired so he received only a portion of the annual salary in the year he retired) for his final four years of employment.
51. Alicia has been working for JMM Corp. for 32 years. Alicia participates in JMM's defined benefit plan. Under the plan, for every year of service for JMM she is to receive 2 percent of the average salary of her three highest years of compensation from JMM. She retired on January 1, 2017. Before retirement, her annual salary was $570,000, $600,000, and $630,000 for 2014, 2015, and 2016. What is the maximum benefit Alicia can receive in 2017? LO 13-1
52. Kim has worked for one employer her entire career. While she was working, she participated in the employer's defined contribution plan [traditional 401(k)]. At the end of 2017, Kim retires. The balance in her defined contribution plan is $2,000,000 at the end of 2016. LO 13-2 tax forms
    a) What is Kim's minimum required distribution for 2017 in 2018 if she is 68 years old at the end of 2017?
    b) What is Kim's minimum required distribution for 2017 if she turns 70½ during 2017 and she has not turned 71 years old by the end of 2017? When must she receive this distribution?
    c) What is Kim's minimum required distribution for 2017 in 2018 if she is 73 years old at the end of 2017?
    d) Assuming that Kim is 75 years old at the end of 2017 and her marginal tax rate is 33 percent, what amount of her distribution will she have remaining after taxes if she receives only a distribution of $50,000 for 2017?
    e) Complete Form 5329, page 2, to report the minimum distribution penalty in part (d). Use the most recent form available.
53. Matthew (48 at year-end) develops cutting-edge technology for SV Inc., located in Silicon Valley. In 2017, Matthew participates in SV's money purchase pension plan LO 13-2

(a defined contribution plan) and in his company's 401(k) plan. Under the money purchase pension plan, SV contributes 15 percent of an employee's salary to a retirement account for the employee up to the amount limited by the tax code. Because it provides the money purchase pension plan, SV does not contribute to the employee's 401(k) plan. Matthew would like to maximize his contribution to his 401(k) account after SV's contribution to the money purchase plan.

a) Assuming Matthew's annual salary is $400,000, what amount will SV contribute to Matthew's money purchase plan? What can Matthew contribute to his 401(k) account in 2017?
b) Assuming Matthew's annual salary is $240,000, what amount will SV contribute to Matthew's money purchase plan? What can Matthew contribute to his 401(k) account in 2017?
c) Assuming Matthew's annual salary is $60,000, what amount will SV contribute to Matthew's money purchase plan? What amount can Matthew contribute to his 401(k) account in 2017?
d) Assume the same facts as part (c), except that Matthew is 54 years old at the end of 2017. What amount can Matthew contribute to his 401(k) account in 2017?

LO 13-2 planning

54. In 2017, Maggy (34 years old) is an employee of YBU Corp. YBU provides a 401(k) plan for all its employees. According to the terms of the plan, YBU contributes 50 cents for every dollar the employee contributes. The maximum employer contribution under the plan is 15 percent of the employee's salary (if allowed, YBU contributes until the employee has contributed 30 percent of her salary).

a) Maggy has worked for YBU corporation for 3½ years before deciding to leave. Maggy's annual salary during this time was $45,000, $52,000, $55,000, and $60,000 (she only received half of her final year's salary). Assuming Maggy contributed 8 percent of her salary (including her 2017 salary) to her 401(k) account, what is Maggy's vested account balance when she leaves YBU (exclusive of account earnings)? Assume YBU uses three-year cliff vesting.
b) Same question as part (a), except YBU uses six-year graded vesting.
c) Maggy wants to maximize YBU's contribution to her 401(k) account in 2017. How much should Maggy contribute to her 401(k) account assuming her annual salary is $100,000 (she works for YBU for the entire year)?
d) Same question as part (c), except Maggy is 55 years old rather than 34 years old at the end of the year.

LO 13-2

55. In 2017, Nina contributes 10 percent of her $100,000 annual salary to her 401(k) account. She expects to earn a 7 percent before-tax rate of return. Assuming she leaves this (and any employer contributions) in the account until she retires in 25 years, what is Nina's after-tax accumulation from her 2017 contributions to her 401(k) account?

a) Assume Nina's marginal tax rate at retirement is 30 percent.
b) Assume Nina's marginal tax rate at retirement is 20 percent.
c) Assume Nina's marginal tax rate at retirement is 40 percent.

LO 13-2

56. Kathleen, age 56, works for MH, Inc., in Dallas, Texas. Kathleen contributes to a Roth 401(k) and MH contributes to a traditional 401(k) on her behalf. Kathleen has contributed $30,000 to her Roth 401(k) over the past six years. The current balance in her Roth 401(k) account is $50,000 and the balance in her traditional 401(k) is $40,000. Kathleen needs cash because she is taking a month of vacation to travel the world. Answer the following questions relating to distributions from

Kathleen's retirement accounts assuming her marginal tax rate for ordinary income is 28 percent.

a) If Kathleen receives a $10,000 distribution from her traditional 401(k) account, how much will she be able to keep after paying taxes and penalties, if any, on the distribution?

b) If Kathleen receives a $10,000 distribution from her Roth 401(k) account, how much will she be able to keep after paying taxes and penalties, if any, on the distribution?

c) If Kathleen retires from MH and then she receives a $10,000 distribution from her traditional 401(k), how much will she be able to keep after paying taxes and penalties, if any, on the distribution?

d) If Kathleen retires from MH and then she receives a $10,000 distribution from her Roth 401(k), how much will she be able to keep after paying taxes and penalties, if any, on the distribution?

e) Assume the original facts except that Kathleen is 60 years of age, not 56. If Kathleen receives a $10,000 distribution from her Roth 401(k) (without retiring), how much will she be able to keep after paying taxes and penalties, if any, on the distribution?

57. In 2017, Nitai (age 40) contributes 10 percent of his $100,000 annual salary to a Roth 401(k) account sponsored by his employer, AY Inc. AY Inc. matches employee contributions to the employee's traditional 401(k) account dollar for dollar up to 10 percent of the employee's salary. Nitai expects to earn a 7 percent before-tax rate of return. Assume he leaves the contributions in the Roth 401(k) and traditional 401(k) accounts until he retires in 25 years and that he makes no additional contributions to either account. What are Nitai's after-tax proceeds from the Roth 401(k) and traditional 401(k) accounts after he receives the distributions, assuming his marginal tax rate at retirement is 30 percent? LO 13-2

58. Marissa participates in her employer's nonqualified deferred compensation plan. For 2017, she is deferring 10 percent of her $320,000 annual salary. Assuming this is her only source of income and her marginal income tax rate is 30 percent, how much *tax* does Marissa save in 2017 by deferring this income (ignore payroll taxes)? LO 13-3 planning

59. Paris participates in her employer's nonqualified deferred compensation plan. For 2017, she is deferring 10 percent of her $320,000 annual salary. Assuming this is her only source of income and her marginal income tax rate is 30 percent, how much does deferring Paris's income save her employer (after taxes) in 2017? The marginal tax rate of her employer is 35 percent (ignore payroll taxes). LO 13-3

60. Leslie participates in IBO's nonqualified deferred compensation plan. For 2017, she is deferring 10 percent of her $300,000 annual salary. Based on her deemed investment choice, Leslie expects to earn a 7 percent before-tax rate of return on her deferred compensation, which she plans to receive in 10 years. Leslie's marginal tax rate in 2017 is 30 percent. IBO's marginal tax rate is 35 percent (ignore payroll taxes in your analysis). LO 13-3 planning

a) Assuming Leslie's marginal tax rate in 10 years (when she receives the distribution) is 33 percent, what is Leslie's after-tax accumulation on the deferred compensation?

b) Assuming Leslie's marginal tax rate in 10 years (when she receives the distribution) is 20 percent, what is Leslie's after-tax accumulation on the deferred compensation?

c) Assuming IBO's cost of capital is 8 percent after taxes, how much deferred compensation should IBO be willing to pay Leslie that would make it indifferent between paying 10 percent of Leslie's current salary or deferring it for 10 years?

LO 13-3 planning

61. XYZ Corporation has a deferred compensation plan under which it allows certain employees to defer up to 40 percent of their salary for five years. For purposes of this problem, ignore payroll taxes in your computations.
   a) Assume XYZ has a marginal tax rate of 35 percent for the foreseeable future and earns an after-tax rate of return of 8 percent on its assets. Joel Johnson, XYZ's VP of finance, is attempting to determine what amount of deferred compensation XYZ should be willing to pay in five years that would make XYZ indifferent between paying the current salary of $10,000 and paying the deferred compensation. What amount of deferred compensation would accomplish this objective?
   b) Assume Julie, an XYZ employee, has the option of participating in XYZ's deferred compensation plan. Julie's marginal tax rate is 40 percent and she expects the rate to remain constant over the next five years. Julie is trying to decide how much deferred compensation she will need to receive from XYZ in five years to make her indifferent between receiving the current salary of $10,000 and receiving the deferred compensation payment. If Julie takes the salary, she will invest it in a taxable corporate bond paying interest at 5 percent annually (after taxes). What amount of deferred compensation would accomplish this objective?

LO 13-4

62. John (age 51 and single) has earned income of $3,000. He has $30,000 of unearned (capital gain) income.
   a) If he does not participate in an employer-sponsored plan, what is the maximum deductible IRA contribution John can make in 2017?
   b) If he does participate in an employer-sponsored plan, what is the maximum deductible IRA contribution John can make in 2017?
   c) If he does not participate in an employer-sponsored plan, what is the maximum deductible IRA contribution John can make in 2017 if he has earned income of $10,000?

LO 13-4

63. William is a single writer (age 35) who recently decided that he needs to save more for retirement. His 2017 AGI is $65,000 (all earned income).
   a) If he does not participate in an employer-sponsored plan, what is the maximum deductible IRA contribution William can make in 2017?
   b) If he does participate in an employer-sponsored plan, what is the maximum deductible IRA contribution William can make in 2017?
   c) Assuming the same facts as in part (b), except his AGI is $75,000, what is the maximum deductible IRA contribution William can make in 2017?

LO 13-4

64. In 2017, Susan (44 years old) is a highly successful architect and is covered by an employee-sponsored plan. Her husband, Dan (47 years old), however, is a Ph.D. student and unemployed. Compute the maximum deductible IRA contribution for each spouse in the following alternative situations.
   a) Susan's salary and the couple's AGI is $190,000. The couple files a joint tax return.
   b) Susan's salary and the couple's AGI is $120,000. The couple files a joint tax return.
   c) Susan's salary and the couple's AGI is $80,000. The couple files a joint tax return.
   d) Susan's salary and her AGI is $80,000. Dan reports $5,000 of AGI (earned income). The couple files separate tax returns.

LO 13-4 tax forms

65. In 2017, Rashaun (62 years old) retired and planned on immediately receiving distributions (making withdrawals) from his traditional IRA account. The balance of his IRA account is $160,000 (before reducing it for withdrawals/distributions described below). Over the years, Rashaun has contributed $40,000 to the IRA.

Of his $40,000 contributions, $30,000 was *nondeductible* and $10,000 was *deductible*. Assume Rashaun did not make any contributions to the account during 2017.

a) If Rashaun currently withdraws $20,000 from the IRA, how much tax will he be required to pay on the withdrawal if his marginal tax rate is 25 percent?

b) If Rashaun currently withdraws $70,000 from the IRA, how much tax will he be required to pay on the withdrawal if his marginal tax rate is 28 percent?

c) Using the information provided in part (b), complete Form 8606, Part I, to report the taxable portion of the $70,000 distribution (withdrawal). Use the most current form available.

66. Brooklyn has been contributing to a traditional IRA for seven years (all deductible contributions) and has a total of $30,000 in the account. In 2017, she is 39 years old and has decided that she wants to get a new car. She withdraws $20,000 from the IRA to help pay for the car. She is currently in the 25 percent marginal tax bracket. What amount of the withdrawal, after tax considerations, will Brooklyn have available to purchase the car? LO 13-4

67. Jackson and Ashley Turner (both 45 years old) are married and want to contribute to a Roth IRA for Ashley. In 2017, their AGI is $188,000. Jackson and Ashley each earned half of the income. LO 13-4

a) How much can Ashley contribute to her Roth IRA if they file a joint return?

b) How much can Ashley contribute if she files a separate return?

c) Assume that Ashley earned all of the couple's income and that she contributed the maximum amount she is allowed to contribute to a Roth IRA. What amount can be contributed to Jackson's Roth IRA?

68. Harriet and Harry Combs (both 37 years old) are married and both want to contribute to a Roth IRA. In 2017, their AGI is $50,000. Harriet earned $46,000 and Harry earned $4,000. LO 13-4

a) How much can Harriet contribute to her Roth IRA if they file a joint return?

b) How much can Harriet contribute if she files a separate return?

c) How much can Harry contribute to his Roth IRA if they file separately?

69. Michael is single and 35 years old. He is a participant in his employer's sponsored retirement plan. How much can Michael contribute to a Roth IRA in each of the following alternative situations? LO 13-4

a) Michael's AGI is $50,000 after he contributes $3,000 to a traditional IRA.

b) Michael's AGI is $80,000 before any IRA contributions.

c) Michael's AGI is $135,000 before any IRA contributions.

70. George (age 42 at year-end) has been contributing to a traditional IRA for years (all deductible contributions) and his IRA is now worth $25,000. He is planning on transferring (or rolling over) the entire balance into a Roth IRA account. George's marginal tax rate is 25 percent. LO 13-4

a) What are the tax consequences to George if he takes $25,000 out of the traditional IRA and puts the entire amount into a Roth IRA?

b) What are the tax consequences to George if he takes $25,000 out of the traditional IRA, pays the taxes due from the IRA distribution, and contributes the remaining distribution to the Roth IRA?

c) What are the tax consequences to George if he takes $25,000 out of the traditional IRA, keeps $10,000 to pay taxes and to make a down payment on a new car, and contributes the remaining distribution to the Roth IRA?

71. Jimmer has contributed $15,000 to his Roth IRA and the balance in the account is $18,000. In the current year, Jimmer withdrew $17,000 from the Roth IRA to pay for a new car. If Jimmer's marginal ordinary income tax rate is 25 percent, what LO 13-4

amount of tax and penalty, if any, is Jimmer required to pay on the withdrawal in each of the following alternative situations?

a) Jimmer opened the Roth account 44 months before he withdrew the $17,000 and Jimmer is 62 years of age.

b) Jimmer opened the Roth account 44 months before he withdrew the $17,000 and Jimmer is age 53.

c) Jimmer opened the Roth account 76 months before he withdrew the $17,000 and Jimmer is age 62.

d) Jimmer opened the Roth account 76 months before he withdrew the $17,000 and Jimmer is age 53.

LO 13-4 planning

72. John is trying to decide whether to contribute to a Roth IRA or a traditional IRA. He plans on making a $5,000 contribution to whichever plan he decides to fund. He currently pays tax at a 30 percent marginal income tax rate but he believes that his marginal tax rate in the future will be 28 percent. He intends to leave the money in the Roth IRA or traditional IRA accounts for 30 years and he expects to earn a 6 percent before-tax rate of return on the account.

a) How much will John accumulate after taxes if he contributes to a Roth IRA (consider only the funds contributed to the Roth IRA)?

b) How much will John accumulate after taxes if he contributes to a traditional IRA (consider only the funds contributed to the Roth IRA)?

c) Without doing any computations, explain whether the traditional IRA or the Roth IRA will generate a greater after-tax rate of return.

LO 13-4

73. Sherry, who is 52 years of age, opened a Roth IRA three years ago. She has contributed a total of $12,000 to the Roth IRA ($4,000 a year). The current value of the Roth IRA is $16,300. In the current year, Sherry withdraws $14,000 of the account balance to purchase a car. Assuming Sherry is in a 25 percent marginal tax bracket, how much of the $14,000 withdrawal will she retain after taxes to fund her car purchase?

LO 13-4

74. Seven years ago, Halle (currently age 41) contributed $4,000 to a Roth IRA account. The current value of the Roth IRA is $9,000. In the current year Halle withdraws $8,000 of the account balance to use as a down payment on her first home. Assuming Halle is in a 25 percent marginal tax bracket, how much of the $8,000 withdrawal will she retain after taxes to fund her house down payment?

LO 13-4 research planning

75. Yuki (age 45 at year-end) has been contributing to a traditional IRA for years (all deductible contributions), and her IRA is now worth $50,000. She is trying to decide whether she should roll over her traditional IRA into a Roth IRA. Her current marginal tax rate is 25 percent. She plans to withdraw the entire balance of the account in 20 years and she expects to earn a before-tax rate of return of 5 percent on her retirement accounts and a 4 percent after-tax rate of return on all investments outside of her retirement accounts. For each of the following alternative scenarios, indicate how much more or less Yuki will accumulate after taxes in 20 years if she rolls over her traditional IRA into a Roth IRA. Be sure to include the opportunity cost of having to pay taxes on the rollover.

a) When she withdraws the retirement funds in 20 years, she expects her marginal tax rate to be 35 percent.

b) When she withdraws the retirement funds in 20 years, she expects her marginal tax rate to be 20 percent.

c) Assume the same facts as in part (b), except that she earns a 3 percent after-tax rate of return on investments outside of the retirement accounts.

d) In general terms, reconcile your answer from part (b) with your answer to part (c) (no numbers required).

76. Sarah was contemplating making a contribution to her traditional individual retirement account for 2017. She determined that she would contribute $5,500 to her IRA and she deducted $5,500 for the contribution when she completed and filed her 2017 tax return on February 15, 2018. Two months later, on April 15, Sarah realized that she had not yet actually contributed the funds to her IRA. On April 15, she went to the post office and mailed a $5,500 (for all) check to the bank holding her IRA. The bank received the payment on April 18. In which year is Sarah's $5,500 contribution deductible? LO 13-4 research

77. Elvira is a self-employed taxpayer who turns 42 years old at the end of the year (2017). In 2017, her net Schedule C income was $130,000. This was her only source of income. This year, Elvira is considering setting up a retirement plan. What is the maximum amount Elvira may contribute to the self-employed plan in each of the following situations? LO 13-5 planning
    a) She sets up a SEP IRA.
    b) She sets up an individual 401(k).

78. Hope is a self-employed taxpayer who turns 54 years old at the end of the year (2017). In 2017, her net Schedule C income was $130,000. This was her only source of income. This year, Hope is considering setting up a retirement plan. What is the maximum amount Hope may contribute to the self-employed plan in each of the following situations? LO 13-5 planning
    a) She sets up a SEP IRA.
    b) She sets up an individual 401(k).

79. Rita is a self-employed taxpayer who turns 39 years old at the end of the year (2017). In 2017, her net Schedule C income was $300,000. This was her only source of income. This year, Rita is considering setting up a retirement plan. What is the maximum amount Rita may contribute to the self-employed plan in each of the following situations? LO 13-5
    a) She sets up a SEP IRA.
    b) She sets up an individual 401(k).

80. Reggie is a self-employed taxpayer who turns 59 years old at the end of the year (2017). In 2017, his net Schedule C income was $300,000. This was his only source of income. This year, Reggie is considering setting up a retirement plan. What is the maximum amount he may contribute to the self-employed plan in each of the following situations? LO 13-5
    a) He sets up a SEP IRA.
    b) He sets up an individual 401(k).

81. Desmond is 25 years old and he participates in his employer's 401(k) plan. During the year, he contributed $3,000 to his 401(k) account. What is Desmond's saver's credit in each of the following alternative scenarios? LO 13-6
    a) Desmond is not married and has no dependents. His AGI after deducting his 401(k) contribution is $34,000.
    b) Desmond is not married and has no dependents. His AGI after deducting his 401(k) contribution is $17,500.
    c) Desmond files as a head of household and has an AGI of $44,000.
    d) Desmond and his wife file jointly and report an AGI of $30,000 for the year.

82. Penny is 57 years old and she participates in her employer's 401(k) plan. During the year, she contributed $2,000 to her 401(k) account. Penny's AGI is $29,000 after deducting her 401(k) contribution. What is Penny's saver's credit in each of the following alternative scenarios? LO 13-6
    a) Penny is not married and has no dependents.
    b) Penny files as a head of household and she has three dependents.

c) Penny files as a head of household and she has one dependent.

d) Penny is married and files a joint return with her husband. They have three dependents.

e) Penny files a separate tax return from her husband. She claims two dependent children on her return.

COMPREHENSIVE PROBLEMS

Select problems are available in Connect®. connect

83. Jacquiline is unmarried and age 32. Even though she participates in an employer-sponsored retirement plan, Jacquiline contributed $3,000 to a traditional IRA during the year. Jacquiline files as a head of household, her AGI before the contribution is $43,000, and her marginal tax rate is 15 percent. What is the after-tax cost of her $3,000 traditional IRA contribution?

84. Ian retired in June 2016 at the age of 69 (he turned 70 in August 2016). Ian's retirement account was valued at $490,000 at the end of 2015 and $500,000 at the end of 2016. He has had all of his retirement accounts open for 15 years. What is Ian's required minimum distribution for 2017 under each of the following alternative scenarios?
   a) Ian's retirement account is a traditional 401(k) account.
   b) Ian's retirement account is a Roth 401(k) account.
   c) Ian's retirement account is a traditional IRA.
   d) Ian's retirement account is a Roth IRA.

85. Alex is 31 years old and has lived in Los Alamos, New Mexico, for the last four years where he works at the Los Alamos National Laboratory (LANL). LANL provides employees with a 401(k) plan and for every $1 an employee contributes (up to 9 percent of the employee's salary) LANL contributes $3 (a 3-to-1 match). The plan provides a six-year graded vesting schedule. Alex is now in his fifth year working for LANL, and his current year salary is $150,000. Alex's marginal tax rate is 28 percent in 2017. Answer the following questions relating to Alex's retirement savings in 2017.
   a) Assume that over the past four years, Alex has contributed $45,000 to his 401(k) and his employer has contributed $115,000 to the plan. The plan has an account balance of $175,000. What is Alex's vested account balance in his 401(k)?
   b) Because Alex considers his employer's matching contributions "free money," he wants to maximize the amount of LANL's contributions. What is the least amount Alex can contribute and still maximize LANL's contribution?
   c) In need of cash to build a home theater, Alex withdrew $30,000 from his traditional 401(k) account. What amount of the withdrawal, after taxes and penalties, will Alex have available to complete his project?
   d) Assume that Alex contributes $10,000 to his traditional 401(k) account this year. Also assume that in 30 years, Alex retires (at age 61) and withdraws the $10,000 contribution made this year *and* all the earnings generated by the contribution. Also assume that his marginal tax rate at the time he retires is 25 percent. Ignore any prior or subsequent contributions to his plan. If Alex earns a 6 percent annual before-tax rate of return, what are his after-tax proceeds from the distribution?
   e) Assume that Alex is 74 years old at the end of the year, retired, and that his marginal tax rate is 25 percent. His account balance in his traditional 401(k) was $1,250,000 at the end of last year. What is the minimum distribution Alex

must receive from his 401(k) account for this year? If Alex receives a $43,000 distribution from his 401(k) account (his only distribution during the year), what amount will he be able to keep after taxes and penalties (if any)?

86. Tommy (age 47) and his wife, Michelle (age 49), live in Columbus, Ohio, where Tommy works for Callahan Auto Parts (CAP) as the vice president of the brakes division. Tommy's 2017 salary is $360,000. CAP allows Tommy to participate in its nonqualified deferred compensation plan in which participants can defer 15 percent of their salary for five years. Tommy also participates in CAP's qualified 401(k) plan. Tommy's current marginal tax rate is 28 percent and CAP's current marginal tax rate is 34 percent.
    a) Assuming Tommy earns a 6 percent *after-tax* rate of return and he expects his marginal tax rate to be 30 percent in five years, what before-tax deferred compensation payment in five years would make him indifferent between receiving the deferred compensation payment or 15 percent of his salary now (ignore payroll taxes)?
    b) Assuming CAP has an 8 percent *after-tax* rate of return and expects its marginal tax rate to be 35 percent in five years, how much would it be willing to pay in five years to be indifferent between paying the deferred compensation or paying 15 percent of Tommy's salary now (ignore payroll taxes)?
    c) Will Tommy and CAP be able to come to an agreement on deferring Tommy's salary?
    d) Assume that Tommy and Michelle have an AGI of $100,000 before IRA deductions by either spouse. The AGI includes $10,000 that Michelle earned working part-time (but she does not participate in an employer-sponsored retirement plan). Tommy and Michelle file a joint return. What is the maximum deductible contribution Tommy and Michelle may make to a traditional IRA?
    e) Tommy has a balance of $55,000 in his traditional IRA. Due to some recent tax cuts, his marginal tax rate is 20 percent, so he would like to roll his traditional IRA into a Roth IRA. What are the tax consequences to Tommy if he takes $55,000 out of the IRA, pays the taxes due from the traditional IRA distribution, and contributes the remaining distribution to the Roth IRA?

87. Gerry (age 56) and Elaine (age 54) have been married for 12 years and file a joint tax return. The couple lives in an apartment in downtown Manhattan. Gerry's father, Mortey, recently retired from Del Boca Vista Corporation (DBVC), where he worked for many years. Mortey participated in DBVC's defined benefit plan. Elaine is an editor and works for Pendent Publishing earning an annual $150,000 salary in 2017. Gerry is a self-employed stand-up comedian and had net business income of $46,000 in 2017. At the advice of their neighbor, Gerry and Elaine have come to you to for help in answering several retirement savings-related questions.
    a) The DBVC defined benefit plan specifies a benefit of 1.5 percent for each year of service, up to a maximum of 30 percent (20 years of service), of the average of the employee's three highest years of salary. Mortey worked for the company for 25 years and earned $75,000, $78,000, and $84,000 over his final three years of service. What is Mortey's annual benefit from DBVC's defined benefit plan?
    b) Elaine has worked at Pendent Publishing since January 1, 2012. The company offers a defined contribution plan. It matches 100 percent of employee contributions to the plan up to 6 percent of her salary. Prior to 2017, Elaine had contributed $40,000 to the plan and her employer had contributed $28,000 to the plan. In 2017, Elaine contributed $17,000 to her traditional 401(k). What is the amount of her employer's matching contribution for 2017? Assuming the company uses a six-year graded vesting schedule, what is Elaine's vested balance in the plan at the end of 2017 (for simplicity, disregard the plan's earnings)?

c) Elaine tells you that her employer has offered her $30,000 in 10 years to defer 10 percent of her current salary (defer $15,000). Assuming that the couple's marginal tax rate is currently 30 percent, they earn an after-tax rate of return of 8 percent, and they expect their marginal tax rate to be 25 percent in 10 years, should Elaine accept her company's offer? What is the minimum amount she should be willing to accept (ignoring nontax factors and payroll taxes)?

d) Gerry has a SEP IRA and would like to contribute as much as possible to this account. What is the maximum contribution Gerry can make to his SEP IRA in 2017?

e) Assuming Gerry had an individual 401(k), what is the maximum amount he could contribute to the plan in 2017?

f) Gerry also has a traditional IRA with an account balance of $42,000. He would like to convert the traditional IRA to a Roth IRA. Gerry would like to pay the least amount of tax possible in rolling the account over. What is the least amount of tax Gerry will be required to pay on the rollover?

g) Assume that Gerry rolled over his traditional IRA into a Roth IRA six years ago (rather than in 2017) and that the account now has a balance of $78,000. The couple is considering buying their first home and would like to pay as much down as possible. They have heard from their friends that they can take the funds from their Roth IRA and use it to buy their first home. Are their friends correct? What would you advise them to do?

h) Assume that Gerry and Elaine made total contributions of $20,000 to their qualified retirement accounts in 2017. Also assume that their AGI is $38,000. What would be the amount of their saver's credit for 2017?

ROGER | *CPA Review*

Sample CPA Exam questions from Roger CPA Review are available in Connect as support for the topics in this text. These Multiple Choice Questions and Task-Based Simulations include expert-written explanations and solutions, and provide a starting point for students to become familiar with the content and functionality of the actual CPA Exam.

chapter 23 State and Local Taxes

Learning Objectives

Upon completing this chapter, you should be able to:

LO 23-1 Describe the primary types of state and local taxes.

LO 23-2 Determine whether a business has sales and use tax nexus and calculate its sales tax withholding responsibilities.

LO 23-3 Identify whether a business has income tax nexus and determine its state income tax liabilities.

© Jupiterimages/Stockbyte/Getty Images

Storyline Summary

Ken Brody

Location: Idaho

Status: Sole owner of Wild West River Runners

Situation: Ken owns retail stores in Idaho and Wyoming that sell merchandise locally; a Wyoming-based Internet store; and provides services in Idaho, Tennessee, Washington, and Wyoming. He must determine the company's state and local tax liabilities.

Ken Brody owns Wild West River Runners Incorporated (Wild West), an Idaho corporation. Wild West offers both guided white-water rafting adventures and retail sales of related equipment. It provides white-water rafting adventures in Idaho, Tennessee, Washington, and Wyoming; operates retail stores in Idaho and Wyoming; and runs an Internet-based retail store from Wyoming. Wild West's retail stores sell only locally (they never ship merchandise), but the salesclerks often refer customers to the Internet store (www.wildwestriverrunners.com). Most employees are seasonal (i.e., teachers or college students). During the off-season, a few guides make sales visits with Ken and operate the retail stores. Also during the off-season, Ken attends the annual Raft and River show for 10 days each year in Phoenix, Arizona, and travels the country promoting Wild West's guided river adventures.

Wild West's federal taxable income for the current year is $53,289, and it must determine its state and local tax liabilities. Because Wild West operates a multistate business, it must determine its sales and use tax withholding responsibilities and identify the states in which it must file returns. Once it makes these determinations, it must also compute taxable income for each relevant state. ■

Like a lot of other businesses, Wild West is a multistate operation. From a business perspective, multistate businesses have access to a larger economic base than those operating in a single state. However, with this economic opportunity comes complexity and additional tax burdens.

LO 23-1

STATE AND LOCAL TAXES

The primary purpose of state and local taxes is to raise revenue to finance state governments. All 50 states and the District of Columbia have some combination of three primary revenue sources: sales and use tax, income or franchise tax, and property tax.[1]

This chapter focuses on sales and use taxes (excise taxes levied on the sale or use of tangible personal property within a state) and taxes based on *net* income (income taxes).[2]

Like federal tax law, state tax law includes the following:

- Legislative law (state constitution and tax code).
- Administrative law (regulations and rulings).
- Judicial law (state and federal tax cases).

While taxpayers deal with a single federal tax code, there are different tax codes for each state in which they are required to pay taxes. This makes state tax research particularly challenging. State tax agencies (such as the California Franchise Tax Board and New York Department of Finance and Taxation) administer the law and promulgate regulations for their particular states.[3] State and federal courts interpret the law when a state's tax authority and taxpayers cannot agree on its interpretation or constitutionality. Because of constitutionality questions, judicial law plays a significantly more important role in state tax law than in federal tax law.

It is impractical, if not impossible, to study each individual state statute in one text. Instead, this chapter addresses the most important state and local tax principles at a conceptual level.

The most important question Wild West, or any other taxpayer, must answer is whether it is subject to a state's taxing regime. The answer depends on the taxpayer's state of commercial domicile and whether the taxpayer has nexus in that state. **Commercial domicile** is the state where a business is headquartered and directs its operations; this location may be different from the place of incorporation.[4] A business must always collect sales tax and pay income tax in the state where it is domiciled. **Nondomiciliary businesses** (businesses not domiciled or headquartered in a state) are subject to tax only where they have nexus. **Nexus** is the sufficient (or minimum) connection between a business and a state that subjects the business to the state's tax system. The requirement for establishing nexus with a state depends on whether the tax is a sales and use tax, an income tax, or a nonincome-based tax. The nexus standard varies because the financial and administrative burdens vary across taxes. Sellers collect sales tax out of administrative convenience, but the sales tax burden belongs to the buyer in most states. In contrast, income tax is both owed and paid by the taxpayer earning the income.

[1]State and local jurisdictions may also tax or levy the following: personal property, capital stock, business licensing, transfer taxes, incorporation, excise, severance, payroll, disability, unemployment, fuel, and telecommunication.

[2]This chapter discusses income and franchise taxes interchangeably. Franchise taxes are imposed for the right to conduct business within a state. Most franchise taxes (such as the California Franchise Tax) are net income based.

[3]A great resource for guidance and forms from specific states can be found on the Federation of Tax Administrator's website, http://www.taxadmin.org/state-tax-forms.

[4]Some companies (e.g., Hewlett-Packard) are incorporated in one state (e.g., Delaware) but domiciled or headquartered in another (e.g., California). These companies pay taxes in both states (although sometimes just a capital stock tax applies in the state of incorporation if there are no activities other than incorporation within a state).

Wild West's commercial domicile is Idaho because it is headquartered there, and it must collect and remit Idaho sales tax and pay Idaho income tax. Yet, as detailed in Exhibit 23-1, it has activities and sales in other states, and therefore must collect sales and use tax and pay income tax in the states in which it has nexus.

EXHIBIT 23-1 Wild West's Activities and Sales by State

Wild West In-State Activities

State	Sale of Goods	Sale of Services	Employees	Property	Commercial Domicile
Arizona	✓				
California	✓				
Colorado	✓				
Idaho	✓	✓	✓	✓	✓
Tennessee	✓	✓	✓	✓	
Washington	✓	✓	✓	✓	
Wyoming	✓	✓	✓	✓	

Wild West Sales

State	Goods	Services	Total
Arizona	$ 89,242	$ 0	$ 89,242
California	132,045	0	132,045
Colorado	75,002	0	75,002
Idaho	167,921	625,003	792,924
Tennessee	45,331	357,061	402,392
Washington	41,982	377,441	419,423
Wyoming	185,249	437,755	623,004
Totals	$736,772	$1,797,260	$2,534,032

When a business sells tangible personal property, which is included in a state's sales tax base, in a state, it must collect and remit the **sales tax** on a periodic basis if it has nexus in that state.[5] Exhibit 23-2 provides an overview of who bears the burden (who

EXHIBIT 23-2 State Sales and Use Tax Process

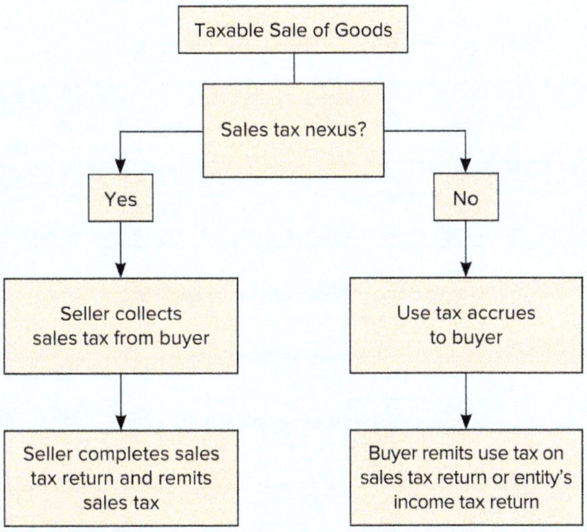

[5]Businesses remit their sales and use tax liability on a monthly, quarterly, or annual basis depending on the size of the liability and the state law thresholds.

must pay and who must collect and remit the tax) of sales and use taxes. Sales tax liability accrues on certain sales of tangible personal property within the state. For example, Wild West's Idaho retail store collects sales tax on goods sold in Idaho stores and remits the tax to the Idaho Department of Revenue. **Use tax** liability accrues in the state where purchased property will be used when no sales tax was paid. The use tax only occurs when a seller in one state ships goods to a customer in a different state and the seller is not required to collect the sales tax (the seller does not have sales and use tax nexus in the state to which the goods are shipped). For example, Colorado customers ordering through Wild West's Wyoming Internet store (which has no Colorado sales tax nexus) are required to accrue and remit the Colorado use tax (usually through their personal income tax returns).[6] Businesses with sales and use tax nexus in a state are responsible for remitting the sales tax even when they fail to collect it.

Businesses engaged in **interstate commerce** must also deal with income-tax related issues. If a business meets certain requirements creating income tax nexus, it may be required to remit income tax to that state. The general process of determining a business's state income tax liability is highlighted in Exhibit 23-3. We compute the **state tax base** by making adjustments to federal taxable income. The adjustments are necessary to account for differences between federal income tax laws and state income tax laws. Then we divide the state tax base into **business income** and **nonbusiness income.** Business income (income from business activities) is subject to **apportionment** among states where nexus exists, based on the extent of the business's activities and property in various states. Nonbusiness income (all income except business income—generally investment income) is subject to **allocation** (assignment) directly to the business's state of commercial domicile. For states in which the business has nexus, state taxable income is the sum of the business income apportioned to that state plus the nonbusiness income allocated to that state. The business computes its state tax liability for that particular state by multiplying state taxable income by the state's tax rate.

Let's now look in more depth at sales and use tax and net income-based taxes, the nexus requirements, and the calculation of each tax.

EXHIBIT 23-3 State Income Tax Process

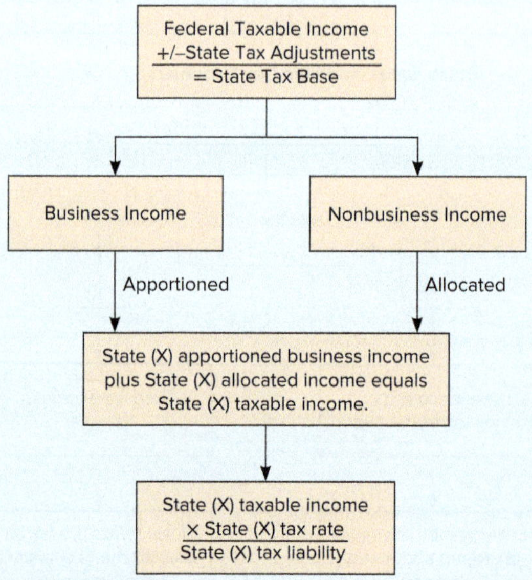

[6]Use tax is paid by individuals completing the use tax liability line on their individual tax return. Alternatively, business entities collecting and remitting sales tax include the use tax on their sales tax return.

SALES AND USE TAXES

LO 23-2

Forty-five states and the District of Columbia impose sales and use taxes; Alaska, Delaware, Montana, New Hampshire, and Oregon do not. Sales tax must be collected on the state's sales tax base. Generally, sales of tangible personal property are subject to the tax. Most states also tax restaurant meals, rental car usage, hotel room rentals (often at higher tax rates than general sales), and some services (which vary by state). Purchases of inventory for resale are exempt from the sales tax. For example, Wild West's rafting equipment purchases for resale are exempt from sales tax because inventory is taxed when sold, but its office furniture purchases for use in the business are taxable because they represent final sales. Taxable items that are included in the sales tax base vary from state to state. Many states exempt food (except prepared restaurant food) because taxing food is considered to be regressive; that is, it imposes a proportionally higher tax burden on lower-income taxpayers that spend a greater proportion of their income on food and other necessities. Most states also exempt sales of real property, intangible property, and services. However, many states are expanding the types of services subject to sales tax in order to increase their sales tax revenue.[7]

THE KEY FACTS

Sales Tax Nexus

- Nexus is the sufficient connection between a business and a state that allows a state to levy a tax on the business.
- Sales tax nexus is established through physical presence of salespeople or property within a state.

TAXES IN THE REAL WORLD Is It Candy or Is It Food?

Items subject to the sales and use tax vary from state to state. Historically, New York taxed the sale of large marshmallows but exempted the sale of small marshmallows. Large and small marshmallows were treated differently because large marshmallows were considered to be candy, which was included in the sales tax base, while small marshmallows were considered to be a food ingredient and therefore excluded from the sales tax base.

The Washington state legislature passed a law subjecting candy to sales taxes a few years ago. Any item containing flour was considered a food item, not candy. As a result, Twix bars were exempt while Starburst candy was subject to sales tax. Within a year, Washington voters repealed the tax on candy through a ballot initiative.

Sales and Use Tax Nexus

Have you ever wondered why sometimes you pay tax on goods purchased over the Internet and sometimes you don't? The answer is nexus. A business is required to collect sales tax from customers in a state only if it has sales and use tax nexus with that state. For example, if you purchased this textbook from your local campus bookstore you paid tax (unless your state exempts educational materials), but if you purchased the book from Amazon.com you didn't pay sales tax (unless you live in Washington or another state where Amazon has nexus).[8] Exhibit 23-4 explains Amazon's position on sales tax collection and indicates that it could have a substantial sales tax liability if a state successfully asserts that its position is wrong.

Businesses that establish sales and use tax nexus with a state but fail to properly collect sales tax can create significant liabilities that may need to be disclosed for financial reporting purposes.[9] As a result, understanding when a business has nexus can be extremely important for profitability, business modeling, and compliance.

[7]For example, Connecticut taxes services such as tax preparation.

[8]Items sold by Amazon.com LLC or its subsidiaries and shipped to destinations in the following states are subject to sales tax withholding: Alabama, Arizona, California, Colorado, Connecticut, District of Columbia, Florida, Georgia, Illinois, Indiana, Kansas, Kentucky, Maryland, Massachusetts, Michigan, Minnesota, New Jersey, New York, Nevada, North Dakota, North Carolina, Ohio, Pennsylvania, South Carolina, Tennessee, Texas, Virginia, Washington, West Virginia, and Wisconsin. https://www.amazon.com/gp/help/customer/display.html?nodeId=468512, accessed December 8, 2016.

[9]Sales tax liabilities are ASC 450 contingencies. Amazon indicated a $407 million potential liability associated with sales taxes.

EXHIBIT 23-4 Excerpt from Amazon's 2015 Annual Report

From the Form 10-K

We Could Be Subject to Additional Sales Tax or Other Indirect Tax Liabilities

U.S. Supreme Court decisions restrict the imposition of obligations to collect state and local sales taxes with respect to remote sales in the U.S. However, an increasing number of states, and certain foreign jurisdictions, have considered or adopted laws or administrative practices that attempt to impose obligations on remote sellers and online marketplaces to collect taxes on their behalf. We support a Federal law that would allow states to require sales tax collection by remote sellers under a nationwide system. More than half of our revenue is already earned in jurisdictions where we collect sales tax or its equivalent.

A successful assertion by one or more states or foreign countries requiring us to collect taxes where we do not do so could result in substantial tax liabilities, including for past sales, as well as penalties and interest. In addition, if the tax authorities in jurisdictions where we already collect sales tax or other indirect taxes were successfully to challenge our positions, our tax liability could increase substantially.

Businesses create sales tax nexus (the sufficient connection with a state that requires them to collect sales tax) when they have a *physical presence* in the state. Businesses have a physical presence in the state if (1) salespeople (or independent contractors representing a business) enter a state to obtain sales or if (2) tangible property (such as a company-owned truck making deliveries) is located within a state.[10] One important planning strategy is that, because nexus is determined on a legal entity basis, nexus can be limited by creating a separate legal entity.

The physical presence requirement is a judicial interpretation of the Commerce Clause of the U.S. Constitution. Designed to encourage interstate commerce, this clause gives Congress power "To regulate Commerce with foreign Nations, and among the several States, and with the Indian Tribes." Because Congress has never exercised its right, the courts have determined the sales tax nexus threshold. In *National Bellas Hess,* the U.S. Supreme Court held that an out-of-state mail-order company did not have a sales tax collection responsibility because it lacked physical presence (even though it mailed catalogs and advertised in the state).[11] The mail-order industry used this decision as a competitive advantage for several decades. In *Quill,* the U.S. Supreme Court reaffirmed that out-of-state (nondomiciliary) businesses must have a physical presence in the state before the state may require a business to collect sales tax from in-state customers.[12]

Example 23-1

Wild West sends promotional brochures from Idaho to its Colorado clients. Wild West generated sales of $75,002 to Colorado customers, but it has never collected Colorado sales and use tax or filed a Colorado sales and use tax return. Wild West has neither employees nor property in Colorado. Does it have sales and use tax nexus in Colorado?

Answer: No. Wild West lacks the physical presence required for Colorado nexus and therefore doesn't have Colorado sales and use tax collection responsibility.

What if: Assume that in addition to mailing promotional brochures, Ken visits Colorado on promotional trips. Does Wild West have sales and use tax nexus in Colorado under these circumstances?

Answer: Yes. The physical presence of Wild West's representatives, even for promotional trips, creates Colorado sales and use tax nexus.

[10] *Scripto, Inc. v. Carson, Sherriff, et al.*, 362 U.S. 207 (1960). Scripto hired independent salesmen to represent the company in Florida. The Supreme Court held that these salesmen were agents of Scripto, who established the physical presence necessary to create nexus.

[11] *National Bellas Hess, Inc. v. Department of Revenue of the State of Illinois,* 386 U.S. 753 (1967).

[12] *Quill Corporation, Petitioner v. North Dakota,* 504 U.S. 298 (1992).

What if: Assume Wild West's representatives (independent contractors), rather than employees, visit Colorado retail stores to solicit additional sales orders. Does Wild West have sales and use tax nexus in Colorado under these circumstances?

Answer: Yes. The physical presence of Wild West's representatives creates Colorado sales and use tax nexus. Thus, the result is the same for employees or independent contractors.

TAXES IN THE REAL WORLD E-Commerce Sales and Use Tax

Businesses selling products over the Internet have been able to avoid collecting sales and use tax because sales tax nexus is created through physical presence in the state of the buyer. In fact, Internet sales represent billions of dollars annually. As a result, the physical presence nexus standard has cost states substantial sales tax revenue. In 2008, New York implemented the so-called "Amazon rule" that requires Internet-based retailers to collect and remit New York sales tax if they have in-state affiliates referring customers to websites; the rule is estimated to increase state revenues by $50 million per year. As you might expect, because this law—often referred to as *click-through nexus*—is potentially inconsistent with the U.S. Supreme Court's decision in *Quill*, Amazon has filed suit against the state of New York but the New York Court of Appeals ruled against Amazon and the U.S. Supreme Court refused to hear the case. Approximately 20 states have now implemented similar laws.

In 2010, Colorado took a different strategy by requiring out-of-state retailers to provide the names, addresses, and taxable purchases of Colorado residents rather than requiring the retailer to collect the sales and use tax. In 2012, this law was determined to be unconstitutional.

Congress is also currently considering three bills that would change the sales and use tax nexus requirements: the Main Street Fairness Act (H.R. 506), the Marketplace Equity Act (H.R. 3179), and the Marketplace Fairness Act (S. 698).

Notwithstanding *Quill* (discussed earlier), it appears that large retailers are losing ground in the nexus fight. Amazon agreed to start collecting sales tax in California in 2013, and voluntarily agreed to start collecting in Utah beginning 2017. While Amazon originally led the fight against sales and use tax nexus, it has changed its position by announcing it would support a federal law implementing a nationwide system. One question is whether Amazon has changed its policy because it believes the legal position to be unsupportable, because it is changing its business model and no longer seeks the competitive advantage of not collecting sales and use taxes, or whether it wishes to prevent others from entering its markets now that it has established itself as the market leader in online sales. Only time will tell how this story will end.

Sales and Use Tax Liability

Typically, sellers with nexus collect customers' sales tax liabilities. For example, Wild West collects sales tax on river rafting equipment it sells from its retail store but not on river guiding *services* it provides. If the seller doesn't have nexus, then the customer is responsible for remitting a use tax (at the same tax rate as sales tax) to the state in which the property is used. If the buyer is charged a sales tax in another state, the buyer will have a use tax liability for an incremental amount if the state where the property is used has a higher sales tax rate.

Example 23-2

Wild West received $3,500 from a customer named Casey Jarvie residing in Sacramento, California. Of this amount, $500 was for personal rafting equipment shipped to Sacramento, where the sales tax rate is 7.75 percent. The remaining $3,000 was payment for a four-day river raft adventure on the Salmon River in Idaho. Wild West has neither salespeople nor property in California. Does Wild West have a responsibility to collect sales tax from Casey?

Answer: No. Wild West lacks physical presence and does not have sales and use tax nexus in California; therefore, it has no California sales tax collection requirement.

(continued on page 23-8)

Because Wild West has no sales tax collection responsibility, does Casey have a use tax liability to the state of California? If so, in what amount?

Answer: Yes. Casey is responsible for remitting $38.75 of use tax ($500 × 7.75%) on his personal California state income tax return for the purchase and use of the personal rafting equipment in California. He is not required to pay California use tax on the river raft adventure purchase because Wild West provided out-of-state *services* (no sales tax is due on the services in Idaho either).

What if: If Casey had Wild West hold the goods until he arrived in Burley, Idaho, to pick them up at the time of the trip (assume the sales tax rate in Burley, Idaho, is 6 percent), would Wild West have sales tax collection responsibility? If so, what is the sales tax amount?

Answer: Yes. Because Wild West has physical presence in Idaho, it is required to collect $30 ($500 × 6%) of sales tax and remit it to Idaho. Casey would also have an $8.75 California use tax liability ($38.75 reduced by the $30.00 remitted to Idaho) in this scenario.

ETHICS

Jill is a Virginia resident who purchased $1,500 of personal property items from Overstock.com and other Internet retailers during the year. While completing her personal tax return using a popular software package, Jill was asked to report her online purchases. After entering these purchases, she noticed that $75 of "use tax" was added to her state tax liability. Jill has never paid this in the past. She decided to delete the online purchase information she had previously entered. What do you think of Jill's failure to report her Virginia use tax?

Large companies often must file sales and use tax returns in all 45 states that have sales and use taxes and the District of Columbia.[13] This administrative burden is further complicated by the fact that there are over 7,500 tax jurisdictions (including counties, cities, school districts, and other divisions) imposing sales and use taxes, and several hundred rates change annually at various times during the year.[14] The sales and use tax administrative burden can also be large for small businesses. For example, a local pizzeria that delivers can sometimes be subject to a half-dozen sales tax rates if its delivery services cross city, county, or school district boundaries.

ETHICS

In 2010, Colorado became the first state to require nondomiciliary businesses without sales tax nexus to report all the necessary information to the Colorado Department of Revenue so that Colorado could collect its use tax from its resident individuals and domiciliary businesses. Assume you are responsible for sales tax issues for an online retailer from another state. You believe that the Colorado tax is unconstitutional based on a seminar you attended and the advice of your accounting firm. Would you recommend that your company comply with the Colorado law? Would your opinion change if the court placed an injunction prohibiting the state from enforcing the new law?

[13]Some counties or political subdivisions of states without state sales taxes (such as Kenal Peninsula Borough in Alaska) impose a county or local sales tax.

[14]Software companies provide sales and use tax solutions that help companies with the administrative burden. However, they generally fail to indemnify or compensate businesses against errors in their software that result in uncollected sales taxes, which creates a liability for the business.

Example 23-3

Recall from Exhibit 23-1 that Wild West has sales in Arizona, California, Colorado, Idaho, Tennessee, Washington, and Wyoming. Also recall that it has property and employees in Idaho, Tennessee, Washington, and Wyoming. In which states does Wild West have sales and use tax nexus and, therefore, sales tax collection responsibility?

Answer: Wild West's physical presence of employees and real and personal property create sales and use tax nexus in Idaho, Tennessee, Washington, and Wyoming.

How much sales and use tax must Wild West remit? Assume the following sales tax rates: Idaho (6.00 percent); Tennessee (9.25 percent); Washington (7.70 percent); and Wyoming (6.00 percent).

Answer: It must remit $28,616, computed as follows:

State	(1) Taxable Sales	(2) Rate	(1) × (2) Sales Tax Due
Idaho	$167,921	6.00%	$10,075
Tennessee	45,331	9.25	4,193
Washington	41,982	7.70	3,233
Wyoming	185,249	6.00%	11,115
Totals	$440,483		**$28,616**

Remember, services are not generally subject to sales tax.

TAXES IN THE REAL WORLD Groupon

Have you ever bought a restaurant meal from Groupon? Did you know there is a tax issue complicating these types of purchases? Suppose you pay $25 for a $50 voucher good at your favorite restaurant. You just scored a great deal. Groupon collects the $25 and pays the restaurant $12.50. You show up, order $50 worth of food, and the server brings you the bill. How much sales tax should the restaurant collect from you on the prepared food (which is a taxable item)? You received $50 worth of prepared food (one possible tax base), but you only paid $25 (another possible tax base), and the restaurant only received $12.50 (a third possible tax base). What is the nature of the $12.50 retained by Groupon? Did it provide a good (taxable) or a service (not taxable)? Most restaurants currently collect tax on the entire $50 benefit you received. They probably collected too much tax, but only time will tell.

INCOME TAXES

LO 23-3

Forty-six states impose an income tax on corporations; Nevada, South Dakota, Washington, and Wyoming do not.[15] Forty-three states tax income from partnerships and S corporations. This chapter focuses on corporations, but the same principles apply to flow-through entities.[16] Businesses must pay income tax in their state of commercial domicile (where they are headquartered). For example, Wild West is both incorporated and domiciled in Idaho and is therefore subject to Idaho's income tax regime. Until a few decades ago, many businesses believed they were virtually exempt from state income taxes in states other than their state of commercial domicile. However, in *Complete Auto Transit,* the U.S.

[15]Several states (such as California and New York) impose a franchise tax rather than an income tax. Since franchise taxes are generally based upon net income, they are essentially the same as income taxes.

[16]Actually, these states tax individuals, including the income that flows through from partnerships and S corporations (although New Hampshire and Tennessee tax only dividends and interest); Alaska, Florida, Nevada, South Dakota, Texas, Washington, and Wyoming do not.

Supreme Court spelled out four criteria for determining whether states can tax nondomiciliary companies and whether the tax imposed is discriminatory against nondomiciliary (domiciled in another state) businesses.[17] First, a sufficient connection or nexus must exist between the state and the business. Second, a state may tax only a fair portion of a business's income. Businesses must be able to divide or apportion income among the states where nexus exists. Third, the tax cannot be constructed to discriminate against nonresident businesses. For example, states cannot impose a higher tax rate on nondomiciliary businesses than domiciliary businesses. Fourth, the taxes paid must be fairly related to the services the state provides. For example, businesses have access to a state's courts, economic base, infrastructure, and so forth.

To determine their state income tax liabilities, businesses must answer the following questions:

- In which states is the business required to file tax returns (in which states does it have nexus)?
- If the business is related to other entities, should it file separate state tax returns, or should it include the activities of the related entities on its state tax returns?
- What adjustments to federal taxable income must the business make to determine state taxable income for each state in which it is required to file?
- If income is taxable (nexus exists) in more than one state, how is income divided among the various states in which the business is required to file tax returns?

THE KEY FACTS

Income Tax Nexus

- Income tax nexus requirements vary depending on whether the business sells tangible personal property, services, or intangibles.
- Sellers of tangible personal property are protected from nexus under Public Law 86-272.
  - Physical presence is protected as long as in-state activities are limited to solicitation.
- Sellers of intangibles, real property, and services establish nexus through physical presence of sales personnel or property.
- Several states are now asserting economic nexus.

Income Tax Nexus

Businesses must file income tax returns in states where they have income tax nexus. However, the determination of whether the business has established income tax nexus within a state depends on the nature of its business's activities in the state. Thus, the rules for determining income tax nexus are not necessarily the same as those for determining sales and use tax nexus. Physical presence creates income tax nexus for service providers, sellers of real property, and businesses licensing intangibles. However, physical presence does not necessarily create nexus for sellers of tangible personal property if their activities within a state are limited to "protected" activities as described by **Public Law 86-272.**

Public Law 86-272 In *Northwestern States Portland Cement,* the U.S. Supreme Court allowed Minnesota to tax an Iowa-based business.[18] By passing Public Law 86-272, Congress placed limits on states' power to impose income taxes on nondomiciliary businesses. Businesses are protected from income tax nexus in a particular state if (and only if) *all* the following apply:

- The tax is based on net income (not gross receipts or revenue).
- The taxpayer sells only tangible personal property in that state.
- The taxpayer's in-state activities are limited to solicitation of sales (see the discussion below for the definition of *solicitation*).
- The taxpayer participates in interstate commerce.
- The taxpayer is nondomiciliary.
- The taxpayer approves orders outside the state.
- The taxpayer delivers goods from outside the state.

[17] *Complete Auto Transit, Inc. v. Brady,* 430 U.S. 274 (1977).

[18] *Northwestern States Portland Cement Co. v. Minnesota,* 358 U.S. 450 (1959). Widespread alarm from the business community following the case led to an intense lobbying effort, and seven months later Congress enacted Public Law 86-272.

Businesses wishing to avoid nexus for taxes based on net income must sell only tangible personal property within the state.[19] Providing services along with property violates the criteria and creates nexus. For example, providing installation services with tangible personal property exceeds solicitation; in-state activities must be limited to solicitation of sales (discussed further in the next section). Only nondomiciliary companies engaging in interstate commerce are protected. Orders taken or received in-state must be sent out of state—say to regional sales offices or headquarters—for approval. The acceptance of orders in the state, or even the power to accept orders, exceeds the protection of Public Law 86-272 and would result in the business being subject to an income tax. Accepted orders must be delivered by common carrier.[20] Delivery using the seller's truck violates the criteria and creates nexus, except as permitted by state law (New Jersey, Rhode Island, and South Carolina are among the states that list delivery by private vehicles as a protected activity).

Example 23-4

What if: Assume that Wild West sends employees to Oregon to visit retail stores and solicit orders of rafting equipment only. Does the presence of Wild West's employees in Oregon create income tax nexus in Oregon?

Answer: No. The physical presence of representatives soliciting sales of tangible personal property is a protected activity under Public Law 86-272. Thus, no income tax nexus for Wild West in Oregon is created. Note, however, that this physical presence *would* create sales and use tax nexus for any sales generated by Wild West in Oregon, unless it has a valid reseller's certificate.

What if: Assume that Ken or other Wild West sales representatives entered Oregon to solicit customers for both rafting equipment and white-water adventures. Does the presence of Wild West's employees create income tax nexus in Oregon?

Answer: Yes. Solicitation of *services* is not a protected activity under Public Law 86-272. Thus, soliciting services creates income tax nexus for Wild West in Oregon and creates an income tax filing requirement.

Solicitation. Public Law 86-272 protects **solicitation** of tangible personal property but doesn't clearly define solicitation. In *Wisconsin v. Wrigley,* however, the U.S. Supreme Court addressed the definition.[21] Wrigley had sales representatives and a regional manager in Wisconsin. Sales meetings were held both in the manager's basement and in a rented hotel space. The sales reps had company cars, a stock of gum, display racks, and promotional literature. The sales activities included handing out promotional materials, free samples, and free display racks; replacing stale gum; handling billing disputes; and occasionally filling orders from their stock of gum and issuing an agency stock check (a bill) to customers. All other orders were sent to Illinois for acceptance and were filled by a common carrier from outside the state. The U.S.Supreme Court determined the following activities meet the definition of solicitation:

- Soliciting by any form of advertising.
- Carrying samples and promotional materials for display or distribution without charge.
- Passing inquiries or complaints to the home office.
- Checking a customer's inventory for reorder.

[19]Taxes calculated based on gross receipts or other bases are not protected by Public Law 86-272.

[20]*Common carrier* is a general term referring to delivery businesses (such as FedEx, UPS, DHL, or USPS).

[21]*Wisconsin Department of Revenue v. William Wrigley, Jr. Co.*, 505 US 214 (1992).

- Maintaining a sample room for two weeks or less; this is known as the **trade show rule.**
- Recruiting, training, and evaluating sales reps using homes or hotels.
- Owning or furnishing personal property and autos used in sales activities.

The U.S. Supreme Court held the following activities do *not* meet the definition of solicitation and, therefore, create income tax nexus with the state in which they take place:

- Making repairs.
- Collecting delinquent accounts.
- Investigating creditworthiness.
- Installing or supervising the installation of property.
- Providing training for employees other than sales reps.
- Approving or accepting orders.
- Repossessing property.
- Securing deposits.
- Maintaining an office (other than an in-home office).

TAXES IN THE REAL WORLD Warranty

One of the biggest current issues for out-of-state retailers is the manner in which warranty work is performed. For example, assume you buy a new laptop for school from an online retailer because the price is unbeatable. Two months later you are told by customer support that the hard drive needs to be replaced and you need to ship the computer to Austin, Texas, for repair. You respond that you cannot go a week without your computer, so the retailer agrees to have a local shop do the repair for you. Many companies wrongly assume that hiring an independent representative to do in-state warranty work does not create nexus. The hiring of the independent contractor is an agency relationship that creates nexus for the out-of-state retailer. The Multistate Tax Commission issued guidance (MTC Nexus Bulletin 95-1) on this issue more than a decade ago—and taxpayers challenging this ruling have lost time and time again. Retailers with these issues quickly find themselves liable for both current and past income as well as sales and use taxes.

If sales reps know and understand these solicitation rules, they can help businesses avoid nexus in states where they want to avoid it.

Example 23-5

Assume that Wild West's Oregon sales reps give store employees free white-water gloves and pass on complaints to the home office. Do these activities create nexus for Wild West in Oregon?

Answer: No. Giving samples (without charge) and passing on complaints, suggestions, and customer inquiries are protected sales activities under Public Law 86-272. Therefore, Wild West is protected from Oregon income tax nexus.

What if: While in Oregon, several sales reps accept checks for down payments on merchandise, repair faulty merchandise, and perform credit checks. Do these activities create nexus in Oregon for Wild West?

Answer: Yes. Each of these activities is an unprotected sales activity, and any or all will create Oregon income tax nexus for Wild West.

Does a one-time sales activity violation create income tax nexus? Technically, yes. However, the *Wrigley* decision indicates that *de minimis* (immaterial) activities may be excluded. The determination of whether an activity is *de minimis* is a subjective one, based on relevant facts and circumstances.

Example 23-6

Assume that Wild West's sales reps occasionally investigate creditworthiness and occasionally repossess property in Oregon. Can Wild West avoid income tax nexus?

Answer: Possibly. Wild West must argue that these unprotected activities are *de minimis* because they were not material to its overall operations within Oregon.

Income Tax Nexus for Other Business Types or Nonincome-Based Taxes

Public Law 86-272 does not protect service providers, sellers of real property, or businesses licensing intangibles. Further, it does not protect businesses from nonincome-based taxes. Establishing income tax nexus for nonprotected activities, and nexus for nonincome-based taxes, requires a physical presence just like establishing sales and use tax nexus. The two most notable nonincome-based taxes are the Texas Margin Tax and the Washington Business and Occupation (B&O) tax. While nonincome-based taxes are beyond the scope of this chapter, a realization that a different nexus standard exists is vitally important.

Example 23-7

What if: Assume that Ken and other Wild West employees visit Colorado retail stores and hold slideshows about summer rafting trips. After the slideshows, Ken and the other guides interact with and gather information from potential white-water rafting customers. Do these solicitation activities create income tax nexus?

Answer: Yes. Because white-water rafting trips are services rather than tangible personal property, the physical presence of Wild West employees creates income tax nexus in Colorado.

Example 23-8

What if: Assume that Wild West sends employees into Texas to visit retail stores and solicit orders of rafting equipment. Texas instituted a new tax, the Margin Tax, beginning in 2008. The tax is calculated on the lesser of gross margin or 70 percent of sales revenue. Would the presence of Wild West employees create nexus for the Texas Margin Tax?

Answer: Yes. Because the tax is nonincome-based (it is not based on *net* income), Wild West is not protected by Public Law 86-272. Therefore, the physical presence of salespeople soliciting sales of tangible personal property creates nexus (but it would *not* have created nexus if the tax were based on net income).

Economic Income Tax Nexus As we have discussed, businesses generally must have a physical presence in a state to establish income tax nexus with that state (Public Law 86-272 is the exception). However, many states currently assert a business without a physical presence in the state may establish income tax nexus if it has an economic presence in the state.[22] South Carolina was the first state to pursue economic nexus. South Carolina disallowed the royalty expenses of Toys 'R' Us South Carolina to Geoffrey (a related Delaware holding company) rather than subject Geoffrey to the South Carolina

[22]The Supreme Court's *Quill* decision created doubt on the standard for income tax nexus because in defining sales tax nexus it said that "nexus for other taxes may be different," which the states have interpreted as meaning that physical presence may not be required for other types of taxes. Several recent cases have given de facto income tax nexus to businesses without the requisite physical presence [*Geoffrey, Inc. v. South Carolina Tax Commission,* S.C. Sup. Ct., 313 S.C. (1992); *Lanco, Inc. v. Director, Division of Taxation,* NJ Sup. Ct., Dkt. No.A-89-05 (2006); and *Tax Commissioner of West Virginia v. MBNA America Bank, N.A.,* 640 SE 2d 226 (WV 2006)].

income tax. States asserting **economic nexus** claim they provide an infrastructure of phone and Internet connections to consumers (an economic base) that nonresident companies use to solicit business (this claim is analogous to providing roads for salespeople to visit the state's customers). For example, West Virginia asserted an income tax liability on a business (MBNA Bank) that merely solicited credit card customers through advertising and phone calls without having physical presence (employees or property) in the state. The West Virginia Supreme Court upheld the assertion, and the U.S. Supreme Court denied MBNA's *writ of certiorari*. However, most experts believe West Virginia's law to be unconstitutional, and the U.S. Supreme Court's refusal to hear the case was designed to urge Congress to resolve the uncertainty surrounding nexus issues.

Example 23-9

What if: Assume that Wild West's Internet store receives and fills an order from a West Virginia customer. Wild West has no physical presence in West Virginia. Does Wild West have West Virginia income tax nexus?

Answer: Perhaps. West Virginia's assertion of economic nexus does not require physical presence. Therefore, Wild West could have economic income tax nexus, which would require it to file an income tax return in West Virginia.

TAXES IN THE REAL WORLD Factor Presence

While several states have asserted economic nexus through state courts, the Multistate Tax Commission adopted the Factor Presence Nexus Standard in 2002 (MTC Policy Statement 02-02). This policy asserts that if any taxpayer exceeds any of the following criteria, substantial nexus is established:

- $50,000 of property
- $50,000 of payroll
- $500,000 of sales, or
- 25 percent of total property, payroll, or sales

A number of states have recently asserted this standard (or a variation) through either legislation or regulation: California, Colorado, Ohio, Oklahoma, and Washington. If upheld, this standard will change the game by making Public Law 86-272 irrelevant, and it should make all companies not filing income tax returns in a state nervous.

Now that we've explored income tax nexus, let's determine Wild West's income tax nexus and filing requirements.

Example 23-10

Wild West is domiciled in Idaho and has physical presence through property and employees whose activities exceed protected solicitation in Idaho, Tennessee, Washington, and Wyoming. Recall from Exhibit 23-1 that Wild West has sales in the following states: Arizona, California, Colorado, Idaho, Tennessee, Washington, and Wyoming. Where does Wild West have income tax nexus?

Answer: Wild West has income tax nexus in Idaho, Tennessee, Washington, and Wyoming. It has nexus in Idaho because of commercial domicile, physical presence of retail stores (where orders are accepted), and provision of services; it has nexus in Tennessee, Washington, and Wyoming because of physical presence of retail stores (where orders are accepted) or provision of services. Where does Wild West have an income tax filing requirement?

Answer: Wild West will be required to file income tax returns in Idaho and Tennessee. Washington and Wyoming do not have a corporate income tax. Instead, Washington has a gross receipts tax (Business & Occupation tax). Wyoming does not tax corporations. As a result, Wild West will also file a Washington gross receipts return, as we discuss in Example 23-21.

Entities Included on Income Tax Return

When a business operates as more than one legal entity, how it files its tax return(s) becomes an issue. Some states require a **separate tax return** for each entity with income tax nexus in the state, and others require a **unitary tax return** (one return) for a group of related entities.[23]

Separate Tax Returns "Separate-return" states require only those businesses with nexus in a state to file an income tax return. This is generally true even when a group of companies files a federal consolidated tax return.[24] Traditionally, most states east of the Mississippi River (except Illinois) are separate-return states.

Example 23-11

Wild West has nexus in Tennessee (a separate-return state) because its employees provide services within the state and it owns property there. Must Wild West file a separate Tennessee income tax return?

Answer: Yes. Wild West must file a separate Tennessee income tax return because it has nexus in Tennessee.

What if: Assume that Wild West splits into two separate corporations: one that runs retail stores (Wild West Retail) and one that provides the guided rafting services (Wild West Services). How would the split affect Wild West's Tennessee income tax filing requirements?

Answer: Wild West would file two separate income tax returns: one for Wild West Retail and one for Wild West Services. Both companies would have nexus in Tennessee because Wild West Retail's stores do more than solicit sales of tangible personal property and Wild West Service's activities are not protected activities under Public Law 86-272.

THE KEY FACTS

Entities Included on a Tax Return

- Separate-return states require a separate return for each entity that has nexus in the state.
- Unitary states require members of a unitary group to file a single tax return reflecting the combined income of the unitary group.
  - Any of three factors determine a unitary group: functional integration, centralization of management, and economies of scale.

While separate tax returns are simple, the income reported on separate tax returns is potentially subject to manipulation through related-entity transactions (transfer pricing, for example). Another important planning technique is the use of *passive investment companies* (PICs). A company simply creates a subsidiary and transfers ownership of its trademarks and patents to a state that does not tax royalties, interest, and other similar types of intangible income. Then the new PIC charges a royalty for use of the intangible, which generates a deductible business expense in the state used and creates income in a little or no taxed state like Delaware or Nevada. States have implemented laws to fight this type of planning, but seven states have adopted unitary filing to avoid this issue. These "tax planning" opportunities are not available if the related entities are required to file a unitary tax return.

Unitary Tax Returns States west of the Mississippi River (and Illinois) are unitary-return states. However, since 2004, Massachusetts, Michigan, New York, Ohio, Texas, Vermont, and Wisconsin have adopted unitary returns. Whether a business must file one tax return with other businesses or entities depends on whether these businesses are considered to be a "unitary" group of entities.

[23]The separate versus unitary discussion is a complex and controversial discussion even at the graduate tax level. However, a basic understanding of the terminology and concepts can be useful for all accounting professionals.

[24]Some states allow combined reporting, a setting where more than one corporation files together on the same income tax return. However, the tax is calculated as if each corporation filed a separate return and was taxed separately.

In *Mobil,* the U.S. Supreme Court identified the following three factors that can be used to determine whether a group of businesses is unitary:

- Functional integration (vertical or horizontal integration or knowledge transfer).
- Centralization of management (interlocking directors, common officers, or rotation of management between companies).
- Economies of scale (group discounts or other efficiencies due to size).[25]

The unitary concept considers the integration and flow of value, rather than the business's legal form and ownership structure, in determining which companies file a tax return together. Taxpayers must consider each of the three factors to determine whether two (or more) businesses will be treated as one for state tax purposes.

The important concept here is that companies filing a federal consolidated tax return can be separated, and companies not filing a federal consolidated tax return can become a unitary group.[26] A unitary tax return group includes all members meeting the unitary criteria—whether they have nexus or not.[27] Unitary businesses usually have a flow of value between the various businesses. For example, raw materials or components can flow between businesses or one entity may borrow funds from another. The unitary concept pervades activities in the entire income tax system, including computing taxable income, computing apportionment percentages (discussed later in the chapter), and determining tax return filing requirements. The primary difference between separate and unitary states is that separate-return states tax the entire apportioned income of each separate business unit with nexus while unitary-return states tax the entire unitary group using a smaller apportioned percentage.

Example 23-12

What if: As in the previous example, assume that Wild West is divided into two separate corporations: Wild West Retail (WWR) and Wild West Services (WWS). Ken owns and manages both companies. The rafting services company purchases all of its rafting equipment from the retail stores company. Guides for the rafting company stop at the retail store before trips so customers can purchase any necessary gear, and the store refers customers looking for guided rafting to the rafting company. Assume the two companies use the same marketing and accounting firms and receive discounts for having multiple bank accounts and insurance policies. Using the *Mobil* factors (functional integration, centralization of management, and economies of scale), are WWR and WWS part of a unitary group?

Answer: Yes. WWR and WWS would likely be considered a unitary group and thus would combine income and file a single tax return. The two companies likely share some integration in that their customer bases have significant overlap, and WWS purchases its equipment from WWR. They share centralization of management in that both are owned and operated by the same individual (Ken). The two companies have some economies of scale because they receive discounts for using the same accounting, banking, insurance, and marketing vendors. Businesses do not have to meet all three factors to be considered a unitary group, but WWR and WWS probably do. As a result, WWR and WWS would likely file a unitary (single) Idaho income tax return.

State Taxable Income

Companies doing business in multiple states must determine tax return due dates, procedures for filing tax return extensions, and other administrative requirements

[25]In *Mobil Oil Corp. v. Vermont Tax Commissioner,* 445 U.S. 425 (1980), the U.S. Supreme Court held that the income of a multistate business can be apportioned if its intrastate and out-of-state activities form a part of a unitary business.

[26]In some cases, different divisions of a single corporation can be separated and in others a partnership and corporation can be joined.

[27]Entities without nexus usually have apportionment factors that are zero. While their incomes increase the unitary group's income, their zero apportionment factors decrease the apportionment factors to the state. Therefore, the inclusion of entities without nexus is usually considered to be nondiscriminatory.

specific to each state. Businesses must also calculate state taxable income for each state in which they must file tax returns. Federal taxable income is generally the starting point for computing state taxable income. Just as corporations reconcile from book income to taxable income (see the Corporate Operations chapter), businesses must reconcile from federal taxable income to state taxable income. This requires them to identify **federal/state adjustments** (differences) for *each specific state* before apportioning the income to a particular state where they have income tax nexus.

Rather than starting from scratch, many states conform to the federal tax law in some way. Most states "piggyback" their state tax laws on the federal tax laws (state tax codes generally follow the Internal Revenue Code).[28] Idaho generally conforms to the current Code. Consequently, Wild West will not report many federal/state adjustments. Other states adopt a specific version of the Code (the Code as of a specific date). For example, California recently adopted the Code as of January 1, 2015 (previously it used the Code as of January 1, 2009). This method requires more federal/state adjustments, because every subsequent change to the Internal Revenue Code results in less conformity between the state law and the federal tax law.

Because states cannot tax federal interest income (interest from Treasury notes, for example), all states require a negative adjustment (reduction in federal income in adjusting to state income) for federal interest income. Most states require a positive adjustment for state income taxes, because they *do not* allow businesses to deduct state income taxes, and they require a positive adjustment for state and local bond interest income if the bond is from another state (i.e., they tax out-of-state bond interest income).[29]

States' tax instruction booklets generally describe common federal/state tax adjustments applicable for that state, but these descriptions are often incomplete and particularly problematic for states with low federal tax conformity. While it is impractical to identify all potential federal/state adjustments, Exhibit 23-5 provides a list of common federal/state adjustments and identifies each as a positive adjustment (state income increasing) or a negative adjustment (state income decreasing).

EXHIBIT 23-5 Common Federal/State Adjustments

Positive Adjustments (Increasing Taxable Income)

State and local income taxes
State and local bond interest income from bonds in other states
Federal dividends received deduction
Federal income tax refunds (only in states where federal tax is allowed as a deduction)
Intercompany expenses associated with related parties (for separate-return states)*
MACRS depreciation over state depreciation
Federal bonus depreciation
Federal domestic production activities deduction

Negative Adjustments (Decreasing Taxable Income)

U.S. obligation interest income (T-bills, notes, and bonds)
State dividends received deduction
Foreign dividend gross-up
Subpart F income
State income tax refunds included on federal return
State depreciation over federal depreciation

*Approximately 20 separate-return states require a positive adjustment of intercompany royalties, interest, and other expenses between related parties. The disallowance prevents companies from extracting profits from high-tax states and placing them in low- or no-tax states.

[28]Also, states may conform or not conform to administrative authority such as Treasury Regulations, Revenue Procedures, and Revenue Rulings.

[29]Thirty-three of the 46 states with an income tax require a positive adjustment for state and local expenses deducted on the federal return.

Example 23-13

Wild West properly included, deducted, or excluded the following items on its federal tax return in the current year:

Item	Amount	Federal Treatment
Idaho income tax	$27,744	Deducted on federal return
Tennessee income tax	18,152	Deducted on federal return
Washington gross receipts tax	6,201	Deducted on federal return
Idaho bond interest income	5,000	Excluded from federal return
Federal T-note interest income	1,500	Included on federal return
Domestic production activities deduction (DPAD)	7,304	Deducted on federal return

Given federal taxable income of $53,289, what is Wild West's state tax base for Idaho and for Tennessee?

Answer: The Idaho state tax base is $97,685; for Tennessee it is $109,989. Bases are calculated as follows:

Federal Taxable Income	Idaho	Tennessee	Source
Wild West	$53,289	$ 53,289	Storyline
Positive Adjustments			
Idaho income tax	$27,744	$ 27,744	Idaho tax is not deducted.
Tennessee income tax	18,152	18,152	Tennessee tax is not deducted.
Washington gross receipts tax	0	0	Washington tax is not a positive adjustment because it is not an income-based tax.
State bond interest	0	5,000	States exempt their own interest only.
DPAD	0	7,304	Idaho conforms to federal law, Tennessee does not.
Total positive adjustments	$45,896	$ 58,200	
Negative Adjustments			
Federal interest	$ 1,500	$ 1,500	Federal interest is not taxable for state purposes.
Total negative adjustments	$ 1,500	$ 1,500	
State tax base	$97,685	$109,989	Federal + Positive − Negative

THE KEY FACTS

Dividing Income among States with Nexus

- Business income is apportioned based on some combination of the following factors:
  - Sales
  - Payroll
  - Property
- Nonbusiness income is allocated.
  - Investment income is allocated to the state of commercial domicile.
  - Rents and royalties are generally allocated to the state where the property is used.

Dividing State Tax Base among States

All state taxable income is taxed in the state of commercial domicile unless the business is taxable in more than one state. An interstate business must separate its business income (earned from business operations) from nonbusiness income (primarily from investments, including rents and royalties). The business must fairly *apportion* its business income among the states in which it conducts business, whereas it *allocates* or assigns nonbusiness income to a specific state (usually the state of commercial domicile).[30]

[30]The Multistate Tax Commission has provided guidance on the division of income between states in Article IV of its Compact. The Compact can be found at www.mtc.gov. Also, see the Uniform Division of Income Tax Purposes Act that many states have adopted.

Business Income Business income includes all revenues earned in the ordinary course of business—sales less cost of goods sold and other expenses. Business income is fairly apportioned or divided across the states with nexus.[31] If a business has nexus with a state, it may apportion income to that state—even if the state does not actually impose a tax.[32]

Example 23-14

Recall from the preceding example that Idaho and Tennessee state tax bases were $97,685 and $109,989, respectively. Wild West's federal tax return shows the following items of investment income: dividends of $6,000, interest income of $16,005 (which includes $14,505 of bank interest and $1,500 of federal government interest but excludes $5,000 from Idaho bond interest), and rental income of $18,000. What is Wild West's business income for Idaho and Tennessee?

Answer: Idaho and Tennessee business income amounts are $59,180 and $66,484, respectively, calculated as follows:

	Idaho	Tennessee	Explanation
(1) State tax base	$ 97,685	$109,989	Example 23-13
(2) Dividends	6,000	6,000	Federal tax return
(3) Interest income	14,505	19,505	$14,505 (bank interest) + $5,000 of Idaho bond interest (for Tennessee only)
(4) Rental income	18,000	18,000	Federal tax return
(5) Nonbusiness income	$ 38,505	$ 43,505	(2) + (3) + (4)
Business income	**$59,180**	**$ 66,484**	(1) − (5)

Apportionment formula. States determine the apportionment formula for income, and most rely on three factors: sales, payroll, and property. For each state in which it establishes income tax nexus, the business determines the factors as the ratio of (1) total sales, payroll, or property in a specific state to (2) total sales, payroll, or property everywhere. For example, the sales factor is

$$\text{Sales factor in state } X = \frac{\text{Total sales in state } X}{\text{Total sales in all states}}$$

The sales factor includes all gross business receipts net of returns, allowances, and discounts.[33] The general rules for determining the amount of sales to include in the sales factor calculation are:

- Sales of tangible personal property are sourced (included) to the destination state (the location where the property is delivered to and used in).
- If the business does not have nexus in the destination state, sales are generally "thrown back" to the state from which the property is shipped; this is called the **throwback rule**.[34] For example, if Wild West ships goods from Idaho to

[31]*Complete Auto Transit, Inc. v. Brady*, 430 U.S. 274 (1977).

[32]Creating nexus in states without an income tax creates "nowhere income"—income that is not taxed anywhere.

[33]There is some variation in the sales factor among states.

[34]Some states don't have a throwback rule and some states such as California have a double-throwback rule. This rule applies to drop shipments from a state without nexus. For example, if a California company ships goods from Arizona into Colorado and has nexus in neither Arizona nor Colorado, the sales are thrown back from Colorado into Arizona and then thrown back again from Arizona to California.

Montana, where it does not have nexus, the sales are treated as if they are Idaho sales.

- Dock sales should be sourced to the good's ultimate destination (sales picked up by an out-of-state buyer at the seller's in-state dock rather than being shipped to the buyer's out-of-state location).
- Sales of services are generally apportioned to the state where the services are performed (Illinois is an exception to this general rule, but the list of states that apportion services to the state where the services are consumed is growing).
- Government sales are sourced in the state from which they were shipped.

TAXES IN THE REAL WORLD The Complexities in Sourcing Receipts from the Sale of Other Than Tangible Personal Property

The last 10 to 15 years have seen a shift from the equally weighted three-factor formula to adopting a single sales factor formula for apportionment purposes. As a result, the computation of the sales factor has gained importance for taxpayers and tax administrators alike. The increased significance of the sales factor coupled with an economic shift towards intangibles and services has shifted the focus of apportionment to sourcing receipts from sales other than sales of tangible personal property. Sales of other than the sale of tangible personal property historically have not been sourced on a destination basis. Rather, most states have generally adopted a method that assigns the sales to the state in which the income producing activity/cost of performance was performed. . . . Recently, states have moved towards a market state or destination approach for sourcing such receipts.

Source: Marilyn A. Wethekam, *Journal of State Taxation*, September–October 2010, p. 39.

Example 23-15

Recall from Exhibit 23-1 that Wild West reported sales of $2,534,032. The sales are split between goods and services and sourced by state as follows:

Wild West Sales

State	Goods	Services	Total
AZ	$ 89,242	$ 0	$ 89,242
CA	132,045	0	132,045
CO	75,002	0	75,002
ID	**167,921**	**625,003**	**792,924**
TN	**45,331**	**357,061**	**402,392**
WA	41,982	377,441	419,423
WY	185,249	437,755	623,004
Totals	**$736,772**	**$1,797,260**	**$2,534,032**

Recall from Example 23-10 that Wild West has nexus in Idaho, Tennessee, Washington, and Wyoming. Washington has a gross receipts tax and Wyoming does not tax corporations. What are the sales apportionment factors for Idaho and Tennessee?

Answer: The apportionment factors for Idaho and Tennessee are 31.29 percent and 15.88 percent, respectively, calculated from figures in the Total column in the sales table above:

Idaho $\frac{\$792,924}{\$2,534,032} = 31.29\%$

Tennessee $\frac{\$402,392}{\$2,534,032} = 15.88\%$

Note the Arizona, California, and Colorado sales are thrown back to Wyoming because the sales were made through the Internet store.

Payroll is generally defined as total compensation paid to employees.[35] The payroll factor is calculated as follows:

- Payroll includes salaries, commissions, bonuses, and other forms of compensation.
- Payroll does not include amounts paid to independent contractors.
- Payroll for each employee is apportioned to a single state (payroll for employees who work in more than one state is sourced to the state where they perform the majority of services).

Example 23-16

Wild West's payments for wages are $737,021, sourced to the states as follows:

Payroll State	Wild West Wages
Idaho	**$201,032**
Tennessee	**148,202**
Washington	115,021
Wyoming	272,766
Total	**$737,021**

What are the payroll apportionment factors for Idaho and Tennessee?

Answer: The payroll apportionment factors for Idaho and Tennessee are 27.28 percent and 20.11 percent, respectively, calculated from the payroll table above:

Idaho $\frac{\$201,032}{\$737,021} = 27.28\%$

Tennessee $\frac{\$148,202}{\$737,021} = 20.11\%$

Property generally includes both real and tangible personal property, but not intangible property.[36] The general rules for determining the property factors are:

- Use the average property values for the year [(beginning + ending)/2].
- Value property at historical cost rather than adjusted basis (do not subtract accumulated depreciation in determining value).

[35]The payroll definition varies by state.

[36]Property definitions may vary slightly by state.

- Include property in transit (such as inventory) in the state of destination.
- Include only business property (values of rented investment properties are excluded).
- Include rented or leased property by multiplying the annual rent by 8 and adding this value to the average owned-property factor.[37]

Example 23-17

The historical cost of Wild West's property (before subtracting accumulated depreciation) owned at the beginning and end of the year and rented during the year, by state, is as follows:

Property			
State	**Beginning**	**Ending**	**Rented**
Idaho	$1,042,023	$1,203,814	$36,000
Tennessee	502,424	531,984	0
Washington	52,327	65,829	60,000
Wyoming	1,420,387	1,692,373	0
Total	$3,017,161	$3,494,000	$96,000

What are the property apportionment factors for Idaho and Tennessee?

Answer: The property apportionment factors for Idaho and Tennessee are 35.07 percent and 12.85 percent, respectively, computed as follows:

Property and Rents Total					
	Owned Property			Rented	
State	**Beginning**	**Ending**	**Average**	**Rents × 8**	**Total**
Idaho	**$1,042,023**	**$1,203,814**	**$1,122,919**	**$288,000**	**$1,410,919**
Tennessee	**502,424**	**531,984**	**517,204**		**517,204**
Washington	52,327	65,829	59,078	$480,000	539,078
Wyoming	1,420,387	1,692,373	1,556,380		1,556,380
Total	**$3,017,161**	**$3,494,000**	**$3,255,581**		**$4,023,581**

Idaho $$\frac{\$1,410,919}{\$4,023,581} = 35.07\%$$

Tennessee $$\frac{\$517,204}{\$4,023,581} = 12.85\%$$

The average amount for each state from the subtotal property table is added to the inclusion amount from the subtotal rent table to reach the total property numerator for each state.

Historically, most states have used an equally weighted three-factor apportionment formula. This method adds together the sales, payroll, and property factors and divides the total by three to arrive at the apportionment factor (percentages) for each state. In recent years, many states have shifted to a double-weighted sales factor (doubling the sales factor, adding the payroll and property factors, and dividing the total by four). Both Idaho and Tennessee use the double-weighted sales factor for apportionment. Recently, some states have moved to a single-weighted sales factor that eliminates the payroll and property

[37]The annual rent is multiplied by 8 to approximate the value of the rental property.

factors altogether. California requires corporations to use a single-weighted sales factor beginning in 2013. All else equal, increasing the weight of the sales factor in the apportionment formula tends to decrease taxes on in-state businesses and increase taxes on out-of-state businesses. The reason is that in-state businesses tend to have higher payroll and property factors relative to their sales factor in the state, and out-of-state businesses tend to have higher sales factors than payroll and property factors.

TAXES IN THE REAL WORLD Apportionment: The Gillette Decision

On December 31, 2015, the California Supreme Court reversed the California Court of Appeal decision in *Gillette Co. v. Franchise Tax Board* (196 Cal. Rptr. 3d 486, 363 P.3d 94 (2015)).

Previously the California Court of Appeals held that a taxpayer could apportion its income to California using the Multistate Tax Compact's evenly weighted three-factor formula, despite statutory language mandating the use of a three-factor, double-weighted sales formula for most corporations for the years at issue.

The California Supreme Court concluded the California Legislature may properly preclude a taxpayer from relying on the Multistate Compact's election provision.

On October 12, 2016, the U.S. Supreme Court denied the *Gillette* appeal.

Similarly, the Michigan Appellate Court reversed a 2015 decision favoring IBM this summer and the Michigan Supreme Court denied the consolidate appeal of IBM and 50 other companies.

Similar cases are progressing in Minnesota, Oregon, and Texas. However, it is unclear whether taxpayers can ultimately win this argument.

Example 23-18

Wild West must apportion its business income to Idaho and Tennessee. Its Idaho sales, payroll, and property factors are 31.29 percent, 27.28 percent, and 35.07 percent, respectively. Its Tennessee sales, payroll, and property factors are 15.88 percent, 20.11 percent, and 12.85 percent, respectively. These factors are aggregated from Examples 23-15 through 23-17. What are Wild West's apportionment factors in both states if they use a double-weighted sales factor?

Answer: The apportionment factors for Idaho and Tennessee are 31.23 percent and 16.18 percent, respectively.

Factor	Idaho	Tennessee	Explanation
(1) Sales	31.29%	15.88%	Exhibit 23-15
(2) Sales	31.29	15.88	Exhibit 23-15
(3) Payroll	27.28	20.11	Exhibit 23-16
(4) Property	35.07	12.85	Exhibit 23-17
Apportionment factor	**31.23%**	**16.18%**	[(1) + (2) + (3) + (4)]/4

What if: Assume Tennessee uses an equally weighted three-factor apportionment formula. What are Wild West's apportionment factors?

Answer: The apportionment factor for Tennessee is 16.28 percent. Tennessee's apportionment factor would now be calculated as follows:

Factor	Tennessee	Explanation
(1) Sales	15.88%	
(2) Payroll	20.11	
(3) Property	12.85	
Apportionment factor	**16.28%**	[(1) + (2) + (3)]/3

Nonbusiness Income We've said nonbusiness income is all income except business income. Here are common types of nonbusiness income and the rules for allocating them to specific states:[38]

- Allocate interest and dividends to the state of commercial domicile (except interest on working capital, which is business income).
- Allocate rental income to the state where the property generating the rental income is located.
- Allocate royalties to the state where the property is used (if the business has nexus in that state; if not, allocate royalties to the state of commercial domicile).
- Allocate capital gains from investment property to the state of commercial domicile.
- Allocate capital gains from selling rental property to the state where the rental property was located.

Example 23-19

Wild West reports nonbusiness income as follows:

Wild West			
	Idaho	Tennessee	
Dividends	$ 6,000	$ 6,000	From Example 23-14
Interest	14,505	19,505	From Example 23-14
Rental income	18,000	18,000	From Example 23-14
Allocable total	$38,505	$43,505	

Wild West's commercial domicile is in Idaho. Its rental income is for real property located in Wyoming. To which state(s) should the firm allocate its nonbusiness income?

Answer: $20,505 to Idaho, and $18,000 to Wyoming, calculated as follows:

Wild West		
Idaho	**$20,505**	$6,000 dividends + $14,505 interest income
Nevada	0	
Tennessee	0	
Washington	0	
Wyoming	**18,000**	Rental income
Total	$ 38,505	

State Income Tax Liability

It is relatively easy to calculate a business's state taxable income and state tax after separating business and nonbusiness income, apportioning business income, and allocating nonbusiness income. Specifically, calculate state taxable income by multiplying business income by the apportionment factor and then adding any nonbusiness income allocated to the state.

[38]Multistate Tax Compact, Article IV, Division of Income, Paragraph 4.

Example 23-20

What if: Assume Idaho and Tennessee have a flat income tax rate of 7.6 percent and 6.5 percent, respectively. What is Wild West's income tax liability for Idaho and Tennessee?

Answer: Its liabilities are $2,963 and $699 in Idaho and Tennessee, respectively, computed as follows:

Description	Idaho	Tennessee	Explanation
(1) State tax base	$ 97,685	$109,989	Example 23-14
(2) Allocable income	$(38,505)	$ (43,505)	Example 23-19
(3) Business income	$ 59,180	$ 66,484	(1) − (2)
(4) Apportionment factor	31.23%	16.18%	Example 23-18
(5) Apportioned income	$ 18,482	$ 10,757	(3) × (4)
(6) Allocable income	$ 20,505	$ 0	Example 23-19
(7) State taxable income	$ 38,987	$ 10,757	(5) + (6)
(8) Tax rate	7.6%	6.5%	
Tax liability	**$ 2,963**	**$ 699**	(7) × (8)

Non (Net) Income-Based Taxes

Several states have nonincome-based taxes. Washington has the Business & Occupation Tax, which is a gross receipts tax. Texas has the Margin Tax (many states are treating the Texas Margin Tax as a tax based on net income), the lesser of a gross margin tax or gross receipts tax. As we discussed earlier, Public Law 86-272 doesn't apply to nexus for non-income-based taxes such as gross receipts taxes or property taxes; these are deductible for calculating taxable income for net income-based taxes.

Example 23-21

Wild West has nexus in Washington and is subject to that state's business and occupation (B&O) tax. The tax is .471 percent of gross receipts for retailers and 1.5 percent of gross receipts on services. Wild West's gross receipts from retail sales and services in Washington are $41,982 and $377,441, respectively (from Exhibit 23-1). Calculate Wild West's B&O tax.

Answer: Wild West's B&O tax is $5,860, calculated as follows:

Activity	(1) Receipts	(2) Rate	(1) × (2) Tax
Retailing	$ 41,982	0.471%	$ 198
Services	377,441	1.500	5,662
B&O tax			**$5,860**

CONCLUSION

In this chapter we discussed the fundamentals of state and local taxation with an emphasis on nexus, sales and use tax, and net income-based corporate taxes. State and local taxes currently make up a significant portion of many businesses' total tax burden and also consume a significant portion of the tax department's time.

Sales and use tax nexus is established through physical presence. Companies selling tangible personal property must collect sales tax from their customers (where nexus exists) and remit it to the various states. Income tax nexus requirements vary based on the type of goods or services provided by a business. Tangible personal property sales are protected from income tax nexus by Public Law 86-272 if certain criteria are met. For all other sales, nexus is created by physical presence, although some states are defining the concept of income tax nexus based on economic rather than physical presence.

Businesses subject to multijurisdictional taxation—taxation by more than one government—have many issues in common. A business located in San Diego, California, but also doing business in Tucson, Arizona, will be subject to California and Arizona tax. If it also does business in Rosarito, Mexico, it will be subject to both U.S. and Mexico taxes. State and local taxation and international taxation bring up many of the same issues. For both, businesses must determine which jurisdiction has the right to tax a transaction (nexus) and determine how to divide income among different jurisdictions. The next chapter examines multinational taxation.

Summary

LO 23-1 Describe the primary types of state and local taxes.

- The primary purpose of state and local taxes is to raise revenue.
- Like federal tax law, state tax law is composed of legislative, administrative, and judicial law.
- Judicial law plays a more important role in state tax law than federal tax law because constitutionality is a primary concern for state tax laws.
- The most important question any taxpayer must answer is whether it is subject to a state's taxing regime.
- Nexus is the connection between a business and a state sufficient to subject the business to the state's tax system.
- When a business sells tangible personal property, either sales or use tax is due. If the seller has nexus, the seller must collect and remit the tax to the state. Otherwise, the buyer is responsible for paying the use tax.
- Businesses engaged in interstate commerce that have nexus must pay income tax.

LO 23-2 Determine whether a business has sales and use tax nexus and calculate its sales tax withholding responsibilities.

- Forty-five states and the District of Columbia impose sales and use taxes.
- The items subject to sales and use tax vary from state to state.
- Businesses are required to collect sales tax on sales only if they have sales and use tax nexus with that state.
- For nondomiciliary businesses, sales and use tax nexus is created through a physical presence (having salespeople or tangible property within the state, for example).

LO 23-3 Identify whether a business has income tax nexus and determine its state income tax liabilities.

- Forty-six states impose an income tax on corporations, and 43 states tax the owners of partnerships and S corporations.
- Businesses must pay income tax in their state of commercial domicile, and nondomiciliary firms are subject to tax if they have nexus in the state.
- Businesses divide or apportion their income among the states where they have established nexus.
- Nexus requirements vary based on the nature of the business's activities: physical presence creates income tax nexus for service providers, sellers of real property, and businesses licensing intangibles; Public Law 86-272 protects solicitation of tangible personal property from nexus.
- Some states require a separate income tax return for each entity with nexus, and others require a unitary (a single) tax return for a group of related entities as long as one of the entities has established nexus in the state.

- Businesses must calculate state taxable income for each state in which they must file a tax return—this requires businesses to identify federal/state adjustments.
- Firms adjust federal taxable income to arrive at their state taxable base.
- The state taxable base of an interstate business is separated into business and nonbusiness income: business income is apportioned across states using a general formula, and non-business income is allocated to specific states using specific rules.
- Business income is apportioned using some variation of sales, payroll, and property factors.

KEY TERMS

allocation (23-4)
apportionment (23-4)
business income (23-4)
commercial domicile (23-2)
economic nexus (23-14)
federal/state adjustments (23-17)
interstate commerce (23-4)
nexus (23-2)
nonbusiness income (23-4)
nondomiciliary business (23-2)
Public Law 86-272 (23-10)
sales tax (23-3)
separate tax return (23-15)
solicitation (23-11)
state tax base (23-4)
throwback rule (23-19)
trade show rule (23-12)
unitary tax return (23-15)
use tax (23-4)

DISCUSSION QUESTIONS

Discussion Questions are available in Connect®. connect

1. Why do states and local jurisdictions assess taxes? LO 23-1
2. Compare and contrast the relative importance of judicial law to state and local and federal tax law. LO 23-1
3. Describe briefly the nexus concept and explain its importance to state and local taxation. LO 23-1
4. What is the difference, if any, between the state of a business's commercial domicile and its state of incorporation? LO 23-1
5. What types of property sales are subject to sales tax and why might a state choose to exclude the sales of certain types of property? LO 23-1
6. In what circumstances would a business be subject to income taxes in more than one state? LO 23-1
7. Describe how the failure to collect sales tax can result in a larger tax liability for a business than failing to pay income taxes. LO 23-1
8. Discuss why restaurant meals, rental cars, and hotel receipts are often taxed at a higher-than-average sales tax rate. LO 23-2
9. Compare and contrast general sales and use tax nexus and the new "Amazon" rule creating nexus in New York. LO 23-2
10. What is the difference between a sales tax and a use tax? LO 23-2
11. Renée operates Scandinavian Imports, a furniture shop in Olney, Maryland, that ships goods to customers in all 50 states. Scandinavian Imports also appraises antique furniture and has recently conducted in-home appraisals in the District of Columbia, Maryland, Pennsylvania, and Virginia. Online appraisals have been done for customers in California, Minnesota, New Mexico, and Texas. Determine where Scandinavian Imports has sales and use tax nexus. LO 23-2
12. Web Music, located in Gardnerville, Nevada, is a new online music service that allows inexpensive legal music downloads. Web Music prides itself on having the fastest download times in the industry. It achieved this speed by leasing server space from 10 regional servers dispersed across the country. Discuss where Web Music has sales and use tax nexus. LO 23-2
13. Discuss possible reasons why the Commerce Clause was included in the U.S. Constitution. LO 23-2

LO 23-2 14. Describe the administrative burden businesses face in collecting sales taxes.

LO 23-3 15. Compare and contrast the rules determining where domiciliary and nondomiciliary businesses must file state income tax returns.

LO 23-3 16. Lars operates Keep Flying Incorporated, a used airplane parts business, in Laramie, Wyoming. Lars employs sales agents that visit mechanics in all 50 states to solicit orders. All orders are sent to Wyoming for approval, and all parts are shipped via common carrier. The sales agents are always on the lookout for wrecked, abandoned, or salvage aircraft with rare parts because they receive substantial bonuses for purchasing and salvaging these parts and shipping them to Wyoming. Discuss the states where Keep Flying has income tax nexus.

LO 23-3 17. Explain changes in the U.S. economy that have made Public Law 86-272 partially obsolete. Provide an example of a company that Public Law 86-272 works well for and one that it does not work well for.

LO 23-3 18. Climb Higher is a distributor of high-end climbing gear located in Paradise, Washington. Its sales personnel regularly perform the following activities in an effort to maximize sales:

- Carry swag (free samples) for distribution to climbing shop employees.
- Perform credit checks of new customers to reduce delivery time of first order of merchandise.
- Check customer inventory for proper display and proper quantities.
- Accept returns of defective goods.

Identify which of Climb Higher's sales activities are protected and unprotected from nexus under the *Wrigley* Supreme Court decision.

LO 23-3 19. Describe a situation in which it would be advantageous for a business to establish income tax nexus in a state.

LO 23-3 20. States are arguing for economic nexus; provide at least one reason for and one reason against the validity of economic nexus.

LO 23-3 21. Explain the difference between separate-return states and unitary-return states.

LO 23-3 22. Explain the rationale for the factors (functional integration, centralization of management, and economies of scale) that determine whether two or more businesses form a unitary group under the *Mobil* decision.

LO 23-3 23. Compare and contrast the reasons why book/tax and federal/state adjustments are necessary for interest income.

LO 23-3 24. Compare and contrast the ways a multistate business divides business and nonbusiness income among states.

LO 23-3 25. Contrast the treatment of government sales and dock sales for the sales apportionment factor.

LO 23-3 26. Most states have increased the weight of the sales factor for the apportionment of business income. What are some possible reasons?

LO 23-3 27. Compare and contrast federal/state tax differences and book/federal tax differences.

PROBLEMS

Select problems are available in Connect®. connect

LO 23-2 28. Crazy Eddie Incorporated manufactures baseball caps and distributes them across the northeastern United States. The firm is incorporated and headquartered in New York and sells to customers in Connecticut, Delaware, Massachusetts, New Jersey, New York, Ohio, and Pennsylvania. It has sales reps only where discussed in the scenarios below. Determine the states in which Crazy Eddie has sales and use tax nexus given the following:

a) Crazy Eddie is incorporated and headquartered in New York. It also has property, employees, salespeople, and intangibles in New York.
b) Crazy Eddie has a warehouse, personal property, and employees in Connecticut.
c) Crazy Eddie has two customers in Delaware. Crazy Eddie receives orders over the phone and ships goods to its Delaware customers using FedEx.
d) Crazy Eddie has independent sales representatives in Massachusetts who distribute baseball-related items for over a dozen companies.
e) Crazy Eddie has salespeople who visit New Jersey. They follow procedures that comply with Public Law 86-272 by sending orders to New York for acceptance. The goods are shipped to New Jersey by FedEx.
f) Crazy Eddie provides graphic design services to another manufacturer located in Ohio. While the services are performed in New York, Crazy Eddie's designers visit Ohio at least quarterly to deliver the new designs and receive feedback.
g) Crazy Eddie receives online orders from its Pennsylvania clients. Because the orders are so large, the goods are delivered weekly on Crazy Eddie's trucks.

29. Brad Carlton operates Carlton Collectibles, a rare-coin shop in Washington, D.C., that ships coins to collectors in all 50 states. Carlton also provides appraisal service upon request. During the last several years the appraisal work has been done either in the D.C. shop or at the homes of private collectors in Maryland and Virginia. Determine the jurisdictions in which Carlton Collectibles has sales and use tax nexus. LO 23-2

30. Melanie operates Mel's Bakery in Foxboro, Massachusetts, with retail stores in Connecticut, Maine, Massachusetts, New Hampshire, and Rhode Island. Mel's also ships specialty breads nationwide upon request. Determine Mel's sales tax collection responsibility and calculate the sales tax liability for Massachusetts, Connecticut, Maine, New Hampshire, Rhode Island, and Texas, based on the following information: LO 23-2
a) The Massachusetts stores earn $500,000 in sales. Massachusetts's sales tax rate is 5 percent; assume it exempts food items.
b) The Connecticut retail stores have $400,000 in sales ($300,000 from in-store sales and $100,000 from catering) and $10,000 in delivery charges for catering activities. Connecticut sales tax is 6 percent and excludes food products but taxes prepared meals (catering). Connecticut also imposes sales tax on delivery charges on taxable sales.
c) Mel's Maine retail store has $250,000 of sales ($200,000 for take-out and $50,000 of in-store sales). Maine has a 5 percent sales tax rate and a 7 percent sales tax rate on prepared food; it exempts other food purchases.
d) The New Hampshire retail stores have $250,000 in sales. New Hampshire is one of five states with no sales tax. However, it has a room and meals tax rate of 8 percent. New Hampshire considers any food or beverage served by a restaurant for consumption on or off the premises to be a meal.
e) Mel's Rhode Island stores earn $300,000 in sales. The Rhode Island sales tax rate is 7 percent and its restaurant surtax is 1 percent. Rhode Island considers Mel's a restaurant because its retail store has seating.
f) One of Mel's best customers relocated to Texas, which imposes an 8.25 percent state and local sales tax rate but exempts bakery products. This customer entertains guests regularly and ordered $5,000 of food items this year.

31. Cuyahoga County, Ohio, has a sales tax rate of 8 percent. Determine the state, local, and transit (a local transportation district) portions of the rate. You can find resources on the State of Ohio website, including the following link: http://www.tax.ohio.gov/portals/0/tax_analysis/tax_data_series/sales_and_use/salestaxmapcolor.pdf LO 23-2 research

LO 23-2 32. Kai operates the Surf Shop in Laie, Hawaii, which designs, manufacturers, and customizes surfboards. Hawaii has a 4 percent excise tax rate, technically paid by the seller. However, the state also allows "tax on tax" to be charged, which effectively means a customer is billed 4.166 percent of the sales price. Determine the sales and use tax the Surf Shop must collect and remit—or that the customer must pay—for each of the following orders:

a) Kalani, a Utah customer, places an Internet order for a $1,000 board that will be shipped to Provo, Utah, where the local sales tax rate is 6.25 percent.

b) Nick, an Alabama resident, comes to the retail shop on vacation and has a $2,000 custom board made. Nick uses the board on vacation and then has the Surf Shop ship it to Tuscaloosa, Alabama, where the sales tax rate is 8.5 percent.

c) Jim, a Michigan resident, places an order for a $2,000 custom board at the end of his vacation. Upon completion, the board will be shipped to Ann Arbor, Michigan, where the sales tax rate is 7 percent.

d) Mike, a Nebraska resident, sends his current surfboard to the Surf Shop for a custom paint job. The customization services come to $800. The board is shipped to Lincoln, Nebraska, where the sales tax rate is 7 percent.

LO 23-2 planning 33. Last year, Reggie, a Los Angeles, California, resident, began selling autographed footballs through Trojan Victory (TV) Incorporated, a California corporation. TV has never collected sales tax. Last year it had sales as follows: California ($100,000), Arizona ($10,000), Oregon ($15,000), New York ($50,000), and Wyoming ($1,000). Most sales are made over the Internet and shipped by common carrier. Determine how much sales tax TV should have collected in each of the following situations:

a) California treats the autographed football as tangible personal property subject to an 8.25 percent sales tax rate. Answer for California.

b) California treats the autographed football as part tangible personal property ($50,000) and part services ($50,000), and tangible personal property is subject to an 8.25 percent sales tax rate. Answer for California.

c) TV has no property or other physical presence in New York (10.25 percent) or Wyoming (5 percent). Answer for New York and Wyoming.

d) TV has Reggie deliver a few balls to fans in Arizona (5.6 percent sales tax rate) and Oregon (no sales tax) while attending football games there. Answer for Arizona and Oregon.

e) Related to part (d), can you make any suggestions that would decrease TV's Arizona sales tax liability?

LO 23-2 34. LeMond Incorporated, a Wisconsin corporation, runs bicycle tours in several states. LeMond also has a Wisconsin retail store and an Internet store that ships to out-of-state customers. The bicycle tours operate in Colorado, North Carolina, and Wisconsin, where LeMond has employees and owns and uses tangible personal property. LeMond has real property only in Wisconsin and logs the following sales:

LeMond Sales

State	Goods	Services	Total
Arizona	$ 34,194	$ 0	$ 34,194
California	110,612	0	110,612
Colorado	25,913	356,084	381,997
North Carolina	16,721	225,327	242,048
Oregon	15,431	0	15,431
Wisconsin	241,982	877,441	1,119,423
Totals	$444,853	$1,458,852	$1,903,705

Assume the following tax rates: Arizona (5.6 percent), California (7.75 percent), Colorado (8 percent), North Carolina (6.75 percent), Oregon (8 percent), and Wisconsin (5 percent). How much sales and use tax must LeMond collect and remit?

35. Kashi Corporation is the U.S. distributor of fencing (sword fighting) equipment imported from Europe. It is incorporated in Virginia and headquartered in Arlington, Virginia; it ships goods to all 50 states. Kashi's employees attend regional and national fencing competitions where they maintain temporary booths to market their goods. Determine whether Kashi has income tax nexus in the following situations: LO 23-3 planning
    a) Kashi is incorporated and headquartered in Virginia. It also has property, employees, salespeople, and intangibles in Virginia. Determine whether Kashi has nexus in Virginia.
    b) Kashi has employees who live in Washington, D.C., and Maryland but perform all their employment-related activities in Virginia. Does Kashi have nexus in Washington, D.C., and Maryland?
    c) Kashi has two customers in North Dakota. It receives their orders over the phone and ships goods to them using FedEx. Determine whether Kashi has nexus in North Dakota.
    d) Kashi has independent sales representatives in Illinois who distribute fencing and other sports-related items for many companies. Does Kashi have nexus in Illinois?
    e) Kashi has salespeople who visit South Carolina for a regional fencing competition for a total of three days during the year. They send all orders to Virginia for credit approval and acceptance, and Kashi ships the goods into South Carolina by FedEx. Determine whether Kashi has nexus in South Carolina.
    f) Kashi has sales reps who visit California for a national fencing competition and several regional competitions for a total of 17 days during the year. They send all orders to Virginia for credit approval and acceptance. The goods are shipped by FedEx into California. Does Kashi have nexus in California?
    g) Kashi receives online orders from its Pennsylvania client. Because the orders are so large, the goods are delivered weekly on Kashi's trucks. Does Kashi have nexus in Pennsylvania?
    h) In addition to shipping goods, Kashi provides fencing lessons in Virginia and Maryland locations. Determine whether Kashi has nexus in Virginia and Maryland.
    i) Given that Kashi ships to all 50 states, are there locations that would decrease Kashi's overall state income tax burden if nexus were created there?

36. Gary Holt LLP provides tax and legal services regarding the tax-exempt bond issues of state and local jurisdictions. Gary typically provides the services from his New York offices. However, for large issuances he and his staff occasionally travel to another state to complete the work. Determine whether the firm has income tax nexus in the following situations: LO 23-3
    a) Gary Holt LLP is a New York partnership and headquartered in New York. It also has property and employees in New York. Does it have income tax nexus in New York?
    b) Gary Holt LLP has employees who live in New Jersey and Connecticut and perform all their employment-related activities in New York. Does it have income tax nexus in New Jersey and/or Connecticut?
    c) Gary Holt LLP has two customers in California. Gary personally travels there to finalize the Alameda County bond issuance. Does it have income tax nexus in California?

LO 23-3

37. Root Beer Inc. (RBI) is incorporated and headquartered in Seattle, Washington. RBI runs an Internet business, makerootbeer.com, and sells bottling equipment and other supplies for making homemade root beer. It also has an Oregon warehouse from which it ships goods. Determine whether RBI has income tax nexus in the following situations:
    a) Root Beer is incorporated and headquartered in Washington and has property and employees in Oregon and Washington. Determine whether RBI has nexus in Oregon and Washington.
    b) Root Beer has hundreds of customers in California but no physical presence (no employees or property). Does it have nexus in California?
    c) Root Beer has 500 New York customers but no physical presence (no employees or property). Remember New York has the new Amazon rule. Determine whether RBI has nexus in New York.

LO 23-3

38. Rockville Enterprises manufactures woodworking equipment and is incorporated and based in Evansville, Indiana. All of its real property is in Indiana. Rockville employs a large sales force that travels throughout the United States. Determine whether each of the following is a protected activity in nondomiciliary states under Public Law 86-272:
    a) Rockville advertises in Wisconsin using television, radio, and newspapers.
    b) Rockville's employees in Illinois check the credit of potential customers.
    c) Rockville maintains a booth at an industry trade show in Arizona for 10 days.
    d) Sales representatives check the inventory of a Tennessee customer to make sure it has enough in stock and that the stock is properly displayed.
    e) Rockville holds a management seminar executive retreat for corporate executives over four days in Florida.
    f) Sales representatives supervise the repossession of inventory from a customer in Maine that is not making payments on time.
    g) Rockville provides automobiles to Idaho and Montana sales representatives.
    h) An Alabama sales representative accepts a customer deposit on a large order.
    i) Colorado sales reps carry display racks and promotional materials that they place in customers' retail stores without charge.

LO 23-3
research

39. Software Incorporated is a sales and use tax software vendor that provides customers with a license to download and use its software on their machines. Software retains ownership of the software. It has customers in New Jersey and West Virginia. Does Software have economic nexus in these states because of the following decisions: *Lanco, Inc. v. Director, Division of Taxation*, 188 N.J. 380, 908 A. 2nd 176 (2006), and *Tax Commissioner of West Virginia v. MBNA America Bank, N.A.*, 640 SE 2d 226 (WV 2006)?

LO 23-3
research

40. Peter Inc., a Kentucky corporation, owns 100 percent of Suvi Inc., a Mississippi corporation. Peter and Suvi file a consolidated federal tax return. Peter has income tax nexus in Kentucky and South Carolina; Suvi has income tax nexus in Mississippi and South Carolina. Kentucky, Mississippi, and South Carolina are separate-return states. In which states must Pete and Suvi file tax returns? Can they file a consolidated return in any states? Explain. (*Hint:* Use South Carolina Form SC 1120 and the related instructions.)

LO 23-3
research

41. Use California Publication 1061 (2014) to identify the various tests California uses to determine whether two or more entities are part of a unitary group.

42. Bulldog Incorporated is a Georgia corporation. It properly included, deducted, or excluded the following items on its federal tax return in the current year: LO 23-3 tax forms research

Item	Amount	Federal Treatment
Georgia income taxes	$25,496	Deducted on federal return.
Tennessee income taxes	13,653	Deducted on federal return.
Washington gross receipts tax	3,105	Deducted on federal return.
Georgia bond interest income	10,000	Excluded from federal return.
Federal T-note interest income	4,500	Included on federal return.
Domestic production activities deduction (DPAD)	15,096	Deducted on federal return.

Use Georgia's Corporate Income Tax Form 600 and Instructions to determine what federal/state adjustments Bulldog needs to make for Georgia. Bulldog's federal taxable income was $194,302. Calculate its Georgia state tax base. Complete Schedule 1, Page 1, of Form 600 for Bulldog.

43. Herger Corporation does business in California, Nevada, and Oregon and has nexus in these states as well. Herger's California state tax base was $921,023 after making the required federal/state adjustments. Herger's federal tax return contains the following items: LO 23-3

Item	Amount
Federal T-note interest income	$ 5,000
Nevada municipal bond interest income	3,400
California municipal bond interest income	6,000
Interest expense related to T-note interest income	1,400
Royalty income	100,000
Travel expenses	9,025

Determine Herger's business income.

44. Bad Brad sells used semi-trucks and tractor trailers in the Texas panhandle. Bad Brad has sales as follows: LO 23-3

Bad Brad	
State	**Sales**
Colorado	$ 234,992
Oklahoma	402,450
New Mexico	675,204
Texas	1,085,249
Totals	$2,397,895

Bad Brad is a Texas corporation. Answer the questions in each of the following alternative scenarios.

a) Bad Brad has nexus in Colorado, Oklahoma, New Mexico, and Texas. What are the Colorado, Oklahoma, New Mexico, and Texas sales apportionment factors?

b) Bad Brad has nexus in Colorado and Texas. Oklahoma and New Mexico sales are shipped from Texas (a throwback state). What are the Colorado and Texas sales apportionment factors?

c) Bad Brad has nexus in Colorado and Texas. Oklahoma and New Mexico sales are shipped from Texas (a throwback state); $200,000 of Oklahoma sales were to the federal government. What are the Colorado and Texas sales apportionment factors?

d) Bad Brad has nexus in Colorado and Texas. Oklahoma and New Mexico sales are shipped from Texas (assume Texas is a nonthrowback state). What are the Colorado and Texas sales apportionment factors?

LO 23-3 45. Nicole's Salon, a Louisiana corporation, operates beauty salons in Arkansas, Louisiana, and Tennessee. These salons' payrolls by state are as follows:

Nicole's Salon	
State	**Payroll**
Arkansas	$ 130,239
Louisiana	309,192
Tennessee	723,010
Total	$1,162,441

What are the payroll apportionment factors for Arkansas, Louisiana, and Tennessee in each of the following alternative scenarios?

a) Nicole's Salon has nexus in Arkansas, Louisiana, and Tennessee.

b) Nicole's Salon has nexus in Arkansas, Louisiana, and Tennessee, but $50,000 of the Arkansas amount is paid to independent contractors.

LO 23-3 46. Delicious Dave's Maple Syrup, a Vermont corporation, has property in the following states:

	Property	
State	**Beginning**	**Ending**
Maine	$ 923,032	$ 994,221
Massachusetts	103,311	203,109
New Hampshire	381,983	283,021
Vermont	873,132	891,976
Total	$2,281,458	$2,372,327

What are the property apportionment factors for Maine, Massachusetts, New Hampshire, and Vermont in each of the following alternative scenarios?

a) Delicious Dave's has nexus in each of the states.

b) Delicious Dave's has nexus in each of the states, but the Maine total includes $400,000 of investment property that Delicious rents out (unrelated to its business).

c) Delicious Dave's has nexus in each of the states, but it also pays $50,000 to rent property in Massachusetts.

LO 23-3 47. Susie's Sweet Shop has the following sales, payroll, and property factors:

	Iowa	**Missouri**
Sales	69.20%	32.01%
Payroll	88.00	3.50
Property	72.42	24.04

What are Susie's Sweet Shop's Iowa and Missouri apportionment factors under each of the following alternative scenarios?

a) Iowa and Missouri both use a three-factor apportionment formula.

b) Iowa and Missouri both use a four-factor apportionment formula that double-weights sales.

c) Iowa uses a three-factor formula and Missouri uses a single-factor apportionment formula (based solely on sales).

48. Brady Corporation is a Nebraska corporation, but it owns business and investment property in surrounding states as well. Determine the state where each item of income is allocated. LO 23-3
    a) $15,000 of dividend income.
    b) $10,000 of interest income.
    c) $15,000 of rental income for South Dakota property.
    d) $20,000 of royalty income for intangibles used in South Dakota (where nexus exists).
    e) $24,000 of royalty income from Kansas (where nexus does not exist).
    f) $15,000 of capital gain from securities held for investment.
    g) $30,000 of capital gain on real property located in South Dakota.

49. Ashton Corporation is headquartered in Pennsylvania and has a state income tax base there of $500,000. Of this amount, $50,000 was nonbusiness income. Ashton's Pennsylvania apportionment factor is 42.35 percent. The nonbusiness income allocated to Pennsylvania was $32,000. Assuming a Pennsylvania corporate tax rate of 8.25 percent, what is Ashton's Pennsylvania state tax liability? LO 23-3

COMPREHENSIVE PROBLEMS

Select problems are available in Connect®. connect

50. Cloud computing is the use of hosted computer facilities through the Internet. Gmail, RIA Checkpoint, and even your iPhone are some applications of cloud computing. research
    a) If HP provides a customized bundle of servers, storage, network and security software, and business application software to a customer in Washington State, how is it taxed?
    b) Is HP leasing tangible personal property, which is taxable, or providing a nontaxable service?
    c) Is the buyer of HP's product subject to Washington sales and use tax?
    d) Is HP subject to Washington's B&O tax?

51. Sharon Inc. is headquartered in State X and owns 100 percent of Carol Corp., Josey Corp., and Janice Corp., which form a single unitary group. Assume sales operations are within the solicitation bounds of Public Law 86-272. Each of the corporations has operations in the following states:

Domicile State	Sharon Inc. State X (throwback)	Carol Corp. State Y (throwback)	Josey Corp. State Z (nonthrowback)	Janice Corp. State Z (nonthrowback)
Dividend income	$ 1,000	$ 200	$ 300	$ 500
Business income	50,000	30,000	10,000	10,000
Sales: State X	70,000	10,000	10,000	10,000
State Y		40,000	5,000	
State Z		20,000	20,000	10,000
State A	20,000			
State B	10,000			10,000
Property: State X	50,000	20,000		10,000
State Y		80,000		
State Z			25,000	20,000
State A	50,000			
Payroll: State X	10,000	10,000		
State Y		40,000		
State Z			3,000	10,000
State A				10,000

Compute the following for State X assuming a tax rate of 15 percent.

a) Calculate the State X apportionment factor for Sharon Inc., Carol Corp., Josey Corp., and Janice Corp.

b) Calculate the business income apportioned to State X.

c) Calculate the taxable income for State X for each company.

d) Determine the tax liability for State X for the entire group.

52. Happy Hippos (HH) is a manufacturer and retailer of New England crafts headquartered in Camden, Maine. HH provides services and has sales, employees, property, and commercial domicile as follows:

Happy Hippos In-State Activities

State	Sales	Employees	Property	Services	Commercial Domicile
Connecticut	✓	✓		✓	
Maine	✓	✓	✓	✓	✓
Massachusetts	✓	✓			
New Hampshire	✓				
Rhode Island	✓	✓			
Vermont	✓	✓	✓	✓	

HH's sales of goods and services by state are as follows:

Happy Hippos Sales

State	Goods	Services	Total
Connecticut	$ 78,231	$ 52,321	$130,552
Maine	292,813	81,313	374,126
Massachusetts	90,238		90,238
New Hampshire	129,322		129,322
Rhode Island	98,313		98,313
Vermont	123,914	23,942	147,856
Totals	$812,831	$157,576	$970,407

HH has federal taxable income of $282,487 for the current year. Included in federal taxable income are the following income and deductions:

- $12,000 of Vermont rental income.
- City of Orono, Maine, bond interest of $10,000.
- $10,000 of dividends.
- $2,498 of state tax refund included in income.
- $32,084 of state net income tax expense, and
- $59,234 of federal depreciation.

Maine state depreciation for the year was $47,923, and Maine doesn't allow deductions for state net income taxes.

The employees present in Connecticut, Massachusetts, and Rhode Island are salespeople who perform only activities protected by Public Law 86-272.

Each of the states is a separate-return state.

HH's payroll is as follows:

Payroll	
State	**Wages**
Connecticut	$ 94,231
Maine	392,195
Massachusetts	167,265
Rhode Island	92,391
Vermont	193,923
Total	$940,005

HH's property is as follows:

Property			
State	**Beginning**	**Ending**	**Rented**
Maine	$ 938,234	$ 937,652	
Vermont	329,134	428,142	$12,000
Total	$1,267,368	$1,365,794	$12,000

a) Determine the states in which HH has sales and use tax nexus.

b) Calculate the sales tax HH must remit assuming the following sales tax rates:

- Connecticut (6 percent)
- Maine (8 percent)
- Massachusetts (7 percent)
- New Hampshire (8.5 percent)
- Rhode Island (5 percent)
- Vermont (9 percent)

c) Determine the states in which HH has income tax nexus.

d) Determine HH's state tax base for Maine, assuming federal taxable income of $282,487.

e) Calculate business and nonbusiness income.

f) Determine HH's Maine apportionment factors using the three-factor method (assume that Maine is a throwback state).

g) Calculate HH's business income apportioned to Maine.

h) Determine HH's allocation of nonbusiness income to Maine.

i) Determine HH's Maine taxable income.

j) Calculate HH's Maine net income tax liability, assuming a Maine income tax rate of 5 percent.

ROGER | CPA Review

Sample CPA Exam questions from Roger CPA Review are available in Connect as support for the topics in this text. These Multiple Choice Questions and Task-Based Simulations include expert-written explanations and solutions, and provide a starting point for students to become familiar with the content and functionality of the actual CPA Exam.

Appendix B

Tax Terms Glossary

§83(b) election a special tax election that employees who receive restricted stock or other property with ownership restrictions can make to accelerate income recognition from the normal date when restrictions lapse to the date when the restricted stock or other property is granted. The election also accelerates the employer's compensation deduction related to the restricted stock or other property.

§162(m) limitation the $1 million deduction limit on nonperformance-based salary paid to certain key executives.

§179 expense an incentive for small businesses that allows them to immediately expense a certain amount of tangible personal property placed in service during the year.

§197 purchased intangibles intangible assets that are purchased that must be amortized over 180 months regardless of their actual useful lives.

§263A Cost (or UNICAP) certain book expenses that must be capitalized into inventory for tax purposes.

§291 depreciation recapture the portion of a corporate taxpayer's gain on real property that is converted from §1231 gain to ordinary income.

§338 election an election by a corporate buyer of 80-percent-or-more of a corporation's stock to treat the acquisition as an asset acquisition and not a stock acquisition.

§338(h)(10) election a joint election by the corporate buyer and corporate seller of the stock of a subsidiary of the seller to treat the acquisition as a sale of the subsidiary's assets by the seller to the buyer.

§481 adjustment a change to taxable income associated with a change in accounting methods.

§1231 assets depreciable or real property used in a taxpayer's trade or business owned for more than one year.

§1231 look-back rule a tax rule requiring taxpayers to treat current year net §1231 gains as ordinary income when the taxpayer has deducted a §1231 loss as an ordinary loss in the five years preceding the current tax year.

§1245 property tangible personal property and intangible property subject to cost recovery deductions.

§1250 property real property subject to cost recovery deductions.

§7520 rate an interest rate set at 120 percent of the applicable federal midterm rate (published monthly by the Treasury) and used to calculate the value of temporal interests.

12-month rule regulation that allows prepaid business expenses to be currently deducted when the contract does not extend beyond 12 months and the contract period does not extend beyond the end of the tax year following the year of the payment.

30-day letter the IRS letter received after an audit that instructs the taxpayer that he or she has 30 days to either (1) request a conference with an appeals officer or (2) agree to the proposed adjustment.

90-day letter the IRS letter received after an audit and receipt of the 30-day letter that explains that the taxpayer has 90 days to either (1) pay the proposed deficiency or (2) file a petition in the U.S. Tax Court to hear the case. The 90-day letter is also known as the *statutory notice of deficiency.*

704(b) capital accounts partners' capital accounts maintained using the accounting rules prescribed in the Section 704(b) regulations. Under these rules, capital accounts reflect the fair market value of property contributed to and distributed property from partnerships.

A

Abandoned spouse a married taxpayer who lives apart from his or her spouse for the last six months of the year (excluding temporary absences), who files a tax return separate from his or her spouse, and who maintains a household for a qualifying child.

Accelerated Cost Recovery System (ACRS) the depreciation system enacted by Congress in 1981 that is based on the concept of set recovery periods and accelerated depreciation methods.

Accelerated death benefits early receipt of life insurance proceeds that are not taxable under certain circumstances, such as the taxpayer is medically certified with an illness that is expected to cause death within 24 months.

Accountable plan an employer's reimbursement plan under which employees must submit documentation supporting expenses to receive reimbursement and reimbursements are limited to legitimate business expenses.

Accounting method the procedure for determining the taxable year in which a business recognizes a particular item of income or deduction thereby dictating the timing of when a taxpayer reports income and deductions.

Accounting period a fixed period in which a business reports income and deductions, generally referred to as a tax year.

Accrual method a method of accounting that generally recognizes income in the period earned and recognizes deductions in the period that liabilities are incurred.

Accrued market discount a ratable amount of the market discount at the time of purchase (based on the number of days the bond is held over the number of days until maturity when the bond is purchased) that is treated as interest income when a bond with market discount is sold before it matures.

Accumulated adjustments account (AAA) an account that reflects the cumulative income or loss for the time the corporation has been an S corporation.

Accumulated earnings and profits undistributed earnings and profits from years prior to the current year.

Accumulated earnings tax a tax assessed on corporations that retain earnings without a business reason to do so.

Acquiescence issued after the IRS loses a trial-level or circuit court case when the IRS has decided to follow the court's adverse ruling in the future. It does not mean that the IRS agrees with the court's ruling. Instead, it simply means that the IRS will no longer litigate this issue.

Acquisition indebtedness debt secured by a qualified residence that is incurred in acquiring, constructing, or substantially improving the residence.

Acquisition subsidiary a subsidiary used by the acquiring corporation in a triangular merger to acquire the target corporation.

Action on decision an IRS pronouncement that explains the background reasoning behind an IRS acquiescence or nonacquiescence.

Ad valorem tax a tax based on the value of property.

Adjusted basis *see* adjusted tax basis.

Adjusted current earnings (ACE) a version of a corporation's current year earnings that more closely represents a corporation's economic income for the year than do regular taxable income or alternative minimum taxable income.

Adjusted gross estate gross estate reduced by administrative expenses, debts of the decedent, losses, and state death taxes.

Adjusted gross income (AGI) gross income less deductions for AGI. AGI is an important reference point that is often used in other calculations.

Adjusted tax basis the taxpayer's acquisition basis (for example, cost) plus capital improvements less depreciation or amortization.

Adjusted taxable gifts cumulative taxable gifts from previous years other than gifts already included in the gross estate valued at date of gift values.

Affiliated group two or more "includable" corporations that are related through common stock ownership and eligible to file a U.S. consolidated tax return. An affiliated group consists of a parent corporation that owns directly 80 percent or more of the voting stock and value of another corporation and one or more subsidiary corporations that meet the 80 percent ownership requirement collectively. Includable corporations are taxable U.S. corporations, excluding real estate investment trusts, regulated investment companies, and life insurance companies.

After-tax rate of return a taxpayer's before-tax rate of return on an investment minus the taxes paid on the income from the investment. The formula for an after-tax rate of return that is taxed annually is the before-tax rate of return × (1 − marginal tax rate) [i.e., $r = R \times (1 - t)$]. A taxpayer's after-tax rate of return on an investment held for more than one tax period is $r = (FV/I)^{1/n} - 1$, where r is the after-tax rate of return, FV is the after-tax future value of the investment, I is the original investment amount, and n is the number of periods the investment is held.

Aggregate approach a theory of taxing partnerships that ignores partnerships as entities and taxes partners as if they directly owned partnership net assets.

Alimony a support payment of cash made to a former spouse. The payment must be made under a written separation agreement or divorce decree that does not designate the payment as something other than alimony, the payment must be made when the spouses do not live together, and the payments must cease no later than when the recipient dies.

All-events test requires that income or expenses are recognized when (1) all events have occurred that determine or fix the right to receive the income or liability to make the payments and (2) the amount of the income or expense can be determined with reasonable accuracy.

All-inclusive income concept a definition of income that says that gross income means all income from whatever source derived.

Allocate as used in the sourcing rules, the process of associating a deduction with a specific item or items of gross income for purposes of computing foreign source taxable income.

Allocation the method of dividing or sourcing nonbusiness income to specific states.

Allowance method bad debt expense is based on an estimate of the amount of the bad debts in accounts receivable at year-end.

Alternative minimum tax (AMT) a tax on a broader tax base than the base for the "regular" tax; the additional tax paid when the tentative minimum tax (based on the alternative minimum tax base) exceeds the regular tax (based on the regular tax base). The alternative minimum tax is designed to require taxpayers to pay some minimum level of tax even when they have low or no regular taxable income as a result of certain tax breaks in the tax code.

Alternative minimum tax adjustments adjustments (positive or negative) to regular taxable income to arrive at the alternative minimum tax base.

Alternative minimum tax base (AMT base) alternative minimum taxable income minus the alternative minimum tax exemption.

Alternative minimum tax exemption a deduction to determine the alternative minimum tax base that is phased out based on alternative minimum taxable income.

Alternative minimum tax system a secondary or parallel tax system calculated on an *alternative* tax base that more closely reflects economic income than the regular income tax base. The system was designed to ensure that taxpayers generating economic income pay some *minimum* amount of income tax each year.

Alternative valuation date the date nine months after the decedent's date of death.

Amortization the method of recovering the cost of intangible assets over a specific time period.

Amount realized the value of everything received by the seller in a transaction (cash, FMV of other property, and relief of liabilities) less selling costs.

Annotated tax service a tax service arranged by code section. For each code section, an annotated service includes the code section; a listing of the code section history; copies of congressional committee reports that explain changes to the code section; a copy of all the regulations issued for the specific code section; the service's unofficial explanation of the code section; and brief summaries (called annotations) of relevant court cases, revenue rulings, revenue procedures, and letter rulings that address issues specific to the code section.

Annual exclusion amount of gifts allowed to be made each year per donee (regardless of the number of donees) to prevent the taxation of relatively small gifts ($14,000 per donee per year in 2017).

Annualized income method a method for determining a corporation's required estimated tax payments when the taxpayer earns more income later in the year than earlier in the year. Requires corporations to base their first and second required estimated tax installments on their income from the first three months of the year, their third installment based on their taxable income from the first six months of the year, and the final installment based on their taxable income from the first nine months of the year.

Annuity a stream of equal payments over time.

Applicable credit also known as the *unified credit*, the amount of current tax on the exemption equivalent; designed to prevent transfer taxation of smaller cumulative transfers.

Applicable tax rate the tax rate or rates used to measure a company's deferred tax asset or liability. In general, it is the enacted tax rate that is expected to apply to taxable income in the period in which the deferred tax asset or liability is expected to be recovered or settled. For U.S. tax purposes, the applicable tax rate is the regular tax rate.

Apportion as used in the sourcing rules, the process of calculating the amount of a deduction that is associated with a specific item or items of gross income for purposes of computing foreign source taxable income.

Apportionment the method of dividing business income of an interstate business among the states where nexus exists.

Arm's-length amount price in transactions among unrelated taxpayers, where each transacting party negotiates for his or her own benefit.

Arm's-length transaction transactions among unrelated taxpayers, where each transacting party negotiates for his or her own benefit.

Articles of incorporation a document, filed by a corporation's founders with the state describing the purpose, place of business, and other details of the corporation.

Articles of organization a document, filed by a limited liability company's founders with the state, describing the purpose, place of business, and other details of the company.

Asset and liability approach the approach taken by ASC Topic 740 that focuses on computing a company's current taxes payable (refundable) and deferred tax assets and liabilities on the balance sheet. The income tax provision recorded on the income statement is the amount needed to adjust the beginning of the year balance sheet amounts to the end of the year balance sheet amounts.

Assignment of income doctrine the judicial doctrine holding that earned income is taxed to the taxpayer providing the service, and that income from property is taxed to the individual who owns the property when the income accrues.

At-risk amount an investor's risk of loss in a worst-case scenario. In a partnership, an amount generally equal to a partner's tax basis exclusive of the partner's share of nonrecourse debt.

At-risk rules tax rules limiting losses flowing through to partners or S corporation shareholders to their at-risk amount.

Average tax rate a taxpayer's average level of taxation on each dollar of taxable income. Specifically,

$$\text{Average tax rate} = \frac{\textit{Total tax}}{\textit{Taxable income}}$$

B

Bargain element (of stock options) the difference between the fair market value of the employer's stock and the amount employees pay to acquire the employer's stock.

Barter clubs organizations that facilitate the exchange of rights to goods and services between members.

Basis a taxpayer's unrecovered investment in an asset that provides a reference point for measuring gain or loss when an asset is sold.

Before-tax rate of return a taxpayer's rate of return on an investment before paying taxes on the income from the investment.

Beneficiary person for whom trust property is held and administered.

Bond a debt instrument issued for a period of more than one year with the purpose of raising capital by borrowing.

Bond discount the result of issuing bonds for less than their maturity value.

Bond premium the result of issuing bonds for more than their maturity value.

Bonus depreciation additional depreciation allowed in the acquisition year for new tangible personal property with a recovery period of 20 years or less.

Book equivalent of taxable income a company's pretax income from continuing operations adjusted for permanent differences.

Book (financial reporting) income the income or loss corporations report on their financial statements using applicable financial accounting standards.

Book–tax difference a difference in the amount of an income item or deduction item taken into account for book purposes compared to the amount taken into account for the same item for tax purposes.

Boot property given or received in an otherwise nontaxable transaction such as a like-kind exchange that may trigger gain to a party to the transaction.

Bracket a subset (or portion) of the tax base subject to a specific tax rate. Brackets are common to graduated taxes.

Branch an unincorporated division of a corporation.

Bright line tests technical rules found in the tax law that provide the taxpayer with objective tests to determine the tax consequences of a transaction.

Brother-sister controlled group a form of controlled group consisting of two or more corporations if five or fewer individuals collectively own more than 50 percent of the voting power or stock value of the corporation on the last day of the year.

Built-in gain the difference between the fair market value and tax basis of property owned by an entity when the fair market value exceeds the tax basis.

Built-in gains tax a tax levied on S corporations that were formerly C corporations. The tax applies to net unrealized built-in gains at the time the corporation converted from a C corporation to the extent the gains are recognized during the built-in gains tax recognition period. The applicable tax rate is 35 percent.

Built-in gains tax recognition period the first 5 years a corporation operates as an S corporation after converting from a C corporation.

Built-in loss the difference between the fair market value and tax basis of property owned by an entity when the tax basis exceeds the fair market value.

Bunching itemized deductions a common planning strategy in which a taxpayer pays two year's worth of itemized expenses in one year to exceed the standard deduction in that year.

Business activity a profit-motivated activity that requires a relatively high level of involvement or effort from the taxpayer to generate income.

Business income income derived from business activities.

Business purpose doctrine the judicial doctrine that allows the IRS to challenge and disallow business expenses for transactions with no underlying business motivation.

Business tax credits nonrefundable credits designed to provide incentives for taxpayers to hire certain types of individuals or to participate in certain business activities.

Bypass provision a provision in the will of a deceased spouse that transfers property to nonspousal beneficiaries to maximize the value of the decedent's applicable credit.

Bypass trust a trust used in lieu of a bypass provision to transfer property to nonspousal beneficiaries to maximize the value of the applicable credit of the first spouse to die.

C

C corporation a corporate taxpaying entity with income subject to taxation. Such a corporation is termed a "C" corporation because the corporation and its shareholders are subject to the provisions of subchapter C of the Internal Revenue Code.

Cafeteria plan an employer plan that allows employees to choose benefits from a menu of nontaxable fringe benefits or receive cash compensation in lieu of the benefits.

Capital account an account reflecting a partner's share of the equity in a partnership. Capital accounts are maintained using tax accounting methods or other methods of accounting, including GAAP, at the discretion of the partnership.

Capital asset in general, an asset other than an asset used in a trade or business or an asset such as an account or note receivable acquired in a business from the sale of services or property.

Capital gain property any asset that would have generated a long-term capital gain if the taxpayer had sold the property for its fair market value.

Capital interest an economic right attached to a partnership interest giving a partner the right to receive cash or property in the event the partnership liquidates. A capital interest is synonymous with the liquidation value of a partnership interest.

Capitalization recording an expenditure as an asset on the balance sheet rather than expensing it immediately.

Carryover basis the basis of an asset the transferee takes in property received in a nontaxable exchange. The basis of the asset carries over from the transferor to the transferee.

Cash method the method of accounting that recognizes income in the period in which cash, property, or services are received and recognizes deductions in the period paid.

Cash surrender value the amount, if any, the owner of a life insurance policy receives when the policy is cashed in before the death of the insured individual.

Cash tax rate the tax rate computed by dividing a company's taxes paid during the year by its pretax income from continuing operations.

Cashless exercise a technique where options are both exercised and at least a portion of the shares are sold in order to facilitate the purchase.

Casualty an unexpected, unforeseen event driven by forces outside the control of the taxpayer (such as "fire, storm, or shipwreck" or other event or theft) that damages or destroys a taxpayer's property.

Casualty loss a loss arising from a *sudden, unexpected,* or *unusual* event such as a "fire, storm, or shipwreck" or loss from theft.

Ceiling limitations that are maximum amounts for adjustments to taxable income (or credits). The amounts in excess of the ceiling are either lost or carried to another tax year.

Certainty one of the criteria used to evaluate tax systems. Certainty means taxpayers should be able to determine when, where, and how much tax to pay.

Certificate of deposit an interest-bearing debt instrument offered by banks and savings and loans. Money removed from the CD before maturity is subject to a penalty.

Certificate of limited partnership a document limited partnerships must file with the state to be formerly recognized by the state. The document is similar to articles of incorporation or articles or organization.

Character of income a type of income that is treated differently than other types of income for purposes of computing a taxpayer's taxable income and income tax liability. For example, one type of income (qualified dividend) may be taxed at a different rate than another type of income (ordinary income).

Charitable contribution limit modified taxable income taxable income for purposes of determining the 10 percent of taxable income deduction limitation for corporate charitable contributions. Computed as taxable income before deducting (1) any charitable contributions, (2) the dividends received deduction, (3) net operating loss carrybacks, and (4) the domestic production activities deduction.

Circular 230 regulations issued by the IRS that govern tax practice and apply to all persons practicing before the IRS. There are five parts of Circular 230: Subpart A describes who may practice before the IRS (e.g., CPAs, attorneys, enrolled agents) and what practicing before the IRS means (tax return preparation, representing clients before the IRS, etc.). Subpart B describes the duties and restrictions that apply to individuals governed by Circular 230. Subparts C and D explain sanctions and disciplinary proceedings for practitioners violating the Circular 230 provisions. Subpart E concludes with a few miscellaneous provisions (such as the Circular 230 effective date).

Citator a research tool that allows one to check the status of several types of tax authorities. A citator can be used to review the history of the case to find out, for example, whether it was subsequently appealed and overturned, and to identify subsequent cases that cite the case. Citators can also be used to check the status of revenue rulings, revenue procedures, and other IRS pronouncements.

Civil penalties monetary penalties imposed when tax practitioners or taxpayers violate tax statutes without reasonable cause—for example, as the result of negligence, intentional disregard of pertinent rules, willful disobedience, or outright fraud.

Claim of right doctrine judicial doctrine that states that income has been realized if a taxpayer receives income and there are no restrictions on the taxpayer's use of the income (for example, the taxpayer does not have an obligation to repay the amount).

Cliff vesting a qualified plan provision allowing for benefits to vest all at once after a specified period of time has passed.

Collectibles a work of art, a rug or antique, a metal or gem, a stamp or coin, an alcoholic beverage, or other similar items held for investment for more than one year.

Combined controlled group a form of a controlled group consisting of three or more corporations each of which is a member of either a parent-subsidiary or brother-sister controlled group and one of which is the parent in the parent-subsidiary controlled group and also is in a brother-sister controlled group.

Commercial domicile the state where a business is headquartered and directs operations; this location may be different from the place of incorporation.

Commercial traveler exception a statutory exception that exempts nonresidents from U.S. taxation of compensation from services if the individual is in the United States 90 days or less and earns compensation of $3,000 or less.

Common-law states the 41 states that have not adopted community property laws.

Community-property states nine states (Arizona, California, Idaho, Louisiana, Nevada, New Mexico, Texas, Washington, and Wisconsin) that automatically equally divide the ownership of property acquired by either spouse during a marriage.

Community property systems systems in which state laws dictate how the income and property is legally shared between a husband and a wife.

Commuting traveling from a personal residence to the place of business.

Complex trust a trust that is not required by the trust instrument to distribute income currently.

Conglomerate a group of corporations in different businesses under common ownership.

Consolidated tax return a combined U.S. income tax return filed by an affiliated group of corporations.

Consolidation the combining of the assets and liabilities of two or more corporations into a new entity.

Constructive dividend a payment made by a corporation to a shareholder that is recharacterized by the IRS or courts as a dividend even though it is not characterized as such by the corporation.

Constructive ownership occurs when the tax laws cause stock not owned by a taxpayer to be treated as owned by the taxpayer for purposes of meeting certain stock ownership tests.

Constructive receipt doctrine the judicial doctrine that provides that a taxpayer must recognize income when it is actually or constructively received. Constructive receipt is deemed to have occurred if the income has been credited to the taxpayer's account or if the income is unconditionally available to the taxpayer, the taxpayer is aware of the income's availability, and there are no restrictions on the taxpayer's control over the income.

Continuity of business enterprise (COBE) a judicial (now regulatory) requirement that the acquiring corporation continue the target corporation's historic business or continue to use a "significant" portion of the target corporation's historic business assets to be tax-deferred.

Continuity of interest (COI) a judicial (now regulatory) requirement that the transferors of stock in a reorganization collectively retain a continuing ownership (equity) interest in the target corporation's assets or historic business to be tax-deferred.

Contribution to capital a shareholder's or other person's contribution of cash or other property to a corporation without receipt of an additional equity interest in the corporation.

Controlled foreign corporation a foreign corporation that is more than 50 percent owned by U.S. shareholders.

Controlled group a group of corporations owned by the same individual shareholders; it can either be brother-sister corporations or parent-subsidiary corporations.

Convenience one of the criteria used to evaluate tax systems. Convenience means a tax system should be designed to facilitate the collection of tax revenues without undue hardship on the taxpayer or the government.

Corporation business entity recognized as separate entity from its owners under state law.

Corporation's effective tax rate the tax rate computed by dividing a company's income tax provision (expense or benefit) for the year by its pretax income from continuing operations.

Corpus the principal or property transferred to fund a trust or accumulated in the trust.

Correspondence examination an IRS audit conducted by mail and generally limited to one or two items on the taxpayer's return. Among the three types of audits, correspondence audits are generally the most common, the most narrow in scope, and least complex. The IRS typically requests supporting documentation for one or more items on the taxpayer's return (e.g., documentation of charitable contributions deducted).

Cost depletion the method of recovering the cost of a natural resource that allows a taxpayer to estimate or determine the number of units that remain in the resource at the beginning of the year and allocate a pro rata share of the remaining basis to each unit of the resource that is extracted or sold during the year.

Cost recovery the method by which a company expenses the cost of acquiring capital assets. Cost recovery can take the form of depreciation, amortization, or depletion.

Coupon rate the interest rate expressed as a percentage of the face value of the bond.

Covenant not to compete a contractual promise to refrain from conducting business or professional activities similar to those of another party.

Criminal penalties penalties commonly charged in tax evasion cases (i.e., willful intent to defraud the government). They are imposed only after normal due process, including a trial. Compared to civil cases, the standard of conviction is higher in a criminal trial (beyond a reasonable doubt). However, the penalties are also much higher, such as fines up to $100,000 for individuals plus a prison sentence.

Current earnings and profits a year-to-year calculation maintained by a corporation to determine if a distribution is a dividend. Earnings and profits are computed for the current year by adjusting taxable income to make it more closely resemble economic income.

Current gifts gifts completed during the calendar year that are not already exempted from the gift tax.

Current income tax expense (benefit) the amount of taxes paid or payable (refundable) in the current year.

Current tax liability (asset) the amount of taxes payable or refundable in the current year.

D

***De minimis* fringe benefit** a nontaxable fringe benefit that allows employees to receive occasional or incidental benefits tax-free.

Debt basis the outstanding principal of direct loans from an S corporation shareholder to the S corporation. Once taxpayers deduct losses to the extent of their stock basis, they may deduct losses to the extent of their debt basis. When the debt basis has been reduced by losses, it is restored by income/gain allocations.

Deceased spousal unused exclusion amount of unused applicable credit from predeceased spouse.

Deductible temporary differences book–tax differences that will result in tax deductible amounts in future years when the related deferred tax asset is recovered.

Deductions amounts that are subtracted from gross income in calculating taxable income.

Deductions above the line *for* AGI deductions or deductions subtracted from gross income to determine AGI.

Deductions below the line *from* AGI deductions or deductions subtracted from AGI to calculate taxable income.

Deferral items, deferred income, or deferrals realized income that will be taxed as income in a subsequent year.

Deferral method recognizes income from advance payments for goods by the earlier of (1) when the business would recognize the income for tax purposes if it had not received the *advance* payment or (2) when it recognizes the income for financial reporting purposes.

Deferred like-kind exchange a like-kind exchange where the taxpayer transfers like-kind property before receiving the like-kind property in exchange. The property to be received must be identified within 45 days and received within 180 days of the transfer of the property given up.

Deferred tax asset the expected future tax benefit attributable to deductible temporary differences and carryforwards.

Deferred tax liability the expected future tax cost attributable to taxable temporary differences.

Defined benefit plan employer-provided qualified plans that spell out the specific benefit employees will receive on retirement.

Defined contribution plan employer-provided qualified plans that specify the maximum annual contributions employers and/or employees may contribute to the plan.

Definitely related deductions deductions that are associated with the creation of a specific item or items of gross income.

Dependency exemption a fixed deduction allowed for each individual who qualifies as a "dependent" of the taxpayer.

Dependent a person for whom a taxpayer may claim a dependency exemption. To qualify as a dependent a person must be a qualifying child or qualifying relative of the taxpayer.

Dependent care benefit a nontaxable fringe benefit that allows employees to receive up to $5,000 of care for children under age 13 or for a spouse or other dependent with physical needs.

Depletion the cost recovery method to allocate the cost of natural resources as they are removed.

Depreciation the cost recovery method to allocate the cost of tangible personal and real property over a specific time period.

Depreciation recapture the conversion of §1231 gain into ordinary income on a sale (or exchange) based on the amount of accumulated depreciation on the property at the time of sale or exchange.

Determination letters rulings requested by the taxpayer, issued by local IRS directors, and generally not controversial. An example of a determination letter is the request by an employer for the IRS to rule that the taxpayer's retirement plan is a "qualified plan."

DIF (Discriminant Function) system the DIF system assigns a score to each tax return that represents the probability that the tax liability on the return has been underreported (a higher score = a higher likelihood of underreporting). The IRS derives the weights assigned to specific tax return attributes from historical IRS audit adjustment data from the National Research Program. The DIF system then uses these (undisclosed) weights to score each tax return based on the tax return's characteristics. Returns with higher DIF scores are then reviewed to determine if an audit is the best course of action.

Direct conversion when a taxpayer receives noncash property rather than a cash payment as a replacement for property damaged or destroyed in an involuntary conversion.

Direct write-off method required method for deducting bad debts for tax purposes. Under this method, businesses deduct bad debt only when the debt becomes wholly or partially worthless.

Disability insurance sometimes called sick pay or wage replacement insurance. It pays the insured for wages lost due to injury or disability.

Discharge of indebtedness debt forgiveness.

Discount factor the factor based on the taxpayer's rate of return that is used to determine the present value of future cash inflows (e.g., tax savings) and outflows (taxes paid).

Disproportionate distributions partnership distributions that change the partners' relative ownership of hot assets.

Disqualifying disposition the sale of stock acquired using incentive stock options prior to satisfying certain holding period requirements. Failing to satisfy the holding period requirements converts the options into nonqualified stock options.

Disregarded entities incorporated entities with one owner that are treated as flow-through entities for U.S. income tax purposes.

Distributable net income (DNI) the maximum amount of the distribution deduction by fiduciaries and the maximum aggregate amount of gross income reportable by beneficiaries.

Distribution deduction deduction by fiduciaries for distributions of income to beneficiaries that operates to eliminate the potential for double taxation of fiduciary income.

Dividend a distribution to shareholders of money or property from the corporation's earnings and profits.

Dividends received deduction a corporate deduction for part or all of a dividend received from other taxable, domestic corporations.

Document perfection program a program under which all tax returns are checked for mathematical and tax calculation errors.

Domestic production activities deduction (DPAD) a deduction for businesses that manufacture goods in the United States.

Donee person receiving a gift.

Donor person making a gift.

Double taxation the tax burden when an entity's income is subject to two levels of tax. Income of C corporations is subject to double taxation. The first level of tax is at the corporate level and the second level of tax on corporate income occurs at the shareholder level. Income of flow-through entities is generally not subject to double taxation.

DRD modified taxable income taxable income for purposes of applying the taxable income limitation for the dividends received deduction. Computed as the dividend receiving corporation's taxable income before deducting the dividends received deduction, any net operating loss deduction, the domestic production activities deduction, and capital loss carrybacks.

Dwelling unit property that provides a place suitable for people to occupy (live and sleep).

Dynamic forecasting the process of forecasting tax revenues that incorporates into the forecast how taxpayers may alter their activities in response to a tax law change.

E

Earmarked tax a tax assessed for a specific purpose (e.g., for education).

Earned income compensation and other forms of income received for providing goods or services in the ordinary course of business.

Earned income credit a refundable credit designed to help offset the effect of employment taxes on compensation paid to low-income taxpayers and to encourage lower income taxpayers to seek employment.

Earnings and profits a measure of a corporation's earnings that is similar to its economic earnings. Corporate dividends are taxable to shareholders to the extent they come from earnings and profits.

Economic nexus the concept that businesses without a physical presence in the state may establish income tax nexus in the state through an economic presence there.

Economic performance test the third requirement that must be met for an accrual method taxpayer to deduct an expense currently. The specific event that satisfies the economic performance test varies based on the type of expense.

Economic substance doctrine doctrine that requires transactions to meaningfully change a taxpayer's economic position *and* to have a substantial purpose (apart from a federal income tax purpose) in order for a taxpayer to obtain tax benefits.

Economy one of the criteria used to evaluate tax systems. Economy means a tax system should minimize its compliance and administration costs.

Educational assistance benefit a nontaxable fringe benefit that allows an employer to provide a certain amount of education benefits on an annual basis.

Effective tax rate the taxpayer's average rate of taxation on each dollar of total income (taxable and nontaxable income). Specifically,

$$\text{Effective tax rate} = \frac{\textit{Total tax}}{\textit{Total income}}$$

Effectively connected income net income that results from the conduct of a U.S. trade or business by a nonresident.

Employee a person who is hired to provide services to a company on a regular basis in exchange for compensation and who does not provide these services as part of an independent business.

Employment taxes taxes consisting of the Old Age, Survivors, and Disability Insurance (OASDI) tax, commonly called the Social Security tax, and the Medical Health Insurance (MHI) tax known as the Medicare tax.

Enacted tax rate the statutory tax rate that will apply in the current or a future period.

Entity approach a theory of taxing partnerships that treats partnerships as entities separate from partners.

Equity one of the criteria used to evaluate a tax system. A tax system is considered fair or equitable if the tax is based on the taxpayer's ability to pay; taxpayers with a greater ability to pay tax, pay more tax.

Escrow account (mortgage-related) a holding account with a taxpayer's mortgage lender. The taxpayer makes mortgage payments to the lender that include payment for the interest and principal and payments for property taxes. The lender maintains the payments for property taxes in the escrow account and uses the funds in the account to pay the property taxes when the taxes are due.

Estate fiduciary legal entity that comes into existence upon a person's death and is empowered by the probate court to gather and transfer the decedent's real and personal property.

Estate tax the tax paid for an estate.

Estimated tax payments quarterly tax payments that a taxpayer makes to the government if the tax withholding is insufficient to meet the taxpayer's tax liability.

Excess net passive income net passive investment income × passive investment income in excess of 25 percent of the S corporation's gross receipts divided by its passive investment income.

Excess net passive income tax a tax levied on an S corporation that has accumulated earnings and profits from years in which it operated as a C corporation if the corporation reports excess net passive income.

Exchanged basis the basis of an asset received in a nontaxable exchange. An exchanged basis is generally the basis of the asset given up in a nontaxable exchange. Exchanged basis may also be referred to as a *substituted basis.*

Excise taxes taxes levied on the retail sale of particular products. They differ from other taxes in that the tax base for an excise tax typically depends on the *quantity* purchased rather than a monetary amount.

Excluded income or exclusions realized income that is exempted from income taxation.

Ex-dividend date the relevant date for determining who receives a dividend from a stock. Anyone purchasing stock before this date will receive current dividends. Otherwise, the purchaser must wait until subsequent dividends are declared before receiving them.

Executor the person who takes responsibility for collecting the assets of the decedent, paying the decedent's debts, and distributing the remaining assets to the rightful heirs.

Exemption a fixed income tax deduction a taxpayer may claim for each person who qualifies as a dependent of the taxpayer. This includes the taxpayer (and spouse on a joint return) who does not qualify as a dependent of another.

Exemption equivalent the amount of cumulative taxable transfers a taxpayer can make without exceeding the applicable credit.

Exercise date the date employees use their stock options to acquire employer stock at a discounted price.

Exercise price the price at which holders of stock options may purchase stock in the corporation issuing the option.

Explicit tax a tax directly imposed by a government.

F

Face value a specified final amount paid to the owner of a coupon bond on the date of maturity. The face value is also known as the *maturity value.*

Facts and circumstances test a test used to make subjective determination such as whether the amount of salary paid to an employee is reasonable. The test requires the taxpayer and the IRS to consider all the relevant facts and circumstances surrounding the situation in order to make a decision. The relevant facts and circumstance are situation-specific.

Family limited partnership a partnership designed to save estate taxes by dividing a family business into various ownership interests representing control of operations and future income and appreciation of the assets.

Favorable book–tax difference a book–tax difference that requires a subtraction from book income in determining taxable income.

Federal/state adjustments amounts added to or subtracted from federal taxable income when firms compute taxable income for a particular state.

Federal short-term interest rate the quarterly interest rate used to determine the interest charged for tax underpayments (federal short-term rate plus 3 percent).

FICA taxes FICA (Federal Insurance Contribution Act) taxes are a term used to denote both the Social Security and Medicare taxes upon earned income. For self-employed taxpayers, the terms "FICA tax" and "self-employment tax" are synonymous.

Fiduciary a person or legal entity that takes possession of property for the benefit of beneficiaries.

Fiduciary duty a requirement that a fiduciary act in an objective and impartial manner and not favor one beneficiary over another.

Field examination the least common audit. The IRS conducts these audits at the taxpayer's place of business or the location where the taxpayer's books, records, and source documents are maintained. Field examinations are generally the broadest in scope and most complex of the three audit types. They can last many months to multiple years and generally are limited to business returns and the most complex individual returns.

FIFO *see* first-in, first-out (FIFO) method.

Filing status filing status places taxpayers into one of five categories (married filing jointly, married filing separately, qualifying widow or widower, head of household, and single) by marital status and family situation as of the end of the year. Filing status determines whether a taxpayer must file a tax return, appropriate tax rate schedules, standard deduction amounts, and several deduction and credit limitation thresholds.

Final regulations regulations that have been issued in final form, and thus, until revoked, they represent the Treasury's interpretation of the Code.

Financial reporting income *see* book (financial reporting) income.

First-in, first-out (FIFO) method an accounting method that values the cost of assets sold under the assumption that the assets are sold in the order purchased (i.e., first purchased, first sold).

Fiscal year a year that ends on the last day of a month other than December.

Fixed and determinable, annual or periodic income U.S. source passive income earned by a nonresident.

Flat tax a tax in which a single tax rate is applied throughout the tax base.

Flexible spending account a plan that allows employees to contribute before-tax dollars that may be used for unreimbursed medical expenses or dependent care.

Flipping a term used to describe the real estate investment practice of acquiring a home, repairing or remodeling the home, and then immediately, or soon thereafter, selling it (presumably at a profit).

Floor limitation a minimum amount that an expenditure (or credit or other adjustment to taxable income) must meet before any amount is allowed.

Flow-through entities legal entities like partnerships, limited liability companies, and S corporations that do not pay income tax. Income and losses from flow-through entities are allocated to their owners.

***For* AGI deductions** deductions that are subtracted from gross income to determine AGI.

For the convenience of the employer benefits nontaxable benefits employers provide to employees and employee spouses or dependents in the form of meals or lodging if provided on the employer's premises and provided for a purpose that is helpful or convenient for the employer.

Foreign joint venture a 50 percent or less owned foreign entity.

Foreign personal holding company income a category of foreign source passive income that includes interest, dividends, rents, royalties, and gains from sale of assets.

Foreign subsidiary a more than 50 percent owned foreign corporation.

Foreign tax credit a credit for income taxes paid to a foreign jurisdiction.

Foreign tax credit limitation the limit put on the use of creditable foreign taxes for the current year.

Form 1065 the form partnerships file annually with the IRS to report partnership ordinary income (loss) and separately stated items for the year.

Form 1120S the form S corporations file annually with the IRS to report S corporation ordinary income (loss) and separately stated items for the year.

Form 2553 the form filed to elect S corporation status.

Form 7004 the form C corporations, partnerships, and S corporations file to receive an automatic extension to file their annual tax return.

Form W-2 used to report wages paid to employees and the taxes withheld from them. The form is also used to report FICA taxes to the Social Security Administration.

Form W-4 a form used by a taxpayer to supply her employer with the information necessary to determine the amount of tax to withhold from each paycheck.

Forward triangular merger an acquisition in which the acquired (target) corporation merges into an acquisition subsidiary of the acquiring corporation, after which the acquired corporation becomes part of the acquisition subsidiary of the acquiring corporation.

Fringe benefits noncash benefit provided to an employee as a form of compensation. As a general rule, fringe benefits are taxable. However, certain fringe benefits are excluded from gross income.

***From* AGI deductions** deductions subtracted from AGI to calculate taxable income.

FTC basket a category of income that requires a separate FTC limitation computation.

Full-inclusion method the method for accounting for advance payments for goods that requires that businesses immediately recognize advance payments as taxable income.

Full-month convention a convention that allows owners of intangibles to deduct an entire month's amortization in the month of purchase and month of disposition.

Functional currency the currency of the primary economic environment in which an entity operates (i.e., the currency of the jurisdiction in which an entity primarily generates and expends cash).

Future interest the right to receive property in the future.

G

GAAP capital accounts partners' capital accounts maintained using generally accepted accounting principles (GAAP).

General category income foreign source income that is not considered passive category income for foreign tax credit purposes (generally income from an active trade or business).

General partnership a partnership with partners who all have unlimited liability with respect to the liabilities of the entity.

Generation-skipping tax (GST) supplemental transfer tax designed to prevent the avoidance of estate and gift taxes through transfers that skip a generation of recipients.

Gift a transfer of property where no, or inadequate, consideration is paid for the property.

Gift tax the tax paid on a gift.

Golsen rule the rule that states that the U.S. Tax Court will abide by the rulings of the circuit court that has appellate jurisdiction for a case.

Goodwill the value of an acquired business in excess of the fair market value of identifiable assets.

Graded vesting a qualified plan rule that requires an increasing percentage of plan benefits to vest with each additional year of employment.

Graduated taxes taxes in which the tax base is divided into a series of monetary amounts, or brackets, where each successive bracket is taxed at a different (gradually higher or gradually lower) percentage rate.

Grant date (stock options) the date on which employees receive stock options to acquire employer stock at a specified price.

Grantor person creating a trust.

Gross estate property owned by the decedent at death and certain property transfers taking effect at death.

Gross income realized income reduced for any excluded or deferred income.

Gross receipts (for purposes of net passive investment income tax calculation) the total amount of revenues (including passive investment income) received or accrued under the corporation's accounting method, not reduced by returns, allowances, cost of goods sold, or deductions. Gross receipts include net capital gains from the sales or exchanges of capital assets and gains from the sales or exchanges of stock or securities (losses do not offset gains).

Group-term life insurance term life insurance provided by an employer to a group of employees.

Guaranteed payments payments made to partners or LLC members that are guaranteed because they are not contingent on partnership profits or losses. They are economically similar to shareholder salary payments.

H

Half-year convention a depreciation convention that allows owners of tangible personal property to take one-half of a year's worth of depreciation in the year of purchase and in the year of disposition regardless of when the asset was actually placed in service or sold.

Head of household one of five primary filing statuses. A taxpayer may file as head of household if s/he is unmarried as of the end of the year *and* pays more than half of the cost to maintain a household for a qualifying person who lives with the taxpayer for more than half of the year; or, s/he pays more than half the costs to maintain a household for a parent who qualifies as the taxpayer's dependent.

Health and accident insurance a fringe benefit provided to employees that provides benefits upon sickness, injury, or death.

Heirs persons who inherit property from the deceased.

Hobby a revenue-generating activity that is motivated by personal motives rather than profit objectives.

Home-equity indebtedness debt (except for acquisition indebtedness) secured by the taxpayer's qualified residence to the extent it does not exceed the fair market value of the residence over the acquisition indebtedness. Interest paid on up to $100,000 of home-equity indebtedness is allowed as an itemized deduction.

Home office deduction deductions relating to the use of an office in the home. A taxpayer must meet strict requirements to qualify for the deduction.

Horizontal equity one of the dimensions of equity. Horizontal equity is achieved if taxpayers in similar situations pay the same tax.

Hot assets unrealized receivables or inventory items defined in §751(a) that give rise to ordinary gains and losses. The exact definition of hot assets depends on whether it is in reference to dispositions of a partnership interest or distributions.

Hybrid entity an entity for which an election is available to choose the entity's tax status for U.S. tax purposes.

I

Impermissible accounting method an accounting method prohibited by tax laws.

Implicit tax indirect taxes that result from a tax advantage the government grants to certain transactions to satisfy social, economic, or other objectives. They are defined as the reduced before-tax return that a tax-favored asset produces because of its tax-advantaged status.

Imputed income income from an economic benefit the taxpayer receives indirectly rather than directly. The amount of the income is based on comparable alternatives.

Inbound transaction a transaction conducted by a foreign person that is subject to U.S. taxation.

Incentive stock option a type of stock option that allows employees to defer the bargain element for regular tax purposes until the stock acquired from option exercises is sold. The bargain element is taxed at capital gains rates provided the stock is retained long enough to satisfy certain holding period requirements. Employers cannot deduct the bargain element as compensation expense.

Income effect one of the two basic responses that a taxpayer may have when taxes increase. The income effect predicts that when taxpayers are taxed more (e.g., tax rate increases from 25 to 28 percent), they will work harder to generate the same after-tax dollars.

Income tax a tax in which the tax base is income. Income taxes are imposed by the federal government and by most states.

Independent contractor a person who provides services to another entity, usually under terms specified in a contract. The independent contractor has more control over how and when to do the work than does an employee.

Indirect conversion the receipt of money or other property as a replacement for property that was destroyed or damaged in an involuntary conversion.

Individual retirement account (IRA) a tax-advantaged account in which individuals who have earned income can save for retirement.

Information matching program a program that compares the taxpayer's tax return to information submitted to the IRS from other taxpayers (e.g., banks, employers, mutual funds, brokerage companies, mortgage companies). Information matched includes items such as wages (e.g., Form W-2 submitted by employers), interest income (e.g., Form 1099-INT submitted by banks), dividend income (e.g., Form 1099-DIV submitted by brokerage companies), and so forth.

Inheritance a transfer of property when the owner is deceased (the transfer is made by the decedent's estate).

Initial public offering the first sale of stock by a company to the public.

Inside basis the tax basis of an entity's assets and liabilities.

Installment sale a sale for which the taxpayer receives payment in more than one period.

Institutional shareholders entities, such as investment companies, mutual funds, brokerages, insurance companies, pension funds, investment banks, and endowment funds, with large amounts to invest in corporate stock entities.

Intangible assets assets that do not have physical characteristics. Examples include goodwill, covenants not to compete, organizational expenditures, and research and experimentation expenses.

Internal Revenue Code of 1986 the codified tax laws of the United States. Although the Code is frequently revised, there have been only three different codes since the Code was created in 1939 (i.e., the IRC of 1939, IRC of 1954, and IRC of 1986).

Interpretative regulations the most common regulation; they represent the Treasury's interpretation of the Code and are issued under the Treasury's general authority to interpret the Code.

Interstate commerce business conducted between parties in two or more states.

Inter vivos transfers gifts made by a donor during his or her lifetime.

Inventory items (for sale of partnership interest purposes) classic inventory defined as property held for sale to customers in the ordinary course of business, but also assets that are not capital assets or §1231 assets, which would produce ordinary income if sold by the entity. There are actually two definitions of inventory items in §751. §751(a) inventory items are defined in §751(d) to include all inventory items. The §751(b) definition includes only substantially appreciated inventory.

Investment activities a profit-seeking activity that is intermittent or occasional in frequency, including the production or collection of income or the management, conservation, or maintenance of property held for the production of income.

Investment expenses expenses such as safe deposit rental fees, attorney fees, and accounting fees that are necessary to produce portfolio income. Investment expenses are allowed for individuals as miscellaneous itemized deductions subject to the 2 percent of AGI floor limitation.

Investment income income received from portfolio type investments. Portfolio income includes capital gains and losses, interest, dividend, annuity, and royalty income not derived in the ordinary course of a trade or business. When computing the deductibility of investment interest expense, however, capital gains and dividends subject to the preferential tax rate are not treated as investment income unless the taxpayer elects to have this income taxed at ordinary tax rates.

Investment interest expense interest paid on borrowings or loans that are used to fund portfolio investments. Individuals are allowed an itemized deduction for qualified investment interest paid during the year.

Involuntary conversion a direct or indirect conversion of property through natural disaster, government condemnation, or accident that allows a taxpayer to defer realized gain if certain requirements are met.

IRS allocation method allocates expenses associated with rental use of the home between rental use and personal use. The percentage of total expenses allocated to rental use is the ratio of the number of rental use days for the property to the total days the property was used during the year.

Itemized deductions certain types of expenditures that Congress allows taxpayers to deduct as *from* AGI deductions.

J

Joint tenancy with the right of survivorship title to property that provides the co-owners with equal rights to it and that automatically transfers to the survivor(s) at the death of a co-owner.

K

Kiddie tax a tax imposed at the parent's marginal rate on a child's unearned income.

L

Last will and testament the document that directs the transfer of ownership of the decedent's assets to the heirs.

Late filing penalty a penalty assessed if a taxpayer does not file a tax return by the required date (the original due date plus extension).

Least aggregate deferral an approach to determine a partnership's required year-end if a majority of the partners don't have the same year-end and if the principal partners don't have the same year-end. As the name implies, this approach minimizes the combined tax deferral of the partners.

Legislative grace the concept that taxpayers receive certain tax benefits only because Congress writes laws that allow taxpayers to receive the tax benefits.

Legislative regulations the rarest type of regulation, issued when Congress specifically directs the Treasury Department to create regulations to address an issue in an area of law. In these instances, the Treasury is actually writing the law instead of interpreting the Code. Because legislative regulations actually represent tax law instead of an interpretation of tax law, legislative regulations have more authoritative weight than interpretative and procedural regulations.

Life estate the right to possess property and/or collect income from property for the duration of someone's life.

Life insurance trust a trust that is funded with an irrevocable transfer of a life insurance policy and gives the trustee the power to re-designate beneficiaries.

LIFO last-in, first-out method; an accounting method that values the cost of assets sold under the assumption that assets are sold in the reverse order in which they are purchased (i.e., last purchased, first sold).

LIFO recapture amount the excess of a C corporation's inventory basis under the FIFO method in excess of the inventory basis under the LIFO method in its final tax year as a C corporation before it becomes an S corporation.

LIFO recapture tax a tax levied on a C corporation that elects to be taxed as an S corporation when it is using the LIFO method for accounting for inventories.

Like-kind exchange a nontaxable (or partially taxable) trade or exchange of assets that are similar or related in use.

Limited liability company (LLC) a type of flow-through entity for federal income tax purposes. By state law, the owners of the LLC have limited liability with respect to the entity's debts or liabilities. Limited liability companies are taxed as partnerships for federal income tax purposes.

Limited partnership a partnership with at least one general partner with unlimited liability for the entity's debts and at least one limited partner with liability limited to the limited partner's investment in the partnership.

Liquidating distributions a distribution that terminates an owner's interest in the entity.

Liquidation value the amount a partner would receive if the partnership were to sell all its assets, pay its debts, and distribute its remaining assets to the partners in exchange for their partnership interests.

Listed property business assets that are often used for personal purposes. Depreciation on listed property is limited to the business use portion of the asset.

Local tax taxes imposed by local governments (cities, counties, school districts, etc.).

Long-term capital gain property property that would generate long-term capital gain if it were sold. This includes capital assets held for more than a year.

Long-term capital gains or losses gains or losses from the sale of capital assets held for more than 12 months.

Luxury automobile an automobile on which the amount of annual depreciation expense is limited because the cost of the automobile exceeds a certain threshold. The definition excludes vehicles with gross vehicle weight exceeding 6,000 pounds.

M

M adjustments *see* Schedule M adjustments.

Majority interest taxable year the common tax year of a group of partners who jointly hold greater than 50 percent of the profits and capital interests in the partnership.

Marginal tax rate the tax rate that applies to the *next additional increment* of a taxpayer's taxable income (or to deductions). Specifically,

$$\text{Marginal tax rate} = \frac{\Delta \mathit{Tax}}{\Delta \mathit{Taxable\ income}} = \frac{(\mathit{New\ total\ tax} - \mathit{Old\ total\ tax})}{(\mathit{New\ taxable\ income} - \mathit{Old\ taxable\ income})}$$

where "old" refers to the current tax and "new" refers to the revised tax after incorporating the additional income (or deductions) in question.

Marital deduction the deduction for transfers of qualified property to a spouse.

Market discount the difference between the amount paid for a bond in a market purchase rather than at original issuance when the amount paid is less than the maturity value of the bond.

Market premium the difference between the amount paid for a bond in a market purchase rather than at original issuance when the amount paid is greater than the maturity value of the bond.

Marriage benefit the tax savings married couples receive by filing a joint return relative to the tax they would have paid had they each filed as single taxpayers. This typically occurs when one spouse is either not working or earns significantly less than the other spouse.

Marriage penalty the extra tax cost a married couple pays by filing a joint return relative to what they would have paid had they each filed as single taxpayers. This typically occurs when both spouses earn approximately the same amount of income.

Married filing jointly one of five primary filing statuses. A taxpayer may file jointly if s/he is legally married as of the end of the year (or one spouse died during the year and the surviving spouse did not remarry) and both spouses agree to jointly file. Married couples filing joint returns combine their income and deductions and share joint and several liability for the resulting tax.

Married filing separately one of five primary filing statuses. When married couples file separately, each spouse reports the income he or she received during the year and the deductions he or she paid on a tax return separate from the other spouse.

Maturity the amount of time to the expiration date, or maturity date, of a debt instrument. The maturity of a debt instrument is generally the life of the instrument at which a payment of the face value is due or the instrument terminates.

Maturity value the amount paid to a bondholder when the bond matures and the bondholder redeems the bond for cash.

Medicare tax the Medical Health Insurance (MHI) tax. This tax helps pay medical costs for qualifying individuals. The Medicare tax rate for employees is 1.45 percent on salary or wages up to $200,000 ($125,000 for married filing separate; $250,000 of combined salary or wages for married filing joint) and is 2.35 percent on salary or wages in excess of $200,000 ($125,000 for married filing separate; $250,000 of combined salary or wages for married filing joint). For employers, the Medicare tax rate is 1.45 percent of employee salary or wages, regardless of the amount of salary or wages. Self-employed taxpayers pay both the employee and employer Medicare tax.

Merger the acquisition by one (acquiring) corporation of the assets and liabilities of another (target) corporation. No new entity is created in the transaction.

Mid-month convention a convention that allows owners of real property to take one-half of a month's depreciation during the month when the property was placed in service and in the month it was disposed of.

Mid-quarter convention a depreciation convention for tangible personal property that allows for one-half of a quarter's worth of depreciation in the quarter of purchase and in the quarter of disposition. This convention must be used when more than 40 percent of tangible personal property is placed into service in the fourth quarter of the tax year.

Minimum tax credit credit available in certain situations for the alternative minimum tax paid. The credit can be used only when the regular tax exceeds the tentative minimum tax.

Miscellaneous itemized deductions deductions representing the sum of certain itemized deductions, such as unreimbursed employee business expenses, investment expenses, and tax preparation fees, that are subject to a special floor limitation.

Mixed-motive expenditures activities that involve a mixture of business and personal objectives.

Modified Accelerated Cost Recovery System (MACRS) the current tax depreciation system for tangible personal and real property. Depreciation under MACRS is calculated by finding the depreciation method, the recovery period, and the applicable convention.

Municipal bond the common name for state and local government debt.

Mutual fund a diversified portfolio of securities owned and managed by a regulated investment company.

N

Negative basis adjustment (for special basis adjustment purposes) the sum of the recognized loss and the amount of the basis increase made by an owner receiving the distribution.

Net capital gain the net gain resulting when taxpayers combine net long-term capital gains with net short-term capital losses.

Net capital loss carryback the amount of a corporation's net capital loss from one year that it uses to offset net capital gains in any of the three preceding tax years.

Net capital loss carryover the amount of a corporation's or an individual's net capital loss from one year that it may use to offset net capital gains in future years.

Net earnings from self-employment the amount of earnings subject to self-employment income taxes. The amount is 92.35 percent of the net income from a taxpayer's Schedule C (for self-employed taxpayers).

Net investment income (for determining deductibility of investment interest expense) gross investment income reduced by deductible investment expenses.

Net investment income tax a 3.8 percent tax on the lesser of (a) net investment income or (b) the excess of modified adjusted gross income over $250,000 for married-joint filers and surviving spouses, $125,000 for married-separate filers, and $200,000 for other taxpayers.

Net long-term capital gain the net gain resulting when taxpayers combine long-term capital gains and losses for the year.

Net long-term capital loss the net loss resulting when taxpayers combine long-term capital gains and losses for the year.

Net operating loss (NOL) the excess of allowable deductions over gross income.

Net operating loss carryback the amount of a current-year net operating loss that is carried back to offset income in a prior year.

Net operating loss carryover the amount of a current-year net operating loss that is carried forward for up to 20 years to offset taxable income in those years.

Net passive investment income passive investment income less any expenses connected with producing it.

Net short-term capital gain the net gain resulting when taxpayers combine short-term capital gains and losses for the year.

Net short-term capital loss the net loss resulting when taxpayers combine short-term capital gains and losses for the year.

Net unearned income unearned income in excess of a specified threshold amount of a child under the age of 19 or under the age of 24 if a full-time student.

Net unrealized built-in gain the net gain (if any) an S corporation that was formerly a C corporation would recognize if it sold each asset at its fair market value. It is measured on the first day of the corporation's first year as an S corporation.

Nexus the connection between a business and a tax jurisdiction sufficient to subject the business to the tax jurisdiction's tax system. Also, the connection that is required to exist between a jurisdiction and a potential taxpayer such that the jurisdiction asserts the right to impose a tax.

No-additional-cost services a nontaxable fringe benefit that provides employer services to employees with little cost to the employer (e.g., airline tickets or phone service).

Nonacquiescence issued after the IRS loses a trial-level or circuit court case when the IRS has decided to continue to litigate this issue.

Nonbusiness income all income except for business income—generally, investment income and rental income.

Nondeductible terminable interests transfers of property interests to a spouse that do not qualify for a marital deduction because the interest of the spouse terminates when some event occurs or a specified amount of time elapses and the property is then transferred to another person.

Nondomiciliary business a business operating in a state other than its commercial domicile.

Nonperformance based compensation compensation paid to an employee that does not depend on the employee's performance or the corporation's performance or success. It usually is straight salary.

Nonqualified deferred compensation compensation provided for under a nonqualified plan allowing employees to defer compensation to a future period.

Nonqualified stock option a type of stock option requiring employees to treat the bargain element from options exercised as ordinary income in the tax year options are exercised. Correspondingly, employers may deduct the bargain element as compensation expense in the tax year options are exercised.

Nonrecaptured net §1231 loss a net §1231 loss that is deducted as an ordinary loss in one year and has not caused subsequent §1231 gain to be taxed as ordinary income.

Nonrecognition provisions tax laws that allow taxpayers to permanently exclude income from taxation or to defer recognizing realized income until a subsequent period.

Nonrecognition transaction a transaction where at least a portion of the realized gain or loss is not currently recognized.

Nonrecourse debt debt for which no partner bears any economic risk of loss. Mortgages on real property are a common form of nonrecourse debt.

Nonrefundable credits tax credits that reduce a taxpayer's gross tax liability but are limited to the amount of gross tax liability. Any credit not used in the current year is lost.

Nonresident alien an individual who does not meet the criteria to be treated as a resident for U.S. tax purposes.

Nonservice partner a partner who receives a partnership interest in exchange for property rather than services.

Nontaxable fringe benefit an employer-provided benefit that may be excluded from an employee's income.

Not definitely related deductions deductions that are not associated with a specific item or items of gross income in computing the foreign tax credit limitation.

O

Office examination the second most common audit. As the name suggests, the IRS conducts these audits at the local IRS office. These audits are typically broader in scope and more complex than correspondence examinations. Small businesses, taxpayers operating sole proprietorships, and middle- to high-income individual taxpayers are more likely, if audited, to have office examinations.

Operating distributions payments from an entity to its owners that represent a distribution of entity profits. Distributions generally fall into the category of operating distributions when the owners continue their interests in the entity after the distribution.

Operating income the annual income from a trade or business or rental activity.

Operating loss the annual loss from a trade or business or rental activity.

Option exercise the use of a stock option to acquire employer stock at a specified price.

Ordinary asset an asset created or used in a taxpayer's trade or business (e.g., accounts receivable or inventory) that generates ordinary income (or loss) on disposition.

Ordinary business income (loss) a partnership's or S corporation's remaining income or loss after separately stated items are removed. It is also referred to as nonseparately stated income (loss).

Ordinary income property property that if sold would generate income taxed at ordinary rates.

Ordinary and necessary an expense that is normal or appropriate and that is helpful or conducive to the business activity.

Organization costs costs associated with legally forming a partnership (such as attorneys' and accountants' fees).

Organizational expenditures expenses that are (1) connected directly to the creation of a corporation or partnership, (2) chargeable to a capital account, and (3) generally amortized over 180 months (limited immediate expensing may be available).

Original issue discount a type of bond issued for less than the maturity or face value of the bond.

Outbound transaction a transaction conducted outside the United States by a U.S. person that is subject to U.S. taxation.

Outside basis an investor's tax basis in the stock of a corporation or the interest in a partnership or LLC.

P

PAL an acronym for "passive activity loss." Losses allocated to partners who are not material participants in the partnership are passive activity losses.

Parent-subsidiary controlled group a form of controlled group consisting of one corporation that owns at least 80 percent of the voting power or stock value of another corporation on the last day of the year.

Partial liquidation a distribution made by a corporation to shareholders that results from a contraction of the corporation's activities.

Partnership agreement an agreement among the partners in a partnership stipulating the partners' rights and responsibilities in the partnership.

Partnership interest an intangible asset reflecting the economic rights a partner has with respect to a partnership, including the right to receive assets in liquidation of the partnership (called a *capital interest*) and the right to be allocated profits and losses (called a *profits interest*).

Passive activity an activity in which the taxpayer does not materially participate.

Passive activity income or loss income or loss from an activity in which the taxpayer does not materially participate.

Passive activity loss rules tax rules designed to limit taxpayers' ability to deduct losses from activities in which they don't materially participate against income from other sources.

Passive category income foreign source personal holding company income, such as interest, dividends, rents, royalties, annuities, and gains from sale of certain assets, that is combined in computing the FTC limitation.

Passive investment income (PII) royalties, rents, dividends, interest (including tax exempt interest), annuities, and gains from the sales or exchanges of stock or securities.

Passive investments direct or indirect investments (other than through a C corporation) in a trade or business or rental activity in which the taxpayer does not materially participate.

Payment liability liabilities of accrual method businesses for which economic performance occurs when the business actually *pays* the liability for, among others: worker's compensation; tort; breach of contract or violation of law; rebates and refunds; awards, prizes, and jackpots; insurance, warranties, and service contracts provided *to* the business; and taxes.

Percentage depletion a method of recovering the cost of a natural resource that allows a taxpayer to recover or expense an amount based on a statutorily determined percentage.

Permanent book–tax differences items of income or deductions for either book purposes or for tax purposes during the year but not both. Permanent differences do not reverse over time, so over the long run, the total amount of income or deduction for the item is different for book and tax purposes.

Permanent establishment generally, a fixed place of business through which an enterprise carries out its business. Examples include a place of management, a branch, an office, and a factory.

Permissible accounting method accounting method allowed under the tax law. Permissible accounting methods are adopted the first time a taxpayer uses the method on a tax return.

Person an individual, trust, estate, partnership, association, company, or corporation.

Personal exemption a fixed deduction allowed for an individual taxpayer (and spouse if filing a joint tax return).

Personal expenses expenses incurred for personal motives. Personal expenses are not deductible for tax purposes.

Personal holding companies closely held corporations generating primarily investment income.

Personal holding company tax penalty tax on the undistributed income of a personal holding company.

Personal property all tangible property other than real property.

Personal property tax a tax on the fair market value of all types of tangible and intangible property, except real property.

Phase-outs limitations that gradually eliminate deductions, credits, or other adjustments to taxable income typically done ratably over a phase-out range (based on AGI or related income measure).

Point one percent of the principal amount of a loan. A home buyer might pay points to compensate the lender for services or for a lower interest rate.

Portfolio investments investments producing dividends, interest, royalties, annuities, or capital gains.

Positive basis adjustment (for special basis adjustment purposes) the sum of the gain recognized by the owners receiving distributed property and the amount of any required basis reduction.

Post-termination transition period (PTTP) the period that begins on the day after the last day of a corporation's last taxable year as an S corporation and generally ends on the later of (a) one year after the last S corporation day, or (b) the due date for filing the return for the last year as an S corporation (including extensions).

Preferential tax rate tax rates lower than the tax rate applied to ordinary income.

Preferentially taxed income income taxed at a preferential rate such as long-term capital gains and qualified dividends.

Present interest right to presently enjoy property or receive income from the property.

Present value the concept that $1 today is worth more than $1 in the future. For example, assuming an investor can earn a 5 percent after-tax return, $1 invested today should be worth $1.05 in one year. Hence, $1 today is equivalent to $1.05 in one year.

Primary authorities official sources of the tax law generated by the legislative branch (i.e., statutory authority issued by Congress), judicial branch (i.e., rulings by the U.S. District Court, U.S. Tax Court, U.S. Court of Federal Claims, U.S. Circuit Court of Appeals, or U.S. Supreme Court), or executive/administrative branch (i.e., Treasury or IRS pronouncements).

Principal partner a partner having a 5 percent interest or more in partnership capital or profits.

Principal residence the main place of residence for a taxpayer during the taxable year.

Private activity bond a bond issued by a municipality but proceeds of which are used to fund privately owned activity.

Private letter rulings IRS pronouncements issued in response to a taxpayer request for a ruling on specific issues for the taxpayer. They are common for proposed transactions with potentially large tax implications. For the requesting taxpayer, a private letter ruling has very high authority. For all other taxpayers, private letter rulings have little authoritative weight.

Private nonoperating foundations privately sponsored foundations that disburse funds to other charities.

Private operating foundations privately sponsored foundations that actually fund and conduct charitable activities.

Probate the process in the probate court of gathering property possessed by or titled in the name of a decedent at the time of death, paying the debts of the decedent, and transferring the ownership of any remaining property to the decedent's heirs.

Probate estate property possessed by or titled in the name of a decedent at the time of death.

Procedural regulations regulations that explain Treasury Department procedures as they relate to administering the Code.

Production of income a for-profit activity that doesn't rise to the level of a trade or business.

Profits interest an interest in a partnership giving a partner the right to share in future profits but not the right to share in the current value of a partnership's assets. Profits interests are generally not taxable in the year they are received.

Progressive tax rate structure a tax rate structure that imposes an increasing marginal tax rate as the tax base increases. As the tax base increases, both the marginal tax rate and the taxes paid increase.

Proportional tax rate structure also known as a *flat tax*, this tax rate structure imposes a constant tax rate throughout the tax base. As the tax base increases, the taxes paid increase proportionally.

Proposed regulations regulations issued in proposed form; they do not carry the same authoritative weight as temporary or final regulations. All regulations are issued in proposed form first to allow public comment on them.

Public Law 86-272 federal law passed by Congress that provides additional protection for sellers of tangible personal property against income tax nexus.

Publicly state traded corporations corporations whose stock is publicly traded on a stock exchange.

Q

Qualified debt (for mortgage interest expense deduction purposes) the amount of debt on which qualified residence interest is paid. This includes up to $1,000,000 of acquisition indebtedness and up to $100,000 of home-equity indebtedness.

Qualified dividends paid by domestic or certain qualified foreign corporations that are eligible for lower capital gains rates.

Qualified educational expenses expenses that consist of tuition and related costs for enrolling the taxpayer, spouse, or a dependent at a post-secondary institution of higher education.

Qualified educational loans loans whose proceeds are used to pay qualified education expenses.

Qualified employee discount a nontaxable fringe benefit that provides employer goods at a discount (but not below the employer's cost) and services to employees at up to a 20 percent discount.

Qualified moving expense reimbursement a nontaxable fringe benefit that allows employers to pay moving-related expenses on behalf of employees.

Qualified nonrecourse financing nonrecourse debt secured by real property from a commercial lender unrelated to the borrower.

Qualified production activities income (QPAI) the *net* income from selling or leasing property that was manufactured in the United States.

Qualified replacement property property acquired to replace property damaged or destroyed in an involuntary conversion. It must be of a similar or related use to the original property even if the replacement property is real property (e.g., rental real estate for rental real estate).

Qualified residence the taxpayer's principal residence and one other residence.

Qualified residence interest interest paid on acquisition indebtedness and on home-equity indebtedness that is secured by a qualified residence.

Qualified retirement accounts plans meeting certain requirements that allow compensation placed in the account to be tax deferred until the taxpayer withdraws money from the account.

Qualified retirement plans employer-sponsored retirement plans that meet government-imposed funding and antidiscrimination requirements.

Qualified small business stock stock received at original issue from a corporation with a gross tax basis in its assets both before and after the issuance of no more than $50,000,000 and with 80 percent of the value of its assets used in the active conduct of certain qualified trades or businesses.

Qualified terminable interest property (QTIP) an exception to the general prohibition against claiming a marital deduction for a transfer of a terminable interest where the surviving spouse is entitled to all of the income from the property payable at least annually and no person has the power to appoint any part of the property to anyone other than the surviving spouse until the death of the surviving spouse.

Qualified transportation fringe benefit a nontaxable fringe benefit provided by employers in the form of mass transit passes, parking, or vanpool benefits.

Qualifying child an individual who qualifies as a dependent of a taxpayer by meeting a relationship, age, residence, and support test with respect to the taxpayer.

Qualifying relative an individual who is not a qualifying child of another taxpayer and who meets a relationship, support, and gross income test and thus qualifies to be a dependent of another taxpayer.

Qualifying widow or widower one of five primary filing statuses. Applies for up to two years after the year in which the taxpayer's spouse dies (the taxpayer files married filing jointly in the year of the spouse's death) as long as the taxpayer remains unmarried and maintains a household for a dependent child.

Question of fact a research question that hinges upon the facts and circumstances of the taxpayer's transaction.

Question of law a research question that hinges upon the interpretation of the law, such as interpreting a particular phrase in a code section.

R

Real property land and structures permanently attached to land.

Real property tax a tax on the fair market value of land and structures permanently attached to land.

Realization gain or loss that results from an exchange of property rights in a transaction.

Realization principle the proposition that income only exists when there is a transaction with another party resulting in a measurable change in property rights.

Realized gain or loss the difference between the amount realized and the adjusted basis of an asset sold or otherwise disposed of.

Realized income income generated in a transaction with a second party in which there is a measurable change in property rights between parties.

Reasonable in amount an expenditure is reasonable when the amount paid is neither extravagant nor exorbitant.

Recapture the recharacterization of income from capital gain to ordinary income.

Recognition gain or loss included in the computation of taxable income.

Recognized gain or loss the gain or loss included in gross income on a taxpayer's tax return. This is usually the realized gain or loss unless a nonrecognition provision applies.

Recourse debt debt held by a partnership for which at least one partner has economic risk of loss.

Recovery period a length of time prescribed by statute in which business property is depreciated or amortized.

Recurring item an election under economic performance to currently deduct an accrued liability if the liability is expected to persist in the future and is either not material or a current deduction better matches revenue.

Refinance when a taxpayer pays off a current loan with the proceeds of a second loan.

Refundable credits credits that are not limited to the amount of the gross tax liability. If the credit exceeds the gross tax liability, the taxpayer receives a refund for the excess credit.

Regressive tax rate structure a tax rate structure that imposes a decreasing marginal tax rate as the tax base increases. As the tax base increases, the taxes paid increase, but the marginal tax rate decreases.

Regulations the Treasury Department's official interpretation of the Internal Revenue Code. Regulations are the highest authority issued by the IRS.

Related-party transaction financial activities among family members, among owners and their businesses, or among businesses owned by the same owners.

Remainder the right to ownership of a property that transfers to a new owner, the remainderman, following a temporary interest.

Remainderman the person entitled to a remainder interest.

Reorganization a tax-deferred transaction (acquisition, disposition, recapitalization, or change of name or place of incorporation) that meets one of the seven statutory definitions found in §368(a)(1).

Requisite service period the period or periods during which an employee is required to provide service in exchange for an award under a share-based payment arrangement (ASC 718, Glossary).

Research and experimentation costs expenses for research including costs of research laboratories (salaries, materials, and other related expenses). Taxpayers can elect to amortize research and development costs over not less than 60 months from the time benefits are first derived from the research.

Residence-based jurisdiction taxation of income based on the taxpayer's residence.

Resident alien an individual who is not a U.S. citizen but is treated as a resident for U.S. tax purposes.

Restricted stock stock employees receive as compensation that may be sold only after the passage of time or after certain performance targets are achieved. Because employees are not entitled to immediately sell the restricted stock they receive, the value of the stock is generally not taxable to employees or deductible by employers until the selling restrictions lapse.

Return of capital the portion of proceeds from a sale (or distribution) representing a return of the original cost of the underlying property.

Revenue procedures second in administrative authoritative weight after regulations. Revenue procedures are much more detailed than regulations and explain in greater detail IRS practice and procedures in administering the tax law. Revenue procedures have the same authoritative weight as revenue rulings.

Revenue rulings second in administrative authoritative weight after regulations. Revenue rulings address the specific application of the Code and regulations to a specific factual situation. Revenue rulings have the same authoritative weight as revenue procedures.

Reverse hybrid entity a "check-the-box" entity owned by multiple persons for which corporation status is elected.

Reverse triangular merger an acquisition in which an acquisition subsidiary of the acquiring corporation merges into the acquired (target) corporation, after which the acquired corporation becomes a subsidiary of the acquiring corporation.

Reversion terms by which ownership of property returns to the original owner following a temporary interest.

Rollover a transfer of funds from a qualified retirement plan to another qualified retirement plan, from a qualified retirement plan to a Roth or traditional IRA, or from a traditional IRA to a Roth IRA.

Roth 401(k) a type of defined contribution plan that allows employees to contribute on an after-tax basis and receive distributions tax-free.

Roth IRA an individually managed retirement plan permitting individuals to contribute on an after-tax basis and receive distributions tax-free.

Royalties payments taxpayers receive for allowing others to use their tangible or intangible property.

S

S corporation a corporation under state law that has elected to be taxed under the rules provided in subchapter S of the Internal Revenue Code. Under subchapter S, an S corporation is taxed as a flow-through entity.

Safe-harbor provision provision of the tax law that reduces or eliminates a taxpayer's liability under the law if the taxpayer meets certain requirements.

Salary a fixed regular payment by an employer to an employee in exchange for the employee's services which is usually paid on a monthly basis, but typically expressed as an annual amount.

Sales tax a tax imposed on the retail sales of goods (plus certain services). Retailers are responsible for collecting and remitting the tax; typically sales tax is collected at the point of sale.

Same-day sale a phrase used to describe a situation where a taxpayer exercises stock options and then immediately sells the stock received through the option exercise.

Schedule C a schedule on which a taxpayer reports the income and deductions for a sole-proprietorship.

Schedule K a schedule filed with a partnership's annual tax return listing its ordinary income (loss) and its separately stated items.

Schedule M adjustments book–tax differences that corporations report on the Schedule M-1 or M-3 of Form 1120 as adjustments to book income to reconcile to taxable income.

Schedule M-1 a schedule on Form 1120 that reconciles book income to taxable income before special deductions. Book–tax differences are reported in a general way.

Schedule M-3 a schedule on Form 1120 that reconciles book income to taxable income for corporations and partnerships with total assets of $10 million or more. The schedule M-3 includes much more detail than the Schedule M-1, including identifying whether each book–tax difference is a temporary difference or a permanent book–tax difference.

Secondary authority unofficial tax authorities that interpret and explain the primary authorities, such as tax research services, tax articles, newsletters, and textbooks. Secondary authorities may be very helpful in understanding a tax issue, but they hold little weight in a tax dispute (hence, the term *unofficial* tax authorities).

Security a financial instrument including an equity interest in business organizations and creditor interests, such as savings accounts, notes, and bonds.

Self-employment taxes Social Security and Medicare taxes paid by the self-employed on a taxpayer's net earnings from self-employment. For self-employed taxpayers, the terms "self-employment tax" and "FICA tax" are synonymous.

SEP IRA a simplified employee pension (SEP) that is administered through an individual retirement account (IRA). Available to self-employed taxpayers.

Separate tax return a state tax return methodology requiring that each related entity with nexus must file a separate tax return.

Separately stated items income, expenses, gains, losses, credits, and other items that are excluded from a partnership's or S corporation's operating income (loss) and disclosed to partners in a partnership or shareholders of an S corporation separately because their tax effects may be different for each partner or shareholder.

Serial gift transfer tax strategy that uses the annual exclusion to convert a potentially large taxable transfer into a tax-exempt transfer by dividing it into multiple inter vivos gifts spread over several periods or donees.

Service partner partners who receive their partnership interest by contributing services rather than cash or property.

Settlement statement a statement that details the monies paid out and received by the buyer and seller in a real estate transaction.

Short-term capital gains or losses gains or losses from the sale of capital assets held for one year or less.

Simple trust a trust that must distribute all accounting income currently and cannot make charitable contributions.

Sin taxes taxes imposed on the purchase of goods (e.g., alcohol, tobacco products, etc.) that are considered socially less desirable.

Single one of five primary statuses available. A taxpayer files as single if s/he is unmarried as of the end of the year and does not qualify for any of the other filing statuses. A taxpayer is considered single if s/he is unmarried or legally separated from his or her spouse under a divorce or separate maintenance decree.

Single member LLC a limited liability company with only one member. Single member LLCs with individual owners are taxed as sole proprietorships and as disregarded entities otherwise.

Social Security tax the Old Age, Survivors, and Disability Insurance (OASDI) tax. The tax is intended to provide basic pension coverage for the retired and disabled. Employees pay Social Security tax at a rate of 6.2 percent on the wage base (employers also pay 6.2 percent). Self-employed taxpayers are subject to a Social Security tax at a rate of 12.4 percent on their net earnings from self-employment. The base on which Social Security taxes are paid is limited to an annually determined amount of wages and/or net earnings from self-employment.

Sole proprietorship a business entity that is not legally separate from the individual owner of the business. The income of a sole proprietorship is taxed and paid directly by the owner.

Solicitation selling activities or activities ancillary to selling that are protected under Public Law 86-272.

Source-based jurisdiction taxation of income based on where the income is earned.

Special allocations allocations of income, gain, expense, or loss, etc., that are allocated to the owners of an entity in a manner out of proportion with the owners' interests in the entity. Special allocations can be made by entities treated as partnerships for federal income tax purposes.

Special basis adjustment an optional (sometimes mandatory) election to adjust the entity asset bases as a result of an owner's disposition of an interest in the entity or of distributions from the entity to its owners.

Specific identification method an elective method for determining the cost of an asset sold. Under this method, the taxpayer specifically chooses the assets that are to be sold.

Split-gift election election that allows spouses to treat all gifts made in a year as if each spouse made one-half of each gift.

Spot rate the foreign currency exchange rate on a specific day.

Spousal IRA an IRA account for the spouse with the lesser amount of earned income. Contributions in this account belong to this spouse no matter where the funds for the contribution came from.

Standard deduction a fixed deduction offered in lieu of itemized deductions. The amount of the standard deduction depends on the taxpayer's filing status.

Stare decisis a doctrine meaning that a court will rule consistently with (a) its previous rulings (i.e., unless, due to evolving interpretations of the tax law over time, it decides to overturn an earlier decision) and (b) the rulings of higher courts with appellate jurisdiction (i.e., the courts to which its cases are appealed).

Start-up costs expenses that would be classified as business expenses except that the expenses are incurred before the business begins. These costs are generally capitalized and amortized over 180 months, but limited immediate expensing may be available.

State tax a tax imposed by one of the 50 U.S. states.

State tax base the federal taxable income plus or minus required state adjustments.

Statements on Standards for Tax Services (SSTS) standards of practice for tax professionals issued by the AICPA. Currently, there are seven SSTS that describe the tax professional standards when recommending a tax return position, answering questions on a tax return, preparing a tax return using data supplied by a client, using estimates on a tax return, taking a tax return position inconsistent with a previous year's tax return, discovering a tax return error, and giving tax advice to taxpayers.

Static forecasting the process of forecasting tax revenues based on the existing state of transactions while ignoring how taxpayers may alter their activities in response to a tax law change.

Statute of limitations defines the period in which the taxpayer can file an amended tax return or the IRS can assess a tax deficiency for a specific tax year. For both amended tax returns filed by a taxpayer and proposed tax assessments by the IRS, the statute of limitations generally ends three years from the *later* of (1) the date the tax return was actually filed or (2) the tax return's original due date.

Step-transaction doctrine judicial doctrine that allows the IRS to collapse a series of related transactions into one transaction to determine the tax consequences of the transaction.

Stock dividend a dividend made by a corporation of its own stock.

Stock-for-stock acquisition an exchange of solely voting stock by the acquiring corporation in exchange for stock of the target corporation, after which the acquiring corporation controls (owns 80 percent or more of) the target corporation. Often referred to as a "Type B reorganization."

Stock redemption a property distribution made to shareholders in return for some or all of their stock in the distributing corporation that is not in partial or complete liquidation of the corporation.

Stock split a stock redemption in which a corporation exchanges a ratio of shares of stock (e.g., 2 for 1) for each share held by the shareholder.

Strike price *see* exercise price.

Structural tax rate the tax rate computed by dividing a company's income tax provision adjusted for nonrecurring permanent differences by its pretax income from continuing operations.

Student loans loans where the proceeds are used for qualified educational expenses, but do not include home-equity loans.

Subchapter K the portion of the Internal Revenue Code dealing with partnerships tax law.

Subchapter S the portion of the Internal Revenue Code containing tax rules for S corporations and their shareholders.

Subpart F income income earned by a controlled foreign corporation that is not eligible for deferral from U.S. taxation.

Substance-over-form doctrine judicial doctrine that allows the IRS to consider the transaction's substance regardless of its form and, where appropriate, reclassify the transaction according to its substance.

Substantial authority the standard used to determine whether a tax practitioner may recommend and a taxpayer may take a tax return position without being subject to IRS penalty under IRC §6694 and IRC §6662, respectively. A good CPA evaluates whether supporting authority is substantial or not based upon the supporting and opposing authorities' weight and relevance. Substantial authority suggests that the probability that the taxpayer's position will be sustained upon audit or litigation is in the 35 to 40 percent range or above.

Substantial basis reduction negative basis adjustment of more than $250,000 resulting from a distribution from an entity taxed as a partnership to its owners.

Substantial built-in loss exists when a partnership's adjusted basis in its property exceeds the property's fair market value by more than $250,000 when a transfer of an interest occurs.

Substantially appreciated inventory (for partnership disproportionate distributions purposes) inventory with a fair market value that exceeds its basis by more than 120 percent.

Substituted basis the transfer of the tax basis of stock or other property given up in an exchange to stock or other property received in return.

Substitution effect one of the two basic responses that a taxpayer may have when taxes increase. The substitution effect predicts that, when taxpayers are taxed more, rather than work more, they will substitute nontaxable activities (e.g., leisure pursuits) for taxable ones because the marginal value of taxable activities has decreased.

Sufficiency a standard for evaluating a good tax system. Sufficiency is defined as assessing the aggregate size of the tax revenues that must be generated and ensuring that the tax system provides these revenues.

Syndication costs costs partnerships incur to promote the sale of partnership interests to the public. Syndication expenses must be capitalized and are not amortizable.

T

Tacks the adding on of the transferor's holding period of property to the transferee in a tax-deferred exchange.

Tax a payment required by a government that is unrelated to any specific benefit or service received from the government.

Tax accounting balance sheet a balance sheet that records a company's assets and liabilities at their tax bases instead of their financial accounting bases.

Tax avoidance the legal act of arranging one's transactions or affairs to reduce taxes paid.

Tax base the item that is being taxed (e.g., purchase price of a good, taxable income, etc.).

Tax basis the amount of a taxpayer's unrecovered cost of or investment in an asset; *see also* adjusted tax basis.

Tax benefit rule holds that a refund of an amount deducted in a previous period is only included in income to the extent that the deduction reduced taxable income.

Tax bracket a range of taxable income taxed at a specified rate.

Tax capital accounts partners' capital accounts initially determined using the tax basis of contributed property and maintained using tax accounting income and expense recognition principles.

Tax carryforwards tax deductions or credits that cannot be used on the current-year tax return and that can be carried forward to reduce taxable income or taxes payable in a future year.

Tax contingency reserve a company's reserve for taxes it has not paid, but it may pay in the future, for uncertain tax positions taken on the current and prior-year income tax returns.

Tax Court allocation method allocates expenses associated with rental use of the home between rental use and personal use. Property taxes and mortgage interest are allocated to rental use of the home based on the ratio of the number of rental use days to the total days in the year. All other expenses are allocated to rental use based on the ratio of the number of rental use days to total days the property was used during the year.

Tax credits items that reduce a taxpayer's tax liability dollar for dollar.

Tax evasion the willful attempt to defraud the government (i.e., by not paying taxes legally owed). Tax evasion falls outside the confines of legal tax avoidance.

Tax haven generally, a country offering very favorable tax laws for foreign businesses and individuals.

Tax rate the level of taxes imposed on the tax base, usually expressed as a percentage.

Tax rate schedule a schedule of progressive tax rates and the income ranges to which the rates apply that taxpayers may use to compute their gross tax liability.

Tax shelter an investment or other arrangement designed to produce tax benefits without any expectation of economic profits.

Tax tables IRS-provided tables that specify the federal income tax liability for individuals with taxable income within a specific range. The tables differ by filing status and reflect tax rates that increase with taxable income.

Tax treaties agreements negotiated between countries that describe the tax treatment of entities subject to tax in both countries (e.g., U.S. citizens earning investment income in Spain). The U.S. president has the authority to enter into a tax treaty with another country after receiving the Senate's advice.

Tax year a fixed period in which a business reports income and deductions, generally referred to as an accounting period.

Taxable estate adjusted gross estate reduced by the marital deduction and the charitable deduction.

Taxable fringe benefit a noncash fringe benefit provided by employers to an employee that is included in taxable income (e.g., auto allowance or group-term life over $50,000).

Taxable gifts the amount left after adjusting current gifts for gift splitting, annual exclusions, the marital deduction, and the charitable deduction.

Taxable income the tax base for the individual income tax.

Taxable temporary differences book–tax differences that will result in taxable amounts in future years when the related deferred tax liability is settled.

Technical advice memorandum ruling issued by the IRS national office, requested by an IRS agent, and generally issued for a completed transaction.

Temporary book–tax differences book–tax differences that reverse over time such that, over the long term, corporations recognize the same amount of income or deductions for the items on their financial statements as they recognize on their tax returns.

Temporary regulations regulations issued with a limited life (three years for regulations issued after November 20, 1988). During their life, temporary regulations carry the same authoritative weight as final regulations.

Tenancy by the entirety ownership by husband and wife similar to joint tenancy with right of survivorship.

Tenancy in common ownership in which owners hold divided rights to property and have the ability to transfer these rights during their life or upon their death.

Tentative minimum tax the tax on the AMT tax base under the alternative minimum tax system.

Terminable interest a right to property that terminates at a specified time or upon the occurrence of a specified event, such as a life estate.

Testamentary transfers transfers that take place upon the death of the donor.

Third-party intermediaries people or organizations that facilitate the transfer of property between taxpayers in a like-kind exchange. Typically, the intermediary receives the cash from selling the property received from the taxpayer and uses it to acquire like-kind property identified by the taxpayer.

Throwback rule the rule that sales into a state without nexus are included with sales from the state the property was shipped from.

Topical tax service a tax service arranged by subject (i.e., topic). For each topic, topical services identify tax issues that relate to each topic and then explain and cite authorities relevant to the issue (code sections, regulations, court cases, revenue rulings, etc.).

Trade or business a profit-motivated activity characterized by a sustained, continuous, high level of individual involvement or effort.

Trade show rule a rule that permits businesses to have physical presence at conventions and trade shows, generally up to two weeks a year, without creating nexus.

Traditional 401(k) a popular type of defined contribution plan with before-tax employee and employer contributions and taxable distributions.

Traditional IRA an individually managed retirement account with deductible contributions and taxable distributions.

Transfer taxes taxes on the transfer of wealth from one taxpayer to another. The estate and gift taxes are two examples of transfer taxes.

Travel expenses expenditures incurred while "away from home overnight," including the cost of transportation, meals, lodging, and incidental expenses.

Treasury bond a debt instrument issued by the U.S. Treasury at face value, at a discount, or at a premium, with a set interest rate and maturity date that pays interest semiannually. Treasury bonds have terms of 30 years.

Treasury note a debt instrument issued by the U.S. Treasury at face value, at a discount, or at a premium, with a set interest rate and maturity date that pays interest semiannually. Treasury notes have terms of 2, 5, or 10 years.

Triple i agreement a 10-year agreement filed with the IRS in which the taxpayer agrees to notify the IRS that he or she has acquired a prohibited interest after waiving the family attribution rules in a complete redemption.

Trust fiduciary entity created to hold and administer the property for other persons according to the terms of a trust instrument.

Trustee the person responsible for administering a trust.

U

Uncertain tax positions a tax return position for which a corporation does not have a high degree of certainty as to its tax consequences.

Underpayment penalty the penalty that applies when taxpayers fail to adequately prepay their tax liability. The underpayment penalty is determined by multiplying the federal short-term interest rate plus three percentage points by the amount of tax underpayment per quarter.

Unearned income income from property that accrues as time passes without effort on the part of the owner of the property.

Unemployment tax the tax that pays for temporary unemployment benefits for individuals terminated from their jobs without cause.

Unfavorable book–tax difference any book–tax difference that requires an add back to book income in computing taxable income. This type of adjustment is unfavorable because it increases taxable income relative to book income.

Unified credit also known as the *applicable credit*, the amount of credit based on the exemption equivalent designed to prevent transfer taxation of smaller cumulative transfers.

Uniform cost capitalization rules (UNICAP rules) specify that inventories must be accounted for using full absorption rules to allocate the indirect costs of productive activities to inventory.

Unitary tax return a state tax return methodology requiring the activities of a group of related entities to be reported on a single tax return. The criteria for determining whether a group of entities must file a unitary tax return are functional integration, centralization of management, and economies of scale.

Unrealized receivables any rights to receive payment for (1) goods delivered, or to be delivered, or (2) services rendered, or to be rendered. Unrealized receivables also include other assets to the extent that they would produce ordinary income if sold for their fair market value.

Unrecaptured §1250 gain a gain from the sale of real estate held by a noncorporate taxpayer for more than one year in a trade or business or as rental property attributable to tax depreciation deducted at ordinary tax rates. This gain is taxable at a maximum 25 percent capital gains rate.

Unrecognized tax benefit a reserve for tax benefits related to a tax position for which the corporation does not have a high degree of certainty as to its sustainability on audit or in a court of law.

U.S. Circuit Courts of Appeal the first level of appeals courts after the trial-level courts. There are 13 U.S. Circuit Courts of Appeal; one for the Federal Circuit and 12 assigned to hear cases that originated from a specific circuit (e.g., the 11th Circuit Court of Appeals only hears cases originating within the 11th Circuit).

U.S. Constitution the founding law of the United States, ratified in 1789.

U.S. Court of Federal Claims one of the three trial-level courts. It is a national court that only hears monetary claims against the federal government.

U.S. District Court one of three trial-level courts. It is the only court that allows a jury trial. There is at least one district court in each state.

U.S. savings bonds debt instruments issued by the U.S. Treasury at face value or at a discount, with a set maturity date. Interest earned from U.S. bonds is paid either at maturity or when the bonds are converted to cash before maturity.

U.S. Supreme Court the highest court in the United States. The Supreme Court hears only a few tax cases a year with great significance to a broad cross-section of taxpayers or cases litigating issues in which there has been disagreement among the circuit courts. For most tax cases, the Supreme Court refuses to hear the case (i.e., the *writ of certiorari* is denied) and, thus, litigation ends with the circuit court decision.

U.S. Tax Court a national court that only hears tax cases and where the judges are tax experts. The U.S. Tax Court is the only court that allows tax cases to be heard *before* the taxpayer pays the disputed liability and the only court with a small claims division (hearing claims involving disputed liabilities of $50,000 or less).

Use tax a tax imposed on the retail price of goods owned, possessed, or consumed within a state that were *not* purchased within the state.

V

Valuation allowance the portion of a deferred tax asset for which management determines it is more likely than not that a tax benefit will not be realized on a future tax return.

Value-added tax a tax imposed on the producer of goods (and services) on the value of goods (services) added at each stage of production. Value-added taxes are common in Europe.

Vertical equity one of the dimensions of equity. Vertical equity is achieved when taxpayers with greater ability to pay tax, pay more tax relative to taxpayers with a lesser ability to pay tax.

Vest to become legally entitled to receive a particular benefit without risk of forfeiture; to gain ownership.

Vesting date the date on which the taxpayer becomes legally entitled to receive a particular benefit without risk of forfeiture.

Vesting period period of employment over which employees earn the right to own and exercise stock options.

W

Wages a payment by an employer to an employee in exchange for the employee's services which is typically expressed in an hourly, daily, or piecework rate.

Wash sale the sale of an investment if that same investment (or substantially identical investment) is purchased within 30 days before or after the sale date. Losses on wash sales are deferred.

Wherewithal to pay the ability or resources to pay taxes due from a particular transaction.

Withholdings taxes collected and remitted to the government by an employer from an employee's wages.

Working condition fringe benefit a nontaxable fringe benefit provided by employers that would be deductible as an ordinary and necessary business expense if paid by an employee (e.g., reimbursement for professional dues).

Writ of certiorari a document filed to request the U.S. Supreme Court to hear a case.

Z

Zero coupon bond a type of bond issued at a discount that pays interest only at maturity.

Appendix D

Tax Rates

2017 Tax Rate Schedule

Schedule X-Single

If taxable income is over:	But not over:	The tax is:
$ 0	$ 9,325	10% of taxable income
$ 9,325	$ 37,950	$932.50 plus 15% of the excess over $9,325
$ 37,950	$ 91,900	$5,226.25 plus 25% of the excess over $37,950
$ 91,900	$191,650	$18,713.75 plus 28% of the excess over $91,900
$191,650	$416,700	$46,643.75 plus 33% of the excess over $191,650
$416,700	$418,400	$120,910.25 plus 35% of the excess over $416,700
$418,400	—	$121,505.25 plus 39.6% of the excess over $418,400

Schedule Z-Head of Household

If taxable income is over:	But not over:	The tax is:
$ 0	$ 13,350	10% of taxable income
$ 13,350	$ 50,800	$1,335.00 plus 15% of the excess over $13,350
$ 50,800	$131,200	$6,952.50 plus 25% of the excess over $50,800
$131,200	$212,500	$27,052.50 plus 28% of the excess over $131,200
$212,500	$416,700	$49,816.50 plus 33% of the excess over $212,500
$416,700	$444,550	$117,202.50 plus 35% of the excess over $416,700
$444,550	—	$126,950.00 plus 39.6% of the excess over $444,550

Schedule Y-1-Married Filing Jointly or Qualifying Widow(er)

If taxable income is over:	But not over:	The tax is:
$ 0	$ 18,650	10% of taxable income
$ 18,650	$ 75,900	$1,865.00 plus 15% of the excess over $18,650
$ 75,900	$153,100	$10,452.50 plus 25% of the excess over $75,900
$153,100	$233,350	$29,752.50 plus 28% of the excess over $153,100
$233,350	$416,700	$52,222.50 plus 33% of the excess over $233,350
$416,700	$470,700	$112,728.00 plus 35% of the excess over $416,700
$470,700	—	$131,628.00 plus 39.6% of the excess over $470,700

Schedule Y-2-Married Filing Separately

If taxable income is over:	But not over:	The tax is:
$ 0	$ 9,325	10% of taxable income
$ 9,325	$ 37,950	$932.50 plus 15% of the excess over $9,325
$ 37,950	$ 76,550	$5,226.25 plus 25% of the excess over $37,950
$ 76,550	$116,675	$14,876.25 plus 28% of the excess over $76,550
$116,675	$208,350	$26,111.25 plus 33% of the excess over $116,675
$208,350	$235,350	$56,364.00 plus 35% of the excess over $208,350
$235,350	—	$65,814.00 plus 39.6% of the excess over $235,350

Basic Standard Deduction Amounts

Filing Status	2016 Amount	2017 Amount
Married Filing Jointly	$12,600	$12,700
Qualifying Widow or Widower	$12,600	$12,700
Married Filing Separately	$ 6,300	$ 6,350
Head of Household	$ 9,300	$ 9,350
Single	$ 6,300	$ 6,350

Amount of Each Additional Standard Deduction

	2016 Amount	2017 Amount
Married taxpayers 65 or over or blind	$1,250	$1,250
Single taxpayer or head of household who is 65 or over or blind	$1,550	$1,550

Personal and Dependency Exemption

2016 Exemption	2017 Exemption
$4,050	$4,050

Corporate Income Tax Rates

Taxable Income	Tax
< $50,000	15% of the taxable income
$50,000–$75,000	$7,500 + 25% of taxable income over $50,000
$75,000–$100,000	$13,750 + 34% of taxable income over $75,000
$100,000–$335,000	$22,250 + 39% of taxable income over $100,000
$335,000–$10,000,000	$113,900 + 34% of taxable income over $335,000
$10,000,000–$15,000,000	$3,400,000 + 35% of taxable income over $10,000,000
$15,000,000–$18,333,333	$5,150,000 + 38% of taxable income over $15,000,000
Over $18,333,333	35% of the taxable income

Code Index

Page numbers followed by n refer to footnotes.

CI-2 Code Index

Subject Index

Page numbers followed by n refer to footnotes.

A

B

C

D

F

G

H

J

K

L

M

N

O

P

Q

R

U

V

W

X

Y

Z

Online Supplements